BUREAU OF INTERNATIONAL RESEARCH
HARVARD UNIVERSITY AND RADCLIFFE COLLEGE

THE MEXICAN CLAIMS COMMISSIONS

1923–1934

THE MACMILLAN COMPANY
NEW YORK · BOSTON · CHICAGO · DALLAS
ATLANTA · SAN FRANCISCO

MACMILLAN & CO., Limited
LONDON · BOMBAY · CALCUTTA
· MELBOURNE

THE MACMILLAN COMPANY
OF CANADA, Limited
TORONTO

THE MEXICAN CLAIMS COMMISSIONS

1923–1934

A Study in the Law and Procedure of International Tribunals

BY

A. H. FELLER

SPECIAL ASSISTANT TO THE ATTORNEY GENERAL OF THE
UNITED STATES; SOMETIME INSTRUCTOR IN INTER-
NATIONAL LAW, HARVARD LAW SCHOOL

NEW YORK

THE MACMILLAN COMPANY

1935

COPYRIGHT, 1935,
BY THE BUREAU OF INTERNATIONAL RESEARCH
Harvard University and Radcliffe College

The Bureau of International Research has aided the author in
carrying on research and in publishing the results. The
Bureau assumes no responsibility for the statements or views expressed.

Set up and printed. Published December, 1935.

To

MANLEY OTTMER HUDSON

PREFACE

THE realm of the procedure of international tribunals is the Antarctica of international law. A few explorers have skirted about its shores; others have surveyed portions of it with more or less thoroughness. Not until its little known territory has been conquered, region by region, will it be possible for some future scholar to draw a complete and revealing map of the entire continent. This book embodies the results of the exploration of one sector—the work of the Mexican Claims Commissions which functioned between 1923 and 1934. This sector may be a relatively small one, yet its topography is so varied and so typical that it may be considered as a model, in miniature, of the continent as a whole. Thus the study of this group of tribunals can furnish a fairly close approximation to the study of the great body of international procedural law. While the detailed exposition of the Mexican Claims Commissions is the major purpose, an attempt has also been made to indicate, by brief sketch maps, so to speak, the place of the Commissions and their practice in the general background of history and of international law.

The matters treated in this study fall into three classes. Some of the chapters are primarily historical, such as the Historical Prelude, the Mexican Revolutions and the Negotiation of the Claims Conventions, and the chapters on the Organization and Work of the Commissions. Other chapters deal with problems more or less peculiar to the Mexican Claims Commissions—Responsibility for Claims Arising out of the Mexican Revolutions, Relation of the International Commissions to the National Claims Commission, and Conflicts of Jurisdiction between the United States–Mexican General and Special Claims Commissions. Most of the chapters are concerned with problems universally encountered in international adjudication. The wealth of material furnished by the work of the Commissions has enabled more extensive exposition of some of these problems than has been possible heretofore.

So much of the material is unpublished that its collection gave some difficulty. For such unpublished and indispensable materials as were secured thanks are due to Green H. Hackworth, Legal Adviser of the Department of State, Professor J. H. W. Verzijl of Utrecht and Señores Eduardo Suarez, Manuel Sierra and Emilio Rabasa of the Mexican Secretariat of Foreign Relations. Special thanks are due to Professor George Grafton Wilson of Harvard University and to the Bureau of International Research of Harvard University and Radcliffe College, without whose aid this voyage of exploration could never have been undertaken. I am particularly indebted to Professor Manley O. Hudson of the Harvard Law School for his unflagging enthusiasm and sympathetic and critical encouragement.

A. H. FELLER.

Washington, D. C.
May 1, 1935.

CONTENTS

Other Kinds of Claimants

CHAPTER 7. RESPONSIBILITY OF STATES FOR OTHER THAN REVOLU-
TIONARY ACTS.

Direct Responsibility

Indirect Responsibility

Failure to Apprehend, Punish and Prosecute

CHAPTER 8. RESPONSIBILITY FOR CLAIMS ARISING OUT OF THE MEXI-
CAN REVOLUTIONS.

CHAPTER 9. JURISDICTION OVER CONTRACT CLAIMS AND RESPONSI-
BILITY OF GOVERNMENTS THEREFOR.

CHAPTER 10. THE CALVO CLAUSE.

CHAPTER 11. RELATION OF THE INTERNATIONAL COMMISSIONS TO THE NATIONAL CLAIMS COMMISSION.

APPENDIX

SOURCES AND FORM OF CITATION OF DECISIONS OF THE MEXICAN CLAIMS COMMISSIONS

PUBLISHED SOURCES

United States-Mexican General Claims Commission

REPORTER	CITED AS
Claims Commission—United States and Mexico—Opinions of Commissioners under the Convention concluded September 8, 1923 between the United States and Mexico—February 4, 1926, to July 23, 1927 (Government Printing Office, Washington, 1927).	Opinions of Commissioners, 1927.
Claims Commission—United States and Mexico—Opinions of Commissioners under the Convention concluded September 8, 1923, as Extended by the Convention Signed August 16, 1927 between the United States and Mexico—September 26, 1928, to May 17, 1929 (Government Printing Office, Washington, 1929)	Opinions of Commissioners, 1929.
Claims Commission—United States and Mexico—Opinions of Commissioners under the Convention Concluded September 8, 1923, as Extended by Subsequent Conventions Between the United States and Mexico—October 1930, to July 1931.	Opinions of Commissioners, 1931.

United States-Mexican Special Claims Commission

REPORTER	CITED AS
Special Claims Commission—United States and Mexico—Opinions of Commissioners under the Convention concluded September 10, 1923, between the United States and Mexico as Extended by the Convention Concluded August 17, 1929—April 26, 1926, to April 24, 1931 (Government Printing Office, Washington, 1931).	Opinions of Commissioners, 1926–1931.

British-Mexican Commission

REPORTER	CITED AS
Claims Commission between Great Britain and Mexico—Decisions and Opinions of the Commissioners in Accordance with the Convention of November 19, 1926, between Great Britain and the United Mexican States—October, 1929, to February 15, 1930 (H. M. Stationery Office, London, 1931).	Decisions and Opinions of Commissioners.
Claims Commission between Great Britain and Mexico—Further Decisions and Opinions of the Commissioners in Accordance with the Conventions of November 19, 1926, and December 5, 1930, between Great Britain and the United Mexican States—Subsequent to February 15, 1930 (H. M. Stationery Office, London, 1933).	Further Decisions and Opinions.

French-Mexican Commission

REPORTER	CITED AS
La Réparation des Dommages causés aux étrangers par des mouvements révolutionnaires—Jurisprudence de la Commission franco-mexicaine des Réclamations (1924–1932) [1] (A. Pedone, Paris, 1933).	Jurisprudence de la Commission franco-mexicaine des Réclamations.

Unpublished Sources

The decisions of the following Commissions have not been published: German-Mexican Commission, Italian-Mexican Commission, Spanish-Mexican Commission, French-Mexican Commission (all except four decisions published by A. Pedone). The decisions of the Italian-Mexican Commission, Spanish-Mexican Commission and of the French-Mexican Commission after its reorganization under the Convention of 1930, are to be found in the archives of the Mexican Secretariat of Foreign Relations. Manuscript copies of the decisions of the German-Mexican Commission and of the unpublished decisions rendered by the first French-Mexican Commission subsequent to the withdrawal of the Mexican Commissioner are in the Harvard Law School Library.

---

[1] This is an unofficial publication containing the French texts of four decisions with an introduction by J. H. W. Verzijl. A dissenting opinion rendered by the Mexican Commissioner in one of these cases is omitted.

FORM OF CITATION

The titles of cases are given as they appear in the official reports. The form of these differs in the various Commissions. Unpublished cases are cited by the number of the decision. It is to be noted that cases decided by the French-Mexican Commission are called "Sentences" following the practice of the Commission which used the term "Decisions" for administrative decisions.

THE MEXICAN CLAIMS COMMISSIONS

1923–1934

CHAPTER 1

HISTORICAL PRELUDE

§1. **Importance of Claims in Mexican History.** The subject of the claims of foreign nationals plays a more important part in the history of the foreign relations of Mexico than in that of any other country. Indeed, it might almost be possible to write that history in terms of international claims. The primary reason for the inordinate importance of this subject in Mexican foreign relations is undoubtedly to be found in the troubled history of Mexico. Where revolution followed upon revolution and governments were sometimes as transitory as the seasons of the year, the lives and property of aliens were subjected to peril in a greater degree than in countries with a more stable political system. On the other hand, the claims which revolutionary disturbances created were sometimes seized upon by foreign states as a pretext for furthering territorial ambitions and economic imperialism. The undeveloped riches of Mexico's natural resources attracted hordes of adventurers to whom the opportunity of collecting on a large claim against the government was an attractive alternative to slower methods of making profits. The military inferiority of Mexico and the subserviency to foreign interests of some transitory government occasionally led to the acknowledgment of fraudulent or inflated claims. Such acquiescence would embitter Mexican public opinion and lead to further antagonism to aliens. The chronic difficulties of the Mexican treasury would make it difficult to liquidate the claims, and the net result would be an increase of ill-feeling between the two countries.

In such circumstances, the submission of claims to an international tribunal offered a way out. Indeed, it may be said that this method of settlement was the only one which reached fairly satisfactory results, though the course of these arbitrations was often a troubled one. Yet, only the history of the relations between the United States and Mexico shows a constant endeavor to resort to this means of settlement.

I

MEXICO AND THE UNITED STATES

§2. **Claims between Mexico and the United States.** The outstanding chapter in the history of foreign claims against Mexico is that of the claims of the United States.[1] Obviously, the proximity of the two countries and the presence of considerable numbers of citizens of the United States in Mexico rendered relations between the two countries particularly sensitive to revolutionary disturbances. Moreover, the disparity in economic and military power between these two neighbors often fostered a greater readiness on the part of the United States to advance claims than the latter would have evinced with regard to more distant or more powerful countries. In the early decades of relations between Mexico and the United States, the latter harbored territorial ambitions in Mexico, and often the support of claims for injury to American citizens was employed as an instrument of pressure to further such territorial designs. Later, when American capital had come to play an important part in Mexican economy, American interests were peculiarly exposed to the vicissitudes of violent political change. Alternating periods of mutual sympathy and distrust in American and Mexican public opinion influenced the vigor with which claims were pressed by the United States and the desire exhibited by Mexico to grant satisfaction to such claims. All these imponderables exercised not only a quantitative influence but were of great importance in determining the legal positions taken by the respective governments.

§3. **United States–Mexican Claims, 1825–1839.** The diplomatic representation of the United States in Mexico began in 1825 with the sending of Joel Poinsett as Minister. In the very next year Poinsett had begun to protest vigorously over the enforcement of Mexican customs regulations in regard to American merchants.[2] During the next decade the claims of the United States against Mexico continued to increase. It was alleged that American vessels had been fired upon, American citizens illegally arrested and maltreated and their property arbitrarily confiscated.[3] Relations between the two countries became

---

[1] On this section see Dunn, The Diplomatic Protection of Americans in Mexico (New York, 1933); Rippy, The United States and Mexico (New York, 1926); Callahan, American Foreign Policy in Mexican Relations (New York, 1932).

[2] Manning, Early Diplomatic Relations between the United States and Mexico (Baltimore, 1918), Ch. VIII.

[3] Dunn, Diplomatic Protection, pp. 18, 19, 20, citing: Butler to McLane, No. 49, July 26, 1833, MS. Desp. Mex., Vol. 6; Butler to McLane, No. 56, Oct. 25, 1833, MS. Desp. Mex., Vol. 6; Instructions of Secretary Forsyth to Ellis, No. 3, Jan. 29, 1836, MS. Inst. Mex., Vol. 15.

increasingly embittered as a consequence of the revolt in Texas. During 1836, the American Minister to Mexico, Ellis, attempted to conclude an agreement for settlement of these claims, but the Mexican government hesitated.[4] By 1837, matters had gone so far that President Jackson in a special message to Congress proposed legislation authorizing the use of the naval forces of the United States to obtain satisfaction for outstanding claims if the Mexican government refused an amicable settlement.[5] Finally, on the proposal of Mexico that the claims be submitted to arbitration,[6] a claims convention was signed April 11, 1839.[7]

§4. The Claims Convention of 1839. Mexico had attempted to include in this convention claims of Mexico against the United States arising out of the support given to the revolt in Texas.[8] The United States declined this proposal, and the convention provided only for the submission of claims arising from injuries to the persons and property of citizens of the United States by Mexican authorities to a board composed of four members; two to be named by the President of each country. Within a period of eighteen months, the Commissioners were to decide upon the justice of the claims and the amount of compensation, if any, due from the Mexican government. In case of difference between the Commissioners, the King of Prussia was to act as Umpire.

Seventy-two cases were finally disposed of under this convention. Eleven awards totalling $439,393.82 were made by the Commissioners and four cases rejected. Fifty-seven cases were referred to the Umpire, who, in fifty-three cases awarded $1,586,745.86, and rejected four cases.[9] The period of eighteen months proved to be too short, and many claims remained undisposed of, a festering focus of irritation for another decade.

§5. The Claims Convention of 1843. In addition to these unsettled claims, it was found to be impossible for Mexico to pay the

---

[4] Dunn, Diplomatic Protection, pp. 22, 23, citing: Ellis to Monasterio, Sept. 25, 1836, enclosure with Ellis to Forsyth, No. 25, Oct. 11, 1836, MS. Desp. Mex., Vol. 7; Monasterio to Ellis, Nov. 15, 1836, enclosure with Ellis to Forsyth, No. 43, Dec. 22, 1836, MS. Desp. Mex., Vol. 8.

[5] Message of Feb. 6, 1827, 3 Richardson, Messages and Papers of the Presidents, p. 278.

[6] Dunn, Diplomatic Protection, p. 26.

[7] 1 Malloy, United States Treaties and Conventions, p. 1101.

[8] 2 Moore, International Arbitrations, p. 1217.

[9] For an account of the work of the Commission of 1839, see Moore, International Arbitrations, p. 1209 et seq. A rather prejudiced recital of the difficulties in the work of the Commission will be found in Cox, Review of the Relations between the United States and Mexico, and of the Claims of the Citizens of the United States against Mexico (1846), p. 62 et seq.

amounts awarded by the Board of Commissioners.[10] On January 30, 1843, a convention was concluded postponing the payment of the awards and binding the two governments to negotiate a new convention for the settlement of the outstanding claims *of the government and citizens of each country against the other*.[11] Though the convention was ratified by both governments, objection arose in the United States to the submission of claims by one government against the other since this would enable the subject of Mexican claims for American support of the Texas revolt to be opened up.[12] A claims convention concluded on November 20, 1843,[13] was ratified by the United States with a reservation which struck out the provision regarding the submission of governmental claims. In view of this reservation, the Mexican government declined to ratify the new claims convention.[14]

§6. The Texas Question. In 1845, the United States annexed Texas, and the subject of settlement of claims became entangled in a web of territorial questions. During 1845 and 1846, the United States attempted to secure a release of Mexico's claim to Texas in return for the assumption by the United States of American claims against Mexico. Additional proposals of cash payments in return for a cession of California were made. The Mexican government refused steadfastly.[15]

§7. The Treaty of Guadalupe Hidalgo and Claims Subsequent Thereto. The next year marked the outbreak of war between Mexico and the United States. The treaty which ended the war (signed at Guadalupe Hidalgo, February 2, 1848) [16] provided for the assumption by the United States of the liquidated claims under the Convention of 1839, and for the satisfaction by the United States of all other claims against Mexico arising prior to the signature of the Treaty of Peace to an amount not exceeding $3,250,000. The United States agreed to set up a board of commissioners to pass on the unliquidated claims. This board was established by the Act of March 3, 1849 [17] and three

---

[10] Dunn, Diplomatic Protection, p. 33.

[11] 1 Malloy, United States Treaties and Conventions, p. 1106.

[12] Dunn, Diplomatic Protection, p. 36.

[13] See Message of the President Transmitting Correspondence Relative to the Claims of Citizens of the United States upon the Mexican Government, House Doc. No. 158, 28th Cong., 2d Sess. (1845).

[14] Dunn, Diplomatic Protection, pp. 40, 42.

[15] Dunn, Diplomatic Protection, pp. 46, 48, citing: Buchanan to Slidell, No. 1, Nov. 10, 1845, MS. Inst. Mex., Vol. 16; Buchanan to Slidell, No. 7, Mar. 12, 1846, MS. Inst. Mex., Vol. 16.

[16] 1 Malloy, United States Treaties and Conventions, p. 1093.   [17] 9 Stat. 393.

commissioners were appointed by the President of the United States. The board awarded $3,208,314.96 in 198 cases and rejected seventy claims.[17a]

No sooner was the Treaty of Guadalupe Hildalgo signed than a new crop of claims began to spring up. American capital had begun to seek a field for investment in Mexico, and the first important claim based on contract had arisen, through the cancellation by Mexico of a concession granted for the building of a railway across the Isthmus of Tehuantepec.[18] In addition, Mexico had advanced a large number of claims against the United States as a result of depredations committed by Indian raids from across the American border, the United States having agreed to suppress such raids under Article 11 of the Treaty of Guadalupe Hidalgo. Again the question of territorial expansion intruded a further complication, the United States desiring to secure a large area on its southwestern boundary.[19]

§8. From the Gadsden Treaty of 1854 to the McLane–Ocampo Treaty of 1859. In 1854, the American Minister Gadsden concluded with Mexico a treaty calling for the cession of certain territory by Mexico and the payment by the United States of fifteen million dollars in consideration of the cession and the extinction of the obligation of the United States under Article 11 of the Treaty of Guadalupe Hidalgo, and of five million dollars in consideration of the assumption by the United States of private claims.[20] However, the United States Senate struck out the provision relating to the settlement of claims.[21] The succeeding years brought forth proposal after proposal by the United States looking toward a settlement; usually coupled with suggestions for further cession of territory.[22] In 1857, the American Minister Forsyth, concluded a claims convention, which was never submitted to the United States Senate.[23] Meanwhile, claims continued to pile up, President Buchanan, in his annual message of 1858, estimating

[17a] See Moore, International Arbitrations, p. 1248 et seq.; Report of the Select Committee of the Senate in Relation to the Proceedings of the Board of Commissioners on the Claims against Mexico, Senate Rep. No. 182, 33rd Cong., 1st Sess. (1854).
[18] See Rippy, The United States and Mexico, p. 42 et seq.
[19] Ibid., p. 68 et seq.
[20] For a very full discussion of the negotiation and ratification of the Gadsden Treaty see ibid., Ch. VII and VIII.
[21] 1 Malloy, United States Treaties and Conventions, p. 1121.
[22] Dunn, Diplomatic Protection, pp. 74, 75; Rippy, The United States and Mexico, p. 214.
[23] Dunn, Diplomatic Protection, pp. 78–79.

them to amount to over $10,000,000.[24] In 1859, the famous McLane-Ocampo Treaty was concluded with Mexico in which the United States in return for certain economic and commercial concessions agreed to pay to Mexico $4,000,000, one-half of which was to be retained in satisfaction of American claims. The United States Senate refused to consent to ratification.[25]

§9. The Claims Convention of 1868. The support given by the United States to republican institutions in Mexico during the French intervention and the episode of the Empire of Maximilian, together with a cessation of American territorial ambitions after the extinction of the slavery issue, led to a comparatively easy conclusion of a claims convention on July 4, 1868.[26] All claims of the citizens of either country against the government of the other arising since the signature of the Treaty of Guadalupe Hidalgo were to be submitted to two commissioners, one to be appointed by each government, these commissioners to name a third person as umpire to decide in case of difference between the commissioners. Before this Commission the United States filed 1,017 claims totalling $470,126,613.40, the Commission awarding $4,125,622.20 in 186 cases and rejecting 831 claims. Mexico filed 998 claims totalling $86,661,891.15, the Commission awarding $150,498.41 in 167 cases and rejecting 831 claims.[27]

The Commission established under the Convention of 1868 terminated its labors on January 31, 1867. The first installment on its awards which fell due on January 31, 1877, was promptly paid by the government of Porfirio Díaz which had come into power shortly before. In the meantime new claims by American citizens against Mexico had been accumulating, particularly as a result of the unsuccessful Díaz revolutions of 1871 and 1872. As a condition to the recognition of the Díaz government, the United States urged the conclusion of another claims convention to settle these new claims.[28] The refusal of the Díaz government delayed recognition for a time, but eventually recognition was extended without the conclusion of such a convention.

[24] Message of Dec. 6, 1858, 5 Richardson, Messages and Papers of the Presidents, p. 512.
[25] Dunn, Diplomatic Protection, pp. 89–90.
[26] 1 Malloy, United States Treaties and Conventions, p. 1128.
[27] For an account of the work of this Commission see 2 Moore, International Arbitrations, p. 1292 et seq.
[28] Dunn, Diplomatic Protection, p. 116, citing: Foster to Evarts, Nos. 558 and 559, June 23, 1877, MS. Desp. Mex., Vol. 59.

§10. **The Díaz Régime.** The thirty-five years of the Díaz régime represented a period of tranquillity in Mexico under a government which exhibited marked hospitality to foreign capital. From time to time claims of American citizens were presented but these were either disposed of through diplomatic channels or permitted to stagnate in Foreign Office files. No further attempt was made to conclude a claims convention until the Díaz régime was brought to an end by the Madero revolt in 1910.

MEXICO AND FRANCE

§11. **The Pastry War.** The problems created by the claims of French nationals against Mexico were serious enough to lead to two wars. The first of these was the so-called Pastry War of 1838.[29] In 1828 a mob had sacked the shops of several French nationals in Mexico City (including the shop of a pastry baker). Negotiations for the settlement of the claims arising out of this event led to no satisfactory results. Mexico proposed arbitration by a third state. The French government rejected this proposition as "laughable." The dignity and the duties of France "could not permit it to leave to a third party (even as regards form, since there could not be two opinions on questions of this kind among civilized nations) the decision as to whether the spoliations, violence and assassinations which its citizenry had suffered could or could not be the subject of sufficient reparation." [30] In 1838 diplomatic relations were broken off and a French fleet was despatched to blockade Mexican ports. The capture of the fortress of San Juan de Ulúa and of the Mexican fleet put an end to the war.

§12. **The Treaty of Peace of 1839.** The treaty of peace signed March 9, 1839,[31] provided for reference to the arbitration of a third power of the questions as to whether Mexico could claim from France the restitution of, or compensation for, the Mexican war vessels captured by the French forces, and whether indemnities should be granted to French nationals who had been expelled from France during the war, and to Mexican nationals who had suffered as a result of the

---

[29] See 5 Bancroft, History of Mexico (San Francisco, 1885), Ch. VIII.
[30] Ultimatum of March 21, 1838, quoted in 1 Lapradelle et Politis, *Recueil des arbitrages internationaux* (Paris, 1905), p. 546. For a criticism of the French position see Lauterpacht, The Function of Law in the International Community (London, 1933), p. 160.
[31] 1 *Derecho internacional mexicano* (Mexico, 1878), p. 415; 29 British and Foreign State Papers, p. 222.

hostilities. A further convention of the same date [32] provided for the payment of 600,000 pesos by Mexico in satisfaction of French claims which had accrued prior to November 26, 1838.

The questions provided for in the Treaty of 1839 were referred to the Queen of Great Britain who handed down an award on August 1, 1844,[33] deciding that France was not bound to make restitution of the captured vessels, and that neither the claims of Mexican nor of French nationals subsequent to November 26, 1838, should be allowed because the injuries complained of resulted from the state of war existing between the two countries.

§13. The Jecker Claims and the Intervention of 1861. In the succeeding decade interest shifted to problems arising out of the Mexican public debt. In 1851, the Mexican government concluded two agreements with the French Minister acknowledging certain debts due to Jecker and Company (a Swiss banking house) and to Serment P. Fort and Company, payment being secured by an assignment of part of the custom's receipts.[34] Subsequently a further assignment was made to secure these and other claims.[35] During the Juárez revolution, the counter-revolutionary government of General Miramón contracted for a loan from Jecker's bank under which, in return for some 1,000,000 pesos in cash and goods, it turned over to the bank bonds amounting to 15,000,000 pesos.[36] When Juárez captured the capital in 1860 he refused to recognize this debt.[37] The following year a law was passed suspending payments for two years on all Mexican obligations. The French, British and Spanish governments immediately broke off diplomatic relations, and on October 31, 1861, concluded a convention for joint intervention in Mexico to enforce their claims.[38]

The intervention began as a joint one in January 1862, but on April 16 France declared war on Mexico. Thus began the adventure which led to the creation of Maximilian's Mexican empire and which

---

[32] 1 *Derecho internacional mexicano*, p. 420; 29 British and Foreign State Papers, p. 224. By an Ordinance of Nov. 30, 1839, the French government set up a commission to pass on the claims of French nationals and distribute the sum paid by Mexico. 29 British and Foreign State Papers, p. 226.

[33] La Fontaine, *Pasicrisie internationale* (Berne, 1902), p. 21. For a criticism of the award see Lapradelle and Politis, *op. cit.*, p. 560 *et seq.*

[34] Turlington, Mexico and her Foreign Creditors (New York, 1930), p. 102.

[35] *Ibid.*, p. 103.

[36] *Ibid.*, p. 117.

[37] *Ibid.*, p. 128.

[38] 51 British and Foreign State Papers, p. 63.

ended when Maximilian was executed by Juárez's soldiers in June 1867.[39]

§14. Claims Conventions of the Government of Maximilian with France. Maximilian's government concluded several conventions relating to claims. By the Convention of April 10, 1864,[40] Mexico agreed to indemnify French subjects for the injuries they had suffered and which had brought about the intervention. The claims were to be submitted to a Commission of three French and three Mexican nationals. After being passed upon by this Commission they were to be submitted for liquidation to a Commission of two French and two Mexican nationals sitting in Paris. A Convention of September 27, 1865, modified May 8, 1866,[41] fixed the total sum due to French claimants at 40,000,000 pesos. Bonds to the par value of 16,440,000 pesos were delivered to the French Government; the balance to be paid later.

§15. Renunciation of French Claims. These conventions were repudiated by the Juárez government soon after it regained power. Diplomatic relations between the two countries were interrupted until 1880. When, in that year France recognized the Díaz government, it agreed not to bring forward or sustain any claims against Mexico arising before the resumption of relations.[42] In 1889 this waiver was re-enforced by a formal statement of the French government.[43]

MEXICO AND GREAT BRITAIN

§16. Claims between Mexico and Great Britain. The history of the relations between Mexico and Great Britain has centered largely around the claims of British bondholders, but claims of other British subjects have also played a part. During the Mexican struggle for independence, quantities of Mexican bonds were sold to British subjects. When the service on these bonds fell into arrears the bondholders appealed for assistance to the British government in 1829.[44] This was refused, but in 1830 the assistance of the British diplomatic

---

[39] The literature on the French intervention is voluminous. See among others, Lefêvre, *Histoire de l'intervention française au Mexique*, 2 vols. (Brussels and London, 1869); *Correspondencia de la legacion mexicana en Washington durante la intervencion extranjera*, 10 vols. (Mexico, 1870–1892); *La intervencion francesa en México*, 10 vols. (Mexico, 1907–1910); Papers relative to Mexican Affairs. Communicated to the Senate June 16, 1894 (Washington, 1865).

[40] 54 British and Foreign State Papers, p. 944.

[41] 2 *Derecho internacional mexicano*, p. 370.

[42] *Correspondencia cambiada entre el gobierno de los Estados Mexicanos y los de varias Potencias Extranjeras*, pp. 180–185.

[43] Turlington, *op. cit.*, p. 217.   [44] *Ibid.*, p. 57.

and consular representatives was given to aid in the transfer of funds to be applied in payment of the debts under an agreement between the Mexican government and the bondholders.[45]

§17. **Claims Conventions from 1842 to 1859.** On various subsequent occasions when the Mexican debt service was suspended, the British government made representations.[46] Meanwhile other claims continued to accrue. Finally, on October 15, 1842, a convention [47] was concluded between the British Minister to Mexico and the Mexican Ministers of Finance and Foreign Affairs under which a charge was placed on the customs duties for the benefit of British subjects to whom the Mexican government acknowledged a liability of 306,931.44 pesos. Still the claims continued to grow. On December 4, 1851, the so-called Doyle Convention [48] was concluded under which Mexico agreed to pay some 5,000,000 pesos for the adjustment of claims and for the redemption of certain bonds of the internal debt. Assignments of customs duties were made under an agreement concluded with the British Minister in 1852,[49] and further Conventions in regard to payment were concluded in 1858 [50] and 1859.[51]

§18. **The Intervention of 1861.** The financial situation of Mexico continued to grow worse and in 1858 the Juárez revolution broke out. In 1860 the Miramón government seized 660,000 pesos which had been placed under official seal in the British legation for the account of British bondholders.[52] The Juárez government refused to recognize a claim for this seizure; in July 1861 payment on all Mexican obligations was suspended, and in October of the same year the British government entered into a treaty of intervention with France and Spain.[53] Nevertheless, a convention was signed on November 21, 1861,[54] relating to the payment of British claims. When ratification was refused by the Mexican Congress, the intervention went forward.

§19. **The Claims Convention of 1862.** The intervention did not prevent the conclusion of a claims convention between Great Britain and the Juárez government on April 28, 1862.[55] The British government failed to ratify this convention, but it is worth notice both for its unusual character and because it was the first attempt to refer

[45] 28 British and Foreign State Papers, p. 971.
[46] 28 ibid., pp. 973–975.
[47] 41 ibid., p. 738.
[48] 41 ibid., p. 740.
[49] 41 ibid., p. 751.
[50] 52 ibid., p. 363.
[51] 49 ibid., p. 1253.
[52] Turlington, op. cit., p. 117.
[53] See supra, p. 8.
[54] 52 British and Foreign State Papers, p. 405.
[55] 53 ibid., 373.

British claims against Mexico to an international tribunal. The claims were to be submitted to a Commission, two of whose members were to be selected by the British and Mexican governments, these Commissioners in turn to name a third person as umpire. After passing on the claims the Commissioners were to issue to the claimants certificates of the sums to be paid, and payment was to be made by the *British* government out of a fund of 2,000,000 pesos to be placed at its disposal in orders on the Treasury of the United States. The reason for this curious arrangement was that a treaty had been concluded between Mexico and the United States [56] providing for a loan of $9,000,000 with a mortgage of certain parts of Mexican territory as security. To guard against the failure to ratify this treaty, the British-Mexican Convention provided that "if the American loan should not be forthcoming the property that has been assigned to the United States by the Treaty . . . shall be converted into cash for the payment of the British claims." An additional article, stipulated on May 12, 1862,[57] provided that the British government could employ its armed forces for the occupation of Mexican ports if the customs authorities failed to pay over the money due under the Convention.

§20. **The Claims Convention of 1866.** After the failure to ratify the Convention of 1862, the British government concluded another Convention with the government of Maximilian on June 26, 1866.[58] A Commission of five was to be set up to pass upon the claims. Only such claims were to be admitted "for which the Mexican government is responsible in accordance with generally admitted principles of international law, and which are in origin, continuity and actuality British." A Convention of October 27, 1866,[59] provided for the issue of bonds by the Mexican government to be exchanged for certificates given by the Commission to the claimants. The Commission sat in Mexico City from August 1866 until March 1867,[60] but it does not appear that any awards were handed down.

[56] See House Executive Document, No. 100, 37th Cong., 2d Sess., 1862, p. 15. This treaty was never ratified.
[57] 53 British and Foreign State Papers, p. 590.
[58] Text published in Memorandum as to How Far Her Majesty's Government are Bound to Support the Claims of British Subjects against Mexico, Foreign Office, Nov. 5, 1881 (Confidential. 4554), p. 19.
[59] 2 *Derecho internacional mexicano*, p. 381.
[60] The Law Officers of the Crown to Earl Granville, Jan. 22, 1884, Further Correspondence Respecting the Renewal of Diplomatic Relations with Mexico, 1884 (Confidential. 5109), p. 2.

§21. **The Settlement of 1884.** From 1867 to 1884 diplomatic relations between Mexico and Great Britain were suspended. They were renewed after the signing, on August 6, 1884, of an Agreement [61] under which Mexico undertook to order an impartial investigation to be made with respect to the pecuniary claims of British subjects based on acts anterior to the exchange of ratifications and to provide for the liquidation of amounts which might be found due as well as for the payments of the claims already recognized by Mexico.[62] Great Britain undertook a similar obligation with respect to the claims of Mexicans against it. At the same time the British Commissioner who signed the Agreement declared that the British government would not invoke in the future "any convention, pact or arrangement for all time anterior to the exchange of ratifications." [63]

The Agreement was ratified by the Mexican Senate on October 21, 1884, with the statement that "the examination, liquidation and payment of the credits of British subjects will be exclusively subject to the dispositions of the laws of Mexico in regard to the settlement of the Public Debt." [64] To this the British government replied that while it admitted the statement it considered "that if the Mexican government should omit to make the inquiry and liquidation provided for in Article I it would be a breach of the Agreement against which Her Majesty's government distinctly reserve their right to protest." [65]

MEXICO AND SPAIN

§22. **The Spanish Claims Fund.** The independence of Mexico was recognized by Spain in the Treaty of December 28, 1836.[66] This Treaty provided for a waiver of all claims by each country against the other in view of the Mexican law of June 28, 1824, by which Mexico had assumed all debts contracted upon the treasury of New

---

[61] 75 British and Foreign State Papers, p. 908.

[62] In 1862 the claims of British subjects against Mexico, excluding the claims of bondholders, were classified as follows: claims recognized by the Mexican government 1,350,833.71 pesos; claims not yet recognized but apparently based on just grounds 849,174.51 pesos; claims supported by the British government 802,411.81. It was pointed out that this "did not represent a final total of the amount of British claims against the Mexican government." Parliamentary Paper No. 727. During the negotiations preliminary to the renewal of relations, the British government submitted, in 1881, a draft Convention referring the claims to a mixed commission. Correspondence Respecting the Renewal of Diplomatic Relations with Mexico, 188–83 (Confidential. 4945), p. 39.

[63] Further Correspondence, *supra*, note 60, p. 34.

[64] *Ibid.*, p. 46.

[65] *Ibid.*, p. 50.

[66] 24 British and Foreign State Papers, p. 864.

Spain prior to 1821. The financial difficulties of Mexico during the succeeding decade led to the conclusion of a Convention on July 17, 1847,[67] which set up a Spanish Claims Fund consisting of 3% of the customs duties. This fund was to be utilized to pay debts of Spanish subjects against Mexico. Claims for confiscation of property and forced loans were to form the subject of special arrangements between the two governments. On November 14, 1851, a Convention [68] was signed providing for the liquidation of these latter claims, as well as for claims of Spanish subjects arising from debts contracted by the treasury of New Spain before 1821. They were to be submitted to the examination of the Spanish Minister to Mexico and the Mexican Minister for Foreign Affairs. After these two officials had agreed on the validity of the claims, they were to be submitted for liquidation to a Commission of three Mexicans. Payment was to be made in bonds delivered to the Spanish government.[69] Certain differences of opinion in regard to the allowance of interest and method of payment of these claims were settled by a Convention of November 12, 1853.[70]

§23. The Convention of 1859. Controversy soon sprang up again in regard to the ownership of various claims submitted under these treaties, leading at one point to the dispatch of a Spanish naval expedition to Vera Cruz.[71] Negotiations tending toward a revision of the Conventions were under way when on December 5, 1856, five Spanish subjects were assassinated.[72] The controversy was reopened again. Finally, on September 26, 1859, the Miramón government concluded a Convention agreeing to indemnify the Spanish subjects injured by the events of December 15, 1856, the amount of the indemnity to be fixed by the French and British governments, and re-establishing the Treaty of 1853 "in all its force and vigor." [73]

§24. The Pacheco Incident and the Intervention of 1861. The Juárez government which captured Mexico City in 1860 felt especially bitter towards the Spanish Ambassador Pacheco whom it accused of having given active support to the rival Miramón government. Among the first acts of Juárez was to hand Pacheco his passports and to

[67] 48 *ibid.*, p. 1301.   [68] 48 *ibid.*, p. 1303.
[69] On Dec. 6, 1851, a Convention was concluded between Spain and Mexico in regard to the claim of Padre Moran, a British subject in charge of certain church interests. 48 *ibid.*, p. 745.
[70] 48 *ibid.*, p. 1307.   [71] See 48 *ibid.*, p. 1311.
[72] 48 *ibid.*, p. 1320 *et seq.* See Lafragua, *Memorandum de los negocios pendientes entre México y España* (Poissy, 1857).
[73] 51 British and Foreign State Papers, p. 926.

declare that Mexico was not bound by the Convention of 1859 "because it was immoral; and because if he acted otherwise, he would have recognized that the reactionary administration had the right to contract in the name of the Republic and to engage its responsibility."[74] These acts led directly to Spanish participation in the tripartite treaty of intervention of October 31, 1861.[75]

After the fall of Maximilian, Juárez declared publicly that Mexico considered its treaties with the intervening powers no longer in force.[76] This declaration was repeated to the Spanish government in 1869 during the negotiations for the renewal of diplomatic relations.[77] Nevertheless, in 1877 a deputy in the Spanish Cortes raised the question as to the subsistence of the Treaty of 1853. The Mexican government protested that it had gone out of force and the Spanish government apparently decided not to press the point.[78]

[74] I Lefêvre, *Histoire de l'intervention française au Mexique*, p. 28.
[75] See *supra*, p. 8, and *de Arboleya, España y Mejico*, 2 vols. (Habana, 1861–1862).
[76] De la Peña y Reyes, *La insubstancia de una convencion de reclamaciones* (Mexico, 1928), p. xxvii.
[77] *Ibid.*, p. 109.
[78] De la Peña y Reyes, *op. cit.*, contains a full documentation of this controversy.

CHAPTER 2

THE MEXICAN REVOLUTIONS OF 1910–1920
AND THE NEGOTIATION OF THE
CLAIMS CONVENTIONS

§25. **The Mexican Revolutions and the Revival of the Subject of Claims.** In 1910 a revolution aimed at the government of Porfirio Díaz ushered in a decade of violence and turmoil for Mexico. Madero, who assumed the presidency in 1911, was overthrown by Huerta in 1913. The Huerta government was in turn faced by revolts led by Carranza, Villa and Zapata. Carranza succeeded in gaining power in 1914, but was overthrown by Obregón in 1920. During this period the United States occupied Vera Cruz and sent an expeditionary force into Mexico in pursuit of Villa. The stake of foreign nationals, particularly of those of the United States, had increased to such an extent that a period of political instability reacted with increased force on their interests.[1] It was inevitable that the subject of claims which had become dormant during the Díaz régime should be revived.

---

[1] "In 1912, Marion Letcher, United States consul at Chihuahua, placed the total American investment at $1,057,770,000 and the British at $321,301,800. As Mexico's total wealth at that time was $2,434,241,422, American investors apparently owned half of it. This investment, according to a subsequent estimate [by the Bureau of Foreign and Domestic Commerce in 1924] was divided approximately as follows:

Oil lands and refineries	478 million
Mines and smelters	300 million
Agricultural and timber lands	200 million
Railroads	160 million
Manufacturing	60 million
Wholesale and retail stores	50 million
Governmental bonds (not including state and municipal bonds)	22 million
Banks, telephones, and telegraphs, light and power companies, tramways	10 million."

Gruening, Mexico and its Heritage (New York, 1928), 559–560.

In 1931, the Bureau of Foreign and Domestic Commerce estimated the total of American direct investments in Mexico at $672,500,000. This estimate took into account the depreciation of the value of petroleum properties, the destruction of property in the revolutionary disturbances, and expropriation of agrarian lands. American Direct Investments

§26. **The Consultative Claims Commission of 1911.** Soon after the accession of Madero, the diplomatic representatives in Mexico of various states began to press upon the new government the necessity of adjusting the claims which had arisen in consequence of the revolution of 1910.[2] The Mexican government responded promptly by setting up a Consultative Claims Commission in June 1911.[3] For a time this satisfied the foreign states, and the United States Department of State called the attention of claimants to the existence of this Commission and suggested that they submit their claims to it.[4] Throughout the ensuing year this Commission considered claims submitted to it and handed down various awards. However, its activities proved most unsatisfactory to the states concerned. The Commission worked slowly, and the Mexican government had taken the position that it could not be held responsible for injuries suffered at the hands of rebels.[5] In fact, only one indemnity was paid during the Madero régime, that being on a German claim which had been the subject of diplomatic negotiations.[6] On August 9, 1912, the United States Congress, by joint resolution, authorized the Secretary of War to appoint a Commission to investigate the claims of American citizens.[7]

§27. **Early Negotiations for Arbitral Tribunals.** The first suggestion for an arbitral tribunal seems to have been made during an interview between Wilson, the American Ambassador to Mexico, and the Mexican Minister for Foreign Affairs in December 1912.[8] The suggestion came from Wilson and only a slight hint of an agreement by the Mexican Minister appears. The Department of State rejected

---

in Foreign Countries, Trade Information Bulletin No. 731 (Washington, 1931), pp. 21–22. A subsequent estimate made in the same year placed the total at $694,576,000. A New Estimate of American Investments Abroad, Trade Information Bulletin No. 767 (Washington, 1931), p. 16. The estimate of investments as of December 31, 1933, was $635,000,-000. The Balance of International Payments of the United States in 1933, Trade Information Bulletin No. 819 (Washington, 1934), p. 56.

[2] Ambassador Wilson to the Secretary of State of the United States, June 7, 1911, 1912 Foreign Relations of the United States, p. 929.

[3] Spanish text in Mariano Salas, *Defensa de Mexico*, p. 61 (Mexico 1920); English translation of the Rules of the Commission in 1912 Foreign Relations, p. 934. The convention of Ciudad Juarez of May 21, 1911, by which Díaz had renounced the Presidency had provided that the new government would accord indemnity for damages caused by the revolution. See Mariano Salas, *op. cit.*, p. 59.

[4] See Circular to American Claimants, Oct. 12, 1911, 1912 Foreign Relations, p. 944.

[5] See 1912 *ibid.*, p. 951 *et seq.*

[6] Chargé d'Affairs O'Shaughnessy to the Secretary of State of the United States, Sept. 1, 1912, 1913 *ibid.*, p. 950. It is there said that the German Minister was stated to have threatened that a warship would be sent to Vera Cruz by the German government if the claims were not settled.

[7] 1912 *ibid.*, p. 966.   [8] 1912 *ibid.*, p. 985.

the suggestion, deeming "it best at present to press individual cases as occasion requires pending that future time when a general settlement with Mexico may be necessary." [9] But after the Madero government had been overthrown by Huerta, Secretary of State Knox instructed Ambassador Wilson to request "that the Mexican government agree in principle to the settlement of all claims resulting in the loss of life by American citizens and damages to American property on account of the recent political disturbances in Mexico by presentation to a mixed international commission which shall award damages therefor." [10]

This position was soon taken up by all the governments concerned. Various members of the Diplomatic Corps having expressed the opinion that an international claims commission ought to be insisted on,[11] a meeting was held between the Mexican Subsecretary for Foreign Affairs and the diplomatic representatives of Spain, France, Great Britain, Italy, Belgium, Germany and Austria-Hungary. There the Mexican Subsecretary advanced a proposal for a new Mexican national claims commission to deal only with the claims of aliens. The foreign representatives present announced that their instructions were to suggest the creation of an international commission, but undertook to transmit the proposal.[12]

§28. The Carranza Decree of 1913. Meanwhile, General Carranza, then Chief of the Constitutionalist Army operating against Huerta, had issued a decree on May 10, 1913,[13] providing for the future creation of a Mexican national claims commission and also of a mixed commission to be appointed by Carranza himself after conferring with the diplomatic representatives of the governments concerned.

§29. Promises of the Carranza Government. When the Carranza government was established, it made great efforts to secure recognition. On June 11, 1915, Carranza declared publicly that the Constitutionalist government would allow to foreigners residing in Mexico "indemnities for the damage which the revolution may have

---

[9] 1913 ibid., p. 924.   [10] 1913 ibid., p. 729.
[11] Ambassador Wilson to the Secretary of State of the United States, March 31, 1913, 1913 ibid., p. 946.
[12] Minutes of the meeting held on July 22, 1913, 1913 ibid., p. 951. The proposal of Mexico was definitely rejected by France and Russia, 1913 ibid., p. 956.
[13] Spanish text in Mariano Salas, op. cit., p. 66; English translation in 1914 Foreign Relations, p. 655.

caused them, in so far as such indemnities may be just, and which are to be determined by a procedure to be established later." [14] On October 19, 1915, *de facto* recognition was accorded to the government of Carranza by the United States, following his declaration that he would "recognize and satisfy indemnities for damages caused by the revolution which shall be settled in due time in terms of justice." [15]

§30. **The American–Mexican Commission of 1916–1917.** The outbreak of violence along the United States–Mexican border in 1916 and the despatch of an American punitive expedition against Villa turned attention away from the question of the settlement of claims. From September 1916 to January 1917 a joint American-Mexican Commission discussed outstanding difficulties between the two countries. The American Commissioners proposed that the Mexican government agree in principle to the establishment of a Mixed Claims Commission, [16] but the conferences broke up without result as a consequence of the failure to agree on the immediate withdrawal of American troops from Mexico.

§31. **The National Claims Commission Legislation of 1917.** On November 24, 1917, the Carranza government enacted a decree setting up a National Claims Commission. [17] The United States objected to certain features of the decree and several other foreign governments entertained decided doubts. [18] Moreover the chief concern of the United States government was now with claims arising out of the Mexican legislation relating to mineral resources and agrarian reform under the Constitution of 1917 rather than with claims for injuries by acts of officials and soldiers. [19]

[14] Manifesto to the Nation, 1914 Foreign Relations, p. 705.

[15] Confidential Agent Arrendondo to the Secretary of State of the United States, Oct. 7, 1915, 1915 *ibid.*, p. 763. The Confidential Agent of the opposing Conventionist Government in a letter to the Secretary of State, Sept. 22, 1915, protested that any obligation entered into by Carranza would lack validity, and stated that the Conventionist Government "admits and accepts as a fact the settlement" of the claims. 1915 *ibid.*, p. 836.

[16] 1917 *ibid.*, p. 921.

[17] Spanish text in 1917 *Leyes y Decretos,* II, p. 181, English translation in 1918 Foreign Relations, p. 793. For subsequent legislation in regard to the National Claims Commission and a discussion of its activities, see below, p. 202.

[18] See 1918 Foreign Relations, p. 800 *et seq;* 1919, II Foreign Relations, p. 632 *et seq.* On July 9, 1919, the Department of State issued a statement to the press warning American claimants that the United States Government "has not advised American claimants to present their claims against Mexico to this Commission." *Ibid.*, p. 636.

[19] On the controversy relating to Mexican petroleum and agrarian legislation see Dunn, Diplomatic Protection, Ch. XI and XII. See also the report of a subcommittee of the Committee on Foreign Relations of the United States Senate appointed to investigate Mexican affairs. Senate Report No. 645, 66th Cong., 2d Sess. (1920).

§32. Negotiations after the Obregón Revolution. In 1920 the Carranza government was overthrown after a revolt led by General Obregón. Soon after its accession to power the new government, desirous of obtaining recognition, evinced a willingness to reach a settlement in regard to the question of claims. Negotiations between the new government and the United States seem to have begun in October 1920,[20] and on the twenty-sixth of the same month the confidential agent of the Mexican government stated in a despatch to the Secretary of State of the United States that:

"The Mexican Government is prepared to establish a joint arbitration commission to pass upon and adjudicate the claims presented by foreigners on account of damages occasioned during the revolution. Any claim that cannot be adjusted by means of direct negotiations between the claimant and the Mexican government will be submitted to the consideration of this commission, whose decisions will be deemed final and binding." [21]

§33. The Circular Telegrams of 1921. On July 12, 1921, the Mexican government sent circular telegrams [22] to the governments of

[20] During a Senatorial investigation of the Teapot Dome oil leases, Mr. George Creel stated that in October 1920 he went down to Mexico at the request of President Wilson and secured the agreement of provisional President de la Huerta and of President-elect Obregón to certain understandings to end the dispute between Mexico and the United States. When he returned about October 20, he brought with him Mr. Oberto Pescara who had ample authority to put these understandings into formal memoranda. Leases upon Naval Oil Reserves, Hearings before the Committee on Public Lands and Surveys, United States Senate, 68th Cong., 1st Sess., pursuant to S. Res. 147, p. 2124 (Washington, 1924).

[21] "The United States and Mexico," International Conciliation, June 1923, No. 187, p. 411.

[22] Following is the text as supplied by the Mexican Secretariat of Foreign Relations:

Telegrama.
Mexico, D. F., 12 de julio 1921.
3079

CIRCULAR

Ponga usted en conocimiento de la Cancillería de ese país que el Gobierno de Mexico esta dispuesto a entrar en arreglos con los Gobiernos extranjeros a fin de indemnizar *ex gratia* a aquellos de sus nacionales que hayan sufrido daños por causa de las revoluciones acaecidas en México desde 1910 hasta la fecha Stop.—Con el proposito indicado, el C. Presidente de la República, fundandose en el articulo quinto del decreto de diez de Mayo de 1913, dado en la ciudad de Monclova por el Primer Jefe del Ejército Constitucionalista, don Venustiano Carranza, y en el articulo trece, reformado, de la ley de venticuatro de diciembre de 1917, que creo la Comisión de Reclamaciones, ha tenido a bien acordar que esta Secretaría invite atentamente a los Gobiernos de cada uno de los países cuyos nacionales hayan sufrido daños por la Revolucion, para que, de comun acuerdo, se proceda a establecer Comisiones Mixtas Permanentes que respectivamente conozcan de las reclamaciones de sus nacionales, ya sea porque éstos hayan quedado inconformes con las resoluciones de la Comisión de Reclamaciónes creada por el referido decreto de 24 de diciembre de 1917, o bien porque prefieran que la Comisión Mixta Permanente respectiva se avoque el conocimiento de sus reclamaciones desde un principio, y que, con tal fin, la Secretaría de Relaciones Exteriores quede facultada para celebrar las Convenciones necesarias, las cuales se

all countries whose nationals might have claims against Mexico (United States, Spain, Italy, France, Germany, Norway, Sweden, Denmark, Austria, Great Britain, Cuba, Japan, China and Belgium), inviting them to participate in the formation of mixed claims commissions to pass on claims incident to the revolutionary disturbances. This is an important event in the history of the negotiation of the claims conventions. For the first time, the Mexican government had extended an invitation to conclude conventions submitting claims to international adjudication.

§34. United States–Mexican Negotiations of 1921: The Pani-Summerlin Conversations. Early in May 1921 conversations were begun between the Mexican Secretary for Foreign Relations and the American Chargé d'Affaires Summerlin in regard to the recognition of the Mexican Government by the United States.[23] The latter desired the conclusion of a commercial treaty, containing clauses relative to the safeguarding of American interests in Mexico acquired prior to the adoption of the Constitution of 1917, as a condition of recognition. A draft of such a treaty, containing also a clause obligating the parties to conclude a claims convention, was transmitted to Mexico on May 27, 1921.[24] The Mexican government not only objected to certain provisions of this draft, but took the position that it would materially injure the dignity of Mexico to receive recognition conditioned on the conclusion of such a treaty.[25] For two years this question of the treaty of commerce and the question of the rights of American nationals in Mexican oil and agricultural lands prevented the recognition of the Mexican government and the conclusion of a claims convention.

§35. The Summerlin Draft of 1921. At no point in these discussions did the settlement of outstanding claims present any great diffi-

---

guiarán en todo por los principios de Dercho Internacional aceptados sobre esta materia Stop.

Para cumplir, pues, este acuerdo del C. Presidente de la República—inspirado en el deseo de normar su conducta por los preceptos del Derecho de Gentes—haga usted cordial invitación al Gobierno de ese pais para el nombramiento de una Comisión Mixta que juzgue en los términos supradichos, de los daños que hayan sufrido sus nacionales residentes en México, suplicando, al mismo tiempo, que al ser considerada tal invitación, se comunique a usted lo que ese Gobierno se sirva resolver respecto a ella.
(Firmado) A. PANI

[23] The correspondence relating to these negotiations was published by the Mexican Government in *La cuestion internacional mexicano-americana durante el gobierno del Gral. Don Alvaro Obregón* (Mexico 1926), and by the United States in Department of State Press Release, May 8, 1926.

[24] *Le cuestion internacional,* p. 16; Press Release, May 8, 1926.

[25] Message of President Obregón to the Congress of Mexico, Sept. 2, 1921, International Conciliation, No. 187, p. 421.

culty. On November 11, 1921, the United States presented a draft claims convention to the Mexican Secretariat of Foreign Relations.[26] The draft provided for the submission to a Commission composed of three members of all claims of citizens of the United States against Mexico and all claims of citizens of Mexico against the United States which had been presented by either government to the other since the signing of the Claims Convention of 1868 as well as any other such claims which might be presented within a specified time. Each government was to appoint one commissioner, the third to be selected by mutual agreement, and in default of such agreement the Queen of the Netherlands was to appoint the third member.

§36. **The Pani Drafts of 1921.** The proposal to submit "all claims" to this Commission proved unacceptable to Mexico. The latter had always maintained that a state could incur no liability under international law for the acts of revolutionary forces which did not succeed in setting up a government, and, while willing to compensate for damages so occasioned, it desired such claims to be given separate treatment. In consequence the Mexican government submitted on November 19, 1921, a counter-proposal embodying drafts of two conventions, one providing for a special claims commission and the other for a general claims commission.[27] Both commissions were to be similarly constituted, one commissioner to be appointed by each of the two governments, the third to be appointed by mutual agreement, failing which the third member was to be designated by "the Tribunal of Arbitration at the Hague." The special claims commission was to have jurisdiction over claims of citizens of the United States against Mexico arising from acts by revolutionary forces between November 20, 1910, and May 31, 1920. The commissioners were to decide all claims "in accordance with the principles of equity, since it is the desire of Mexico that its responsibility shall not be fixed in accordance with the general principles of international law, but from the point of view of magnanimity, it being sufficient that the alleged damage may exist and that it may have been due to one of the causes enumerated . . . that Mexico may feel morally obliged to make indemnification." The general claims commission was to have jurisdiction over all claims

[26] *La cuestion internacional,* p. 33. The text of this draft was not published by the United States.
[27] Pani to Summerlin, Nov. 19, 1921, *La cuestion internacional,* pp. 38–50; Press Release, May 8, 1926.

of citizens of each country against the other excepting claims arising from acts incident to the revolutions. The commissioners were to decide "in accordance with the principles of public law, justice or equity."

It is evident that the proposal of these conventions was made with a view to securing recognition while avoiding the previous conclusion of a commercial treaty. The Mexican government urged the immediate signature of the special claims convention, which, in its opinion would constitute an "implicit" recognition of the government. Recognition being once granted, the two governments could then proceed to sign the general claims convention. In short, the Mexican government was offering as the price of recognition the settlement of those claims for which it had contended that it had no liability under international law.

§37. **Position of the United States towards the Pani Drafts.** During the subsequent negotiations little comment was devoted to these drafts. The United States still continued to press for a commercial treaty, but it retreated from its previous stand that the signing of this treaty must precede recognition. On April 20, 1922, Chargé d'Affaires Summerlin wrote:

All objections to recognition through the signing of a treaty having disappeared, the only remaining question is: What shall the treaty be? You suggest that it should be simply the proposed Convention No. 1 as to claims. The Department of State has suggested that it should be the proposed Treaty of Amity and Commerce which contains provisions as to the adjustment of claims. My Government is indifferent to a mere matter of procedure and it has no objection to satisfactory conventions relating to claims being embodied in separate documents. It is, however, quite as much concerned with the importance of suitable assurances for the adequate protection of American citizens and their property rights as it is with the desirability of a convention as to claims; and it is unable to see any reason why assurances should not be given as to the adjustment of claims and not be given in the same manner with respect to the protection of fundamental interests.

It will be quite satisfactory to my Government to have the Claims Convention, or Conventions, signed first, provided it is clearly understood that the signing of a Treaty of Amity and Commerce, with provisions previously agreed upon and put in draft form (as in the case of the Claims Convention), shall follow without delay.[28]

[28] Press Release, May 8, 1926.

§38. The "Bucareli" Conference of 1923 and the Drafting of the Claims Conventions. Matters remained at this stage until the appointment of a United States–Mexican Commission to discuss outstanding questions between the two countries. This Commission met in Mexico City between May 4 and August 15, 1923.[29] The formal meetings were taken up with a discussion of questions relating to Mexican petroleum and agrarian legislation. The claims conventions were drawn up by Charles Beecher Warren and Fernando González Roa during recesses from July 2 to 18 and July 23 to 26, 1923.[30] Two draft conventions were prepared following, with some changes, the drafts proposed by the Mexican government in 1921. At the final meeting of the Commission, the Commissioners of both countries declared that the texts of the general and special claims conventions which were incorporated in the minutes were approved by their respective governments.[31] On August 31, 1923, the United States and Mexico announced the resumption of diplomatic relations.

§39. Signature and Ratification of the United States–Mexican Claims Conventions. The General Claims Convention was signed at Washington September 8, 1923, ratified by the President of the United States February 4, 1924, and by Mexico February 16, 1924; ratifications were exchanged March 1, 1924. The Special Claims Convention was signed at Mexico City September 10, 1923, ratified by the President of the United States February 4, 1924, and by Mexico February 16, 1924; ratifications were exchanged February 19, 1924.

§40. Claims Conventions between Mexico and the European States. The Obregón government had invited twelve states other than the United States to participate in the settlement of claims, but conventions were finally concluded only with France, Germany, Great Britain, Italy and Spain. All these conventions provided only for the settlement of claims arising out of revolutionary disturbances and follow the text of the Special Claims Convention with the United

[29] See Proceedings of the United States–Mexican Commission, convened in Mexico City May 14, 1923 (Washington 1925). The Conference of the Commissioners is frequently called the "Bucareli Conference" since the sessions were held at 85 Bucareli St. in Mexico City.

[30] Ibid., pp. 36, 45. The most important change was in the Special Claims Convention. The Mexican draft had included four categories of forces whose acts were to give rise to responsibility. The new draft added a fifth: "revolutionary forces as a result of the triumph of whose cause governments de facto or de jure have been established, or by revolutionary forces opposed to them."

[31] Ibid., p. 51.

States. A convention of a different character was concluded with Belgium.[32]

§41. The French–Mexican Claims Convention: Early Negotiations. The first move of the Obregón government to secure recognition from France appears to have been made in August 1920. At that time the French government requested, among other things, that a draft convention for the submission of French claims to an arbitral tribunal be drawn up.[33] It does not appear that any such draft had been prepared when diplomatic relations were resumed. After the Mexican circular telegram of July 12, 1921,[34] the Mexican Chargé d'Affaires at Paris addressed a note to the French Minister for Foreign Affairs on July 15, 1921, repeating the invitation extended in the circular telegram.[35] This telegram referred to the Carranza decree of November 24, 1917, which had provided for the establishment of mixed commissions to be appointed by the Mexican government and the diplomatic agents of the countries whose nationals were involved. The French government seems to have been puzzled by this provision and on July 27, 1921, the French Minister for Foreign Affairs replied to the Mexican Chargé d'Affaires that: "Before making the designation which you request, I should like to know under exactly what conditions the proposed mixed commissions will function, since they seem to be like those which President Carranza established as commissions of appeal or of second instance."[36] During the next month correspondence continued about the question of the relationship between the proposed commissions and the Mexican National Claims Commission, but no definite results were achieved.[37]

§42. The Same: Negotiations in 1923 and the Signature of the Convention. Negotiations were resumed on May 19, 1923 when Señor Pani, Mexican Minister for Foreign Relations, submitted to the French diplomatic representative in Mexico a draft claims convention, apparently similar to the United States–Mexican Special Claims Convention.[38] On March 21, 1924, the French Minister to Mexico officially

---

[32] See *infra*, p. 28.

[33] Director of Political and Commercial Affairs Peretti de la Roca to the Mexican Confidential Agent Palvicini, Aug. 17, 1920, 3 *Revista mexicana de derecho internacional* (1923), Annex, p. 226.

[34] See *supra*, p. 19.

[35] République française (Georges Pinson) *v.* Etats-unis mexicains, Sentence No. 1, Jurisprudence de la Commission franco-mexicaine des réclamations, p. 9.

[36] *Ibid.*, p. 11.

[37] *Ibid.*, pp. 12–14.   [38] *Ibid.*, p. 16.

accepted the invitation extended in the note of July 15, 1921.[39] The French Minister accepted the Pani draft of May 19, 1923, as a basis for a convention but pointed out the necessity of a provision for the inclusion of the claims of French Syrian and Lebanese protégés.[40] This was acceded to by the Mexican Minister for Foreign Relations on March 29, 1924,[41] and the French Minister transmitted a draft containing such a provision on June 12, 1924.[42] The Mexican Minister for Foreign Relations replied on June 30, 1924, by sending a new draft containing the suggested provision.[43]

The Convention was signed in Mexico City on September 25, 1924; ratified by France on November 19, 1924, and by Mexico on December 5, 1924. Ratifications were exchanged in Mexico City December 29, 1924.

§43. **The Claims Convention between Germany and Mexico.** On July 14, 1921, the Mexican government extended to Germany an invitation to participate in the settlement of claims.[44] The course of the subsequent negotiations cannot be traced because of the absence of published sources. The German legation at Mexico City received a draft convention from the Mexican Secretariat for Foreign Relations sometime before February 7, 1925. On that date the German legation suggested various modifications in the draft,[45] some of which were accepted in a note of the Mexican secretariat of February 13, 1925.[46] The text of the Convention as finally adopted while substantially similar to that of the United States–Mexican Convention, differs from the latter in several important particulars. The Convention was signed in Mexico City March 16, 1925; ratified by Mexico January 8, 1926, and by Germany October 6, 1925. Ratifications were exchanged in Mexico City February 1, 1926.

§44. **The Claims Convention between Spain and Mexico.** The Spanish-Mexican Claims Convention was signed in Mexico City November 25, 1925; ratified by Mexico January 15, 1926, and by Spain

---

[39] *Ibid.*, p. 16.
[40] République française (Pablo Nájera) *v.* Etats-unis mexicains, Sentence No. 30—A, Jurisprudence de la Commission franco-mexicaine des réclamations, p. 165.
[41] *Ibid.*, p. 166.
[42] *Id.*
[43] *Id.*
[44] The preamble of the German-Mexican Claims Convention states that the Convention was concluded in consequence of the invitation of July 14, 1921.
[45] Reproduced in Republica Alemana (Ketelsen y Degetau Sucs.) *v.* Estados Unidos Mexicanos, Decision No. 53, German-Mexican Commission (unpublished).
[46] *Loc. cit.*

March 1, 1926. Ratifications were exchanged in Mexico City July 7, 1926.

§45. **The Convention with Great Britain: Early Negotiations.** In July 1920 an agent of the De la Huerta government arrived in London and began negotiations with a view towards recognition by Great Britain. He was informed that the British government would not require the payment of all the claims of British subjects as a condition of recognition, nor would it press for the payment of such claims before they were examined by an impartial commission. Nevertheless it would await the election of a Mexican President before taking any definite steps.[47] Yet in spite of this initial friendly attitude five years passed before the Obregón government was recognized. Throughout this period there was considerable British sentiment for recognition. The government, however, continued to resist this sentiment. At first it sought sufficient evidence of stability of the Mexican government.[48] The emphasis then shifted to the settlement of outstanding claims by Mexico, the government considering that recognition would be premature "until some practical suggestion can be made by the Mexican government for settling these questions." [49] Negotiations towards the conclusion of a claims convention were begun in October 1921.[50]

§46. **The Same: Negotiations in 1922.** On March 4, 1922, the Mexican government sent two draft conventions to the British Foreign Office.[51] A few days later it was announced in the House of Commons that the British government was preparing a draft with certain modifications of the Mexican proposals,[52] and this draft was transmitted to Mexico later in the month.[53] Apparently, the draft which was then

[47] R. Sperling of the British Foreign Office, to Señor Palvecini, Mexican Confidential Agent, July 22, 1920, 3 *Revista Mexicana de derecho internacional* (1921), Annex, p. 223.

[48] Mr. F. G. Kellaway, Additional Parliamentary Under-Secretary of State, in the House of Commons, March 1, 1921, 138 H. C. Deb. 5s., p. 1585.

[49] Mr. Cecil Harmsworth, Under-Secretary for Foreign Affairs, in the House of Commons May 11, 1921, 141, H. C. Deb. 5s., p. 1837: "In September last, the Mexican Government stated that, as soon as they had been fully recognized by other countries, they would be prepared to agree to the appointment of a mixed commission to negotiate concerning British claims." See also Mr. Harmsworth in the House of Commons, June 27, 1921, 143 H. C. Deb. 5s., p. 1836.

[50] Major C. Lowther in the House of Commons, March 16, 1922, 151 H. C. Deb. 5s., pp. 2530–2531.

[51] République française (Georges Pinson) *v.* Etats-Unis mexicains, Sentence No. 1, Jurisprudence de la Commission franco-mexicaine des réclamations, p. 16.

[52] Sir P. Lloyd-Greame, in the House of Commons, March 15, 1922, 151 H. C. Deb. 5s., p. 2157.

[53] Mr. Cecil Harmsworth in the House of Commons, March 27, 1922, 152 H. C. Deb. 5s., p. 949.

under discussion was similar to the draft United States–Mexican General Claims Convention since it applied equally to the claims of British nationals against Mexico and Mexican nationals against Great Britain.[54] "The negotiations broke down at the end of 1922 because the Mexican government demanded recognition before any Commission was set up, and insisted on the exclusion of certain categories of claims from the purview of the Commission. Among these categories were claims arising out of expropriations carried out under the Mexican agrarian laws, and also those of the British holders of certain bonds, including the Mexican National Packing Company, or De Kay bonds, which the Mexican government did not recognize." [55]

§47. **The Hohler Mission and the Cummins Incident.** No further progress was made until May 1924 when Sir Thomas Hohler was appointed on a special mission to report on conditions in Mexico. At this point negotiations were interrupted by a controversy over the expropriation by the Mexican authorities of the estate of a British national, Mrs. Evans. When the British Chargé des Archives Cummins protested, he was asked to leave the country, and all relations between Great Britain and Mexico were broken off on June 20, 1924.[56]

§48. **Conclusion of the British–Mexican Claims Convention.** Relations were resumed on August 28, 1925.[57] On September 2 of the same year it was officially announced that an agreement had been reached for the submission to a mixed commission of British claims arising from revolutionary disturbances. The announcement went on to state:

"With regard to claims of British subjects of a more general nature, that is, any claims not arising from revolutionary causes, the two governments have agreed that such claims shall be dealt with through the diplomatic channel. Any such claims of a general nature as have not been settled by diplomatic discussion within a period of one year (to be prolonged by mutual consent if necessary to 18 months) from the date of presentation of the first claim will be submitted to a Mixed Claims Commission, or, if the two governments are unable to agree to the constitution of such a Commission, to the Permanent Court of Arbitration at The Hague. The necessary convention

---

[54] Mr. Ronald McNeill, Under-Secretary of State for Foreign Affairs, in the House of Commons, March 14, 1923, 161 H. C. Deb. 5s., p. 1522.

[55] *Loc. cit.*

[56] On the Evans and Cummins incidents see 1925 Survey of International Affairs, II, pp. 421–422. Cmd. 2225.

[57] The Times (London), August 29, 1925, p. 10.

to settle details of such arbitration will be signed before the expiration of the above-mentioned period of one year or 18 months as the case may be." [58]

The Claims Convention was not signed until September 10, 1926, and no provision was made for the general claims, nor has any agreement in regard to such claims been brought into force at the date of this writing.

§49. **The Claims Convention between Italy and Mexico.** The Italian-Mexican Claims Convention was signed in Mexico City January 13, 1927; ratified by Mexico October 25, 1927, and by Italy April 26, 1928. Ratifications were exchanged in Mexico City November 27, 1928.

§50. **The Agreement between Belgium and Mexico.** The Belgian claims against Mexico were few in number and it was apparently thought that the elaborate machinery of a Commission was unnecessary. Consequently, it was agreed by an exchange of notes between the Mexican Secretary of Foreign Relations and the Belgian Minister to Mexico on May 14, 1927, to set up an "administrative arbitral tribunal." This tribunal was to consist of two members who, in case of disagreement, could call upon an umpire. These persons were to pass upon the claims submitted by the Belgian Legation to the Mexican Secretariat of Foreign Relations. No provision was made for the representation of the governments before the tribunal nor for any proceedings before it.

[58] The Times (London), September 3, 1925, p. 9.

CHAPTER 3

GENERAL SURVEY OF THE MEXICAN CLAIMS CONVENTION

§51. Introductory. Three different types of Claims Conventions were concluded by Mexico. The United States–Mexican General Claims Convention provided for a Commission having jurisdiction over all claims both against the United States on the part of Mexican citizens and against Mexico on the part of American citizens, with certain exceptions. The United States–Mexican Special Claims Convention, the British-Mexican, French-Mexican, Spanish-Mexican and Italian-Mexican Conventions provided for jurisdiction only over claims against Mexico arising out of the revolutions. The agreement between Belgium and Mexico provided for an "Administrative Arbitral Tribunal" to pass on claims against Mexico arising out of the revolutions, the tribunal to consist of two persons who were to call on an umpire in case of disagreement. This tribunal was of minor importance, and it will be dealt with only occasionally in this work. Where reference is made to "all the Commissions" or Conventions it is to be understood that the Belgian-Mexican Tribunal is not included.

§52. Designation of Commissioners. All of the Conventions provided the same method for the designation of the Commissioners.[1] Each government party to the Convention was to appoint one Commissioner. The third, who was to preside over the Commission, was to be selected by mutual agreement of the governments, failing which he was to be designated by the President of the Permanent Administrative Council of the Permanent Court of Arbitration. All of the Conventions, excepting those with the United States, provided that this third member should not be a national of a country having similar claims against Mexico. In case of death, absence or incapacity of a member of the Commission the same procedure was to be followed for filling the vacancy as was followed in appointing him.

---

[1] Art. I of all the Conventions.

29

§53. Meetings of the Commissions. Each of the Conventions provided that the Commission was to meet within six months following the exchange of ratifications. The United States–Mexican General Claims Commission was to meet first in Washington, and might thereafter meet either in the United States or in Mexico as might be convenient, subject to the special instructions of the two governments.[2] The other Commissions were to meet in Mexico City.[3] Before entering upon his duties each Commissioner was required to make and subscribe to a solemn declaration. In the General Claims Commission the declaration was to be to the effect that "he will carefully and impartially examine and decide, according to the best of his judgment and in accordance with the principles of international law, justice and equity, all claims presented for decision."[4] In the other Commissions the declaration was to be in the same form except for the omission of the words "international law."[5]

§54. Jurisdictional Provisions. (1) *The United States–Mexican General Claims Convention.* Article I of the General Claims Convention provided for three seemingly distinct categories of claims. The first clause of this Article read: "All claims (except those arising from acts incident to the recent revolutions) against Mexico of citizens of the United States, whether corporations, companies, associations, partnerships or individuals, for losses or damages suffered by persons or by their properties, and all claims against the United States of America by citizens of Mexico, whether corporations, companies, associations, partnerships or individuals, for losses or damages suffered by persons or by their properties; . . ." This clause confers jurisdiction over all claims (except those arising from the revolutions) by citizens of either country against the other. It is broad enough to have served as the only jurisdictional provision. The second clause, however, served a useful purpose. It read: "all claims for losses or damages suffered by citizens of either country by reason of losses or damages suffered by any corporation, company, association or partnership in which such citizens have or have had a substantial and bona fide interest, provided an allotment to the claimant by the corporation, company, association or partnership of his proportion of the loss or damage suffered is presented by the claimant to the Commission here-

---

[2] U. S.–Mexican General Claims Convention, Art. II.
[3] Art. II of all the Conventions.   [4] *Supra,* note 2.   [5] *Supra,* note 3.

inafter referred to; . . ." This covers claims by American or Mexican citizens who had interests in corporations of a different nationality which had suffered damage. It removed once for all the difficult question as to whether State A could advance a claim on behalf of persons of its nationality who were stockholders or bondholders in a corporation having the national character of State B. However, in making use of the word "allotment" without giving any explanation of just what it meant, it raised a group of new problems.[6]

The third clause of Article I read: "and all claims for losses or damages originating from acts of officials or others acting for either Government and resulting in injustice, and which claims may have been presented to either Government for its interposition with the other since the signing of the Claims Convention concluded between the two countries July 4, 1868, and which have remained unsettled, as well as any other such claims which may be filed by either Government within the time hereinafter specified, shall be submitted to a Commission consisting of three members for decision in accordance with the principles of international law, justice and equity." The mention of a third class of claims in the first phrase of this clause is most puzzling. The present writer cannot conceive of any claim based on acts of officials which would be valid unless these acts resulted in injustice. It seems obvious that the claims here mentioned are covered by the first clause of the Article. However, the Commission managed to find it possible to give a meaning to this phrase.[6a] The two following phrases (from "and which claims" to "time hereinafter specified") are equally puzzling. They are separated from the first phrase by a comma, yet it seems that they must be taken to qualify the whole of the Article. Nor do they seem to serve any purpose. They may have been intended to indicate that claims barred by the 1868 Convention were not to be revived, but a much simpler form of statement could have been used. The inartistic draftsmanship of the second and third clauses is to be noted. The first clause contains the exception of claims arising from acts incident to revolutionary disturbances and the stipulation that the claims must be "of citizens." Neither the exception nor the stipulation as to ownership of claims are repeated in the second and third clauses and the punctuation renders it impossible to refer back to the first clause. Fortunately, the inclusion of

[6] See *infra*, p. 118.　　　　　　[6a] See *infra*, p. 141.

these limitations in the preamble obviated the embarrassing necessity of determining the consequences of the omissions.

(2) *The Other Conventions.* The jurisdiction of all the other Commissions was limited to claims for losses or damages caused during the period included between November 20, 1910, and May 31, 1920, by an act of one or any of a number of enumerated "forces." The enumeration of the United States–Mexican Special Claims Commission may serve as an example.

1. By forces of a Government *de jure* or *de facto*.

2. By revolutionary forces as a result of the triumph of whose cause governments *de facto* or *de jure* have been established, or by revolutionary forces opposed to them.

3. By forces arising from the disjunction of the forces mentioned in the next preceding paragraph up to the time when the government *de jure* established itself as a result of a particular revolution.

4. By federal forces that were disbanded, and

5. By mutinies or mobs, or insurrectionary forces other than those referred to under subdivisions 2, 3 and 4 above, or by bandits, provided in any case it be established that the appropriate authorities omitted to take reasonable measures to suppress insurrectionists, mobs or bandits, or treated them with lenity or were in fault in other particulars.

This enumeration was the same in all the Conventions though there is some slight difference in wording. The Conventions with the European states contained in addition the following paragraph:

The Commission shall also deal with claims for losses or damages caused by acts of civil authorities provided such acts were due to revolutionary events and disturbed conditions within the period referred to in this Article, and that the said acts were committed by any of the forces specified in subdivisions 1, 2 and 3 of this article.

These provisions may appear clear to the casual glance. Read in the light of Mexican history between 1910 and 1920 they are seen to be full of ambiguities. Around these provisions revolved some of the bitterest controversies which troubled the work of the Commissions. The disruption of two of the Commissions is in large part due to the failure to provide in these articles a firm jurisdictional foundation. The story of these controversies and of the defects in the jurisdictional provisions will be told in subsequent chapters.[7]

[7] See *infra,* Chs. 5 and 8.

§55. The Law to be Applied. We have seen that the Commissioners of the General Claims Commission were to decide "in accordance with the principles of international law, justice and equity," while the Commissioners of the other Commissions were to decide "in accordance with the principles of justice and equity." The reason for the latter form of statement is set forth in each of the Conventions relating to claims for revolutionary acts in a form somewhat like the following: [8]

The Mexican Government desires that the claims shall be so decided because Mexico wishes that her responsibility shall not be fixed according to the generally accepted rules of international law, but *ex gratia* feels morally bound to make full indemnification and agrees, therefore, that it will be sufficient that it be established that the alleged loss or damage in any case was sustained and was due to any of the causes enumerated in Article III hereof. [Article III contained the enumeration of forces.]

The German-Mexican Convention set forth a somewhat different form. The words "generally accepted rules of international law" were replaced by "Article XVIII of the Treaty of Amity, Commerce and Navigation in force between the United Mexican States and the German Republic." This Convention also contained a solemn declaration by Germany recognizing that the Claims Convention did not modify the Treaty of Commerce in whole or in part, tacitly or expressly, and agreeing not to invoke the Convention as a precedent.

§56. Provisions relating to Procedure. The United States–Mexican Conventions provided that "in general," the Commissions should adopt "as the standard" for their proceedings the rules of procedure of the United States–Mexican Claims Commission of 1868, but that the Commissions could by majority decision establish such other rules as might be deemed expedient and necessary, not in conflict with any of the provisions of the Conventions.[9] It was not wise to attempt to bind the Commissions to a procedure used more than half a century before, and as will be seen the Commissions paid only lip-service to this provision.[10] The Conventions with the European states merely stated: "The Commission shall determine their own methods of procedure, but shall not depart from the provisions of this present

[8] Art. II of all the Conventions.
[9] Art. III, U. S.–Mexican General Claims Convention; Art. IV, U. S.–Mexican Special Claims Convention.   [10] See *infra*, p. 229.

Convention." [11] Each of the Conventions provided for the appointment of agents and counsel by the governments who were to present evidence and arguments orally or in writing. The United States–Mexican and British-Mexican Conventions also provided for the offering of documentary evidence by agents and counsel and for the examination of witnesses. In every Convention, except that with Germany, it was provided that the language of either contracting party might be employed in the proceedings and in judgments. The German-Mexican Convention provided for the use either of Spanish or English. Decisions were to be rendered by a majority of the Commission.

Each Commission was to keep records of claims submitted and minutes of its proceedings.[12] For this purpose each government was permitted to appoint a secretary. The secretaries were to act as joint secretaries and were to be subject to the Commission's instructions. Provision was also made for the furnishing of periodical reports to the governments by the Commissions.

§57. **Exhaustion of Local Remedies.** Each of the Conventions contained a provision to the effect that no claims should be disallowed or rejected on the ground that legal remedies had not been exhausted prior to the presentation of the claim.[13] This was a remarkable concession on the part of Mexico which was willing to waive an established requirement of international law in order to reach an equitable settlement.

§58. **Time Limits for Filing and Deciding of Claims.** The time limits for filing and deciding of claims differ in each of the Conventions, the time limit always being counted from the date of the first meeting of the Commission. The effect of these time limits will be discussed elsewhere.[13a] For the purposes of comparison we may list here these various periods.

United States–Mexican General Claims Convention: [14] filing—one year for claims accruing prior to the signing of the Convention, three years for claims accruing subsequently; deciding—three years.

United States–Mexican Special Claims Convention: [15] filing—two years; deciding—five years.

---

[11] Art. V of the German-Mexican Convention; Art. IV of other Conventions.

[12] Art. IV, U. S.-Mexican General Claims Convention; Art. VI, German-Mexican Convention; Art. V of all other Conventions.

[13] Art. V, U. S.-Mexican General Claims Convention; Art. VII, German-Mexican Convention; Art. VI of all other Conventions.

[13a] See *infra*, Ch. 5.   [14] Art. VI.   [15] Art. VII.

British-Mexican Convention: [16] filing—nine months; deciding—two years.

French-Mexican Convention: [17] filing—nine months; deciding—two years.

German-Mexican Convention: [18] filing—six months; deciding—two years.

Italian-Mexican Convention: [19] filing—four months; deciding—one year.

Spanish-Mexican Convention: [20] filing—nine months; deciding—three and one half years.

§59. **Measure of Damages.** The Conventions with the European states provided that "in order to determine the amount of compensation to be granted for damage to property, account shall be taken of the value declared by the interested parties for fiscal purposes except in cases which in the opinion of the Commission are really exceptional." The amount of compensation for personal injuries was not to exceed "that of the most ample compensation granted by" the claimant state in similar circumstances.[21] The provision as to property damage is one to which no exception can be taken, but the provision as to damages for personal injuries seems altogether meaningless. It is impossible to tell whether it refers to compensation awarded by municipal courts in suits between individuals, or by administrative authorities in proceedings against the government, or by the Foreign Office in international claims. No decision of any of the Commissions gives any indication that this provision was taken into account in fixing damages. Neither of these provisions was contained in the Conventions with the United States.

§60. **Effect of Decisions.** Each of the Conventions contained provisions wherein the parties agreed to consider the decision of the Commission on each claim decided as final and conclusive and to give effect to such decisions.[22] In the Conventions dealing with claims arising out of revolutionary acts the parties further agreed to consider the result of the labors of the Commission as a full, final and perfect settlement of all claims within the jurisdiction of the Commission

---

[16] Art. VII.
[17] Art. VII.
[18] Art. VIII.
[19] Art. VII.
[20] Art. VII.
[21] Art. VII, German-Mexican Convention; Art. VI of other Conventions.
[22] Art. IX, German-Mexican Convention; Art. VIII of all other Conventions.

whether or not such claims were presented to the Commission, provided that those claims which had been presented had been examined and decided. The General Claims Convention provided that claims for loss or damage sustained prior to the exchange of ratifications were to be considered as settled as a result of the proceedings of the Commission. It will be remembered that this Commission had jurisdiction also over claims arising subsequent to the exchange of ratifications and such claims were not to be barred if they had not been presented.

§61. **Payment of Awards.** The General Claims Convention contained elaborate provisions with respect to the payment of awards.[23] The total amount awarded to the citizens of one country was to be deducted from the total amount awarded to the citizens of the other, and the balance paid in gold coin or its equivalent at Washington or at Mexico City. In any case the Commission might decide that a property or right be restored to the claimant in addition to the amount awarded for loss or damage sustained. At the same time the Commission was required to determine the value of such property or right, and the government affected was given an election to pay this amount rather than to restore the property or right. If that government chose to pay the amount fixed it was agreed that notice should be filed with the Commission within thirty days after the decision and the amount fixed was to be paid immediately. Upon failure so to pay the amount the property or right was to be restored. Apparently, these provisions for *restitutio in integrum* were inserted with a view to the settlement of the many claims arising out of Mexican oil and agrarian legislation.

The Special Claims Convention [24] and the French-Mexican Convention [25] provided that payment was to be made to the claimant government in gold or its equivalent. The other Conventions provided that the form in which the Mexican government should make payment was to be determined by both governments after termination of the work of the Commission, such payment to be made in gold or its equivalent to the claimant government.[26]

§62. **Expenses of the Commissions.** The same method of paying expenses was provided in all the Conventions. Each government was to pay its own Commissioner and bear its own expenses, and half

---

[23] Art. IX. [24] Art. IX. [25] Art. IX.
[26] Art. X, German-Mexican Convention; Art. IX, British-Mexican, Italian-Mexican and Spanish-Mexican Conventions.

of the expenses of the Commission, including the salary of the third Commissioner.[27]

§63. **Language of the Conventions.** In the French-Mexican,[28] German-Mexican,[29] and Italian-Mexican [30] Conventions it was stated that the Convention had been drawn up in Spanish and in the language of the other party and an indication was given as to which version was to prevail in case of divergence (French in the French-Mexican Convention; Spanish in the German-Mexican and Italian-Mexican). The British-Mexican Convention stated merely: "This Convention is drawn up in English and Spanish." [31] The United States–Mexican Conventions contained no statement at all. These two Conventions were drawn up at the "Bucareli" Conference between Commissioners from the United States and Mexico which met in 1923. The minutes of the final meeting of this Conference contain the following declarations:[32]

The American Commissioners stated in behalf of their Government that the text in English of the special claims convention and the text in English of the general claims convention as hereinafter written as a part of these proceedings are approved by the President of the United States and in the event that diplomatic relations are resumed between the two Governments these conventions as hereinafter set forth will be signed forthwith by duly authorized plenipotentiaries of the President of the United States.

The Mexican Commissioners stated in behalf of their Government that the text in English of the special claims convention and the text in English of the general claims convention as hereinafter written as a part of these proceedings are approved by the Mexican Government and in the event that diplomatic relations are resumed between the two Governments these conventions as hereinafter set forth will be signed forthwith by duly authorized plenipotentiaries of the President of the United Mexican States. . . .

The negotiations connected with the formulating and drafting of the general claims convention and the special claims convention were conducted in English. The texts of such conventions as hereinafter set forth in the records of these proceedings were prepared in English and are approved as the originals.

In a case arising before the Special Claims Commission involving a provision susceptible of different constructions in each version, it

[27] Art. XI, German-Mexican Convention; Art. X of all other Conventions.
[28] Art. XI.   [29] Art. XIII.   [30] Art. XI.   [31] Art. XI.
[32] Proceedings of the United States–Mexican Commission convened in Mexico City May 14, 1923, p. 51.

was argued by the American agent that the English version ought to prevail in view of these declarations at the "Bucareli" Conference.[33] This problem will be discussed later,[34] but the mere fact that it arose is evidence of the danger of failing to designate an authentic text particularly when statements of the kind quoted above are contained in the *travaux préparatoires*.

§64. **Ratification of the Conventions.** All the Conventions were to be ratified by the contracting parties "in accordance with their respective constitutions." Ratifications were to be exchanged as soon as practicable and the Conventions were to come into force from the date of exchange of ratifications.

§65. **Registration of the Conventions.** While Mexico was not a member of the League of Nations at the time these Conventions were concluded, five of the contracting states (France, Germany, Great Britain, Italy and Spain) were members. Nevertheless only the Conventions with Germany, Great Britain and France were registered with the Secretariat of the League of Nations as required by Article 18 of the Covenant of the League.[35]

A question with respect to the non-registration of a convention was raised before the French-Mexican Commission by the Mexican Agent during the oral arguments on the *Nájera* case.[36] These arguments took place between July 2–12, 1928, before the Convention had been registered. Exactly what the contention of the Mexican agent was does not appear: the Presiding Commissioner understood it to be not that registration had not been effected but that it had not been duly proved before the Commission. The French Agent declared officially that the

---

[33] U. S. A. (Naomi Russell) *v.* United Mexican States, Opinions of Commissioners, 1926–1931, p. 44, at 64–66.   [34] See *infra*, p. 163.

[35] German-Mexican Convention of March 16, 1925, registered August 3, 1926, 52 League of Nations Treaty Series, p. 93; French-Mexican Convention of September 25, 1924, registered August 4, 1928, 79 *ibid.*, p. 417; British-Mexican Convention of November 29, 1926, registered November 11, 1929, 85 *ibid.*, p. 51. The following supplementary conventions were also registered: German-Mexican Supplementary Convention of December 20, 1927, registered August 4, 1928, 79 *ibid.*, p. 229; French-Mexican Supplementary Convention of March 12, 1927, registered August 8, 1928, 79 *ibid.*, p. 424; British-Mexican Supplementary Convention of December 5, 1920, registered July 3, 1931, 119 *ibid.*, p. 261. Two of the United States–Mexican Supplementary General Claims Conventions were communicated by the United States: Convention of Aug. 16, 1927, communicated Nov. 30, 1927, 68 *ibid.*, p. 451; Convention of Sept. 2, 1929, communicated Nov. 27, 1929, 101 *ibid.*, p. 541.

[36] Rep. française (Pablo Nájera) *v.* Etats-Unis mexicains, Jurisprudence de la Commission franco-mexicaine des réclamations, p. 156, at 157–162. For a discussion of this and other cases involving Article 18 of the Covenant see Hudson, "Legal Effect of Unregistered Treaties in Practice, under Article 18 of the Covenant," 28 Amer. Journal of International Law (1934), p. 546.

formality required by Article 18 of the Covenant had been observed;
it does not appear whether this declaration was made before or after
August 4, the date on which the Convention was registered. The
opinion of the Presiding Commissioner was rendered on October 19,
1928. He took the position that, "since as a general rule, treaties
concluded by members of the League are regularly registered and
their registration is a matter of common knowledge, . . . an international tribunal may properly hold as the most reasonable rule . . .
that the tribunal may limit itself to requiring proof of registration only
when it is not convinced of it." [37] Apparently the Presiding Commissioner was convinced of the registration since he required no proof,
although he does not state directly that the Convention had been registered. The opinion contains an elaborate exposition of the theory
of the binding effect of non-registered treaties, though this discussion
was hardly germane in view of the position taken by the Presiding
Commissioner.[38] The essence of this exposition is that a non-registered
convention between members of the League cannot be considered as
binding even by an international tribunal independent of the League,
but that the sanction of Article 18 of the Covenant cannot be applied
to conventions concluded with a non-member state.[39]

---

[37] *Ibid.*, p. 160.

[38] The French Commissioner concurred with the statement that it did not seem to him
necessary to formulate his personal opinion on the question of registration which the
Mexican agency appeared to have raised only incidentally. The dissenting opinion of the
Mexican Commissioner makes no mention of the question.

[39] "La raison pour laquelle, entre membres de la Société des Nations, une convention
non-enregistrée ne saurait être considérée comme obligatoire, pas même par un tribunal
international indépendant de la Société, consiste en ceci que les Parties contractantes sont,
l'une et l'autre, liées par la même règle de droit impérative (*jus cogens*), qui prévaut sur
leur liberté d'agir en matière de traités internationaux. Mais cette raison n'existe pas, en
ce qui concerne les traités conclus entre un Etat membre et un Etat non-membre, et non
enregistrés. Il va de soi qu'un tribunal international indépendant n'a pas, comme les
organes de la Société des Nations, la mission de coopérer *ex officio* à l'accomplissement,
par les membres de ladite Société, de leurs obligations vis-à-vis de celle-ci, et d'en frapper
l'inobservation par des sanctions, qui ne découlent pas également des principes généraux
du droit. Or, il me paraît impossible d'interpréter la sanction prévue à l'article 18 du
Pacte, comme constituant l'application d'un principe général de droit. Cela pourrait être
le cas, si la disposition dudit article 18 impliquait une *capitis deminutio* des membres de la
Société des Nations, en ce sens que, après la naissance de celle-ci, ses membres seraient
limités dans leur capacité juridique traditionelle de contracter des engagements internationaux (*internationale Handlungsfähigkeit*), comme c'est le cas, par exemple, d'Etats
souverains entrés dans une fédération, ou s'étant soumis au protectorat d'un autre Etat.
Mais évidemment, pareille situation ne se présente pas ici. L'article 18 ne limite en rien
ladite capacité juridique. Il frappe seulement d'une sanction nouvelle, une règle de droit
nouvelle qui ne produit ses effets, *erga omnes,* et notamment vis-à-vis d'un tribunal arbitral
indépendant, qu'entre membres de la Société, mais qui, entre un Etat membre et un Etat
non membre, ne les produit qu'en ce qui concerne la seule Société et ses organes." *Ibid.*,
pp. 161–62.

CHAPTER 4

THE ORGANIZATION OF THE COMMISSIONS

§66. Designation of Members of International Tribunals. The choice of the method of organization of an international tribunal often involves a delicate question, yet one which is surpassed in delicacy by the question of designation of the members. The first problem may be met in a variety of ways. A single arbitrator may be designated.[1] Or the parties may decide on the establishment of what might be called the "umpire" type of tribunal.[2] Here two or more national commissioners are designated. In the first instance these commissioners hear and decide all claims. In case of disagreement, a third or neutral person, the umpire, is called upon to decide the disputed point. The umpire may have been chosen beforehand or he may be chosen only after the disagreement arises. Lastly, the parties may set up a collegiate tribunal, where the third person sits with the national commissioners as presiding member and takes part in the hearing and deciding of all cases.[3]

§67. The "Umpire" and the "Collegiate" Types of Tribunals. The umpire type of tribunal has more or less gone out of fashion. It has the disadvantage of emphasizing the national character of the national commissioners, often resulting in reducing them to the position of mere advocates for their governments. The modern trend has been towards emphasizing the judicial character of claims adjudication and

---

[1] An example of a tribunal consisting of a single arbitrator is the Islands of Palmas Arbitration between the United States and the Netherlands. Agreement of Jan. 23, 1925, U. S. Treaty Series No. 711.

A recent example of arbitration by a single arbitrator is the Shufeldt Claim between the United States and Guatemala. Exchange of notes, Nov. 2, 1929. Shufeldt Claim (Washington, 1932), p. 9.

[2] Examples of the "umpire" type of tribunal are the Venezuelan Protocols of 1903, Ralston, Venezuelan Arbitrations of 1903, *passim,* and the United States–German Mixed Claims Commission, Convention of August 10, 1922, U. S. Treaty Series No. 665.

[3] The Alabama Claims Arbitration, Treaty of May 8, 1871, U. S. Treaty Series, No. 133, and the North Atlantic Fisheries Arbitration, Agreement of Jan. 27, 1909, U. S. Treaty Series, No. 521, furnish examples of this type of tribunal.

the creation of collegiate tribunals analogous to municipal courts is in line with this trend.[4] It is true that the national members of such tribunals have not always succeeded in displaying a complete detachment from their governments, and for this reason the choice of a single, neutral arbitrator is greatly to be preferred. One of the difficulties with regard to this, is that a single arbitrator would find the task of writing opinions in a multitude of cases too arduous.[5] Of course, this difficulty could be obviated by choosing three or five neutral members to serve on the tribunal. Unfortunately, the imponderable elements of national pride and lack of confidence in the ability and impartiality of neutral arbitrators continue to prevent such consummation.

§68. **Provisions in the Summerlin and Pani Drafts of 1921.** The first draft claims convention presented in the negotiations between the United States and Mexico (the Summerlin draft of November 11, 1921) suggested the creation of a collegiate tribunal. There were to be three members, two national commissioners, and a neutral commissioner. There was no specific indication that the latter was to preside over the Commission.[6] This form of organization was adhered to in all the succeeding negotiations, except that the presidential function of the neutral member was clearly indicated. Only the method of designating the neutral member gave some difficulty. The Summerlin draft proposed that he be designated by mutual agreement between the two governments, and failing such agreement by the Queen of the Netherlands. The Mexican draft of November 19, 1920,[7] proposed that, in case of disagreement, the choice was to be made by the "Tribunal of Arbitration of The Hague." This is patently absurd since there is no institution so called. In the draft convention drawn up at the Bucareli Conference in 1923,[8] the designation was to be made

---

[4] Among the recent examples of claims arbitration by the judicial type of tribunal may be mentioned: British-American Claims Arbitration under the Convention of Aug. 18, 1910, U. S. Treaty Series No. 573; United States–Panama Claims Convention of July 28, 1926, U. S. Treaty Series No. 842; The Salem Claim between the United States and Egypt under the Agreement of Jan. 20, 1931, Salem Claim, Case of the United States (Washington, 1933), p. 29.

[5] Compare, however, the Arbitration Agreement of May 29, 1923, between Great Britain and Spain under which a number of claims of British subjects against the Spanish authorities for damage to life or property were submitted to Max Huber "for examination and report," the parties agreeing that the report "shall be accepted as an arbitral award." Williams and Lauterpacht, Annual Digest of Public International Law Cases, 1923–1924, p. 359.

[6] *La cuestion internacional,* p. 34.   [7] *Ibid.,* p. 47.

[8] Proceedings of the United States–Mexican Commission convened in Mexico City, May 14, 1923, p. 58, Art. 1.

by the "President of the Permanent Tribunal of Arbitration of The Hague." This is another absurdity since there is no such person. Finally, by subsequent negotiation between the governments, the clause was rectified to read: "the President of the Permanent Administrative Council of the Permanent Court of Arbitration at The Hague." [9]

§69. **Provisions in the Conventions with the United States.** As finally concluded, the two conventions between Mexico and the United States provide that the claims specified "shall be submitted to a Commission consisting of three members." And further:

"Such Commission shall be constituted as follows: One member shall be appointed by the President of the United States; one by the President of the United Mexican States; and the third, who shall preside over the Commission, shall be selected by mutual agreement between the two Governments. If the two Governments shall not agree within two months from the exchange of ratifications of this Convention in naming such third member, then he shall be designated by the President of the Permanent Administrative Council of the Permanent Court of Arbitration at The Hague described in Article XLIX of the Convention for the pacific settlement of international disputes concluded at The Hague on October 18, 1907. In case of the death, absence, or incapacity of any member of the Commission, or in the event of a member omitting or ceasing to act as such, the same procedure shall be followed for filling the vacancy as was followed in appointing him." [10]

§70. **Provisions in Conventions with France, Germany, Great Britain, Italy and Spain.** The conventions with France, Germany, Great Britain, Italy and Spain contain similar provisions for the organization of the commissions and the designation of personnel. All of them, however, contain two further sentences of some importance. The provision in the Convention with Great Britain may be cited as typical:

"The request for this appointment by the President of the Per-

---

[9] In effect, this left the designation to the Minister for Foreign Affairs of the Netherlands who is *ex officio* President of the Permanent Administrative Council of the Permanent Court of Arbitration.

[10] Art. 1, General Claims Convention and Special Claims Convention. A similar method of designating the third member of the tribunal is embodied in the Arbitration Agreement of January 20, 1931, between the United States and Egypt in regard to the Salem Claim, Salem Claim, Case of the United States (Washington, 1933), p. 29, and in the United States–Panama Claims Convention of July 28, 1926, U. S. Treaty Series No. 842.

manent Administrative Council of the Permanent Court of Arbitration shall be addressed by both Governments to the President of the aforesaid Council, within a further period of one month, or after the lapse of that period by the Government which may first take action in the matter. In any case the third arbitrator shall be neither British nor Mexican, nor a national of a country which may have claims against Mexico similar to those which form the subject of this convention." [11]

§71. **Designation of Presiding Commissioner by President of the Permanent Administrative Council.** On only two occasions does it appear to have been necessary to resort to the President of the Permanent Administrative Council for the designation of a third member. Kristian Sindballe of Denmark was designated in this manner to serve on the United States–Mexican General and Special Commissions,[12] and Jan W. H. Verzijl of the Netherlands was designated to serve on the French-Mexican Commission.

§72. **The Mexican–Belgian Administrative Arbitral Tribunal.** Not all of the Mexican Claims Commissions were of the collegiate type. The Convention of May 20, 1927 between Belgium and Mexico provided for an "Administrative Arbitral Tribunal" to consist of two arbitrators to be chosen by the governments. In case of disagreement these arbitrators were to call upon the governments to appoint an umpire to decide upon the point of disagreement. The French-Mexican Commission was originally constituted as a collegiate tribunal. Various difficulties arose in its work,[13] and, by a Convention of August 2, 1930,[14] the Commission was reconstituted in a form like that of the Belgian-Mexican Tribunal. Similarly, as a result of difficulties encountered in its work, the United States–Mexican General Claims Commission was reconstituted by the Protocol of April 24, 1934.[15] Only two national Commissioners were provided for, with provision for the eventual designation of an Umpire by the governments.

---

[11] Art. 1 of the British-Mexican Claims Convention. Similar provisions in Art. 1 of the French-Mexican, German-Mexican, Italian-Mexican and Spanish-Mexican Claims Conventions.

[12] It has been said that Dr. Sindballe's designation was preceded by "long and fruitless efforts to agree upon a successor." Dunn, Diplomatic Protection, p. 404. Dr. Sindballe was appointed on June 16, 1928, his predecessor, Cornelis van Vollenhoven, having resigned on Aug. 30, 1927.

[13] See *infra*, p. 70 et seq.

[14] *Memoria de la Secretaría de Relaciones Exteriores,* 1929–1930, p. 36.

[15] See *infra*, p. 61 et seq.

The Personnel of the Commissions

§73. **Importance of Proper Choice of Personnel.** Today, we are familiar enough with the role which the abilities, personality, habits and temperament of judges play in the judicial process. Important as these factors are in municipal courts, they are often greatly enhanced in the international forum. Training in different systems of law, national pride, patriotism, the special character of international law, all these contribute to making the choice of arbitrators a question of paramount importance. It is, therefore, a great and justified temptation to embark on a discussion of the backgrounds and personalities of the men who sat on the Mexican Claims Commissions. Unfortunately, we are too close to these Commissions, the sources of information too meagre to make an excursion into judicial psychology possible. All that can be done here is to set down the bare names of the Commissioners. After we have seen how the Commissions did their work, it will be possible for us to attempt an appraisal of the influence of the personality of the Commissioners on the results achieved.

TABLE I

MEMBERS OF THE UNITED STATES–MEXICAN GENERAL CLAIMS COMMISSION

A. UNDER THE CONVENTION OF SEPTEMBER 8, 1923

Mexican Commissioner

Genaro Fernandez MacGregor. Served continuously from 1924.

American Commissioners

Joseph R. Baker, served from 1924 to May 31, 1925. Did not take part in the decision of any cases.

Nathan L. Miller, served from 1925 to January 5, 1926. Did not take part in the decision of any cases.

Edwin B. Parker. Resigned July 17, 1926. Took part in the decision of seventeen cases.

Fred Kenelm Nielsen. Appointed July 31, 1926. Served continuously thereafter.

Presiding Commissioners

Cornelis van Vollenhoven. Netherlands. Appointed by agreement of the two governments. Served from 1924 to August 30, 1927.

Kristian Sindballe. Denmark. Appointed by the President of the Permanent Administrative Council of the Permanent Court of Arbitration. Served June 16, 1928–July 1, 1929.

Horacio F. Alfaro. Panama. Appointed by agreement of the two governments. Served continuously after May 27, 1930.

B. UNDER THE PROTOCOL OF APRIL 24, 1934

Mexican Commissioner

Genaro Fernandez MacGregor. Appointed in 1934.

American Commissioner

Oscar Underwood, Jr. Appointed in 1934.

TABLE II

MEMBERS OF THE UNITED STATES–MEXICAN SPECIAL CLAIMS COMMISSION

Mexican Commissioner

Fernando González Roa. Served continuously from 1924.

American Commissioners

Ernest B. Perry. Served from 1924 to November 30, 1930. Took part in the decision of one case.

Fred Kenelm Nielsen. Served continuously from January 6, 1931.

Presiding Commissioners

Rodrigo Octavio. Brazil. Appointed by agreement of the two governments. Served from 1924 to July 9, 1926.

Kristian Sindballe. Denmark. Appointed by the President of the Permanent Administrative Council of the Permanent Court of Arbitration. Served June 16, 1928–July 1, 1929.

Horacio F. Alfaro. Panama. Appointed by agreement of the two governments. Served continuously after January 6, 1931.

TABLE III

MEMBERS OF THE FRENCH-MEXICAN CLAIMS COMMISSION

A. UNDER THE CONVENTION OF SEPTEMBER 25, 1924

Mexican Commissioner

Fernando González Roa. Served 1925–1929.

French Commissioners

E. Lagarde. Served 1925–1928.

Victor Ayguesparsse. Served 1928–1929.

Presiding Commissioners

Rodrigo Octavio. Brazil. Appointed by agreement of the two governments. Served 1925–1927.

Jan H. W. Verzijl. Netherlands. Appointed by the President of the Permanent Administrative Council of the Permanent Court of Arbitration. Entered into functions March 26, 1928. Resigned August 29, 1929.[16]

B. UNDER THE CONVENTION OF AUGUST 2, 1930

Mexican Commissioner

Eduardo Suarez.

French Commissioner

René Delage.

TABLE IV

MEMBERS OF THE GERMAN-MEXICAN CLAIMS COMMISSION

Mexican Commissioner

F. Iglesias Calderón. Served continuously from 1926.

German Commissioner

Siegfried Hofman. Served continuously from 1926.

Presiding Commissioner

Miguel Cruchaga Tocornal. Chile. Appointed by agreement of the two governments. Served continuously from 1926.

TABLE V

MEMBERS OF THE BRITISH-MEXICAN CLAIMS COMMISSION

Mexican Commissioners

Benito Flores. Served from 1927 to January 1932.
Genaro Fernandez MacGregor. Served after January 1932.

British Commissioners

Artemus Jones. Served from 1927 to December 6, 1929.
Sir John Percival. Served December 6, 1929–February 1930.
W. H. Stoker. Served after February 15, 1930.

Presiding Commissioner

Alfred Rudolf Zimmerman. Netherlands. Appointed by agreement of the governments. Served continuously from 1927.

TABLE VI

MEMBERS OF THE SPANISH-MEXICAN CLAIMS COMMISSION

Mexican Commissioner

Fernando González Roa. Served continuously from 1927.

[16] On May 7, 1929, the Mexican government stated that it considered M. Verzijl's functions as Presiding Commissioner to have terminated on Dec. 26, 1928. See *infra.* p. 72.

Spanish Commissioners

Antonio Bernaben. Served 1927–1929.

José Garcia Acuna. Served 1929–1930.

Emilio Zapico. Served from 1930.

Presiding Commissioner

Miguel Cruchaga Tocornal. Chile. Appointed by agreement of the two governments. Served continuously from 1927.

TABLE VII

MEMBERS OF THE ITALIAN-MEXICAN CLAIMS COMMISSION

Mexican Commissioner

Isidro Fabela. Served continuously from 1930.

Italian Commissioner

Mario Serra di Cassano. Served continuously from 1930.

Presiding Commissioner

Miguel Cruchaga Tocornal. Chile. Served continuously from 1930.

TABLE VIII

MEMBERS OF THE BELGIAN-MEXICAN ADMINISTRATIVE ARBITRAL TRIBUNAL

Mexican Arbitrator

Julio Garcia.

Belgian Arbitrator

Edmond Adolphe Bouchot.

SECRETARIES OF THE COMMISSIONS

§74. **Provisions in the Conventions Concerning Secretaries.**
The preliminary drafts of the Claims Convention between the United States and Mexico contained no mention of a secretariat to serve the commission. Obviously, a commission would have difficulty in functioning without such a body, and all the Claims Conventions concluded by Mexico contained a provision similar to the following:

The Commission shall keep an accurate record of the claims and cases submitted, and minutes of its proceedings with the dates thereof. To this end, each Government may appoint a Secretary; these Secretaries shall act as joint Secretaries of the Commission and shall be subject to its instructions. Each Government may also appoint and employ any necessary assistant secretaries

and such other assistance as may be deemed necessary. The Commission may also appoint and employ any person necessary to assist in the performance of its duties.

This provision is badly drafted. While the secretaries are expressly made subject to the instructions of the Commission, the assistant secretaries are not. The latter are to be appointed and employed by the governments, which would imply full control by the latter.[17] Such divided control might well have led to unpleasant consequences, though none are disclosed by the records.

§75. **The Question of the Control over Secretaries.** On at least one occasion, however, the question was raised as to who had control of the secretaries. During the controversy between the Mexican government and M. Verzijl, President of the French-Mexican Commission over the regularity of the constitution of that Commission, a meeting of the latter was called by M. Verzijl (on May 24, 1929). In a letter of May 27, 1929, the Mexican Sub-secretary of Foreign Relations, Señor Cienfuegos, informed M. Verzijl that the Mexican government no longer considered him to be President and stated that the Mexican secretary had been ordered to absent himself from the Commission. In reply, M. Verzijl protested that under the Convention the secretaries were subject to the orders of the Commission. It is, of course, true that the Convention so provides. But whether or not the action of the Mexican government was improper would depend on the validity of the contention of that government that M. Verzijl had no authority to convene the Commission.

§76. **Duties of Secretaries.** All the Rules of Procedure imposed substantially the same duties on the secretaries. They were custodians of all documents and records of the Commission; they had to keep the Docket, Minute Book, Notice Book, Order Book, Register of Awards and other books and documents which the Commission might order; indorse the date of filing on documents presented to the Commission, and enter a minute thereof in the Docket; enter in the Notice Book all notices required by the Rules to be filed by the agents and give notice thereof to the agent required to be notified; furnish copies of pleadings, motions, notices and other papers filed to the agent of

---

[17] That the Commissions, in practice, did not exercise control over the assistant secretaries may perhaps be inferred from the absence of any mention of such functionaries in any of the Rules of Procedure.

the opposite party; and perform such other duties as the Commission might prescribe.[18] In addition, the British-Mexican and Italian-Mexican Rules provided that the secretaries should render reports on the work of the Commission to their respective governments at such a time as the Commission might not be sitting.[19]

A unique function was conferred on the secretaries by the Rules of the Spanish-Mexican Commission. Both secretaries were given the duty of examining witnesses under oath or affirmation "in accordance with the tenor of interrogatories presented by the agents." [20]

§77. **Minor employees.** Only in the Rules of the Spanish-Mexican, Italian-Mexican and United States-Mexican General Claims Commissions was any reference made to minor employees.[20a] It was there provided that persons employed in making translations for the Commission and interpreters employed at hearings were placed under the jurisdiction of the secretaries, subject to the direction of the Commission.[20b]

EXPENSES OF THE COMMISSIONS

§78. **Provisions in the Conventions for Payment of Expenses.** The Mexican preliminary draft of the Claims Convention with the United States provided for a unique method of paying for the expenses of the Commission.[21] Each government was to pay its own commissioner and bear its own expenses. The expenses of the Commission, including the salary of the third commissioner, were to be paid by deducting 5% of the total sum awarded by the Commission to each government. If this were not sufficient, the remainder was to be paid

---

[18] The question as to whether secretaries could refuse to receive a document does not seem to have arisen before any of the Mexican Claims Commissions. In the United States-German Mixed Claims Commission, the German secretary on one occasion refused to receive a petition for rehearing. In a suit in a United States court against the government of Germany, it was contended that the claims attempted to be reheard were not pending because of this refusal. The Rules of the Commission with regard to the duties of secretaries were similar to those of the Mexican Claims Commission. It was held that: "The joint secretaries are under the control of the commissioners, and it is not within the power of the secretaries to determine what documents are to be filed." U. S. on behalf of Lehigh Valley R. R. Co. v. Government of Germany, 5 Fed. Supp. 97 (E.D.N.Y. 1933).

[19] British-Mexican Rule 53 (h) ; Italian-Mexican Rules, Art. 48 (h).

[20] Spanish-Mexican Rules, Art. 33.

[20a] U. S.-Mexican General Rule XII 2; Spanish-Mexican Rules, Art. 53; Italian-Mexican Rules, Art. 49.

[20b] The United States-Mexican General Rules originally provided that minor employees should "be placed under the exclusive control and direction of the secretaries." In 1926 this provision was amended by adding the words: "subject to the direction of the Commission."

[21] *La cuestion internacional,* p. 50.

equally by both governments. This proposal had the merit of apportioning the expenses in accordance with the advantage which each of the governments derived from the work of the Commission. It would, of course, have meant that Mexico's share would have been much less than that of the United States. However, the proposal possessed the singular vice of failing to make any provision for payment of expenses before the termination of the Commission's work. It is obvious also, that such a scheme could not be applied to the Special Claims Commissions where no claims by Mexico were to be entertained.

As finally concluded each of the Claims Conventions provided that each government was to pay its own commissioner and bear its own expenses and that the expenses of the Commission, including the salary of the third commissioner, were to be borne equally by the two governments.[22] It may be observed that this equal division of expenses imposed a rather heavy burden on Mexico, which was not only party to all the Commissions, but also would have to bear the eventual burden of paying the sums awarded.

§79. **Cost of the Commissions to the Governments.** No exact indication of the cost of the Commissions to the various governments can be found in the public documents. In the case of Italy and Germany no information is available from the published budgetary estimates. The estimates of other governments furnish some approximation of the cost of the Commissions.

The appropriations made by the United States may be set out in some detail. Unfortunately, it is not possible to determine what sums were expended for each of the two Commissions, and for the agency of the United States.

§80. **Appropriations by the Congress of the United States.** The first appropriation of $171,930.00 for the fiscal year 1925 was contained in the Second Deficiency Act, 1924.[23] This appropriation was made:

"For the expenses of the settlement and adjustment of claims by the citizens of each country against the other under a convention concluded September 8, 1923, and of citizens of the United States against Mexico under a convention concluded September 10, 1923, between the United States and

---

[22] Art. X of the United States-Mexican Convention, British-Mexican Convention, French-Mexican Convention, Spanish-Mexican Convention and Italian-Mexican Convention; Art. XI of the German-Mexican Convention.
[23] Act of Dec. 5, 1924, 43 Stat. 672, at 691.

Mexico, including the expenses which, under the terms of the two conventions, are chargeable in part to the United States, the expenses of the two commissions and the expenses of an agency of the United States to perform all necessary services in connection with the preparation of the claims and the presenting thereof before the said Commissions, as well as defending the United States in cases presented under the general convention by Mexico, including salaries of an agent and necessary counsel and other assistants and employees in the District of Columbia and elsewhere, rent, law books and books of reference, printing and binding, contingent expenses, traveling and subsistence expenses, and such other expenses in the United States and elsewhere as the President may deem proper."

By the Act of February 27, 1925,[24] $275,000.00 was appropriated for the same purposes for the fiscal year 1926, of which $100,000 was to be immediately available. By the Second Deficiency Act, 1925,[25] the Secretary of State was authorized to allow out of the appropriation for 1925 "the payment of per diem in lieu of subsistence for foreign travel at not to exceed $8." Further appropriations were as follows: for the fiscal year 1927, $350,000; [26] deficiency appropriation for the fiscal year 1926, $10,800; [27] for the fiscal year 1928, $350,000; [28] for the fiscal year 1929, $350,000; [29] for the fiscal year, 1930, $350,000; [30] for the fiscal year 1931, $350,000; [31] for the fiscal year 1932, $367,-000.[32] By the Act of May 29, 1928 [33] the appropriation for the fiscal years 1928 and 1929 were made available "for the payment of special counsel, translators, and other technical experts heretofore or hereafter employed by contract without regard to the provisions of any other statute, and for contract stenographic services without regard to section 3709 of the Revised Statutes of the United States." Subsequent appropriations were also made available for such purposes. The First Deficiency Act, 1932,[34] provided that $50,000 of the $367,000 appropriation for the fiscal year 1932, should be available "for such expenses, in addition to those now enumerated in the appropriation, as in the

[24] 43 Stat. 1014, at 1024.
[25] Act of March 4, 1925, 43 Stat. 1313, at 1340.
[26] Act of April 29, 1926, 44 Stat. 330, at 340.
[27] Second Deficiency Act, 1926, Act of July 3, 1926, 44 Stat. 841, at 865.
[28] Act of Feb. 24, 1927, 44 Stat. 1178, at 1190.
[29] Act of Feb. 15, 1928, 45 Stat. 64, at 74.
[30] Act of Jan. 25, 1929, 45 Stat. 1094, at 1105.
[31] Act of April 18, 1930, 46 Stat. 173, at 184.
[32] Act of Feb. 23, 1931, 46 Stat. 1309, at 1319.
[33] 45 Stat. 883, at 913.
[34] Act of Feb. 2, 1932, 47 Stat. 15, at 25.

discretion of the Secretary of State may be necessary in closing up the affairs of the agency of the United States, including expenses incurred on and after October 15, 1931." By the Second Deficiency Act, 1932,[35] the unexpended balance of the appropriation for the fiscal year 1932 was made available until June 30, 1933.

TABLE IX

RECAPITULATION

APPROPRIATION BY THE CONGRESS OF THE UNITED STATES FOR THE EX-
PENSES OF THE GENERAL AND SPECIAL CLAIMS COMMISSIONS AND OF THE
AGENCY OF THE UNITED STATES.

Fiscal year	Appropriations
1925	$ 171,930
1926	275,000
1926 deficiency	10,800
1927	350,000
1928	350,000
1929	350,000
1930	350,000
1931	350,000
1932	367,000
Total	$ 2,574,730

TABLE X

COST TO THE MEXICAN GOVERNMENT OF THE COMMISSIONS AND THE MEX-
ICAN AGENCY.

Year		Appropriations in Pesos	
1925 [36]	U.S.-Mexican General Comm. and U.S.-Mexican Special Comm.		310,000
1926 [37]	U.S.-Mexican General Comm.	250,000	
	U.S.-Mexican Special Comm.	175,000	
	French-Mexican Comm.	95,000	
	Spanish-Mexican Comm.	150,000	
	German-Mexican Comm.	110,000	
	Total		780,000
1927 [38]	U.S.-Mexican General Comm.	265,000	
	U.S.-Mexican Special Comm.	125,000	
	Spanish-Mexican Comm.	85,000	
	German-Mexican Comm.	58,000	
	French-Mexican Comm.	12,000	

[35] Act of July 1, 1932, 47 Stat. 525, at 538.
[36] *Memoria de la Secretaría de Relaciones Exteriores*, 1925–6, p. 289.
[37] *Memoria*, 1925–26, p. 288.   [38] *Memoria*, 1926–27, p. 652.

Additional appropriations [39]

Appropriations in Pesos

U.S.-Mexican General Comm.	50,000	
U.S.-Mexican Special Comm.	3,000	
Total		598,000

1928 [40]

U.S.-Mexican General Comm.	313,240	
U.S.-Mexican Special Comm.	127,040	
Spanish-Mexican Comm.	77,540	
German-Mexican Comm.	60,540	
French-Mexican Comm.	60,540	
Italian-Mexican Comm.	26,940	
British-Mexican Comm.	55,540	
Total		721,380

1929 [41]

U.S.-Mexican General Comm.	250,000	
U.S.-Mexican Special Comm.	120,000	
Spanish-Mexican Comm.	54,995	
German-Mexican Comm.	41,509	
French-Mexican Comm.	30,000	
Italian-Mexican Comm.	12,575	
British-Mexican Comm.	57,076.50	
Total		566,155.50

1930 [42]   Appropriated for all Commissions   551,637.50

1931 [43]   Appropriated for all Commissions   510,671.44

1932 [44]   Appropriated for all Commissions   347,499.60

[39] *Memoria,* 1927–28, p. 878.
[40] *Memoria,* 1927–28, p. 890.
[41] *Memoria,* 1929–30, Annex 9.
[42] *Memoria,* 1930–31, Annex 21. For 1930 and subsequent years the appropriations for each Commission are not separately listed. The total listed is made up of the following items:

Salaries	75,737.50
Technical personnel	333,500.00
Supernumerary employees, substitutes and extra pay for personnel in United States	130,000.00
Service of dependencies	12,400.00
Total	551,637.50

[43] *Memoria,* 1931–32, table facing p. 1072. The total given is made up:

Salaries	72,271.44
Services of personnel	430,000.00
Services of dependencies	8,400.00
Total	510,671.44

[44] *Memoria,* 1931–32, table facing p. 1072. The total given is made up of:

Salaries	51,099.60
Services of personnel	285,000.00
Services of dependencies	11,400.00
Total	347,499.60

TABLE XI

RECAPITULATION OF APPROPRIATIONS BY MEXICO FOR ALL COMMISSIONS.

Year	Appropriations in Pesos
1925	310,000.00
1926	780,000.00
1927	598,000.00
1928	721,380.00
1929	566,155.50
1930	551,637.50
1931	510,671.44
1932	347,499.60
Total	4,385,344.04

TABLE XII

COST TO THE BRITISH GOVERNMENT OF THE BRITISH–MEXICAN CLAIMS COMMISSION AND THE BRITISH AGENCY.

Year	Provisions in Pounds
1927 [45]	6,000
1928 [46]	3,500
1929 [47]	6,470
1930 [48]	4,380
1931 [49]	4,500
1932 [50]	10
Total	£24,860

TABLE XIII

COST TO THE FRENCH GOVERNMENT OF THE FRENCH–MEXICAN CLAIMS COMMISSION AND THE FRENCH AGENCY.

Fiscal year	Appropriations in Francs
1926 [51]	580,000
1927 [52]	778,500
1928 [53]	656,700
1929 [54]	791,600
1930 [55]	nothing
1931–32 [56]	395,800
Total	3,202,600

[45] Civil Estimates, 1927. A provision of £6,000 was made for 1926 but it was not required and a revote was taken for 1927.
[46] Civil Estimates, 1928.
[47] Civil Estimates, 1929. Of this amount, £1,118 was an additional vote due to inadequate provision for travelling and general expenses.
[48] Civil Estimates, 1930.   [49] Civil Estimates, 1931.   [50] Civil Estimates, 1932.
[51] Projet de loi présenté à la Chambre des Députés portant fixation du Budget Général de l'exercice 1926—Affaires Etrangères.
[52] Ibid., 1927.   [54] Ibid., 1929.   [56] Ibid., 1931–32.
[53] Ibid., 1928.   [55] Ibid., 1930.

TABLE XIV

COST TO THE SPANISH GOVERNMENT OF THE SPANISH–MEXICAN CLAIMS
COMMISSION AND THE SPANISH AGENCY.

Year	Appropriations in Pesos
1927 [57]	181,300
1928 [58]	221,300
1929 [59]	150,000
1930 [60]	150,000
1931 [61]	150,000
1932 [62]	150,000
Total	1,002,600

[57] *Resúmens generales de los presupuestos del Estado*, 1927.
[58] *Ibid.*, 1928.　　　[60] *Ibid.*, 1930　　　[62] *Ibid.*, 1932.
[59] *Ibid.*, 1929.　　　[61] *Ibid.*, 1931.

CHAPTER 5

THE WORK OF THE COMMISSIONS: HEREIN OF THE SUPPLEMENTARY CONVENTIONS

§81. Difficulties Encountered in the Work of International Tribunals. The colorless phrases of the official documents which tell of the life of international institutions do not often reveal the human factors which have influenced this life. The work of international tribunals, like that of all human institutions, is affected by the short-comings and emotions of those who create and direct the tribunals. No matter how skillfully conventions and rules of procedure are drawn up, no matter how carefully chosen the personnel may be, friction and disagreement are bound to arise. Obviously, however, such hindrances to efficient work must be kept at a minimum. It is essential, first of all that the period during which claims are to be decided be so fixed that the tribunal should be able to finish its work within that period. Sufficient time for filing claims should be provided so that the Foreign Offices will be able to sort out those claims which are worthy of consideration. The Convention and the rules of procedure should be carefully drafted so as to obviate haggling and delay over petty technicalities. Lastly, the members of the tribunal should be carefully chosen.

As will appear later, many of these counsels were overlooked in the organization of the Mexican Claims Commissions. The result was much confusion and delay and not a little bitterness. The difficulties engendered by procedural and jurisdictional provisions will be related in other chapters. Here we are concerned with the business of the Commissions—what their tasks were, how they accomplished them and some of the obstacles which were met.

UNITED STATES-MEXICAN GENERAL CLAIMS COMMISSION

§82. The First Three Years of the United States–Mexican General Claims Commission. The General Claims Convention pro-

vided that the Commission should meet for organization within six months after the exchange of ratifications. All claims accruing prior to the signing of the Convention were to be filed within one year from the date of the first meeting.[1] The Commission was bound to hear and to decide all these claims within a period of three years from the date of the first meeting. During this period of three years, the governments were permitted to file additional claims accruing after the signing of the Convention. If any such claims were not decided during the three year period, the governments agreed to extend the life of the Commission to permit decision.

The period of one year for the filing of claims was lamentably short. Neither government had adequate opportunity to sort out the meritorious claims in its files. Since all claims, whether presented to the Commission or not, were to be considered as settled, the two governments proceeded figuratively to dump the contents of their claims files on the desks of the Commission.[1a] The United States filed 2,781 claims amounting to $513,694,267.17 and Mexico filed 836 claims amounting to $245,158,395.32.

With so huge a mass of claims before it, the three year period of life given to the Commission proved far too brief. The Commission met for organizational purposes on August 30, 1924. Thus its life should have expired on August 30, 1927. During this period five sessions, including the inaugural session, were held. The inaugural session was devoted to preparing the rules of procedure. In the second session, from June 1 to June 30, 1925, various amendments to the rules were adopted and discussion was had with regard to the extension of time for filing claims. No cases were argued. It was in the third session, from February 1 to March 31, 1926, that the Commission began to hear and decide cases. Nineteen opinions were handed down, fifteen of these being interlocutory decisions.[2] In the fourth session (October 1

---

[1] "Unless in any case reasons for the delay, satisfactory to the majority of the Commissioners shall be established, and in any such case the period for filing the claim may not be extended to exceed six additional months." Art. VI.

[1a] This practice has been all too common in claims arbitrations. The American Commissioner in the United States-Mexican Commission of 1868 once stated: "The Mexican Department (of Foreign Affairs) emptied the contents of its waste baskets on the Commission, just as the U. S. Department sent every scrap of paper with 'Mexico' marked on it, to the same reservoir of defunct claims." Perez Case, Docket No. 79, cited in American and Panamanian General Claims Arbitration, Report of Bert L. Hunt (Washington, 1934), p. 11.

[2] The opinions handed down in the third and fourth sessions were rendered in the name of the Commission without indication of the author of the opinion. In the fifth session the practice was adopted of the rendering of opinions by individual commissioners.

to December 6, 1926) twenty-six opinions [3] were handed down, and in the fifth session (March 10 to July 23, 1927) forty-five opinions.[4]

§83. The General Claims Commission under the Supplementary Convention of August 16, 1927. The life of the Commission was about to expire with only sixty claims decided. Obviously, an extension of this life was necessary. On August 16, 1927, a Convention was signed [5] extending the duration of the Commission until August 30, 1929. The Commission was also to decide claims accruing between September 8, 1923, and August 30, 1927, if filed before the latter date.

Simultaneously with the expiration of the first period, Dr. Van Vollenhoven, the presiding Commissioner, resigned. Months were taken up by a fruitless effort to secure agreement on a successor.[6] Finally, reference was made to the President of the Permanent Administrative Council of the Permanent Court of Arbitration, who, on June 16, 1928, appointed Dr. Kristian Sindballe. Two sessions were held under the presidency of the latter, both in Mexico City.[7] Twenty-five opinions were handed down in the first of these (from September 7 to October 18, 1928), and thirty-eight opinions in the second (from March 1 to May 17, 1929).

§84. The Commission under the Supplementary Convention of September 2, 1929. Again the life of the Commission was approaching expiration with comparatively few cases decided. On September 2, 1929, a Convention further extending the duration of the Commission to August 30, 1931, was signed.[8] Dr. Sindballe had resigned on July 1, 1929. A long period of negotiations between the governments followed until they agreed upon Horacio F. Alfaro as Presiding Commissioner. The eighth session began in Mexico on August 13, 1930. Twenty-five cases were argued and twenty-three opinions were handed down. On October 29, the Presiding Commissioner announced a decision to the effect that the Commission would adjourn and would meet again in Washington on December 3, 1930.[9] Commissioner MacGregor dissented. The Mexican agent expressed doubt as to whether a majority

---

[3] A number of these opinions were merely rectifications of previous awards.
[4] A number of these opinions were interlocutory decisions or rectifications of previous awards.
[5] See Appendix, p. 330. Ratifications were exchanged Oct. 12, 1927.
[6] See Dunn, Diplomatic Protection, p. 404.
[7] All the previous sessions had been held in Washington.
[8] See Appendix, p. 333. Ratifications were exchanged October 10, 1929.
[9] *Memoria de la Secretaría de Relaciones Exteriores*, 1930–1931, p. 604.

of the Commission could change the place of meeting without the consent of the two governments.[10] The Presiding Commissioner stated that he would be disposed to follow the instructions of the governments concerned. No further announcement was made of the confirmation or revocation of the decision of October 29, and the Commission continued in session until November 5, 1930. Subsequently it was agreed by direct negotiations between the governments that the ninth session would be held in Washington from May 5 to July 15, 1931.

This ninth session was the last under the 1929 Convention for Further Extension and it appears to have been a troubled one. Three cases were argued, but the Commission did not announce any decisions while the session was in progress. Subsequently the United States Government Printing Office published the text of the opinions in the *International Fisheries* Case which had been argued at this session and in the *Dickson Car Wheel Company* Case which had been argued at the previous session. Both of these opinions bear the date line: "July —, 1931," and the dissenting opinions of the American Commissioner conclude with the following remarks:

"I consider it to be important to mention an interesting point that has arisen since the instant case was argued—Rule XI, 1, provides: 'The award or other judicial decision of the Commission in respect of each claim shall be rendered at a public sitting of the Commission.' The other two Commissioners have signed the 'Decision' in this case. However, no meeting of the Commission was ever called by the Presiding Commissioner to render a decision in this case, and there has never been any compliance with the proper rule above quoted." [11]

The *Memoria* of the Mexican Secretariat of Foreign Relations [12] hints at a more serious disagreement: "As a consequence of an incident provoked (*provocado*) by the American Commissioner, the ninth session of the Commission was, at first, suspended, and then declared terminated in August 1931." The published sources do not reveal what the character of this "incident" was.

The life of the Commission expired on August 30, 1931, no conven-

---

[10] Art. II of the Convention of 1923 provided: "The Commission may fix the time and place of its subsequent meetings, either in the United States or in Mexico, as may be convenient, subject always to the special instructions of the two governments.

[11] Opinions of Commissioners, 1931, pp. 206, 286.

[12] *Memoria de la Secretaría de Relaciones Exteriores,* 1931–1932, p. 268.

tion for a further extension of duration having been concluded. At that time, after some eight years of existence, the balance sheet of the Commission was as follows:

TABLE XV

WORK OF THE UNITED STATES-MEXICAN GENERAL CLAIMS COMMISSION
TO AUGUST 30, 1931

American Claims

Claims filed	2,781,	amounting to	$513,694,267.17
Claims disallowed or dismissed	50		
Awards made	89,	amounting to	$4,607,926.59

Mexican Claims

Claims filed	836,	amounting to	$246,158,395.32
Claims disallowed or dismissed	4		
Awards made	5,	amounting to	$39,000.00

§85. **The Convention and Protocol of June 18, 1932.** On December 10, 1931, President Hoover, in a special message to Congress,[13] stated that negotiations looking towards a renewal of activities of both the General and Special Commissions were under way. Previously, on February 17, 1931, the Senate of the United States had passed a resolution requesting the president to conclude agreements for extending the duration of the two Commissions.[14] Two Conventions and two protocols were signed on June 18, 1932.[15] One of those Conventions provided for an extension of the duration of the General Claims Commission for two years from the date of the exchange of ratifications. The accompanying protocol contained certain provisions intended to speed up the work of disposing of the claims. The two governments were to proceed to discuss in an informal manner the pending agrarian claims with a view to reaching an agreement with respect to them consistent with equity and with the rights of the claimants and the rights

[13] 75 Congressional Record (72nd Cong., 1st Sess.), p. 299.
[14] "The President is requested, in his discretion, to negotiate and conclude with the Mexican Government such agreement or agreements as may be necessary and appropriate for the further extension of the duration of the General Claims Commission provided for by the Convention of September 8, 1923, and of the Special Claims Commission provided for by the Convention of September 10, 1923, between the United States and Mexico, in order to permit of the hearing, examination, and decision of all claims within the jurisdiction of said commissions under the terms of said conventions, and to make such further arrangements as in his judgment may be deemed appropriate for the expeditious adjudication of such claims." 74 Congressional Record (71st Cong., 3rd Sess.), p. 6410.
[15] Texts in *Memoria de la Secretaría de Relaciones Exteriores*, 1931–1932, Appendix, p. 7 *et seq.*

and obligations of the Mexican government. During this discussion no agrarian claims were to be submitted to the Commission for decision. The meetings of the Commission were to be held partly in Mexico City and partly in Washington. The Presiding Commissioner was to be requested to keep the Commission in continuous session except for short vacations. The agents of the two governments were to be instructed to secure the amendment to the Rules of Procedure with a view to speeding up the presentation of claims, shortening oral argument, and facilitating the settlement of claims by agreement of the agents.

§86. **The Protocol of April 24, 1934.** The Convention of June 18, 1932, came into force, by exchange of ratifications on December 13, 1934. Previous to this coming into force there was concluded on April 24, 1934, a protocol relating to the general claims.[16] Under this protocol it was agreed to preserve the *status quo* of the General Claims Convention of 1923 and of the Convention of June 18, 1932, extending the duration of the former. However, fundamental changes were made in the organization of the Commission and in procedural method. The preamble set forth the advisability of effecting "a more expeditious and more economical disposition of the claims, either by means of an *en bloc* settlement or a more simplified method of adjudication." Since the available information at the time of the signing of the Protocol was not such as to permit the two governments to appraise the true value of the claims presented "with sufficient accuracy to permit of the successful negotiation of an *en bloc* settlement," the following method of procedure was agreed upon. Each government was to designate promptly from among its own nationals an outstanding jurist to serve as Commissioner. Each Commissioner, individually, was to proceed to appraise claims, on their merits, as rapidly as possibly. The two commissioners were to meet six months before the termination of the period agreed upon for the completion of the pleadings and briefs. The two Commissioners were to attempt to reconcile their appraisals, and were then, not later than six months from the date of the completion of the pleadings and briefs, to submit to the two governments a joint report of their conferences. This report was to indicate those cases in which they should be unable to agree with respect to the merits or the amount of liability.

Upon the basis of this joint report, the two governments were then

---

[16] See Appendix, p. 340.

to conclude, with the least possible delay, a convention for the final disposition of the claims; this convention to take one of the following forms: either an agreement for *en bloc* settlement, or an agreement for the disposition of the claims on their individual merits. If the latter alternative were adopted, the two Commissioners were to be required to record their agreements with respect to individual claims and the bases upon which their conclusions had been reached. The convention to be concluded, was to accept the report as final and conclusive disposition of the cases on which the two Commissioners had reached an agreement. With respect to those cases in which the Commissioners should not have been able to reach agreements, the two governments were to agree, by the convention to be concluded, that the pleadings and briefs in such cases, together with the written views of the two Commissioners, should be referred to an Umpire, whose written decisions were to be accepted by both governments as final and binding.

The Protocol of 1934 also contained various provisions relating to procedure. Pleadings and briefs were to be limited to four in number—Memorial, Answer, Brief and Reply Brief. All pleadings and briefs were to be filed at the Embassy of the respective government; the Joint Secretaries being thus dispensed with. The time for filing briefs and pleadings was to be two years counting from a date agreed upon between the two governments in an exchange of notes to take place not later than November 1, 1934.[16a] There were to be no oral proceedings. For the purposes of the pleadings and briefs and for the appraisals and decisions of the two Commissioners and the decisions of the Umpire, the provisions of the General Claims Convention of 1923 were to be considered as fully effective and binding upon the two Governments, except in so far as matters of procedure were concerned.

Provision was also made in the Protocol of 1934 with respect to agrarian claims. It was agreed that the two governments would proceed to an informal discussion of the agrarian claims pending before the General Claims Commission, "with a view to making an adjustment thereof that shall be consistent with the rights and equities of the claimants and the rights and obligations of the Mexican Government, as provided by the General Claims Protocol of June 18, 1932. Pending such discussion no agrarian claims were to be presented to the Commis-

---

[16a] The writer is informed by the American Agency that the date for completing the filing of pleadings and briefs has been set at Feb. 1, 1937.

sioners or to the Umpire; but memorials of cases not yet memorialized might be filed in order to regularize the awards made upon the agreed adjustments. Consequently, the other provisions of the Protocol of 1934 were to apply to agrarian claims only in so far as these provisions should not conflict with the status of the agrarian claims "as exclusively fixed" by Article I of the Protocol of 1932.

The result of these provisions is to leave the status of the agrarian claims curiously vague. Apparently, if the informal discussion of these claims should be terminated before the Commissioners file their report, then appraisal and decision of these claims will be proceeded with. Otherwise, it is to be presumed that agrarian claims would be taken care of in an *en bloc* settlement if at all. The relationship between the Protocol of 1934 and the Protocol of 1932 is exceedingly difficult to determine. The former clearly envisages the remaining in force of Article I of the 1932 Protocol. At the same time every word in this Article I is repeated in the 1934 Protocol. It is, therefore, uncertain what is meant by the status of the agrarian claims "as exclusively fixed" by the terms of Article I of the 1932 Protocol. All in all, it would seem as if the 1932 Protocol has a mere formal existence and none of its provisions could have any applicability.

United States-Mexican Special Claims Commission

§87. **The First Five Years of the Commission.** The Special Claims Convention contained rather liberal time provisions. All claims were to be filed within two years from the date of the first meeting of the Commission, and the duration of the Commission was to extend to five years from the date of the first meeting. Apparently it was assumed that many more claims would be filed before this Commission than before the General Claims Commission. In fact, fewer claims were filed, 3,176 for an aggregate amount of $421,300,132.41. Yet, though there were fewer claims and the period for decision was longer, the Special Claims Commission accomplished much less than the General Claims Commission.

The Commission first met in Mexico City from August 18, 1924, to August 22, 1924, when the Rules of Procedure were adopted. The second session (January 23 and 24, 1925) was taken up with discussion of amendments to the rules. The next session did not take place until a year later, January 5 to February 10, 1926. It was devoted

mainly to arguments on the *Santa Isabel* claims, and marked the beginning of a series of unfortunate disagreements which were destined to hamper seriously the work of the Commission. At one point, the American agent moved to strike out a portion of the Mexican answer on the ground that it was offensive to the United States. When the Commission, with the American Commission dissenting, denied the motion, the American agent entered a protest. The Presiding Commissioner then answered that the decision had been an impartial one and that the protest would be admitted only as evidence of the liberality of the Commission.[17] On February 8, the American agent (Col. Henry H. Anderson) gave a statement to the press to the effect that the attitude of the American agent in denying liability for acts of Villa forces "in effect negatives the entire convention and is a repudiation of liability on the part of Mexico."[18] This was followed by rumors of serious difficulties and by press reports that the Commission would probably dissolve if the Mexican viewpoint were sustained.[19] On February 11, the Mexican agent found it necessary to deny statements that serious difficulties had arisen because of the position of the American agent.[20] On March 5, an Associated Press despatch stated that the Presiding Commissioner (Dr. Rodrigo Octavio) had formally notified the American Commissioner (Judge Perry) that he intended to resign for reasons of health.[21] Rumors persisted that the Commission had rendered a decision favorable to Mexico, and on March 10 the Mexican agent issued a statement to this effect.[22] In the meantime the Presiding Commissioner had gone to Havana and, from there, issued a call for the Commission to meet at Tampico on April 12. The Mexican government agreed, but since the United States insisted that the meetings must be held in Mexico City, a new call was sent out for a meeting to be held in the latter place on April 26.[23]

On that date the Commission handed down a decision dismissing the claims, the American Commissioner dissenting. Before the de-

---

[17] *Memoria de la Secretaría de Relaciones Exteriores,* 1925–1926, p. 41.
[18] New York Times, Feb. 9, 1926, p. 1.
[19] New York Times, Feb. 10, 1926, p. 12. See also editorial, New York Times, Feb. 11, 1926, p. 20, commencing: "It is unbelievable that the Mexican Government . . . will persist in ignoring claims for damages sustained by Americans in the Villa and Zapata revolts."
[20] New York Times, Feb. 12, 1926, p. 11.
[21] New York Times, March 6, 1926, p. 3.
[22] New York Times, March 11, 1926, p. 2.
[23] New York Times, April 13, 1926, p. 9.

cision was read, the American Commissioner charged that he had never been consulted about the opinion and that a copy of it had been given to the Mexican Commissioner beforehand but not to him.[24] Following the reading of the decision, the Assistant Agent of the United States presented in writing a reservation of rights against the decision. Thereupon the Mexican Agent moved to strike out the protest as contrary to Article VIII of the Convention relating to the finality of decisions. After hearing the opinions of the national Commissioners, the Presiding Commissioner declared that it was a constant practice of international arbitral commissions not to reject immediately any protest or reservation of rights, and that therefore, although in his opinion it was irregular, he agreed that a written protest should be received.[25] On July 7, 1926, the Presiding Commissioner resigned for reasons of health.

[24] See New York Times, April 27, 1926, p. 9, giving a highly dramatic description of the meeting. The Presiding Commissioner found it necessary to refute this account in the following letter (New York Times, May 8, 1926, p. 17):

"To the Editor of the New York Times:

"The reports published by the press about the last meeting of the Mexican-American Claims Commission, held in Mexico City on March 26, and which have just reached me on my arrival here from Mexico, are so fantastic and without foundation that I feel I must ask you to rectify them.

"That meeting was not characterized by any disagreeable incidents such as were circulated in the press. The condition of my health not permitting of my remaining in Mexico City, I arrived in that capital from Tampico on the morning of the 26th, for which date a meeting of the commission had been called.

"My intention was to have a private meeting with my associate Commissioners in order to acquaint them with my decision on the Santa Ysabel claims, which I had prepared in accordance with the written opinions of the Commissioners. On my arrival in Mexico City I was informed that the Commission had been called to a public meeting to be held at 11 A.M. of that day. Notwithstanding the pressure of time, I went to that meeting, having invited my colleagues to a private meeting, which Judge Perry refused to attend. At the public meeting I again invited Judge Perry to participate in the private session and as he refused to do so I took a seat and opened the public meeting.

"I then explained that, having received the written opinions of the Commissioners on the Santa Ysabel claims, I took them with me to Havana, where I was compelled to go by the condition of my health, and where I wrote my decision in accordance with the opinion of the majority. Upon my arrival in Tampico, where I thought the commission meeting would be held, I sent to my secretary in Mexico City the English and Spanish texts of my decision both written by me, in order that copies might be made therefrom, as required by the rules of procedure.

"The private meeting to which I had invited my colleagues was for the purpose of explaining the aforesaid and to acquaint them with the text of my decision before it would be signed and published in the public meeting. With the refusal of Judge Perry to take part in the private meeting, I offered to each of my associate Commissioners a copy of the decision and adjourned the meeting until 3 o'clock so they might take cognizance of it. At 3 o'clock in the afternoon the meeting was held, the decision signed, and the dissenting opinion of Judge Perry read. The Commissioners then agreed to adjourn until the next meeting, set for Sept. 1, 1926, at Tampico, subject to instructions of the interested Governments.   RODERIGO OCTAVIO

"Presiding Commissioner, Mexican-American Claims Commission. New York, May 7, 1926."

[25] *Memoria de la Secretaría de Relaciones Exteriores*, 1925-1926, p. 44.

It is difficult to evaluate the merits of this controversy from the accounts available. The action of the American Agent in making a public protest against the attitude of the Mexican Agent before a decision was rendered was hardly proper. Who was responsible for the leaking out of the decision cannot now be ascertained, but the Commission should have made every effort to prevent such an occurrence. The publicity attending the matter was particularly unfortunate. Yet, it must not be forgotten that these incidents took place in the midst of a serious diplomatic controversy between the United States and Mexico with respect to agrarian and petroleum legislation. Undoubtedly, this latter controversy produced a supercharged atmosphere which contributed a good deal to the irritation displayed in the *Santa Isabel* matter.

The *Santa Isabel* decision caused considerable dissatisfaction in the United States.[26] The result was that several years passed before a successor to Señor Octavio was named. In April 1928 when the two governments agreed to call upon the President of the Permanent Administrative Council of the Permanent Court of Arbitration to designate a presiding commissioner for the General Claims Commission, it was agreed that the person so designated should also serve as presiding commissioner of the Special Claims Commission.[27] Dr. Sindballe was thus designated, but the Special Claims Commission did not meet at any time during his presidency.

§88. **The Commission under the Supplementary Convention of August 17, 1929.** By a Convention signed August 17, 1929,[28] the duration of the Commission, which was to expire on that same day, was extended for two years. Horacio F. Alfaro was subsequently designated as the presiding commissioner, and the Commission met again in February 1931, after a lapse of five years. At this session, a large number of motions for the filing of late claims were passed upon, but the chief matter disposed of was the *Russell* claim.[29] This seems to have aroused an extraordinary passion in the Commissioners, of which the opinions rendered are a sufficient indication. Three opinions were written, one by each of the Commissioners. These are followed by a

---

[26] See, *e.g.*, Editorial in the New York Times, April 28, 1926, p. 24.
[27] U. S. Department of State Press Release, April 24, 1928.
[28] See Appendix, p. 393. Ratifications were exchanged Oct. 29, 1929.
[29] U. S. A. (Naomi Russell) *v.* United Mexican States, 1926-1931, p. 44.

decision dated April 24, 1931, disallowing the claim, signed by the Presiding Commissioner with the Mexican Commissioner concurring. Commissioner Nielsen then filed a dissenting opinion under date of June 20 in which he takes exception to the method followed in arriving at the decision of the Commission.[30] The Mexican Commissioner then filed, under date of July 11, 1931, a document entitled "Supplementary Observations in Regard to the Decision in the Russell Case" wherein he stated that he had "been surprised by the arguments advanced by the Commissioner of the United States, to the effect that the procedure followed is, under the Convention of September 10, 1923, irregular, as the President should abstain from stating his points of view in writing until after knowing the opinions of the other two Commissioners." Commissioner Nielsen then replied with a document headed "Comments on 'Supplementary Observations, etc.'" commencing in this fashion: "There has come to my notice some kind of an opinion filed by the Mexican Commissioner, Dr. Gonzalez Roa, in relation to the Russell case. The opinion is a combination of strange statements made by himself and by the Mexican agent, Dr. Elorduy. It appears to be a reply to my dissenting opinion written in that case."

Shortly after this somewhat heated interchange of views between the two national Commissioners, the duration of the Commission came to an end. After some eight years of existence, its work could be summarized as follows:

[30] "The reasons why I dissent from the decision disallowing this claim are indicated by the opinion which I wrote under the plan adopted by the Commissioners to express their views respecting the issues involved in the case. However, when I formulated the opinion I had not before me the views of the Presiding Commissioner nor those of the Mexican Commissioner. . . .

"The Convention of September 10, 1923, provides for a Commission of three members. The decision in each case must be reached, in my opinion, by discussion among those members respecting the question of liability or non-liability of the respondent government. The discussion of that question requires a comparison of the views of all the members and not solely a comparison of the views of the two Commissioners appointed, respectively, by each of the Governments parties to the arbitration. If such an interchange of views is to be effected, as was done in the instant case, to some extent by an exchange of written opinions, it seems to me that the Commissioners should have before them the opinions of all three members, and that the Presiding Commissioner should not refrain from expressing any views in writing until after the submission of written opinions by the other two Commissioners. The instant case was promptly dismissed following the preparation of the third opinion. The procedure following in this case seems to me to conform in its fundamental features to that prescribed by arbitration treaties which provide for two Commissioners and an Umpire, rather than with that established by a Convention creating a Commission of three members. Undoubtedly the former may at times possess certain advantages, but the latter is that which is prescribed by the Convention of September 10, 1923." *Ibid.*, pp. 152–153.

TABLE XVI

WORK OF THE UNITED STATES-MEXICAN SPECIAL CLAIMS COMMISSION TO AUGUST 1931

Claims filed   3,176, amounting to $421,300,132.41
Claims disallowed   18
Awards made   None.

§89. The Unratified Convention and Protocol of June 18, 1932.
Following the resolution of the Senate of the United States referred to earlier, a Convention and Protocol were concluded on June 18, 1932.[31] The Convention provided for an extension of the duration of the Commission for two years following the exchange of ratifications. The Protocol provided for amendments to the Rules of Procedure similar to those contained in the Protocol of the same date relating to the General Claims Commission. It was also provided that all meetings of the Commission should be held in Mexico City, that the Presiding Commissioner should be requested to have the Commission sit continuously, with only short and occasional vacations, and that the governments would instruct their respective Commissioners to admit the terms of the renewed Claims Conventions between Mexico and France, Great Britain and Spain as an interpretation of the Convention and to give consideration to the decisions of the Mexican-German, Mexican-French and Mexican-British Commissions. The Convention and Protocol were ratified by Mexico but not by the United States.

§90. The Convention of April 24, 1934. On April 24, 1934, a new Convention[32] was signed providing for the payment of a lump sum of money which should equal the same proportion of the total amount claimed by the United States as the proportion represented by the total amount awarded on the same class of claims to the governments of Belgium, France, Germany, Great Britain, Italy and Spain. The definite amount of this liability was to be computed and determined by a joint committee, composed of one representative of each government, whose joint report was to be accepted by the two governments as final. In computing the total amount claimed by the United States there was to be deducted (1) claims decided; (2) one half of the amount represented by the total claimed in all cases in which the same claim had been filed twice with the Special Claims Commission;

[31] Texts in *Memoria de la Secretaría de Relaciones Exteriores,* 1931–1932, Appendix, p. 12 *et seq.*
[32] See Appendix, p. 395.

(3) the total amount of claims registered with both Commissions which in fact or apparently should have been registered only with the General Claims Commission. The amount provided for was to be paid at Washington, in dollars, at the rate of $500,000 a year beginning January 1, 1935. All payments made after January 2, 1935, were to bear interest at the rate of one half of one per cent for the first year, and an additional one fourth of one per cent until a maximum of one per cent. For the purpose of facilitating a proper distribution of the money by the United States to the claimants, the Mexican government agreed to deliver to the United States, upon request, all evidence in its possession bearing on the merits of particular claims, and to procure, at the cost of the United States, such additional evidence as the latter might indicate to be necessary.

At the time of the signing of the Convention it was announced that it was contemplated that the special claims would be referred for adjudication on their individual merits to a domestic claims commission in the United States to be established by an Act of Congress.[32a] Ratifications were exchanged on December 13, 1934. On January 3, 1935, the first payment of $500,000 due under the Convention was made.[32b] Thus, the efforts to adjudicate the special claims against Mexico ended with the clear confession that the method of international adjudication had failed.

French-Mexican Commission

§91. The First Two Years of the Commission. The French-Mexican Commission had an unhappy history. Under the Convention of September 25, 1924, all claims were to be filed within nine months after the first meeting of the Commission, and all claims were to be decided within two years from the first meeting. This meeting was held on March 14, 1925. During the first session, which ended on

---

[32a] Press Release, April 28, 1934. The domestic commission (known as the Special Mexican Claims Commission) was established by the Act of April 10, 1935, Public No. 30, 74th Cong. The Commission was to consist of three members appointed by the President, and was to have jurisdiction to hear and determine "conformable to the terms of the Convention of September 10, 1923, and justice and equity, all claims against the Republic of Mexico, notices of which were filed with the Special Claims Commission . . . in which the said Commission failed to award compensation, except such claims as may be found by the Committee provided for in the Special Claims Convention of April 24, 1934 to be General Claims and recognized as such by the General Claims Commission." For the text of the Act of April 10, 1935 see Appendix, p. 539.

[32b] New York Times, January 4, 1935, p. 17. The total amount due under the Convention had not yet been computed at that time.

March 23, 1925, the Rules of Procedure were drawn up. One other session was held but no cases were argued or decided.

§92. **The French–Mexican Commission under the Convention of March 12, 1927.** On March 12, 1927, an additional Convention [33] was signed extending the duration of the commission to nine months following its first meeting after the ratification of this additional convention. If the Commission were not to finish within this period, then a further extension not to exceed nine months could take place by a simple exchange of notes between the two governments.

The Commission reassembled on March 26, 1928. Rodrigo Octavio, the Presiding Commissioner, had resigned previously and had been replaced by Prof. J. H. W. Verzijl of the Netherlands, designated by the President of the Permanent Administrative Council of the Permanent Court of Arbitration. The Commission had before it 251 claims amounting to 43,883,434.14 pesos. During this session which lasted until October 19, 1928, a number of cases were argued and three decisions were handed down, in all three of which the Mexican Commissioner dissented. At the end of the session it was orally agreed among the Commissioners that they would exchange the drafts of their opinions on the other cases which had been argued at this session and on which the oral proceedings had been declared terminated.[34] During the next four months the Presiding Commissioner and the French Commissioner prepared and exchanged draft opinions, but they received no communication from the Mexican Commissioner. The nine months' period provided for in the additional Convention of 1927 expired on December 26, 1928. The exchange of notes, which was necessary in order to extend the duration of the Commission for another nine months, did not take place until April 17, 1929.[35] In the meantime there was serious danger that the Commission would be precluded from passing upon the claims which had previously been argued, and upon which the oral arguments had been declared closed.[36] In consequence, the Presiding Commissioner and the French Commissioner

---

[33] See Appendix, p. 420. Ratifications exchanged Oct. 22, 1927.

[34] The minutes of the final meeting which were inspected by the present writer contain no mention of this agreement. M. Verzijl stated to the present writer that such an agreement had been made.

[35] *Memoria de la Secretaría de Relaciones Exteriores*, 1928–1929, p. 656.

[36] Article VII of the Convention of 1924 provided that the Commission must decide each claim within six months following the termination of the hearing thereon. The hearings on several claims had been declared closed on September 6, 1928. There was nothing in the Additional Convention of 1927 to indicate that a lapse between the expiration of

met in Paris on March 5, 1929 [37] and handed down a decision (Decision No. 20) reopening the proceedings in these cases.[38]

On March 23, 1929, M. Verzijl, in agreement with the French Commissioner, wrote to the Mexican Commissioner proposing that a session be called in Mexico City on May 13, 1929. Receiving no reply, M. Verzijl officially convoked the Commission for May 16, 1929, after having been informed, on April 23, by the French government that the two governments had proceeded to exchange the notes of prorogation provided for in the Convention of 1927. On May 2, as M. Verzijl was about to depart from Utrecht, he received a telegram from the Mexican government, addressed to him in his capacity as Presiding Commissioner, requesting that the session be postponed because of the inability of the Mexican Commissioner to attend. In view of the fact that only five months remained to complete the work of the Commission, M. Verzijl refused to accede to this request, and on his arrival in Mexico on May 15, requested the Mexican government to

---

the nine months' period and the exchange of notes for extending duration would interrupt the running of the six months' period. Hence, decisions would have to be rendered before March 6, 1929.

[37] According to M. Verzijl, the Mexican Commissioner was not informed of this meeting because of the lack of time. Telegrams and letters had been sent to him previously in regard to the draft opinions which he had agreed to send, but no answer had been received from him.

[38] The text of this decision is as follows (manuscript copy furnished by M. Verzijl):

Le Commissaire Président de la Commission franco-mexicaine et le Commissaire de la République Française, réunis à Paris, en vue d'examiner la situation créée par l'expiration éventuelle du delai de 6 mois visé à l'Article VII (dernier alinéa) de la Convention franco-mexicaine des Réclamations du 25 Septembre 1924 concernant une série d'affaires plaidées et déclarées closes au cours de la première période des sessions, prévue dans la Convention additionelle du 12 mars 1927 et,

Considérant qu'à ce jour les Commissaires soussignés n'ont pas reçu l'opinion de leur collègue mexicain relative à aucune des affaires déclarées closes et que par déférence pour lui ils désirent ne pas rendre de sentence à la majorité, avant que ce dernier ait pu donner son avis,

Considérant qu'un supplément d'information parait nécessaire sur les affaires déjà plaidées et qu'il n'a pas été possible de l'obtenir dans les delais voulus,

Considérant qu'à ce jour les Commissaires soussignés ne savent pas si les deux périodes de neuf mois prévues dans la Convention du 12 mars 1927 seront séparées par une interruption de plusieurs mois, ou si au contraire, aucune solution de continuité n'est à envisager,

Considérant que dans l'éventualité où aucune interruption de travaux de la Commission ne serait admise, le délai prévue à l'article VII arrive à expiration du 6 de ce mois pour deux affaires et dans les jours suivants pour plusieurs autres réclamations et que par conséquent les Commissaires soussignés ne peuvent plus différer leur résolution,

En conséquence, les Commissaires soussignés, vu l'article 39 du Règlement de procédure et se prononçant à la majorité en l'absence de leur collègue mexicain,

Decident rouvrir les débats et poursuivre l'examen de la cause dans toutes les affaires déjà plaidées et déclarées closes et dans lesquelles une sentence n'est pas encore intervenue.

Fait à Paris le 5 mars, 1929.

Le Commissaire de la
République Française   Le Commissaire Président
(Signed)   (Signed)

designate a substitute Commissioner in accordance with the procedure established by the Convention. However, the Mexican government had, on May 7, 1929, informed the French government that it considered M. Verzijl's functions as Presiding Commissioner to have terminated on December 26, 1928 (the date of the termination of the Convention of 1927), and no reply was made to M. Verzijl's request.

On May 24, 1929, M. Verzijl definitely convoked the Commission to meet on May 29. The French Minister to Mexico signified his assent to this meeting, but the Mexican Secretariat of Foreign Relations replied (on May 27) by informing M. Verzijl that he was no longer Presiding Commissioner.

Nevertheless, the Commission met on June 3, with the Mexican Commissioner, Agent and Secretary absent. Two decisions were handed down, one (Decision No. 21) [39] affirming that M. Verzijl still

---

[39] The text of this decision (manuscript copy furnished by M. Verzijl) is as follows:

La Commission franco-mexicaine des réclamations, à la suite d'un premier échange de vues à la date du 29 mai dernier, après convocations régulièrement faites.

Considérant que, d'accord avec le Commissaire français, le Président de la Commission a tout d'abord, le 23 mars 1929, proposé au Commissaire mexicain la date du 13 mai pour l'ouverture de la nouvelle session, et ensuite, en l'absence de toute réponse du Commissaire mexicain, a convoqué officiellement la Commission pour le 16 mai 1929,

Considérant que le Gouvernement mexicain, qui à la date du 20 avril 1929 avait adressé une communication à M. Verzijl en sa qualité de Président, a demandé le 2 mai 1929 par voie diplomatique à M. Verzijl toujours considérée comme Président, d'adjourner la réunion de la Commission, vu l'empêchement du Commissaire mexicain,

Considérant que étant donné l'état des travaux en suspens, le Président n'a pas estimé possible de déférer à ce désir et que, dès son arrivé à Mexico, le 15 mai 1929, il a demandé au Gouvernement mexicain de lui indiquer la personnalité designée pour remplacer M. Gonzalez Roa,

Considérant que, aucune réponse n'ayant été faite à cette demande à date du 24 mai 1929, le Président a définitivement convoqué la Commission pour le 29 mai, convocation notifiée, d'une part, au Secrétariat des Relations Extérieures et au Ministre de France, et, d'autre part, au Commissaire français, aux Agents et aux Secrétaires,

Considérant qu'en réponse à cette communication M. Verzijl a reçu, d'une part, une lettre du Ministre de France donnant sa conformité et déclarant qu'il inviterait le Commissaire, l'Agent et le Secrétaire français à se rendre à cette convocation et d'autre part, une lettre du Ministère des Relations Extérieures lui faisant connaître qu'il ne le considerait plus comme Président depuis le 26 décembre 1928 et qu'en conséquence l'Agent et le Secrétaire mexicain seraient invités à ne pas se rendre à sa convocation, sans faire allusion au Commissaire mexicain,

Considérant que, devant ces deux réponses contradictoires, M. Verzijl estime que la Commission ne saurait reprendre ses travaux sous sa présidence qu'après avoir examiné la question et s'être prononcée,

Considérant que, de l'examen des conditions dans lesquelles M. Verzijl à été nommé tiers arbitre, il resort que, ayant été designé, en février 1927, par le Président du Conseil d'Administration de la Cour Permanente d'Arbitrage à la Haye et ayant accepté alors cette fonction, mais sans l'avoir effectivement remplis par suite de l'expiration de la Convention d'arbitrage du 25 septembre 1924, M. Verzijl a été invité, vers la fin de 1927, par des notes identiques des Représentants diplomatiques des deux Gouvernements à la Haye, à continuer à se charger de cette fonction prévue par la Convention additionnelle du 12 mars 1927,

Considérant que s'il est exact que deux périodes de neuf mois sont prévues par

continued to be Presiding Commissioner, since the Mexican government could not unilaterally withdraw its consent to his functioning, and declaring the session to be a regular one. The other decision (Decision No. 22) [40] declared the oral proceedings which had been reopened by

ladite Convention additionnelle pour l'achèvement des travaux de la Commission, aucune modification dans la composition de la Commission à la fin de la première n'est stipulée et qu'aucune réserve à ce sujet n'a été faite non plus dans les notes d'invitation conjoint ci-dessus visées,

Considérant que le désir manifesté par le Gouvernement mexicain de ne pas laisser d'intervalle entre les deux périodes des sessions a eu pour conséquence d'amener le Gouvernement français à insister auprès de M. Verzijl, Président, pour l'amener à hâter son retour à Mexico,

Considérant que l'échange des lettres de prorogation entre les deux Gouvernements, à la date du 17 avril 1929, a été également pur et simple, sans aucune allusion à un changement de Président,

Considérant que postérieurement encore, le Gouvernement mexicain s'est adressé deux fois, les 20 avril et 2 mai 1929, à M. Verzijl en sa qualité de Président, la dernière communication contenant la demande officielle de différer la convocation de la Commission,

Considérant que c'est seulement le 7 mai, dans une note communiqué au Président le 27 mai, que le Gouvernement mexicain a demandé au Gouvernement français de choisir un autre tiers arbitre, alors que M. Verzijl était sur le point d'arriver à Mexico,

Considérant que si une telle demande aurait pu s'expliquer le 26 décembre 1928 à la fin de la première période, ou même le 17 avril 1929 au moment de l'échange des lettres de prorogation, cette demande faite le 7 mai et qui fixe la fin des fonctions de M. Verzijl au 26 décembre 1928, est incompatible avec la demande adressée, cinq jours auparavant, le 2 mai, par le Gouvernement mexicaine, et officiellement, à M. Verzijl en sa qualité de Président,

Considérant que jusqu'à ce jour le Gouvernement français n'a pas accédé à la demande du Gouvernement mexicain de remplacer le tiers arbitre,

Considérant que, si on ne peut nier à un Gouvernement le droit de proposer à tout moment le remplacement du tiers arbitre en fonctions, une telle proposition ne peut produire d'effet juridique tant qu'elle n'a pas été acceptée par l'autre gouvernement et tant qu'une décision conjointe n'est pas intervenue et, par suite une destitution unilatérale ne saurait être que nulle et de nul effet,

Considérant que, en effet, la designation conjointe d'un tiers arbitre est un acte juridique international bilatéral, ayant les effets d'une Convention internationale et comportant notamment l'engagement réciproque des Etats de conserver le tiers arbitre dans ses fonctions jusqu'à ce que se soit manifestée la volonté communes des deux Parties de le destituer,

Pour ces motifs, la Commission, statuant à la majorité des membres de la Commission et à l'unanimité des Commissaires présents, *Décide,* de déclarer que, M. Verzijl n'ayant pas cessé d'être Président de la Commission, la convocation de la Commission faite par lui en cette qualité est valable et la présente réunion est régulière.

Fait à Mexico, le 3 juin 1929.

Le Commissaire Français	Le Commissaire Président	Le Secrétaire Français
(Signed)	(Signed)	(Signed)

[40] The text of this decision (manuscript copy furnished by M. Verzijl) is as follows:

La Commission franco-mexicaine des réclamations,

Vu la décision No. 21, constatant la regularité de la présente session,

Vu les conclusions présentées par l'Agent du Gouvernement français le 15 mai 1929 relativement aux réclamations plaidées au cours de la troisième session,

Vu l'article VII de la Convention franco-mexicaine, fixant un délai de 6 mois pour rendre des sentences sur les affaires dont les débats ont été déclarés clos.

Considérant qu'au cours de la troisième session de la Commission, un certain nombre d'affaire on été plaidées, que pour la plupart, les débats ont déjà été déclarès clos et que, pour les autres, ils peuvent encore l'être sans inconvénient,

Considérant qu'il avait été entendu entre les Commissaires, avant l'interruption des travaux en octobre dernier, que les Commissaires français et mexicain feraient parvenir

Decision No. 20 (the Paris Decision) to be terminated and announced that the Commission would proceed to render awards in these cases.

At its meetings between June 3 and June 22, the Commission handed down awards in 23 claims, these awards being notified to the respective secretaries, agents and governments. The meetings were held in private quarters, the Mexican government having refused the use of a room in the Secretariat of Foreign Relations, and the Mexican

---

aussitôt que possible au Président leurs opinions respectives, et si possible communes, sur chaque affaire declarée close,

Considérant que le Commissaire français a effectivement remis ses opinions, sous la forme de projets de sentence, aux Secrétaires le 20 décembre 1928, pour être communiquées au Commissaire mexicain, et qu'ultérieurement, le 22 février 1929, lesdites opinions ont été notifiées au Président,

Considérant que le Président, de son côté, a fait connaître aux Secrétaires, par lettre en date du 25 décembre 1928, qu'il avait lui-même préparé ses opinions sur toutes les affaires plaidées, mais qu'à cette date il n'avait encore reçu aucune opinion de ses deux collègues et que, pour ce motif, il différait encore l'expédition des sentences,

Considérant que, malgré une lettre adressée au Commissaire mexicain par le Président le 15 décembre 1928, ledit Commissaire n'a ni envoyé ses opinions, ni manifesté ses opinions,

Considérant qu'en mars 1929, étant donné l'incertitude existant sur la date de la reprise des délais, et en l'absence de toute opinion du Commissaire mexicain, il a parue nécessaire au Président et au Commissaire français, afin de remplir l'obligation fait à la Commission de rendre des sentences dans un certain délai tout en permettant au Commissaire mexicain de faire encore connaître son opinion, de prendre en date du 5 mars 1929, à Paris, une décision (No. 20), tendant à rouvrir les débats déclarés clos précédemment,

Attendu que tous les délais ayant été effectivement interrompus entre le 27 décembre 1928 et le 17 avril 1929, date à laquelle les deux Gouvernements ont échangé des notes au sujet de la prorogation de neuf mois prévue par la Convention additionnelle du 12 mars 1927, la décision ci-dessus est sans utilité pratique, le délai de six mois visé à l'article VII n'étant pas épuisé,

Attendu que, conformément à l'article 44 du règlement de procédure, la Commission est libre de fixer le mode de préparation des sentences, et qu'elle se trouve en présence actuellement des opinions du Commissaire français déjà communiquées au Commissaire mexicain et qui constituent une base de discussion pour la rédaction definitive des sentences,

Attendu que ni l'abstention du Commissaire mexicain de faire connaître ses opinions, ni la non-représentation du Mexique dans la Commission après la reprise des travaux ne mettent d'obstacle juridique à rendre des sentences à la majorité sur les affaires plaidées antérieurement, en présence des trois Commissaires,

Vu les article 42 et suivante du règlement de procédure,

La Commission, a l'unanimité des membres présents et à la majorité des Commissaires
Décide:

1. de considérer les débats sur les affaires plaidées au cours de la troisième session et visées dans la décision No. 20 comme définitivement clos et, en tant que besoin, les déclarer a nouveau clos;

2. de déclarer clos les débats sur les autres affaires plaidées au cours de la troisième session;

3. de rendre en conséquence, dans les délais prévus par la convention, et en tant que les circonstances le permettront, des sentences sur toutes les affaires plaidées, qui seront notifiées non seulement aux Secrétaires, mais encore (en copies certifiées conformes) aux Agents et aux Gouvernements.

Fait à Mexico le 3 Juin 1929

Le Commissaire Français   Le Commissaire Président
    (Signed)   (Signed)
                    Le Secrétaire Français
                        (Signed)

Commissioner absented himself throughout. On June 24, the Commission decided (Decision No. 23) [41] that the session be suspended until the Commission could be regularly reconstituted. On August 29, 1929, M. Verzijl presented his resignation to the French government.[42]

[41] The text of this decision (manuscript copy furnished by M. Verzijl) is as follows:
La Commission franco-mexicaine des réclamations.
Vu la décision No. 21, constatant la régularité de la présente session.
Vu les lettres adressées par le Gouvernement mexicain à M. Verzijl le 7 et 27 mai et 20 juin 1929 et
Considérant que le Gouvernement mexicain, par lesdites lettres a renouvelé à trois reprises et d'une manière non équivoque son refus de reconnaître M. Verzijl comme Président de la Commission,
Considérant que le Gouvernement mexicain n'a pas désigné de Commissaire en remplacement de M. Gonzalez Roa,
Considérant que dans ces conditions l'agent du Gouvernement français demande à la Commission, au nom de son Gouvernement, de constater officiellement que l'absence du Commissaire mexicain met la Commission dans l'impossibilité de fonctioner et qu'il la prie de déclarer la session en cours interrompue jusqu'à ce que, soit par voie diplomatique, soit autrement le tribunal ait pu être régulièrement complété.
Dans ces conditions
Opinion du Commissaire Français:
Le Commissaire français se déclare favorable à l'interruption de la session en cours en raison du refus trois fois réitéré du Gouvernement mexicain de reconnaître M. Verzijl comme Président et de l'abstention manifeste du Commissaire mexicain.
Opinion du Commissaire Président:
Le Commissaire Président se déclare également favorable à l'interruption de la session en cours, mais non sans avoir exprimé, dans l'intérêt de l'arbitrage international en général, son opinion que, malgré l'attiude doublement illegitime du Gouvernement mexicain ci-dessus signalée, la Commission serait parfaitement en droit de continuer a remplir sa mission, attendre en effet que:
d'une part le refus unilatéral de reconnaître un tiers arbitre régulièrement designé et étant régulièrement en fonctions, ainsi que l'a constaté la decision No. 21, est contraire au droit international et ne saurait mettre d'obstacle juridique au fonctionnement régulier de la Commission;
d'autre part, que le refus d'envoyer un Commissaire siéger dans la Commission constitue un manquement des Etats Unis Mexicains à leur engagement international découlant de l'article Ier de la Convention du 25 sept. 1924; que si, dans ces conditions, une Commission internationale d'arbitrage se déclaraient incompétente, par suite de la défaillance de l'une des Parties, pour continuer à remplir la mission que les deux Parties lui ont confiée conjointement, elle porterait une grave atteinte à l'institution de l'arbitrage internationale en méconnaissant le principe général de droit suivant lequel personne ne saurait se prévaloir en sa faveur du non-accomplissement de ses obligations juridiques; que par conséquent, aucune impossibilité juridique ne s'opposerait à la continuation des travaux.
Pour ces motifs
La Commission
statuant à la majorité de ses membres et à l'unanimité des Commissaires présents
Décide
que la session en cours est interrompue à la date de ce jour, jusqu'à ce que, soit par voie diplomatique, soit autrement, la Commission ait pu être régulièrement complétée.
Fait à Mexico, le 24 juin 1929.
Le Commissaire Français   Le Commissaire Président
(Signed)   (Signed)
Le Secrétaire Français
(Signed)

[42] M. Verzijl's report to the French Ministry of Foreign Affairs, August 29, 1929, gives the following reasons which had been given him for his dismissal:
"Jusqu'ici on m'a donné le choix entre plusieurs raisons ou prétextes supposés ou

§93. **The Convention of August 2, 1930.** During the succeeding year efforts were directed towards concluding a new Convention. This Convention, signed August 2, 1930,[43] departed radically from the previous Convention. A Commission of two members was set up who were to pass on the claims, and were to call upon the two governments to designate an umpire in case of disagreement. The Commission was to pass only upon the claims listed in an appendix to the Convention. The decisions rendered by the Commission under the Convention of 1924 were to be binding, but it is noteworthy that the governments did not consider the decisions rendered after the Mexican Commissioner had been withdrawn as decisions of the Commission, since every one of the claims there involved was listed in the appendix referred to. Thus, only two of the awards given by the previous Commission were considered binding.[44]

The new Commission, consisting of Eduardo Suarez, Mexican Commissioner, and René Delage, French Commissioner, met in Mexico City from March 16 to November 3, 1931. It completed all its work during this period. At no time was it found necessary to have recourse to an umpire.[44a]

TABLE XVII

SUMMARY OF THE WORK OF THE FRENCH-MEXICAN COMMISSION

Claims filed	251,	amounting to 6,169,086.52 pesos
Claims withdrawn	108	
Claims disallowed or dismissed	50	
Awards made	93,	amounting to 1,300,000 pesos

allégués à titre plus ou moins officiel, tels que: la sentence no. 30-A prononçant la recevabilité des réclamations de Syriens et de Libanais; la façon trop ouverte dont j'ai signalé certaines méthodes de défense mexicaine; mon refus de considérer l'examen juridique des réclamations comme une espèce de négociations diplomatiques poursuivies; certaines théories de droit international inadmissible que j'aurais émises; certains ressentiment de mon collègue mexicain, dont je n'ai pas pu approuver le système fragile de défense; ma volonté trop ferme de terminer l'examen des réclamations avant l'expiration du terme de dix-huit mois; la crainte mexicaine des précédents et de leurs conséquences financières et la nécessité imperieuse de m'empêcher de juger, même au moyen d'une violation ouverte des obligations internationales du Mexique; le prétendu charactère arbitraire de la décision no. 20, prise à Paris le 5 mars 1929, à la suite du silence prolongé du Commissaire mexicain . . . ; le reproche qui m'a été fait semi-officielement d'être 'plus Français que les Français.' " (Copied from manuscript.)

[43] See Appendix, p. 423.

[44] The Pinson and Bimar awards. These were the only final decisions rendered by the Commission prior to the withdrawal of the Mexican Commissioner.

[44a] The following table shows the disposition by the reorganized Commission of the

GERMAN-MEXICAN COMMISSION

§94. **The German–Mexican Commission.** The German-Mexican Commission seems to have had a happier life than those previously discussed. The Convention fixed a period of two years for decision which expired on March 5, 1928, the Commission having first met on March 6, 1926. One hundred and forty claims, totalling 6,169,086.52 pesos, were filed by Germany. Only a single decision, an interlocutory one, was rendered during this two year period. A supplementary Convention extending the duration of the Commission for nine months was signed on December 20, 1927.[45] A second supplementary Convention was signed on December 15, 1928,[46] and a third supplementary Convention was signed on August 14, 1929,[47] each of these extending the duration of the Commission for a further period of nine months. The Commission completed its work on March 5, 1930, having held 65 meetings during its four year period of existence.

TABLE XVIII

SUMMARY OF THE WORK OF THE GERMAN-MEXICAN CLAIMS COMMISSION

Claims filed	140,	amounting to 6,169,086.52 pesos
Claims withdrawn	68	
Claims disallowed or dismissed	38	
Awards made	34,	amounting to 508,912.31 pesos

cases passed on by the first Commission after the withdrawal of the Mexican Commissioner:

Claim	Award of First Commission	Award of Reorganized Commission
Pellat	10,000	1,500
Mériniac	700	700
Talavero	10,000	10,000
Lambreton	6,000	5,500
Prodeau	3,000	3,000
Chaurand	7,000	6,500
Gustave Caire	8,000	7,000
Pietri	3,000	Rejected in consequence of change in Convention
Turin	125,000	55,000
Matty	100,000	40,000
Gomes	Rejected	Rejected
Feuillebois	6,000	4,000
Albrand	1,800	1,000
Bellon	30,000	18,000
Estrayer	17,000	15,000
Maurin	Rejected	Rejected
Esclangon y Cía	Rejected	3,000
Fabre	1,500	1,000
Bourillon, Jacques et Cía	60,000	60,000
Lombard Hermanos	220,000	200,000
Soc. du Paraíso Novello	150,000	30,000

[45] See Appendix, p. 452.   [46] See Appendix, p. 454.   [47] See Appendix, p. 455.

BRITISH-MEXICAN COMMISSION

§95. The First Two Years of the Commission. The work of the British-Mexican Commission seems to have been carried through with efficiency and despatch and with a minimum of irritation. This Commission also suffered from too short a period of duration. The Convention of November 19, 1926, provided for a duration of two years which, since the Commission first met on August 22, 1928, expired August 21, 1930. One hundred and twenty-eight claims amounting to 138,605,063.97 pesos were filed. During this period, 21 decisions were handed down.

§96. The Supplementary Convention of December 5, 1930. The British government began negotiations for a supplementary Convention in June 1930. But the Mexican government was apparently unwilling to agree to an extension of the duration of the Commission unless certain of the provisions of the Convention of 1926 were modified. The supplementary Convention was not signed until December 5, 1930.[48] It provided for a further extension of nine months as from August 22, 1930, this period to be extended for another nine months, if necessary, by a simple exchange of notes, and provided for various amendments of the original Convention.

These amendments are of interest in that they illustrate some of the major difficulties which had been encountered in the application of the various Conventions. Article 2 of the Convention of 1926 provided for the oath to be taken by the Commissioners and stated that Mexico desired that her responsibility should not be established in conformity with international law. It was to be sufficient "that it be established that the alleged damage actually took place, and was due to any of the causes enumerated in Article 3 of this Convention, for Mexico to feel moved *ex gratia* to afford" compensation. The supplementary Convention added to this article after the words "Article 3 of this Convention" the following: "that it was not a lawful act and that its amount be proved." This amendment was probably made in order to dispose of the difficulties engendered by the question as to whether Mexico was liable for acts of a *de jure* or *de facto* government engaged in military operations necessary for the suppression of insurrection.[49]

[48] See Appendix, p. 476. Ratifications were exchanged, March 9, 1931.
[49] See *infra*, p. 162.

Article 3 of the Convention of 1926 enumerated the categories of forces whose acts would engage the responsibility of Mexico. One of the categories read: "By revolutionary forces which, after the triumph of their cause, have established a government *de jure* or *de facto,* or by revolutionary forces opposed to them." Considerable controversy had arisen before some of the Commissions as to whether the opposing revolutionary forces referred to were forces opposed to a government *de jure* or *de facto* or opposed to other revolutionary forces which succeeded in setting up a government.[50] The supplementary Convention cut the Gordian knot by striking out the words "or by revolutionary forces opposed to them." The supplementary Convention also omitted the category which, in the original Convention, had followed the one just quoted: "By forces arising from the disjunction of those mentioned in the next preceding paragraph up to the time when a *de jure* government had been established, after a particular revolution."

Several other important amendments were made. The original Convention provided for jurisdiction over claims of British subjects "or persons under British protection." The *Nájera* case [51] before the French-Mexican Commission had revealed a sharp difference of opinion as to whether inhabitants of a territory under mandate were included under the term *"protégés."* It was doubtless in order to obviate another such conflict that the words "or persons under British protection" were stricken out by the supplementary Convention. That Convention also provided as follows:

"The claims within the competence of the Commission shall not include those caused by the forces of Victoriano Huerta or by the acts of his régime.

"The Commission shall not be competent to admit claims concerning the circulation or acceptance, voluntary or forced, of paper money."

The first paragraph marked the settlement of a controversy which had troubled almost all of the Commissions.[52] It had been contended on behalf of claimant governments that Mexico was liable for the acts of the Huerta forces as forces of a government *de facto.* Mexico had argued strenuously that Huerta was not the head of either a gov-

[50] See *infra,* p. 163.
[51] Rep. française (Pablo Nájera) *v.* Etats-Unis mexicains, Jurisprudence de la Commission franco-mexicaine des réclamations, p. 156. See *infra,* p. 102.
[52] See *infra,* p. 160.

ernment *de facto* or *de jure*, but was a mere *detentador del poder*, a usurper. With this amendment Mexico succeeded in excluding such claims from the jurisdiction of the Commission.

The origin of the second paragraph is probably due to the immense number of claims based on the acceptance of depreciated paper money. These claims would have imposed a heavy burden on Mexico.

§97. **Work of the British–Mexican Commission under the Supplementary Convention.** After the supplementary Convention had come into force, the Commission reassembled on March 11, 1931. Fifty-nine meetings were held between this date and May 22, 1931. Decisions were handed down in seventy-seven cases, but the Commission had not been able to complete its work and it was necessary to extend the duration of the Commission for another nine months by an exchange of notes.[53] Two more sessions were held, one from May 23 to July 21, 1931, and the other from January 18 to February 15, 1932, when the work of the Commission was finally completed. This conclusion was hastened by the adoption of the practice of settling cases by agreement of the agents with the consent of the Commission.[54] Eleven claims in which 21,310,360.83 pesos were asked for were disposed of in this manner, the total awards amounting to 2,760,300 pesos.

TABLE XIX

SUMMARY OF THE WORK OF THE BRITISH-MEXICAN CLAIMS COMMISSION

Claims filed	128,	amounting to 138,605,063.97 pesos
Claims withdrawn	18	
Claims disallowed or dismissed	60	
Awards made	50,	amounting to 3,795,897.53 pesos

ITALIAN-MEXICAN COMMISSION

§98. **The Italian–Mexican Commission.** The Italian-Mexican Convention of January 13, 1927, provided an exceedingly short period for the duration of the Commission: only one year. The Commission first met on November 29, 1930, and continued in session until December 8, 1930. The one task accomplished was the adoption of the Rules of Procedure. One hundred and fifty seven claims, amounting to 7,842,500.37 pesos, were filed, and, in the normal course of events, all these would have had to be decided by November 29, 1931. Yet with this task before it, the Commission did not meet for the hearing

[53] *Memoria de la Secretaria de Relaciones Exteriores,* 1930–31, p. 629.
[54] See *infra,* p. 287.

of claims until July 6, 1931. A supplementary Convention extending the duration of the Commission seemed necessary, yet it was never concluded. Both governments merely agreed to interpret the words "first meeting" in the Convention as meaning "first meeting for the hearing, examination and decision of claims." [55] Thus, with unique simplicity the life of the Commission was extended to July 6, 1932. Surely, this is a perfectly proper interpretation of these words and fully in accord with the purposes of the Convention, the only objection being that such an interpretation was not placed on exactly the same words in the other Claims Conventions.[55a] Unfortunately, this reprieve did not suffice. By July 6, 1932, the Commission had heard all the claims, but it had handed down only eight decisions. Another provision of the Convention was then subjected to interpretation. The Convention provided that: "The Commission shall give its decision [Sp.—*dará su fallo;* It.—*emetterá la sua decisione*] on every claim presented within three months counting from the conclusion of the hearing relative to such claim." This was obviously designed to speed up proceedings by requiring decisions to be handed down within a relatively short time after hearing. But, this provision was interpreted to mean that the Commission could take an extra three months, *i. e.,* until October 6, 1932, to hand down its decisions. This seems to be a flagrant disregard of the provision that: "The Commission shall hear, examine and *decide* all claims presented to it within a period of one year from the date of its first meeting." (Italics inserted.) Yet, no objection was made, and this interpretation enabled the Commission to get through with its work without the delay incident to the conclusion of a new convention. The Commission held its last session from October 3 to October 6, 1932.

TABLE XX

SUMMARY OF THE WORK OF THE ITALIAN-MEXICAN COMMISSION

Claims filed,	157,	amounting to 7,842,500.37 pesos
Claims withdrawn	51	
Claims disallowed or dismissed	63	
Awards made	43,	amounting to 315,098.75 pesos

[55] Information furnished by Lic. Manuel Sierra of the Mexican Secretariat of Foreign Relations in a letter to the present writer, May 25, 1934.

[55a] Even the Italian-Mexican Commission originally placed a different interpretation on these words. The Convention provided that all claims were to be filed within four months "counting from the day of the first meeting." The Italian-Mexican Rules (Art. 9) provided that all claims were to be filed within four months "contados desde el 29 de noviembre de 1930, fecha en que se instaló la Comisión."

Spanish-Mexican Commission

§99. The Spanish–Mexican Commission. The Spanish-Mexican Claims Convention of November 25, 1925, provided that the Commission should decide all claims within a period of three and a half years from the date of the first meeting. This was the longest period provided by any of the Conventions, but even this proved insufficient. The Commission first met on January 7, 1927, the prescribed period thus terminating on July 6, 1920. A considerable number of claims were filed—1,268. The published records disclose no evidence of any friction in the work of the Commission, and there is no apparent explanation for the failure of the Commission to hand down a single award during three and a half years of existence. Although the life of the Commission expired on July 6, 1930, it was not until December 5, 1930, that a supplementary Convention for extending its duration was signed.[56] Again this Convention was unusual in the liberality of the time provisions. The duration of the Commission was extended for 18 months counting from July 6, 1930, and further extension for one year could be arranged for by a simple exchange of notes. Various amendments to the original Convention were also stipulated, these amendments being identical with those in a Convention between Mexico and Great Britain signed on the same day.[57]

The Commission met again on July 6, 1931, and concluded its work sometime in 1932.[58]

[56] See Appendix, p. 525.
[57] These amendments are discussed *supra*, p. 78 *et seq.*
[58] At the time of publication it was found impossible to secure details of the amount awarded by the Spanish-Mexican Commission.

CHAPTER 6

CLAIMANTS

§100. **The Bases of the Law Relating to International Claims.**
The orthodox theory underlying the law relating to international claims
has been clearly expressed by the Permanent Court of International
Justice.

"It is an elementary principle of international law that a State is entitled
to protect its subjects, when injured by acts contrary to international law
committed by another state, from whom they have been unable to obtain
satisfaction through the ordinary channels. By taking up the case of one
of its subjects and by resorting to diplomatic action of international judicial
proceedings on his behalf, a State is in reality asserting its own rights—its
right to ensure, in the person of its subjects, respect for the rules of international law.

"The question, therefore, whether the present dispute originates in an
injury to a private interest, which in point of fact is the case in many international disputes, is irrelevant from this standpoint. Once a State has taken
up a case on behalf of one of its subjects before an international tribunal, in
the eyes of the latter the State is sole claimant." [1]

To put it in other terms, an injury to an alien committed by a
state in violation of international law is an injury to the state of which
he is a national. The alien himself has no claim under international
law although he may have a claim under the municipal law of his
state of residence. When his own state "espouses" the claim (*i. e.,*
demands that the state which has injured him grant reparation) then
it becomes a national public claim over which the espousing state has
full control.[2] The principle here expressed has a double origin. On
the one hand it springs from a primitive feeling of clannishness, the

[1] Mavrommatis Palestine Concessions, Publications of the Court, Series A, No. 2, p. 12.
[2] See Borchard, Diplomatic Protection of Citizens Abroad, p. 355, *et seq.;* 2 Phillimore,
International Law (3d ed., 1882), p. 4; 1 Westlake, International Law (1904), p. 327,
et seq.

necessity of protecting a member of the clan and of avenging him when he is injured. The classic statement of Vattel is an expression of this motivation:

> "Whoever ill-treats a citizen indirectly injures the State, which must protect that citizen. The sovereign of the injured citizen must avenge the deed and, if possible, force the aggressor to give full satisfaction or punish him, since otherwise the citizen will not obtain the chief end of civil society, which is protection."[3]

On the other hand, this primitive conception has acquired a nineteenth century legal polishing. Under the positivist theory of international law an alien could not advance a claim against a state which injured him because he has no rights or duties under international law. Only states are the subjects of that law. The notion of the injury to the state coincided neatly with positivist theory. Since a violation of international law can be committed only as against a state, then when a state advances a claim alleging such a violation it must be because it has itself been injured. Certain of the rules developed in practice bear out the orthodox theory. A state may refuse to advance a claim;[4] it may compromise it;[5] it may, in theory, retain the proceeds of the award or distribute them as it desires.[6]

Unfortunately, the orthodox theory is not broad enough to cover all the facts as we see them in international practice. Consider the

---

[3] 3 Vattel, The Law of Nations (text of 1758, 3d ed., 1916), p. 136.

[4] ". . . whether the individual has a legal right to compel his state to espouse the claim is a matter of internal law, not of international law . . . so far as the writer is aware, no state gives the individual a legal right to compel such espousal and prosecution, which is dependent entirely upon the discretion and good will of his government." Borchard, "The Protection of Citizens Abroad and Change of Original Nationality," 43 Yale Law Journal (1934), p. 359, at 372.

[5] See Borchard, Diplomatic Protection of Citizens Abroad, pp. 366–375.

[6] See Opinion of the Solicitor of the Department of State on the Distribution of the Alsop Award (Washington, 1912); Frelinghuysen v. Key, 110 U. S. 63 (1884); Rustomjee v. The Queen, 1 Q.B.D. 487 (1876), 2 Q.B.D. 69 (1876); Civilian War Claimants Association v. The King, [1932] A.C. 14, Heirs of Oswald v. Swiss Government, 52 Bundesgerichts-entscheidungen (Switzerland), II, pp. 235, 599, digested in Annual Digest of Public International Law Cases, 1925–1926, p. 244. Cf., however, Umpire Parker of the United States-German Mixed Claims Commission in Administrative Decision No. V, Consolidated Edition of Decisions and Opinions, p. 190: "Even if payment is made to the espousing nation in pursuance of an award, it has complete control over the fund so paid to and held by it and may, to prevent fraud, correct a mistake or protect the national honor, at its election return the fund to the nation paying it or otherwise dispose of it. But where a demand is paid on behalf of a designated national, and an award and payment is made on that specific demand, the fund so paid is not a national fund in the sense that the title vests in the nation receiving it entirely free from any obligation to account to the private claimant, on whose behalf the claim was asserted and paid and who is the real owner thereof."

logical consequences of the theory. The state is injured because a violation of international law has been committed. Supposing the individual national who suffered the primary injury dies before the presentation of the claim leaving no heirs. His state has suffered an independent injury; why should it not be entitled to demand reparation for it? Or, supposing the national dies and leaves an heir who is a national of a third state. Surely the same considerations should apply, and the state of the deceased be permitted to advance its independent claim.[7] And what of the reparation? That would have to be in such a form as would be necessary to repair whatever wrong were done to the state itself. It might be a salute to the flag or it might be pecuniary, but it would be immaterial whether the injured national were a pauper supported by his relatives or an engineer earning a huge salary. Or, to go to the uttermost extreme of logic—what difference does it make whether the injured alien is a national of the complaining state? All states have an interest in the enforcement of international law. Every state is injured by such a violation and should have the right to complain.[8]

All of these contentions follow logically from the positivist premise. They have proved unavailing to pierce through the web of rules woven by long practice, not around the state, but around the injured individual. Firstly, it is well established that a state may advance a claim only where the individual injured was its national at the time of injury.[9] This is a definite indication of the dominance of the primitive conception. The injury to the state lies not primarily in the violation of international law in the abstract. It lies in the violation of international law committed on the person of its national. Secondly, the

---

[7] This argument was made by British counsel in the Stevenson Case, British-Venezuelan Claims Commission of 1903, Ralston, Venezuelan Arbitrations, p. 438, in the following words: "The principle upon which the British Government ask compensation is that underlying the diplomatic presentation of all claims of foreign subjects by their governments. Compensation in such cases is demanded and granted in respect of an international wrong, committed to the property of the subject of the demanding state by the state on which the demand is made. The injury done to the subject is an injury done to the state and remains unatoned until the claim is satisfied. . . . The claim, then, being a claim on behalf of a British subject in its inception has not been satisfied. The injury done to the state therefore remains and is not affected by the death of the person injured and the vesting of the estate in another." The Umpire rejected this contention and dismissed the claim with respect to the non-British heirs.

[8] It is to be noted that states may by treaty agree to permit one state to complain of violations of international law injuring nationals of another state. This was done in the Minorities Treaties of 1919–1920.

[9] See citations in Borchard, "The Protection of Citizens Abroad and Change of Nationality," *op. cit., supra*, note 4, at 373 note.

reparation awarded is measured by the injury to the individual and not by the injury to the state.[10] Thirdly, the claim must be "national" in character continuously from the time of origin at least to the time of presentation.[11] Fourthly (as a corollary of the preceding rule but not as well established), the "beneficial interest" in the claim must be "national" at the time of presentation.[12] This last rule presents a particularly difficult problem for the positivist theory. If the claim is that of the state, how can an international tribunal be concerned with the "beneficial interest" which can arise only under the municipal law of the claimant state? If, as is admitted, the state may keep the proceeds, why should it be precluded from recovering because if it wanted to distribute the proceeds its own municipal law would direct that they go to an alien heir or legatee? These rules do not all fit in with the fundamental theory. Their justification lies chiefly in the fact that they are established. Moreover they are "practical"; they interpose a check on an indiscriminate pressing of claims upon weaker governments, and the consequent financial burden which might be imposed.

With such a conglomerate of inconsistent rules before us, a satisfactory theory is impossible. The most that can be attempted is a working hypothesis which we might state as follows: An injury to a national of State A committed in violation of international law by State B, gives rise to a right of State A to receive reparation equivalent to the amount of loss suffered by its national. This right does not become complete unless at the time of the presentation of the claim, and at all times since the injury, the injured person has remained a national of A, or if he has died, unless State A could, if it so desired, distribute the proceeds to persons who are its nationals

---

[10] "It is a principle of international law that the reparation of a wrong may consist in an indemnity corresponding to the damage which the nationals of the injured State have suffered as a result of the act which is contrary to international law. This is even the most usual form of reparation; it is the form selected by Germany in this case and the admissibility of it has not been disputed." The Factory at Chorzów, Publications of the Permanent Court of International Justice, Series A, No. 17, p. 27.

This rule is, perhaps, not altogether inconsistent with the fundamental theory. We might say that although reparation more in accord with a state injury (e.g., a salute to the flag) might be awarded, a more effective sanction is the imposition of a pecuniary penalty which, for reasons of convenience, is computed as equivalent to what the individual would receive if he were suing in a municipal forum. See further, infra, p. 307.

[11] See Borchard, "The Protection of Citizens Abroad and Change of Original Nationality," op. cit., supra, note 4; Hurst, "Nationality of Claims," British Year Book of International Law, 1926, p. 162.

[12] See articles cited in previous note.

under the municipal law relating to succession. This statement, it is believed, covers the generally accepted rules developed by international tribunals. Our task will now be to see to what extent the practice of the Mexican Claims Commissions is consistent with this statement.

§101. **The State and the Individual: Provisions of the Mexican Claims Conventions and of the Rules of Procedure.** The Mexican Claims Conventions dealt only with claims arising out of injuries to individuals. Thus the United States-Mexican General Claims Commission was given jurisdiction over claims "against Mexico of citizens of the United States . . . for losses or damages suffered by persons or by their properties," and over claims "against the United States of America by citizens of Mexico . . . for losses or damages suffered by persons or by their properties." [13] The claims to be considered are those "of" or "by" citizens of one country against the other country. The British-Mexican Convention did not emphasize the role of the individual so strongly: "The Commission shall deal with all claims against Mexico for losses or damages suffered by British subjects or persons under British protection. . . ." [14] On the other hand, the control of the state over these claims is clearly apparent. The preamble of the General Claims Convention stated the desire of the contracting parties "to settle and adjust amicably claims by the citizens of each country against the other," and similar statements were made in the preambles of the other Conventions (excepting the German-Mexican Convention). The designation of the Commissioners was wholly within the control of the governments. That the proceedings were under the control of the state is evident from the provision that the agents and counsel were to be appointed by the governments.[15] Finally, the contracting parties agreed to consider the decisions of the Commission as final and conclusive, and the proceedings of the Commission as a final settlement of all claims within the

[13] Article I of the General Claims Convention. Similar provision in Art. I of the United States-Mexican Special Claims Convention ("claims against Mexico of citizens of the United States . . . for losses or damages suffered by persons or by their properties"). The Spanish version is slightly different in both Conventions: "las reclamaciones . . . en contra de México, de ciudadanos de los Estados Unidos . . . por pérdidas o daños sufridos en sus personas o en sus propriedades."

[14] Article III.

[15] U. S.-Mexican General Claims Convention, Art. III; U. S.-Mexican Special Claims Commission, Art. IV; British-Mexican Commission, Art. IV; French-Mexican Convention, Art. IV; German-Mexican Convention, Art. V; Italian-Mexican Convention, Art. IV; Spanish-Mexican Convention, Art. IV.

terms of the Convention,[16] and payment was to be made to the government and not to the individual claimant.[17]

The Rules of the United States-Mexican Commissions demonstrate most strikingly the control of the state. "All claims must be filed by the respective Governments by or in the name of the agents thereof." [18] And again: "No . . . statements, documents, or other evidence will be received or considered by the Commission if presented by any other channel" than by the agents or in the name of the agents by assistant agent or counsel.[19] These provisions are not found in the Rules of the other Commissions, but other provisions show how completely the proceedings were controlled by the agents. These provisions will be discussed elsewhere, but attention might here be called to the power given to the agents to settle claims by agreement.[20] The one provision which assigned any part at all to the individual claimant was that requiring him to sign the memorial.[21]

§102. **The Same: Statements by the Commissions.** The most forthright avowal of adherence to the orthodox theory of state responsibility was made by the General Claims Commission:

"The relation of rights and obligations created between two States upon the commission by one of them of an act in violation of International Law, arises only among those States subject to the international juridical system. There does not exist, in that system, any responsibility between the transgressing State and the injured individual for the reason that the latter is not subject to international law. The injury inflicted upon an individual, a national of the claimant State, which implies a violation of the obligations imposed by International Law upon each member of the Community of Nations, constitutes an act internationally unlawful, because it signifies an offense against the State to which the individual is united by the bond of nationality." [22]

[16] U. S.-Mexican General Claims Convention, Art. VIII; U. S.-Mexican Special Claims Commission, Art. VIII; British-Mexican Convention, Art. VIII; French-Mexican Convention, Art. VIII; German-Mexican Convention, Art. IX; Italian-Mexican Convention, Art. VIII; Spanish-Mexican Convention, Art. VIII.
[17] U. S.-Mexican General Claims Convention, Art. IX; U. S.-Mexican Special Claims Commission, Art. IX; British-Mexican Convention, Art. IX; French-Mexican Convention, Art. IX; German-Mexican Convention, Art. X; Italian-Mexican Convention, Art. IX; Spanish-Mexican Convention, Art. IX.
[18] U. S.-Mexican General Rule III 1; U. S.-Mexican Special Rule III 1.
[19] U. S.-Mexican General Rule VIII 1; U. S.-Mexican Special Rule VIII 1.
[20] See *infra*, p. 287.
[21] See *infra*, p. 233.
[22] U. S. A. (Dickson Car Wheel Co.) *v.* United Mexican States, Opinions of Commissioners, 1931, p. 175, at 187–188.

Here is a whole-hearted acceptance of the principle stated by Vattel. Yet, in its practical application to the adjudication of claims, the principle must of needs be tempered to accord with the traditions of international practice.

"The control of the Government, which has espoused and is asserting the claim before the Commission, is complete. In the exercise of its discretion it may espouse a claim or decline to do so. It may press a claim before this Commission or not as it sees fit. Ordinarily a nation will not espouse a claim on behalf of its national unless requested to do so by such national. When, on such request, a claim is espoused, the nation's absolute right to control it is necessarily exclusive. In exercising such control, it is governed not only by the interest of the particular claimant but by the larger interests of the whole people of the nation, and must exercise an untrammeled discretion in determining when and how the claim will be presented and pressed or withdrawn and compromised, and the private owner will be bound by the action taken. *But the private nature of the claim inheres in it and is not lost or destroyed so as to make it the property of the nation,* although it becomes a national claim in the sense that it is subject to the absolute control of the nation espousing it." [23] (Italics inserted.)

The italicized words in this quotation represent an attempt to set forth the most troublesome aspect of the theory: the relationship of the interest of the individual to the claim. One Commissioner stated this fact somewhat more directly: "Rights successfully asserted by the claimant Government under international law in cases of this character inure to the benefit of the nationals of the contracting parties." [24] In view of such statements it is idle to pretend that the relationship between the individual claimant and the government asserting the claim is a matter of indifference to an international tribunal.[24a]

[23] U. S. A. (William A. Parker) *v.* United Mexican States, General Claims Commission, Opinions of Commissioners, 1927, p. 35, at 36.
[24] Commissioner Nielsen, concurring in U. S. A. (Jennie L. Corrie) *v.* United Mexican States, General Claims Commission, Opinions of Commissioners, 1927, p. 213, at 216.
[24a] In the Case of the Mexican Union Railway, British-Mexican Commission, Decisions and Opinions of Commissioners, p. 157, it was urged that a government could present a claim notwithstanding the presence of a Calvo Clause, since the latter could only bind the individual. The Commission said:
"But the Commission is bound to consider the object for which it was created, the task it has to fulfill and the treaty upon which its existence is based. It has to examine and to judge the claims contemplated by the convention. These claims bear a mixed character. They are public claims in so far as they are presented by one government to another government. But they are private in so far as they aim at the granting of a financial award to an individual or to a company. The award is claimed *on behalf* of a person or a

§103. **Must the Private Claimant Consent to the Presentation of a Claim?** In a case before the General Claims Commission it was contended that the record should contain some evidence that the claimant had invoked the assistance of his government. To this, the Commission replied:

". . . it may be said that the Commission has repeatedly rendered awards in cases containing no evidence of this character. There can be no doubt that in international law and practice and under the terms of the Convention of September 8, 1923, either Government has a right to press claims before the Commission on proper proof of nationality. It may be assumed that it would be very unusual for a government to press a claim in the absence of any desire on the part of the claimant." [24b]

A different view was taken by the Italian-Mexican Commission in a case of unusual interest.[25] Claim was made for damages arising out of the murder of the claimant's husband by revolutionary forces. The claimant refused to sign the memorial and informed the Italian agent that she did not desire to have the claim presented. The Commission disallowed the claim. It stated that since under the Convention Mexico's responsibility was, in many cases, purely *ex gratia,* the Italian government could not advance a claim in its own behalf in the absence of proof that the claim was one for which Mexico was liable under international law. Under the Convention it was a condition *sine qua non* that the private claimant should initiate the suit and the sole function of the Italian agent was to prosecute the claim as representative of one of the contracting parties. The power of the government to espouse or not to espouse a claim and the wide powers granted to agents before international commissions were explained as deriving from a general principle that the members of a state exercise their rights in the international forum through the political authority to which they have

corporation, and, in accordance therewith, the Rules of Procedure prescribe that the memorial shall be signed by the claimant or his attorney or otherwise clearly show that the alien who suffered the damage, agrees to his government's acting in his behalf. For this reason the action of the government cannot be regarded as an action taken independently of the wishes or the interests of the claimant. It is an action the initiative of which rests with the claimant."

[24b] U. S. A. (Melczer Mining Company) *v.* United Mexican States, Opinions of Commissioners, 1929, p. 228. The Commission relied on the Cayuga Indians Case, American and British Arbitration of 1910, Nielsen's Report, at pp. 272–273, in which it was held that a private claimant had no power to withdraw a claim after it was presented.

[25] Case of Emilia Marta Viuda de Giovanni Mantellero, Decision No. 3 (unpublished).

delegated their international representation.[26] This represents an almost complete repudiation of the theory that the claim is that of the state—not quite complete because the Commission limits itself to the peculiar circumstances of the Convention, *viz.:* the assumption of responsibility *ex gratia.* Because Mexico has no liability under international law Italy cannot advance a claim in its own behalf and consequently cannot advance a claim on behalf of an individual who refuses to consent to the espousal. The conclusion is logical enough but it is not consistent with the positivist theory. Mexico may not have been under an international obligation when the injury was committed, but it assumed an obligation to pay for the injury. This obligation was assumed as against the Italian government. The Convention does not expressly require the consent of the individual. To read the necessity for such consent into the Convention amounts to holding that the individual acquired a right against Mexico under an international instrument. Nonetheless, it is submitted that from a practical standpoint the result is sound. The requirement of securing the consent of the injured individual is a wise limitation on the presentation of unfounded claims. In fact, the claim could have been dismissed on the narrow ground of noncompliance with the Rules in that the memorial was not signed as required.

§104. **Must there be a Private Claimant?** In a number of cases before the Italian-Mexican Commission, the Italian government

[26] "Conviene recordar que, en términos generales, México ha accedido graciosamente al establecimiento de su responsabilidad por ciertos y determinados actos lesivos del patrimonio de súbditos italianos durante un período fijado en la Convención. Muchos de los daños y pérdidas por los cuales México accede a indemnizar, pueden serlo sólo en virtud de la aplicación de la equidad, y no han podido, ni podrían, por lo tanto, ser objeto de acción intergubernamental, tales las representaciones diplomáticas fundadas en el quebrantamiento de una obligación de justicia al extranjero residente en otro Estado.

"En la secuela de esta reclamación no se han aducido pruebas para demonstrar que la existido quebrantamiento de una obligación internacional que pudiera poner en juego, *ipso jure,* el derecho del Gobierno italiano para entablar una acción de *jure proprio.* Queda, pues, limitada la esfera de acción al campo de la equidad, y para requerir un pronunciamiento dentro de los términos de la Convención de 13 de enero de 1927, es condición *sine qua non,* la de que sea el interesado mismo quien inicie la acción correspondiente, pues, en los términos del convenio precitado, el señor Agente de Italia no tiene otra función que la de patrocinar, como personero de una de la Altas Partes Contratantes ante una jurisdicción internaciónal, reservada al ejercicio de las atribuciones representatives del Estado, la expectativa o el derecho de uno de sus mandantes particulares.

"Esta facultad que los Gobiernos se reservan de patrocinar o no una reclamación privada, y las amplias atribuciones otogardas a sus Agentes ante las Comisiones Internacionales, derivan del concepto generalmente aceptado, de que fuera de la jurisdicción nacional, propria o ajena, los miembros de la comunidad moral erigida en Estado, sólo ejercitan sus derechos por conducto de la autoridad política en quien han delegado su representación internaciónal." *Ibid.*

claimed *on its own behalf* by reason of the killing of Italian citizens by revolutionary forces.[27] In these cases it was found impossible to identify the heirs of the deceased and the government contended that it could claim as ultimate successor. The Commission dismissed these claims holding that under the Convention a claim could be made only on behalf of designated persons whose nationality must be proved. A similar problem arose in another case before the same Commission.[28] Claim was made on behalf of the widow of an Italian who had been killed. No proof of the nationality of the widow was presented, but Italy argued that this was unnecessary since, in any event, it could claim on its own behalf on account of the murder of an Italian. Again the Commission dismissed the claim, saying:

"We do not consider that a claim thus formulated falls within the limits set up for our Commission. The latter was established to study and decide claims for losses and damages suffered by individuals of Italian nationality, and the loss resulting to a government from the murder of one of its subjects cannot be included within these terms."

These holdings are beyond cavil. The Conventions are limited to claims of nationals and governmental claims are clearly excluded. It is essential that there be some designated person of proper nationality entitled to receive the award. But does it follow that this person must have been designated at the time the memorial was filed? In a case before the United States-Mexican General Claims Commission a memorial was filed on behalf of a person who was dead at the time, his death being unknown to the agency. A motion was made to substitute the name of another claimant. The Commission stated:

"Article 1 of the Convention requires not only the existence of a claim against either Government, but a claim vesting in a specific claimant at the time of its being filed. The Commission in either accepting claims or assuming jurisdiction over them is obligated to look behind the claim as espoused by either Government, and to determine whether there are individual claimants and who they are. . . . The mere fact, therefore, that a private claimant . . . did not exist at the time the claim was filed would, if nothing else could be brought forward, necessarily render acceptance of the claim impossible." [29]

[27] Case of Giovanni Priva (Herederos), Decision No. 35 (unpublished); Case of Giovanni Gusti, Decision No. 40 (unpublished).
[28] Case of Pietro Gebbia, Decision No. 46 (unpublished). *Accord:* Case of Francesco Osti y Hermanos, Decision No. 81 (unpublished).
[29] U. S. A. (Jennie L. Corrie) *v.* United Mexican States, Opinions of Commissioners, 1927, p. 213, at 214.

Yet the Commission allowed the motion to substitute stating that:

"However, important though the status of the individual claimant may be, Articles I, VI, VII, and VIII of the Convention in dealing with the presentation, filing, hearing, and decision of claims apparently attach more importance to the *claims* as such than to the claimants behind them. The Commission, evidently, must carefully see to it that additions or substitutions of claimants do not modify the nature, amount, or nationality of the claim presented and accepted; but if such a modification is not involved, a change in the parties claimant does not necessarily give the claim the character of a new claim."

In another case involving the same situation a motion to substitute claimants was also granted, but the Mexican agent then argued that the fact of the death of the originally designated claimant prior to the filing "alone would suffice in itself to consider the claim as nonexistent from the time the error incurred by the American Agency had been detected, that is to say, from the time in which it was found that the claim had been presented in behalf of a person who did not exist." The Commission granted an award, saying:

"We are not concerned in the instant case with a situation in which there is no national who may be entitled to receive the benefits of an award. The change in the name of the beneficiary does not involve as regards the merits of the case any new assertion of rights under international law nor any change or amplification of fact or legal contentions with respect to liability." [30]

It is essential therefore that a proper claimant be designated at the time award is rendered, but at the time of filing it would seem sufficient if some claimant has been designated in compliance with the Rules even though this person be not the proper claimant. Of course, this would not justify an agent in filing a case in the name of a nominal claimant while searching for the claimant who would be entitled to recover.

§105. **When Does a Claim Arise?** Ordinarily it would seem absurd to ask the question as to when a claim arises — obviously it would be at the time the injury was inflicted. Yet, in the case of those Mexican Claims Conventions which dealt with revolutionary claims the answer is not so obvious. It will be remembered that in these Con-

---

[30] U. S. A. (Mary E. A. Munroe) *v.* United Mexican States, Opinions of Commissioners, 1929, p. 314, at 315. *Cf.* U. S. A. (Flora Lee) *v.* United Mexican States, Opinions of Commissioners, 1927, p. 3; U. S. A. (Wells Fargo Bank) *v.* United Mexican States, *ibid.*, p. 71; and see *infra*, p. 239.

ventions Mexico's liability was stated to be *ex gratia* and not based on international law. It might be said then that a claim under one of these Conventions could not exist (at least as far as international law was concerned) until the Convention was concluded. But, the claim might be such that Mexico would have been liable for it under general principles of international law. In such a case it would seem that the claim must be held to have arisen at the time the injury was inflicted, the Convention serving only to organize the tribunal for redress and not creating a right.

The practical importance of this problem is illustrated in two cases before the British-Mexican Commission. One case [30a] involved these facts: A was murdered by revolutionaries in 1914. His father, B, who was dependent on him, married C in 1920 and died in 1925, leaving a will under which C became sole executrix. Claim was made on behalf of B. The Commission dismissed the claim on the ground that there was no showing of legal relationship or dependency between A and C. No claim against Mexico could form part of the estate of B until the right to present it had accrued to him. This right did not arise until the Convention was signed and ratified. In the second case,[30b] a partnership had suffered property loss at the hands of revolutionaries in 1919. In 1920 the partnership conveyed all its assets, including its claim, to a corporation on whose behalf the claim was brought. The Mexican agent contended that the corporation had no standing because the right to claim had not come into existence until the signing of the Convention. The Commission, however, held that "the right to claim was not created by the signing of the Convention but existed as a marketable asset from the time the loss occurred."

It is impossible to reconcile these two cases. They are squarely contradictory. In neither of them was any attempt made to base the decision on the nature of the claim, although this would seem to be the all-important criterion.

NATIONALITY OF THE CLAIM [31]

§106. **Nationality at the Origin of the Claim.** We have seen that under general principles it is essential that the claim should have

---

[30a] Case of Ada Ruth Williams, Decisions and Opinions of Commissioners, p. 67.
[30b] Case of William E. Bowerman, Decisions and Opinions of Commissioners, p. 141.
[31] Problems relating to proof of nationality are discussed in the chapter on "Evidence." See *infra*, p. 271 *et seq.*

been a national one at its inception. In the words of the British-Mexican Commission:

". . . a long course of arbitral decisions has established the principle that no claim falls within a treaty which is not founded upon an injury or wrong done to a citizen of the claimant Government." [32]

Most of the Mexican Claims Conventions gave express embodiment to this principle. The British-Mexican Convention, for example, provided that: "The Commission shall deal with all claims against Mexico for losses or damages suffered by British subjects or persons under British protection." The corresponding provision in the United States-Mexican and Spanish-Mexican Conventions was somewhat different. Thus the United States-Mexican General Claims Convention provided for jurisdiction over "claims against Mexico of citizens of the United States . . . for losses or damages suffered by persons or by their properties. . . ." It might be arguable from this wording that the United States could present a claim not American in inception. If a German national were injured by Mexico and subsequently became naturalized in the United States, there would be a claim "against Mexico of a citizen of the United States." No such argument was ever made before the Commission; a testimony, perhaps, to the force of the "nationality at inception" principle. This provision in the United States-Mexican Convention contains a more serious defect. It will be noted that it provides for claims of "citizens" of the United States. Thus, it would seem that the claims of Filipinos, who are "nationals" of the United States but not "citizens" thereof, were excluded. Whether or not this was done intentionally or whether the United States Department of State had been presented with any such claims does not appear. Probably, the use of this word represents a slavish copying from earlier claims conventions concluded when "national" and "citizen" of the United States were coterminous. Draftsmen of future conventions of this character should see to it that the term "nationals" is employed.[33]

So well settled is the principle that the claim must be national in origin that the question arose in only one case. A claim of a Mexican

---

[32] Case of W. H. Gleadell, Decisions and Opinions of Commissioners, p. 55, at 56.

[33] In the U. S.-Panama Claims Convention of July 28, 1926, U. S. Treaty Series No. 842, one of these errors was corrected and the other left standing. Art. I of this Convention provided for jurisdiction over all claims "which at the time they arose were those of citizens of the United States of America."

company against the Mexican government had been assigned to an Italian company. Claim was made on behalf of the latter before the Italian-Mexican Commission. The Commission dismissed the claim holding that it had no jurisdiction over claims which were Mexican in origin.[34]

§107. **Continuity of Nationality.** Until recently, there was little doubt that an award could not be rendered on a claim which had not remained a national one from the time of origin to the time of presentation.[35] Of recent years some attempt has been made to overthrow this rule and permit a claim to be advanced on behalf of a person who had changed his nationality subsequent to the inception of the claim.[36] The Mexican Claims Commissions followed the traditional rule without deviation. The rule is implicit in the provision in all the Rules of Procedure requiring the nationality of the owner or owners of the claim from the time of origin to the date of filing to be set forth in the memorial.[37] The British-Mexican Commission expressly stated that "a claim must be founded upon an injury or wrong to a citizen of the claimant Government, and that the title to that claim must have remained continuously in the hands of citizens of such Government until the time of its presentation for filing before the Commission."[38] In one case this Commission dismissed a claim for damage to property which had belonged to a British subject at the time of the injury but which had been left by will to a Mexican national before the filing of the claim.[39] The Italian-Mexican Commission dismissed a claim where the claimant had become a naturalized Mexican between the time of the injury and the time of filing.[40]

While there is general agreement on the requirement of continuity of nationality until the filing of the claim, there is considerable disagreement as to whether this nationality must continue beyond filing.[41]

[34] Case of Lange & Co., Decision No. 13 (unpublished).
[35] See citations in Borchard, "The Protection of Citizens Abroad and Change of Original Nationality," 43 Yale Law Journal (1934), p. 359, particularly note 38.
[36] See discussions of the Oslo session of the Institute of International Law, 1931 Annuaire de l'Institut de Droit International, p. 479 et seq.
[37] See infra, p. 232.
[38] Case of F. W. Flack, Decisions and Opinions of Commissioners, p. 80, at 81.
[39] Case of W. H. Gleadell, Decisions and Opinions of Commissioners, p. 55.
[40] Case of Edgardo Trucco, Decision No. 1 (unpublished).
[41] Both Borchard, Diplomatic Protection of Citizens Abroad, pp. 664, 666, and Ralston, Law and Procedure of Arbitral Tribunals, p. 162, state that a claim must have remained continuously in the hands of a citizen of the claimant government until the time of its presentation. On the other hand, the Preparatory Committee of the Conference on Codification of International Law drew up the following Basis of Discussion (No. 28)

In a case before the British-Mexican Commission the claimant lost her British nationality after the claim had been filed.[42] The Commission was impressed with the advantages of adhering to the rule requiring continuity only until filing.

"It might be argued that international jurisdiction would be rendered considerably more complicated if the tribunal had to take into account changes supervening during the period between the filing of the claim and the date of the award. Those changes may be numerous and may even annul one another. Naturalisation may be applied for, and obtained, and may be voluntarily lost. Marriages may be concluded and dissolved. In a majority of cases, changes in identity or nationality will escape the knowledge of the tribunal, and often of the Agents as well. It will be extremely difficult, even when possible, to ascertain whether at the time of the decision all personal elements continue to be identical to those which existed when the claim was presented. Jurisdiction would undoubtedly be simplified if the date of filing were accepted as decisive, without any of the events that may very frequently occur subsequently to that date, having to be traced up to the very date of rendering judgment." [43]

Nevertheless, the Commission dismissed the claim, stating:

"On the other hand it cannot, however, be denied that when it is certain and known to the tribunal, that a change of nationality has taken place prior to the date of the award, it would hardly be just to obligate the respondent Government to pay compensation to a citizen of a country other than that with which it entered into a convention." [44]

The French-Mexican Commission also took the view that the claimant must have retained French nationality until the rendering of the award.[45] This was decided in a case in which the loss of the French nationality of the claimant occurred not only subsequent to the filing but also after the specific claim had been listed as receivable in the Supplementary French-Mexican Convention of 1930.

---

on the basis of replies received from the various governments: "A State may not claim a pecuniary indemnity in respect of damage suffered by a private person on the territory of a foreign State unless the injured person was its national at the moment when the damage was caused and retains its nationality *until the claim is decided.*" League of Nations Document, Vol. III—C.75.M.69.1929.V.

[42] Case of Minnie Stevens Eschauzier, Further Decisions and Opinions, p. 177.

[43] *Ibid.*, at 180.

[44] *Ibid.*, at 180.

[45] Case of Maria Guadalupe A. Vve. Markassuza, Sentence No. 38 (unpublished; reorganized Commission).

§108. Dual Nationality. It is well established that an international tribunal has no jurisdiction over a claim advanced on behalf of a person who, although possessing the nationality of the claimant state, also possesses the nationality of the respondent state.[46] This is based on the obvious principle that a state can have no responsibility under international law towards its own nationals. This rule was reaffirmed by several of the Mexican Claims Commissions.[47] Of course, the mere fact that the claimant has a dual nationality is immaterial so long as he does not have the nationality of the respondent state.[48]

§109. Mexican Nationality of Claimants. On many occasions Mexican agents contended that claimants on whose behalf claims were advanced against Mexico had Mexican nationality. This necessitated an examination of Mexican law on the part of the Commission.[49] The most difficult problem under this head was that of the effect of Article 30 of the Constitution of 1857 providing:

"The following are Mexicans: . . . (3) Aliens who acquire immovable property in the Republic or have Mexican children, provided they do not express the wish to preserve their nationality."

This provision has had a history in international tribunals. Mexico's contention has always been that under this provision an alien acquiring land in Mexico or having children born there became *ipso facto* a Mexican national. Tribunals have invariably held against this contention.[50] The problem came up before three of the Mexican

---

[46] The Canevaro Case, Tribunal of the Permanent Court of Arbitration (1912), Scott, Hague Court Reports (1916), p. 284.

[47] Case of Carlos L. Oldenbourg, British-Mexican Commission, Decisions and Opinions of Commissioners, p. 97; Case of Coralie Davis Honey, British-Mexican Commission, Further Decisions and Opinions, p. 13. See also Rep. française (George Pinson) v. Etats-Unis mexicains, Jurisprudence de la Commission franco-mexicaine des réclamations, p. 1, at 59.

[48] Rep. Alemana (Enrique Rau) v. Estados Unidos Mexicanos, German-Mexican Commission, Decision No. 51 (unpublished): Claimant had German and Russian nationalities but the claim was allowed.

[49] For commentaries on the Mexican law of nationality see Vallarta, *Exposición de motivos del projecto de Ley sobre extranjería y naturalización* (Mexico, 1890); Rodriguez, *Codigo de extranjería* (Mexico, 1903); Azpíroz, *Codigo de extranjería de los Estados Unidos Mexicanos* (Mexico, 1876); Gertz, *La nacionalidad y los derechos de los extranjeros en Mexico* (Mexico, 1927); Zavala, *Elementos de derecho internaciónal privado. Apéndice: Examen y exposición de la ley de extranjería de 28 mayo de 1886* (Mexico, 1889).

[50] See the following decisions of the U. S.-Mexican Claims Commission of 1868: Case of Anderson and Thompson, Moore, International Arbitrations, p. 2479; Case of Benjamin Elliott, *ibid.*, p. 2481; Case of Emilio Robert, *ibid.*, p. 2468; Case of George W. Morton, *ibid.*, p. 2477; Case of Smith Bowen, *ibid.*, p. 2482. *Cf.* Case of James B. C. Prim, *ibid.*, p. 2482.

Claims Commissions. The most elaborate opinion was by the Presiding Commissioner of the French-Mexican Commission in the *Pinson* case in which the claimant's father had had children born to him in Mexico.[51] The Mexican contention was to the effect that Article 30 resulted in an automatic acquisition of Mexican nationality, and that the provisions of the Law of 1886 [52] which provided that such nationality was not automatically acquired, but that the alien was required to fulfill certain formalities, were unconstitutional. The Presiding Commissioner expressed some doubts as to whether the Commission should attempt to pass on the constitutionality of the law in view of the fact that the Mexican government could have secured a decision from Mexican courts. Apparently these courts had never passed on the constitutionality of this law. But he had no doubts of the power of the Commission to do so, and after examination he held the law to be constitutional.[53] The decision, however, was not based on the Law of 1886 but on an interpretation of the Constitution of 1857, it being held that the law did not force citizenship upon the alien. The alien in question had, in the certificate of birth of his son, inscribed himself as being of French nationality. This, the Presiding Commissioner held, was a tacit expression of the intention to retain his original nationality and a full compliance with the Constitution. "I refuse to believe that the legislator desired to impose a nationality on an alien who did not wish to acquire it, and to punish him because he had not 'manifested the intention to preserve his nationality' in an express form but only in a tacit form." [54] Having reached this conclusion, he found it unnecessary to determine whether the interpretation contended for by Mexico was in conformity with international law.

[51] Rep. française (Georges Pinson) *v.* Etats-Unis mexicains, Jurisprudence de la Commission franco-mexicaine des réclamations, p. 1, at 59–76.

[52] "The following are Mexicans . . . (10) Aliens acquiring real estate in the Republic, provided they do not declare their intention of retaining their nationality. At the time of making the declaration the alien shall declare to the officiating notary or judge whether he does or does not wish to acquire Mexican nationality as granted him by Section III of Article 30 of the Constitution, and the alien's decision on this point shall appear in the document. If he chooses Mexican citizenship, or if he omits making any declaration on the subject, he may, within one year, apply to the Department of [Foreign] Relations, in order to comply with the requirements of Article 19, and be deemed a Mexican. (11) Aliens having children born in Mexico, provided they do not prefer to retain their alien character. . . ." Flournoy and Hudson, Nationality Laws (New York, 1929), p. 428.

[53] In the Case of Santos Barcena, Spanish-Mexican Commission, Decision No. 11 (unpublished) it was held that the Commission had no power to pass on the constitutionality of the Law of 1886.

[54] Pinson case, *supra*, note 51, at 70.

The possibility of so narrow a holding was apparently not present in the cases brought before the German-Mexican, Italian-Mexican and Spanish-Mexican Commissions. These Commissions held squarely that Article 30 of the Constitution did not impose Mexican nationality automatically on the alien, since it was intended to confer a privilege on the alien to enable him to acquire Mexican nationality more easily if he so desired, and that if Article 30 were interpreted in line with the Mexican contention it would be contrary to international law.[55] These decisions are of considerable general importance. They establish the proposition that even though the conferring of nationality is a matter within the domestic jurisdiction of a state, international law imposes certain limits on the conferring of nationality without the consent of the person concerned.

Other problems requiring the consideration of the Mexican law of nationality are of lesser importance. The General Claims Commission held that children born in Mexico of an American father did not acquire Mexican nationality where they left Mexico before coming of age.[56] The Commission relied on the Constitution of 1917 providing that persons born in Mexico of foreign parents are to be considered Mexicans by birth if they elect Mexican citizenship within one year after coming of age. The persons in question were born before 1917 and it is doubtful whether the Constitution was applicable to their case, but the same result would be reached under the Law of 1886.[56a] Applying this law, the British-Mexican Commission held that a son born in Mexico of British subjects was a Mexican national because of failure to opt for British nationality after attaining his majority.[57]

---

[55] *German-Mexican Commission*—Rep. Alemana (Enrique Rau) *v.* Estados Unidos Mexicanos, Decision No. 51 (unpublished).
   Italian-Mexican Commission—Case of Luis Occelli, Decision No. 67 (unpublished); Case of Vincenzo y Vespasiano Sarli, Decision No. 75 (unpublished); Case of Alphonso y Leopoldo Martello, Decision No. 105 (unpublished).
   Spanish-Mexican Commission—Case of Santos Barcena, Decision No. 11 (unpublished).
   [56] U. S. A. (Lily J. Costello) *v.* United Mexican States, General Claims Commission, Opinions of Commissioners, 1929, p. 252.
   [56a] "Article 2. The following are aliens: . . . (2) The children of an alien, or of an alien mother and unknown father, born in the national territory, until they reach the age at which, according to the law of the nationality of the father or of the mother, as the case may be, they come of age. At the expiration of the year following that age they shall be regarded as Mexicans, unless they declare before the civil authorities of the place where they reside that they follow the citizenship of their parents." Flournoy and Hudson, Nationality Laws (New York, 1929), p. 429.
   [57] Case of Coralie Davis Honey, Further Decisions and Opinions, p. 13.

The Italian-Mexican Commission held that the minor child of an Italian who became a naturalized Mexican also acquired Mexican nationality. [58] In the arguments on the *Pinson* case before the French-Mexican Commission considerable discussion was had as to whether service in a foreign army resulted in a loss of Mexican nationality. Article 37 of the Constitution of 1857 provided: "La calidad de ciudadano se pierde: . . . II. Por servir officialmente el gobierno de otro pais . . ." The Mexican agent argued that such service deprived the person in question of Mexican *citizenship* and not of Mexican *nationality*. The Presiding Commissioner held otherwise. [59]

§110. **Loss of Nationality.** The General Claims Commission was presented with the knotty problem of the meaning of the American statutory provision of presumption of loss of citizenship of a naturalized citizen by residence abroad. [60] Claim was made on behalf of the heirs of Costello who had been naturalized in the United States and had then resided for over ten years in Mexico. In 1920 the Department of State instructed the Consul General in Mexico to cancel Costello's registration on the ground that he had failed to overcome the presumption of loss of citizenship. Costello was killed in 1922. The claim was dismissed for lack of evidence, but the American Commissioner took the view that the statute merely created a presumption of loss which deprived the person in question of the right to claim protection but did not deprive him of his citizenship.

"According to a ruling of the Department of State, Timothy J. Costello evidently was not considered to be entitled to protection of his Government at the time he was killed in Mexico. But he was an American citizen at that time. He was not a Mexican. And he had not by any action of his Government been outlawed as a man without a country. There was nothing in any established rule of domestic policy that would have precluded his Government from extending protection to him at some future date after he had returned to his own country to reside.

"But the precise case before this Commission is one in which complaint

[58] Case of Florindo Demenghi, Decision No. 90 (unpublished).
[59] Rep. française (Georges Pinson) *v.* Etats-Unis mexicains, *supra*, note 51, at 76–91.
[60] "When any naturalized citizen shall have resided for two years in the foreign state from which he came, or for five years in any other foreign state, it shall be presumed that he has ceased to be an American citizen, and the place of his general abode shall be deemed his place of residence during said years: *Provided, however,* that such presumption may be overcome on the presentation of satisfactory evidence to a diplomatic or consular officer of the United States, under such rules and regulations as the Department of State may prescribe." Act of March 2, 1907, 34 Stat. 1228.

is made that proper steps were not taken to apprehend and punish the murderers of an American citizen. That the Department of State might have been unwilling to protect Costello had he sought its protection shortly before his death can in no way be determinative of the right of the United States at this time to invoke the rule of international law requiring effective measures with respect to apprehension and punishment of persons who injure an alien. That rule is invoked in this case with a view to obtaining compensation for three American claimants now resident in the United States." [61]

The two other Commissioners took a different view. While authoritative pronouncements in the United States are at variance,[62] it is believed that the view of the American Commissioner as to the effect of the statute is the better one.

§111. "Protégés." Three of the Mexican Claims Conventions provided for jurisdiction over the claims of *"protégés"*: the British-Mexican Convention ("persons under British protection"), the French-Mexican Convention (*"protégés français"*), and the Spanish-Mexican Convention (*"protegidos españoles"*). Only one case involving this provision was decided: the *Nájera* case before the French-Mexican Commission.[63] Claim was made by France on behalf of a person of Syrio-Lebanese nationality. The memorial was filed June 15, 1926. Claimant's option for Syrio-Lebanese nationality had been executed November 5, 1925, submitted to the French High Commissioner for Syria and Lebanon on June 9, 1926, and acceptance notified to the French consular authorities in Mexico on December 29, 1927. It was contended by Mexico that the Commission had no jurisdiction because *"protégés"* means subjects of a protectorate, while Syria and Lebanon was a territory under mandate. France contended that its *"protégés"* were all persons to whom it was obliged and to whom it had the right to extend diplomatic protection. The Presiding Commissioner very properly rejected the Mexican contention. He found no warrant in international usage for restricting the term in this manner. A *"protégé"* might be the subject of a state under protectorate, or under mandate, or of a vassal state under the suzerainty of another,

[61] U. S. A. (Lily J. Costello) *v.* United Mexican States, Opinions of Commissioners, 1929, p. 252, at 263.

[62] See Opinion of Attorney General Wickersham, Dec. 1, 1910, 28 Ops. Atty. Gen. 504; U. S. *v.* Howe, 231 Fed. 546 (D.C.N.Y. 1916); Thorsch *v.* Miller, 5 Fed. (2d) 118 (C. of A.D.C. 1925).

[63] Rep. française (Pablo Nájera) *v.* Etats-Unis mexicains, Jurisprudence de la Commission franco-mexicaine des réclamations, p. 156.

or of a state which was none of these but whose foreign relations were conducted by another state (Danzig). Or it might be a personal relationship of the subject of one state to another state as under the Convention of Madrid of July 30, 1880. Long before the Treaty of Lausanne, France had, in fact, protected the Syrians and Lebanese and this relationship had been recognized by the Turkish government. Under the Treaty of Lausanne and the Mandate France had been given the function of conducting the foreign relations of Syria and Lebanon.

The Presiding Commissioner admitted that the claimant could not be said to have had Syrio-Lebanese nationality at the time the claim was filed. The statements contained in the declaration of option indicated that it was not intended to be retroactive. But the traditional relation of protection between the French government and inhabitants of Syria and Lebanon had existed long before that time. This relation would be sufficient to support jurisdiction. Furthermore it was obvious to the Mexican government at the time the Convention was negotiated that the provision was intended to apply to such persons and that a new relation of protection growing out of the mandate was in process of evolution. With the concurrence of the French Commissioner, the jurisdiction of the Commission was sustained.

The dissenting opinion of the Mexican Commissioner argues that mandates being *sui generis,* the relation of protection does not exist between the mandatory and the inhabitants of the territory. He casts some doubts also on the statement that inhabitants of Syria and Lebanon were under French protection before the mandate. This opinion is not altogether convincing. The strongest argument in favor of the decision of the Commission is that the records of the negotiation of the Convention indicate rather clearly that the parties understood the term *"protégés"* to refer to such persons as the claimant.

Nevertheless, this decision seems to have caused the Mexican government particular dissatisfaction. In the French-Mexican Supplementary Convention of August 2, 1930, all references to *protégés* were omitted and, in the annex to the Convention containing all claims upon which the reorganized Commission was to pass, only one Syrio-Lebanese claim was included, this being the *Nájera* claim. When this claim came up for the decision before the reorganized Commission it

was dismissed on the ground that the Commission had jurisdiction only over the claims of French nationals.[64]

In the Supplementary Conventions with Great Britain, December 5, 1930, and with Spain, December 5, 1930, references to *protégés* were also omitted although no case involving the application of these provisions had arisen before these Commissions.

WHO MAY CLAIM

§112. **Analysis of the Problems.** It is obvious that a claim may be made only on behalf of a person who has suffered a loss as the result of the injury complained of. Yet there may be considerable difficulty in applying this simple principle in cases in which the person who suffered the primary injury is dead at the time the claim is filed. These cases fall into two main categories: (1) cases involving a person who has sustained personal or property injury and who dies before the claim is filed; (2) cases involving a person who has been killed under circumstances entailing the responsibility of the respondent state. In the first category the questions which arise are: (a) does the particular claim for damages survive the death of this person? and (b) on whose behalf may claim be made? In the second category of cases the question is one of damages: which persons have suffered such an injury by the death of the person killed that they are entitled to receive redress? Outside of these two categories lies an indefinite penumbra embracing various persons who claim to have suffered loss because of a property injury inflicted against a third person—creditors, pledgees, lessees, etc.

§113. **Survival of Claims.** There is no question that a claim for injuries to property survives the death of the claimant. The problem of survival arises in the case of personal injuries. In the *Dujay* case [65] before the United States-Mexican General Claims Commission claim was made on behalf of the executrix of the estate of Dujay who had been wrongfully imprisoned in Mexico in 1884. Dujay had died before the memorandum was filed. Mexico invoked the common law rule *actio personalis moritur cum persona* and also contended that under international law a claim of this kind could not be advanced because

---

[64] Case of Pablo Nájera, Sentence No. 13 (unpublished). Article IV of the Supplementary Convention permitted the Commission to reject any claim listed in the Annex if it did not come within its jurisdiction as defined in Article III.

[65] U. S. A. (Fannie P. Dujay) v. United Mexican States, Opinions of Commissioners, 1929, p. 180.

the claimant had suffered no pecuniary injury. The Commission felt that municipal law could not be applied because it would lead to the absurd result that the claimant might not recover if he were a national of a common law country but could recover if he were a national of a civil law country. It then examined the cases in which international tribunals had held that claims for personal injuries had survived [66] and held that a rule of international law to that effect existed. It also pointed out that to hold otherwise would put a premium on delays with the hope that the claimant would die. The claim was allowed.

The *Beolchi* case [67] before the Italian-Mexican Commission seems to follow a different path. Memorandum was filed on behalf of Beolchi claiming compensation for the wrongful killing of his son by revolutionaries. Beolchi died and the case was continued on behalf of his heirs. The Commission dismissed the claim. It found that the injury to Beolchi consisted of mental suffering for the loss of his son (for which, under the Convention, the Commission had held no damages could be awarded), and loss of support. The claim for loss of support was extinguished by the death of Beolchi, and the heirs who were not dependent on the decedent son could not recover.[68] It is difficult to distinguish this from the *Dujay* case. All the considerations which the General Claims Commission took into account apply here. The few precedents which exist in international practice are contrary to this holding.[69] Nor does it seem possible to distinguish the

---

[66] See Metzger Case, German-Venezuelan Commission of 1903, Ralston, Venezuelan Arbitrations, p. 578; Plumer Case, U. S. Board of Commissioners on Mexican Claims of 1849, 1 Commissioners on Claims Against Mexico, Opinions, p. 182; Hughes Case, U. S. Board of Commissioners on Mexican Claims of 1849, 2 Moore, International Arbitrations, p. 1285; 3 *ibid.*, p. 2972; Webster Case, U. S.-Mexican Commission of 1868, 3 *ibid.*, p. 3004; De Luna Case, U. S.-Spanish Commission of 1871, 4 Moore, p. 3276.

[67] Case of Herederos de Giuseppe Beolchi, Decision No. 4 (unpublished).

[68] "El daño que experimenta un padre por la muerte por asesinato de su hijo tiene dos caracteres que se distinguen bien claramente: 1° el sufrimiento moral que no es indemnizable, especialmente dentro de los términos de la Convención que declara indemnizables las péridas o daños sufridos por el reclamente en su persona o en sus bienes, con lo cual quedan excluídos los sufrimientos morales y sentimentales; y 2° la pérdida material que para el padre significa el asesinato de su hijo, como quiera que, por virtud de la muerte anormal de éste, aquél se vé privado del beneficio material que habría reportado de su hijo en el caso de que el asesinato no hubiera terminado violentamente con su vida y de que, por las circunstancias económicas en que se hubiera desarrollado la vida de uno y otro, hubiera tenido necesidad el padre de ejercitar su derecho legal y natural de pedir alimentos a su hijo." *Ibid.*

[69] See U. S. A. (Macpherson Crichton) *v.* Germany, U. S.-German Mixed Claims Commission, Consolidated Edition of Decisions and Opinions, p. 493; U. S. A. (Frank J. Proctor) *v.* Germany, *ibid.*, p. 542. In these cases awards were made on behalf of the estates of persons who had suffered injury as a result of the wrongful death of another person on whom they had been dependent.

cases on the basis of the loss caused. If Dujay had recovered for his wrongful imprisonment his estate would have been larger. Similarly, if Beolchi had recovered for the death of his son his estate would have been larger.

A view similar to that in the *Beolchi* case was taken by the British-Mexican Commission in the *Williams* case.[70] George Ernest Williams, a bachelor, was killed by a mob in 1914. The father of Williams was partially dependent on him for support. In 1920 the father married the claimant and died in 1925 leaving the claimant as sole executrix. The British government advanced the contention that the estate of the father from 1914 had been impoverished by the loss of the son's contributions and that the father's widow, as the executrix of the estate, was entitled to recover the money. The Commission allowed a motion to dismiss, and said:

"In order to succeed in the claim, Mrs. Williams must establish legal relationship or dependency as between herself and the late Mr. G. E. Williams, and there is no evidence of this in the facts set out in the Memorial, or in the oral argument. No claim against the respondent Government could form part of the estate of Major Williams until the right to present it had accrued to him. That right did not arise until the Anglo-Mexican Treaty was signed in 1926 and ratified in 1928, whereas Major Williams died in 1925, and with his death all his personal rights expired." [71]

The latter part of this reasoning can hardly be sustained. The question of the right of the claimant depended on whether or not the claim survived the death of the father, and this should be decided on the nature of the claim and not on the mere accident of whether the death of the father occurred before or after the signature of the Convention. The notion of a claim "accruing" on the signing of a claim's convention seems an empty legalism.

§114. **Claims on Behalf of Decedents' Estates.** Once it has been determined that the claim is one which survives the death of the person primarily injured, the question arises as to who may claim—the estate or the individual heirs. The Rules of the British-Mexican Commission supplied an answer in the following provision:

[70] Case of Ada Ruth Williams, Decisions and Opinions of Commissioners, p. 67.
[71] *Ibid.*, p. 68.

"Claims presented solely for the death of a British subject shall be filed on behalf of those British subjects considering themselves personally entitled to present them. Any claims presented for damage to a British subject already deceased at the time of filing such claim, if for damage to property, shall be filed on behalf of his estate and through his legal representative, who shall duly establish his legal capacity therefor." [72]

The rules of the other Commissions also embodied this distinction between claims which might be presented on behalf of individuals and those which had to be presented on behalf of a decedent's estate, although it was not given such clear expression.[73] This distinction was carefully preserved in practice,[74] but it was preserved because of its procedural convenience and not because a distinction in substance between the two kinds of claims was intended. This is shown by the *Gleadell* case [75] before the British-Mexican Commission.

The wife of the claimant had been compelled to subscribe to a forced loan by revolutionary forces. On her death, she bequeathed all her real and personal property in Mexico to her daughter who was an American citizen. The husband, a British subject, was made residuary legatee and executor. Claim was made on behalf of the husband on the ground that the right to reparation was vested in him. The Commission sustained a motion to dismiss. It held that since the will was made in England by a British subject, the intention of the testatrix must be interpreted in accordance with British law. Under this

---

[72] British-Mexican Rule 11.

[73] U. S.-Mexican General Rule IV 2 (i) provided: "Claims put forward on behalf of a claimant who is dead, either for injury to person or loss of or damage to property, shall be presented by the personal or legal representative of the estate of the deceased. The memorial shall set out with respect to both the claimant and such representative the facts which, under these Rules, would be required of the former were he alive and presenting his claim before the Commission; and the claim shall be accompanied by documentary evidence properly certified of the authority of such representative." See also U. S.-Mexican Special Rule IV 2 (i); French-Mexican Rules, Art. 12; Spanish-Mexican Rules, Art. 13 (i); Italian-Mexican Rules, Art. 11 (i); German-Mexican Rules, Art. 12.

[74] Note the Case of Edith Henry, British-Mexican Commission, Further Decisions and Opinions, p. 299. Claim was made on behalf of Mrs. Henry for the murder of her husband and the theft of his property. The first part of the claim was allowed but not the second, the Commission saying: "Mrs. Henry's claim as regards the loss of her husband's personal property is not brought by her as representing, or on behalf of her husband's estate, and she has not shown any legal authority for so claiming it, as provided by the Rules of Procedure." *Cf.* Rep. Alemana (Laura Z. Vda. de Plehn) *v.* Estados Unidos Mexicanos, German-Mexican Commission, Decision No. 13 (unpublished). Claim was made on behalf of a widow for wrongful death of her husband. The Mexican agent contended that the claim should have been brought on behalf of the estate. It was held that the claim was properly brought since the widow was claiming for a loss which was personal to her.

[75] Case of Captain W. H. Gleadell, Decisions and Opinions of Commissioners, p. 55.

law the claim must be considered part of the estate situate in Mexico since it was a debt which is situated where the debtor resides.[76] The right to the claim was therefore vested in the daughter who was not a British subject. The claim had lost its British character even though the executor of the estate was British.

This case lays down two rules: (1) that the construction of a will is a matter of domestic law; [77] (2) that the nationality of an executor or administrator is not material since the Commission will look to the nationality of the heirs or legatees.[78] These two propositions find abundant support in international jurisprudence and in other decisions of the Commissions. One of the rare expressions of a contrary opinion was by British Commissioner Stoker, dissenting in the *Eschauzier* case.[79] William Eschauzier, who had suffered property losses at the hands of revolutionaries, died and appointed Francis Eschauzier as his sole heir and executor. The latter died in 1914 and left a will appointing his wife as sole heir and executrix. William and Francis were British subjects, but the wife ceased to be a British subject after the presentation of the claim by marrying an American citizen. The majority of the Commission allowed a motion to dismiss. The British Commissioner, however, was of the opinion "that the true test to be applied is the nationality of the person who sustained the injury and damage, and whether the claim is made on behalf of his estate or by an alien assignee of the original claim." He then went on to say:

"These should be the sole considerations, irrespectively of what may be the ultimate destination of the beneficial interest in the estate. Supposing, for instance, that the deceased owed debts, and left either no assets beyond the existing claim for injuries and damage to his estate, or left assets insufficient except for such claim, to pay his debts, then his solvency, and the pay-

[76] The Commission cited Dicey, Conflict of Laws, p. 318, for this much disputed proposition.

[77] *Accord:* Case of Ruth Mabel Raeburn, British-Mexican Commission, Further Decisions and Opinions, p. 54, at 55: "It is a principle universally admitted in International Law, that as regards the form or external formalities of contracts, wills and all public instruments, the laws of the country where they are executed are the ones that should govern, '*lex loci regit actum.*' "

[78] *Accord:* U. S. A. (Belle M. Hendry) *v.* United Mexican States, U. S.-Mexican General Claims Commission, Opinions of Commissioners, 1931, p. 97 at 98; Case of F. W. Flack, British-Mexican Commission, Decisions and Opinions of Commissioners, p. 80, at 81.

For decisions holding that the nationality of the heirs must be shown see: Rep. Alemana (Herederos de Sr. Arnoldo Vogel) *v.* Estados Unidos Mexicanos, German-Mexican Commission, Decision No. 38 (unpublished); Case of Constantino Rivero, Spanish-Mexican Commission, Decision No. 17 (unpublished).

[79] Case of Minnie Stevens Eschauzier, Further Decisions and Opinions, p. 177.

ment of his debts, even to creditors of his own nationality, would depend on the recovery on behalf of his estate of such damages. To defeat recovery thereof because his Executor or Administrator, or the ultimate beneficiary (after payments of debts and pecuniary or other legacies), might be of a different nationality, would in my opinion be an injury and injustice to such creditors, and to legatees, as well as to the reputation of the deceased, by causing him to have died insolvent." [80]

The Commissioner admitted that this view might seem to be in contradiction with other decisions of international tribunals. But in his opinion, "if the nationality attaches and remains attached or is deemed to attach to the *estate* on behalf of which the claim is really brought, there is no such contradiction. The nationality of a mere assignee of the original claim is of course a different matter."

This opinion is, of course, only a restatement of the view which holds that there should not be a requirement of continuity of nationality. All the objections to the latter view apply here. The attempt to refute the objections by invoking a fiction of nationality attaching to the estate is obviously futile. Substantively there is no difference between holding that a change in nationality does not affect the status of the claim or holding that nationality attaches to the estate and the nationality of the heirs is immaterial. Either form of statement goes beyond existing rules as established by decisions of tribunals, while the latter form of statement has the added disadvantage of introducing the conception that an estate may have nationality, a conception hitherto unknown to international law.

The reason for requiring a claim to be submitted on behalf of a decedent's estate is for procedural convenience. It is necessary to have the claims of all the heirs and legatees before the tribunal in order to determine the amount of damages and whether or not all the persons claiming are of proper nationality. The one practicable way in which to get all these claims before the tribunal is by requiring the claim to be filed on behalf of the executor or administrator. It is regrettable to find tribunals which have misconceived the purpose of such a requirement. Thus the French-Mexican Commission had before it a claim on behalf of an undivided estate (*succession indivise*).[81] Two of the heirs were French, each of these having a one-sixth right

[80] *Ibid.*, p. 183.
[81] Case of Succession de M. Tomas de la Torre y Mier, Sentence No. 53 (unpublished; reorganized Commission).

in the estate. The other heirs were not French. The Commission held that the provision in the Convention which gave the Commission jurisdiction over corporations, associations, etc., "or other groupings of interests" provided that French nationals held an interest greater than 50% of the capital was applicable. The undivided estate was held to be a "grouping of interests" and the claim was dismissed. This holding is an extraordinary misinterpretation of the provision in the Convention which was obviously intended to apply only to business organizations.

§115. **Evidence of Status as Legal Representative.** The Rules of Procedure made no express provision for the sort of evidence necessary to establish the status of a claimant as executor or administrator. In practice the authority of a legal representative was rarely questioned. A few exceptions are to be found. In a case before the Spanish-Mexican Commission, claim was made on behalf of the *albacea* (executor) of an estate.[82] The will of the decedent was produced but not a court order appointing the claimant as *albacea*. A motion to dismiss was made on the ground that the claimant was not a proper representative. The Commission denied the motion but ordered the Spanish agent to produce an order of a judge at the place of last domicile of the testator before final decision.

In the *Raeburn* case [83] before the British-Mexican Commission the memorial was filed on behalf of the heir of a decedent who had sustained damage. Mexico moved to dismiss on the ground that it was not shown that the claimant was the executor of the decedent's estate. The British agent then attempted to amend the claim to read on behalf of one Watson, the executor under decedent's will. He also presented the will which had been probated in Edinburgh. The Commission found that the decedent had been domiciled in Mexico and that the will had been executed there, but that it was not a valid will under Mexican law because it had not been executed before a notary. Therefore the appointment of the executor and the naming of an heir were invalid and the motion to dismiss was sustained.

§116. **Claims Arising out of Wrongful Death.** Where a claim is presented on behalf of a person who is alleged to have suffered damage as a result of the death of another person, the question of the standing of the claimant to prosecute the claim is closely connected

[82] Case of Constatino Rivero, Decision No. 17 (unpublished).
[83] Case of Ruth Mabel Raeburn, Further Decisions and Opinions, p. 54.

with the question of damages. As we shall see later, two categories of damages for wrongful death are recognized, one being damages for loss of support, and the other being damages for grief and indignity.[84] Generally, international tribunals have been reluctant to award damages for grief and indignity alone but have required a showing of pecuniary loss. As a general rule, therefore, a claimant in order to recover for wrongful death must show that he was dependent in some way on the deceased. Under this rule, the Mexican Claims Commission made awards in favor of parents,[85] widows,[86] children [87] and brothers.[88] Occasionally, however, Commissions have been willing to go further, as is shown in the *Stephens* case [89] before the United States-Mexican General Claims Commission. Claim was made on behalf of two brothers of the deceased. One brother suffered from a mental disorder and had not sustained any pecuniary damage. The other brother suffered a remote pecuniary loss by the death in that the deceased, together with this brother, supported an aged aunt by contributing $75 a month, an amount which the surviving brother alone paid after the death. The Commission awarded $7,000 on behalf of *both* claimants stating that "if in the present case injustice for which Mexico is

---

[84] See *infra*, Ch. 17.

[85] U. S. A. (J. W. and N. L. Swinney) *v.* United Mexican States, U. S.-Mexican General Claims Commission, Opinions of Commissioners, 1927, p. 131; United Mexican States (Francisco Quintanilla) *v.* U. S. A., *ibid.*, 1927, p. 136; United Mexican States (Teodoro García) *v.* U. S. A., *ibid.*, 1927, p. 163; U. S. A. (Margaret Roper) *v.* United Mexican States, *ibid.*, p. 205; U. S. A. (Ida R. S. Putnam) *v.* United Mexican States, *ibid.*, 1927, p. 222.

[86] U. S. A. (Laura M. B. Janes) *v.* United Mexican States, U. S.-Mexican General Claims Commission, Opinions of Commissioners, 1927, p. 108; United Mexican States (D. Guerrero Vda. de Falcón) *v.* U. S. A., *ibid.*, 1927, p. 140; U. S. A. (Mamie Brown) *v.* United Mexican States, *ibid.*, 1927, p. 211; Rep. Alemana (Laura Z. Vda. de Plehn) *v.* Estados Unidos Mexicanos, German-Mexican Commission, Decision No. 13 (unpublished); Case of Edith Henry, British-Mexican Commission, Further Decisions and Opinions, p. 165; Case of Ventura Torres Vda. de Antonio Orio, Italian-Mexican Commission, Decision No. 98 (unpublished).

[87] U. S. A. (Thomas H. Youmans) *v.* United Mexican States, U. S.-Mexican General Claims Commission, Opinions of Commissioners, 1927, p. 150; U. S. A. (Lily J. Costello) *v.* United Mexican States, Opinions of Commissioners, 1929, p. 252; U. S. A. (Jesús Navarro Tribolet) *v.* United Mexican States, Opinions of Commissioners, 1931, p. 68.

In the following cases claims were presented on behalf of guardians of children of deceased persons: U. S. A. (Laura M. B. Janes) *v.* United Mexican States, U. S.-Mexican General Claims Commission, Opinions of Commissioners, 1927, p. 108; U. S. A. (Gertrude Parker Massey) *v.* United Mexican States, *ibid.*, 1927, p. 228; U. S. A. (Lillian Greenlaw Sewall) *v.* United Mexican States, Opinions of Commissioners, 1931, p. 112.

[88] U. S. A. (Agnes Connelly) *v.* United Mexican States, U. S.-Mexican General Claims Commission, Opinions of Commissioners, 1927, p. 160; U. S. A. (Daisy Sanders) *v.* United Mexican States, *ibid.*, 1927, p. 212; U. S. A. (Lily J. Costello) *v.* United Mexican States, Opinions of Commissioners, 1929, p. 252; U. S. A. (Mary E. A. Munroe) *v.* United Mexican States, *ibid.*, 1929, p. 314.

[89] U. S. A. (Charles S. Stephens) *v.* United Mexican States, Opinions of Commissioners, 1927, p. 397.

liable is proven, the claimants shall be entitled to an award in the character of satisfaction, even when the direct pecuniary damages suffered by them are not proven or are too remote to form a basis for allowing damages in the character of reparation." This decision goes to the very verge of the existing law and it may perhaps be considered as an aberration from an otherwise well-established rule that collateral relatives may recover for wrongful death only on a showing of direct pecuniary injury.[90]

§117. **Assignment of Claims.** International tribunals have generally held that the assignee of a claim may recover on it if both he and his assignor are of proper nationality.[91] The Mexican agent before the British-Mexican Commission made an attempt to overthrow this rule.[92] Loss was suffered by a British partnership. In 1920 all the assets of the partnership, including this claim for damages, were sold to a British corporation. The Mexican agent contended that no right to the claim existed at that time and that it came into existence only with the signing of the Convention in 1926. The Commission granted an award and said:

"The majority of the Commission is . . . of opinion that the right to claim was not created by the signing of the Convention, but existed as a marketable asset from the time when the loss occurred, even though it might subsequently turn out to be worthless. This is shown by the fact that such rights may be assigned or inherited as appears from the decisions of numerous International Commissions, and the same principle is implicit in Article 10 (paragraphs (f) and (g)) of the Rules of Procedure, which show that the eventuality of an assignment of the right to claim after the time when it had its origin, i.e., the date of the loss, has been taken into consideration." [93]

CORPORATE CLAIMS

§118. **Provisions in the Conventions.** International tribunals have frequently been faced with difficult problems arising out of

---

[90] Cf. the Connelly case, supra, note 88, in which the Commission pointed out that the deceased, before his death, was contributing towards the support of his brother and sisters who were the claimants in the case.

[91] U. S. A. (Williams A. Parker) v. United Mexican States, U. S.-Mexican General Claims Commission, Opinions of Commissioners, 1927, p. 82; U. S. A. (G. W. McNear, Inc.) v. United Mexican States, Opinions of Commissioners, 1929, p. 68; Case of Lange & Co., Italian-Mexican Commission, Decision No. 13 (unpublished) (dismissing claim of an Italian company which had been assigned to it by a Mexican company).

[92] Case of William E. Bowerman, Decisions and Opinions of Commissioners, p. 141.

[93] Ibid., at 144.

claims on behalf of groupings of interests. In the Mexican Claims Convention an attempt was made to do away with these problems by specifying the jurisdiction over claims of this nature. Two categories of claims were dealt with: (1) claims of corporations and associations having the national character of the claimant state; (2) claims of nationals of the claimant state for losses suffered as a result of injury to corporations or associations having the national character of another state. The first category was covered by defining "citizen" or "national" to include "corporations, companies, associations, partnerships or individuals." [94] The second category was treated differently in the Conventions with the United States and in the Conventions with the European states. Thus the United States-Mexican General Claims Convention provided for jurisdiction over:

"all claims for losses or damages suffered by citizens of either country by reason of losses or damages suffered by any corporation, company, association or partnership in which such citizens have or have had a substantial and bona fide interest, provided an allotment to the claimant by the corporation, company, association or partnership of his proportion of the loss or damage suffered is presented by the claimant to the Commission."

The French-Mexican Convention may serve as an example of the contrasting provision in the Conventions with the European states. Jurisdiction was granted over all claims:

"a raison . . . des pertes ou dommages causés aux intérêts de Français ou de protégés français dans des sociétés, compagnies, associations ou autres groupements d'intérêts, pourvus que l'intérêt du lésé, dès avant l'époque du dommage ou du perte, soit supérieur à cinquante pour cent du capital total de la société ou association dont il fait partie, et qu'en outre, le dit lésé présente à la Commission une cession, consentie à son profit, de la proportion qui lui revient dans les droits à indemnité dont peut se prévaloir ladite société ou association." [95]

[94] This is the language of the United States-Mexican Conventions (Sp.—*corporaciones, compañías, asociaciones, sociedades o individuos particulares*). Other Conventions read: French-Mexican—"*sociétés, compagnies, associations ou personnes morales françaises ou sous la protection française*"; British-Mexican—"British partnerships, companies, associations or British judicial persons or those under British protection"; German-Mexican—"*Gesellschaften, Unternehmungen, Vereinigungen oder deutsche juristische Personen*"; Italian-Mexican—"*società, compagnie, associazione o persone morali italiane*"; Spanish-Mexican—"*sociedades, compañias, asociaciones o personas morales españoles.*"

[95] The German-Mexican, Italian-Mexican and Spanish-Mexican Conventions were substantially the same as this. The British-Mexican Convention was somewhat different: ". . . for losses or damages suffered by British subjects or persons under British

It will be noted that the right to claim in cases coming within th
first category was based solely on the national character of the cor
poration. Even if all the stockholders were of a different nationalit
the claim on behalf of the corporation could be validly presented. Nev
ertheless, the American Agency seems to have adopted the commenc
able practice of refusing to present claims on behalf of corporation
incorporated in the United States in which there was no beneficia
American interest.[95a]

§119. **National Character of Corporations.** Since the Conver
tions defined "nationals" as including corporations, associations an
partnerships," the question arose as to how the national character o
nationality of a corporation on whose behalf a claim was presente
was to be determined. Numerous criteria [96] have been suggested i
the voluminous writings [97] on the subject of nationality of corpor
tions, and the decisions of international tribunals show much confu
sion and many contradictions.[98] It is curious to note that the fashio
in this subject has changed from time to time. In the decade befor
the World War, considered opinion was strongly in favor of using th

---

protection, by reason of losses or damages suffered by any partnership, company or asso
ciation in which British subjects or persons under British protection have or have had a
interest exceeding fifty per cent of the total capital of such partnership, company c
association, and acquired prior to the time when the damages or losses were sustaine
But in view of certain special conditions in which some British concerns are placed in suc
societies which do not possess that nationality it is agreed that it will not be necessary tha
the interest above mentioned shall pertain to one single individual, but it will suffice tha
it pertains jointly to various British subjects, provided that the British claimant o
claimants shall present to the Commission an allotment to the said claimant or claimant
of the proportional part of such losses or damages pertaining to the claimant or claiman
in such partnership, company or association."

[95a] See reference to this in Case of the British Shareholders of the Mariposa Company
British-Mexican Commission, Further Decisions and Opinions, p. 304.

[96] Among the criteria suggested have been the following:
1. Place of incorporation.
2. Place of main offices (*siège social*).
3. Place of doing business (*lieu d'exploitation*).
4. Nationality of shareholders.
5. Nationality of "control."
6. Place where shares were sold.

[97] See in particular Mamelok, *Die juristische Person in internationalen Privatrech*
(Zürich, 1900); Young, Foreign Companies and Other Corporations (Cambridge, 1912)
Isay, *Die Staatsangehörigkeit der juristischen Personen* (Tübingen, 1907); League o
Nations Committee of Experts on Progressive Codification of International Law, Na
tionality of Commercial Corporations and their Diplomatic Protection, League of Nation
Document, C.207.M.81.1927.V.

[98] The cases are collected in Borchard, Diplomatic Protection of Citizens Abroad
pp. 617-625, and in Ralston, Law and Procedure of International Tribunals, pp. 149-15
On the cases in the Mixed Arbitral Tribunals see Feller, Note on *Staatsangehörigke*
juristischer Personen, 2 *Zeitschrift für ausländisches öffentliches Recht und Völkerrech*
(1930-31), II, p. 55.

place of the main offices (*siège social*) as the decisive criterion for determining national character.[99] During the war, the test of "control" was clearly in the ascendant.[100] Since then, opinion has shifted towards ascribing to a corporation the national character of the state under whose laws it was incorporated.[101] This last criterion is the one which seems to have been applied in the practice of the Mexican Claims Commission.[102] It is the criterion adopted in the only case in which the problem was discussed.

This was a case before the German-Mexican Commission.[103] Claim was made on behalf of the Mexico Plantagen G.m.b.H., a limited liability company established under the laws of Germany doing business in Mexico, with main offices in Hamburg. The Mexican agent contended that the company must be considered as Mexican because it did business in Mexico, and also that it had no standing as a claimant because it had failed to publish its balance sheet as required by Mexican law. The opinion of Presiding Commissioner Cruchaga, a lengthy exposition of theory and practice, accepted the notion that companies have a nationality and the theory that this nationality is that of the state under whose laws the company is established. He held further that, under Mexican law, failure to publish the balance sheet does not result in depriving a foreign company of juristic personality but merely exposes it to liability for a penalty.

Whatever may be the merits of the rival criteria for determination of national character, it would seem that the criterion of the state under whose laws the corporation was established is the only one which is in accord with the spirit of the Conventions. Normally, a corporation which had a claim would have been one which either did business in Mexico or had its main office there. To have used either of these two factors as the criterion would have resulted in depriving most of these corporations of their remedy in the international forum.

[99] See in particular Young, Foreign Companies and Other Corporations (Cambridge, 1912).

[100] The "control" theory was first stated in Daimler Co. *v.* Continental Tyre & Rubber Co., [1916] 2A.C. 307. It was incorporated into the Peace Treaties of 1919–1920 and into various post-war conventions. See Case Concerning Certain German Interests in Polish Upper Silesia, Publications of the Permanent Court of International Justice, Series A, No. 7, pp. 56, 68, 70, 74.

[101] See Feilchenfeld, "Foreign Corporations in International Public Law," 8 Journal of Comparative Legislation (3d Series, 1926), pp. 81, 260.

[102] In no case in which a claim was presented on behalf of a corporation does it appear that the corporation was incorporated elsewhere than in the claimant state.

[103] Rep. Alemana (Mexico Plantagen, G.m.b.H.) *v.* Estados Unidos Mexicanos, Decision No. 27 (unpublished).

§120. **National Character of Parnerships.** The question of the national character of a partnership was involved in a case before the British-Mexican Commission.[104] A claim was filed on behalf of a partnership. The Mexican agent filed a demurrer on the ground that although the British nationality of the two partners had been established, there was no proof that the firm was a British partnership. The Commission sustained the demurrer, and said:

"The Commission have come to the conclusion that the partnership of Messrs. D. J. and D. Spillane and Company, having been formed under the Mexican law and being domiciled and working in Mexico, possesses Mexican nationality. For this reason the claim in the name of the partnership cannot be put forward under the Special Claims Convention. . . . The Commission, while realizing that they are not competent to take cognizance of the claim, as long as preferred on behalf of the partnership, see no objection to declare that a claim filed in the name of the partners individually will be taken into consideration." [105]

It will be noted that the Commission made no attempt to distinguish which of the three criteria it invoked (establishment, domicile, doing business) should be decisive. The decision merely holds that the nationality of the partners is immaterial.[106] Since the Conventions do not distinguish between corporations and partnerships, it would seem that the same criterion should be applied in both cases, even where the partnership does not constitute a legal person under municipal law.

§121. **Receivers of Corporations.** A number of claims on behalf of corporations in liquidation or receivership were presented to the Commissions. In only one case was any question raised with respect to a receiver's authority.[107] Claim was made before the United States-Mexican General Claims Commission on behalf of a receiver of a Delaware corporation which had its main office in Texas. The receiver had been appointed by a Texas court. It was urged that the claim should be dismissed because the nationality of the receiver had not been

---

[104] Case of Messrs. D. J. and D. Spillane and Co., Further Decisions and Opinions, p. 72.

[105] *Ibid.*, p. 79.

[106] *Cf.* U. S. A. (Adolph Deutz and Charles Deutz, a Copartnership) *v.* United Mexican States, General Claims Commission, Opinions of Commissioners, 1929, p. 213, in which it was held sufficient to show the nationality of the partners. The place of formation and the domicile of the firm did not appear.

[107] U. S. A. (W. C. Greenstreet, Receiver) *v.* United Mexican States, Opinions of Commissioners, 1929, p. 199.

shown and because, according to American law, his authority as receiver was limited to Texas. The Commission held that the nationality of the receiver was immaterial since he was only a representative of the insolvent corporation, and stated:

". . . even if it be considered as doubtful whether, according to American law, Greenstreet has the authority to dispose of the present claim on behalf of the Burrowes Rapid Transit Company, which, from a legal point of view must be considered as still existing as a going concern in the State of Delaware, where it is incorporated, the Commission is of the opinion that from the point of view of international law the claim, as having been espoused by the Government of the United States, is duly presented." [108]

§122. **Claims of Nationals Having Interests in Foreign Corporations.** The Conventions with the United States and the Conventions with the European states differed in an important respect with regard to the conditions under which claims on behalf of nationals who had interests in corporations of another nationality might be presented. The Conventions with the United States required that the national have "a substantial and bona fide interest" in the corporation; the Conventions with the European states required that he have "an interest exceeding fifty per cent of the total capital" of the corporation. The latter is, of course, a much more practicable standard. It eliminates difficult questions as to what is "substantial." Yet it has the disadvantage of any arbitrary rule in that it may work hardship in individual cases. One or two examples of such hardship did occur.[109] It is possible that the word "interest" in the Conventions with the United States was intended to have a broader meaning than capital, *i.e.*, to include bondholders and creditors as well as stockholders. However, no attempt seems to have been made to urge this interpretation. A further difference appeared between the British-Mexican Convention and the other Conventions. The former specifically provided that the interests of various British subjects could be added together to make up the necessary majority interest,[110] while other Conventions made no such provision. In the German-Mexican Commission it was contended that since the Convention made use of the

---

[108] *Ibid.*, p. 200.
[109] See case of Carlos L. Oldenbourg, British-Mexican Commission, Further Decisions and Opinions, p. 163, where the case turned on whether or not the failure to refund a loan made by a firm to one of the partners had reduced the capital.
[110] See *supra*, note 95.

singular (*"el interés del damnificado"*) various interests could not be cumulated. The Commission rejected the contention.[111]

It would seem too obvious for argument that it was intended in the Mexican Claims Conventions to give national shareholders in *any* corporation a standing to claim. Nevertheless, this intention was drawn into question before the German-Mexican Commission. In cases in which damage had been suffered by companies in which German nationals were interested, it was the practice of the German Agency to file the claim in the name of the company.[112] To all these claims the Mexican agency interposed the objection that these companies were Mexican and that the Commission had no jurisdiction. The German agency thereupon moved to amend the pleadings by substituting the names of the associates. It was then met with the argument that such amendments were inadmissible because the nationality of the claimants was changed, and that in any event, the Commission had no jurisdiction over claims by German nationals for losses suffered by Mexican companies. In reply the German agency laid great stress upon the difference in wording between the American and German Conventions, the former reading: "all claims against Mexico *of* citizens of the United States," and the latter: "all claims against Mexico for losses or damages *suffered by* German nationals." In most of these cases the Commission allowed the amendment and assumed jurisdiction, without expressly adopting the German argument based on the difference in wording.[113] Indeed this argument seems quite unnecessary. If it were valid, the two United States-Mexican Commissions would have had jurisdiction only over claims by American nationals for damages suffered by American corporations, which would have meant that much of the Conventions was merely superfluity.

§123. The Problem of "Allotment." All of the Convention provided that the supervision of claims on behalf of nationals having

---

[111] Rep. Alemana (Juan Laue y Cía., en Liquidación) *v.* Estados Unidos Mexicanos Decision No. 35 (unpublished). The German Agent quoted from a memorandum prepared by the Mexican Secretariat for Foreign Relations during the negotiation of the Convention, which bears out his interpretation: "Cuando se habla en singular en términos generales, queda comprenido el plural por lo que incurriria en una rendundancia in necesaria."

[112] See, *e.g.,* Rep. Alemana (Rademacher, Müller y Cía., Sucs., en Liquidación) Decision No. 25 (unpublished); Rep. Alemana (E. Puttkamer, S. en C.) *v.* Estados Unidos Mexicanos, Decision No. 29 (unpublished); Rep. Alemana (Delires y Cia.) *v.* Estados Unidos Mexicanos, Decision No. 31 (unpublished).

[113] See, particularly, Rep. Alemana (Juan Laue y Cía., en Liquidación) *v.* Estados Unidos Mexicanos, Decision No. 44 (unpublished).

terests in corporations of another nationality was conditioned on
ne presentation to the Commission of an "allotment" (Sp.—*asigna-
ión;* Fr.—*cession;* Ger.—*Abtretung;* It.—*atto di cessione*) to the
laimant by the corporation of his proportion of the loss or damage
uffered.[114] The purpose of this condition is clear enough—it was
ntended to protect the respondent state against a claim for the whole
mount of loss by a corporation after an award for part of the loss
ad been made to a shareholder. Two serious problems, however, were
reated by this provision: (1) What should be the form of an allotment? (2) What should be a shareholder's proportion of the loss suf-
ered?

The question of the form of an allotment gave rise to lively con-
roversies. Here is a description of such a controversy before the
'rench-Mexican Commission:

"During the preparatory conferences held by the two agencies before
he introduction of the first important pleadings, the French agent attempted
o reach an agreement with his Mexican colleague on the exact tenor which
he 'allotments' must have in the different possible cases of dissolved com-
anies, companies continued with a new organization, and companies continu-
ng in their original form. Unfortunately these attempts led to no practical
esult, and this failure subsequently led to a veritable torrent of procedural
locuments in which all sorts of writings, under public and private seal, of dis-
olution, of assignment, of cession, etc., were presented by the French agent
s satisfying the conditions required by Article III, but constantly declined
y the Mexican Agent as not satisfying it. The only thing on which the
gencies seemed to have reached an agreement consisted in this, that they
vere in accord in considering that the word *'cession'* which appears in Ar-
icle III need not necessarily be considered in the strict technical sense of
rivate law." [115]

It would seem futile to attempt to apply any private law concepts
o an "allotment." The term is an invention of the negotiators of the
Conventions. It cannot be an assignment since, first of all, there is
nothing to assign, the corporation not having any right at all to claim,

[114] The provision in the British-Mexican Convention (Art. III) is so awkwardly
rafted that it seems to require an allotment only in cases of joint owners, *i.e.,* where the
nterests of several British subjects are cumulated to make up the required majority.
;ut see Case of the Sonora (Mexico) Land and Timber Co., British-Mexican Commission,
'urther Decisions and Opinions, p. 171.

[115] Presiding Commissioner Verzijl in Rep. française (Intérêts français dans la
ociété en nom collectif José Esclangon y Cia.) *v.* Etats-Unis mexicains, Sentence No. 50
unpublished, Mexican Commissioner absent).

and since, secondly, it would be absurd to speak of an "assignment" of a loss.[116] All that can be required is that some document be presented drawn up by a competent officer of the company [117] indicating the proportion of the company's loss to which the claimant is entitled. It does not appear that any of the Commissions insisted that allotments have any particular form.[118]

More difficult is the question of the substance of the allotment. Before various of the Commissions, Mexico contended that an allotment must set forth not the claimant's proportionate share of the damages suffered by the corporation, but of the claimant's proportionate share of the assets in event of liquidation. It was also urged that an allotment must be accompanied by a copy of the corporation's balance sheet.[119] The basis of these contentions was that the claimant could not receive such a share of the damages as is proportionate to his share in the capital of the corporation, since allowance must be made for the rights of creditors. Thus, suppose the balance sheet of a Mexican corporation reads:

	Assets			*Liabilities*	
Merchandise	90,000	pesos	Capital stock	20,000	pesos
Accounts receivable	10,000		Debts	80,000	
Total	100,000	pesos	Total	100,000	pesos

[116] See Case of the Sonora (Mexico) Land and Timber Co., British-Mexican Commission, Further Decisions and Opinions, p. 292. Certain British subjects owned the shares of a Mexican company. These individuals were merely the nominees of a British Company. The following procedure was adopted: the Mexican company allotted to each British shareholder the proportional part of its losses pertaining to the number of shares held. Each British shareholder then in turn *assigned* the rights allotted to him to the British company.

[117] In Case of the British Shareholders of the Mariposa Company, British-Mexican Commission, Further Decisions and Opinions, p. 304, an allotment executed in the form of an affidavit by the president of the company and attested by the secretary was accepted. In U. S. A. (H. G. Venable) *v.* United Mexican States, General Claims Commission, Opinions of Commissioners, 1927, p. 331, the allotment was made by the Board of Directors of the company.

[118] The controversy in the French-Mexican Commission referred to above was settled by a series of agreements between the agents in twenty-eight cases involving French interests in non-French companies to the effect that these claims should be admissible because more than 50% of the capital in these companies belonged to French nationals. No mention was made of the requirement of an allotment. In effect this was an agreement by the Mexican agent to waive this requirement. These agreements were ratified by the Commission by a series of decisions on September 11, 1928. Sentences Nos. 2A–29A (unpublished).

[119] This contention was made before the French-Mexican Commission in the Esclangon case, *supra,* note 115, and before the British-Mexican Commission in Case of Alfred Mackenzie, Further Decisions and Opinions, p. 203. From the discussion in Nielsen, International Law Applied to Reclamations, pp. 56–61, it would appear that it was also made before the United States-Mexican Commissions.

A French shareholder, on whose behalf claim is made by France, holds 75% of the capital stock. All the merchandise is destroyed by revolutionary troops. The corporation, if it were entitled to claim, could be awarded 90,000 pesos, and its creditors could have recourse to this fund. But, if the shareholder could be given the right to receive 75% of 90,000 pesos the transaction would be in fraud of the creditors. He can only be awarded 75% of the net assets, 20,000 pesos.

While this reasoning may be sound it disregards the provision of the Convention which clearly calls for an allotment of a proportionate share of the *damages suffered*. If the allotment conforms to that requirement the jurisdiction of the Commission is complete. Nonetheless, the question of the amount of damages still remains when the case comes up for decision on the merits. If the corporation is insolvent, then an award to the shareholder of a proportionate share of the damage caused to the corporation will unquestionably operate in defraud of creditors. It would seem that Commissions should exercise great caution in such cases and should demand the production of a balance sheet in all cases in which there is a *prima facie* showing that the corporation may be insolvent. If it is insolvent, the Commission would be justified in granting a small award commensurate with whatever it may believe the value of the shareholder's interest to be.[120] No such case seems to have arisen in the practice of the Mexican Claims Commission.

In general, the Commissions tended to apply the allotment requirement with considerable liberality. Thus, the British-Mexican Commission held that where a partnership had been dissolved no allotment would be required.[121] Similarly, the German-Mexican Commission did not require an allotment where all the assets of a Mexican company were acquired by one of two German associates.[122] The same Commission permitted an allotment to be made after the claim was filed and after the expiration of the time for filing claims.[123] Where

---

[120] *Cf*. Nielsen, *ibid.*, pp. 59–61, taking a different view from that adopted in the text.

[121] Case of Mrs. Frederick Adams, Further Decisions and Opinions, p. 199, at 201: "The partnership no longer exists and it is therefore impossible to obtain the allotment. By those same facts the eventual possibility of a claim by the partnership of the amounts already awarded to a partner is excluded. The reason for producing an allotment has therefore disappeared." *Accord:* Case of James R. A. Stevens, *ibid.*, p. 191.

[122] Rep. Alemana (Schauenburg y Meyer, Sucs.) *v*. Estados Unidos Mexicanos, Decision No. 59 (unpublished).

[123] Rep. Alemana (Juan Laue y Cía., en Liquidación) *v*. Estados Unidos Mexicanos, Decision No. 35 (unpublished).

a memorandum had been filed on behalf of two partners and the memorial subsequently filed on behalf of only one of them because the nationality of the other partner could not be established, the General Claims Commission held that no allotment was necessary since the non-claimant partner had indicated his agreement to presentation of the claim.[123a]

Other Kinds of Claimants

§124. **Mortgagees.** The few decisions of international tribunals which deal with the claims of mortgagees who allege that they have been damaged by injury to the mortgaged property have generally tended towards disallowing such claims.[124] Two decisions of the Mexican Claims Commissions are in line with this tendency. In a case before the British-Mexican Commission, claim was made on behalf of the debenture holders of the A Company. The latter held a mortgage on cattle owned by B which were alleged to have been stolen by revolutionary forces. The Commission sustained a motion to dismiss, saying:

"Even assuming, then, that the cattle whose value is claimed had been stolen, the loss would have been sustained by [B], who was the owner thereof . . . ; but not by the debenture holders, who are only free to take action against the company, and the latter, in turn against [B], in order to collect their loan by having the mortgaged property put up for sale at auction, should this be necessary, as no proof has ever been shown of insolvency on the part of the principal debtor." [125]

Another case before the French-Mexican Commission involved a claim on behalf of the shareholders of a bank.[126] The bank held mortgages on rural property and damages were claimed because the security had been damaged by depredations of revolutionary forces. The Commission held that only the owners of the property might claim. The bank had suffered only a *"préjudice,"* not a *"dommage"* and the Commission only had jurisdiction in cases of *"pertes et dom-*

[123a] U. S. A. (Samuel Davies) *v.* United Mexican States, Opinions of Commissioners, 1929, p. 282.

[124] See Borchard, Diplomatic Protection of Citizens Abroad, p. 645.

[125] Case of Debenture Holders of the San Marcos and Pinos Co., Further Decisions and Opinions, p. 135, at 138. The point was raised but not decided in Case of Debenture Holders of the New Parral Mines Syndicate, *ibid.*, p. 281.

[126] Case of Société civile des Porteurs d'obligations du Crédit Foncier Mexicain, Sentence No. 79 (reorganized Commission, unpublished).

mages." Even if the security had depreciated the bank still had its rights against the debtors.

§125. **Unsecured Creditors.** If such is the attitude of international tribunals towards mortgagees, it is to be expected that the claims of unsecured creditors would be looked upon even more unfavorably.[127] Yet, the *Dickson Car Wheel* case [128] before the United States-Mexican General Claims Commission revealed a sharp difference of opinion. The claimant, an American corporation, had sold car wheels to the National Railways of Mexico in 1912. In 1914 the Mexican government took over the lines of the National Railways and retained them until 1925. No payment for the wheels was ever made. The United States contended that the government had become substituted for the rights and obligations of the National Railways, that the taking over of the lines had prevented the National Railways from fulfilling its contract, and that the government had obtained an unjust enrichment. There was some conflict as to whether the National Railways, as a corporation, had any assets after the lines had been taken from it. The majority of the Commission stated that it did have assets, but it was shown that the National Railways had excused its failure to pay on the ground that all its assets has been taken over by the government. The Commission disallowed the claim. It showed that the National Railways had continued to exist at all times as a juridical entity against which the claimant possessed a legal remedy. With respect to the contention that Mexico was liable because the government had prevented the National Railways from fulfilling its contract, the Commission held that "a State does not incur international responsibility from the fact that an individual or company of the nationality of another state suffers a primary injury as the corollary or result of an injury which the defendant State has inflicted upon an individual or company irrespective of nationality when the relations between the former and the latter are of a contractual nature." The conclusion was buttressed by the analogy of the lack of remedy of an alien for damage resulting to him from an injury

[127] In U. S. A. (W. C. Greenstreet, Receiver) *v.* United Mexican States, General Claims Commission, Opinions of Commissioners, 1929, p. 199, at 200, it was held that the nationality of the creditors of an insolvent corporation need not be shown, "the nationality of the creditors being just as immaterial as is that of the stockholders of an insolvent company."

[128] U. S. A. (Dickson Car Wheel Co.) *v.* United Mexican States, Opinions of Commissioners, 1931, p. 175.

inflicted upon a relative of his who is a national of the state inflicting the injury.

The American Commissioner (Nielsen), dissenting, based his opinion upon the theory that a contractual right is property and that its destruction involves international responsibility. He went on to say:

"It is said that the problem in the instant case is to determine if a damage caused to a Mexican national and which affects an American national, causing remote damage, constitutes an act violative of the law of nations.

"This brief sentence to my mind is a total fallacy. In the first place, the United States has not complained of an injury to a Mexican national. It does not predicate its claim on any such ground. It might indeed be considered that the Mexican national was benefited in that it was not obliged to pay its debts, since the Mexican Government prevented the payment. The damage caused to the American national was not remote. It was a very specific loss directly consequent upon the action of the Mexican Government. The issue is whether acts of Mexican authorities in causing directly an injury, namely the destruction of property rights, impose responsibility on Mexico." [129]

It is apparent that the debate reduced itself to a discussion as to whether the damage was "direct" or not. Certainly the decision should not be permitted to turn on a word so incapable of exact definition. Perhaps the element of intention may be summoned to assist in reaching a decision. If the Mexican government had taken over the lines because it wanted to prevent the fulfillment of this or other contracts, it would be easier to say that the damage was "direct" and to hold Mexico responsible. But where an entirely different purpose was evinced in the taking over of the lines, it is difficult to escape holding that this situation fits into the traditional legal pattern of "indirect" or "remote" damage. At any rate, the notion that the prevention of the fulfillment of a contract is a taking of property, goes beyond the existing limits of the law and opens up an unbounded and unexplored range of state responsibility. Even the constitutional law of the United States, with its meticulous conceptions of "due process of law" has not gone that far.[130]

[129] Ibid., p. 202.
[130] Federal statutes which result in an impairment of existing contracts are not invalid under the due process clause of the Fifth Amendment to the Federal Constitution. Philadelphia, Baltimore and Washington R.R. v. Schubert, 224 U. S. 603 (1911); Legal Tender Cases, 12 Wallace 457 (1870). A state statute having the same effect might be held invalid under the impairment of contracts clause of the Constitution which does not bind the Federal government. New York v. United States, 257 U. S. 591 (1922).

§126. **Manager of Farm.** In a case before the British-Mexican Commission claim was made for depredations committed on a farm by revolutionary forces. The claimant was the son of the owner who had conferred upon his son the right to administer the farm. The Commission said:

"The father being the owner, it seems clear that the son is not entitled to claim in his own name for losses, which fall upon the legal ownership, such as the reduction of the value of the land, the fencing, the buildings and the wells.

"A different conclusion must, however, be arrived at when those losses pertaining to the operation of the ranch, such as the loss of mules, agricultural equipment and products are concerned.

"As regards this part of the claim, the Commission have acquired the conviction that the property was in reality farmed for the account and the risk of the son." [131]

§127. **Sharecroppers.** A case before the Italian-Mexican Commission involved the following facts: The claimant had contracted to cultivate a vineyard and was to receive 15% of the product. The vines were destroyed by revolutionary forces. The Commission held that since the claimant was not the owner of the vines he had not suffered any damage by their destruction. Nevertheless, a small award was made on equitable grounds.[132] The holding is consistent with the general trend of decisions to disallow the claims of persons other than legal owners, though the case might have gone off on the ground that no damages could be awarded for growing crops, a rule followed by this and other Commissions.[133]

§128. **Pledgees.** Another decision of the Italian-Mexican Commission shows a definite departure from the general trend exemplified in the cases discussed above. The claimant was the proprietor of a pawnshop from which various pawned objects were taken by bandits. The Commission allowed the claim, stating that although in "strict law" the claimant still retained his rights against the pledgor, these rights might turn out to be illusory. He had lost his security and, in equity, at least a part of the damages should be awarded to him.[134]

---

[131] Case of Patrick Grant, Further Decisions and Opinions, p. 194, at 196.
[132] Case of Vittorio Rocchietti, Decision No. 19 (unpublished).
[133] See *infra*, p. 305.
[134] Case of Andres Ardito, Decision No. 61 (unpublished).

This case is hardly distinguishable from the mortgagee cases discussed above and it must be considered as inconsistent with them. Perhaps the Commission was influenced by the fact that the property was physically in the possession of the claimant and was taken out of his hands.

§129. **Insurance Companies.** The problem of the standing of insurance companies to claim for losses incurred by insured persons is one of great complexity. The problem is easier as regards life insurance, since wrongful death merely results in accelerating the maturity, and it has been held that no claim may be made by an insurer of life.[135] In the case of property insurance, however, the loss might never have occurred but for the fault of the respondent government. The insurer, then, has suffered a loss as a result of an act entailing international responsibility. But what is the extent of that loss? The insurer has been partially compensated by the payment of premiums. These premiums may have been fixed with a view towards just this kind of loss. Furthermore, the practice of reinsurance may have cut down the loss of the particular claimant.[136] All these problems were present in the *Home Insurance* case [137] before the United States-Mexican General Claims Commission. Yet, surprisingly enough, they were not considered, and an award was made in favor of the claimant. The only other claim by an insurance company was in the British-Mexican Commission.[138] Here, the insured persons were Mexicans, the insurers being British. The insured property had been destroyed by revolutionary forces. A motion to dismiss was allowed. The holding is to the effect that no recovery can be had where the primary loss was suffered by a Mexican national, but the language of the case is broad

---

[135] Life Insurance Claims, U. S.-German Mixed Claims Commission, Consolidated Edition of Decisions and Opinions, p. 103.

[136] *Cf.* the language of Umpire Parker in Life Insurance Claims, *supra*, note 135, at p. 135: "The aggregate amount of the *property loss* became fixed when the ship sank and is neither increased nor diminished nor in any wise influenced by the amount of the insurance or re-insurance thereon. The insurance becomes material only in determining who really suffered the loss. This is because a contract of marine or war-risk insurance is a contract of indemnity ingrafted on and inhering in the property insured. The extent of the liability thereunder is limited by the economic loss suffered. The insured suffers no loss to the extent of payments made him by the insurer, who is the real loser to the extent of such payments not reimbursed by re-insurance."

[137] U. S. A. (Home Insurance Co.) *v.* United Mexican States, Opinions of Commissioners, 1927, p. 51.

[138] Case of the Eagle Star and British Dominions Insurance Co., Further Decisions and Opinions, p. 32.

enough to cast doubt on the right of an insurer to recover even where the primary loss was suffered by a national of the respondent state.[139]

[139] "The Commission sees a great difference between the position of insurers and that of other claimants, although they are in a similar position in so far as the losses suffered by both of them can be traced to certain events. But that is where the similarity ends.

"Other claimants—assuming that the facts are proved—have suffered losses indirectly as a consequence of a contract, into which they have entered voluntarily, professionally, in the normal and ordinary course of their business and in consideration of certain payments. They suffer losses not in the first place and just because certain events have occurred, but because, in their legitimate desire to subserve their own financial interests, they have undertaken to run the risk of those events.

"It seems difficult to look at insurers in the same light as at other claimants. They who, as a professional act and with a view to make profit, undertake risks, to which other persons are exposed, who direct an entire organization based on the existence of risks, which would be useless in the case of their absence, and who are finally able to assume such chances and to calculate such premiums as will ultimately result in a profit on the whole volume of their transactions, cannot be regarded as entitled to compensation on the same footing as persons to whom the occurrences which give rise to the claim were an unforeseen calamity. . . .

"In the case now under consideration, the insured party was a Mexican firm not entitled to claim compensation from their Government under the terms of the Claims Convention. By declaring themselves competent to adjudicate upon this claim, the Commission would grant to the insurance companies a right which the first that suffered the loss did not have. There would be laid upon the Mexican Government a liability towards another Government, which would not have arisen out of the events had not the said firm entered into a contract to which the Mexican Government were not a party." *Ibid.*, pp. 34, 35.

CHAPTER 7

RESPONSIBILITY OF STATES FOR OTHER THAN REVOLUTIONARY ACTS

§130. **General Principles.** The responsibility of states for injuries committed against aliens is a subject on which a voluminous literature has been written.[1] It would be futile and confusing to rehearse the contents of this literature here. Nor would it be wise to commence with an analysis of the precedents of international practice. Let us just seek to answer the question: Why should states be held responsible for injuries to aliens? The answer must be based on a consideration of the ever-present antinomies of contemporary international life. On one side is the fact of the sovereignty of states, on the other side the interest of the community of nations in freedom of intercourse. The reconciliation of the antinomies is at the same time an answer to our question: While a state's jurisdiction over aliens within its borders is plenary, the interest in maintaining a reasonable freedom of international intercourse demands that every member of the international community maintain a governmental system adequate to protect the lives and properties of such aliens as it admits to its territories. With this as a fundamental postulate, it would be possible to construct a system of rules of international responsibility. Unfortunately, they would not, in many respects, coincide with the rules developed by international tribunals. It will not be denied that taken as a whole these latter rules may be rationalized into a system with

---

[1] The more important works are: Anzilotti, *Teoria generale de la responsabilita dello Stato nel diritto internazionale* (Florence, 1902); Tchernoff, *Le droit de protection exercé par un état à l'égard de ses nationaux résidant à l'étranger* (Paris, 1898); Decencière-Ferrandière, *La responsibilité internationale des Etats à raison des dommages subis par des étrangers* (Paris, 1925); Borchard, Diplomatic Protection of Citizens Abroad (New York, 1915); Eagleton, The Responsibility of States in International Law (New York, 1928); Dunn, The Protection of Nationals (Baltimore, 1932); Strupp, *Das völkerrechtliche Delikt* (Stuttgart, 1920); Research in International Law, Harvard Law School, Convention on Responsibility of States for Damage Done in their Territory to the Person or Property of Foreigners. Bibliographies will be found in Borchard and Eagleton.

such an ideological basis as we have posited. But this system is at best only a distorted image of the ideal. Taken singly the rules now enforced often reveal a baser origin, the primitive revenge motive. Criticism of the decisions of the Mexican Claims Commissions will therefore more often be *de lege ferenda* than *de lege lata*.

§131. **The Terminology of International Responsibility: "Denial of Justice."** Nothing has been more conducive to confusion of thought on the subject of international responsibility than the vagueness with which the term "denial of justice" has been used.[2] At least three different meanings have been given to this term. (1) It has been used to denote any sort of international delinquency committed by an organ of the state.[3] This usage has long been out of favor since, as as Presiding Commissioner van Vollenhoven has put it: "If 'denial of justice' covers not only governmental acts implying so-called indirect liability, but also acts of direct liability, and if, on the other hand, 'denial of justice' is applied to acts of executive and legislative authorities as well as to acts of judicial authorities—as is often being done—there would exist no international wrong which would not be covered by the phrase 'denial of justice,' and the expression would lose its value as a technical distinction."[4] (2) The more popular meaning of denial of justice is that it is such action or inaction of the judicial authorities of the state as constitutes an international delinquency. This is the usual narrower meaning of the term.[5] Yet, it still seems too broad to serve as a useful designation. As thus used, it covers failure to punish an offender who has injured an alien. This is an unfortunate usage since it emphasizes disproportionately the interest of the victim in the punishment of his assailant. Offenders are pun-

---

[2] "A book could be written on the various meanings that have been given to the term 'denial of justice.' It is perhaps the most frequently used term in the whole vocabulary of the law of diplomatic protection, and the one that is the least understood. The high emotional content that the word 'justice' carries with it seems to shut off all conscious intellectual processes in dealing with the term. One is impressed with the mental paralysis that seems to follow upon the mere pronouncement of the term 'denial of justice' in connection with a particular situation." Dunn, The Protection of Nationals, p. 147. See also Fitzmaurice, "The Meaning of the Term Denial of Justice," British Year Book of International Law, 1932, p. 93.

[3] "A denial of justice, in a broad sense, occurs whenever a state, through any department or agency, fails to observe with respect to an alien, any duty imposed by international law or by treaty with his country." 1 Hyde, International Law, p. 491.

[4] In U. S. A. (B. E. Chattin) v. United Mexican States, General Claims Commission, Opinions of Commissioners, 1927, p. 422 at 427.

[5] Borchard, Diplomatic Protection of Citizens Abroad, p. 330; Eagleton, Responsibility of States, p. 112.

ished in the interest of the community as a whole and not for purposes of private revenge.[6] It would be preferable to narrow the meaning of the term still further. (3) Denial of justice would then be applied only where a direct injury is inflicted by the judicial authorities on an alien. Typical examples would be illegal arrest, illegal detention and prolonged delay or misconduct in the trial of an alien. It is in this sense that we shall use the term, although the second usage seems to have been favored by the Mexican Claims Commission.

§132. **The Same: "Direct" and "Indirect" Responsibility.** The distinction between "direct" and "indirect" responsibility has been thought to be of fundamental importance. An elaborate exposition of the distinction is to be found in the opinion of the United States-Mexican General Claims Commission in the *Chattin* case,[7] an opinion which deserves quotation at length.

"In the *Kennedy* case . . . before this Commission it was contended that, a citizen of either country having been wrongfully damaged either by a private individual or by an executive official, the judicial authorities had failed to take proper steps against the person or persons who had caused the loss or damage. A governmental liability proceeding from such a source is usually called 'indirect liability,' though considered in connection with the alleged delinquency of the government itself, it is quite as direct as its liability for any other acts of its officials. The liability of the government may be called remote or secondary only when compared with the liability of the person who committed the wrongful act (for instance, the murder) for that very act. Such cases of *indirect governmental liability* because of lack of proper action by the judiciary are analogous to cases in which a government might be held responsible for denial of justice in connection with nonexecution of private contracts, or in which it might become liable to victims of private or other delinquencies because of lack of protection by its executive or legislative authorities.

"Distinct from this so-called indirect government liability is the *direct responsibility* incurred on account of acts of the government itself, or of its officials, unconnected with any previous wrongful act of a citizen. If such governmental acts are acts of *executive* authorities, either in the form of breach of governmental contracts made with private foreigners, or in the form of other delinquencies of public authorities, they are at once recognized as acts

---

[6] *Cf.* Dunn, Protection of Nationals, p. 151.

[7] U. S. A. (B. E. Chattin) *v.* United Mexican States, Opinions of Commissioners, 1927, p. 422.

involving direct liability; for instance, collisions caused by public vessels, reckless shooting by officials, unwarranted arrest by officials, mistreatment in jail by officials, deficient custody by officials, etc. . . .

"The practical importance of a consistent cleavage between these two categories of governmental acts lies in the following. In cases of direct responsibility, insufficiency of governmental action entailing liability is not limited to flagrant cases such as cases of bad faith or wilful neglect of duty. So, at least, it is for the nonjudicial branches of government. Acts of the *judiciary*, either entailing direct responsibility or indirect liability (the latter called denial of justice, proper [8]), are not considered insufficient unless the wrong committed amounts to an outrage, bad faith, wilful neglect of duty, or insufficiency of action apparent to any unbiased man. Acts of the executive and legislative branches, on the contrary, share this lot only then, when they engender a so-called *indirect* liability in connection with acts of others; and the very reason why this type of acts often is covered by the same term 'denial of justice' in its broader sense may be partly in this, that to such acts or inactivities of the executive and legislative branches engendering *indirect* liability, the rule applies that a government cannot be held responsible for them unless the wrong done amounts to an outrage, to bad faith, to wilful neglect of duty, or to an insufficiency of governmental action so far short of international standards that every reasonable and impartial man would readily recognize its insufficiency. With reference to *direct* liability for acts of the executive it is different. . . .

". . . It is true that *both* categories of government responsibility—the direct one and the so-called indirect one—should be brought to the test of international standards in order to determine whether an international wrong exists, and that for *both* categories convincing evidence is necessary to fasten liability. It is moreover true that, so far as acts of the *judiciary* are involved, the view applies to *both* categories that 'it is a matter of the greatest political and international delicacy for one country to disacknowledge the judicial decision of a court of another country' (*Garrison's* case; Moore, 3129) and to both categories the rule applies that state responsibility is limited to judicial acts showing outrage, bad faith, wilful neglect of duty, or manifestly insufficient governmental action. But the distinction becomes of importance whenever acts of *other* branches of government are concerned; then the limitation of liability (as it exists for *all* judicial acts) does not apply to the category of direct responsibility, but only to the category of so-called indirect or derivative responsibility for acts of the executive and legislative branches, for instance on the ground of lack of protection against acts of individuals."

[8] Note that the Commission is here using "denial of justice" in the second of the three meanings discussed *supra* on p. 129.

A close reading of this quotation reveals that the Commission fails entirely to make out a case for the practical consequence of the distinction between direct and indirect liability. From a practical standpoint the true distinction should be between acts of the judiciary and acts of other branches of the government. The distinction between direct and indirect is useful for purposes of classification. Our use of it in this chapter will be solely for analysis of the cases. It is not admitted that any practical consequences should follow on such a distinction.

DIRECT RESPONSIBILITY

§133. **Introductory.** We have stated our fundamental postulate of responsibility as being based on an international interest in freedom of intercourse. Following this postulate we would have to say that not every injury which a state committed against an alien should entail direct responsibility. Only such acts as indicated that the governmental system of the respondent state was insufficient to provide a reasonable degree of safety to aliens would have this effect. Ordinarily it would hardly be necessary to go into this question for the reason that an international tribunal would not have jurisdiction unless the claimant had exhausted all local remedies. If an injury has been committed by the respondent state and adequate means for redressing such injury are not available, it can be said that the conditions of our fundamental postulate are fulfilled. But, the Mexican Claims Conventions all provided that no claim should be disallowed or dismissed because of failure to exhaust local remedies. International responsibility must thus be shown irrespective of the presence or absence of an adequate system of redress. Our inquiry will therefore be directed towards determining the extent to which the decisions of the Mexican Claims Commissions fit in with the fundamental postulate.[9]

§134. **Acts of Administrative Officials.** In a number of cases decided by the United States-Mexican General Claims Commission, Mexico was held responsible for various acts on the part of adminis-

---

[9] At this point, we may note that a state is not relieved of responsibility because an injury was committed by officials of a political subdivision instead of by officials of the central government. This rule was repeatedly applied by the Mexican Claims Commissions without discussion. See, *e.g.*, United Mexican States (Francisco Mallén) *v.* U. S. A., General Claims Commissions, Opinions of Commissioners, 1927, p. 254, at 260.

trative officials. Two cases involved confiscation by Mexican authorities, one of a pipe line [10] and the other of a shipment of wood,[11] Mexico being held responsible in both cases. In another case,[12] A, the claimant, had sold wheat on conditional sale to B. Various shipments of wheat sent to B were seized by Mexican authorities on the ground that B was a smuggler. It was contended that A had an adequate remedy under Mexican law since he could have instituted a court proceeding to determine his title to the wheat. The Commission held that Mexico was liable because the authorities could easily have recognized from the shipping documents that the title to the wheat remained in A. There three cases fall into the conventional category of "confiscation," liability for which is well established in international law. The first two were perhaps of a flagrantly arbitrary nature. The third, however, can hardly be so classified. The authorities who seized the wheat were mistaken, or at the worst negligent. The claimant had an easy remedy in the Mexican courts. Yet, an injustice had been committed and under the terms of the Convention the Commission had to grant an award. A similar problem was presented in a case [13] in which the claimant had imported sheep after receiving a letter from the Mexican Department of Finance informing him that he could import the sheep "without the collection of any charges." Upon importation, he was forced to pay consular and inspection fees. Mexico contended that under its law officials had no power to remit the payment of fees and that the quoted words were merely intended to inform the claimant that the law did not impose any customs duties. The Commission held that responsibility for the misunderstanding lay with the Mexican officials and granted an award for the amount of the consular fees.

In contrast to these cases are three others in which the provisions of domestic law were applied to relieve the respondent state of liability. In one case,[14] hay was shipped by the claimant to Mexico. The con-

---

[10] U. S. A. (Melczer Mining Co.) v. United Mexican States, Opinions of Commissioners, 1929, p. 228.
[11] U. S. A. (Samuel Davies) v. United Mexican States, Opinions of Commissioners, 1929, p. 282.
[12] U. S. A. (G. W. McNear, Inc.) v. United Mexican States, Opinions of Commissioners, 1929, p. 68.
[13] U. S. A. (John B. Okie) v. United Mexican States, Opinions of Commissioners, 1927, p. 61.
[14] U. S. A. (Toberman, Mackey & Co.) v. United Mexican States, Opinions of Commissioners, 1927, p. 306.

signee refused to accept the hay and it was left in the customs house until it deteriorated. The claim was disallowed, the Commission stating that international law did not impose any obligation to take care of goods in a customs house, that Mexican law was applicable and that this law imposed no liability. Similarly, Mexico was held not liable for destruction of goods shipped on a railway operated by the Mexican government.[15] Private carriers were not liable under Mexican law in such circumstances and the government could not be held to a greater liability. In a third case, a claim for taxes imposed on property claimed to be tax exempt, was disallowed, the Commission holding that the exemption did not exist under the applicable Mexican law.[16]

Two interesting cases on the responsibility for acts of administrative officials arise out of the occupation of Vera Cruz by American forces.[17] In one case,[18] a Mexican corporation had shipped coffee out of the port of Vera Cruz through New Orleans with a destination in Northern Mexico. It was forced to pay two export duties, one to the Mexican authorities at Orizaba (where a temporary customs station had been established) and another to the American authorities at Vera Cruz who were enforcing Mexican customs laws. It was alleged that under Mexican law the claimant was entitled to a refund of export duties for shipments passing out of Mexico in transit to final destination in Mexico, that the Mexican government had made such a refund but that the American government had not. A motion to dismiss was overruled, the Commission saying:

"The American military forces in occupying Veracruz and in establishing all proper rules and regulations for the government of the occupied territory saw fit to adopt and enforce the laws then prevailing in Mexico for levying and collecting customs duties. Had Mexico on behalf of the claimant merely alleged that the American authorities were not entitled to perform any act of administration at Veracruz, and stopped there, then the Commission would have dismissed this claim; not, to be sure, because of the political background

---

[15] U. S. A. (Home Insurance Co.) *v.* United Mexican States, Opinions of Commissioners, 1927, p. 51.

[16] U. S. A. (George W. Cook) *v.* United Mexican States, Opinions of Commissioners, 1931, p. 61.

[17] In addition to the two cases here discussed see United Mexican States (Armando Cobos Lopez) *v.* U. S. A., Opinions of Commissioners, 1927, p. 12; United Mexican States (Fabian Rios) *v.* U. S. A., *ibid.*, 1927, pp. 59, 70.

[18] United Mexican States (El Emporio del Cafe) *v.* U. S. A., Opinions of Commissioners, 1927, p. 7.

of said occupation. . . . Neither does the mere fact that the occupation had been directed by the President of the United States, whose action was approved by Congress, affect the question presented, for in determining the jurisdiction of this Commission the rank, be it high or low, of the national authorities whose acts are made a basis for complaint is immaterial.

"While the individual claimant was twice compelled to pay customs duties on the basis of the Mexican tariff laws which, according to these very laws, were due only once; and while one of these payments must have been unlawfully enforced, the Commission is not clothed, by the terms of this Convention under which it is constituted, with jurisdiction to inquire and decide which payment was legal and which illegal. A controversy of this character, constituting a controversy between the Governments themselves, does not change its nature when presented by either Government in the shape of the claim of an individual, and such a controversy has not been submitted to this Commission by the provisions of the Convention under which it is acting.

"But the administrative acts of the American representatives during such occupation can and must be examined to determine to what, if any extent they invaded the rights of Mexican nationals to their damage. The Memorial alleges that while the Mexican tariff laws which the American authorities undertook to administer authorized the collection of import duties which were actually collected, they also required that the duties so paid should be refunded to the shipper when and if the shipments on which duties were paid were reshipped into Mexico. Assuming the truth of said allegations, it follows that the claimant was entitled to such refund from the American authorities, which has not been made."

The principle here expressed was applied later in a case in which the sole ground of claim was that the claimant had been forced to pay import duties both to the American authorities at Vera Cruz and to the Mexican authorities at Orizaba. The claim was dismissed.[19]

§135. **Acts of Soldiers and Police Officials.** Cases imposing responsibility for acts of administrative officials are often difficult to

[19] United Mexican States (David Gonzalez) v. U. S. A., Opinions of Commissioners, 1927, pp. 9, 69.

Two cases of considerable interest from the standpoint of international law may be mentioned at this point. In U. S. A. (Oriental Navigation Co.) v. United Mexican States, Opinions of Commissioners, 1929, p. 23, the Commission disallowed a claim by the owner of a vessel which had been prevented by a Mexican gunboat from unloading at a port in the hands of insurgents, even though there was no effective blockade. The dissenting opinion of Commissioner Nielsen presents a considered view of this difficult question of the law of neutrality. In U. S. A. (George W. Johnson) v. United Mexican States ("Daylight" Case), Opinions of Commissioners, 1927, p. 241, a claim arising out of a collision between an American vessel and a Mexican gunboat was disallowed because of lack of evidence of negligence. The opinions contain interesting discussions of the law applicable in cases of collision.

reconcile with our fundamental postulate. Where acts of soldiers and police officials are involved the difficulty is lessened. These officials are entrusted with the duty of protecting persons and property. It is clearly the duty of the state to furnish an adequate system of such protective forces. Acts of individual officials may indicate such an inadequacy of the protective system as will involve the responsibility of the state. The *Youmans* case [20] before the General Claims Commission is an illustration of this. Several American citizens had been killed by a mob in which Mexican soldiers had participated. These soldiers were under the command of an officer and had been sent to the scene with orders to subdue the mob. It was argued by Mexico that the soldiers having disobeyed their orders they must be held to have acted in a private capacity and Mexico was therefore not liable. The Commission granted an award stating that: "It cannot properly be said that adequate protection is afforded to foreigners in a case in which the proper agencies of the law to afford protection participate in murder." [21]

Contrast the *Gordon* case [22] before the same Commission with this. Two Mexican officers had engaged in target practice in a fort without troubling to ascertain whether anyone was in the line of fire. Several shots hit an American vessel anchored in the harbor beyond the fort and the claimant, who was on the vessel, was injured. After considerable delay, the officers were prosecuted on a charge of inflicting injuries through negligence. They were acquitted on the ground that it could not be established which of the two had fired the shot which injured the claimant. The Commission disallowed the claim on the ground that the officers were not engaged in prescribed target practice but in a private act.

"Not every act of an official is binding upon the Governments; it is necessary that it 'result in injustice' and this phrase is merely another manner of saying that the act is unjust according to International Law. The principle is that the personal acts of officials not within the scope of their authority do not entail responsibility upon a State. It has already been said that the Mexican officials in question acted outside the line of their duty. Therefore no responsibility attaches to the Mexican Government on this count." [23]

[20] U. S. A. (Thomas H. Youmans) *v.* United Mexican States, Opinions of Commissioners, 1927, p. 150.   [21] *Ibid.*, at 157.
[22] U. S. A. (Louis B. Gordon) *v.* United Mexican States, Opinions of Commissioners, 1931, p. 50.   [23] *Ibid.*, at 53.

The American Commissioner, dissenting, sought to base the responsibility of Mexico on a theory of "control" by the state.

". . . it would seem to be clear that if private soldiers had engaged in target practice from the fort or from environs belonging to the fort there would be responsibility on the part of the government. And this would be so, even though the soldiers were engaged in target practice at some hour not specifically prescribed, or in some manner not required by army regulations. The soldiers in this situation would be in the position in which it is considered responsibility would attach for their acts; they would be under some form of control or authority of officers. It therefore seems to me that if officers themselves engaged in some kind of target practice in the same circumstances there should be responsibility on the part of the government for their acts." [24]

It is apparent that an exceedingly thin line separates acts performed within the scope of functions and acts performed outside this scope. Innumerable municipal courts have struggled with these problems of agency, and it cannot be expected that an all embracing formula can readily be found by international tribunals. The theory of "control" is not sufficient. In the very case in which it was advanced, it would seem to be inadequate to support an award. The only element of "control" was the fact that the firing was done from a fort. If the officers had gone outside the walls and fired, Mexico would clearly not have been liable. Again we are faced with a situation in which the lawyer must say, despairingly, that each case must be decided on its own facts.

When it has been determined that soldiers were acting within the scope of their functions, it then becomes necessary to determine whether the act complained of was lawful. The General Claims Commission, which decided a number of cases of shooting by soldiers, held such shootings to be unlawful under two circumstances: (1) where the soldiers violated army regulations regarding the use of firearms; (2) where the shooting was "reckless." [25] The second is an even vaguer concept than "scope of functions." In some cases the Commission held that the shooting was "reckless," [26] in others that it was

---

[24] *Ibid.*, at 58.
[25] United Mexican States (D. Guerro Vda. de Falcón) *v.* U. S. A., Opinions of Commissioners, 1927, p. 140.
[26] U. S. A. (Margaret Roper) *v.* United Mexican States, Opinions of Commissioners, 1927, p. 205; U. S. A. (J. W. and N. L. Swinney) *v.* United Mexican States, *ibid.*, 1927, p. 131.

a legitimate act of police power.[27] The opinions do not indicate any very solid basis for distinction. Possibly the Commission acted on judicial "hunches" which may be all that any court can do in such cases.

§136. The Same: The Teodoro García Case. The most interesting of these cases is the *Teodoro García* case.[28] Several members of a Mexican family, none of whom carried firearms, were engaged in crossing the Rio Grande on a raft at a place where crossing was unlawful. A troop of American soldiers under the command of an officer, saw the raft, and thinking the persons on it were engaged in smuggling, fired in order to bring the raft to a halt. A bullet which ricocheted from the water killed a little child, whose parents were the claimants before the Commission. The officer who ordered the firing had been court-martialed for disobeying army regulations which provided that: "firing on unarmed persons supposed to be engaged in smuggling or crossing the river at unauthorized places, is not authorized." The court-martial's decision was reversed by the President of the United States on the ground that these regulations should be interpreted to authorize firing where the officer has reasonable grounds for assuming that the delinquents are armed; the presumption being in favor of their carrying arms. The Commission stated that no denial of justice had been committed by the United States.

"In order to assume such a denial there should be convincing evidence that, put to the test of international standards, the disapproval of the sentence of the court-martial by the President acting in his judicial capacity amounted to an outrage, to bad faith, to wilful neglect of duty, or to an insufficiency of governmental action so far short of international standards that every reasonable and impartial man would readily recognize its insufficiency. None of these deficiencies appears from the record." [29]

Nevertheless, in spite of the lack of a denial of justice and in spite of the fact that in view of the President's decision the shooting was proper under the army regulations, the Commission granted an award. Its reasoning was as follows:

[27] U. S. A. (J. & O. L. B. Nason) *v.* United Mexican States, Opinions of Commissioners, 1927, p. 106; U. S. A. (James H. McMahan) *v.* United Mexican States, Opinions of Commissioners, 1929, p. 235.

[28] U. S. A. (Teodoro García) *v.* United Mexican States, Opinions of Commissioners, 1927, p. 163.

[29] *Ibid.,* at 169.

"The only problem before this Commission is whether, *under international law,* the American officer was entitled to shoot in the direction of the raft in the way he did.

"The Commission makes its conception of international law in this respect dependent upon the answer to the question, whether there exists among civilized nations any international standards concerning the taking of human life. The Commission not only holds that there exists one, but also that it is necessary to state and acknowledge its existence because of the fact that there are parts of the world and specific circumstances in which human practice apparently is inclined to fall below this standard. . . .

"If this international standard of appraising human life exists, it is the duty not only of municipal authorities but of international tribunals as well to obviate the use of firearms. . . .

"In order to consider shooting on the border by armed officials of either Government (soldiers, river guards, custom guards) justified, a combination of four requirements would seem to be necessary: (*a*) the act of firing, always dangerous in itself, should not be indulged in unless the delinquency is sufficiently well stated; (*b*) it should not be indulged in unless the importance of preventing or repressing the delinquency by firing is in reasonable proportion to the danger arising from it to the lives of the culprits and other persons in their neighborhood; (*c*) it should not be indulged in whenever other practicable ways of preventing or repressing the delinquency might be available; (*d*) it should be done with sufficient precaution not to create unnecessary danger, unless it be the official's intention to hit, wound, or kill. In no manner can the Commission endorse the conception that a use of firearms with distressing results is sufficiently excused by the fact that there exist prohibitive laws, that enforcement of these laws is necessary, and that the men who are instructed to enforce them are furnished with firearms." [30]

These are fine words, but how can such talk by a transitory international "obviate" the use of firearms? The Commission seems to have been misled by its excellent humanitarian impulses. Surely, it is not the business of such a tribunal to attempt to lay down detailed rules for such a situation. If we look through this veil of words, it is apparent that what the tribunal really held was that the American army regulations, as interpreted by the President, were below the international standard. The American Commissioner (Nielsen) saw this quite clearly and he urged that Mexico be required to show this by a comparison to the laws of other countries. The failure of the Commission to do this is perhaps explainable by a very understandable desire to

[30] *Ibid.,* at 165 *et seq.*

render an award in favor of the bereaved parents and by a reluctance to be forced into a position of stating boldly that the regulations were below the international standard.

§137. **Distinction between Superior and Minor Officials.** Writers and international tribunals have long struggled with the question as to whether the acts of so-called minor officials involve the responsibility of the state.[31] We need not enter into the tangled maze of this controversy here. The distinction between acts of superior and minor officials played but a small part in the cases before the Mexican Claims Commission. The *Massey* case [32] before the General Claims Commissions is one of the few in which it was involved. Massey was killed by a Mexican who was arrested and confined to jail from which he escaped due to the negligence of the jailer. The jailer was punished. The claim was predicated on a failure to punish adequately the murder of Massey. It will be noted that this was a case of alleged indirect responsibility and that the guilty official had been punished. An award was granted, the Commission (by Commissioner Nielsen) saying:

"An examination of the opinions of international tribunals dealing with the question of a nation's responsibility for minor officials reveals conflicting views and considerable uncertainty with regard to rules and principles to which application has been given in cases in which the question has arisen. To attempt by some broad classification to make a distinction between some 'minor' or 'petty' officials and other kinds of officials must obviously at times involve practical difficulties. Irrespective of the propriety of attempting to reach any such distinction at all, it would seem that in reaching conclusions in any given case with respect to responsibility for acts of public servants, the most important considerations of which account must be taken are the character of the acts alleged to have resulted in injury to persons or to property, or the nature of functions performed whenever a question is raised as to their proper discharge . . . it appears to be a proper construction of provisions in Article I of the Convention of September 8, 1923, that uncertainty with respect to a point of responsibility was largely eliminated by the two Governments when they stipulated that the Commission should pass upon 'all claims for losses or damages originating from acts of officials or others acting for either Government and resulting in injustice.' . . .

[31] See Borchard, Diplomatic Protection of Citizens Abroad, p. 185 *et seq.;* Eagleton, Responsibility of States, p. 45 *et seq.;* Dunn, Protection of Nationals, p. 125 *et seq.*
[32] U. S. A. (Gertrude Parker Massey) *v.* United Mexican States, Opinions of Commissioners, 1927, p. 228.

"In considering the question of a nation's responsibility for acts of persons in its service, whether they be acts of commission or of omission, I think it is pertinent to bear in mind a distinction between wrongful conduct resulting in direct injury to an alien—to his person or to his property—and conduct resulting in the failure of a government to live up to its international obligations. The cases which have been cited in the Mexican brief are concerned with the former; the instant case with the latter.

"I believe that it is undoubtedly a sound general principle that, whenever misconduct on the part of any such persons, whatever may be their particular status or rank under domestic law, results in the failure of a nation to perform its obligations under international law, the nation must bear the responsibility for the wrongful acts of its servants." [33]

Several points in this quotation are to be noted. Responsibility for acts of minor officials is predicated on a provision in the General Claims Convention relating to responsibility for "acts of officials or others acting for either Government and resulting in injustice." [34] The Commission had previously relied on this provision on three occasions. In one case it was said that it "should be so construed as to include all claims against one Government by the nationals of the other for losses or damages suffered by such nationals or by their properties, even when there is no evidence that they originate from acts of competent authorities, whether officials or others with a limited jurisdiction, but where there is merely evidence that they originate from acts of others acting for either Government." [35] In the other cases [36] it was relied on to reach the same result as in the *Massey* case, *i.e.*, to impose liability for the acts of minor officials (in those cases, policemen). It was undoubtedly legitimate to seize on this provision of the Convention as a way out of the dilemma created by the confused state of the law on the subject, even though this rather vague provision may not have been intended to cover such cases. However, it means that the decisions of the General Claims Commission on the subject of responsibility for acts of minor officials cannot be cited as embodying general propositions of international law.

[33] *Ibid.*, at 230–231, 233–234.
[34] U. S.-Mexican General Claims Convention, Art. I.
[35] U. S. A. (William A. Parker) *v.* United Mexican States, Opinions of Commissioners, 1927, p. 35, at 41.
[36] United Mexican States (Francisco Quintanilla) *v.* U. S. A., Opinions of Commissioners, 1927, p. 136; U. S. A. (Margaret Roper) *v.* United Mexican States, *ibid.*, 1927, p. 205.

It is also to be noted that the opinion in the *Massey* case attempted to draw a distinction between direct and indirect responsibility based upon acts of minor officials. The reason for this is not apparent. The Commission had previously based direct responsibility upon acts of minor officials.[37]

§138. **Illegal Arrest and Detention.** The General Claims Commission dealt with a considerable number of cases where illegal arrest or detention, or maltreatment by police officials, was alleged. In general, these cases follow a relatively simple pattern. A number of examples may be taken for comparison. In the *Knotts* case,[38] claim was made on account of illegal arrest and humiliating treatment during detention. An award was made on the ground that the arrest was illegal because made in contravention of Mexican law, but it was held that there was no evidence of hardship during detention. In the *Franke* case [39] a similar claim was dismissed on the ground that there was probable cause for arrest. In the *Cibich* case [40] the claimant had been arrested while drunk and his money, which had been taken from him by the police, was stolen. The claim was dismissed on the ground that the claimant had been lawfully taken into custody, his money had been properly taken by the police for safekeeping, and the evidence failed to disclose lack of reasonable care on the part of the Mexican authorities in guarding the money. In contrast with this is the *Quintanilla* case [41] which seems to be predicated on the theory that the government is liable as an insurer when a prisoner is taken into custody. A Mexican national was arrested by a Texas deputy sheriff and two accusers. Some time later he was found dead by the roadside. The accusers were arrested but were released. An award was made on the ground that when an officer of a state takes an alien into custody, the government must account for him.[42] No decision was made as to

[37] See cases cited in previous note.

[38] U. S. A. (Joseph D. Knotts) *v.* United Mexican States, Opinions of Commissioners, 1929, p. 312.

[39] U. S. A. (Oscar C. Franke) *v.* United Mexican States, Opinions of Commissioners, 1931, p. 73.

[40] U. S. A. (Nick Cibich) *v.* United Mexican States, Opinions of Commissioners, 1927, p. 65.

[41] United Mexican States (Francisco Quintanilla) *v.* U. S. A., Opinions of Commissioners, 1927, p. 136.

[42] *Cf.* U. S. A. (Mary Ann Turner) *v.* United Mexican States, Opinions of Commissioners, 1927, p. 416, in which Mexico was held responsible for the death as a result of illness contracted in jail by an American citizen who had been illegally arrested. It was said (at p. 420): "If having a man into custody obligates a government to account for him, having a man in *illegal* custody doubtless renders a government liable for dangers and disasters which would not have been his share, or in a less degree, if he had been at liberty."

whether the United States would be liable for a "denial of justice" in failing to prosecute the supposed murderers.

A special ground for international responsibility is the keeping of a prisoner *incommunicado* for a long period.[43] It was held, however, that there was no international delinquency in keeping a prisoner *incommunicado* only during the seventy-two hours period permitted by Mexican law.[44] Similarly, it was held "that a foreigner not familiar with the laws of the country where he temporarily resides, should be given the opportunity" of communicating with his consul when arrested.[45]

A number of cases involving charges of brutality by arresting officers or cruel treatment were decided. The only one of interest is the *Roberts* case [46] in which it was contended that Mexico was not liable because the claimant had been confined in an insanitary jail since he had been accorded the same treatment as other prisoners. The Commission rejected this contention, saying:

"Facts with respect to equality of treatment of aliens and nationals may be important in determining the merits of a complaint of mistreatment of an alien. But such equality is not the ultimate test of the propriety of the acts of authorities in the light of international law. That test is, broadly speaking, whether aliens are treated in accordance with ordinary standards of civilization."

§139. Acts of Judicial Authorities. It has been shown previously that the proper use of the term "denial of justice" is in connection with improper action of judicial authorities with regard to an alien who is involved in a judicial proceeding. The *Chattin* case [47] before the General Claims Commission is one which may properly be classified as a

---

[43] U. S. A. (Daniel Dillon) *v.* United Mexican States, Opinions of Commissioners, 1929, p. 61.

[44] U. S. A. (Jacob Kaiser) *v.* United Mexican States, *ibid.,* 1929, p. 80. See also U. S. A. (Joseph A. Farrell) *v.* United Mexican States, *ibid.,* 1929, p. 157, at 161, in which it was said: "The Commission is not prepared to state that a law which permits the *incomunicación* of an accused in a manner implying neither cruelty nor interference with the right of defense, is in violation of international law."

[45] U. S. A. (Walter H. Faulkner) *v.* United Mexican States, Opinions of Commissioners, 1927, p. 86 at 90.

[46] U. S. A. (Harry Roberts) *v.* United Mexican States, Opinions of Commissioners, 1927, p. 100.

[47] U. S. A. (B. E. Chattin) *v.* United Mexican States, Opinions of Commissioners, 1927, p. 422. The following cases grew out of the same events: U. S. A. (John W. Haley) *v.* United Mexican States, *ibid.,* 1927, p. 465; U. S. A. (G. A. Englehart) *v.* United Mexican States, *ibid.,* 1927, p. 471; U. S. A. (C. W. Parrish) *v.* United Mexican States, *ibid.,* 1927, p. 473.

case of denial of justice. Chattin was one of several American citizens employed as conductors on a Mexican railway, who were arrested on a charge of embezzlement, sentenced by a court and kept in prison for ten months until released by Madero forces. The claim was predicated on illegal arrest, improper trial and cruel treatment in jail. The illegal arrest and cruel treatment were found not to be proven but with respect to the charge of improper trial it was held that irregularities in the proceedings were sufficiently shown to justify an award. The summary of the Commission's inquiry into these proceedings is worth quoting as an illustration of the factors which enter into a judgment that judicial proceedings fall below the international standard:

"The whole of the proceedings disclose a most astonishing lack of seriousness on the part of the Court. There is no trace of an effort to have the two foremost pieces of evidence explained. . . . There is no trace of an effort to find one Manuel Virgen, who, according to the investigations of July 21, 1910, might have been mixed in Chattin's dealings, nor to examine one Carl or Carol Collins, a dismissed clerk of the railroad company concerned, who was repeatedly mentioned as forging tickets and passes and as having been discharged for that very reason. One of the Mexican brakemen, Batiz, stated on August 8, 1910, in court that 'it is true that the American conductors have among themselves schemes to defraud in that manner the company, the deponent not knowing it for sure'; but again no steps were taken to have this statement verified or this brakeman confronted with the accused Americans. No disclosures were made as to one pass, one 'half-pass' and eight perforated tickets shown to Chattin on October 28, 1910, as pieces of evidence; the record states that they were the same documents as presented to Ramirez on July 9, 1910, but does not attempt to explain why their number in July was eight (seven tickets and one pass) and in October was ten. No investigation was made as to why Delgado and Sarabia [two witnesses who testified as to Chattin's alleged embezzlement] felt quite certain that June 29 was the date of their trip, a date upon the correctness of which the weight of their testimony wholly depended. No search of the houses of these conductors is mentioned. Nothing is revealed as to a search of their persons on the day of the arrest; when the lawyer of the other conductors, Haley and Engelhart, insisted upon such an inquiry, a letter was sent to the Judge at Culiocán, but was allowed to remain unanswered. Neither during the investigations nor during the hearing in open court was any such thing as an oral examination or cross-examination of any importance attempted. It seems highly improbable that the accused have been given a real opportunity during the hearings in open court,

freely to speak for themselves. It is not for the Commission to endeavor to reach from the record any conviction as to the innocence or guilt of Chattin and his colleagues; but even in case they were guilty, the Commission would render a bad service to the Government of Mexico if it failed to place the stamp of its disapproval and even indignation on a criminal procedure so far below international standards as the present one. If the wholesome rule of international law as to respect for the judiciary of another country . . . shall stand, it would seem of the utmost necessity that appellate tribunals when, in exceptional cases, discovering proceedings of this type should take against them the strongest measures possible under constitution and laws, in order to safeguard their country's reputation. . . .

"Bringing the proceedings of Mexican authorities against Chattin to the test of international standards . . . there can be no doubt of their being highly insufficient. Inquiring whether there is convincing evidence of these unjust proceedings . . . the answer must be in the affirmative. Since this is a case of alleged responsibility of Mexico, it is necessary to inquire whether the treatment of Chattin amounts even to an outrage, to bad faith, to wilful neglect of duty, or to an insufficiency of governmental action recognizable by every unbiased man . . . and the answer here again can only be in the affirmative.

". . . Irregularity of court proceedings is proven with reference to absence of proper investigations, insufficiency of confrontations, withholding from the accused the opportunity to know all of these charges brought against him, undue delay of the proceedings, making the hearings in open court a mere formality, and a continued absence of seriousness on the part of the Court." [48]

The *Dyches* case [49] is another example of a "denial of justice" properly speaking. Dyches had been arrested on a charge of stealing a horse. He was kept in jail for one year before being sentenced to imprisonment for six years and nine months. After another year and a half had passed, the Supreme Court of Mexico held that Dyches had been guilty only of the crime of entering another's premises without permission, and Dyches was released from jail. Various allegations of illegality in the trial were made. The Commission held that it could not be urged that there had been a denial of justice in the trial since any defects had been cured by the decision of the Supreme Court. However, it held that the lengthy delay in finally disposing of the case —two years and six months—constituted a denial of justice and an

---

[48] Chattin case, *supra,* note 47, at p. 435 *et seq.*
[49] U. S. A. (Clyde Dyches) *v.* United Mexican States, Opinions of Commissioners, 1929, p. 193.

award was made. In a concurring opinion, the American Commissioner Nielsen stated:

"No doubt it is a general rule that a denial of justice cannot be predicated upon the decision of a court of last resort with which no grave fault can be found. It seems to me, however, that there may be an exception, when during the course of legal proceedings a person may be the victim of action which in no sense can ultimately be redressed by a final decision, and that an illustration of such an exception may be found in proceedings which are delayed beyond all reason and beyond periods prescribed by provisions of constitutional law." [50]

In a later case,[51] the American Agency advanced the contention that this decision had established a rule that certain irregularities of procedure cannot be redressed even when a final sentence doing justice is rendered. This was a case in which an American had been convicted in a lower court and the conviction had been reversed by an appellate court. It was argued that the decision of the appellate court could be examined because the evidence submitted against the claimant was so unsatisfactory as to warrant his immediate release. The Commission very properly rejected this contention and pointed out that the *Dyches* case must be limited to the factual situation there presented, *i.e.*, an undue delay of judicial proceedings in violation of Mexican law.

§140. **Appreciation of Decisions Dealing with Direct Responsibility.** Only a few of the decisions which we have discussed can be fitted into our fundamental postulate. Rarely was any attempt made by the Commission to determine whether the particular act complained of was symptomatic of a disease of the governmental system. Instead, the approach was highly particularistic. The decisions relating to shooting by soldiers may perhaps form an exception. It might be urged that it is unfair to criticize the Commission for lacking a standard of social ends; that certain rules of direct responsibility have become crystallized in international law; that these rules have grown up about the primitive revenge motive enunciated by Vattel; [52] and that though they may express some empirical fumbling toward

---

[50] *Ibid.*, at 198.
[51] U. S. A. (Joseph A. Farrell) *v.* United Mexican States, Opinions of Commissioners, 1913, p. 157.
[52] See *supra,* p. 84.

a social end in accord with modern conditions and ideals, it is difficult to shape them into a coherent system. There is some force in these contentions, yet it is submitted that much more desirable results could have been reached within the traditional framework. The Commission should have adhered rigidly to what might be called the rule of local inquiry. Not every injury committed by an official involves the responsibility of the state. The latter can arise only where there has been a failure to punish the offending official. This principle is certainly not to be denied application because the convention does away with the local remedy rule. The fact that the individual claimant need not seek his own redress in a municipal forum does not excuse the Commission from examining in every case whether the respondent government has, of its own motion, disciplined the offender. If it has failed to do so, the imposition of liability is justified because of the danger of repetition of such acts. The end of every inquiry into responsibility is whether or not an adequate system for the protection of aliens is being maintained.[52a]

INDIRECT RESPONSIBILITY

§141. **Introductory.** The crystallization of rules concerning indirect responsibility has not advanced as far as in cases of direct responsibility. Indirect responsibility is largely of modern growth. Psychologically it is more difficult to express in terms of "fault" or "culpa," and the result has been that some writers and tribunals have resorted to such fictions as "condonation" to support this liability. Of course, these fictions are wholly unnecessary. Our fundamental postulate of a governmental system adequate to protect the lives and properties of aliens furnishes all the basis necessary for supporting indirect liability.

§142. **Failure to Protect.** Numerous claims before the General

---

[52a] "It is of course often difficult to draw a line between personal and official acts. On the other hand, not every wrongful act of an official can be deemed evidence of a failure of the government to prevent, or evidence of governmental international liability. Otherwise, every wrongful act of an administrative official within the scope of his authority would automatically impose liability on the government. There is no such rule either in municipal law or in international law. It is only when the government as an administrative system is so negligently constituted as to invite such wrongs, or fails to discipline the wrongdoing officer thereafter, thus indicating connivance, approval, or indifference, that international responsibility can be said to arise." Borchard, "Recent Opinions of the General Claims Commission, United States and Mexico," 25 Amer. Journal of International Law (1931), p. 735 at 736.

Claims Commission were based on alleged failure to afford protection. The liability for such failure is clear enough, and the decisions generally turn on questions of evidence.[53] A number of cases deal with the question as to whether special protection must be afforded to consular officers. The *Mallén* case [54] is the chief of these. Mallén was a Mexican consul at El Paso, Texas, who was twice assaulted by Franco, a deputy consul of the State of Texas. The General Claims Commission in granting an award said:

"The question has been raised whether consuls are entitled to a 'special protection' for their persons. The answer depends upon the meaning given these two words. If they should indicate that, apart from prerogatives extended to consuls either by treaty or by unwritten law, the government of their temporary residence is bound to grant them other prerogatives not enjoyed by common residents (be it citizens or aliens), the answer is in the negative. But if 'special protection' means that in executing the laws of the country, especially those concerning police and penal law, the Government should realize that foreign Governments are sensitive regarding the treatment accorded their representatives, and that therefore the Government of the consul's residence should exercise greater vigilance in respect to their security and safety, the answer as evidently shall be in the affirmative." [55]

However, when it came to awarding damages, the Commission said:

"When accepting as the basis for an award, in so far as compensatory damages are concerned, the physical injuries inflicted upon Mallén on October 13, 1907, only those damages can be considered as losses or damages caused by Franco which are direct results of the occurrence. While recognizing that an amount should be added as satisfaction for indignity suffered, for lack of protection, and for denial of justice, as established heretofore, account

[53] One of the debated questions is whether a government can be held responsible for lack of protection where no request for protection has been made. The following statement by Commissioner Nielsen is believed to represent the better view:
"The fact that a request for protection has not been made does not relieve the authorities of a government from protecting inhabitants. Protection is a function of a state, and the discharge of that function should not be contingent on requests of the members of a community. On the other hand, in determining whether adequate protection has been afforded in a given case, evidence of a request for protection may be very pertinent in showing on the one hand that there was a necessity for protection and on the other hand that the warning of possible injury was given to the authorities." Concurring opinion in U. S. A. (F. M. Smith) *v.* United Mexican States, Opinions of Commissioners, 1929, p. 208, at 210.
[54] U. S. A. (Francisco Mallén) *v.* United Mexican States, Opinions of Commissioners, 1927, p. 254.
[55] *Ibid.,* at 257.

should be taken of the fact that the very high sums claimed or paid in order to uphold the consular dignity related either to circumstances in which the nation's honor was involved, or to consuls in backward countries where their position approaches that of the diplomat." [56]

Thus, the duty of special protection is robbed almost entirely of practical significance in the assessment of damages. This result is an interesting commentary on the orthodox theory that the basis of international claims is the injury committed against a state when its citizens suffer damage. Here, a special duty was owed to the claimant's state, yet where redress was sought in the form of compensation to the injured official, the award was limited almost entirely to the injuries which he himself suffered.

Somewhat more significance was given to this duty in the *Chapman* case.[57] Chapman was American consul at Puerto Mexico. A threat, growing out of a Sacco-Vanzetti demonstration, was made against the consulate. Chapman informed the municipal authorities and asked for adequate protection. None was furnished and shortly thereafter Chapman was shot at in the consular premises and wounded. The Commission granted an award and laid emphasis on the duty of special protection, particularly in circumstances where the consul had warned the authorities of threatened danger.[58]

FAILURE TO APPREHEND, PUNISH AND PROSECUTE

§143. Introductory. We now come to the most difficult problem in the subject of state responsibility. The rule we are about to consider is this—if a private individual injures an alien, the state of the alien has a claim against the state on whose territory the injury was committed if the latter has failed to apprehend and properly punish the assailant. Why such a rule should exist is a question of some difficulty. Let it be remembered that the injured alien will receive the sum awarded as reparation. If the respondent state has properly punished the assailant then the victim receives money. Obviously it is all to his advantage if there was a failure to punish. The only

---

[56] *Ibid.*, at 264.

[57] U. S. A. (William E. Chapman) *v.* United Mexican States, Opinions of Commissioners, 1931, p. 121.

[58] But *cf.* U. S. A. (Victor A. Ermerins) *v.* United Mexican States, Opinions of Commissioners, 1929, p. 219. An award was made in favor of an American consular agent under circumstances very much like those of the Chapman case. However, the Commission did not even mention the duty of special protection of consular officers.

interest which the victim can have in the punishment of his assailant is a desire of revenge, an emotion which a modern system of law should certainly not encourage. Yet, the rule is clearly designed to do just that. On the other hand, the claimant state may have an important interest—that of seeing that the lives and property of its nationals are adequately protected. An inadequate system of punitive justice in the respondent state would violate this duty owed by the one state to the other. The inquiry must then, as in other cases of state responsibility, be directed towards a determination of the adequacy of the governmental system.

True, even this method of approach has several faults. If the governmental system is inadequate, why should the individual victim be compensated? Ideally, he should not be; whatever reparation is granted should go to the state. While the distribution of the award is a matter of municipal law with which the arbitral tribunal can have no concern, it is true that the measure of reparation is determined by the injury to the individual. In the present imperfect state of the organization of international justice we might say that this is a rough and ready means of enforcing a sanction. The award is in form compensatory, but in substance punitive. Another difficulty is that modern criminology has rejected the idea that punishment prevents crime. If this were true then there would be no reason for requiring a state to provide a strict standard of punitive justice—we could only require an adequate police system for purposes of prevention. However, we can hardly ask international tribunals to accept a theory which only a very few national systems of criminal law have accepted.

Enough has been said to indicate the confusion which exists in this branch of the law of responsibility. An examination of the decisions of the United States-Mexican General Claims Commission will bear this out.

§144. **Failure to Apprehend.** The General Claims Commission consistently applied the rule that a state is responsible for failure to make a diligent effort to apprehend the assailant of an alien; [59] but

---

[59] United Mexican States (Catalina Balderas de Díaz) *v.* U. S. A., Opinions of Commissioners, 1927, p. 143; U. S. A. (Hazel M. Corcoran) *v.* United Mexican States, Opinions of Commissioners, 1929, p. 211; U. S. A. (S. J. Stallings) *v.* United Mexican States, *ibid.*, 1929, p. 224; U. S. A. (Richard A. Newman) *v.* United Mexican States, *ibid.*, 1929, p. 284; U. S. A. (Sarah Ann Gorham) *v.* United Mexican States, Opinions of Commissioners, 1931, p. 132.

it did not take the position that it could impose liability merely because the steps taken by the local authorities were not as active or efficient as they might have been. In the *Neer* case [60] one of the first which it considered, the Commission stated that: "the grounds of liability limit its inquiry to whether there is convincing evidence either (1) that the authorities administering the Mexican law acted in an outrageous way, in bad faith, in wilful neglect of their duties, or in a pronounced degree of improper action, or (2) that Mexican law rendered it impossible for them properly to fulfill their tasks." [61] In that case the Commission refused an award even though the Governor of the State of Durango had proposed the removal of the local judge because of his inefficiency in conducting the investigation.

This is an excellent rule and is quite in accord with our fundamental postulate which looks towards the adequacy of the system of punitive justice. Yet it is easy to permit such a rule to become a lifeless formula. Thus in the *Austin* case [62] the Commission granted an award because of failure to apprehend the murderer of an American even though it was apparently admitted that apprehension of the murderer was impossible because he had escaped into rebel territory. The ground for the decision was that the Mexican authorities had failed to institute any form of judicial proceedings which, it was said, "constitutes a form of denial of justice." In such a decision the salutary rule of the *Neer* case has degenerated into a rule-of-thumb formula requiring the local authorities to do "something" even though it is obviously useless.

§145. **Failure to Prosecute.** Where the assailant of an alien has been apprehended, he must be prosecuted with due diligence. A general amnesty which renders this assailant immune from prosecution has the same effect as a failure to punish, even though there may be reasons of national policy for granting the amnesty.[63] It is not enough

[60] U. S. A. (L. F. Neer) *v.* United Mexican States, Opinions of Commissioners, 1927, p. 71.
[61] *Ibid.*, at 73.
[62] U. S. A. (Martha Ann Austin) *v.* United Mexican States, Opinions of Commissioners, 1921, p. 108.
[63] U. S. A. (F. R. West) *v.* United Mexican States, Opinions of Commissioners, 1927, p. 404. However, the majority of the United States-Mexican Special Claims Commission took a different view with respect to the amnesty granted to General Villa. In the Santa Isabel Cases, Opinions of Commissioners, 1926–1931, p. 1, at 11, it was said: "The agreement of July 28, 1920, as concluded with Villa on behalf of the Provincial Government of señor Adolfo de la Huerta and through which, in consideration of his being granted

merely to commence a prosecution—it must be carried through. Thus in the *Galván* case [64] the murderer of a Mexican citizen was indicted in Texas, but the trial was postponed for six years and was never held. An award was granted. Similarly in the *Chase* case,[65] the assailant of an American citizen had been arrested and placed on trial but was subsequently released on bond and nothing further was done. The Commission granted an award saying:

"International justice is not satisfied if a government limits itself to instituting and prosecuting a trial without reaching the point of defining the defendant's guilt and assessing the proper penalty." [66]

A curious problem arose in the *Richards* case.[67] An American citizen was killed by bandits. Several persons were apprehended and indicted. On March 17, 1922, they were released because of an alibi. On March 22, 1922, the prosecuting attorney filed an appeal which was not acted upon until March 2, 1925, when the accused were ordered to be retried. The claim had been filed on December 17, 1924, and Mexico contended that no claim had accrued at that time because no deficiencies in the procedure appeared before 1925. The Commission rejected this contention on the ground that the appeal should have been decided soon after it was filed. This case presents somewhat of a dilemma.[68] If Mexican law did not provide for an appeal by the prosecution (as in the United States) it would not have been held liable. But where it does provide for such an appeal it is liable if the procedure is not carried through with due diligence.[69]

certain favors, Villa undertook to lay down his arms, however strange it may seem, represents a supreme effort for achieving, by any means whatsoever, the pacification of the country, already weary of long years of serious disturbances, and it cannot be looked upon as an act of lenity in connection with the events of Santa Isabel." See *infra*, p. 167.

[64] United Mexican States (Salomé Lerma de Galván) *v.* U. S. A., Opinions of Commissioners, 1927, p. 408.

[65] U. S. A. (John D. Chase) *v.* United Mexican States, Opinions of Commissioners, 1929, p. 17.

[66] *Ibid.*, p. 19.

[67] U. S. A. (George David Richards) *v.* United Mexican States, Opinions of Commissioners, 1927, p. 412.

[68] The decision of the Commission can be supported on another ground—that of failure to apprehend some of the bandits.

[69] The General Claims Commission also granted awards, based on failure to prosecute diligently, in the following cases: U. S. A. (J. J. Boyd) *v.* United Mexican States, Opinions of Commissioners, 1929, p. 78; U. S. A. (Louise O. Canahl) *v.* United Mexican States, *ibid.*, 1929, p. 90; U. S. A. (A. L. Harkrader) *v.* United Mexican States, *ibid.*, 1929, p. 66; U. S. A. (Laura A. Mecham) *v.* United Mexican States, *ibid.*, 1929, p. 168; U. S. A. (Elvira Almaguer) *v.* United Mexican States, *ibid.*, 1929, p. 291.

§146. **Failure to Punish Adequately.** The decisions which ground liability on the failure to apprehend or to prosecute are not, in general, open to any serious criticism. The decisions grounding liability on the failure to inflict adequate punishment are much less satisfactory. We may grant that some penalty should be inflicted for crime. But is not the Commission going too far when it lays down the rule that "the imposition of a penalty inadequate to the crime committed constitutes a denial of justice?" [70] Where, as in the *Kennedy* case,[71] a Mexican who shot and seriously wounded an American received only a two months' sentence, an award may well be justified. Other illustrations of the application of this rule, however, may serve to bring out its defects.

In the *Connolly* case,[72] several Mexicans had killed and robbed a number of Americans. The assailants were duly arrested and prosecuted and were convicted of homicide during a fight, which under Mexican law carried a penalty of five years' imprisonment. The Commission granted an award of $2,500 on the ground that Mexico was responsible for a denial of justice for failure to prosecute these assailants for robbery. Surely this is most extraordinary. A fairly severe punishment in accordance with Mexican law had been imposed, and yet Mexico is held responsible for failure to punish for another and lesser offense.

In the *Sewell* case [73] one of the grounds for granting an award was that the penalties imposed on the assailants of an American citizen were not in accord with the provisions of the Penal Code for the Federal District of Mexico.[74] The Commission undertook an elaborate study of a technical question of statutory construction in order to reach this result. It is submitted, that an international tribunal should not undertake to interpret local law for the purpose of determining any such question as adequacy of punishment.

[70] U. S. A. (Lillian Greenlaw Sewell) *v.* United Mexican States, Opinions of Commissioners, 1931, p. 112, at 119.

[71] U. S. A. (George Adams Kennedy) *v.* United Mexican States, Opinions of Commissioners, 1927, p. 289. *Cf.* U. S. A. (Ethel Morton) *v.* United Mexican States, Opinions of Commissioners, 1929, p. 151, in which the murderer of an American citizen had been sentenced to four years' imprisonment.

[72] U. S. A. (Norman T. Connolly) *v.* United Mexican States, Opinions of Commissioners, 1929, p. 87.

[73] U. S. A. (Lillian Greenlaw Sewell) *v.* United Mexican States, Opinions of Commissioners, 1931, p. 112.

[74] Other grounds for the decision were lack of diligence in pursuit and apprehension.

Closely allied to the problem of adequacy of punishment are the cases in which a convicted prisoner escapes without serving his entire sentence. In the *Putnam* case [75] an award was rendered under such circumstances on the ground that Mexico must account for the prisoner and since he had escaped, "Mexico is responsible for the denial of justice resulting from such conduct." Undoubtedly, given the premises on which responsibility for failure to punish is predicated, this decision is correct. Permitting the escape of a criminal lets loose a menace to society. But compare the *Davies* case.[76] Here an American citizen had been killed by a Mexican who was brought to trial but was acquitted on the ground of insanity and ordered to be confined to an asylum. The authorities failed to confine him. A claim was disallowed on the ground that the international duty of Mexico was fulfilled with the apprehension and trial, there being no provision of Mexican law requiring the committal of insane persons acquitted of murder.

The *Davies* case illustrates the fallacious foundation of the principle of liability in all these cases. It is just as dangerous, if not more so, to let loose an insane murderer on the community as to fail to punish a sane criminal. But this criterion of public safety, the only criterion which could give the rule any sure basis, is hardly ever considered. The conception seems to be almost purely one of revenge. A crime has been committed and the criminal must be punished to the full extent of the law. If he is, then the claimants may rest content. They have received their just due. If a similar act is committed by an insane man then there has been no crime committed. *Ergo,* there can be no liability.[77]

---

[75] U. S. A. (Ida R. S. Putnam) *v.* United Mexican States, Opinions of Commissioners, 1927, p. 222.

[76] U. S. A. (Jane Joynt Davies) *v.* United Mexican States, Opinions of Commissioners, 1931, p. 146.

[77] Compare the trenchant criticism by Rice, "State Responsibility for Failure to Vindicate the Public Peace," 28 American Journal of International Law (1934), p. 246.

CHAPTER 8

RESPONSIBILITY FOR CLAIMS ARISING OUT OF THE MEXICAN REVOLUTIONS [1]

§147. History of the Mexican Revolutions. The problems with respect to claims for revolutionary acts arising under the Mexican Claims Conventions cannot be properly understood without a preliminary glimpse into the history of Mexico between 1910 and 1920.[2] The Mexican revolution was launched on November 20, 1910, the date on which Francisco Madero issued the "Plan of San Luis Potosi," formally proclaiming a revolution against the government of Porfirio Díaz. A revolutionary army at once gathered under the banner of Madero, re-enforced by deserters from the Federal troops. These were the forces known as *Maderistas*. On May 25, 1911, Díaz resigned pursuant to an agreement under which Francisco de la Barra became Provisional President. The de la Barra Presidency lasted until November 30, 1911. No military movements against this government occurred until the very end of this period when on November 28, 1911, Emiliano Zapata announced his "Plan of Ayala" embodying a revolutionary agrarian program. His forces (the *Zapatistas*) had fought side by side with the *Maderistas* during the first stage of the revolution.

---

[1] In view of the provisions of the Mexican Claims Conventions, there is no occasion here to discuss the general principles relating to responsibility for damages arising out of revolutionary acts. The literature on this subject is voluminous. See in particular: Borchard, Diplomatic Protection of Citizens Abroad, p. 228 *et seq.;* Goebel, "The International Responsibility of States for Injuries Sustained on Account of Mob Violence, Insurrections and Civil War," 8 Amer. Journal of Int. Law (1914), p. 812; Strupp, *Das völkerrechtliche Delikt* (Stuttgart, 1920); Muszack, *Über die Haftung einer Regierung für Schäden welche Ausländer gelegentlich innerer Unruhen in ihren Landen erlitten haben* (Strassburg, 1905); Sadoul, *De la guerre civile en droit des gens* (Nancy, 1905); Podesta Costa, *El extranjera en la guerra civil* (Buenos Aires, 1913).

[2] See Gruening, Mexico and Its Heritage (New York, London, 1928); Priestly, The Mexican Nation, A History (New York, 1923); Beals, Mexico: An Interpretation (New York, 1923); Breceda, *México Revoluccionario 1913-1917* (Madrid, 1920); Rabasa, *L'Evolution Historique du Mexique* (Paris, 1924); Obregón, *Ocho Mil Kilómetres en Campana* (Mexico, 1917).

Madero assumed the Presidency (by election) on November 30, 1911. Zapata continued in armed opposition, and two further revolts sprang up. General Pascual Orozco (leader of the *Orozquistas*) proclaimed a revolution with reactionary aims on March 25, 1912, and in October of the same year a military uprising under General Félix Díaz took place in Vera Cruz. Both were crushed, but the elements which had composed them remained dangerous opponents of Madero.

On February 8, 1913, General Félix Díaz was released from prison by disloyal troops, and another revolt began. The rebellious forces occupied the Ciudadela in Mexico City. The government placed General Victoriano Huerta in charge of the suppression of the revolt. Huerta, however, entered into a conspiracy with General Díaz to overthrow Madero. For ten days (*la Decena Trágica*) the contending forces kept up a constant bombardment, the artillery of the government troops being so placed as not to hit the rebels. "The purpose of this wanton destruction was to create the picture of an irreconcilable civil war, of Madero's inability to end chaos, and to predispose the suffering public, totally in the dark concerning the inwardness of the fake conflict, toward the solution which the generals would offer."[3] The end of this bloody comedy was the arrest of Madero, his resignation on February 19, and his murder on February 22.

Huerta now became President, but armed opposition sprang up all over the country at the moment of his assumption of power. The revolting forces, united under the "Plan of Guadalupe" proclaimed March 26, 1913, were known as *Constitutionalistas* and acknowledged Venustiano Carranza as "First Chief." The *Zapatistas* also continued in opposition to the Huerta government but never acknowledged the leadership of Carranza.[4] During the Huerta Presidency, the United States sent forces to occupy Vera Cruz, and Huerta was forced to resign on July 15, 1914. From July 15 to August 13, 1914, Francisco Carbajal governed as Provisional President. The Constitutionalist forces entered Mexico City, and Carranza, on August 22, announced that he had taken over the executive power of the Republic, refusing to recognize the proclamation of General Gutierrez as Provisional President. Within a few days he was driven out of the capital by

---

[3] Gruening, *op. cit., supra*, note 1, p. 305.

[4] The *Zapatistas* have often been described as being Constitutionalists during the Huerta régime. The statement in the text is based on a quotation from an unpublished letter of Zapata in Gruening, *op. cit., supra*, note 1, p. 98, note 4.

General Francisco Villa, whose forces had formed part of the Constitutionalist army but who now rejected Carranza's authority and joined hands with Zapata. This took place in September 1914. In the next month a group of Constitutionalist generals known as the "Convention" appointed a commission of five to take over the government. On November 9, 1914, Carranza disowned the Conventionist government and continued to claim that he was head of a government *de facto* established at Vera Cruz.

During the next eleven months Mexico was in a state which can only be described as anarchy. The Constitutionalists fought the Conventionists (who included the Villa and Zapata forces), Yaqui Indians committed depredations in the North, and bandits ranged throughout the country. Within three weeks in July 1915, control of Mexico City passed from one group of forces to another five times. On October 19, 1915, the United States accorded *"de facto"* recognition to the Carranza government. The Conventionist forces melted away. Villa suffered severe defeats at the hands of Alvaro Obregón, a Constitutionalist general, and withdrew into the mountains. But these defeats had not destroyed him. On January 10, 1916, a group of Villistas held up a train near Santa Isabel and murdered sixteen American mining engineers. On March 9, Villa crossed the American border and raided the town of Columbus, New Mexico. Presumably these outrages were committed by him because of pique at the failure of the United States to recognize his government. The United States despatched a punitive expedition into Mexico in pursuit of Villa. This expedition was withdrawn on February 5, 1917, having accomplished nothing.

Carranza was inaugurated as President on March 12, 1917, following the adoption of a constitution. No revolutionary movements of any consequence took place for some three years. Then, in 1919, General Alvaro Obregón rose in revolt. The remnants of the Conventionists joined him and on April 22, 1920, he promulgated the "Plan of Agua Prieta." Carranza was killed on May 21, 1920, Adolfo de la Huerta becoming Provisional President on May 24.

§148. Provisions in the Conventions. It will be recalled that, during the negotiations preceding the adoption of the United States-Mexican Conventions, Mexico took the position that it was not responsible for injury caused by revolutionary forces which did not

succeed in setting up a government,[5] but that it was willing to grant reparation as a matter of grace. As a result two separate conventions were concluded, one for general claims and the other covering "special" or revolutionary claims. The Special Claims Convention provided for an *ex gratia* payment by Mexico if it were proved that the alleged damage was caused by one of a number of "forces." These forces were enumerated in Article III, reading:

The claims which the Commission shall examine and decide are those which arose during the revolutions and disturbed conditions which existed in Mexico covering the period from November 20, 1910, to May 31, 1920, inclusive, and were due to any act by the following forces:

(1) By forces of a Government *de jure* or *de facto*.

(2) By revolutionary forces as a result of the triumph of whose cause governments *de facto* or *de jure* have been established, or by revolutionary forces opposed to them.

(3) By forces arising from the disjunction of the forces mentioned in the next preceding paragraph up to the time when the government *de jure* established itself as the result of a particular revolution.

(4) By federal forces that were disbanded, and

(5) By mutinies, mobs, or insurrectionary forces other than those referred to under subdivisions (2), (3) and (4) above, or by bandits, provided in any case it be established that the appropriate authorities omitted to take reasonable measures to suppress insurrectionists, mobs, or bandits, or treated them with lenity or were in fault in other particulars.

A similar article was incorporated in the Conventions with the European states with the addition of another paragraph reading:

The Commission shall also deal with claims for losses or damages caused by acts of civil authorities provided such acts were due to revolutionary events and disturbed conditions within the period referred to in this article, and that the said acts were committed by any of the forces specified in subdivisions 1, 2, and 3 of this article.

It will be readily noted that this article establishes two different types of liability. In the case of an act committed by any of the forces enumerated in subdivisions (1) to (4), Mexico's liability arises

---

[5] The position taken by Mexico is in accord with the general rule now followed with respect to injuries inflicted by rebels. ". . . the doctrine which has now received general support is that on principle the state is not responsible for the injuries sustained by aliens at the hands of insurgents in civil war unless there is proven fault or a want of due diligence on the part of the authorities in preventing the injury or in suppressing the revolution." Borchard, Diplomatic Protection, p. 229.

merely by virtue of proof that damage was suffered. In the case of an act committed by one of the forces mentioned in subdivision (5), Mexico's liability arises only after there has been a showing of fault. In these latter cases Mexico would, of course, have been liable under general principles of international law, even though the Convention purports to treat all types of liability as *ex gratia*. On a number of occasions, some of the Commissions adverted to the fact that in a particular case Mexico's liability might either be one which arose on the basis of international law, or one which arose on the basis of the Convention, *i.e.*, *ex gratia*.[6]

§149. **Positions of the States.** The scope of the jurisdiction granted by the Conventions was a matter of much controversy before all the Commissions. Generally speaking the claimant states contended that Mexico was liable for losses caused by all the governments which had been effectively established during the revolutionary period and for losses caused by all military forces which had taken part in the civil wars. The Mexican Government, on the other hand, contended that it had assumed liability only for the acts of *legitimate* governments and for the acts of forces which had emerged victorious out of the struggle and had succeeded in establishing governments. All other forces, it was urged, fell into the category of insurrectionists, rebels or bandits for the acts of which Mexico was responsible only if negligence or lenity could be shown.[7] The practical consequences of the Mexican thesis bade fair to be momentous. To choose a few examples: Mexico would not be liable for the acts of the Huerta government because it was not "legitimate," nor for the acts of the Conventionists, Villistas and Zapatistas after their secession from the Constitutionalists except on a showing of negligence or fault.

Many reasons were advanced by Mexico for this position. It was argued that the obligation assumed by Mexico was an exception to international law and should therefore be interpreted as strictly as possible. It was urged that grammatically speaking an armed uprising

---

[6] It was suggested that the basis of liability might make some difference in determining whether interest should be awarded. In Rep. Alemana (Frederico Griese) *v.* Estados Unidos Mexicanos, German-Mexican Commission, Decision No. 8 (unpublished), the German Commissioner urged that interest should be awarded where liability arose out of international law, but not where it arose *ex gratia*. This view did not prevail. See *infra*, p. 311.

[7] The fullest exposition of the Mexican viewpoint is given in Rep. française (Georges Pinson) *v.* Etats-Unis mexicains, Sentence No. 1, Jurisprudence de la Commission franco-mexicaine des réclamations, at pp. 103–105.

could only be called a "revolution" if it succeeded and that two "revolutions" could not exist at the same time. Particular stress was laid upon the wording of the Conventions and upon certain grammatical difficulties which will appear hereafter. Eventually, the Mexican thesis was successful. Some of the Commissions adopted it in whole or in part; in other cases the Conventions were modified so as to embody this thesis.

§150. **Forces Comprehended under the Conventions.** (1) *"By forces of a Government de jure or de facto."*

On its face, this phrase is clear enough, and the difficulties which arose in its application were due to the facts of Mexican history rather than to any ambiguity of draftsmanship. It was clear that the phrase included the acts of at least these forces: (*a*) the forces of Porfirio Díaz between November 20, 1910, and May 25, 1911; [8] (*b*) the forces of Madero between May 25, 1911, and February 19, 1913; [9] (*c*) the forces of Carranza between September 1915 (when the *de facto* Carranza government was set up) and May 21, 1920.[10] The salient difficulty was whether or not the acts of the forces of Victoriano Huerta could be included in this category.

It will be remembered that Huerta had been in undisputed control of the capital and of a considerable portion of the country and that his government had been recognized as *de jure* by a number of European states. Nevertheless, Mexico contended strenuously that it could not be held liable for acts of the Huerta government. It was argued that this was neither a government *de facto* nor *de jure*. Huerta was a usurper; he had seized the power through murder; therefore he was a mere *"detentador del poder,"* and not the head of a government. In a case before the German-Mexican Commission,[11] the Mexican Commissioner attempted to support this extraordinary contention by the following argument. A *de jure* government is one which comes into power in accordance with the constitution and which has the support of the nation. A *de facto* government is a régime which ripens into a *de jure* government. Consequently the Huerta government was neither *de jure* nor *de facto*. That such an argument could be seriously

---

[8] Rep. française (Georges Pinson) *v.* Etats-Unis mexicains, *supra*, note 7, at p. 148 (dictum).

[9] Case of Michele Barra, Decision No. 21, Italian-Mexican Commission (unpublished).

[10] Case of Caterina Capiteruccio Viuda de Rafael Bello, Decision No. 62, Italian-Mexican Commission (unpublished).

[11] Rep. Alemana (Adolfo Stoll) *v.* Estados Unidos Mexicanos, Decision No. 47 (unpublished).

advanced shows that the Mexican contention was not based on the logic of traditional international law concepts. It was, most people would say, irrational. Yet it seems to have sprung from so deep rooted a conviction of disgust and repudiation of Huerta that it finally succeeded in forcing its way past the barrier of logic. In the German-Mexican Commission, the Presiding Commissioner (Cruchaga) denied liability for acts of Huerta forces on the ground that where compensation is given *ex gratia* it would be inequitable to impose liability for the acts of a usurper. *"Una Comisión de equidad . . . no puede consagrar la violación de la moralidad política como uno medio de asumir el poder representativo en una República."* [12] The same view was taken by the Italian-Mexican Commission of which Señor Cruchaga was also Presiding Commissioner. [13] The latter Commission went so far as to disallow a claim for injuries inflicted by Huerta forces after the Mexcan National Claims Commission had granted an award.[14]

The Mexican contention with respect to non-liability for acts of the Huerta forces was definitely rejected by the French-Mexican Commission.[15] The British-Mexican Commission was presented with a case involving such acts but was able to decide on other grounds.[16] When the French, British and Spanish Conventions were revised in 1930 and 1931, it was expressly provided in each of these Conventions that:

> The claims within the competence of this Commission shall not include those caused by the forces of Victoriano Huerta or by the acts of his régime.[17]

[12] Rep. Alemana (Adolfo Stoll) *v.* Estados Unidos Mexicanos, *supra,* note 11. *Accord:* Rep. Alemana (Karl Schulte) *v.* Estados Unidos Mexicanos, Decision No. 32 (unpublished).

[13] Case of Lange & Co., Decision No. 13 (unpublished); Case of Viuda e Hijos de Vincenzo Pasquali, Decision No. 28 (unpublished); Case of Daniel Baldi, Decision No. 66 (unpublished).

[14] Case of Michele Giacomino, Decision No. 30 (unpublished). The position taken by the Italian-Mexican and German-Mexican Commissions should be compared with the far more reasoned opinion of the United States-Mexican Claims Commission in U. S. A. (George W. Hopkins) *v.* United Mexican States, Opinions of Commissioners, 1927, p. 42. This was a claim for non-payment of postal money orders issued during the Huerta régime. The Commission had no "doubt but that the assumption of power by Huerta was pure usurpation." It then pointed out the evident distinction between transactions of a "personal" character in support of the particular agencies administering the government for the time being (*e.g.,* a loan to furnish supplies to the army) and transactions of an "impersonal" character taking place in the course of ordinary government routine. It concluded that acts of the latter character were binding upon Mexico.

[15] Rep. française (Georges Pinson) *v.* Etats-Unis mexicains, Sentence No. 1, Jurisprudence de la Commission franco-mexicaine des réclamations, p. 106.

[16] Case of Alfred Hammond Bromly, Further Decisions and Opinions, p. 235.

[17] This provision was also made applicable to the interpretation of the United States-Mexican Special Claims Convention by the Protocol of June 18, 1932. The latter, however, never came into force.

Another problem raised by the first subdivision of the jurisdictional article was whether Mexico was liable for so-called "lawful acts" committed by a *de jure* or *de facto* government. Mexico took the position that it could not be held liable for acts committed by a government in the exercise of its duty to maintain law and order.[18] The contention certainly seems just although the wording of the Conventions is broad enough to include liability for such acts. The Mexican contention was accepted by several Commissions which considered claims arising out of the *Decena Trágica,* it being held that Mexico was not liable for damage caused by the bombardment carried on by the Madero forces on that occasion.[19]

When the French, British and Spanish Conventions were revised in 1930 and 1931, it was provided that Mexico should be liable only if it were shown that the damage "was not the consequence of a lawful act," and the controversy was thus settled in favor of Mexico.[20]

(2) *"By revolutionary forces as a result of the triumph of whose cause governments de facto or de jure have been established, or by revolutionary forces opposed to them."*

This clause proved to be a source of much trouble. Two groups of forces were mentioned: (*a*) successful revolutionary forces; (*b*) opposing revolutionary forces. The greatest difficulty was experienced in dealing with the latter group. The first group presented no unusual problems.

[18] See Mexico City Bombardment Claims, British-Mexican Commission, Decisions and Opinions of Commissioners, p. 100, at 106, in which, however, no decision was rendered on this point.

[19] *German-Mexican Commission:* Rep. Alemana (Walter Heyn, G. A. Wislicenus y Carlos Schmidt) *v.* Estados Unidos Mexicanos, Decisions Nos. 1, 2, and 3 (unpublished).
    Italian-Mexican Commission: Case of Leonida Prosdocini, Decision No. 9 (unpublished).
    Compare, however, Rep. Alemana (Frederico Griese) *v.* Estados Unidos Mexicanos, Decision No. 8 (unpublished) where Mexico was held liable for damages caused by the bombardment by insurgents of a house which Madero forces had used as a fort.

[20] A number of decisions involving the meaning of "lawful acts" were rendered by the British-Mexican and French-Mexican Commissions subsequent to the revision of the Conventions.
    British-Mexican Commission: Occupation for military purposes of a house situated on a firing line between Federal forces and rebels was a "lawful" act. Case of Robert John Lynch, Further Decisions and Opinions, p. 101. Burning of a station as a result of attack by Federal troops held a "lawful" act. Case of Central Agency (Ltd.), *ibid.,* p. 258. An act committed by Carranzistas at a time before they had established a *de facto* government could not be a "lawful" act. Case of El Palmar Rubber Estates (Ltd.), *ibid.,* p. 316.
    French-Mexican Commission: In the following cases it was held that Mexico was not liable for damage resulting from the bombardment during the *Decena Trágica.* Case of Joseph Simon, Sentence No. 35 (unpublished); Case of Léon Gas, Sentence No. 44 (unpublished); Case of Julian Lévy, Sentence No. 45 (unpublished); Case of Sidonie Brunet, Sentence No. 46 (unpublished).

(a) *Successful Revolutionary Forces.* Certain groups of forces could obviously be placed in this category. The Maderistas, Carranzistas and Obregónistas had all succeeded in establishing *de jure* or *de facto* governments and any acts committed by these forces before the establishment of the respective governments would fall within this subdivision.[21] It was held uniformly that acts committed by forces forming part of the forces above named but which subsequently separated therefrom were also included within this category. Consequently Mexico was held responsible for acts committed by the Zapatistas [22] and by the Villistas [23] while they formed part of the Constitutionalist forces.

(b) *Opposing Revolutionary Forces.* We have said before that this category was productive of much difficulty. Indeed, it was the cause of a great deal of the irritation which hindered the work of some of the Commissions. It was the Mexican contention that, despite the use of the words "revolutionary forces opposed to them," no liability could arise for Mexico under this phrase because no forces answering this description existed.[24] This conclusion was arrived at in the following fashion. It was argued that the opposing forces referred to were such as were opposed to revolutionary forces which later succeeded in setting up a government. That is to say, forces opposed to a *government* were not included, only forces opposed to other forces. It was pointed out that the Spanish version read: *"o por fuerzas revolucionarias contrarias a aquéllas."* [25] The word *"aquéllas"*

---

[21] *Maderistas:* Case of Mazapil Copper Co. (Ltd.), British-Mexican Commission, Decisions and Opinions of Commissioners, p. 132; Case of the Palmarejo and Mexican Gold Fields (Ltd.), Further Decisions and Opinions, p. 347; Case of Michele Barra, Decision No. 21, Italian-Mexican Commission (unpublished).

Carranzistas: Case of Mrs. Jessie Watson, British-Mexican Commission, Further Decisions and Opinions, p. 93; Case of George Henry Clapham, *ibid.,* p. 159; Case of Nicholas Freda, Decision No. 71, Italian-Mexican Commission (unpublished).

Obregonistas: Case of Frederick W. Stacpoole, British-Mexican Commission, Decisions and Opinions of Commissioners, p. 124.

[22] Case of Augustin Melliar Ward, British-Mexican Commission, Further Decisions and Opinions, p. 107; Case of Désiré Hermitte, Sentence No. 66, reorganized French-Mexican Commission (unpublished).

[23] Case of the Buena Tierra Mining Co. (Ltd.), British-Mexican Commission, Further Decisions and Opinions, p. 259, at 261; Case of Lorenzo Elissetche, Sentence No. 50, reorganized French-Mexican Commission (unpublished).

[24] An elaborate exposition of the Mexican contention is contained in the various opinions in U. S. A. (Naomi Russell) *v.* United Mexican States, United States-Mexican Special Claims Commission, Opinions of Commissioners, 1926–1931, p. 44. See also Rep. française (Georges Pinson) *v.* Etats-Unis mexicains, Jurisprudence de la Commission franco-mexicaine des réclamations, at p. 103 *et seq.*

[25] French version: "par les forces révolutionnaires qui, à la suite de leur triomphe, ont

is feminine and agrees in gender with *"fuerzas"* but not with *"gobiernos."* Thus it was argued that the English version ("them") was ambiguous while the Spanish version (*"aquéllas"*) indicated clearly that the reference was to "forces" and not to "governments." The argument then proceeded as follows: It is impossible to speak of revolutionary forces opposed to other revolutionary forces because (*a*) "revolutionary" implies successful; until a movement becomes successful it is merely an insurrection; and (*b*) there cannot be two revolutions at the same time in one country.

The result of this argument is to render the words "or by revolutionary forces opposed to them" entirely without meaning.[26] Consequently the forces of Villa and Zapata (subsequent to their separation from the Constitutionalists), the forces of the Conventionists, and the forces of Orozco would not be comprehended within this subdivision and Mexico would be liable for injuries committed by them only in the event of a showing of negligence or fault.

Again the Mexican contention was successful. Some of the Commissions accepted this viewpoint in their decisions. In the case of the French, British and Spanish Commissions, the revision of the Conventions in 1930 and 1931 struck out the words "or by revolutionary forces opposed to them." The story of the victory of the Mexican thesis can best be followed by considering each of the groups of forces in question.

(i) *Orozquistas.* The leading case involving acts of Orozco forces is the *Russell* case [27] before the United States-Mexican Special Claims Commission. Over the vigorous dissent of the American Commissioner (Nielsen) it was held that these forces were not comprehended within

---

établi des Gouvernements *de jure* ou *de facto,* ou par les forces révolutionnaires qui leur étaient opposées."

German version: "von revolutionären Streitkräften, die beim Siege ihrer Sache eine Regierung *de jure* oder *de facto* eingesetzt haben, oder von den gegnerischen revolutionären Streitkräften."

Italian version: "da forze rivoluzionare che abbiano costituito, al triunfo della lora causa, un Governo *de jure* o *de facto* o da forze rivoluzionare contrarie alle predette."

[26] A written statement filed by the Mexican agent in the Pinson case, *supra,* note 24, at p. 153, explains this phrase as follows: "Deben considerarse como fuerzas revolucionarias contrarias a otras revolucionarias que establecieron gobiernos *de jure* o *de facto,* es decir, contrarias a las especificados en la sección 2 que antecede, todos aquellas que hubiesen organizado *una revolución distinta* de las fuerzas mencionadas. Como en México nunca se ha admitido la existencia de dos revoluciones a la vez, la fracción que se está comentando no tiene aplicación desde este punto de vista. Nosostros creemos que la frase 'fuerzas revolucionarias contrarias a aquellas,' se puso en la convención, para abarcar, en términos generales, los casos de varias revoluciones simultáneas por si los hechos historicos fueren susceptibles de esa interpretación, lo que, repetimos, nunca se ha aceptado."

[27] *Supra,* note 24.

the subdivision referred to because they were forces opposed to a government (that of Madero). The majority of the Commission adopted the Mexican contention with respect to the meaning of the contested phrase. The original French-Mexican Commission found the Orozquistas to be within this subdivision,[28] but after the elimination of this phrase from the Convention, the reorganized Commission held that Mexico could be liable for acts of these forces only if negligence or fault were shown.[29]

(ii) *Zapatistas*. These forces do not lend themselves easily to categorizing. Zapata supported the Madero revolution for a time but he remained in opposition to other factions for many years. At the same time it was evident that he was animated by a desire for social and economic reform rather than by any such desire for gain or personal power as would permit him to be classified with mutineers or bandits. The Mexican agents before the commissions contended that the career of the Zapatistas (and of the Villistas) fell into three periods.[30] In the first period, prior to November 1914, the Zapatistas formed part of the Constitutionalist army[31] and Mexico was therefore liable for their acts as those of forces which set up a government *de facto*. In the second period, November 1914 to September 1915, there was no government in Mexico. The Zapatistas could not be classed as an opposing revolutionary force since no such forces existed, and they could not be classed as insurrectionaries, rebels, etc., because there being no government there could be no insurrection. Therefore, Mexico could not be liable *even if negligence or fault could be proved*, within the meaning of subdivision (4) of the jurisdictional article. In the third period, subsequent to September 1915, a government did exist, and Mexico would therefore be liable for acts of the Zapatistas if negligence or fault should be shown.

This elaborate analysis seems to have been adopted only by the British-Mexican Commission; this being after the phrase "or by revolutionary forces opposed to them" had been eliminated from the Convention. In the *Patton* case[32] it took the extreme view of complete non-liability for acts of Zapata forces (excepting acts of brig-

---

[28] Dictum in the Pinson case, *supra*, note 24, at p. 149.
[29] Case of Dorcasberro et Jannet, Sentence No. 65 (unpublished); Case of Thomé et Cie., Sentence No. 76 (unpublished).
[30] See in particular Case of Mrs. Edith Henry, British-Mexican Commission, *Further Decisions and Opinions*, p. 165.
[31] This may not be historically accurate. See *supra*, note 4.
[32] Case of Mrs. Christina Patton, *Further Decisions and Opinions*, p. 215.

andage) committed in March 1915. The Commission apparently felt driven to this conclusion because of the elimination of the reference to opposing forces.[33] The French-Mexican Commission (after its reorganization) took the more moderate view of non-liability except on a showing of negligence or fault.[34] A similar view was taken by the Italian-Mexican Commission whose decisions were rendered under a Convention which at all times contained the phrase relating to opposing forces.[35]

(iii) *Villistas.* In general, the forces of Pancho Villa were classified in the same fashion as the forces of Zapata.[36] However, a special

---

[33] ". . . during the second period, the two contending factions (Zapatistas and Villistas) were fighting with the same character for political aims, and . . . as neither of the two had been able to establish a government, neither of them could be regarded as being in mutiny, rising or insurrection against the other. From that point of view their acts are not covered by the Convention, since by the last revision, the words *'or by revolutionary forces opposed to them'* have been eliminated. The Commission wish it, however, to be clearly understood that this opinion of theirs goes only to those acts, which were of a political or military nature, or directed towards political or military aims. While acts of that description seem to have been excluded when the treaty was amended, this cannot be maintained as regards acts of brigandage." *Ibid.,* at p. 218.

[34] Case of Compania Azucarera del Paraiso Novello, Sentence No. 70 (unpublished): "Attendu qu'à partie du 25 novembre 1914, les forces villistes et les forces zapatistes se sont séparées du parti constitutionaliste et sont entrées en lutte contre celui-ci; qu'elles n'ont réussi a former ni Gouvernement *de jure,* ni Gouvernement *de facto* et que, pendant cette seconde période, elles doivent être considérées conformément au paragraphe 4 de l'article III de la Convention, comme des 'forces insurrectionnelles autres que celle qui sont indiquées aux paragraphes 2 et 3' du même article; qu'en conséquence leurs actes, pendant cette période, ne peuvent donner droit à indemnité que s'il est établi que les autorités compétentes ont omis de prendre des mesures raisonnables pour les réprimer ou pour en punir les auteurs."

While both the French and Mexican Commissioners signed this opinion, the Mexican Commissioner made the following statement in addition:

"Le Commissaire mexicain, entièrement d'accord avec l'opinion antérieure, considère cependant qu'aux termes de la Convention des Réclamations entre la France et le Mexique, signée le 2 août 1930, le Gouvernement de son pays n'est responsable dans aucun cas, même si la négligence était invoquée et prouvée pour des actes des factions villiste et zapatiste, depuis le 25 novembre 1914 jusqu'à la date où fut constitué le Gouvernement *de facto* de Carranza."

[35] Case of Francesco Vetrano, Decision No. 24 (unpublished); Case of Luis Occelli, Decision No. 67 (unpublished); Case of Francesco Motta, Decision No. 72 (unpublished). But in the Case of Attilio Bellato, Decision No. 38 (unpublished), an award was granted on equitable grounds because other persons who had suffered injury at the hands of the same troop of Zapatistas had been indemnified by the National Claims Commission.

[36] In the following cases involving acts of Villa forces prior to November 1914, it was held that Mexico was liable as for acts of forces which succeeded in setting up a government: Rep. Alemana (Ernesto H. Goeldner) *v.* Estados Unidos Mexicanos, Decision No. 14, German-Mexican Commission (unpublished); Case of Vincenzo Rotunno, Decision No. 29, Italian-Mexican Commission (unpublished); Case of Lorenzo Elissetche, Sentence No. 50, reorganized French-Mexican Commission (unpublished).

In the following cases involving acts of Villa forces subsequent to November 1914, it was held that Mexico was not liable for such acts without a showing of negligence or fault: Rep. Alemana (A. Stallforth) *v.* Estados Unidos Mexicanos, German-Mexican Commission, Decision No. 58 (unpublished); Case of Antonio Ranauro, Italian-Mexican Commission, Decision No. 16 (unpublished).

interest exists in the problem of liability for the acts of the Villistas because of the fateful decision in the *Santa Isabel* cases [37] which nearly brought about the disruption of the United States-Mexican Special Claims Commission.[38] On January 10, 1916, a number of American mining engineers who were proceeding to a mine were taken from a train near Santa Isabel by a group of armed men and murdered. The murderers were under the command of a Villa officer. A claim brought by the United States was dismissed by the majority of the Commission on the ground that Mexico was not liable under the Convention. The basis of this holding was that in January 1916, Villa was a bandit and Mexico could be liable for the acts of his forces only if negligence or fault on the part of the authorities could be shown. It will be noted that this result was not reached on a construction of the Convention as had been done in the case discussed heretofore. It would have been possible to hold that the Villa forces could not be included under the second subdivision of the jurisdictional article for the same reasons that led this Commission to deny liability for acts of the Orozquistas. However, the result was reached by a consideration of the character of the Villa movement. The historical fact which was given paramount importance was that Villa was considered a "bandit" by public opinion in Mexico and in the United States and that he had been so denominated in public documents of both governments. This sort of reasoning is not particularly impressive. If the character of the Villa movement is to be considered it must not be forgotten that Villa had fought for years with a political motive and that shortly before the Santa Isabel massacre he had attempted to secure recognition as the head of a *de facto* government. The massacre may not have been animated by any political motive but there is nothing in the Convention which relieves Mexico of liability for acts of banditry committed by revolutionary forces.

After deciding that Villa was a bandit, the Special Claims Commission was faced with the question as to whether there had been any negligence, or fault or lenient treatment on the part of the authorities. It decided that nothing of the kind had taken place and that Mexico was therefore not liable. The most interesting problem in this connection is furnished by the amnesty which was granted to Villa in an agreement made in 1920 with the provisional de la Huerta

---

[37] Opinions of Commissioners, 1926–1931, p. 1.   [38] See *supra*, p. 64.

government. The Commission says of this that "however strange it may seem [the agreement of 1920] represents a supreme effort for achieving, by any means whatsoever, the pacification of the country, already weary of long years of serious disturbances, and it cannot be looked upon as an act of lenity in connection with the events at Santa Isabel." [39]

This decision may be compared with a far better reasoned opinion of the British-Mexican Commission [40] in a case involving a claim for confiscation by Villa forces of various objects in 1915, 1916 and 1919. This Commission accepted the division of Villa's career into the three periods which it had followed with regard to Zapata in the *Patton* case.[41] In considering the nature of the acts of the Villa forces in the third period, *i.e.*, subsequent to October 1915, the Commission said:

"It is clear, in the opinion of the Commission, that, speaking generally, the Villista movement and Villa's activities continued as a political factor until the conclusion of the Agreement of the 28th July, 1920. In this respect they differ from the view of the Mexican Agent that during the third period Zapata and Villa could no longer be considered as political factors. Therefore they will have to consider the category within which the various acts complained of in this case fall. In the opinion of the Commission, these acts, with possibly the exception of the train assault and gold taking in September 1919, were *prima facie* of a political or military character, done in pursuance or in aid of political aims, and they can find no evidence sufficient to establish that the acts were pure brigandage. . . .

"The Commission (on the whole) take the view that the Villa Agreement was an act of political expediency on the basis of the Villistas being regarded as belligerents, and does not in itself involve the Mexican Government in financial liability for acts done by Villistas of a political or military nature in pursuance and in aid of their political aims. . . . The Commission desire, however, to make clear that they are not speaking here of acts such as wanton murder or other crimes committed with no possible legitimate excuse or reason of military necessity." [42]

This seems an excellent solution of the problem. It recognizes that the amnesty to Villa was a matter of serious national policy and

[39] *Op. cit., supra*, note 37, at p. 11.
[40] Case of the Buena Tierra Mining Co. (Ltd.), Further Decisions and Opinions, p. 259.
[41] See *supra*, p. 165. The same division into periods was adopted by the Commission in the following cases: Case of William Alexander Kennedy, Further Decisions and Opinions, p. 242; Case of Thomas Pulley Mallard, *ibid.*, p. 250; Case of Fanny Graves, *ibid.*, p. 254.
[42] Case of the Buena Tierra Mining Co. (Ltd.), *supra*, note 40, at pp. 263, 265.

should not involve Mexico in liability for all acts of Villa forces. At the same time, it recognizes that the granting of the amnesty does have the effect of lenient treatment with respect to acts of brigandage and wanton murder. Had this principle been applied to the Santa Isabel cases by the Special Claims Commission, Mexico would have been held liable.

(3) *"By forces arising from the disjunction of the forces mentioned in the next preceding paragraph up to the time when the government de jure established itself as a result of a particular revolution."*

(4) *"By federal forces that were disbanded."*

Neither of these two subdivisions appear to have given rise to any problems. They are interesting as showing the comprehensive scope of the jurisdiction which the negotiators of the Conventions attempted to confer on the Commissions.

(5) *"By mutinies or mobs, or insurrectionary forces other than those referred to under subdivisions (2), (3) and (4) above, or by bandits, provided in any case it be established that the appropriate authorities omitted to take reasonable measures to suppress insurrectionists, mobs or bandits, or treated them with lenity or were in fault in other particulars."*

This subdivision was obviously designed as a catch-all. After the enumeration of various forces whose acts would result in the automatic *ex gratia* liability of Mexico, all other revolutionary acts of armed groups were to be judged in accordance with principles of liability apparently intended to be the same as those laid down by general international law. We have seen that at least one of the Commissions, the British-Mexican, destroyed the comprehensive character of the jurisdictional article by holding that the acts of the Zapata and Villa forces between November 1914 and September 1916 could not impose any liability on Mexico under any circumstances.[43]

Generally speaking, the decisions of the Commissions dealing with negligence or fault on the part of the authorities are not of any great interest. In most cases, the question presented would be one of evidence. Only the British-Mexican Commission laid down a general rule regarding the questions of evidence required in such cases. This rule was phrased as follows:

[43] See *supra*, p. 165.

In a great many cases it will be extremely difficult to establish beyond any doubt the omission or the absence of suppressive or punitive measures. The Commission realizes that the evidence of negative facts can hardly ever be given in an absolutely convincing manner. But a strong *prima facie* evidence can be assumed to exist in those cases in which *first* the British Agent will be able to make it acceptable that the facts were known to the competent authorities, either because they were of public notoriety or because they were brought to their knowledge in due time, and *second* the Mexican Agent does not show any evidence as to action taken by the authorities.[44]

The most interesting cases decided under this subdivision are those dealing with mob violence. In a case before the British-Mexican Commission claim was made for injuries resulting from acts of a mob which had sacked a factory in Saltillo on the occasion of the American occupation of Vera Cruz.[45] The Commission rejected the claim saying:

The Commission regard the occurrences, referred to in these parts of the claim, as the consequence of a popular demonstration of a violent nature. They cannot view them as revolutionary acts, nor as a mutiny, a rising, an insurrection, nor as acts of banditry. The movement was not directed against the Government or against public authorities, but against the foreigners residing at Saltillo. Regrettable as the events were, they cannot, under the wording of the Convention, justify the granting of compensation.

The same result was reached by the Italian-Mexican Commission in a case in which rioters had sacked the claimant's shop after Villa forces had withdrawn from the town.[46] However, instead of resting its decision on so unimpeachable an interpretation of the Convention, as the British-Mexican Commission had done, this Commission decided the case by resort to general principles of international law, without even considering whether or not the Convention was applicable. It was held that Mexico was not liable because, under gen-

---

[44] Mexico City Bombardment Claims, Decisions and Opinions of Commissioners, p. 100, at p. 104. For applications of this rule see: Case of Mrs. A. H. Francis, *ibid.*, p. 131; Case of William E. Bowerman, *ibid.*, p. 141; Case of Santa Gertrudis Jute Mill Co. (Ltd.), *ibid.*, p. 147, at p. 151; Case of Annie B. G. Kidd, Further Decisions and Opinions, p. 36; Case of James F. Bartlett, *ibid.*, p. 51; Case of John Gill, *ibid.*, p. 85, at p. 88; Case of William McNeil, *ibid.*, p. 96; Case of George Creswell Delamain, *ibid.*, p. 222; Case of Alfred Hammond Bromly, *ibid.*, p. 235.

[45] Case of William J. Russell, Further Decisions and Opinions, p. 341, at p. 342.

[46] Case of Rafael Ferrigno, Decision No. 10 (unpublished).

eral international law a government is not liable for acts of mob violence.[47]

The British-Mexican Commission also held that acts of thievery committed by private individuals did not come within the Convention,[48] this decision being based on the requirement that the acts be those of "forces," which would imply groups of men rather than single individuals. The same Commission also held that the consequences of a strike and the acts of violence accompanying a strike did not fall within the terms of the Convention.[49]

§151. Acts of Civil Authorities. It will be remembered that the Conventions with the European States contained an additional provision conferring jurisdiction over claims for losses or damages caused by acts of civil authorities "provided such acts were due to revolutionary events and disturbed conditions within the period referred to in this article, and that the said acts were committed by any of the forces specified in subdivisions 1, 2 and 3 of this article." Thus circumscribed, this provision amounted to very little in practice. In a case involving a seizure of property, the British-Mexican Commission explained this provision as follows:

> This seizure in itself, . . . does not make the Mexican Government liable according to the Convention. Property can be confiscated at all times, in all kinds of circumstances and on different grounds. To establish an obligation on the part of Mexico, it is necessary that it be proved that the act was committed by one of the forces enumerated in Article 3 of the Convention; in other words, the seizure must not have been an administrative act or an act ordered by purely civil authorities, but must have emanated from the elements which the article has in view, or, even if ordered by civil authorities, have been due to revolutionary events and disturbed conditions and committed by the forces already enumerated (last words of Article 3).[50]

Subsequently, the Commission held that the failure to allege that acts of confiscation by civil authorities were carried out through the intervention of military authorities rendered a memorial subject to

---

[47] The Commission said that losses caused by acts of rioters "son considerados como obra de fuerza mayor y no dan derecho a reclamaciones aceptables. Ellos no son imputable al Gobierno porque no fueron cometidos por los elementos a su orden sino por la plebe que aprovecha del desconcierto en tales circunstancias anormales."

[48] Case of Frederick Adams, Further Decisions and Opinions, p. 289.

[49] Case of the Tomnil Mexican Mining Co. (Ltd.), Further Decisions and Opinions, p. 321, at p. 322.

[50] Case of Norman Tucker Tracey, Decisions and Opinions of Commissioners, p. 118, at p. 121.

a motion to dismiss.[51] A contention by the British agent that when a confiscation took place during the revolutionary period, it was to be presumed that the military authorities "were behind" the civil authorities, was rejected.

A curious case involving this problem arose before the Italian-Mexican Commission.[52] The claimant had concluded a contract with the Díaz government in 1910 undertaking to furnish agricultural information. Payments were continued by the Madero and Huerta governments, but in October 1914 the Secretariat of Agriculture refused to pay for services previously rendered. The Commission held that Mexico was not liable because the claim did not arise out of revolutionary acts. Nevertheless, in view of the contractual relationship, the Commission recommended that the Mexican government pay the amount due for services rendered.

§152. **Appreciation of the Decisions of the Commissions.** Two facts are readily apparent from a consideration of the foregoing discussion: (1) the jurisdictional article of the Conventions was very badly drafted; (2) generally speaking, the Commissions showed a marked tendency to relieve Mexico of liability. We may add, that the history of the problem of liability for revolutionary acts as it developed through these decisions and through revisions of various of the Conventions records a series of steady victories for Mexico. It is not altogether easy to pass judgment on these developments. It would not have been difficult to draft a more satisfactory convention. For example it would have been possible to name the various commanders of forces in the convention itself. Yet, it may be that the difficulties in the way of arriving at a satisfactory text were such that the negotiators preferred to leave the text obscure. The tendency to relieve Mexico of liability is more difficult to evaluate. It does not seem in accord with the spirit of the Conventions which seem to embody a notion of an exceedingly generous compensation for injuries suffered as a result of the revolutions. On the other hand, the firmness with which the Mexican representatives pressed their fundamental theories was such that the Commissioners are not to be blamed too much for failing to resist them more effectively. After all, the loose language of the Conventions furnished rather weak bulwarks.

---

[51] Case of John Walker, Further Decisions and Opinions, p. 18.
[52] Case of Giovanni Rossi, Decision No. 7 (unpublished).

CHAPTER 9

JURISDICTION OVER CONTRACT CLAIMS AND RESPONSIBILITY OF GOVERNMENTS THEREFOR

§153. The Problem. International tribunals whose jurisdiction extends to "all claims for losses or damages" have often been perplexed by the question as to whether their jurisdiction includes so-called contractual claims. This question is inextricably interwoven with the question of the responsibility of governments for claims of this nature. Contractual claims fall readily into three classes: claims arising out of contracts between nationals of different states; claims arising out of contracts between an alien and a state; claims arising out of contracts between states. Only the second category need be considered here. Responsibility for claims arising out of contracts between private individuals can be predicated only where a state fails to provide adequate redress in its courts.[1] Claims arising out of contracts between states have on occasion been submitted to arbitration,[2] but the Mexican Claims Conventions excluded "governmental" claims.

§154. Basis of International Responsibility for Contractual Claims. What is the basis of international responsibility for breach by a government of a contract which it has concluded with an alien?[3] One possible basis is that the breach of contract is in and of itself a confiscation of property. It is thus violative of international law and the responsibility of the government arises immediately. This is the view taken by American Commissioner Nielsen in the General Claims

---

[1] Of course, an international tribunal may, by express stipulation, be given jurisdiction over contracts between private persons, as in the case of the Mixed Arbitral Tribunals set up under the Treaties of Peace. See, *e.g.*, Art. 304 of the Treaty of Versailles.

[2] *E.g.*, The Russian Indemnity Case, Tribunal of the Permanent Court of Arbitration (1912), Scott, Hague Court Reports, p. 297.

[3] See generally, Eagleton, Responsibility of States in International Law, Ch. VII; Borchard, Diplomatic Protection of Citizens Abroad, Ch. VII; 6 Moore, Digest of International Law, §§995–997; Hoijer, *Responsabilité internationale des Etats* (Paris, 1930), pp. 117–155; J. C. Witenberg, *"La recevabilité des réclamations devant les juridictions internationales,"* 1932—III *Recueil des Cours de l'académie de Droit International,* pp. 56–63.

Commission [4] and by one or two international tribunals.[5] The over-whelming weight of opinion, both of writers and tribunals, has been, however, to the effect that international responsibility for a breach of contract does not arise until there has been a "denial of justice," *i.e.*, until the alien has applied to the local authorities and courts and adequate redress has been denied him.[6] The one apparent exception has been with respect to "confiscatory" breaches of contract, where, it is said, international responsibility arises immediately. On examination these "confiscatory" breaches resolve themselves into cases where no means of local redress exist and the denial of justice is therefore established without the necessity of going through the futile forms of seeking redress, or where there has been an arbitrary annulment of the contract by the Executive without resort to judicial procedure.[7] In short then, as far as international responsibility is concerned, there

[4] "In the ultimate determination of responsibility under international law I think an international tribunal in a case grounded on a complaint of a breach of contract can properly give effect to principles of law with respect to confiscation. International tribunals in dealing with cases growing out of breaches of contract are not concerned with suits on contracts instituted and conducted conformably to procedure prescribed by the common law or statutes in countries governed by Anglo-Saxon law, nor conformably to corresponding procedure in countries in which the principles of the civil law obtain. International law does not prescribe rules relative to the forms and the legal effect of contracts, but that law is, in my opinion, concerned with the action authorities of a Government may take with respect to contractual rights. If a Government agrees to pay money for commodities and fails to make payment, it seems to me that an international tribunal may properly say that the purchase price of the commodities has been confiscated, or that the commodities have been confiscated, or that property rights in a contract have been destroyed or confiscated." Commissioner Nielsen dissenting in U. S. A. (International Fisheries Co.) *v.* United Mexican States, Opinions of Commissioners, 1931, p. 207, at pp. 241-242. See also U. S. A. (George W. Cook) *v.* United Mexican States, Opinions of Commissioners, 1929, p. 266, at p. 269.

[5] "A claim is none the less a claim because it originates in contract instead of in tort. The refusal to pay an honest claim is no less a wrong because it happens to arise from an obligation to pay money instead of originating in violence offered to persons or property." Commissioner Findlay in the Venezuelan Bond Cases, U. S.-Venezuelan Claims Commission of 1885, 4 Moore, International Arbitrations, at p. 3649. See also the Rudloff Case, U. S.-Venezuelan Claims Commission of 1903, Ralston, Venezuelan Arbitrations of 1903, p. 182, at p. 188; the Oliva Case, Italian-Venezuelan Claims Commission of 1903, *ibid.*, p. 771, at p. 781.

[6] See Harvard Research in International Law, "Draft Convention on Responsibility of States for Damage Done in Their Territory to the Person or Property of Foreigners," Art. 8, 23 Amer. Journal of Int. Law (1929), Special Supplement, p. 167 *et seq.*, Eagleton, *loc. cit., supra*, note 1; Borchard, *loc. cit., supra*, note 1; Hyde, International Law, p. 545 *et seq.*; 1 Westlake, International Law, p. 331 *et seq.*

[7] "Cases have frequently occurred in which the contracts of citizens of the United States with foreign governments were arbitrarily annulled by the contracting government without recourse to a judicial determination of the contract or of the legitimacy of its act. An act of this kind has generally been held by the Department of State to be a confiscatory breach of the contract and to warrant diplomatic interposition as in cases of tort. Any weakening of the judicial remedy of the citizen has been held equally to relieve the government from the ordinary rule of non-interposition in contract cases. . . . The forcible deprivation of the property and franchises of a citizen of the United States without

is little difference between a "contractual" claim and a "tort" claim.[8]

§155. **The Jurisdictional Question before International Tribunals.** In the ordinary case then of an international tribunal having jurisdiction over "all claims," the question of jurisdiction over contractual claims should present no difficulty, and the majority of tribunals have readily taken jurisdiction.[9] If local remedies have been exhausted or if no such remedies are afforded, then the tribunal will take cognizance of the claim as for a "denial of justice." Where, however, there is an express waiver of the requirement of exhaustion of local remedies, as in the Mexican Claims Conventions, the problem is more complicated.

§156. **The Illinois Central Railroad Case.** The *Illinois Central Railroad* case [10] before the General Claims Commission involved a

---

due process of law and a fair trial is considered as a tort and the claim will be pressed on that ground regardless of its contractual origin." Borchard, Diplomatic Protection of Citizens Abroad, pp. 292, 293.

"If one examines the cases carefully, one finds that, so far as they can be said to contain any common ground at all, it is the feature of the use of governmental power to defeat the obligations of the contract. The types of cases set forth are as follows: (1) failure to provide adequate remedies in the local courts against breaches by the state; (2) arbitrary annulment by the contracting government without recourse to a judicial determination of the terms of the contract or of the legality of the government's act; and (3) various other 'arbitrary' acts by the contracting government resulting in loss to the private contractor. In all of these cases the distinguishing feature is an interjection of governmental power to alter the situation envisaged in the contract. To the extent that one party to a contract is able to do this without the consent of the other party, the expectations created by the contractual relation are defeated." Dunn, Protection of Nationals, p. 167.

[8] *Cf.* the statement by Hall, International Law (6th ed.), p. 276: "there is no difference in principle between wrongs inflicted by breach of monetary agreement and other wrongs for which the state, as itself the wrongdoer, is immediately responsible." Borchard criticizes this statement as "technically correct," but "apt to be misleading." . . . "in the case of contractual claims the active notice taken by the state of the wrong done its citizen is deferred until he has exhausted his local judicial remedies and a denial of justice is established, whereas in claims arising out of tort, if chargeable to a government authority, interposition is generally immediate." Borchard, *op. cit.*, p. 282.

[9] See cases before the United States-Mexican Claims Convention of 1839, 4 Moore, International Arbitrations, pp. 3425–3428; Case of Hudson's Bay Co., United States-British Claims Commission of 1853, *ibid.*, p. 3458; Eldredge's Case, United States-Peruvian Claims Commission of 1863, *ibid.*, p. 3460; De Witt's Case, United States-Mexican Claims Commission of 1868, *ibid.*, p. 3466; Kearny's Case, United States-Mexican Claims Commission of 1868, *ibid.*, pp. 3467–3468. *Contra:* Hubbell's Case, U. S.-British Mixed Commission of 1871, *ibid.*, p. 3484. The United States-Spanish Claims Convention of Feb. 12, 1871, provided that the arbitrators were not to have jurisdiction of claims growing out of contract. U. S. Treaty Series, No. 328—1.

[10] U.S.A. (Illinois Central R. R. Co.) *v.* United Mexican States, Opinions of Commissioners, 1927, p. 15. In two cases arising earlier on motion to dismiss the Commission had held that, "although the allegation of nonperformance of contractual obligations is apparent on the face of the record, it does not necessarily follow as a legal conclusion that the claim does not fall within the General Claims Convention." U.S.A. (Thomas O. Mudd *v.* United Mexican States, *ibid.*, p. 10; U. S. A. (Joseph E. Davies) *v.* United Mexican States, *ibid.*, p. 13. This holding seems quite meaningless. On a motion to dismiss the Commission was under a duty to decide whether or not it had jurisdiction.

claim for the balance alleged to be due on a number of locomotive engines sold by the claimant to the Government Railway Administration of the National Railways of Mexico. The Mexican agent moved to dismiss on the grounds that the claim was based on an alleged nonperformance of contractual obligations and was therefore not within the jurisdiction of the Commission, and that, the obligation itself not being denied by Mexico, no controversy existed for decision. The Commission quite properly refused to base its decision upon the decisions of other international tribunals,[11] but rather upon an interpretation of the Claims Convention. The salient question was whether the opening words of Article I ("all claims for losses or damages suffered by persons or by their properties") must be construed in the light of the closing words of the same article, providing that claims should be decided "in accordance with the principles of international law, justice and equity," to the effect that "all claims" must mean all claims for which either government is responsible according to international law. This conclusion, the Commission felt, would go too far. The only permissible inference would be that they must be claims of an international character, not that they must be claims entailing international responsibility of governments. It went on to say:

"International claims, needing decision in 'accordance with the principles of international law' may belong to any of four types:
"*a*. Claims as between a national of one country and a national of another country. These claims are international, even in cases where interna-

---

[11] The refusal was proper but the reasons given are hardly valid: "Before entering upon this examination the Commission feels bound to state that any representation of international jurisprudence, and especially of the jurisprudence of the Mexican Claims Commission of 1868, intended to proclaim in a general way that such jurisprudence was either in favor of jurisdiction over contract claims or disclaimed jurisdiction over contract claims, is contrary to the wording of the awards themselves. Whatever statements from authors in this respect it may be possible to quote, a perusal of the very awards clearly shows that not only either allowance or disallowance of contract claims is not their general and universal feature but that it is even impracticable to deduce from them one consistent system. A rule that contract claims are cognizable only in case denial of justice or any other form of governmental responsibility is involved is not in them; nor can a general rule be discovered according to which mere non-performance of contractual obligations by a government in its civil capacity withholds jurisdiction, whereas it grants jurisdiction when the non-performance is accompanied by some feature of the public capacity of the government as an authority. . . . The Treaty is this Commission's charter. It must look primarily to the language of that Treaty . . . to discover the scope and limits of its jurisdiction." *Ibid.*, p. 16. The decisions of other tribunals are not applicable, not because no rule of law can be deduced from them, but because they were rendered under Conventions which did not contain a waiver of exhaustion of local remedies. *Cf.* the comments of Dunn, Protection of Nationals, p. 221.

tional law declares one of the municipal laws involved to be exclusively applicable; but they do not fall within Article I.

"*b*. Claims as between two national governments in their own right. These claims also are international and also are outside the scope of Article I.

"*c*. Claims as between a citizen of one country and the government of another acting in its public capacity. These claims are beyond doubt included in Article I.

"*d*. Claims as between a citizen of one country and the government of another country acting in its civil capacity. These claims too are international in character, and they too must be decided 'in accordance with the principle of international law,' even in cases where international law should merely declare the municipal law of one of the countries involved to be applicable.

"It seems impossible to maintain that legal pretensions belonging to this fourth category are not 'claims.' It seems equally impossible to maintain that they are not 'international claims.' . . . The Commission concludes that the final words of Article I, which provide that it shall decide cases submitted to it 'in accordance with the principles of international law, justice and equity,' prescribe the rules and principles which shall govern in the decision of claims falling within its jurisdiction, but in no wise limit the preceding clauses, which do fix this Commission's jurisdiction." [12]

§157. Law Applicable to Contractual Claims.

Since, in addition, the Commission believed that the wording of Article I indicated "a broad and liberal spirit underlying and permeating this Treaty," it being "well known to have been the purpose of the negotiators to have by this Convention removed a source of irritation between the two nations and a constant menace to their friendly intercourse," it disallowed the motion to dismiss.[13]

All this is commendable so far as it goes. The Commission has jurisdiction over claims which are international in character. A claim for breach of a contract between a government of one country and a national of another is certainly international in character. The re-

---

[12] Pp. 17–18.
[13] With respect to the contention that no controversy existed for decision because Mexico did not deny the obligation, the Commission said: "Non-performance of a contractual obligation may consist either in the denial of the obligation itself and non-performance as a consequence of such denial, or in acknowledgment of the obligation itself and non-performance notwithstanding such acknowledgment. In both cases such non-performance may be the basis of a claim cognizable by this Commission." P. 20. When the case came up for decision on the merits, the Commission awarded $1,807,531.36 plus interest. U. S. A. (Illinois Central R. R. Co.) *v.* United Mexican States, Opinions of Commissioners, 1927, p. 187.

quirement of decision "in accordance with the principle of international law" merely indicates the source of the law to be applied and does not constitute a limitation on jurisdiction.[14] But, granted the jurisdiction, how is such a claim to be decided "in accordance with the principles of international law"? International law contains no rules for the decision of controversies involving breach of such contracts. All that can be found in international law is a reference back to municipal law. Under the usual type of convention all the Commission could do would be to tell the claimant to take the controversy into the municipal courts, to exhaust his local remedies. Under this Convention it cannot do so. Therefore the Commission itself must apply a municipal, in this case Mexican, law.[15] It may either be said then that the Commission in this case acts as a Mexican tribunal, or that it acts as an international tribunal applying Mexican law which, for this purpose, has been incorporated into international law. The Commission failed to point this out in the *Illinois Central* case, but in several later cases it expressly stated that the law applicable to contractual claims was Mexican law.[16]

[14] A similar problem arose in the Serbian Loans Case before the Permanent Court of International Justice. It was argued that, notwithstanding the consent of the parties, the court had no jurisdiction, because the case could not be decided by the application of rules of international law. The court said: "Article 38 of the statute cannot be regarded as excluding the possibility of the court's dealing with disputes which do not require the application of international law. . . . All that can be said is that cases in which the court must apply international law will, no doubt, be more frequent, for it is international law which governs relations between those who may be subject to the court's jurisdiction." Publications of the Court, Series A, No. 20, p. 20. *Cf.* the dissenting opinion of Judge Pessoa, *ibid.*, at p. 62.

[15] International law will refer the matter to municipal law. But will it give an answer to the question of *which* municipal law? This question arose in the Serbian Loans Case before the Permanent Court of International Justice. The Court said: "Any contract which is not a contract between States in their capacity as subjects of international law is based on the municipal law of some country. The question as to which this law is forms the subject of that branch of law which is at the present day usually described as private international law or the doctrine of the conflict of laws. The rules thereof may be common to several states and may even be established by international conventions or customs, and in the latter case may possess the character of true international law governing the relations between States. But apart from this it has to be considered that these rules form part of municipal law. The Court, which has before it a dispute involving the question as to the law which governs the contractual obligations at issue, can determine what this law is only by reference to the actual nature of these obligations and to the circumstances attendant upon their creation, though it may also take into account the expressed or presumed intention of the parties." Publications of the Court, Series A, No. 20, p. 41. The Court decided that the contracts were subject to Serbian law taking into account that the loans were contracted by a sovereign state, that the Serbian laws under which the bonds were issued were printed in the bonds, that the bonds were issued to bearer, and that they were not issued at one place.

[16] U. S. A. (George W. Cook) *v.* United Mexican States, Opinions of Commissioners, 1927, p. 318, at p. 320; U. S. A. (George W. Cook) *v.* United Mexican States, Opinions of Commissioners, 1929, p. 266, at p. 268. In a claim arising out of legal services rendered by the claimant to the Mexican government, it was argued that the contract was void under Mexican law. The American agent contended that the contract was governed by

Supposing now that an examination of Mexican law reveals that the claimant cannot recover on the contract under that law. It does not necessarily follow that the Claims Commission may not make an award. The provisions of Mexican law in question may be beneath the international standard of justice. The municipal legislation may be in violation of a rule of international law as where it provides for non-liability for the contracts of a former revolutionary government. Or, even where no violation of international law is involved the Commission may give an award on equitable grounds where there has been an "unjust enrichment."

§158. **Claims for Non-payment of Postal Money Orders.** The decisions of the General Claims Commission are not always consistent with this analysis as a comparison of contractual claims granted and disallowed will show. The majority of contractual claims filed fall into two classes: claims for non-payment of postal money orders and claims arising out of goods sold and delivered or services rendered. Most of the money order claims were granted. The first question raised under these claims was whether Mexico was under an obligation to redeem money orders issued by the Huerta administration. The Carranza government had, by degrees, annulled all acts of the government of Huerta. The Commission held that irrespective of whether the Huerta government was legal or illegal, Mexico was liable under international law for its routine governmental acts, even though the result would be that aliens would be placed in a better position than nationals.[17] It was then argued that the Mexican Statute of Limitations imposing a two-year prescriptive period should be applied to deny recovery. The Commission held that the period of limitation would not be applied where the claimant had made demand of the Mexican authorities before this period expired.[18] Two cases involved

---

American law because concluded in the United States. The Commission held that the contract was valid under either law. U. S. A. (Joseph E. Davies) v. United Mexican States, Opinions of Commissioners, 1927, p. 197.

[17] U. S. A. (George W. Hopkins) v. United Mexican States, Opinions of Commissioners, 1927, p. 42.

[18] U. S. A. (George W. Cook) v. United Mexican States, Opinions of Commissioners, 1927, p. 318. In U. S. A. (Francis J. Acosta) v. United Mexican States, Opinions of Commissioners, 1929, p. 121, it was argued that there was no proof that the money orders had been presented for payment during the two year period. The Commission held that since there was no doubt that during the time in question money orders were not paid when presented, the declaration of the claimant that presentation had been made was sufficient. Cf. U. S. A. (George W. Cook) v. United Mexican States, Opinions of Commissioners, 1927, p. 311. Claim was made with regard to postage stamps which claimant had purchased. The Mexican authorities had cancelled the stamps without giving the three months' notice required by the Mexican Postal Code. The claim was granted.

the following facts. A purchased a money order and indorsed it to B. Claim was made on behalf of C who, it was alleged, was the undisclosed principal of A. It appeared that under Mexican law a money order would be paid only to the drawee or to indorsees. The Commission held that it would look to the real party in interest and grant recovery in favor of an undisclosed principal, but that it would require convincing evidence of the relationship between A and C.[19] The only other question with regard to these money order claims was as to the rate of exchange for calculating the awards.[20]

§159. Claims for Goods Sold and Delivered and Services Rendered. In claims arising out of goods sold and delivered and services rendered the contention was also made that Mexico was not liable because the contract was made with an illegal or revolutionary government. The Commission held Mexico liable for goods sold to the Huerta government [21] and to a representative of the Carranza government,[22] and for services rendered to a representative of the Carranza Constitutionalists.[23] Several claims were dismissed on a construction of the contract,[24] and others were dismissed for lack of evidence to establish the existence of a contract.[25] In one of the latter cases the Commission enunciated the rule that "to establish before any tribunal the existence of a contract with a government, the require-

---

[19] U. S. A. (John A. McPherson) v. United Mexican States, Opinions of Commissioners, 1927, p. 325, recovery allowed; U. S. A. (George W. Hopkins) v. United Mexican States, ibid., p. 329, recovery denied because of lack of evidence of legal relationship between claimant and drawee or indorsee.

[20] U. S. A. (George W. Cook) v. United Mexican States, Opinions of Commissioners, 1927, p. 318; U. S. A. (Parsons Trading Co.) v. United Mexican States, ibid., p. 324; U. S. A. (Francis J. Acosta) v. United Mexican States, Opinions of Commissioners, 1929, p. 121; U. S. A. (Singer Sewing Machine Co.) v. United Mexican States, ibid., p. 123; U. S. A. (Esther Moffit) v. United Mexican States, ibid., p. 288.

[21] U. S. A. (Peerless Motor Car Co.) v. United Mexican States, Opinions of Commissioners, 1927, p. 303; U. S. A. (Parsons Trading Co.) v. United Mexican States, Opinions of Commissioners, 1929, p. 135.

[22] U. S. A. (Amer. Bottle Co.) v. United Mexican States, Opinions of Commissioners, 1929, p. 162.

[23] U. S. A. (United Dredging Co.) v. United Mexican States, Opinions of Commissioners, 1927, p. 394. In the following cases also awards were made on contractual claims: goods sold and delivered—U. S. A. (Adolph Deutz and Charles Deutz) v. United Mexican States, Opinions of Commissioners, 1929, p. 213; U. S. A. (Lee A. Craw) v. United Mexican States, ibid., p. 1; U. S. A. (William A. Parker) v. United Mexican States, Opinions of Commissioners, 1927, p. 82; services rendered—U. S. A. (J. Parker Kirlin) v. United Mexican States, Opinions of Commissioners, 1927, p. 162; U. S. A. (Joseph E. Davies) v. United Mexican States, ibid., p. 197.

[24] U. S. A. (W. C. Greenstreet) v. United Mexican States, Opinions of Commissioners, 1929, p. 199; U. S. A. (Harry H. Hughes) v. United Mexican States, Opinions of Commissioners, 1931, p. 99.

[25] U. S. A. (Macedonio J. García) v. United Mexican States, Opinions of Commissioners, 1927, p. 146.

ments are more rigorous and exacting than when the contract is between private persons." [26] Several cases involved the question as to whether the person with whom the contract was made had authority to bind the Mexican government.[27] A group of cases involved the discharge of American employees of the Mexican National Railways during the occupation of Vera Cruz by American forces. The Commission properly held that the discharge of these employees was a legitimate measure of defense during an emergency, irrespective of whether or not a technical state of war could be said to exist.[28]

§160. **The Cook Case.** Two cases are of particular interest and deserve extended consideration. The *Cook* case [29] involved a claim for school benches sold to the Mexican Ministry of Public Instruction and Fine Arts. The contract was made with Solórzano, a salesman employed by the firm of Mosler, Bowen & Cook. The firm was not mentioned in the contract but it was known to the Ministry that the firm was the principal and would make deliveries. The Commission disallowed a claim on behalf of the owner of the firm. It stated that under Mexican law a principal could not recover on a contract made by an agent in his own name unless the agent were a "factor," which Solórzano was not. Whether or not this was a proper construction of the Mexican law,[30] it would seem that an award should have been

---

[26] U. S. A. (Pomeroy's El Paso Transfer Co.) *v.* United Mexican States, Opinions of Commissioners, 1931, p. 1. See *infra*, p. 278.

[27] Contracts were made with the Industrial Agent of the Mexican National Railways. Claims dismissed. U. S. A. (American Short Horn Breeders' Ass.) *v.* United Mexican States, Opinions of Commissioners, 1927, p. 280; U. S. A. (Waukesha County Holstein-Friesian Breeders' Ass.) *v.* United Mexican States, *ibid.*, p. 285.

[28] U. S. A. (E. R. Kelley) *v.* United Mexican States, Opinions of Commissioners, 1931, p. 82; U. S. A. (Halifax C. Clark) *v.* United Mexican States, *ibid.*, p. 94; U. S. A. (J. E. Dennison) *v.* United Mexican States, *ibid.*, p. 96; U. S. A. (Belle M. Hendry) *v.* United Mexican States, *ibid.*, p. 97.

[29] U. S. A. (George W. Cook) *v.* United Mexican States, Opinions of Commissioners, 1929, p. 266.

[30] There are three types of agents under Mexican law: *mandatario, comisionista* and *factor*. The *mandato* is a relationship under the civil law. In the Federal Civil Code of 1883 it was defined as a power given to the agent (*mandatario*) to act on behalf of his principal in the name of the latter (Art. 2342). No provision was made for the case where the *mandatario* contracts in his own name. In the Federal Civil Code of 1932 it is expressly provided that where the *mandatario* contracts in his own name, his principal may not sue the third party (Art. 2561). The Commercial Code provides that "the *mandato* applicable to concrete acts of commerce is called *comisión mercantil*," the agent being known as *comisionista* (Art. 273). No express provision is made as to the rights of the principal to sue the third party when the *comisionista* contracts in his own name, but in other civil law countries it is clear that the principal has no right of action. 3 Lyon-Caen et Renault, Traité de droit commercial (5th ed., Paris, 1923), p. 474; Netherlands Commercial Code, Art. 78; Italian Commercial Code, Art. 381; Spanish Commercial Code, Art. 246. A *factor* may contract in his own name and give his principal a right of suit, but a *factor* is defined by the Mexican Commercial Code as one who has the management

made on equitable grounds. Mexico had received the benches and had been unjustly enriched. This decision is clearly contrary to the decisions of the Commission in the money order cases.[31]

§161. The Dickson Car Wheel Case. In the *Dickson Car Wheel* case [32] the claimant had sold car wheels to the National Railways of Mexico in 1912. In 1914 the Mexican government took possession of the lines of the National Railways and kept possession until 1925. No payment for the wheels was ever made. The United States contended that the government became substituted for the rights and obligations of the National Railways, that the taking over of the lines had prevented the National Railways from fulfilling its contract, and that the government had obtained an unjust enrichment. The Commission disallowed the claim. It showed that the National Railways continued to exist at all times as a juridical entity against which the claimant possessed a legal remedy. With respect to the contention that Mexico was liable because the government had prevented the National Railways from fulfilling its contract, the Commission held that, "a state does not incur international responsibility from the fact that an individual or company of the nationality of another state suffers a primary injury as the corollary or result of an injury which the defendant State has inflicted upon an individual or company irrespective of nationality when the relations between the former and the latter are of a contractual nature." The holding was supported by the demonstration that there had not been any internationally illegal act on the part of Mexico, which had only taken possession of the property of its own nationals. It was also said that no unjust enrichment existed because the government had agreed to indemnify the National Railways when the lines were returned to private management.

---

of the establishment or is authorized to enter into contracts with regard to all matters referring to the establishment (Art. 309). Solórzano appears to have been merely a salesman employed by the firm and was clearly neither a *comisionista* nor a *factor*. It would seem that the Mexican law in force at the time did not expressly exclude suit by the principal. The Commission admits that whether suit could be brought by the latter must depend on the intention of the parties. It is significant in this respect that the contract was prepared by the firm, that the claimant agreed that Solórzano should sign the contract, and that Solórzano was present. The Commission placed some weight on the curious case of Elbinger Actien Gesellschaft *v.* Claye, L. R., 8 Q.B. 313 (1873), which refused to permit suit to be brought by an alien principal of an English agent who had contracted in his own name. But, an English case would hardly seem to be applicable in the construction of a Mexican contract.   [31] Particularly the McPherson case, *supra*, note 19.
    [32] U. S. A. (Dickson Car Wheel Co.) *v.* United Mexican States, Opinions of Commissioners, 1931, p. 175.

It is difficult to form an opinion of the correctness of the decision in view of the conflict of testimony as to whether the National Railways had any assets. The majority of the Commission stated that it did have assets, but it was shown that the National Railways had excused its failure to pay on the ground that all its assets had been taken over by the government. The interesting question as to the liability of a government to alien creditors of a national whose property has been taken away by it has been discussed elsewhere.[33]

§162. The Howard Case. With one exception, the Mexican Claims Commissions dealing with revolutionary claims had no occasion to consider the question of jurisdiction over contractual claims.[34] The exception is the *Howard* case [35] before the British-Mexican Commission. The claimant owned a house which had been occupied by various revolutionary leaders who paid him rent. Claim was made for the difference between the rental value and the amount paid. Mexico moved to dismiss on the ground that the acceptance of rent gave rise to a contractual relationship over which the Commission had no jurisdiction. The Commission disallowed the motion to dismiss on the ground that no contractual relationship had arisen because the acceptance of the rent by the claimant was not voluntary but had been forced upon him by the revolutionary leaders.[36] At the same time the Commission thought it necessary to state "that until now it has not yet had to deal with the question whether it is competent to take cognizance of claims arising out of contractual relations. This question will have to be examined and decided as soon as a claim of this nature comes up for decision." Apparently, the Commission forgot this promise. A subsequent case involved a claim for compensation

---

[33] See *supra*, p. 123.

[34] Two cases involving contract claims were decided by the Italian-Mexican Claims Commission. In one of these, the claimant had contracted to furnish information on agriculture to the Mexican government in 1910. Payments were continued under the Madero and Huerta governments, but on October 15, 1914, the Secretary of Agriculture refused to pay for services previously rendered. The Commission held that no award could be rendered because the cancellation of the contract was not a revolutionary act, but recommended that the claimant be paid 840 pesos as a matter of grace. Case of Giovanni Rossi, Decision No. 7 (unpublished). The other case involved a claim by an Italian company on a contractual claim assigned to it by a Mexican company. The Commission held that it had no jurisdiction over a claim which was Mexican in origin. Case of Lange & Co., Decision No. 13 (unpublished). In neither case was there any discussion of jurisdiction over contract claims.

[35] Case of James Hammet Howard, British-Mexican Commission, Further Decisions and Opinions, p. 15.

[36] Subsequently, an award was made in favor of the claimant. Case of James Hammet Howard, British-Mexican Commission, Further Decisions and Opinions, p. 226.

for wood and timber supplied by the claimant to revolutionary and counter-revolutionary forces. The Commission disallowed the claim, stating very briefly that it found nothing to prove that the claimant company, in supplying wood and timber, acted under violence and not voluntarily in the course of business, and that it could not regard an order to supply fuel as an act of forces covered by the Convention.[37]

[37] Case of the Suchi Timber Co., Ltd., British-Mexican Commission, Further Decisions and Opinions, p. 246.

CHAPTER 10

THE CALVO CLAUSE

§163. **Definition of the Calvo Clause.** In 1870 the Argentinian writer Calvo enunciated the doctrine that aliens are not entitled to more than national treatment.[1] This is the Calvo Doctrine, a conception which has failed to receive recognition as a principle of international law, but one which fathered the ubiquitous and difficult problem of the Calvo Clause. The Calvo Clause, in its various manifestations, represents an attempt by the Latin-American nations to give concrete embodiment to the Doctrine. In its most typical form, the Calvo Clause is a stipulation in a contract between an alien and a government whereby the alien agrees not to call upon his government for protection in all matters arising out of the contract. The form of the Clause shows many variants. It may be an agreement to resort to private arbitration or to the local courts with regard to disputes arising out of the contract; or a promise not to seek diplomatic protection under any circumstances; or an agreement that the alien shall be considered as a national for the purposes of the contract. Nor is the Clause limited to contracts. It is to be found in constitutions and statutes.

§164. **History of the Calvo Clause.** The history of the Calvo Clause in international case-law previous to the Mexican Claims Conventions is a confused one.[2] In eight cases the Clause was held to be a bar to an international claim.[3] Three of these were decisions by

---

[1] See 1 *Le droit international* (Paris, 1870), sec. 290. The doctrine was elaborated in subsequent editions. See the compendium of statements from the fifth edition of Calvo's work in Borchard, Diplomatic Protection of Citizens Abroad, p. 792.

[2] See generally, Borchard, Diplomatic Protection of Citizens Abroad, Ch. IV; Eagleton, Responsibility of States in International Law, pp. 168–176; Ralston, Law and Procedure of International Tribunals (rev. ed.), pp. 58–72; Summers, "The Calvo Clause," 19 Virginia Law Rev. (1933), p. 459.

[3] Case of Beales, Noble & Garrison, United States-Venezuelan Commission of 1885, 4 Moore, International Arbitrations, p. 3548 (dictum); Case of Flanagan, Bradley, Clark & Co., United States-Venezuelan Commission of 1885, *ibid.*, p. 3564; Case of Tehuantepec Ship Canal Co., United States-Mexican Commission of 1868, *ibid.*, p. 3132; Woodruff Case, United States-Venezuelan Commission of 1903, Ralston, Venezuelan Arbitrations of 1903, p. 151; Orinoco Steamship Co. Case, United States-Venezuelan Commission of

Umpire Barge of the American-Venezuelan Commission of 1903 [4] and exhibit such contradictions and confusion of thought that they are entitled to little weight.[5] In two other cases,[6] the question of the validity of the Calvo Clause was not involved in the decision. In another case [7] serious doubts were expressed as to whether the Clause would be valid in the event of a denial of justice, and in still another case [8] it was said that the Clause did not "obligate foreign governments." Eleven cases have denied the validity of the Calvo Clause.[9]

1903, *ibid.*, p. 72; Turnbull Case, United States-Venezuelan Commission of 1903, *ibid.*, p. 200; Kunhardt Case, United States-Venezuelan Commission of 1903, *ibid.*, p. 63 (dictum); Nitrate Railway Co. Case, Anglo-Chilean Commission of 1893, 2 Reclamaciones presentados al Tribunal Anglo-Chileno, p. 320. *Cf.* Case of Roferio & Co., Brazilian-Bolivian Commission of 1903, Helio Lobo, O Tribunal Arbitral Brasiliero-Boliviano (Rio de Janeiro, 1910), p. 72, abstracted in Ralston, Law and Procedure of International Tribunals (rev. ed.), p. 69.

[4] The Woodruff, Orinoco Steamship and Turnbull cases. *Supra,* note 3.

[5] The following is a typical comment on the Barge opinions: "These contradictory decisions, absurdly reasoned, and resulting in mutually destructive conclusions, fit only for *opera bouffe*, would afford material for the gaiety of nations, were it not that the ripple of laughter dies on the lips when we consider the gross injustice thus perpetrated on private claimants." Clarke, "Intervention for Breach of Contract or Tort Committed by a Sovereignty," Proceedings of the Amer. Society of International Law, 1910, p. 162; and see Correspondence Relating to Wrongs Done to American Citizens by the Government of Venezuela, Senate Doc. 413, 60th Cong., 1st Sess. (1908), pp. 79–84.

[6] The Beales, Noble & Garrison, and Kuhnhardt cases. *Supra,* note 3.

[7] The Flanagan case. *Supra,* note 3.

[8] The Nitrate Railway case. *Supra,* note 3.

[9] Borchard, Diplomatic Protection of Citizens Abroad, pp. 805–808, has divided these cases into three classes. (1) Those in which the decision was on the ground that it is beyond the competence of an individual to contract away the superior right of his government to protect him: Rudloff Case, United States-Venezuelan Commission of 1903, Ralston, Venezuelan Arbitrations of 1903, p. 182; Martini Case, Italian-Venezuelan Commission of 1903, *ibid.*, p. 819; Selwyn Case, British-Venezuelan Commission of 1903, *ibid.*, p. 322. (2) Those in which the decision was on the ground that the action of the government in annulling the contract without first appealing to the local courts relieved the claimant from the stipulation not to make the contract a subject of international claim: McMurdo Case, United States-Portuguese Commission of 1891, Moore, International Arbitrations, p. 1865; North and South American Construction Co. Case, United States-Peruvian Commission of 1868, *ibid.*, p. 1643; Milligan Case, United States-Peruvian Commission of 1868, *ibid.*, p. 1643. (3) Those in which the decision was reached by holding that the claim arose out of some violation of property rights: American Electric and Manufacturing Co. Case, United States-Venezuelan Commission of 1903, Ralston, Venezuelan Arbitrations of 1903, p. 246; Del Genovese Case, United States-Venezuelan Commission of 1903, *ibid.*, p. 174; Coro and La Vela Ry. and Improvement Co. Case, United States-Venezuelan Commission of 1903, Report of Robert C. Morris, Senate Doc. 317, 58th Cong., 2d Sess. (1904), p. 69; Antofagasta and Bolivia Ry. Co. Case, Anglo-Chilean Commission of 1893, 3 Reclamaciones presentados al Tribunal Anglo-Chileno, p. 699; Stirling Case, Anglo-Chilean Commission of 1893, 1 *ibid.*, p. 128. In some of the cases cited two of these grounds are given as the basis for the decision.

In several cases before the Mixed Arbitral Tribunals set up under the Treaty of Peace, it was held that an arbitration clause in a private contract did not deprive the Mixed Tribunal of jurisdiction. Petit et Cie. *v.* Thuss, German-Belgian Mixed Arbitral Tribunal, 1 *Recueil des Decisions des Tribunaux Arbitraux Mixtes*, p. 401 (1922); Goulley *v.* S. A. Bosphore, Franco-Bulgarian Mixed Arbitral Tribunal, 3 *ibid.*, p. 410 (1925); Gouvernement hellenique *v.* Vulcan Werke, Greco-German Mixed Arbitral Tribunal, 3 *ibid.*, p. 887 (1925).

§165. The North American Dredging Case. Several cases involving the Calvo Clause were decided by the recent Mexican Claims Commissions. The first of these was the *North American Dredging* [10] case before the United States-Mexican General Claims Commission. The claimant had entered into a contract with the Mexican government to dredge a harbor. Article 18 of the contract read as follows:

The contractor and all other persons who, as employees or in any other capacity, may be engaged in the execution of work under this contract, either directly or indirectly, shall be considered as Mexicans in all matters, within the Republic of Mexico, concerning the execution of such work and the fulfilment of this contract. They shall not claim nor shall they have, with regard to the interests and the business connected with this contract, any other rights or means to enforce the same than those granted by the laws of the Republic to Mexicans, nor shall they enjoy any other rights than those established in favor of Mexicans. They are consequently deprived of any rights as aliens, and under no conditions shall the intervention of any foreign diplomatic agents be permitted, in any matter related to this contract.[11]

The United States, on behalf of the Dredging Company, asked for the recovery of damages alleged to have been suffered by the claimant in consequence of various acts of Mexican officials. The Commission assumed that the claim was based merely on a breach of contract; a misleading assumption, which, as will be shown below, resulted in far-reaching consequences. The Commission unanimously sustained a motion by the Mexican agent to dismiss the claim. An alien, it said, may not deprive "the government of his nation of its undoubted right of applying international remedies to violations of

---

[10] U. S. A. (North American Dredging Co.) *v.* United Mexican States, 1927, p. 21. For comments on this case see Borchard, "Decisions of the Claims Commission, United States and Mexico," 20 Amer. Journal of Int. Law (1926), p. 536; Hyde, "Concerning Attempts by Contract to Restrict Interposition," 21 *ibid.* (1927), p. 298; Summers, "The Calvo Clause," 19 Virginia Law Rev. (1933), p. 459; Case note, 27 Columbia Law Rev. (1927), p. 741.

[11] The Spanish text as produced by the American Commissioner in U. S. A. (International Fisheries Co.) *v.* United Mexican States, Opinions of Commissioners, 1931, p. 206, at 260 reads:

"El contratista y todas las personas que como empleados o con cualquier otro carácter, tomaron parte en la construcción de la gran obra objeto de este contrato, directa o indirectamente, serán considerandos como mexicanos en todo lo que se relacione, dentro de la República, con la ejecución de tal obra y con el cumplimiento de este contrato; sin que puedan alegar con respecto a los intereses o negocios relacionados con éste, ni tener otros derechos ni medios de harcerlos valer, que los que las leyes de la República conceden a los mexicanos, ni disfrutar de ostros más que los establecidos a favor de éstos; quedando, en consecuencia, privados de todo derecho de extranjería, y sin que por ningún motivo sea de admitirse la intervención de agentes diplomáticos extranjeros en ningún asunto que se relacione con este contrato."

international law committed to his damage." Article 18 of the contract did not amount to a waiver of the right of the claimant "to apply to his government for protection against the violation of international law (internationally illegal acts) whether growing out of this contract or out of other situations." This clause in the contract is merely a promise by the alien not to invoke or accept "the assistance of his government with respect to the fulfillment of his contract and the execution of his work thereunder." The Calvo Clause, then, is interpreted to be a contractual stipulation to exhaust local remedies within a limited sphere.

§166. **The Same: Interpretation of the Contractual Stipulation.** This interpretation of Article 18 of the contract is a crucial point of the case. The Commission stated emphatically that: "If it were necessary to so construe Article 18 of the contract as to bind the claimant not to apply to its government to intervene diplomatically or otherwise in the event of a denial of justice to the claimant growing out of the contract declared upon or out of any other situation, then this Commission would have no hesitation in holding such a clause void *ab initio* and not binding on the claimant." [12] Such, the Commission thought, was not the meaning of this contractual clause.

"Reading this article as a whole, it is evident that its purpose was to bind the claimant to be governed by the laws of Mexico and to use the remedies existing under such laws. The closing words 'in any matter connected with the contract' must be read in connection with the preceding phrase 'in everything connected with the execution of such work and the fulfillment of this contract' and also in connection with the phrase 'regarding the interests or business connected with this contract.' In other words, in executing the contract, or in putting forth any claim 'regarding the interests or business connected with this contract,' the claimant should be governed by those laws and remedies which Mexico had provided for the protection of its own citizens." [13]

This, it is submitted, is a rather disingenuous construction. Of course, the company agreed to be governed by Mexican law on an equality with Mexican citizens. The first two sentences of Article 18 are clear. But the last sentence states that: "They are consequently deprived of any rights as aliens, and under no conditions shall the

[12] Opinions of Commissioners, 1927, at p. 33.
[13] *Ibid.*, p. 27.

intervention of foreign diplomatic agents be permitted, in any matter related to this contract." It would be absurd to conceive that the intention of the parties was to bar foreign diplomatic agents from intervening in matters before Mexican courts. Diplomatic intervention would normally take place in the event of a denial of justice or "confiscatory" breach of contract, and it seems a perversion of language to say that such a situation would not be the result of matters related to the contract.[14]

§167. The Same: Exhaustion of Local Remedies. Having interpreted Article 18 to be merely a contractual stipulation to exhaust local remedies, the Commission met a real hurdle in the provisions of the Claims Convention. Article V of the Convention reads:

The high contracting parties, being desirous of effecting an equitable settlement of the claims of their respective citizens, thereby affording them just and adequate compensation for their losses or damages, agree that no claim shall be disallowed or rejected by the Commission by the application of the general principle of international law that the legal remedies must be exhausted as a condition precedent to the validity or allowance of any claim.

If all the Calvo Clause requires is an exhaustion of local remedies before invoking diplomatic protection, is not Article V of the Convention decisive in requiring the Commission to take jurisdiction? [15] The Commission bounded over the hurdle with admirable nonchalance. Article V is applicable only to claims which are "rightfully" presented to the claimant's government.[16] Where the claimant by his act of

[14] Dunn, Protection of Nationals, p. 17, offers a theory which would support the General Claims Commission's interpretation: "Private contractors are usually not unwilling to include clauses binding them to have recourse to local remedies in the event of non-performance by the government. But it is hardly to be supposed that this is a conscious, voluntary acceptance by the individual contractor of all the risks of losses arising under the contractual relation, including those which may be brought about by action of the government outside of its rôle as a contracting party. The chances are that the private contractor, in signing a contract containing a Calvo Clause, foresees only those types of possible loss that are commonly associated with the contractual relation in general."

[15] In Rep. française (Georges Pinson) *v.* Etats-Unis mexicains, Jurisprudence de la Commission franco-mexicaine des Réclamations, at p. 24, Presiding Commissioner Verzijl stated by way of *obiter* that the parallel article of the French-Mexican Claims Convention "expressly" excluded the principle of the Calvo Clause.

[16] It is conceivable that the word "rightfully" is here used with a moral rather than a legal connotation. This is strengthened by the language of the Commission throughout the opinion: the claimant "wilfully ignores" his agreement; he had "waived his right to conduct himself as if no competent authorities existed in Mexico; as if he were engaged in fulfilling a contract in an inferior country subject to a system of capitulations." The present writer agrees that a moral argument may have considerable force in view of the provision that the decision is to be "in accordance with the principles of international law,

presentation violates a contractual stipulation with the respondent government, the presentation cannot be called "rightful." The *ratio decidendi* is then stated in language which charmingly mingles legal doctrine and rhetorical argumentation:

> Where a claim is based on an alleged violation of any rule or principle of international law, the Commission will take jurisdiction notwithstanding the existence of such a clause in the contract subscribed by the claimant. But where a claimant has expressly agreed in writing, attested by his signature, that in all matters pertaining to the execution, fulfillment, and interpretation of the contract he will have resort to local tribunals, remedies and authorities, and then wilfully ignores them by applying in such matters to his government, he will be held bound by his contract and the Commission will not take jurisdiction of his claim.[17]

At first glance the principle thus stated has all the merits of compromise. No need to enter into discussion of the extent to which the alien can bind his government. His government cannot be bound. But he has violated a provision of his contract by calling upon his government to intervene and he must suffer the consequences. Unfortunately, the Commission's actions do not fit its words. It holds itself to be without jurisdiction. Yet can a failure to observe a term of a contract vitiate jurisdiction? The question seems to bear its own answer. One must probe deeper to find support for the rule.

To begin with, we need to know how it comes about that the Commission is called upon to decide a case supposedly involving nothing more than a breach of contract. As we have seen[18] the crux of the matter lies in Article V of the Convention which, by obviating the requirement of local redress, permits the Commission to decide cases by resort to municipal law where international law provides for a reference back. Apply this to the *North American Dredging* case. The Dredging Company agreed not to call upon its government before

---

justice and equity." The Commission, however, does not clearly place its holding on such moral grounds. Prof. Borchard doubts whether Article V of the Convention is susceptible of the interpretation given it by the Commission, but thinks the conclusion may be sustained "as a matter of expediency and justice." See Borchard, "Decisions of the Claims Commissions, United States and Mexico," 20 Amer. Journal of International Law (1926), p. 536, at p. 540. Moreover, it does not seem that the Commission was justified in saying that the claimant "wilfully ignored" the agreement since the case came up on motion to dismiss, and the Memorial had alleged the presentation of the claim to various Mexican authorities including the Departments of Hacienda and Communications and Public Works.

[17] Opinions of Commissioners, 1927, p. 31.
[18] *Supra*, p. 178.

exhausting local remedies. Let us accept the Commission's interpretation that this is what the company undertook. The contract is governed by Mexican law, and it is to that law that the Commission must look in deciding whether there has been a breach. The Dredging Company has assumed an obligation *under Mexican law* to exhaust local remedies. It so happens that an international law rule operating between the two governments concerned has the same content. Article V provides that no claim shall be disallowed "by the application of the *general principle of international law* that the legal remedies must be exhausted as a condition precedent to the validity or allowance of any claim." This removes the application of the *international law* principle. The principle of *Mexican law* embodied in the contract still operates as between the claimant and the Mexican government. The result achieved by the Commission is then easily supported by saying that the Commission has no jurisdiction because Article V of the Convention is not applicable, and the logical consequences of the *Illinois Central* case permit jurisdiction to be taken only where the article can be applied.

Such a justification of the rule in the *North American Dredging* case bears the unfortunate stigmata of *ex posto facto* rationalization, but it has at least the merit of making the rule there enunciated something more than a restatement of a settled principle of international law, and the greater merit of avoiding the curious conception of claims "rightfully" presented. It means, however, that the North American Dredging Case can only be applicable in a situation where a Commission functions under a provision like that of Article V.

§168. The Same: Allegations in the Memorial. A more serious defect in the *Dredging* case remains to be considered. It has been mentioned above that the General Claims Commission assumed that the claim was based on breach of contract. This assumption colors the whole of the decision. However, a study of the memorial of the United States shows this assumption to have been wrong. The United States alleged not only a failure of payment by Mexico, but also the stopping of work "by arbitrary orders of the Inspector of the Mexican Federal Government," and the illegal detention of a dredge and some scows.[19] The case came up for decision on the Mexican agency's

[19] This was pointed out by the Mexican Commissioner in his opinion in the International Fisheries Case: "It is worthy of note that in this case as in that of the North American Dredging Company, the American Agency maintained that the question was

motion to dismiss, under which all the allegations of the memorial must be taken as confessed.[20] The failure to take into account these allegations cannot but result in a substantial weakening of the force of the decision.

§169. **Influence of the North American Dredging Case.** Despite the criticism to which the opinion in the *North American Dredging* case is open, it has had an important influence. It has generally been accepted to this extent: a contractual stipulation which purports to bind the claimant not to apply to his government to intervene in the event of a denial of justice or in respect of violations of international law is void, but a contractual stipulation that the local courts shall have exclusive jurisdiction over all matters pertaining to the contract is valid and binding on an international tribunal.[21] This, in effect, is nothing more than a restatement of the well-settled rule that local remedies must be exhausted.[22]

---

not one of non-fulfillment of contract, but one of international delinquency incurred directly by the state, of a denial of justice, of a wrongful act, and thus the memorial of said claim spoke of interruptions to the work owing to *arbitrary orders* given by Mexican officials, of the *wrongful detention* of a dredge and its accessories, and of two launches which were a total loss. Notwithstanding the aspect given to them by the American Agency, the facts were held by this Commission to be matters relating to the contract to which the North American Dredging Company of Texas was a party." Opinions of Commissioners, 1931, p. 220.

[20] United Mexican States (El Emporio del Cafe) *v.* U. S. A., Opinions of Commissioners, 1927, p. 7.

[21] The League of Nations Preparatory Committee for the Conference on Progressive Codification of International Law sent out a questionnaire to various governments containing the question: "What are the conditions which must be fulfilled when the individual concerned has contracted not to have recourse to the diplomatic remedy?" The British Government replied: "His Majesty's Government in Great Britain accept as good law and are content to be guided by the decision of the Claims Commission between the United States of America and Mexico in the case of the North American Dredging Company of Texas of March 31st, 1926, printed in the volume of the 'Opinions of Commissioners,' page 21. It is laid down in this opinion that a stipulation in a contract which purports to bind the claimant not to apply to his Government to intervene diplomatically or otherwise in the event of a denial of justice or in the event of any violation of the rules or principles of international law is void, and that any stipulation which purports to bind the claimant's Government not to intervene in respect of violations of international law is void, but that no rule of international law prevents the inclusion of a stipulation in a contract between a Government and an alien that in all matters pertaining to the contract the jurisdiction of the local tribunals shall be complete and exclusive, nor does it prevent such a stipulation being obligatory in the absence of any special agreement to the contrary between the two Governments concerned, upon any international tribunal to which may be submitted a claim arising out of the contract in which the stipulation is inserted." Conference for the Codification of International Law, Responsibility of States for Damage Caused in Their Territory to the Person or Property of Foreigners, League of Nations Document C. 75. M. 69. 1929. V, p. 134. And see Eagleton, Responsibility of States, p. 175, note 43, where it is said that the Dredging case opinion "seems to offer the most complete exposition of the Calvo Clause in contracts which has yet been made."

[22] In consequence, Eagleton says that the Calvo Clause "must be regarded as a superfluous statement of the rules upon which responsibility is founded." Responsibility of States, p. 168.

§170. The International Fisheries Case. The *International Fisheries* case [23] also arose before the General Claims Commission. A contract-concession, containing a Calvo Clause [24] essentially similar to that involved in the *Dredging* case, had been concluded with a Mexican company, La Pescadora, S. A., in which the claimant owned 985 out of the 1000 shares. The concession had been cancelled by the Mexican Government in 1917 in reliance on a provision in the concession. The American agent argued that the Calvo Clause was not binding on the claimant because it had been agreed to by a Mexican national and not by it, and that the cancellation of the contract constituted an arbitrary act and a denial of justice. The Commission (with the American Commissioner dissenting) dismissed the claim for lack of jurisdiction. It pierced the corporate veil to hold that the claimant was bound by the agreement made by La Pescadora, and it found that under the contract the Mexican government could properly cancel the contract by administrative decree. There was no denial of justice, it felt, since judicial remedies were open to the claimant.

§171. The Mexican Union Railway Case. The *Mexican Union Railway* case [25] before the British-Mexican Commission is more interesting. The claimant constructed and operated a railway under a concession from the Mexican government, containing the following clause:

The Company shall always be a Mexican Company even though any or all of its members should be aliens, and it shall be subject exclusively to the jurisdiction of the courts of the Republic of Mexico in all matters whose cause and right of action shall arise within the territory of said Republic. The said Company and all aliens and successors of such aliens having any interests in its business, whether as shareholders, employees or in any other capacity, shall be considered as Mexicans in everything relating to said company. They shall never be entitled to assert, in regard to any titles and business connected with the company, any rights of alienage under any pretext whatso-

<hr>

[23] U. S. A. (International Fisheries Co.) *v.* United Mexican States, Opinions of Commissioners, 1931, p. 207.
[24] "The Concessionary Company or whosoever shall succeed in its rights, even though all or some of its members may be aliens, shall be subject to the jurisdiction of the Courts of the Republic in all matters the cause and action of which take place within its territory. It shall never claim, with respect to matters connected with this contract, any rights as an alien, under any form whatsoever, and shall enjoy only the rights and measures for enforcing them that the laws of the Republic afford to Mexicans, foreign diplomatic agents being unable therefore, to intervene in any manner with relation to the said matters."
[25] Decisions and Opinions of Commissioners, p. 157.

ever. They shall only have such rights and means of asserting them as the laws of the Republic grant to Mexicans, and foreign diplomatic agents may consequently not intervene in any manner whatsoever.[26]

The claimant alleged a long series of acts resulting in loss, including lack of protection, depredations by government and rebel forces, forced acceptance of paper currency, requisitions, and arbitrary threats to cancel the concession. A majority of the Commission allowed a motion to dismiss.

The decision is largely based on the *Dredging* case, the considerations of which the Commission enthusiastically adopted "not thinking it necessary to repeat them, or possible to express them better." Yet, the Commission stated that it was aware that this case differed in some respects. The differences are striking. The claim is based, not on a breach of contract, but on revolutionary acts. There is no necessity here of resorting to Mexican law; the acts alleged, if proven, would clearly result in an award in favor of the claimant. The Commission admits that some of these acts "may in themselves constitute a breach of international law." "But even if this were so, the Commissioners cannot see that it would justify the ignoring of Article 11 (the Calvo Clause). It is one of the recognized rules of International Law that the responsibility of the State under International Law can only commence when the persons concerned have availed themselves of all remedies open to them under the national laws of the State in question." But Article 6 of the Convention expressly excludes the rule of local redress in the following terms:

The Government of Mexico being desirous of reaching an equitable agreement in regard to the claims specified in article 3 and of granting to the claimants just compensation for the losses or damages they may have sustained, it is agreed that the Commission shall not set aside or reject any claim on the grounds that all legal remedies have not been exhausted prior to the presentation of such claim.

[26] The Spanish text reads:
"La empresa será siempre mexicana aún cuando todos o algunos de sus miembros fueron extranjeros y estará sujeta exclusivamente a la jurisdicción de los Tribunales de la República Mexicana en todos los negocios cuya causa y acción tengan lugar dentro de su territorio. Ella misma y todos los extranjeros y los sucesores de éstos que tomaran parte en sus negocios, sea como accionistas, empleados o con cualquier otro carácter, serán considerados como mexicanos en todo cuanto a ella se refiera. Nunca podrán alegar respecto de los títulos y negocios relacionados con la empresa, derechos de extranjería bajo cualquier pretexto que sea. Sólo tendrán los derechos y medios de hacerlos valer que las leyes de la República conceden a los Mexicanos, y por consiguiente no podrán tener ingerencia alguna los Agentes Diplomáticos extranjeros."

Following blindly in the footsteps of the General Claims Commission, the opinion of the majority can only say that this article does not apply because the claim was not "rightfully" presented. It is to be noted that not even the theory of two rules of local redress, one of international law and one of Mexican law, which we invoked to support the *Dredging* case [27] can be applied here. The General Claims Convention provides for a waiver "of the general principle of international law that the legal remedies must be exhausted." The British-Mexican Convention directs the Commission categorically not to set aside or reject any claim "on the grounds that all legal remedies have not been exhausted."

Furthermore, the wording of the Calvo Clause in the Mexican Railway contract was much broader than in the Dredging company contract. The latter had forbidden recourse to diplomatic intervention "in any matter related to the contract." The General Claims Commission was able to support the validity of the clause by interpreting it to be an agreement not to request diplomatic intervention in matters pertaining to the execution, fulfillment and enforcement of the contract. The Calvo Clause of the Mexican Railway contract included "all matters whose cause and right of action shall arise within the territory" of Mexico, "everything relating to" the company, and "any titles and business connected with the company." The Commission accepts the *Dredging* case dictum that a Calvo Clause which was intended to bar all recourse to diplomatic intervention would be void *ab initio*. But it saw no essential difference between the two Calvo Clauses. On this point the British Commissioner, dissenting, stated:

"It appears to me impossible to doubt, from the terms of Article 11 of the contract, that it was the intention of the Mexican Government to prevent the claimant's government from interfering diplomatically or otherwise in any case in which the company might have suffered loss in relation to its existence, business, or property, even though such loss had arisen through breach of the rules or principles of international law." [28]

If this interpretation is the correct one, then it is clear that, accepting the applicability of the *Dredging* case dictum, the clause in the contract is invalid. And, if it were possible to limit the scope of the clause to the contract itself as was done in the *Dredging* case,

---

[27] See *supra*, p. 191.
[28] Decisions and Opinions of Commissioners at p. 170.

then the case would be decided in favor of the claimant, since the claim is not based on breach of contract but on damage caused by revolutionary acts.

§172. Other Calvo Clause Cases in the British-Mexican Commission. The *Mexican Railway* decision was followed by the British-Mexican Commission in two other cases [29] involving Calvo Clauses identical with that in the first case. One of the cases [30] shows that the Clause may be a bar even when the claimant does not "wilfully ignore" it. The claimant had strictly complied with Mexican law; it had applied to the Department of Hacienda, had waited six years without result, and had then filed a claim with the National Claims Commission. At the time of decision by the British-Mexican Commission the claim had been pending about a year and a half. It was held that this delay did not constitute a denial of justice and the claim was dismissed. A later case,[31] however, showed that some limitations were to be applied. The claimant had applied to the National Claims Commission which had failed to render an award after nine years. It was held that this was such a delay as constituted a denial of justice, and a motion to dismiss was denied.

One more case [32] remains to be considered. A concession granted by a Mexican municipality contained the following clause:

The concessionaries, or the company which they may organize, may transfer their rights to another company or to an individual with the approval of the corporation, under the precise condition that the business will preserve its Mexican character and without rights of foreigners, even if it may be sustained by foreign capital.

A majority of the Commission disallowed a motion to dismiss on two grounds: (1) that the wording of this clause did not clearly reveal an intention to stipulate a Calvo Clause,[33] (2) that the Mexican government had nothing to do with the concession and could not derive rights from a contract to which it was not a party.

§173. The Pitol Case. The Italian-Mexican Commission was pre-

---

[29] Case of the Vera Cruz (Mexico) Railway, Ltd., Further Decisions and Opinions, p. 207; Case of the Interoceanic Railway of Mexico, *ibid.*, p. 118.

[30] The Interoceanic Railway case, *supra*, note 29.

[31] Case of El Oro Mining and Railway Co., Further Decisions and Opinions, p. 141.

[32] Case of Douglas G. Collie MacNeill, Further Decisions and Opinions, p. 21.

[33] "The majority holds the view that a so-called Calvo Clause to be respected in international jurisprudence, must be drafted in such a way as not to allow any doubt as to the intentions of both parties." *Id.*, at p. 24.

sented in the *Pitol* case [33a] with a Calvo Clause situation of an unusual character. The claimant had acquired land in Mexico as a colonist under a contract with the government, in which he agreed to cultivate the land for ten years, at the end of which time he became full owner of the land. This contract was concluded by virtue of the General Colonization Law of 1883 which contained the following provision (Article 13):

"The colonists shall be considered as having all the rights and obligations which the Federal Constitution imposes on Mexicans and aliens respectively, and shall enjoy the temporary exemptions provided by the present law; but in all questions which may arise, they shall be of the class which remains subject to the decisions of the courts of the Republic, with absolute exclusion of all foreign intervention." [33b]

The ten year period provided in the contract had expired and the claimant had become the owner of the land. Claim was made for losses suffered through depredations by revolutionary forces.

The majority of the Commission had so little doubt that the statutory provision was an effective bar to its jurisdiction that it did not even stop to discuss it. Its sole concern was as to whether the Calvo Clause undertaking survived the expiration of the ten year colonization period. It held that the status imposed by Article 13 of the statute was a permanent one and that it had no jurisdiction. The question of the duration of the Calvo Clause obligation need not concern us here; it is a pure question of Mexican law. The question of the effectiveness of the Clause as a bar to international reclamation is another matter. Superficially the holding seems out of line with the dicta of the other Mexican Claims Commissions. The Calvo Clause is as broad as it could possibly be; "all questions which may arise" are covered by it. The injury done is clearly one for which Mexico is liable under the Convention. Yet it is necessary to point out the distinguishing fact—this was a case in which the claimant had received a special privilege, that of colonizing on government land. As a price of the privilege it might well be held that Mexico could require such a promise as was made. This is quite different from the attempt which

---

[33a] Case of Ornato Pitol, Decision No. 107 (unpublished).

[33b] "Los colonos serán considerados con todos los derechos y obligaciones que a los mexicanos y a los extranjeros, en su caso, concede e impone la Constitución Federal, gozando de las exenciones temporales que les otorga la presente ley; pero en todas las cuestiones que se susciten, sean de la clase que fueren quedarán sujetos a las decisiones de los tribunales de la República, con absoluta exclusión de toda intervención extraña."

was formerly made by Mexico to impose its nationality on aliens acquiring any land in the country. Here the land was acquired from the government as a special favor.

§174. **Arguments in Support of the Calvo Clause.** The foregoing discussion of the Calvo Clause cases in the Mexican Claims Commission has been limited to a criticism of the decisions on logical grounds. All these cases have proceeded from the premise that the intention of the parties was to restate the rule of exhaustion of local remedies. There remains the larger question of the validity of a Calvo Clause which attempts to achieve the result which is really desired, *viz.*, to obviate any appeal at all to diplomatic intervention. The decisions we have discussed follow the weight of international opinion to the effect that such a clause is invalid. This opinion, it is believed, has not been sufficiently sympathetic to the case which may be made out in favor of the Calvo Clause. There can be no question that international claims have not infrequently been used as a pretext to advance imperialistic ambitions. A country like Mexico may not possess the capital requisite to exploit its natural resources. It permits aliens to come into the country for that purpose, but the interests of its people require that some protection be afforded against an unregulated servitude to foreign capital.[34] The Calvo Clause is perhaps the only means of protection available. Mexico could keep out aliens altogether. Why should she not be able to let them in on condition that they be treated in all respects like nationals?[35] And

---

[34] An illustration of the importance which some governments attach to the Calvo Clause may be found in the statement in the Mexican Union Railway case that the question of the Calvo Clause was a vital one to the Mexican government, and that if the Commission should take jurisdiction, the Mexican government would register a protest against such decision and would make a reservation as to its rights. Decisions and Opinions of Commissioners, p. 173.

[35] "States possessing great natural resources which they are desirous to see developed, or wishing to improve the means of communication between different parts of the country, or to promote the exploitation of public services may follow different methods.

"They can, when faced with a decision as to what persons or concerns a concession is to be given make no discrimination whatever between aliens and nationals, and impose no special conditions when dealing with the former. They may also reserve the exploitation of the wealth of the country and of public services for their own subjects and decline to give interests of vital importance into the hands of the subjects of foreign governments. And they may in the third place consider that they must not deprive their country of the advantages accruing from the investment of foreign capital and from foreign technical knowledge, and yet at the same time see to it that the presence of huge foreign interests within their boundaries does not increase their international vulnerability.

"It is this third method which has been chosen by the Mexican Republic." Case of the Mexican Union Railway Co., Decisions and Opinions of Commissioners, at p. 160.

where the alien has expressly agreed to the condition why should he not abide by his agreement?

§175. **Arguments Opposed to the Calvo Clause.** To this argument, international lawyers have opposed two others. Only states can have rights and duties under international law. The right of interposition in the event of a violation of international law is a right of the alien's state. In the nature of things, he cannot by his agreement, deprive his state of that right. Even if we accept the orthodox theory that individuals may not have rights and duties under international law, this argument does not seem a complete answer. The law of international claims is replete with inherent contradictions, rules which do take into account the position of the individual claimant in spite of the fact that the state is theoretically the only claimant. It is submitted, that the desire for logical symmetry should not be sufficient to overcome the desire for self-protection which the Calvo Clause embodies. The second argument is based on policy. International law has laboriously constructed a series of rules designed to protect aliens from injury. The community of nations has a great interest in providing for some measure of freedom of movement of aliens. If a state were permitted to impose whatever conditions it chose on the admission of aliens into its territory the result might well be a destruction of these rules and a frustration of the interests of the international community.[36]

As far as Calvo Clauses in statutes are concerned, *i.e.*, imposition of national status without the express consent of the alien, this argument is certainly compelling. Even in cases of contracts for the rendering of services, as in the *Dredging* case, the same argument should control. But is not the situation different with respect to concessions? Here the argument based on protection of national resources is of great potency. Should not an international tribunal be much more reluctant to invalidate a Calvo Clause in a concession than in an ordinary commercial contract? It is on this basis, perhaps, that the *Mexican Union Railways* case is to be sustained. The question of the validity of the Calvo Clause should not be answered categorically for

---

[36] An analogy may be found in American law. A state of the United States may refuse to admit the corporations of other states, or it may admit them on conditions. But certain conditions, *e.g.*, that the corporation shall not remove suits brought against it to the federal courts, are "unconstitutional," even though stipulated in a contract. Home Insurance Co. *v.* Morse, 20 Wall. 445 (1874); Barron *v.* Burnside, 121 U. S. 186 (1887); Southern Pacific Co. *v.* Denton, 146 U. S. 202 (1892).

all cases. Each case should be treated on its merits with particular regard to the subject matter of the contract.

§176. **Limitation of the Calvo Clause Decisions of the Mexican Claims Commissions.** One thing more. Both the General Claims Commission and the British-Mexican Commission agreed that a Calvo Clause which attempted to prevent diplomatic intervention in all circumstances would be void *ab initio*. Such a rule may be applicable under a convention which contains a waiver of the rule of local redress; that is, if the Clause is valid then local remedies must be exhausted despite the waiver in the convention, whereas the waiver remains operative if the Clause is void. Stated as a general rule it would be meaningless If all any Calvo Clause can do is to restate the general rule of local redress, then whether or not the Clause is void, local remedies must nevertheless be exhausted before an international tribunal could render an award, if the convention does not contain a waiver.

CHAPTER 11

RELATION OF THE INTERNATIONAL COMMISSIONS TO THE NATIONAL CLAIMS COMMISSION

§177. History of the National Claims Commission. The efforts of Mexico to dispose of claims through a National Claims Commission have already been adverted to. Some of the international commissions were confronted with the problem of the scope of their jurisdiction over claims which had previously been presented to the National Commission.[1] A sketch of the history of the National Commission is of interest in connection with this problem.

§178. The Consultative Commission of 1911. The "Convention" of Ciudad Juarez of May 21, 1911,[2] by which Diaz had renounced the presidency had provided that the new government would accord indemnities for damages caused directly by the revolution. The first "Law of Claims" was enacted on May 31, 1911,[3] directing the Executive to appoint a commission to consider claims for indemnification in consequence of the revolution. A decree of June 30, 1911,[4] set up a Consultative Commission to take charge "of the examination and elucidation of claims . . . and to consult with the Department of Finance with reference to the legal foundation or non-foundation of said claim, and upon the amount of indemnity, if any, to which claimants may be entitled." This Commission worked very slowly and only a single indemnity was paid during the Madero régime.[5]

§179. The Decree of Monclova. The Huerta *coup d'état* swept

---

[1] This problem does not seem to have arisen in the United States-Mexican Commissions. However, the United States-Mexican General Claims Commission held that though the fact of the pendency of a similar claim before a Mexican court was apparent on the face of the record it did not "necessarily follow as a legal conclusion" that the claim did not fall within the jurisdiction of the General Claims Commission. U. S. A. (Pine King Land and Lumber Co.) *v.* United Mexican States, Opinions of Commissioners, 1927, p. 4.

[2] Text in Mariano Salas, *Defensa de México* (Mexico 1920), p. 59.

[3] Text in Salas, *op. cit.*, p. 61.

[4] English translation in 1912, Foreign Relations, p. 934.

[5] See *supra,* p. 16.

the Consultative Commission into the discard. The next step was th
Decree of Monclova of May 10, 1913,[6] issued by General Carranza
First Chief of the Constitutionalist Army. This decree acknowledge
the right of all nationals and foreigners to enter claims for damage
sustained during the revolution of 1910 (more specifically from No
vember 21, 1910, to May 31, 1911) and for damages which they migh
suffer from February 19, 1913, until the constitutional order shoul
be restored. In addition, foreigners were granted the right to mak
claim for the payment of damages caused to them by revolutionar
forces between May 31, 1911, and February 19, 1913. The decre
provided for the establishment of a commission of Mexican citizen
to pass on claims when Carranza should assume the Executive Powei
and stated that at that time, Carranza would confer with the foreig
diplomatic representatives with a view to setting up mixed commis
sions to pass on the claims of foreigners.

§180. **The Law of Claims of 1917.** The Decree of Monclova wa
carried out by the enactment of the Law of Claims of November 21
1917.[7] This created a commission under the Department of the Treas
ury, consisting of five Mexican citizens appointed by the President
The commission was to accept only such claims as were based or
damages caused by: (1) revolutionary forces or forces recognized
as such by the legitimate governments established upon the triumpl
of the respective revolutions; (2) by forces of the before-mentione
governments in the performance of their duties and during the struggl
against rebels; (3) by forces of the Federal Army up to the time o
its dissolution. After a claim had been decided by the commission
it was to be placed before the President of the Republic for fina
decision. In the case of foreign claimants who objected to the finding
of the commission, the findings were to be submitted for arbitratiot
to three persons, one to be appointed by the President of Mexico
another by the diplomatic representative of the claimant's country
and the third by the two persons so selected. The decision of the arbi
tral commission was to be final.

§181. **The Decree of August 30, 1919.** This law was supersede
by the Decree of August 30, 1919,[8] which retained the main provi

[6] Text in Salas, *op. cit.*, p. 66; English translation in 1914, Foreign Relations, p. 656.
[7] Text in Salas, *op. cit.*, p. 69; English translation in 1918, Foreign Relations, p. 793.
[8] Text in Salas, *op. cit.*, p. 75.

ions of the Law of 1917 and also required the commission to accept
laims for losses caused by outlaws (*foragidos*) or rebels, provided
hat it be proved that the loss was caused in consequence of an act,
:nity or omission imputable to the legitimate authorities. It was also
rovided that the arbitral commissions which were to pass on claims
f foreigners were to have cognizance only of the case for which they
vere appointed except where the Executive should conclude interna-
ional conventions for the formation of permanent mixed commissions.

The commission established under the Law of 1919 continued to
xist beyond the Obregón revolution under the name of the National
Claims Commission. By a decree of July 29, 1924,[9] its jurisdiction
vas extended to include losses caused by acts of forces serving under
he Conventionist government from the time of the disavowal of the
'irst Chief of the Constitutionalist Army until June 30, 1920, and
)sses caused by acts of mutinies, mobs, or insurrectionists distinct
rom the forces mentioned, from November 20, 1910, to June 30,
920, provided that it be proved that the authorities omitted to grant
rotection to the claimant or acted with lenity.

§182. **Provisions in the Claims Conventions.** The National
Claims Commission had thus been in existence for a number of years
vhen the Claims Conventions were concluded. It should have been
bvious that some provision defining the relations between the Na-
ional Claims Commission and the international Commission was nec-
ssary. Yet, only in the German-Mexican Convention was any pro-
ision made. Article XII of that Convention provided as follows:

Claims submitted by German nationals to the National Claims Commision in accordance with the decree of August 30, 1919, and the regulations
1 execution thereof, shall be subject to the following provisions:

I. In so far as they have been decided upon and not disputed by the
laimants within the time-limit fixed by the law, they shall come under Ar-
icle IX of the present arrangement and their payment shall be regulated in
ccordance with the terms of Article X.

II. In so far as they have been decided upon but have been disputed by
he claimants in virtue of Article XII of said decree, they shall, in execu-
ion of that decree, be submitted for confirmation, modification or annul-
ent to the decision of the Commission appointed in accordance with the
resent arrangement.

[9] *Diario Oficial,* Aug. 7, 1924.

III. In so far as they are under consideration and not yet decided upon they shall be submitted to the Commission established by the present arrangement and be subject to the terms of this arrangement.

Thus, claims decided by the National Claims Commission and not disputed by the claimants were to be considered as final; claims decided but disputed by the claimants were to be submitted to the German-Mexican Commission for confirmation, modification or annulment; pending claims were to be treated in all respects as claims not submitted to the National Claims Commissions. The reference in paragraph 2 of Article XII of the decree of 1919 is interesting. That article had provided that claims of foreigners decided by the National Commission should be submitted to an arbitration commission if objection was made. Evidently, the Claims Convention envisaged that the German-Mexican Commission was in substitution of the arbitral commission provided for in the law.

§183. **Problems before the German–Mexican Commission** Few problems of any consequence arose from this provision of the German-Mexican Convention. In a number of cases the Commission was called upon to decide whether the claimant had properly entered an objection to the decision of the National Claims Commission.[10] It held that the decision could not be upset if the claimant had not entered an objection in accordance with the terms of the Mexican law. In a case where a claim had been dismissed by the National Commission, the German agent argued that the words "and their payment shall be regulated in accordance with the terms of Article X" in paragraph 1 of Article XII of the Convention indicated that paragraph 1 was applicable only to cases in which the National Commission had made an award and the amount of this was contested. This contention was rejected, and it was held that paragraph 1 applied to cases where the National Commission had dismissed the claim as well as where it had rendered an allegedly inadequate award.[11] In two cases[12] the National Commission had fixed the amount of damages

---

[10] Rep. Alemana (Guillermo Fink) v. Estados Unidos Mexicanos, Decision No. 12 (unpublished); Rep. Alemana (Peters y Cía.) v. Estados Unidos Mexicanos, Decision No. 4 (unpublished).
[11] Rep. Alemana (Ernesto Tillman) v. Estados Unidos Mexicanos, Decision No. 1 (unpublished).
[12] Rep. Alemana (Peters y Cía.) v. Estados Unidos Mexicanos, Decision No. 4 (unpublished); Rep. Alemana (Luis Andresen y Carlos Hardt), Decision No. 7 (unpublished).

but had held that the claimants were Mexicans. The claimants had properly objected to the decision on their nationality, but had entered no objection to the amount of damages fixed. The German-Mexican Commission held that it had no competence to pass on the abstract question of nationality of the claimants, and that the amount of damages not having been objected to, the decision of the National Commission was *res judicata*.[13]

§184. **Attitude of the German–Mexican Commission towards Decisions of the National Commission.** In view of the close connection established by the Convention between the National Commission and the German-Mexican Commission, it is surprising to find cases in which the latter passed upon claims dismissed by the National Commission without giving any weight expressly to the decision of that Commission.[14] This is in decided contrast to the practice of other Commissions whose Conventions contained no reference to the National Commission. An exception is to be found in the *Rau* case.[15] The National Commission had made an award on one of the elements of the claim to which the claimant objected as being inadequate. The Mexican agent contended that although the National Commission had approved part of the claim, the German-Mexican Commission should examine and evaluate the evidence furnished by the claimant on this point *de novo* and render its own decision. The Commission held that, although it was dissatisfied with the evidence furnished, the sum approved by the National Commission should, "in equity" be included in the total sum awarded.

§185. **The Problem before the First French–Mexican Commission.** The French-Mexican Commission was faced with the problem of its relation to the National Claims Commission in the first case

---

[13] "The Commission was not established for the purpose of declaring nationality in the abstract, but in order to judge losses or damages, and it may deal with nationality only in order to determine whether the claimant had German nationality, an indispensable prerequisite for establishing the claim. If it were considered possible to divide the decision of the National Commission into a part objected to and a part not objected to, this Mixed Commission would, in the present case, have to limit itself to deciding on the nationality of the claimants, a matter with which it would deal only in connection with a claim for losses or damages, which is not the real case here." Presiding Commissioner Cruchaga in Rep. Alemana (Luis Andresen y Carlos Hardt) *v.* Estados Unidos Mexicanos, *supra,* note 12.

[14] See, *e.g.,* Rep. Alemana (Laura Z. Vda. de Plehn) *v.* Estados Unidos Mexicanos, Decision No. 12 (unpublished); Rep. Alemana (Juan Andresen) *v.* Estados Unidos Mexicanos, Decision No. 20 (unpublished).

[15] Rep. Alemana (Enrique Rau) *v.* Estados Unidos Mexicanos, Decision No. 51 (unpublished).

presented for its decision.[16] The Convention contained no reference to the National Commission. Consequently, the Mexican agent argued that no relation at all existed and that every claim submitted must be examined *de novo*. It was urged that the findings of the National Commission were not judicial decisions since they were subject to the approval or disapproval of the President of the Republic and that the National Commission was nothing more than an administrative tribunal.[17] On the other hand, the French agent contended that a very close connection existed between the two, based on the history of the negotiation of the Convention. Indeed, he argued that the French-Mexican Commission was a tribunal of appeal from the National Commission and that the provisions of the Mexican Federal Code of Civil Procedure applied.[18] Article 424 of this Code provided that: "If a judgment or decree should consist of several propositions, a party may consent with respect to one or more and appeal with respect to the others. In such case, the appellate court shall decide only on the propositions appealed from." If this provision were applicable, the position of the French agent would have been extremely comfortable. The Commission would have been able to decide only those parts of decisions of the National Commission with which the French claimant was dissatisfied.

The Commission rejected both these alternatives. The majority [19] found from an examination of the history of the Conventions that a connection did exist between the National Commission and the French-Mexican Commissions.[20] The international Conventions were the final realization of the program announced by the Decree of Monclova, but these Conventions have worked a sort of novation. "The procedure provided by the Convention and the Rules of Procedure present the essential characteristics of a new examination of the claims in all their aspects, on the basis of a perfect equality of the two parties litigant, and it excludes any idea of a procedure under which, as the

[16] Rép. française (Georges Pinson) *v.* Etats-Unis mexicains, Jurisprudence de la commission franco-mexicaine des réclamations, p. 1.

[17] *Id.*, at pp. 6, 7.

[18] *Id.*, at p. 17 *et seq.*

[19] The majority consisted of the Presiding Commissioner and the French Commissioner. The Mexican Commissioner took the position that the findings of the National Claims Commission were to be treated in all respects like the decisions of a court and that they could only be upset if they involved a denial of justice. See *id.*, at p. 7.

[20] This conclusion was based mainly on the fact that the circular telegram sent out by Mexico on July 12, 1921, to various governments referred to the Carranza decrees. For the history of the negotiation of the claims conventions see Chapter 2.

Mexican agent has well characterized it, the international Commission would be an automaton only able to open its mouth when the French agent permitted it." [21] The conclusion was then drawn that though the French-Mexican Commission could not be bound by the decisions of the National Commission, it would give great weight to the latter.

"As regards the points which have found a solution in the Claims Convention, such as: the enumeration of the persons and associations which have a standing to present themselves as claimants before the French-Mexican Commission, the conditions on which the admissibility of the claim depend, the list of authors of damages for which Mexico has *ex gratia* assumed responsibility, the revolutionary period which the Convention embraces and the basis on which the decisions of the Commission must rest, the Convention is decisive, and France cannot invoke in its favor . . . the fact that with regard to one of these points the National Commission has decided in a particular way.

"The same is true with regard to those points which are regulated in the Rules of Procedure. . . . Nevertheless, as regards other points, the fact that a lower tribunal has already examined the claims can and should have a considerable interest for our Commission. This is particularly the case with regard to evidence introduced by claimants in support of their claim and accepted as convincing proof by the National Commission. . . . Since the National Commission has always decided at a time which is closer to the revolutionary events than the French-Mexican Commission; since the former was able to use all elements of information which might neutralize the evidence produced in favor of the claim; since in passing on a claim, the National Commission generally undertook a minute examination of the facts and since the possibility of decisions unduly favorable to foreign claimants is highly unlikely, the findings of the national tribunal . . . necessarily have a very considerable persuasive force." [22]

§186. Attitude of the First French–Mexican Commission towards the Decisions of the National Commission.

But, it is to be noted that in spite of this language, the majority of the Commission did not conceive that its sole concern with the decisions of the National Commission was to take them into account for their persuasive force. The Presiding Commissioner considered the Commission to be a tribunal of "revision" using the latter term "in an indeterminate sense, without technical color, and only in order to indicate that

---

[21] Presiding Commissioner Verzjil in the Pinson case, *supra,* at p. 18.
[22] *Id.,* at pp. 21–22.

the French-Mexican Commission is sometimes called upon to enter into a new examination of certain claims on which there already exists a decision of an inferior tribunal." [23] Nevertheless, the practice of the Commission in drawing up the operative part of several decisions shows that it used the term "revision" in a rather more technical sense. Thus the operative part of the decision in the *Pinson* case reads in part: "The Commission . . . II. Confirms, *en instance de révision,* the findings of the National Claims Commission . . . in so far as they had declared proven the materiality of the facts alleged by the claimant in support of his claim; II. Modifies the said findings in the sense that not only that part of the damages imputable to the Constitutionalist forces, but also that imputable to the Zapatist forces, are to be included in the category of damages giving rise to indemnity, and the sum of the latter should be increased." [24]

§187. **The Problem before the Reorganized French–Mexican Commission.** After the French-Mexican Commission was reorganized under the supplementary Convention of August 2, 1930, the problem arose again in one of the cases which had been passed on by the previous Commission. Claim was made on account of depredations committed by Constitutionalist forces in 1914 and by Zapatista forces in 1915. The National Claims Commission had decided that the acts of these forces entailed the responsibility of Mexico and awarded 85,500 pesos. The first French-Mexican Commission awarded 100,000 pesos ("par reformation du dictamen de la Commission Nationale"). [25] This decision was not recognized as binding by the Convention of 1930 and the case came up for decision before the reorganized French-Mexican Commission which stated that there was nothing in the Convention which required it to follow the decisions of the National Claims Commission. Under the Convention of 1930 Mexico was not liable for acts of Zapatista forces and therefore only 40,000 pesos for dam-

---

[23] *Id.,* at p. 19.

[24] *Id.,* at p. 141. *Cf.* the following forms adopted for the operative part of decisions: "The Commission . . . decides *par réformation du dictamen de la Commission Nationale* . . . ," Rep. française (Succession de Mme. Veuve Matty) *v.* Etats-Unis mexicains, Sentence No. 43 (unpublished, Mexican Commissioner absent), and Rep. française (Pablo Nájera) *v.* Etats-Unis mexicains, Jurisprudence de la Commission franco-mexicaine des réclamations, p. 156, at 226; "The Commission decides *de reformer la dictamen de la Commission Nationale des réclamations* . . . ," Rep. française (Etienne Albrand) *v.* Etats-Unis mexicains, Sentence No. 46 (unpublished, Mexican Commissioner absent).

[24] Rep. française (Succession de Mme. Veuve Matty) *v.* Etats-Unis mexicains, Sentence No. 43 (unpublished, Mexican Commissioner absent).

ages caused by the Constitutionalists would be awarded.[26] This decision was clearly proper under the Convention of 1930, but the Commission perhaps said more than it desired with respect to its complete independence from the decisions of the National Claims Commission. In a subsequent case the claimant asked for the execution of an award in the amount of 5,000 pesos rendered by the National Commissions. The French-Mexican Commission awarded 5,000 pesos "attendu que, dans des cas semblables, les commissions mexicano-allemande et mexicano-anglaise ont confirmé les decisions [of the National Claims Commission] et ont ordonné le paiement des sommes allouées."[27] This reference to the German-Mexican Commission is not in point since the German-Mexican Convention made express provision for the treatment of decisions of the National Commission. Nor is the reference to the British-Mexican Commission correct. As will be seen below, that Commission did not "confirm" decisions of the National Commission and "order payment of the sums awarded." In two cases it adopted the view taken by the National Commission and awarded similar amounts.

§188. The Problem before the Italian–Mexican Commission. The Mexican agent before the Italian-Mexican Commission advanced the contention that in cases where the National Claims Commission had rendered an award which had not yet received the approval of the President of Mexico, the international Commission had no jurisdiction because of the operation of the principle of litispendence. The international Commission could only acquire jurisdiction if the claimant withdrew his claim before the National Commission. This argument was disposed of by the Italian-Mexican Commission with the observation that the Convention contained no reference to the National Commission and that its jurisdiction over claims coming within the Convention was plenary.[28] At the same time it strongly stressed its readiness to take into consideration the decisions of the National Commission, even though not bound by them.[29] More than that, it

---

[26] Case of Mme. Beaurang Veuve Matty, Decision No. 117 (unpublished).

[27] Case of Samuel Blum, Sentence No. 64 (unpublished).

[28] Case of Vincenzo y Lorenzo Vecchio, Decision No. 63 (unpublished); case of Bello Hermanos, Decision No. 64 (unpublished).

[29] Case of Alfonso Pelfini, Francesso Martiniani y Mariano A. Gregori, Decision No. 42 (unpublished): "Esta Comisión Mixta habrá de tomar en cuenta los antecedents que hayan servido a las Comisiones Nacionales para formar su concepto y habrá de considerar los opiniones que sobre ellos hayan emitido y los juicios que se hayan formado

readily admitted in evidence the records of claims submitted to the National Commission.[30] In only two cases did it refuse to give any weight to decisions of the National Commission. In one of these the reason was that no grounds for the decision had been set forth; [31] in the other the National Commission had rendered an award holding Mexico responsible for acts of Huerta forces, whereas the Italian-Mexican Commission had adopted the view that Mexico was not responsible for such acts.[32]

§189. The Problem before the British–Mexican Commission. When the same question arose before the British-Mexican Commission, the Mexican agent adopted a somewhat different standpoint.[33] This was a case in which the National Claims Commission had rendered a decision to which the claimant had expressly agreed. The Mexican agent moved to dismiss on the ground that the Commission was incompetent. He argued that the decision of the National Commission was *res judicata* and that the claimant could not now claim compensation for losses or damages but only the execution of a judgment which fell outside the competence of the British-Mexican Commission. The majority of the Commission, in disallowing the motion, took the view that the absence of any clause in the convention establishing a connection between the two Commissions meant that no such connection existed. "In this respect the Convention gave to British subjects a right which they did not possess under the Decree which created the National Commission, and one not possessed by Mexican citizens either. . . . Had the two governments desired to exclude from these rights British subjects who had already applied to the National Commission, this would certainly have been expressed in the treaty." [34] The claimants' agreement to the award could not

---

sobre las reclamaciones presentadas a su deliberacion. No está, sin embargo, constreñida a adoptar sus resoluciones o indicaciones." *Accord:* Case of Biagio Limongi, Decision No. 68 (unpublished).

[30] Case of Giuseppe Marasco, Decision No. 69 (unpublished); Case of Nicolas Freda, Decision No. 71 (unpublished).

[31] Case of Ferando Vignola, Decision No. 101 (unpublished).

[32] Case of Michele Giacomino, Decision No. 30. *Cf.*, however, case of Attilio Bellato, Decision No. 38 (unpublished). Claim was made for losses suffered at the hands of Zapata forces. It was held that, although Mexico was not liable for the acts of such forces in the absence of a showing of negligence on the part of the authorities, yet an award would be made on equitable grounds because the National Claims Commission had granted awards to other persons who had suffered loss on the same occasion through acts of these forces.

[33] Case of David Roy, British-Mexican Commission, Further Decisions and Opinions, p. 39. The Mexican Commissioner dissented without opinion.

[34] *Id.*, at p. 41.

affect the result in this case because the agreement was given before the Claims Convention was concluded, at a time when no other means of redress existed.[35]

But the Commission, while denying any legal connection with the National Commission, went on to say:

"In taking the view that the jurisdiction of the National Commission can have no legal or other bearing, originating in the treaty, on the acts of this Commission, the majority at the same time fully realize that the judgment of the former may have great weight for the decisions of the latter, principally because the examination of claims by the National Institution took place at a time less remote from the occurrence underlying the claim. . . . At the same time the Commission wish it to be understood that the amount already received by claimants, will of course be taken into consideration in fixing any award which the Commission may feel justified in allowing."

This is the same result which the French-Mexican Commission reached in the *Pinson* case. But the British-Mexican Commission did more than pay lip service to the doctrine of giving weight to these decisions. In two cases it awarded the claimants exactly the same amounts which had been awarded by the National Commission.[36] In another case it disallowed a claim which had been disallowed by the National Commission.[37]

§190. **Appreciation of the Handling of the Problem by the Commissions.** While both the French-Mexican and British-Mexican Commissions reached the same result with respect to the problem of relations to the National Claims Commission, the British-Mexican Commission came to the result by a much more direct route. The French-Mexican Commission professed to find a historical connection; the Claims Conventions were the "final realization of the Decree of Monclova." Yet, the net result of a lengthy historical demonstra-

---

[35] This statement of the Commission is not convincing. Art. XII of the Mexican decree of 1919 provided for the institution of arbitral tribunals in cases where alien claimants objected to the decisions of the National Commission. It may well be argued that the Commission should have given some weight to the failure of the claimant to take advantage of the right of objection accorded to him by the decree.

[36] *Id.*, at pp. 41–42.

[37] Case of David Roy, British-Mexican Commission, Further Decisions and Opinions, p. 198; Case of the Anzures Land Co., Ltd., British-Mexican Commission, Further Decisions and Opinions, p. 202. In both these cases it was said that: "The Commission see no reason why they should not declare themselves satisfied with the evidence and the considerations which led the National Tribunal to the granting of their award, the less so because that court rendered judgment in 1925, *i.e.*, a time less remote from the events than the present moment."

tion is that serious consideration should be given to the decisions of the National Commission, a result which common sense would have required in any event. Whatever the historical connection, it was of a most tenuous kind. The Claims Commissions set up by the Conventions are of quite a different character from the arbitral tribunals envisaged in the Mexican claims legislation. All the conventions contained a provision waiving the requirement of exhaustion of local remedies. Were it to be held that a claimant should be bound by the decision of the National Claims Commission, then he would be in a worse position than one who had failed to have recourse to the agencies provided by Mexico. In the absence of an express stipulation the Commissions were justified in holding that their jurisdiction over claims submitted to the National Commission was unfettered.

CHAPTER 12

CONFLICTS OF JURISDICTION BETWEEN THE UNITED STATES–MEXICAN GENERAL AND SPECIAL CLAIMS COMMISSIONS

§191. **Provisions in the Special and General Claims Conventions.** Since conflicts of jurisdiction between international tribunals are of rare occurrence,[1] the numerous problems raised by the simultaneous existence of the United States-Mexican General and Special Claims Commissions are of particular interest. The preamble of the General Claims Convention set forth the desire of the contracting parties to settle and adjust amicably claims by the citizens of each country against the other "without including the claims for losses or damages growing out of the revolutionary disturbances in Mexico, which form the basis of another and separate Convention," and Article I provided for jurisdiction over all claims "except those arising from acts incident to the recent revolutions." The preamble of the Special Claims Convention set forth the desire of the Parties to settle and adjust amicably claims arising from losses or damages suffered by American citizens "through revolutionary acts within the period from November 20, 1910, to May 31, 1920, inclusive." Article III of the same Convention provided that: "The claims which the Commission shall examine and decide are those which arose during the revolutions and disturbed conditions which existed in Mexico covering the period from November 20, 1910, to May 31, 1920, inclusive and were due to any act" by five enumerated categories of forces.

---

[1] The Permanent Court of International Justice has stated that the principle of Art. 36, par. 1, of its Statute ("The jurisdiction of the Court comprises all cases which the parties refer to it and all matters specially provided for in treaties and conventions in force.") "only becomes inoperative in those exceptional cases in which the dispute which States might desire to refer to the Court would fall within the exclusive jurisdiction reserved to some other authority." Rights of Minorities in Upper Silesia, Publications of the Court, Series A, No. 15, p. 23. In several cases it was contended that the Court had no jurisdiction because exclusive jurisdiction had been conferred on some other tribunal. The Court held otherwise in all these cases. See German Interests in Polish Upper Silesia (Merits), Series A, No. 7, p. 33; The Factory at Chorzów (Indemnity, Jurisdiction), Series A, No. 9, pp. 26, 30; The Mavrommatis Palestine Concessions, Series A, No. 2, p. 32.

It is obvious that the phraseology of the two Conventions is not consistent. Conceivably there might be claims which did "grow out of" revolutionary disturbances or which arose "from acts incident" to the revolutions and yet were not "due to any act" by the forces enumerated in the Special Claims Convention. Conversely, there might be claims for acts committed by forces of a government *de jure* or *de facto* which did not "grow out of" revolutionary disturbances and which did not arise "from acts incident to the" revolutions. On the other hand, there might be claims which could fall under the description in either Convention. No ready answer being possible on the face of the Conventions, the Agency of the United States filed several hundred claims with both Commissions.[2]

§192. Interpretation of the Conventions. In the first ten years of its existence, the Special Claims Commission did not consider any case involving a conflict, but the General Claims Commission had before it a number of such cases.

The fundamental question presented was whether the two Conventions should be read together for the purpose of interpreting the provisions of the General Claims Convention. The Conventions were concluded between the same parties, they were both part of a general settlement of claims, and the preamble of the General Claims Convention makes reference to "another and separate" Convention. Clearly, then, the Commission was justified in referring to the provisions of the Special Claims Convention for the purpose of determining the scope of its own jurisdiction,[3] though its interpretation of the scope

---

[2] See U. S. A. (Clara W. Roney and George E. Boles) *v.* United Mexican States, General Claims Commission, Opinions of Commissioners, 1927, p. 5, at p. 6.

[3] See U. S. A. (Genie Lautman Elton) *v.* United Mexican States, Opinions of Commissioners, 1929, p. 301, at p. 306 *et seq.* In one of its earliest opinions the General Claims Commission stated that, "it will prove helpful to the Commission to have before it, in considering such claims, the opinion of the Special Claims Commission in the series of test cases, already submitted to it, in which it is believed opinions will be rendered at an early date. Such opinions on legal points are entitled to and will have great consideration and will be given great weight by this Commission in construing the exceptions contained in Art. I and VIII and in the preamble of the General Claims Convention." U. S. A. (Clara W. Roney and George E. Boles) *v.* United Mexican States, *supra,* note 2, at p. 6. In a later case, when Mexico contended that the hearing of the case should be suspended until it should be known whether or not the Special Claims Commission would be of the opinion that the claim was within its jurisdiction, the Commission stated: "There is . . . no rule in international law, nor no provision in the Conventions entered into between the United States and Mexico or in the rules of this Commission, that precludes the United States from presenting a claim to this Commission because of its having been previously filed by Memorial before the Special Claims Commission." U. S. A. (American Bottling Co.) *v.* United Mexican States, Opinions of Commissioners, 1929, p. 162, at p. 164.

of the Special Claims Convention could not bind the Special Claims Commission.

§193. **Various Cases of Conflicts.** Reference to the Special Claims Convention established that the phrase "recent revolutions" included only the period between November 29, 1910, and May 31, 1920. Thus a claim arising out of acts done by the de la Huerta revolutionary forces in 1924 was held to be within the jurisdiction of the General Claims Commission.[4] On the other hand, the mere fact that a claim arose between 1910 and 1920 did not take it out of the jurisdiction of the General Claims Commission if it was not incident to the revolutions.[5] Where a claim was based on an act committed during this period the Commission directed its attention towards the character of the act and the agency committing it. Routine governmental acts of a government established in consequence of a revolution were clearly within the jurisdiction of the General Claims Commission, and the Commission took jurisdiction over a claim involving the purchase of ambulances by the Huerta government in 1913.[6] Similarly the Commission took jurisdiction over a claim involving a routine governmental act which had a certain connection with a revolution: the stabling of horses in El Paso by the Mexican Post Office in order to prevent their capture by revolutionary forces.[7] Nor was the Commission deprived of jurisdiction because the act complained of, though that of an established government, had its origin in revolutionary disturbances, as where claim was made for harsh and oppressive treatment by the Mexican government in 1911 of an American citizen who had been arrested because of complicity in the Madero revolution.[8] On the other hand, where the gravamen of the claim was a confiscation of property and the confiscation was carried out by one of the enumerated forces, then the General Claims Commission held it did not have jurisdiction.[9]

[4] U. S. A. (Bond Coleman) v. United Mexican States, Opinions of Commissioners, 1929, p. 56.
[5] U. S. A. (Jacob Kaiser) v. United Mexican States, Opinions of Commissioners, 1929, p. 80.
[6] U. S. A. (Peerless Motor Car Co.) v. United Mexican States, Opinions of Commissioners, 1927, p. 303.
[7] U. S. A. (Pomeroy's El Paso Transfer Co.) v. United Mexican States, Opinions of Commissioners, 1931, p. 1.
[8] U. S. A. (Jacob Kaiser) v. United Mexican States, supra, note 5.
[9] U. S. A. (Frank La Grange) v. United Mexican States, Opinions of Commissioners, 1929, p. 309.
This rule placed American Commissioner Nielsen in peculiar difficulties with respect

A series of cases involved claims based on events which occurred both before and after May 31, 1920. In these cases the Commission endeavored to isolate that element of the facts upon which the claim was based. Thus, in one case an American citizen had been murdered in Mexico on May 1, 1920. Mexico contended that the murder had been committed by bandits and therefore the claim was not within the jurisdiction of the General Claims Commission. The Commission held otherwise on the ground that the claim was based on the failure of the Mexican authorities to prosecute the murderers, this failure occurring after May 31, 1920.[10] The most curious of these cases involved a claim for non-payment of a loan which had been made on or about March 20, 1920, to Adolfo de la Huerta, then "Supreme Chief of the Sonora Revolution." The claimant produced a "receipt" for the amount of the loan, signed by Huerta, stating that the loan "should be paid when the federal public Hacienda is found to be in a favorable situation for making this reimbursement." The receipt was dated May 31, 1920. It was held that the Commission had jurisdiction because payment was not due until subsequent to May 31,

---

to claims based on non-payment of contractual obligations. Nielsen had always contended that non-payment of an obligation amounted to confiscation of property. See, *e.g.,* U. S. A. (International Fisheries Co.) *v.* United Mexican States, Opinions of Commissioners, 1931, p. 207, at p. 242. A claim was presented to the Commission on behalf of an American company which had sold bottles to a Mexican brewery in 1914, at a time when the brewery was administered by an official of the Carranza government which had seized the brewery because of revolutionary activity on the part of its management. It was alleged that the Carranza official with whom the contract had been made failed to pay for the bottles. The majority of the Commission found no difficulty in holding that the claim was within the jurisdiction of the General Claims Commission. The claim was not for seizure of the brewery but for non-payment of an obligation which could not be said to constitute an act incident to the revolution. Under Nielsen's view, however, non-payment was confiscation, it was committed by an official of a revolutionary government, and the claim would thus seem to fall within the jurisdiction of the Special Claims Commission. Yet he was able to reach the same result as the majority of the Commission by a consideration of the "peculiar facts" of the case. The United States had filed this claim with both Commissions and in both Commissions the Mexican agent had contended that there was no jurisdiction. "The United States, by prosecuting the claim to a hearing before this Commission, seems to have acquiesced in the Mexican government's contention that the Special Commission has not jurisdiction, which therefore must be vested in the General Claims Commission." This was an "interpretation" of the Conventions by the two governments which the Commissions ought to follow. U. S. A. (American Bottling Co.) *v.* United Mexican States, Opinions of Commissioners, 1929, p. 162 at p. 167. A most ingenious solution, but several difficulties are apparent. The United States had never withdrawn its claim before the Special Commission, and it had prosecuted the claim to a hearing before the General Commission because the Special Commission was dormant at the time. A similar problem was presented in U. S. A. (Pomeroy's El Paso Transfer Co.) *v.* United Mexican States, *supra,* note 7, but there was no possibility of escape as in the Bottling case. Nielsen there said that the Commission should take jurisdiction because such action would be "in harmony with past decisions of the Commission." *Id.* at p. 11.

[10] U. S. A. (Lillian Greenlaw Sewell) *v.* United Mexican States, Opinions of Commissioners, 1931, p. 112.

1920, and the claim did not therefore arise within the revolutionary period.[11]

This attempt to isolate the element upon which the claim was based involved the Commission in apparently inconsistent decisions. Two cases involve attacks on American citizens during the Díaz régime, the arrest and imprisonment of the assailant and his subsequent release from prison by revolutionary forces. In one case the Commission held Mexico responsible for a denial of justice resulting from the failure to reapprehend the murderer of an American citizen without even discussing the jurisdictional point.[12] In the other case, the Commission held that it had no jurisdiction because the alleged responsibility of Mexico was based "exclusively" upon the failure to punish the assailant resulting from his release by the revolutionary forces.[13]

American Commissioner Nielsen, dissenting, attempted to set forth a rule for the isolation of the element on which the claim was based. The definition of the nature of the claim, he said, must be sought in the allegations of the memorial, provided these allegations are not colorable or fictitious. Jurisdiction attaches with the filing of the memorial, and matters pleaded in defense with respect to the merits of the case are not relevant to the question of jurisdiction.[14] The memorial did not allege the release of the assailant by revolutionists; this fact was first stated in the Mexican answer. Since the memorial contained allegations of lack of protection and of improper action by a court during the Díaz régime, the Commission should take jurisdiction. The adoption of this viewpoint would have made the task

[11] U. S. A. (Macedonio J. García) v. United Mexican States, Opinions of Commissioners, 1927, p. 146.

[12] U. S. A. (Ida Robinson Smith Putnam) v. United Mexican States, Opinions of Commissioners, 1927, p. 222. Cf. U. S. A. (Hazel M. Corcoran) v. United Mexican States, Opinions of Commissioners, 1929, p. 211.

[13] U. S. A. (C. E. Blair) v. United Mexican States, Opinion of Commissioners, 1927, p. 107. This case may be distinguished on the ground that the assailant was killed in battle after his release from prison.

[14] Cf. the rule in the United States federal courts, that a defendant cannot remove a suit from a state court to a federal court on the ground that a federal question is involved where the existence of a federal question does not appear on the face of the plaintiff's declaration or bill. Tennessee v. Union & Planters' Bank, 152 U. S. 454 (1894). Cf. also this statement of the United States-German Mixed Claims Commission: "When the allegations in a petition or memorial presented by the United States bring a claim within the terms of the Treaty, the jurisdiction of the Commission attaches. If these allegations are controverted in whole or in part by Germany, the issue thus made must be decided by the Commission. Should the Commission so decide such issue that the claim does not fall within the terms of the Treaty, it will be dismissed for lack of jurisdiction." Administrative Decision No. I, Consolidated Edition of Decisions and Opinions, p. 1, at p. 7.

of the Commission much easier and would have been in line with its general tendency to refrain from dismissing cases for lack of jurisdiction wherever possible.

In this case the American agent argued that it was necessary to distinguish between the act which caused injury to the claimant and the act which gave rise to responsibility of the Mexican government. The Special Claims Commission envisaged responsibility of Mexico for injuries caused by acts of forces. In this case, the claimant was injured by the act of a single person; the acts of the revolutionary forces did not injure the claimant who had already been injured, it gave rise to the international responsibility of Mexico. This argument is not altogether satisfactory. It is true that the indemnity paid by Mexico will be measured by the injury inflicted by the assailant. But Mexico is not rendered responsible by reason of the fact that the claimant was assaulted. Something more is necessary, in this case the failure to punish, which is due to acts of revolutionary forces.

§194. Cases Involving "Bandits." Most difficult of the problems of conflicting jurisdiction was that arising out of acts committed by "bandits." The Special Claims Commission was to decide claims due to acts by bandits provided it were established that the appropriate authorities omitted to take reasonable measures to suppress bandits, or treated them with lenity or were at fault in other particulars.[15] The word "bandits" is not a term of art, and in diplomatic correspondence it had not infrequently been used to describe any sort of criminal. Thus, when claims arising out of non-punishment of murderers of American citizens committed between 1910 and 1920 were pressed, it was possible for Mexico to contend that they were committed by "bandits" and therefore, being within the jurisdiction of the Special Commission, were outside that of the General Commission. In answer to this contention the United States took the position that in order that the question of the jurisdiction of the Commission could be raised it must appear on the face of the record that more than one man joined in inflicting the injury [16] since the acts of bandits referred to in the Special Claims Convention meant acts of groups of men acting in the manner of organized banditry. The Commission stated that "there appeared to be some force" in this argument, but never accepted it

---

[15] U. S.-Mexican Special Claims Convention, Art. III(5).
[16] U. S. A. (C. E. Blair) v. United Mexican States, supra, note 13, at p. 113.

definitely.[17] Indeed, no clear indication of the basis for the solution of this problem was ever given. In the *Gorham* case, [18] the husband of the claimant had been murdered in 1919 by a number of persons who had looted the body. The claim was based on failure to prosecute the murderers. The latter had been described as "bandits" in various documents accompanying the memorial. The decision of the Commission holding the claim to be within its jurisdiction is vague and confused. At once place it is said that: "To attempt in the light of the record . . . to ascribe the losses which it is alleged the claimant suffered as growing out of a revolutionary disturbance, or as incident to recent revolutions, would seem to be entering into a field of speculation and of strained reasoning which neither Convention requires or justifies." [19] Subsequently it is said that: "It is also proper to take account of the precise nature of the claims within our jurisdiction as distinct from claims in which Mexico has undertaken to make compensation *ex gratia* on the basis of direct responsibility, so to speak. The instant case is based on contentions as to the failure of Mexico to live up to the obligations of the rule of international law with respect to punishment of persons who murdered the claimant's husband. Its merits must be determined by the application of the rule of international law pertaining to a complaint of that nature." [20]

The latter statement hints towards approval of the position taken by the United States in another case [21] that where a claim could be decided by the application of rules of international law the General Claims Commission had jurisdiction over it, because under the Special Claims Convention Mexico had undertaken to make compensation for claims *ex gratia* and not on the basis of international law. But, this contention of the United States had been expressly disapproved by the Commission, to which it seemed "to be clear that the jurisdiction of each Commission was not primarily defined on the basis of some grouping of claims from the standpoint of susceptibility of determination under international law." [22]

§195. Appreciation of the Decisions. While the Commission failed to set forth any coherent body of rules for resolving conflicts

---

[17] U. S. A. (Sarah Ann Gorham) *v.* United Mexican States, Opinions of Commissioners, 1931, p. 135, at p. 136.
[18] *Supra,* note 17, at p. 136. [19] *Id.,* at p. 136. [20] *Loc. cit.*
[21] U. S. A. (Genie Lautman Elton) *v.* United Mexican States, Opinions of Commissioners, 1929, p. 301, at p. 304. [22] *Id.,* at p. 305.

of jurisdiction, most of its decisions are to be commended. It started with the propositions that it would read both Conventions together and that, unless a claim fell clearly within the jurisdiction of the Special Commission, it was within the jurisdiction of the General Commission.[23] The result was a decided reluctance to dismiss claims for lack of jurisdiction.[24] Clearly this was the proper course to follow. Since the Special Commission could not be bound by the decisions of the General Commission, it might well have been that a claim which the latter dismissed for lack of jurisdiction might also be dismissed by the former.

[23] *Cf.* this statement of the Permanent Court of International Justice: "The Court, when it has to define its jurisdiction in relation to that of another tribunal, cannot allow its own competence to give way unless confronted with a clause which it considers sufficiently clear to prevent the possibility of a negative conflict of jurisdiction involving the danger of a denial of justice." The Factory at Chorzów (Jurisdiction), Series A, No. 9, p. 30.

[24] "Pleas to the jurisdiction of this Commission have often been invoked; they have seldom been sustained." Commissioner Nielsen in U. S. A. (Genie Lautman Elton) *v.* United Mexican States, *supra,* note 21, at p. 301.

CHAPTER 13

THE LAW TO BE APPLIED BY THE COMMISSIONS

§196. **Provisions of the General Claims Conventions.** The United States-Mexican General Claims Convention provided that the Commissioners were to decide "in accordance with the principles of international law, justice and equity." [1] This is a provision common to a multitude of claims conventions. The one significant problem raised by the provision was whether it merely indicated the source of the law to be applied or whether it also constituted a limitation on jurisdiction. The problem was squarely raised in the *Illinois Central* case [2] involving the question of jurisdiction over contract claims. It was argued by Mexico that the words "all claims" in Article I must be construed in the light of the provisions indicating the source of law, in such a manner that "all claims" must mean claims for which either government is responsible according to international law. We have seen that the Commission rejected this view and held that its jurisdiction extended over all claims of an international character, saying:

"The Commission concludes that the final words of Article I, which provide that it shall decide cases submitted to it 'in accordance with the principles of international law, justice and equity,' prescribe the rules and principles which shall govern in the decision of claims falling within its jurisdiction, but in no wise limit the preceding clauses which do fix the Commission's jurisdiction." [3]

We have also seen that in certain situations the Commission might apply municipal law. [4] This was due to the inclusion in the Convention of the provision that "no claim shall be disallowed or rejected by the Commission by the application of the general principles of international law that the legal remedies must be exhausted as a condition precedent to the validity or allowance of any claim." [5] If, in a particu-

---

[1] Article I.
[2] U. S. A. (Illinois Central R. R. Co.) *v.* United Mexican States, 1927, p. 15. See the discussion of this case, *supra,* p. 175.
[3] *Ibid.,* p. 18.   [4] See *supra,* p. 178.   [5] Article V.

lar case, international law required the exhaustion of legal remedies
the Commission, not being able to reject the claim, would be required
to turn to municipal law as a source of decision.

§197. **Provisions in the Conventions Dealing with Revolutionary Claims.** All of the Conventions dealing with revolutionary
claims (excepting the German-Mexican Convention) contained a provision similar to the following:

> "Each member of the Commission, before entering upon his duties, shall
> make and subscribe a solemn declaration in which he shall undertake to ex-
> amine with care, and to judge with impartiality, in accordance with the prin-
> ciples of justice and equity, all claims presented, since it is the desire of
> Mexico *ex gratia* fully to compensate the injured parties, and not that her
> responsibility should be established in conformity with the general principles
> of International Law; and it is sufficient therefore that it be established that
> the alleged damage actually took place, and was due to any of the causes
> enumerated in Article 3 of this Convention, for Mexico to feel moved *ex gratia*
> to afford such compensation." [6]

The German-Mexican Convention differed from this in that the
words "general principles of international law" were replaced by "Article XVIII of the Treaty of Amity, Commerce and Navigation in
force between the United Mexican States and the German Republic." [7]

---

[6] This provision is Article II of the British-Mexican Convention. Article II of the
French-Mexican, Italian-Mexican and Spanish-Mexican Conventions were substantially
identical. Article II of the United States-Mexican Special Claims Conventions provided
in part:

"... each member of the Commission, before entering upon his duties, shall make
and subscribe a solemn declaration stating 'that he will carefully and impartially examine
and decide, according to the best of his judgment and in accordance with the principles
of justice and equity, all claims presented for decision,' and such declaration shall be
entered upon the record of the proceedings of the Commission.

"The Mexican Government desires that the claims shall be so decided because Mexico
wishes that her responsibility shall not be fixed according to the general accepted rule
and principles of international law, but *ex gratia* feels morally bound to make full
indemnification and agrees, therefore, that it will be sufficient that it be established that
the alleged loss or damage in any case was sustained and was due to any of the causes
enumerated in Article III hereof."

[7] Article XVIII of the Treaty of Commerce, signed December 5, 1882, provided:

"The contracting parties mutually agree to allow envoys, ministers, and other public
agents to enjoy the same privileges, exemptions and immunities as are granted, or may
hereafter be granted, to the representatives of the most favored nation. Moreover, the
contracting parties, animated by the desire of avoiding the discussion of questions which
may disturb friendly relations, agree further that as regards complaints brought forward by private individuals in connection with civil, criminal or administrative matters
their diplomatic agents shall interfere in these cases only where there has been a denial
of justice, or some unusual or unwarranted delay in giving effect to the verdict of a court
or where, after all legal means have been tried, there has been a direct violation either of

The significant fact in these provisions is that cases were to be decided "in accordance with the principles of justice and equity." [8]

Several possibilities of interpretation can be imagined. It might be said that recourse to the principles of international law is forbidden and that all questions presented for decision must be decided on the basis of "justice and equity." This raises the further problem of the meaning of the word "equity." It could be urged that, since Mexico had voluntarily undertaken the obligation to indemnify, all doubtful questions must be decided in favor of Mexico. It could be urged with equal persuasiveness that justice and equity must incline the scales of doubt in favor of the innocent victims of revolutionary disturbances. On the other hand, it is arguable that the principles of justice and equity are to be the sole basis only for determining the question of the responsibility of Mexico, but that the principles of international law should be resorted to for determining other questions.

It is submitted that the view last set forth is the correct one. The justification for it may be stated as follows: It is a generally accepted principle that an international tribunal is bound to follow the rules of international law even when no express direction to that effect is contained in the Convention. [9] True, the Mexican Claims Conventions

---

existing treaties or of international law, public and private, as generally recognized by civilized nations.

"By agreement between the two parties, it is also stipulated that, except in cases where there has been culpable negligence or want of due diligence on the part of the Mexican authorities or of their agents, the German Government shall not hold the Government of Mexico responsible for such losses, damages, or exactions as, in time of insurrection or civil war, German subjects may suffer on Mexican territory at the hands at insurgents, or from the acts of those tribes of Indians which have not yet submitted to the authority of the Government." 73 British and Foreign State Papers, p. 709.

The reference to Article XVIII of the Treaty of Commerce necessitated the addition of the following article to the German-Mexican Claims Convention:

"Article III. The German Republic appreciates the friendly attitude adopted by the United Mexican States in consenting to its responsibility being fixed for the purposes of the present arrangement only, in accordance with principles of equity, and in refraining from basing a dismissal of these claims on Article XVIII of the Treaty of Friendship, Commerce and Navigation now in force between the two countries and signed on December 5, 1882, at Mexico City.

"Accordingly the German Republic solemnly declares that it agrees that the present arrangement shall not modify the treaty in question either wholly or in part or either tacitly or expressly, and that it undertakes not to refer to the present arrangement as a precedent."

[8] "Probably this passage does not mean that in the opinion of the parties international law is not compatible with justice and equity." Lauterpacht, The Function of Law in the International Community (Oxford, 1933), p. 313, note 2. This is so obviously a truism that it is surprising to find Dr. Lauterpacht making such a statement.

[9] See Scott, Hague Court Reports, p. ix; Ralston, Law and Procedure of Arbitral Tribunals, p. 53. The Venezuelan Protocols of 1903 required cases to be decided "upon

provided affirmatively that it was "the desire of Mexico that its liability should not be determined in accordance with the principles of
international law." But this affirmative direction went only to the
question of liability. While it is clear that on this question the rules of
international law could not be resorted to, the general principle set
forth above required resort to international law for the decision of
other questions. This reasoning can be buttressed by the practical
advantages of being able to decide questions in accordance with more
or less definite rules of law rather than in accordance with the vague
standard of equity. The questions which could be decided on the basis
of international law would be, among others: nationality of claims,
the admissibility of corporate claims, relative responsibility for acts of
superior and minor officials, measure of damages, interest on awards,
rules of evidence. Finally, all the provisions of the Convention, including the provisions relating to responsibility, would have to be interpreted in the light of the rules of international law for the interpretation of treaties.

§198. **Practice of the Commissions.** It cannot readily be said
what the practice of the Commissions in this respect was. In three of
the Commissions elaborate discussions of the meaning of equity were
had; but two of these represented only the views of individual commissioners. We have seen, however, that time and again the Commissions applied international law to the decision of problems before them.
It may be inferred, therefore, that the Commissions proceeded on the
view that "equity" was to be restricted to the decision of the question
of Mexico's responsibility, and that as to all other questions the rules
of international law were to be applied.[10]

---

a basis of absolute equity, without regard to objections of a technical nature or of the
provisions of local legislation." Nevertheless several umpires considered that they were
bound to apply international law. See, *e.g.*, Umpire Plumley in the Aroa Mines Case,
Ralston, Venezuelan Arbitrations of 1903, pp. 344, 379, 386.

[10] Only the most meagre references to "equity" are to be found in the decisions of
the British-Mexican and Italian-Mexican Commissions.

British-Mexican Commission: In Case of the British Shareholders of the Mariposa
Company, Further Decisions and Opinions, p. 304, at 306, it was said to be "a postulate
of equity" to award compensation for cattle confiscated by revolutionary forces in order
to supply the population of a town with meat.

Italian-Mexican Commission: In Case of Francisco Barra, Decision No. 20 (unpublished), it was said: "La equidad no puede, en ninguna forma, autorizar a modificar el
marco de la competencia y de la jurisdicción."

In Case of Vittoria Rocchietti, Decision No. 19 (unpublished), it was said: ". . . la
equidad consiste en no aplicar en toda su extensión el rigor de la ley, pero nunca puede
autorizar a salirse de la ley, que, en este caso, está constituída por el Convenio internacional que ha creado a este Tribunal."

With this in mind, it becomes clear that the requirement of decision "in accordance with justice and equity," without reference to international law, is unwise and often futile. If the negotiators of arbitral conventions desire that arbitrators should reach their decisions by the process of negotiation and compromise, they should say so in unmistakable language. The members of international tribunals usually have a justifiable reluctance to drifting about in the mists of "equity" without guidance from the rule of law.

§199. **The Meaning of "Equity."** Assuming the rules of international law are to be applied to the decision of some questions, what meaning does the word "equity" have? Commissioner Nielsen argued forcibly in the *Russell* case [11] that "equity" meant that responsibility was fixed by treaty and not by international law.

"The Convention, instead of prescribing the application of international law, requires that in determining responsibility in each case two questions must be ascertained in the light of evidence, namely whether loss or damage was sustained, and whether such loss or damage was due to any of certain causes specified in the Convention. The determination of these two points is therefore what is meant by the determination of responsibility in accordance with equity. The Commission must therefore not decide cases in accordance with the individual notions of members as to what equity may be in any given case. . . . It must apply the provisions of the Convention, which prescribes how responsibility is to be determined." [12]

Presiding Commissioner Verzijl of the French-Mexican Commission took essentially the same view:

"Le rôle de l'équité dans le présent arbitrage . . . consiste donc à rendre impossible au Mexique de faire valoir devant la Commission franco-mexicaine l'exception déclinatoire du défaut d'avoir épuisé préalablement les recours légaux, et de charger ladite Commission de mettre a la base de ses décisions les principes équitables admis par les Hautes Parties Contractantes elles-

---

[11] U. S. A. (Naomi Russell) *v.* United Mexican States, Special Claims Commission, Opinions of Commissioners, 1926–1931, p. 44.

[12] *Ibid.,* p. 81. *Cf.,* the views of Mexican Commissioner Roa in the same case (p. 119): "Mexico . . . considers that equity is also applicable to it, as well as to the claimant party, and that if International Law provides for an excessive remedy, when it is applicable it must be reduced in Mexico's benefit. Mexico considers that its obligation is *ex gratia* and that the two contracting parties established the situation even in those cases in which the practice of nations would bind the Nation. In other words, the obligation is based on the fact of having admitted the existence of gratuitous obligation and not on a right. This enlightens the whole Convention. The undersigned, therefore, considers that all extensive interpretations not subject to the terms strictly applied to the Convention, is contrary to the spirit of the High Contracting Parties."

mêmes dans la Convention, au lieu de les fonder, soit sur la négation absolue de toute responsabilité internationale pour dommages révolutionnaires, soit sur un examen approfondi de la teneur des règles de droit international relatives a cette matière." [13]

At the same time the Presiding Commissioner remarked that this did not prevent the invocation of equity either as a supplementary principle of decision in cases where international law was silent, or as a corrective in exceptional cases where the application of strict law would lead to manifestly unjust results.[14] This latter statement is a necessary supplement to the views of Commissioner Nielsen. The word "equity" has been used too long in claims conventions to permit an interpretation which might rob it of any essential meaning. While, if at all possible, it should not be so construed as to do away entirely with the rule of law, it can serve the purpose of providing a principle of flexibility and of moderation of undesirably harsh results.[15]

Señor Cruchaga, Presiding Commissioner of the German-Mexican Commission, gave a much broader meaning to the term "equity" than was given to it by these Commissioners. He defined equity as follows: [16]

"La equidad es . . . la justicia natural por oposición a la letra de la ley, la moderación de la ley positiva atendiendo mas a la intención del legislador que a la lettra de ella, o sea, le predominio de la conciencia en la resolución de un Juez. Un tribunal puede 'conceder por equidad aquello que no constituye obligación,' y fallar 'sin sujeción a la Ley.' "

He then went on to say that a tribunal authorized to decide only in accordance with the principles of equity should put aside the rules of international law and decide in accordance with simple equity as appears fair to the members of the tribunal.[17] This is, in effect, to

[13] République française (Georges Pinson) v. Etats-unis mexicains, Jurisprudence de la Commission franco-mexicaine des réclamations, p. 26.

[14] "Enfin, je tiens à faire remarquer que les conclusions formulée ci-dessus n'empêchent pas que l'équité soit invoquée encore comme principe supplémentaire de décision dans les cas où le droit positif est silencieux, ou comme correctif dans le cas où le droit positif, comme tout œuvre humaine, est imparfaite et que, pour cela, il a quelquefois besoin de correction par un principe supérieur, qu'on l'indique par justice on par équité." Ibid., p. 30.

[15] See the Cayuga Indians Case, U. S.-British Claims Arbitration under the Agreement of 1910, Nielsen's Report, p. 307.

[16] Republica Alemana (Testamentaria del Señor Hugo Bell) v. Estados Unidos Mexicanos, Decision No. 67 (unpublished).

[17] "Una Comisión Mixta autorizada a fallar con sujeción sólo dos dictados de la equidad, deberá dejar de lado las reglas aceptadas del Derecho International y resolver

give the word "equity" the broadest meaning possible and to deprive an international tribunal so governed of every vestige of judicial character.

It may be doubted whether Señor Cruchaga intended to go as far as these words indicate. The very decision in connection with which they were used serves to belie them. Claim was made on behalf of the estate of a German who had been killed by insurrectionists. The question was whether Mexico could be held guilty of fault or negligence. The Commission found that Mexico was not guilty but proceeded to recommend that compensation be paid as a matter of grace. The discussion of the meaning of equity was had in order to determine whether the Commission could recommend payment. It was, therefore, quite unnecessary. No one doubts that any arbitral tribunal may *recommend* an award as a matter of grace.[18] The Commission held that Mexico was not liable as a matter of law and did not attempt to say that the application of equitable principles alone could render Mexico liable to pay an award. We have discussed many instances of the application of international law principles by the German-Mexican Commission, and it is obvious that this Commission did apply international law despite these dicta of Señor Cruchaga. At the same time, numerous decisions of this Commission are expressed as having been based on equitable principles. The result is that these decisions must often be scrutinized with great caution to determine what the principles of decision really were.

---

los reclamos, dentro de su competencia, con arreglo a la *mera equidad,* tal como aparezca de los antecedentes al honrado criterio de los miembros que la componen." *Ibid.*

[18] For instances of recommendation as a matter of grace, see Ralston, Law and Procedure of Arbitral Tribunals, p. 57.

CHAPTER 14

PROCEDURE

§200. General Considerations. Primarily the procedure of an international tribunal is governed by the treaty under which it functions and by the Rules of Procedure which it draws up. When questions arise to which these documents give no answer, a difficult problem may arise as to the sources to be drawn upon.[1] The most obvious source would seem to be the practice of other international tribunals. It is true that the practice has developed only the rudiments of a law of procedure.[2] Yet, the extent to which the Rules of one tribunal have been patterned on those of other tribunals [3] is a significant indication of the similarity of the procedural problems presented. A second possible source is municipal procedural law. But here great caution is necessary. Where countries having different legal systems are represented before a tribunal, the use of technical procedural concepts from the one or the other legal system is a dangerous matter. Under some circumstances it may be useful by way of analogy but in general it should not be employed. It is important to bear in mind that the parties are sovereign states and that the freest and most flexible procedure possible should be provided.[4] The combative and sporting

---

[1] The provision in the Rules of the United States-Mexican Commissions, Rule XV ("In, or in reference to, any matter as to which express provision is not made in these rules, the commission will proceed as international law, justice and equity require."), is not particularly helpful but has the advantage of leaving the Commission a wide latiture. A similar provision was made in the Italian-Mexican Rules, Art. 52.

[2] See generally, Ralston, Law and Procedure of International Tribunals, Ch. VI; Merighnac, *Traité théorique et pratique de l'arbitrage international* (Paris, 1895); Lammasch, *Die Lehre von der Schiedsgerichtsbarkeit in ihrem ganzen Umfange* (Stuttgart, 1914). For an early attempt to provide a set of rules of general application see Rules of the Institut de Droit International, adopted 1875, 1 *Annuaire de l'institut de droit international* (1877), p. 126.

[3] On the similarity of the Rules of Procedure of various Commissions to which the United States was a party see Ralston, Law and Procedure of International Tribunals, p. 198.

[4] *Cf.* the following statement by the Permanent Court of International Justice: "The Court, whose jurisdiction is international, is not bound to attach to matters of form the same degree of importance which they might possess in municipal law." The Mavrommatis Palestine Concessions, Publications of the Court, Series A, No. 2, p. 34. See also Interpretation of Judgments No. 7 and 8 (The Chorzów Factory), Series A, No. 13, p. 16.

aspects of the trial may still flourish in municipal procedure; in international procedure with its freedom from traditional concepts and methods they must be ruled out. The subsequent discussion will show that many of the forms of municipal procedure have been borrowed from municipal systems, yet in the process of adaptation they have lost many of their technical fine points and have become more flexible instruments for the promotion of the convenience of the litigants and the ends of justice.

§201. **The Rules of Procedure.** All the Mexican Claims Conventions expressly conferred authority on the Commissions to promulgate Rules of Procedure.[5] The United States-Mexican Conventions provided:

In general, the Commission shall adopt as the standard for its proceedings the rules of procedure established by the Mixed Claims Commission created under the Claims Convention between the two Governments signed July 4, 1868, in so far as such rules are not in conflict with any provisions of this Convention. The Commission, however, shall have authority by the decision of the majority of its members to establish such other rules for its proceedings as may be deemed expedient and necessary, not in conflict with any of the provisions of this Convention.[6]

The first sentence soon became a dead letter. The General and Special Claims Commissions did not attempt to let themselves be guided by the Rules of the 1868 Commission. Instead, they made use of the authority given them in the second sentence to promulgate entirely new Rules which bear only a distant resemblance to the Rules of the 1868 Commission.[7] The other Mexican Claims Conventions

[5] Ralston has stated that: "From the very nature of things arbitral courts have the right to adopt ordinary rules to govern their procedure and determine the privileges and duties of litigants before them. This right exists whether expressed in the protocol or not, but always limited by its provisions." Law and Procedure of International Tribunals, p. 197.

[6] The Pani Draft of Nov. 19, 1920, provided only that "the Commissioners will adopt as the standard in their proceedings, in general, the rules established by the Mixed Commission created in 1869." *La cuestion internacional*, p. 48. The Summerlin Draft of Nov. 11, 1921, provided that: "The commissioners may adopt any rule of procedure which shall be in accordance with justice and equity and designate the order and the manner in which each party shall set forth its arguments and may provide for all the formalities required for the examination of evidence." *Ibid*, p. 35.

[7] During the first session the General Claims Commission "was chiefly occupied in drawing up the rules under which all affairs before it were to be carried on. The question immediately arose as to how the provision of Article III of the Convention, obliging the Commission to govern itself in accordance with the Rules adopted in 1868, should be interpreted. After discussion, it was unanimously concluded that the Rules

provided merely that: "The Commission shall determine their own methods of procedure, but shall not depart from the provisions of the present Convention." The Commissions adopted Rules of Procedure substantially similar to those of the United States-Mexican Commissions.

§202. **Language of Proceedings.** With the exception of the Spanish-Mexican Commissions, the proceedings in all the Commissions were bi-lingual. In the German-Mexican Commission either English or Spanish could be used; [8] in all the other Commissions the language of both parties had to be used, except in oral argument.[9] All pleadings were to be filed in both languages, and either agent could require the translation of documents submitted by the other agent. Records were kept in both languages, and decisions were also rendered in both languages without any indication as to which text was authentic except in the French-Mexican Commission.[10]

§203. **Filing and Docketing of Claims.** Two methods of filing claims were provided for: by memorandum or by memorial.[11] The

---

of 1868 should serve as a guide, but that the Commission had complete liberty to amend these Rules or adopt others, provided they are not contrary to the Convention of 1923." *Memoria de la Secretaría de Relaciones Exteriores,* 1925–1925, p. 29.

The Rules of the 1868 Commission will be found in Moore, International Arbitrations, p. 2153. They may be summarized as follows: (1) Entering of claims into dockets to be kept by the secretaries. (2) Claims to be presented through the respective governments on or before March 31, 1870, unless at a later day for special cause. (3) Persons having claims were to file memorials with the secretaries. Memorial to be signed and verified by the claimant or his attorney and to set forth the origin, nature and amount of the claim, with other circumstances substantially like those required by the Rules of the 1923 Commissions. (4) All motions and arguments to be made in writing. Brief verbal explanations might be made by the agents at the opening of each day's session. (5) Twenty printed copies of the memorial in English and Spanish to be filed. Documents and proofs might be filed in manuscript. (6) Adverse proofs and arguments to be filed within four months after filing of proofs and argument by claimant.

Except for the contents of the memorial, the Rules of the 1868 Commission and of the 1923 Commissions differ in every important respect. Note that under the 1868 Rules the memorial is filed by the *claimant;* oral arguments are all but suppressed; no provision is made for pleadings beyond the memorial, nor for production of evidence, nor for examination of witnesses, nor for inspection of documents in archives, nor for the conduct of secretaries, nor for the rendering of awards.

[8] German-Mexican Rules, Arts. 47–49. Apparently English was hardly ever used, if at all. The decisions are drawn up only in Spanish.

[9] U. S.-Mexican General Rules II 1, III, V, IX 3, XI 5; U. S.-Mexican Special Rules II, III, V, IX 3, XI 5; British-Mexican Rules 49–51; French-Mexican Rules, Arts. 47–49; Italian-Mexican Rules, Arts. 45–47.

[10] The French-Mexican Rules were amended in 1928 by the insertion of the following sentences in Art. 49: "The Commission shall indicate in each decision which of the two texts is authentic. It reserves the liberty to publish only one of these texts." Nevertheless, the decisions rendered by the reorganized Commission under the supplementary Convention of 1930 were drawn up in Spanish and French without any indication as to which text is authentic.

[11] U. S.-Mexican General Rule III; U. S.-Mexican Special Rule III; French-Mexican

memorandum (sometimes called "statement" or "declaration") was required to contain merely the name of the claimant, a brief statement of the nature of the claim and the amount thereof. Upon the presentation to the secretaries of the memorandum in duplicate signed by the agent, the claim was deemed to be formally filed. The reason for providing for filing by memorandum was the impossibility of preparing memorials on all the claims within the period provided for presentation, but the ease with which memoranda could be prepared encouraged the indiscriminate filing of claims without regard to their validity. In all claims filed by memorandum, a memorial was also required before the claim could be heard. Upon receipt of the memorandum or memorial, the secretaries were required to make an endorsement of filing thereon and immediately docket the claim under the appropriate number.

PLEADINGS

§204. **Order of Pleadings.**[12] The written pleadings (Sp.—*escritos fundamentales;* Fr.—*pièces fondamentales*) consisted of the memorial (Sp.—*memorial;* Fr.—*mémoire*), the answer (Sp.—*contestación;* Fr.—*contre-mémoire*), the reply [13] (Sp.—*réplica;* Fr.—*réplique*), the rejoinder [14] (Sp.—*dúplica;* Fr.—*duplique*), amendments (Sp.—*reformas;* Fr.—*modifications*), and motions. Other pleadings could be had if the agents agreed or if the Commission so ordered.[15]

§205. **The Memorial.**[16] The memorial as the first pleading had to set forth the claim and all facts necessary to establish the jurisdic-

---

Rules, Arts. 6–9; German-Mexican Rules, Arts. 6–9; Spanish-Mexican Rules, Arts. 7–11; Italian-Mexican Rules, Arts. 7–9. The British-Mexican Rules 6–8 provided for filing only by memorial.

[12] U. S.-Mexican General Rule IV 1; U. S.-Mexican Special Rule IV 1; British-Mexican Rule 9; French-Mexican Rules, Art 10; German-Mexican Rules, Art 10; Spanish-Mexican Rules, Art 12; Italian-Mexican Rules, Art 10.

[13] The reply was always optional with the agent for the claimant government.

[14] The Rules of the U. S.-Mexican Commissions made no express provision for a rejoinder.

[15] In the U. S.-Mexican General Claims Protocol of April 24, 1934, it was provided that the pleadings should be limited in number to four—Memorial, Answer, Brief and Reply Brief. Paragraph Sixth (c).

Cf. the order of pleadings in the procedure of the Permanent Court of International Justice; in proceedings instituted by special agreement—a case by each party, a counter-case by each party, a reply by each party; in proceedings instituted by application—the case by the applicant, the counter-case by the respondent, the reply by the applicant, the rejoinder by the respondent. Rules of the Court, Art. 39.

[16] U. S.-Mexican General Rule IV 2; U. S.-Mexican Special Rule IV 2; British-Mexican Rule 10; French-Mexican Rules, Art. 11; German-Mexican Rules, Art 11; Spanish-Mexican Rules, Art 13. Italian-Mexican Rules, Art. 11.

tion of the Commission.[17] Consequently the Rules of Procedure required that the memorial contain a clear and concise statement of the facts upon which the claim was based, and in addition:

(*a*) *To establish jurisdiction over the subject matter*—facts showing that the losses or damages for which claim was made resulted from one of the causes enumerated in the Convention and occurred within the time limit specified (*i.e.*, under the General Claims Convention—subsequent to July 4, 1868; under the other Conventions—between November 20, 1910 and May 31, 1920).

(*b*) *To enable the damages to be fixed*—the amount of the claim, time and place where it arose, kinds and amount and value of property lost or damaged itemized so far as possible, personal injuries if any, the facts and circumstances attending the loss or damage to person or property.

(*c*) *To determine who the claimant is*—for and on behalf of whom the claim was preferred, and if in a representative capacity, the authority of the person preferring the claim.

(*d*) *To determine the nationality of the claim*—Here the Rules differ somewhat. The United States-Mexican and Spanish-Mexican Rules required the statement of the citizenship of the owner or owners of the claim from the time of its origin to the date of filing and whether such citizenship was derived from birth, naturalization, or other act, and all facts in relation thereto. The Rules of the other Commissions required a statement of the nationality in virtue of which the claimant considered himself entitled to invoke the provisions of the Convention. The Rules provided that where it appeared that there had entered into the chain of title to the claim the rights or interests of any person or corporation of any country other than that of the claimant, the facts in relation to such rights or interest had to be fully set forth.

(*e*) *To determine the ownership of the claim*—whether the entire amount of the claim belonged solely and absolutely to the claimant at the time of filing, and did so belong at the time when it had its origin,

---

[17] Ralston distinguishes between "case" and "counter-case" which are "used in the larger arbitrations involving the greater questions between nations" and "memorial" and "answer" which are used in claims commissions and which involve a lesser degree of formality. Law and Procedure of International Tribunals, pp. 198–199. While it may be true that some claims commissions have permitted a degree of informality in the presentation of claims, the distinction cannot validly be applied to the Mexican Claims Commissions. The difference in terminology seems purely accidental, and it is to be noted that the French terms "memoire" and "contre-memoire" are used both in larger arbitrations and in claims commissions.

and if any other person was or had been interested therein, then who such other person was and what was or had been the nature and extent of his interest, and whether the claimant, or any other person who might have been entitled to the amount claimed had ever received any indemnification in any form from all or part of the loss, and if so, when and from whom.

(*f*) *Where the claim arises out of damage to a corporation*—the nature and extent of claimant's interest in the corporation which suffered the loss, and documentary evidence of an allotment.

(*g*) *To establish any resort to local remedies*—whether the claim had ever been presented or complaint with respect to it lodged with either government or any official thereof.

The memorial had to be accompanied by copies of all documents and other proofs in support of the claim then in possession of the agent presenting it.

§206. **The Briefs.** It is to be noted that no provision was made for the inclusion in the memorial of statements of, or arguments on, law. Indeed, the Rules of the United States-Mexican General Commission were amended in 1926 by the addition of the following sentence: "All statements concerning and discussion of matters of law shall be confined to such briefs as may be filed or oral arguments as may be made in support or in defense of a claim." Nor was it required that the memorial contain submissions or conclusions.[18] Arguments on the law and conclusions were set forth in briefs (Sp.—*alegatos;* Fr.— *conclusions*) which were filed by both parties when a case came up for hearing before the Commission. Under the United States-Mexican Rules the brief might be prepared by the agent or his counsel, or by the private claimant or his attorney if countersigned by the agent or counsel.

§207. **Signing of the Memorial.** Under all the Rules, excepting the British-Mexican, it was required that the memorial be signed by the claimant or his attorney in fact and by the agent.[19] Under the

---

[18] The rules of the Permanent Court of International Justice require that the case contain: (1) a statement of the facts on which the claim is based; (2) a statement of law; (3) a statement of conclusion; (4) a list of the documents in support. Rules of the Court, Art. 40.

[19] The Rules of the U. S.-Mexican Commissions also required verification by the claimant and signature by the solicitor or counsel, if any, of the claimant. On the amendment of the U. S.-Mexican General Rules in 1926 all provisions for signature and verification were stricken out. In a case arising subsequently it was argued that the verification of the memorial by the claimant was sufficient to permit the facts

British-Mexican Rules, the memorial could be signed in this manner or by the agent alone, provided that in the latter case the memorial contained a statement of the claim signed by the claimant. This provision was the origin of a number of difficulties in the British-Mexican Commission. In one case in which the claimant was a British company, the memorial was signed "Roberto Craig, per pro Diego S. Dunbar, Sucr." An annex to the memorial contained an affidavit by the secretary of the company alleging that Diego S. Dunbar, Sucr., were the agents of the company and authorized to make the claim. On the objection of the Mexican agent that this did not constitute compliance with the rules, the British agent produced a power of attorney executed by Diego S. Dunbar, Sucr., in favor of Craig. A majority of the Commission disallowed a motion to dismiss, being satisfied from the documents that the secretary was the secretary of the company, that Dunbar, Sucr., were the agents of the company, and that Craig was an authorized agent.[20] In another case involving a claim on behalf of a British company the authority of a general manager to sign for the company was held to be sufficiently established by reason of the fact that a declaration made by the general manager before a Mexican notary public recited that the latter had seen a power of attorney.[21] In another case, the Commission accepted as sufficient a power of attorney executed after the memorial had been signed by an agent of the claimant ratifying the acts done by the agent.[22] In all these cases [23] the Commission took the wise course of refraining from holding the claimant too strictly to the provisions of the Rules and of admitting the memorial whenever it was satisfied that the claimant desired the claim to be submitted.[23a] Only one claim was dismissed for failure to comply with this provision, this being one in which the

---

sworn to be used as evidence. The Commission held otherwise. U. S. A. (National Paper and Type Co.) *v.* United Mexican States, Opinions of Commissioners, 1929, p. 3. The Spanish-Mexican Rules also provided that the memorial must be signed by the solicitor or counsel, if any, of the claimant (*deberá estar suserito*). Under the Italian-Mexican Rules the solicitor or counsel *might* sign (*podrá estar suserito*).

[20] Case of Central Agency, Ltd., Decisions and Opinions of Commissioners, p. 68.

[21] Case of Santa Gertrudis Jute Mill Co., Ltd., Decisions and Opinions of Commissioners, p. 147.

[22] Case of Mazapil Copper Co., Ltd., Decision and Opinions of Commissioners, p. 132.

[23] See also Case of William E. Bowerman and Messrs. Burberry Ltd., Decisions and Opinions of Commissioners, p. 141; Case of Anzures Land Co., Ltd., Further Decisions and Opinions of Commissioners, p. 169.

[23a] The same liberality was shown by the Italian-Mexican Commission. In the Case of Michele Barra, Decision No. 21 (unpublished), a memorial not signed by the claimant was held admissible after the agency had presented various letters from the claimant showing his desire that the claim be presented.

memorial failed to contain a statement of the claim signed by the claimant.[24]

§208. **Variation between Memorandum and Memorial.** The memorandum is a rather informal document used for the purpose of saving time in filing. As a result, an agent might find, when he came to draw up the memorial, that the facts were not accurately stated in the memorandum. In a case before the General Claims Commission, the Mexican agent moved to reject a memorial filed by the United States on the ground that the memorial was at variance with the memorandum. The Commission disallowed the motion, holding that divergences between a memorandum and a memorial are allowable in all cases "in which it is apparent that the modified claim is identical with the original claim." The Rules were construed to the effect that the amount of a claim as set forth in a memorandum should be considered as an approximate amount even in cases where the memorandum did not expressly so state, it being allowable to set forth the amount more accurately in subsequent pleadings.[25]

§209. **The Answer.**[26] It was required that the answer be directly responsive to each of the allegations of the memorial and clearly announce the attitude of the respondent government with respect to each of the various elements of the claim. In addition, it might contain any new matter or affirmative defense which the respondent government might desire to assert within the scope of the Convention. The answer had to be accompanied by copies of the documents and other proof on which the respondent government intended to rely in defense of the claim.[27]

---

[24] Mexico City Bombardment Claims—Claim of Daniel John Tynan, Decisions and Opinions of Commissioners, p. 105.

[25] U. S. A. (Globe Cotton Oil Mills) v. United Mexican States, Opinions of Commissioners, 1927, p. 1. In several cases the American agency asked for leave to file a memorial on behalf of another claimant than the one named in the memorandum. The Commission held the proper procedure to be the filing of the memorial in the name of the original claimant, and then the filing of a motion to amend the memorial by substituting a new claimant. U. S. A. (Flora Lee) v. United Mexican States, Opinions of Commissioners, 1927, p. 3; U. S. A. (Wells Fargo Bank) v. United Mexican States, ibid., p. 71.

[26] U. S.-Mexican General Rule IV 3; U. S.-Mexican Special Rule IV 3; British-Mexican Rule 12; French-Mexican Rules, Art. 14; German-Mexican Rules, Art. 14; Spanish-Mexican Rules, Art. 14; Italian-Mexican Rules, Art. 12.

[27] The rules of the Permanent Court of International Justice provide that the counter-case shall contain: (1) the affirmation or contestation of the facts stated in the case; (2) a statement of additional facts, if any; (3) a statement of law; (4) conclusions based on the facts stated; these conclusions may include counter-claims; (5) a list of the documents in support. Rules of the Court, Art. 40.

§210. **The Reply** [28] **and the Rejoinder.** [29] The reply had to dea
only with the allegations in the answer which presented facts or con
tentions not adequately met and dealt with in the memorial and with
new matter or affirmative defenses, if any, set up in the answer. I
had to be accompanied by copies of documents and other proof upon
which the claimant relied in support thereof, not filed with the memo
rial. The rejoinder was subject to the same rules.

§211. **The Way Case.** The *Way* case [30] before the General Claims
Commission involved two important procedural questions: (1) If a
memorial sets out a "cause of action," is the claimant government
bound thereby so that it cannot ask for recovery on another theory?
(2) What sort of arguments may be introduced under a general allega
tion in an answer? Claim was made by the United States on the basis
of the following facts. Way had been wrongfully arrested under the
orders of Torres, an Alcade, *i.e.*, a minor judicial officer. While Way
was being conveyed to jail he was murdered by two deputies of Torres
alleged to be acting on the latter's instigation. Torres was brought to
trial charged with aggravated homicide, but the court held that there
was not sufficient evidence to sustain this charge, and he was sentenced
to imprisonment for one year and fifteen days, apparently for illega
arrest. The memorial, after setting forth the facts in detail, concluded
that Torres "should have been punished for the crime of murder and
the failure so to punish him was a miscarriage and denial of justice
for which the Government of Mexico is responsible." The American
brief began with the following sentence: "This claim is based upon
the failure of authorities of the State of Sinaloa to punish one Hermo
loa Torres, Alcade of Baca, Sinaloa, for complicity in the murder of
Clarence Way." Thus, the pleadings of the United States proceeded
upon the theory of a denial of justice through failure to punish ade
quately the murderer of an American citizen. However, counsel for
the United States, at the outset of his oral argument announced that
one of the grounds of the claim was the direct responsibility of Mexico
for the acts committed by, and at the instigation of, Torres as a judi

[28] U. S.-Mexican General Rule IV 4; U. S.-Mexican Special Rule IV 4; British-
Mexican Rule 13; French-Mexican Rules, Art 15; German-Mexican Rules, Art. 15
Spanish-Mexican Rules, Art. 15; Italian-Mexican Rules, Art 13.

[29] British-Mexican Rule 14; French-Mexican Rules, Art. 16; German-Mexican Rules
Art. 16; Spanish-Mexican Rules, Art. 16; Italian-Mexican Rules, Art. 14. The U. S.
Mexican General and Special Rules made no provision for a rejoinder.

[30] U. S. A. (William T. Way) *v.* United Mexican States, Opinions of Commissioners
1929, p. 94.

cial officer of the State of Sinaloa. Counsel for Mexico then objected that neither the memorial nor the brief mentioned this point and he had therefore not been given a proper opportunity to meet it. The argument of counsel for the United States on the question of direct responsibility was then deferred pending consideration of the objection made by counsel for Mexico.

Meanwhile, counsel for Mexico proceeded to make a lengthy argument in which he discussed questions of nationality, the right of a half-brother to claim an indemnity, the theory that one of the claimants was illegitimate, and other matters. All of these, he asserted, had their foundation in the allegation in the answer that: "It is expressly denied that William T. Way and John M. Way, Jr., have any standing to claim an award or indemnification for the death of Clarence Way." This action of the Mexican counsel was seized upon by the Commission as a means out of the procedural dilemma. It considered that counsel for Mexico could properly object to the United States raising the issue of direct responsibility in oral argument.

"The sufficiency of a memorial cannot be solely determined on the basis of some quantitative measure of the allegations. The allegations must make clear the complaint presented. This was very aptly clarified by the use by counsel for Mexico for purpose of illustration, of a term of domestic law when he stated that the Memorial must clearly reveal the 'cause of action,' or as may be said with reference to proceedings before an international tribunal, the precise character of the wrong of which complaint is made. The difficulty in the instant case is that the Memorial, so far from doing this with respect to the issue of direct responsibility, by the language employed indicated . . . that the claimant Government had chosen to rely on the sole complaint of failure of adequate punishment of the wrongdoers, and counsel for Mexico was justified in making his defense on that theory." [31]

But, since the counsel for Mexico had departed from the answer, the Commission held that it would consider the question of direct responsibility and, after giving the Mexican agent time to present an argument on the point, it held for the claimant.

§212. The "Cause of Action." It will be noted that the Commission expressed the view that the memorial must "clearly reveal . . . the precise character of the wrong of which complaint is made," and that it accepted the analogy of the "cause of action" in domestic

[31] *Ibid.*, p. 102.

law.[32] The Rules offer no warrant for this. All that is required to be stated in the memorial are certain facts with reference to the cause of loss, amount of claim, personality of the claimant, etc. No requirement of a statement of submissions or conclusions as in the procedure of the Permanent Court of International Justice is made.[33] Perhaps it would have been better if the Rules had required some statement of the theory on which recovery was demanded, but the Commission should not have read it in *ex post facto*. Supposing, however, that the agent sets forth a "theory" or "cause of action" in the memorial, even though not required to do so. May he advance a different theory subsequently? It is submitted that he should be permitted to do so. A narrow and technical view of procedural requirements is out of place in international procedure. If the agent for the respondent claims surprise the Commission should give him sufficient time to prepare a defense.

§213. **What May be Introduced under a General Allegation.** The Rules provided that the answer should be directly responsive to each of the allegations of the claim and might in addition contain any new matter. The general allegation of the Mexican answer that the claimants had "no standing to claim an award," could hardly be said to be a compliance with this provision. Undeniably, counsel for the United States could claim surprise when this allegation was used as a foundation for arguments on the most diverse points. The way out here would have been to permit an amendment to the answer, or a postponement to permit the American agent to prepare a reply to these arguments.

AMENDMENTS TO PLEADINGS

§214. **Provisions of the Rules.** The matter of amendments to pleadings is often of considerable moment. By means of amendments, escape may often be had from oversight or mistakes in technical requirements. A liberal policy with respect to amendments is typical of modern procedural systems.[34] The Rules of the Mexican Claims Commissions made provision for amendment of pleadings at any time before

---

[32] The "cause of action" in American Codes of Procedure has provoked many difficulties and furious controversy. See Harris, "What is a Cause of Action?" 16 California Law Review (1928), p. 549; McCaskill, "Actions and Causes of Actions," 34 Yale Law Journal (1925), p. 614; Gavit, "A Pragmatic Definition of the Cause of Action," Univ. of Pennsylvania Law Review (1933) p. 129; Clark, "The Cause of Action," 82 *ibid.* (1934), p. 354.

[33] See Feller, "Conclusions of the Parties in the Procedure of the Permanent Court of International Justice," 25 Amer. Journal of Int. Law, p. 490 (1931).

[34] See Feller, *op. cit., supra,* note 33.

final award either (1) by stipulation between the agents confirmed by the Commission, or (2) by leave of the Commission in its discretion, such leave to be granted only upon motion, after due notice and upon such terms as the Commission should impose.[35] A provision similar to the following was set forth:

> The Commission will not consider any matter of claim or defense not set up in appropriate pleadings or amendments thereto made as herein provided; but the Commission may in its discretion at any time before final award direct amendments to pleadings which it may deem essential to a proper consideration of any claim or to meet the ends of justice.[36]

The fundamental problem involved in amendment of pleadings is this: Does the amendment constitute so radical a change that it can be said that a new claim is being presented? Since all hearings were held after the time for filing claims had expired, it is obvious that if an amendment of such a nature were to be permitted the time limit would be evaded.

§215. **Practice of the General Claims Commission.** The leading case on this problem is the *Corrie* case [37] before the United States-Mexican General Claims Commission. A memorial had been filed on behalf of Jennie L. Corrie on account of the murder of her son. At the time of filing this person was dead, but her death was unknown to the American agency. After the time for filing claims had expired, a motion was made to amend the memorial by substituting the name of Alexander St. J. Corrie, the husband of the late claimant. It was objected that this constituted a new claim. The Commission allowed the amendment, stating that a substitution of claimants does not necessarily give the claim the character of a new claim if neither the nature, the amount nor the nationality of the claim is changed. This trinity of nature, amount and nationality runs through other cases in which substitution of claimants was permitted.[38]

---

[35] U. S.-Mexican General Rules IV 5–6; U. S.-Mexican Special Rules IV 5–6; British-Mexican Rule 15; French-Mexican Rules, Art. 17; German-Mexican Rules, Art. 17; Spanish-Mexican Rules, Arts. 17–18; Italian-Mexican Rules, Art. 15.

[36] This provision is from the British-Mexican Rules. The U. S.-Mexican Rules differed somewhat. In the amendment of the U. S.-Mexican General Rules in 1926 this provision was stricken out.

[37] U. S. A. (Jennie L. Corrie) v. United Mexican States, Opinions of Commissioners, 1927, p. 213.

[38] U. S. A. (Flora Lee) v. United Mexican States, Opinions of Commissioners, 1927, p. 3; U. S. A. (Wells Fargo Bank) v. United Mexican States, *ibid.*, p. 71. See also U. S. A. (Mary E. A. Munroe) v. United Mexican States, Opinions of Commissioners, 1929, p. 314.

§216. **Practice of the German–Mexican Commission.** This trinity was not accepted altogether by the German-Mexican Commission. In a series of cases in which damage had been suffered by companies in which German nationals were interested, the German agency adopted the practice of filing the claim in the name of the company.[39] To all these claims the Mexican agency interposed the objection that these companies were Mexican and that the Commission had no jurisdiction. The German agency thereupon moved to amend the pleadings by substituting the names of the associates. It was then met with the argument that such amendments were inadmissible because the nationality of the claimants was being changed. In all of these cases the Commission granted the motion, holding that amendments were not subject to the rules of the municipal law of either party, that the Commission had full liberty to decide on the allowance of amendments, and that although these motions involved a change in the nationality of the claimant, the substance of the claim remained the same.[40] The Commission took the same view in a case where the German agent moved to amend the memorial by adding a prayer for the inclusion of interest in the amount of the award, thus permitting the amount of the claim to be increased.[41]

§217. **Appreciation of the Problem.** The doctrine of the General Claims Commission that amendment will not be permitted if the nature, amount or nationality of the claim will be changed thereby is rather too much of a rule of thumb. The claim arises out of a certain fact situation which has resulted in injury to a national of the claimant state. In orthodox theory the state is the claimant because the injury to its national is an injury to it. The exact identity of the injured national is therefore inconsequential at the time the memorial is filed,

---

[39] Cases of Rademacher, Müller y Cía., Sucr., en Liquidación, Decision No. 25; E. Puttkamer, S. en C., Decision No. 29; Delires y Cía., Decision No. 31; Juan Laue y Cía., en Liquidación, Decisions Nos. 35 and 44; Ketelsen y Degetau, Sucs., Decision No. 54. All unpublished.

[40] "Article 17 of the Rules has given the parties the means of amending memorials prior to submission for final decision and this faculty has not been subjected to limitations taken from the procedural law of the nations which signed the Convention of March 16, 1925, but is subject only to the agreement of the parties or the decision of the Commission.

"For these reasons the Commission should decide on a request for a change in the name of the claimant without being bound by any other criterion than that resulting from the spirit of the Convention and the rules of equity, which should inspire its decisions." Presiding Commissioner Cruchaga in Rep. Alemana (Juan Laue y Cía., en Liquidacion) v. Estados Unidos Mexicanos, Decision No. 35 (unpublished).

[41] Rep. Alemana (Federico Griese) v. Estados Unidos Mexicanos, Decision No. 8 (unpublished).

though it becomes indispensable when the award is rendered because the amount of damages is measured by the injury to the individual. If the respondent has received due notice of the fact situation and of the injury, within the established time limit, it should not be heard to complain of any substitution of claimants thereafter. The practice of the German-Mexican Commission is to be supported on this ground. The injury had been committed against German nationals, and this fact was readily apparent from the memorials even though the formal claimants were Mexican companies. Despite this criticism of the General Commission's formula, it is to be remembered that it remained little more than a formula and that all the Commissions which were presented with the problem of amendment administered the rules in a spirit of wide liberality.[42]

DILATORY PLEAS

§218. **General Considerations.** A dilatory plea is a pleading used for the purpose of raising matters in bar to another pleading or bringing before the tribunal for decision defects apparent on the face of the pleadings. The various forms of dilatory pleas used in international procedure have been borrowed from municipal procedure [43] and the result has been great diversity of practice. This is particularly true in the Mexican Claims Commissions where all of the Rules differ in terminology in this respect, several of them also differing in substance. Nevertheless, an international tribunal should not attempt to tie down its practice to the technical rules of municipal procedure even though its own forms may have been borrowed from that procedure.[44]

§219. **Practice of the United States–Mexican Commissions.** The Rules of the United States-Mexican Commissions provided for

[42] See Case of Gervase Scrope, British-Mexican Commission, Further Decisions and Opinions, p. 269.

[43] For dilatory pleas in various Civil Law countries see: France, Code de Procedure Civile, Arts. 166–192; Germany, Zivilprozessordnung, §§ 274–275; Italy, Codice di Procedura Civile, Arts. 187–192; Spain, Ley de Enjuiciamiento Civil of February 3, 1881, Arts. 532–539; Mexico, Codigo de Procedimientos Civiles vigente en el Distrio Federal y Territorios, Arts. 26–35.

[44] Cf. this statement by the Permanent Court of International Justice: "The Court has not to ascertain what are, in the various codes of procedure and in the various legal terminologies the specific characteristics of such an objection, in particular it need not consider whether 'competence' and jurisdiction, *incompetence* and *fin de non-recevoir* should invariably and in every connection be regarded as synonymous expressions." The Mavrommatis Palestine Concessions, Publications of the Court, Series A, No. 2, p. 10.

two sorts of dilatory pleas: the motion to dismiss and the motion to reject or strike out.[45] The motion to dismiss a claim (Sp.—*moción para desechar una reclamación*) might be made at any time after docketing and before final submission to the Commission for good cause shown in the motion, and apparent on the face of the record, going to the jurisdiction of the Commission or the merits of the claim. A motion to reject or strike out a pleading (Sp.—*moción para rechazar o eliminar un escrito fundamental*) might be made at any time after the filing of the pleading and before final submission of the claim to the Commission for any cause apparent on the face of the pleading. All motions were to be in writing and filed with the secretaries as in the case of original pleadings. If a motion was sustained, the Commission might in its discretion permit amendment. In the early days of the functioning of the General Claims Commission motions to dismiss were used for the following purposes: to raise the issue of the jurisdiction of the Commission over contract claims,[46] over claims based on title to real estate,[47] over claims based on revolutionary acts, [48] over claims based on contracts containing a Calvo Clause; [49] to challenge the nationality of the claimant; [50] to raise the question as to whether the acts of the Huerta administration were binding on Mexico [51] and whether the United States was responsible for losses arising out of the occupation of Vera Cruz in 1914.[52] No procedural difficulties seem to have been encountered in the administration of the Rules. It was early held that for the purpose of a motion to dismiss the allegations of the memorial must be taken as confessed,[53] and this type of pleading might have developed into a useful instrument for the speedy dis-

[45] U. S.-Mexican General Rule VII; U. S.-Mexican Special Rule VII.

[46] U. S. A. (Illinois Central R. R. Co.) v. United Mexican States, Opinions of Commissioners, 1927, p. 15.

[47] U. S. A. (Pine King Land & Lumber Co.) v. United Mexican States, Opinions of Commissioners, 1927, p. 4.

[48] U. S. A. (Clara W. Roney and George E. Boles) v. United Mexican States, Opinions of Commissioners, 1927, p. 5.

[49] U. S. A. (North American Dredging Co.) v. United Mexican States, Opinions of Commissioners, 1927, p. 21.

[50] U. S. A. (William A. Parker) v. United Mexican States, Opinions of Commissioners, 1927, p. 14.

[51] U. S. A. (George W. Hopkins) v. United Mexican States, Opinions of Commissioners, 1927, p. 42.

[52] United Mexican States (El Emporio del Cafe) v. U. S. A., Opinions of Commissioners, 1927, p. 7; United Mexican States (David Gonzalez) v. U. S. A., *ibid.*, p. 9; United Mexican States (Armando Cobos Lopez) v. U. S. A., *ibid.*, p. 12.

[53] United Mexican States (Fabian Rios) v. U. S. A., Opinions of Commissioners, 1927, p. 59; United Mexican States (El Emporio del Cafe), *ibid.*, p. 7.

position of cases. However, when the Rules of the General Claims Commission were amended in 1926 it was provided that thereafter no motion should be made by one government to dismiss a claim or to reject or strike out a pleading submitted by the other. The issues which had heretofore been raised by motion were then considered together with the merits of the claim. No dilatory pleas were considered by the Special Claims Commission.

§220. **Practice of the British–Mexican Commission.** A somewhat more complex system of dilatory pleas was provided by the British-Mexican Rules.[54] There were three types of pleas: the demurrer, the motion to dismiss and the motion to reject. The demurrer (Sp.—*excepción dilatoria*) might be interposed by the respondent "so as not to take up the merits of the claim." It might be filed in the form of a special answer prior to any pleading in defense on the merits and within the term fixed for the answer, or when answering the claim upon its merits, at the choice of the agent for the respondent. Upon the filing of a demurrer in the form of a special answer the course of the proceedings were stayed in so far as the study of the merits were concerned. There were, in that event, no pleadings other than the memorial, the demurrer and the reply thereto. If the demurrer were overruled, the respondent was obliged to answer the memorial within thirty days. The motion to dismiss a claim (Sp.—*moción para desechar una reclamación*) might be made at any time after registration of the claim and before final submission "for good cause shown in the motion." The motion to reject or strike out a pleading (Sp.— *moción para rechazar or eliminar un escrito fundamental*) might be made at any time after filing of the pleading and before submission of the claim "for any cause apparent on the face of the pleading." The provisions with regard to filing and the discretion of the Commission to permit amendment were similar to those in the United States-Mexican Rules.

No clear distinction between the demurrer and the motion to dismiss is apparent from the Rules, except that a demurrer must be filed within the time set for answering and a motion to dismiss might be filed at any time before final submission of the claim. In practice, however, a distinction was established. The demurrer was used chiefly for raising the issue that evidence of nationality presented with the

[54] British-Mexican Rules 16, 17, 19–22.

memorial was insufficient,[55] it being held by the Commission that the respondent was not bound to answer the memorial so long as the nationality of the claimant was not established.[56] Subsidiarily, it was used to indicate formal defects in the memorial.[57] All demurrers were apparently filed in the form of special answers. The motion to dismiss was used chiefly in order to raise the issue of lack of jurisdiction (whether acts of one of the forces enumerated in the Convention had been the cause of loss,[58] whether the Commission had jurisdiction in the event of a Calvo Clause [59]). It was also used to raise questions of law as to the nationality of the claimant [60] and to raise the question as to whether the claimant was the person entitled to be indemnified.[61] Occasionally, formal defects in the memorial were also indicated by motion to dismiss.[62] Yet, in other cases, all these issues were raised in the discussion of the merits, and except in a few instances where the use of a dilatory plea resulted in the laying down by the Commission of a doctrine of general import, the dilatory pleas do not seem to have been of much utility. Indeed, the Commission evinced a decided tendency to suspend decision on dilatory pleas until the examination of the merits.[63]

§221. **Practice of the German-Mexican Commission.** The Rules of the German-Mexican Commission with respect to dilatory pleas were identical with those of the British-Mexican Commission.[64] The equivalent of the demurrer was the *excepción,* the equivalent of the motion to dismiss, the *moción para desechar,* and the equivalent of the motion to reject, the *moción para rechazar.* Dilatory pleas turned out to be of little importance in the practice of this Commission, the reason being that the Commission rendered only a single interlocutory decision on a dilatory plea. This was in the first case considered.[65] Thereafter

[55] Case of Robert John Lynch, Decisions and Opinions of Commissioners, p. 20; Case of Virginia Lessard Cameron, *ibid.,* p. 33; Case of Annie B. G. Kidd, *ibid.,* p. 50; Case of Mary Hale, Further Decisions and Opinions, p. 26; Case of Webster Welbanks, *ibid.,* p. 28; Case of J. H. Henderson, *ibid.,* p. 30.

[56] Case of F. W. Flack, Decisions and Opinions of Commissioners, p. 80.

[57] Case of Virginia Lessard Camerson, *supra,* note 55.

[58] Case of John Walker, Further Decisions and Opinions, p. 18.

[59] Case of Mexican Union Railway, Ltd., Decisions and Opinions of Commissioners, p. 157.

[60] Case of Coralie Davis Honey, Further Decisions and Opinions, p. 13.

[61] Case of W. H. Gleadell, Decisions and Opinions of Commissioners, p. 55.

[62] Case of Central Agency, Ltd., Decisions and Opinions of Commissioners, p. 65.

[63] See case of Vera Cruz Telephone Construction Syndicate, Decisions and Opinions of Commissioners, p. 74, at 77.

[64] German-Mexican Rules, Arts 18, 19, 21-24.

[65] Case of Carlos Klemp, 24 Amer. Journal of International Law (1930), p. 610.

dilatory pleas were considered only in connection with the merits on final decision.[66] Only one *excepción* was filed in the form of a special answer.[67] In other cases the *excepciones* were included in the answer on the merits, which meant that they simply became allegations in the answer rather than independent pleadings.

§222. **Practice of the French–Mexican Commission.** Provisions with respect to dilatory pleas similar to those in the British-Mexican Rules were contained in the Rules of the French-Mexican Commission.[68] The terminology was borrowed from French procedure—the equivalent of the demurrer being the *exception* or *fin de non recevoir,* the equivalent of the motion to dismiss, *conclusions tendant au rejet d'une réclamation,* and the equivalent of the motion to reject, *conclusions tendant au rejet d'une pièce fondamentale.* One decision was rendered on a *fin de non recevoir* raising the issue as to whether the claim of a Lebanese was within the terms of the Convention.[69] In another case in which the Mexican agent had filed a *fin de non recevoir,* he refrained from requesting the suspension of proceedings on the merits, and both the *fin de non recevoir* and the merits were dealt with in one decision.[70]

§223. **Practice of the Spanish–Mexican Commission.** The Rules of the Spanish-Mexican Commission did not embody any of the complicated systems described above. Only a single motion to declare a claim inadmissible (*moción parar declarer inadmissible una reclamación*) was provided for.[71] Such a motion could be made at any time after docketing of the claim and before final submission to the Commission, for any justifiable cause appearing on the face of the record, going to the jurisdiction of the Commission or the merits of the claim.

The Commission handed down five decisions on motions. These

---

[66] Motions to dismiss were filed in several cases but consideration of them was postponed until decision on the merits. Rep. Alemana (Luis Andresen y Carlos Hardt) *v.* Estados Unidos Mexicanos, Decision No. 7 (unpublished); Rep. Alemana (Frederico Griese) *v.* Estados Unidos Mexicanos, Decision No. 8 (unpublished).

[67] In the Klemp Case, *supra,* note 65.

[68] French-Mexican Rules, Arts. 18, 19, 21–24.

[69] Rep. français (Pablo Nájera) *v.* Etats-unis mexicains, Jurisprudence de la Commission franco-mexicaine des réclamations, p. 156.

[70] Rep. française (Jean Baptiste Caire) *v.* Etats-unis mexicains, Jurisprudence de la Commission franco-mexicaine des réclamations, p. 207. In a group of cases involving claims of French nationals in Mexican corporations, the Mexican agent filed *fins de non recevoir* which were withdrawn after the agents of both governments had agreed on the admissibility of the claims. Sentences Nos. 2—A to 29—A, September 11, 1928 (unpublished).

[71] Spanish-Mexican Rules, Arts. 25–27.

motions were made on the ground that the claimant was not of Mexican nationality,[71a] that a certificate of baptism was not sufficient proof of nationality,[71b] that a provision in the supplementary Convention cutting down the jurisdiction of the Commission applied retroactively to claims previously filed,[71c] and that a claimant was not the proper representative of a deceased person's estate.[71d]

§224. **Practice of the Italian–Mexican Commission.** The Rules of the Italian-Mexican Commission provided for an *excepción dilatoria* identical with the demurrer of the British-Mexican Rules.[71e] In addition provision was made for a motion to declare a claim inadmissible. This motion could be made "for justifiable cause" at any time subsequent to the filing of the claim.[71f] No provision was made for a motion to reject a pleading. The Commission did not render any decisions on motions, always dealing with motions when cases were up for decision on the merits.

§225. **The Utility of Provisions for Dilatory Pleas.** It has been seen that dilatory pleas played a small part in the procedure of the Mexican Claims Commission. They may be useful in expediting proceedings under some circumstances, but on the whole they probably are a hindrance rather than a help. It is submitted that the experience of these Commissions shows that elaborate provisions for dilatory pleas are unnecessary in rules of procedure of international tribunals.[72]

§226. **Submission of Cases to the Commission.** All of the Rules made elaborate provision for the bringing up of cases for submission. In the United States-Mexican,[73] British-Mexican[74] and German-

---

[71a] Case of Santos Bárcena, Decision No. 1 (unpublished); Case of Santos Bárcena, Decision No. 11 (unpublished).

[71b] Case of Santos Bárcena, Decision No. 7 (unpublished).

[71c] Case of Angel Lopez, Decision No. 9 (unpublished).

[71d] Case of Constantino Rivero, Decision No. 17 (unpublished).

[71e] Italian-Mexican Rules, Arts. 19–20.

[71f] Italian-Mexican Rules, Arts. 25–26.

[72] It may be noted that the Rules of the Permanent Court of International Justice contain no provisions for dilatory pleas. "Neither the statute nor the Rules of Court contain any rule regarding the procedure to be followed in the event of an objection being taken *in limine litis* to the Court's jurisdiction. The Court therefore is at liberty to adopt the principle which it considers best calculated to ensure the administration of justice, most suited to procedure before an international tribunal and most in conformity with the fundamental principles of international law." The Mavrommatis Palestine Concessions, Publications of the Court, Series A, No. 2, p. 16.

[73] U. S.-Mexican General Rule X 1, 2; U. S.-Mexican Special Rules X 1, 2. In 1926 the U. S.-Mexican General Rules were amended so as to provide for a "trial calendar" in which were to be listed for hearing all cases which either government should submit for that purpose. When the agent presenting a claim desired to proceed to hearing, he had to file notice with the Secretaries and might file a brief at the same time. On receipt of the notice the Secretaries were to list the claim on the trial calendar.

[74] British-Mexican Rules 40–41.

Mexican [75] Commissions the order in which cases were to come up for submission was to be determined either by agreement between the agents, subject to revision in the discretion of the Commission, or by order of the Commission. The French-Mexican [76] Rules provided that the order should be fixed by the Commission either of its own motion or taking into account the agreement of the agents. Under the Spanish-Mexican and Italian-Mexican Rules [77] the cases were submitted in the order in which the agent for the claimant government gave notice that they were ready for submission, but this order could be changed by agreement of the agents, confirmed by the Commission. If there were no cases listed as ready for submission, the Commission could itself order them listed after consulting both agents. In some instances, Commissions do not seem to have exercised any real control over the order of submission.[78]

The procedure followed in submitting a case was for the agent of the claimant government to file notice and a brief with the secretaries, together with such documentary proofs in addition to those already filed by him as he might desire. The agent of the respondent government was required to file a reply brief within a stipulated period (30 days in some Rules, 20 days in others). A counter brief might then be submitted by the agent of the claimant government within 10 or 15 days, and the agent of the respondent was then given a short

---

[75] German-Mexican Rules, Arts. 36–37.
[76] French-Mexican Rules, Arts. 36–37.
[77] Spanish-Mexican Rules, Arts. 40–42; Italian-Mexican Rules, Arts. 35–36.
[78] Note the following account of the proceedings at the opening of one of the sessions of the United States-Mexican General Claims Commission:

"Con anteriodad a la celebración de la sesión inaugural, el Licenciado Rabasa, Sub-agente de México, obrando con instrucciones expreses del Agente, y el Señor Bouvé, Agente de los Estados Unidos de America, se pusieron de acuerdo respecto de los casos en que ambas Agencias estaban preparadas para someterlos desde luego al conocimiento y fallo de la Comisión, y de conformidad con los Reglas de Procedimiento presentaron une lista de los primeros trece casos que deberian ser discutidos. La Comisión, en el acuerdo mencionado [un acuerdo dictado por la Comisión referente a los primeros casos que deberian sometidos en discusión oral al fallo de la Comisión], pretendia que se vieran y fallaran un grupo de reclamaciones que no estaban comprendidas en la lista presentada por ambos Agentes ye como semejante disposición trastornaba fundamentalmente lo pactado por ellas y el plan de preparación formulado por dichas agencias, el Subagente de México y el Agente de los Estados Unidos de América se opusieron a la mencionada orden dictada por la Comisión y al fin se convino en que se procedaria a la vista de dos reclamaciones que aparecián en la lista arreglada por las Agencias y en que posteriormente la Comisión consultaría el paracer de ambos Agentes respecto de la conveniencia de que se sometieran a discusión los casos propuestos por la Comisión, y si esto no fuere aprobado, se procedería a la audiencia de las reclamaciones que figuraban en la lista antes citada." *Memoria de la Secretaría de Relaciones Exteriores,* 1930–31, p. 589.

Nielsen, International Law Applied to Reclamations (Washington, 1933), p. 5, says that the General Claims Commission was "permitted to decide" but relatively few cases.

time (5 days or 15 days) to answer any new matter in the reply brief.

§227. **Oral Proceedings.** There was some difference of practice among the Commissions with respect to oral proceedings. The Rules of the General Claims Commission [79] and of the Spanish-Mexican Commission [80] provided that the agent of the government presenting the claim, or his counsel, should open the case, and the agent of the other government might reply. Further discussion was within the discretion of the Commission which was also to fix the time allowed for oral argument. When a case was submitted in pursuance of these provisions, the proceedings were to be deemed closed unless opened by order of the Commission. Similar provisions were made in the Rules of the Special Claims Commission,[81] excepting that the case was always to be opened by the agent of the United States or his counsel. The Rules of the British-Mexican,[82] French-Mexican [83] and German-Mexican [84] Commissions provided that the agent of the claimant government or his counsel should open the case and that the Mexican agent, or his counsel, should reply. When a case was submitted in pursuance of these provisions, the proceedings before the Commission were to be deemed closed, but, notwithstanding this, the Commission might again hear the agents on any points it might deem necessary. Attendance at the hearings could be waived by either one or both agents. In the case of persons having no connection with the Commission, permission from the Presiding Commissioner was required before they could be present at any hearing. Under the Italian-Mexican Rules [85] the proceedings were to be terminated with the exchange of the written pleadings. Oral proceedings could be had only by agreement of the two agents or by order of the Commission on the request of one of them. If oral proceedings were ordered the Commission was to fix rules for their conduct.

§228. **Rendering of Awards.** The Rules of the various Commissions differed considerably with respect to the practice of rendering awards. The Rules of the General Claims Commission [86] and of the Spanish-Mexican [87] and Italian-Mexican [88] Commissions provided that

---

[79] Rule X 3–4.
[80] Arts. 43–44.
[81] Rules X 3–4.
[82] Rules 42–45.
[83] Arts. 38–41.

[84] Arts. 38–41.
[85] Arts. 37–38.
[86] Rules XI.
[87] Arts. 45–51.
[88] Arts. 39–44.

awards were to be rendered at a public sitting of the Commission.[88a]
Awards were to set out fully the grounds on which they were based, and
were to be signed by at least two members of the Commission. Any
member might render a dissenting opinion. The Secretaries were required to furnish copies of awards and dissenting opinions, to the Agents.
Within a stipulated period after the Agents had been furnished with
copies of an award, the Commission could interpret or rectify the decision if it were obscure, or incomplete, or contradictory, or contained
any errors in expression or calculation, or in which the two texts did
not correspond.[89] Two printed copies of all awards and dissenting
opinions were to be forwarded to the International Bureau of the Permanent Court of Arbitration. The Rules of the Special Claims Commission [90] were somewhat briefer. Awards were to be delivered at public sessions "as soon after the hearing of such claim has been concluded as may be possible." Any member who dissented might make
and sign a dissenting report. Copies of the awards and dissenting
opinions were to be furnished to the agents. Substantially similar provisions were contained in the British-Mexican Rules,[91] with the addition of a provision authorizing the Commission, in its discretion or
on the request of either agent, to "make clear or correct" any award.

The necessity of rendering awards at public sessions was done away
with in the German-Mexican [92] and French-Mexican [93] Rules. It was
provided instead that awards should be "public" and should be notified
to the agents. In addition provision was made for the drawing up of
awards. The Presiding Commissioner was to designate a Commissioner
to make a report for each case. The latter was to draw up a list of
the points which should be treated and communicate this to the other
Commissioners. If the opinion of the reporting Commissioner pre-

---

[88a] This provision seems to have been violated in the rendering of the Dickson Car
Wheel and International Fisheries cases by the General Claims Commission. The dissenting opinions of the American Commissioner in each of these cases conclude with the following remarks: "I consider it to be important to mention an interesting point that has
arisen since the instant case was argued. Rule XI, 1, provides: 'The award or other judicial decision of the Commission in respect of each claim shall be rendered at a public sitting of the Commission.' The other two Commissioners have signed the 'Decision' in this
case. However, no meeting of the Commission was ever called by the Presiding Commissioner to render a decision in this case, and there has never been any compliance with the
proper rule above quoted." Opinions of Commissioners, 1931, pp. 206, 286.
[89] For instances of rectification of minor errors see: U. S. A. (Walter H. Faulkner) v.
United Mexican States, Opinions of Commissioners, 1927, p. 193; U. S. A. (Thomas H.
Youmans) v. United Mexican States, ibid., p. 196.
[90] Rule XI.   [92] Arts. 42–46.
[91] Rules 46–48.   [93] Arts. 42–46.

vailed, he was to draw up the decision of the Commission. If he were in the minority, the Commissioner whose opinion prevailed was to draw up the decision. If there were three opinions, the decision of the Commission was to be drawn up by the Presiding Commissioner.[94] It may be inferred that this arrangement did not work very well in practice. In 1928 the French-Mexican Rules were amended to provide that: "The Commission reserves to itself full discretion with regard to the procedure to be followed in the preparation and drawing up of its decisions." The German-Mexican Rules were not amended but it is significant to note that the great majority of opinions were rendered in the name of the Presiding Commissioner even where the Commission was unanimous.

[94] For the practice followed by the Permanent Court of International Justice in arriving at decisions, see Hudson, Permanent Court of International Justice (1934), Ch. 26

CHAPTER 15

EVIDENCE

§229. The Conflict of Systems of Evidence. The great differences between the Anglo-American and Civil Law systems of evidence result in peculiar difficulties when countries belonging to both systems face each other in the forum of international law. It is a commonplace that the Common Law system contains a vastly greater body of exclusionary rules than the Civil Law system.[1] Yet, it will be found that American and British arbitrators and agents have been much readier to abandon the application of exclusionary rules in international procedure than have their colleagues trained in the Civil Law. Perhaps this attitude is due to the fact that the governments of Great Britain and the United States have more often been claimants than respondents and that it has been to the interest of their representatives to proclaim a greater liberality in respect to the admission of evidence. More probably, the basing of Common Law rules of evidence on the existence of the jury has led American and British lawyers more readily to an acceptance of the view that rules for the exclusion of evidence have little place where the erratic actions of a jury are not to be feared. On the other hand, while the Civil Law systems contain relatively few exclusionary rules, the rules which exist are generally directed to the proper authentication of documents and other formal requirements. Being accustomed to seeing documentary evidence presented in certain forms, Civil Law lawyers have been led to insist on such forms in international procedure, and at the same time, to protest against the use of forms novel to them (*e.g.*, affidavits). In arbitration between countries of similar legal systems, the conflict over exclusionary rules of evidence is less acute. That these conflicts are not irreconcilable is due to the evolution through practice of a series of

---

[1] See Feller, "Evidence in the Modern Civil Law," 5 Encyclopedia of the Social Sciences, p. 646.

standards for the admission and appreciation of evidence peculiarly adapted to international procedure.

§230. **Documentary Evidence: Provisions in the Conventions** The provisions in the Mexican Claims Conventions concerning the introduction of documentary evidence contained no hint of any ex clusionary rules. The United States-Mexican Conventions were the most detailed permitting agents and counsel to offer to the Commis sion "any documents, affidavits, interrogatories, or other evidence de sired in favor of or against any claim." [2] The British-Mexican Con vention contained a similar provision except that the word "affidavits' was omitted.[3] The other Conventions provided merely that agents and counsel "shall present to the Commission, orally or in writing, the evidence . . . which they shall desire to invoke in favor of or against any claims." [4]

§231. **Documentary Evidence: Provisions in the Rules.** Only the Rules of the United States-Mexican and Spanish-Mexican Com missions contained any important additions to the meagre provisions of the Conventions, as far as documentary evidence was concerned.[5] These Rules provided that the Commissions would "receive and con sider all written statements, documents, affidavits, or other interroga tories . . ." presented by the governments.[6] For the United States- Mexican Commissions this was merely a repetition of the provisions of the Conventions, but no such enumeration was contained in the Spanish-Mexican Convention, and the enumeration of these kinds of evidence is significant, particularly since express mention is made

[2] United States-Mexican General Claims Convention, Art. III; United States-Mexican Special Claims Convention, Art IV.

[3] British-Mexican Convention, Art. IV.

[4] French-Mexican Convention, Art. IV; German-Mexican Convention, Art. V; Spanish Mexican Convention, Art. IV; Italian-Mexican Convention, Art. IV.

[5] U. S.-Mexican General Rule VIII 1; U. S.-Mexican Special Rule VIII 1; Spanish Mexican Rules, Art. 28. The British-Mexican Rules (Rule 23) and the German-Mexican Rules (Art. 25) provided that: "The Commission will receive and consider all written statements, documents and other evidence which may be presented to it by the respective agents"; the French-Mexican Rules (Art. 25) that: "The Commission will examine the documents presented by the agents"; the Italian-Mexican Rules (Art. 27) that: "The Commission will receive and consider all written statements, documents, interrogatories or other evidence which may be presented to it by the Agents, within the periods fixed by these Rules, in support of or in opposition to any claim."

[6] The Spanish-Mexican Rules provided for documents presented "by either govern ment"; the United States-Mexican Rules provided for documents presented "by the respective agents or in the name of such agents by an assistant agent or counsel." The Rules of these Commissions also provided that: "no such statement, documents, or other evidence will be received or considered if presented through any other channel." The latter provision was also contained in the Italian-Mexican Rules.

of "affidavits," a species of evidence all but unknown outside of Anglo-American law. More important is the provision in these Rules that the Commission "will give such weight to the documents presented as in its judgment such evidence is entitled in the circumstances of the particular case." This is the principle of the free appreciation of evidence, repeatedly affirmed by international tribunals, and yet requiring constant reaffirmation in the practice of the Commissions. The Rules of all the Commissions contained elaborate provisions regarding the protection of documents on file in governmental archives.[7]

§232. **Oral Testimony.** The taking of oral testimony before an international tribunal is of rare occurrence.[8] Despite elaborate provisions therefor in the Rules of the Mexican Claims Commissions, only a few instances of the appearance of witnesses are recorded.[9] Nevertheless, the provisions are worthy of note as an indication of some problems which may be presented in international adjudication. The United States-Mexican Conventions gave to agents and counsel

[7] If an original paper on file in governmental archives could not conveniently be withdrawn, certified copies thereof might be received. If an agent did not possess a copy of a document on file in the archives of the government on the other side which he desired to present in support of allegations in his pleadings, he could notify the agent of the other government of his desire to inspect the document. Refusal to accede to the request was to be reported to the Commission, which would take note of the refusal together with the reasons assigned therefor. Even though only a part of such a document was brought forward in support of or in answer to a claim, the right to inspect the original extended to the whole of the document but not to any enclosures, annexes, minutes or endorsements, if these were not adduced as evidence or specifically referred to in the pleadings. U. S.-Mexican General Rules VIII 3–5; U. S.-Mexican Special Rules VIII 3–5; British-Mexican Rules 24–26; French-Mexican Rules, Arts. 26–28; German-Mexican Rules, Arts. 26–28; Spanish-Mexican Rules, Arts. 29–31; Italian-Mexican Rules, Arts. 28–29.

In a case before the Italian-Mexican Commission, the Italian agent applied for the production of documents in the archives of the National Claims Commission. The Mexican agent argued that the Rules did not apply to such documents but only to documents which were the property of the claimant or of the requesting agency. The matter was settled by agreement of the agents and was not passed on by the Commission. Case of Michele Ferrara Volpe, Decision No. 31 (unpublished).

[8] On the practice of the Permanent Court of International Justice with respect to the taking of oral testimony see Hudson, Permanent Court of International Justice (1934), p. 502 et seq.

[9] In the following cases it appears that witnesses were heard by the Commission: Rep. français (Th. Gendrop) v. Etats-Unis mexicains, Jurisprudence de la Commission franco-mexicaine des réclamations, p. 203 (unpublished, Mexican Commissioner absent); Rep. française (Hélène Bimar) v. Etats-Unis mexicains, French-Mexican Commission, Sentence No. 31 (unpublished); Case of Santa Gertrudis Jute Mill Co., British-Mexican Commission, Decisions and Opinions of Commissioners, p. 147, at 151; Case of Carl Olof Lundholm, British-Mexican Commission, Further Decisions and Opinions of Commissioners, p. 43; Case of Cecil A. Burns, British-Mexican Commission, ibid., p. 104, at 106. In an opinion rendered on October 3, 1928, it was said by the United States-Mexican General Claims Commission that: "No oral testimony has heretofore been offered to the Commission." U. S. A. (G. L. Solis) v. United Mexican States, Opinions of Commissioners, 1929, p. 48, at 49.

"the right to examine witnesses under oath or affirmation before the Commission in accordance with such rules of procedure as the Commission shall adopt." [10] A similar right was conferred by the British-Mexican Convention except that the witnesses were to be examined "under affirmation before the Commission, in accordance with Mexican Law and such rules of procedure as the Commission shall adopt." [11] No such right was expressly conferred by the other Conventions, but it can be derived from the provision that agents "shall present to the Commission, orally or in writing, the evidence which they shall desire to invoke in favor of or against any claim." [12]

This right to examine witnesses was restated in the Rules of all the Commissions and procedures varying in some degree were provided.

§233. **The Same: United States–Mexican General and Special Rules.**[13] An agent desiring to take oral testimony before the Commission was required to file notice to that effect with the secretaries within fifteen days from the expiration of the time for the filing of the claimant's reply; the notice to state the number, names and addresses of the witnesses and the date on which the application would be made to the Commission to fix a time and place to hear the testimony. No oral testimony would be heard except in pursuance of such notice, unless the Commission were to allow it for good cause shown. Examination of witnesses was to be within the control and discretion of the Commission. Any member of the Commission might, in his discretion and "in the interest of justice" question a witness at any point in the giving of his testimony. A witness produced on behalf of one party could be cross-examined by the agent or counsel of the other. The testimony was to be reported verbatim in writing, the report or a manuscript to be made part of the records, and copies to be furnished to the agents. A witness might testify either in English or Spanish, or, if necessary, in any other language. Translations were to be made, under the direction of the Commission, into Spanish, English, or both languages.

---

[10] U. S.-Mexican General Claims Convention, Art. III; U. S.-Mexican Special Claims Convention, Art. IV.

[11] Art. IV.

[12] French-Mexican Convention, Art. IV; German-Mexican Convention, Art. V; Italian-Mexican Convention, Art. IV; Spanish-Mexican Convention, Art. IV.

[13] U. S.-Mexican General Rules VIII 2, IX; U. S.-Mexican Special Rules VIII 2, IX.

§234. **The Same: British–Mexican Rules.**[14] The same sort of notice of the intention to produce witnesses was required as under the United States-Mexican Rules. Examination of witnesses was to be conducted in accordance with the procedure and in such manner as the Commission might determine. No provision was made for questioning by the Commissioners, but the opposing agent was given the right to cross-examine witnesses. The testimony was to be made a part of the record and copies furnished to the agents. Provision was also made for calling the claimant to give testimony either on the request of the agents or in the discretion of the Commission. After the filing of the last pleading and at any time prior to the award, the Commission might order that the opinion of one or more experts be heard on matters requiring special knowledge, and it might likewise order views of premises. If it were not possible for any witness or claimant to appear before the Commission, he might be examined by means of letter rogatory issued by the Commission or any competent judicial authority at the seat of the Commission. Such testimony was to be received in accordance with the formalities required by law at the place of residence of the witness or claimant. No provision was made with regard to the language in which testimony was to be given.

§235. **The Same: German–Mexican and French–Mexican Rules.**[15] These were identical with the British-Mexican Rules except that provision was also made for a special form of examination by the Commission. The agents could draw up a questionnaire and the witnesses examined in accordance therewith by the Commission. Such examination was to take place after the filing of the final pleading, the witness to be summoned by the agent desiring his testimony.

§236. **The Same: Spanish–Mexican**[16] **and Italian–Mexican**[17] **Rules.** The procedure under the Spanish-Mexican Rules was substantially different from that of the other Commissions. After notice given as under the United States-Mexican Rules, the witnesses would be examined by both secretaries in accordance with interrogatories presented by the agents. The opposing agent had the right of cross-examination. The time for the taking of testimony was to be fixed

---

[14] British-Mexican Rules 27–32.
[15] German-Mexican Rules, Arts. 29–35; French-Mexican Rules, Arts. 29–35.
[16] Spanish-Mexican Rules, Arts. 33–38.
[17] Italian-Mexican Rules, Art. 30.

by the secretaries, and the transcript of the testimony was to be signed by the witness. The Commission might, in its discretion, receive testimony at any stage of the proceedings, and it, or any of its members, might require the appearance, previous to oral argument, of any witness who had testified before the secretaries. Provisions regarding language of testimony similar to those in the United States-Mexican Rules were included; in other respects (testimony of experts and claimant, letters rogatory) the Rules were similar to the British-Mexican Rules. The Italian-Mexican Rules were substantially the same, excepting that the examination of witnesses was to be conducted by the Commission instead of by the secretaries.

§237. **Appreciation of Provisions Concerning Oral Testimony.** The salient defect of the Conventions in this respect is the failure to make any provision for compelling the attendance of witnesses, a defect which is shared by all other arbitral conventions. The problem of compelling testimony before international tribunals is a serious one, as the history of the United States-German Mixed Claims Commission and recent American legislation show.[17a] It would be a simple

---

[17a] The Act of July 3, 1930 (46 Stat. 1005), provides that whenever any claim in which the United States or any of its nationals is interested is pending before an international tribunal established pursuant to an agreement between the United States and a foreign government, each member of the tribunal or a clerk or secretary thereof shall have authority to administer oaths. Every person swearing falsely in any proceedings before such a tribunal *whether held within or outside the United States,* is subject to punishment for perjury. The tribunal is given power to issue subpoenas requiring the attendance of witnesses or the production of documents; failure to obey a subpoena may be regarded as contempt of the authority of the tribunal and may be punished in any United States federal court. Subpoenas are to be served by United States marshals. The tribunal is also empowered to appoint commissioners for the taking of testimony under rules promulgated by the tribunal. Such commissioners may exercise the general duties of special masters in suits in equity. This Act was amended by the Act of June 7, 1933 (Public No. 31), empowering the agent of the United States before an international tribunal to apply to a federal district court to issue subpoenas for the examination of witnesses or the production of documents. The court is empowered to appoint a commissioner or referee for the taking of testimony. The examination is to be conducted by the agent of the United States and witnesses may be cross-examined by the agent of the opposing government who is to be given reasonable notice of the proceedings. Penalties for perjury and for failure to obey subpoenas are provided.

This legislation was occasioned by the "Black Tom" and "Kingsland" cases (U. S. A. (Lehigh Valley R. R. Co., *et al.*) *v.* Germany) before the United States-German Mixed Claims Commission. The United States claimed that German agents had caused the explosion of munitions depots in 1916. On Nov. 13, 1930, the Commission handed down a decision dismissing these cases. The United States then moved for a rehearing on the ground that the Commission had misapprehended the facts and committed errors of law. A supplemental petition alleged newly discovered evidence. On Dec. 3, 1932, the Umpire (Owen J. Roberts) rendered a decision dismissing the petition for a rehearing on the ground that the new evidence was not sufficient to change the original findings. On May 4, 1933, the American agent filed another petition for rehearing alleging (1) "That certain important witnesses for Germany, in affidavits filed in evidence by Ger-

matter for the parties to future conventions of this character to permit the service of compulsory process on witnesses in their respective territories. Witnesses so served might either be compelled to appear before the tribunal or to give testimony before a local court. Such provisions should be supplemented by national legislation, but the problem cannot be solved by national legislation alone. The provisions in the Rules of some of the Mexican Claims Commissions for the issuing of letters rogatory were not binding on the contracting states since they are not stipulated in the Conventions, and such letters could not have the force of compelling testimony.[17b]

§238. General Principles Applicable to the Admission and Evaluation of Evidence. Each of the Mexican Claims Commissions was faced with the problem as to whether it was obliged to follow the rules of some municipal law in the admission and evaluation of evidence. Various principles were pressed in argument: Mexican law must be applicable by reason of the applicability of the *lex loci*

---

many, furnished fraudulent, incomplete, collusive and false evidence . . . ," (2) "That there are certain witnesses within the territorial jurisdiction of the United States . . . who have knowledge of the facts and can give evidence adequate to convince the Commission of the liability of Germany for the destruction of the Black Tom Terminal and the Kingsland plant, but whose testimony cannot be obtained without authority to issue subpoenas and to subject such witnesses to penalties for failure to testify fully and truthfully. . . ." On Dec. 15, 1933, the Umpire rendered a decision to the effect that the Commission had power to reopen the cases and that it should do so in view of the allegations made by the United States. In the meantime, the Act of June 7, 1933, was passed to remedy the defect described in the petition of the American agent. Examination of witnesses was then had under orders of the various United States Courts. See U. S. on behalf of Lehigh Valley R. R. Co. *v.* Government of Germany, 5 Fed. Sup. 97 (D.C.N.Y., 1933).

"Legislation of this kind may point the way to methods of improving procedure before international tribunals. But it also illustrates the difficulties of effecting such a desirable purpose. It is of course purely a matter of speculation as to what might be accomplished by such legislation in dealing with thousands of cases in the course of proceedings interrupted for long intervals from time to time. It is also interesting to consider the question whether one nation can confer on a Commissioner appointed by one nation, or on another Commissioner selected by both nations, power to issue subpoenas, and whether it can empower an international tribunal, constituted in the conventional way, to punish for 'contempt.' It is further interesting to consider whether such powers could be of any use to a commission when sitting in one country, to obtain the testimony of persons in another country. And in any event with respect to the use of a measure of this kind, in connection with pending arbitration proceedings between Mexico and the United States, it seems to be obvious that such legislation could be of little or no purpose, unless identical legislation should be enacted by Mexico, and the two Governments should in effect make the law a common law applicable to the proceedings of the Commission." American Commissioner Nielsen in U. S. A. (Naomi Russell) *v.* United Mexican States, U. S.-Mexican Special Claims Commission, Opinions of Commissioners, 1926–1931, p. 44, at 90.

[17b] Some use was made of letters rogatory. In case of Pietro Gebbia, Decision No. 46 (unpublished), the Italian-Mexican Commission sent commissions rogatory to various Mexican courts to secure testimony of witnesses.

or *lex fori;* the special Mexican legislation relating to the National Claims Commission must be applicable when revolutionary claims were dealt with; Mexican law must be applicable to authentication of documents; when the nationality of the claimant was involved, the rules relating to proof of nationality of the country whose national he claimed to be must be applied. Each of the Commissions gave the same answer: an international tribunal is not bound by any rules of municipal law either in the admission or evaluation of evidence. The statement of the United States-Mexican General Claims Commission has become classic:

"For the future guidance of the respective agents, the Commission announces that, however appropriate may be the technical rules of evidence obtaining in the jurisdiction of the United States or Mexico as applied to the conduct of trials in their municipal courts, they have no place in regulating the admissibility of and in the weighing of evidence before this international tribunal. There are many reasons why such technical rules have no application here, among them being that this Commission is without power to summon witnesses or issue processes for the taking of depositions with which municipal tribunals are usually clothed. The Commission expressly decides that municipal restrictive rules of adjective law or of evidence cannot be here introduced and given effect by clothing them in such phrases as 'universal principles of law' or 'the general theory of law,' and the like. On the contrary, the greatest liberality will obtain in the admission of evidence before this Commission with a view of discovering the whole truth with respect to each claim submitted." [18]

Similar statements were made by each of the other Commissions.[19] There is little need to linger over the evident wisdom of this prin-

---

[18] U. S. A. (William A. Parker) *v.* United Mexican States, Opinions of Commissioners 1927, p. 35, at 38. These words have been frequently quoted. In the Case of Virginia Lessard Cameron, British-Mexican Commission, Decisions and Opinions of Commissioners, p. 33, at 38, British Commissioner Jones stated that in his judgment the reasons advanced in the Parker case "ought to be adopted by this and every other international Commission."

[19] In the Case of Virginia Lessard Cameron, British-Mexican Commission, *supra,* note 18, at p. 34, it was said: ". . . the Commissioners consider that there is no limitation in the terms of the treaty to restrict them in the evidence they receive. The Commissioner is independent of both of the Mexican and the British law and there is nothing in the treaty to suggest the contrary. As an international tribunal the function of the Commission is fundamentally different from the function of a civil national tribunal. The Commission has been created by two sovereign states for the purpose of carrying out a determinate object and both states have selected experienced lawyers who possess their confidence." The Commission then went on to quote from the Parker case, *supra,* note 18, with approval,

"I hold, as a fundamental principle of procedure in regard to evidence, the com-

ciple. Freedom in the admission and evalution of evidence is a hall-
mark of modern procedural systems,[20] and it would seem the only
principle possible of application in international procedure.[21] But,
it is necessary to emphasize the distinction between admission and
evaluation: freedom in admission of evidence means that any evidence
at all will be admitted, *i.e.,* it will go into the record and be considered by the tribunal; freedom in evaluation of evidence means that
the tribunal will be enabled to give to the evidence admitted such
weight as it desires. Yet the latter does not necessarily mean a complete absence of standards for evaluation. Such standards are not

---

plete liberty of the French-Mexican Commission to admit such kinds of proof as it shall
deem it desirable to admit and to evaluate such evidence freely in each particular case,
without being bound in any respect by the legal provisions in force in Mexico. This
being the case, I agree, without any reservation, with the unanimous opinion of the
United States-Mexican General Claims Commission [in the Parker case]." Presiding
Commission Verzijl in Rep. française (Georges Pinson) *v.* Etats Unis mexicains, Jurisprudence de la Commission franco-mexicaine des réclamations, at p. 94.

"As far as the kind of evidence is concerned, our Commission is not bound by any
rule of the Convention and . . . it has the greatest freedom of appreciation in this regard; . . . it considers the testimony, declarations and expert opinions in the record
as amply sufficient to establish the nature and the importance of the losses of which
claimants complain." Case of the Compañía Azucarera del Paraiso Novello, reorganized
French-Mexican Commission, Decision No. 70 (unpublished).

"In accordance with the provisions of Art. 25 of the Rules, the Commission will
receive and consider all declarations, documents and other written evidence presented
by the agents; consequently, the evaluation of these documents, declarations and other
evidence is subject to the judgment of the Commission in every case, without subjection
to special rules of procedure." Rep. Alemana (Juan Andresen) *v.* Estados Unidos Mexicanos, German-Mexican Commission, Decision No. 17 (unpublished).

". . . the appreciation of the evidence and of the facts lies completely within the
judgment of the Commissioners, who are obliged to account only to their consciences."
Case of Santos Bárcena, Spanish-Mexican Commission, Decision No. 1 (unpublished).

[20] The principle of freedom in the appreciation of evidence (*freie Beweiswürdigung*)
has found its most complete expression in Sec. 286 of the German *Zivilprozessordnung:*
"The court shall decide, in consideration of the entirety of the proceedings and the
result of any testimony which may be given, according to its free conviction, whether
a statement of fact is to be considered as true or as false. . . . The court is bound by
legal rules of evidence only in the cases indicated in this Law." For comment see
1 Seuffert-Walsmann, *Zivilprozessordnung* (Munich, 1932), p. 471 *et seq.*

[21] "The commission . . . is not limited in the adjudication of the claims submitted
to it to only such evidence as may be competent under the technical rules of the common
law, but may also investigate and decide claims upon information furnished by or on
behalf of the respective governments. It has indeed been found impossible in proceedings
of this character to adhere to strict judicial rules of evidence. Legal testimony presented
under the sanction of an oath administered by a competent authority will undoubtedly
be awarded greater weight than unsworn statements contained in letters, informal
declarations, etc., but the latter are, under the protocol, entitled to admission and such
consideration as they may seem to deserve." Lasry Case, U. S.-Venezuelan Commission
of 1903, Ralston, Venezuelan Arbitrations, p. 38.

". . . Alors le tribunal arbitral demeurera libre d'employer, pour s'eclairer, tous les
genres de preuve qu'il croira nécessaires; et il ne sera lié, à cette égard, par aucune des
restrictions qu'on rencontre dans les lois positives, spécialement quant à l'administration
de la preuve testimonial." Merignhac, *Traité de l'arbitrage international*, p. 269, cited
with approval in the Franqui Case, Spanish-Venezuelan Commission of 1903, Ralston,
Venezuelan Arbitrations, p. 934.

imposed upon the tribunal, but the latter may, in its own practice, follow certain standards which seem to it advisable, although it will be free to depart from them when circumstances render it desirable. This distinction between freedom of admission and freedom of evaluation was occasionally overlooked in the practice of some of the Commissions, and standards relating to the weight to be given to certain types of evidence were applied as if they were exclusionary rules, in contradiction to the fundamental principles set forth above.

§239. **Applicability of Local Law to Documents Submitted.** In a few cases, Mexican agents objected to the admission of documents because they had not been authenticated in accordance with the requirements of Mexican law. The Commissions before which this objection was made overruled it in every case.[21a] This is definitely in accord with the general principle of freedom from exclusionary rules. A similar application of the general principle is shown in a problem which arose before the German-Mexican Commission. In this Commission evidence was often submitted in the form of depositions taken before Mexican courts. The Mexican agent objected to the admission of such of these depositions as were not taken before Federal courts on the ground that the acts of local courts could not, under Mexican law, bind the Federal government unless a representative of the latter entered an appearance. The Commission rejected this contention and relied freely on such depositions.[21b]

§240. **Burden of Proof.** With respect to the burden of proof, the United States-Mexican General Claims Commission also rejected any application of municipal rules, and established a general principle

---

[21a] *United States-Mexican General Claims Commission:* U. S. A. (Edgar A. Hatton) *v.* United Mexican States, Opinions of Commissioners, 1929, p. 6, at 9: Mexican agent objected that a receipt for military requisitions had not been authenticated as required by Mexican law. The Commission said: "No formalities required by domestic law as to the form of authentication of a receipt for requisitioned property, or the failure of a military commander to comply with those formalities could render such a receipt nugatory as a record of evidential value before this Commission."

German-Mexican Commission: Rep. Alemana (Rademacher, Müller y Cía., Sucs., en Liquidación) *v.* Estados Unidos Mexicanos, Decision No. 25 (unpublished): Mexican agent objected to the admission of a power of attorney executed before a notary public in New York on the ground that it "carece de legalización y protocolización, requisitos indispensables para que surta efectos en la República"; the document was admitted. In Rep. Alemana (Max Müller) *v.* Estados Unidos Mexicanos, Decision No. 37 (unpublished) a statement authenticated by a consul of the United States was accepted without question.

[21b] Case of Guillermo Buckenhofer, Decision No. 5 (unpublished). The same contention was made before the French-Mexican Commission which refused to decide on it. See Rep. française (Georges Pinson) *v.* Etats-Unis mexicains, Jurisprudence de la Commission franco-mexicaine des réclamations, p. 1, at 98.

based on the nature of international procedure,[22] *viz.*, the duty of the agents on both sides to present to the Commission all the evidence which they could discover.[23]

"As an international tribunal, the Commission denies the existence in international procedure of rules governing the burden of proof borrowed from municipal procedure. On the contrary, it holds that it is the duty of the respective Agencies to co-operate in searching out and presenting to this tribunal all facts throwing any light on the merits of the claim presented. The Commission denies the 'right' of the respondent merely to wait in silence in cases where it is reasonable that it should speak." [24]

This does not mean that the failure of the respondent to rebut evidence introduced by the claimant will result in a decision for the former. Nor does it mean that the claimant is obliged to prove its case beyond a reasonable doubt.

"On the other hand, the Commission rejects the contention that evidence put forward by the claimant and not rebutted by the respondent must necessarily be considered as conclusive. But, when the claimant has established a *prima facie* case and the respondent has offered no evidence in rebuttal the latter may not insist that the former pile up evidence beyond a reasonable doubt without pointing out some reason for doubting. While ordinarily it is incumbent upon the party who alleges a fact to introduce evidence to establish it, yet before this Commission this rule does not relieve the respondent from its obligation to lay before the Commission all evidence within its possession to establish the truth, whatever it may be." [25]

Thus, the failure to produce evidence does not automatically decide the case one way or the other.

"In any case where evidence which would probably influence its decision is peculiarly within the knowledge of the claimant or of the respondent Government, the failure to produce it, unexplained, may be taken into account by the Commission in reaching a decision." [26]

---

[22] Ralston, Law and Procedure of International Tribunals, p. 220, states that: "Undoubtedly the burden of proof falls upon the claimants before commissions as in other cases, except in so far as such burden may be removed by the provisions of the protocol." Only the Feuilleton Case, British-Venezuelan Commission of 1903, Ralston, Venezuelan Arbitrations, p. 406, is cited in support. The present writer cannot believe that such is "undoubtedly" the rule, and would consider it highly undesirable if it were.

[23] U. S. A. (William A. Parker) *v.* United Mexican States, Opinions of Commissioners, 1927, p. 35.

[24] *Ibid.*, at p. 39.   [25] *Ibid.*, at p. 39.   [26] *Ibid.*, at p. 40.

To the cynical observer of the habits of lawyers all this may seem nothing more than a pious wish. Is it possible that lawyers, even when representing governments in international disputes, will "co-operate in searching out and presenting . . . all facts throwing any light on the merits of the claim presented"? [27] A final answer to this question is hardly possible, yet the impression gained from a study of the cases is that the agents generally complied with the duty laid upon them. Occasionally it was found necessary to resort to the sanction laid down by the Commission: the drawing of an inference from the non-production of evidence peculiarly within the knowledge of one of the governments. In several instances, evidence presented by the claimant was held sufficient to establish the claim in view of the failure of the respondent government to introduce rebutting evidence.[28] This did not become crystallized into an inflexible rule: in one case it was expressly stated that the respondent had not fully complied with its duty to produce all available evidence, and yet the evidence offered by the claimant was held to be insufficient.[29]

---

[27] Art. 75 of the Hague Convention of 1907 for the Pacific Settlement of International Disputes provides: "The parties undertake to supply the tribunal, as fully as they consider possible, with all the information required for deciding the case."

[28] U. S. A. (National Paper & Type Co.) v. United Mexican States, Opinion of Commissioners, 1929, p. 3: claimant introduced receipts for goods sold, respondent government failed to introduce evidence of person who had signed the receipts; U. S. A. (Edgar A. Hatton) v. United Mexican States, ibid., p. 6; claimant introduced receipt for cattle requisitioned from the A ranch, receipt did not mention name of claimant, respondent government failed to introduce evidence that claimant was not owner of ranch; U. S. A. (G. L. Solis) v. United Mexican States, ibid., p. 48: "In the absence of any evidence from the civilian or military authorities of Mexico destroying the value of the affidavits preserved by the United States, the Commission would not be justified in considering them without evidential value"; U. S. A. (L. J. Kalklosch) v. United Mexican States, ibid., p. 126: dispute as to whether claimant had been wrongfully arrested and mistreated. Mexican agent alleged that court and police records had been destroyed by fire. This was held not to be a satisfactory explanation because some of the records were in another town. "In the absence of official records the non-production of which has not been satisfactorily explained, records contradicting evidence accompanying the Memorial respecting wrongful treatment of the claimant, the Commission cannot properly reject the evidence"; U. S. A. (Lillie S. Kling) v. United Mexican States, Opinion of Commissioners, 1930, p. 36: question as to whether Mexico had been negligent in failing to prosecute assailants of deceased Americans. No evidence as to whether an investigation had been made was introduced.

[29] U. S. A. (Pomeroy's El Paso Transfer Co.) v. United Mexican States, Opinions of Commissioners, 1930, p. 1.
    Cf. U. S. A. (Melczer Mining Co.) v. United Mexican States, Opinions of the Commissioners, 1929, p. 228, at 233, in which it was said: ". . . it may be taken for granted that Mexico could have furnished evidence with respect to the amount and value of the property taken. And it may therefore be assumed that such evidence as could have been produced on this point would not have refuted the charge in relation thereto which is made in the memorial. However, even though this assumption be justified, the Commission would not be warranted in awarding the amount claimed for the pipe line. The evidence produced by the United States is altogether too uncertain."

Only the French-Mexican Commission followed the General Claims Commission in laying down a general principle with respect to the burden of proof.[30] All of the Commissions, however, at one time or another took into account the failure of the respondent government to introduce evidence rebutting that offered by the claimant.[31] Apparently, the one exception to this practice was the rule laid down by the Italian-Mexican Commission to the effect that the burden of proving lenity or negligence on the part of the Mexican government rested on the claimant.[31a]

§241. **Judicial Notice.** No general statement was made by any of the Commissions as to when notice would be taken of facts of public notoriety or of history.[32] There are a number of instances where such

---

[30] Rep. française (Georges Pinson) v. Etats-Unis mexicains, Jurisprudence de la Commission franco-mexicaine des réclamations, at pp. 94–95. In this case, after quoting with approval from the Parker case, Presiding Commissioner Verzijl went on to say: "Indeed, international relations are of such importance and the observation of justice in their development is so necessary, that it would be a crime against humanity to wish to degrade international suits from their elevated position to the level at which so many suits between individuals are unfortunately carried on. Furthermore, I am absolutely convinced that the honor of their countries would prevent the French and Mexican Agencies from acting contrary to the principles enunciated in the passages above cited i.e., from the Parker case]."

[31] *British-Mexican Commission:* Mexico City Bombardment Claims, Decisions and Opinions of Commissioners, p. 100, at 104: "In a great many cases it will be extremely difficult to establish beyond any doubt the omission or the absence of suppressive or punitive measures. The Commission realizes that the evidence of negative facts can hardly ever be given in an absolutely convincing manner. But a strong *prima facie* case can be assumed to exist in these cases in which *first* the British agent will be able to make it acceptable that the facts were known to the competent authorities, either because they were of public notoriety or because they were brought to their knowledge in due time, and *second* the Mexican agent does not show any evidence as to action taken by the authorities."

German-Mexican Commission: Rep. Alemana (Laura Z. Vda. de Plehn) v. Estados Unidos Mexicanos, Decision No. 13 (unpublished): Mexico pleaded that assailants of deceased German had been adequately punished, but failed to produce the court record. The Commission said: "La exhibición del expediente habría permitido determinar la diligencia empleada por los autoridades para el castigo de los culpables, y no puede perjudicar a la reclamante la ausencia de esta pieza probatoria, que no estaba en su mano presentar y que correspondía a la Agencia demandada exhibir para comprobar su aseveración de que no hubo lenidad o falta de diligencia de parte de las autoridades."

[31a] "La prueba de lenidad o negligencia del Gobierno debe ser suministrada por la parte reclamante. Esta regla establecida por la Convención, que es la ley que crea la jurisdicción de este Tribunal, hace difícil, sin duda, para un reclamante acreditar el hecho de tal lenidad o negligencia; pero hay que atenerse a lo que al respecto la Convención dispone." Case of Francisco Barra, Decision No. 20 (unpublished). *Accord:* Case of Salvatore Lammoglia, Decision No. 58 (unpublished).

[32] In 1926 the Rules of the U. S.-Mexican General Claims Commission were amended by inserting the following paragraph in Rule VIII: "Printed or published copies of any public document, reports, and evidence taken in connection therewith, and printed or published under or by authority of either Government may be filed with the Commission and referred to from time to time by either Agent in support of or defense to claims without being proved, where the portion thereof so relied upon is properly identified in pleadings or briefs. Matter so filed and referred to will be given such weight as the

notice was taken of the character of military forces and of the districts in which certain forces operated, and in these cases, the claimant was not required to present evidence on these points.[33]

§242. **Affidavits.** As has been seen, all of the Commissions adhered in general terms to the principle of freedom from exclusionary rules of evidence. Nonetheless, it was contended at various times that affidavits were not admissible in evidence. The affidavit, a statement sworn to by the declarant before an official known as a notary public or commissioner of oaths, is unknown in the procedure of Civil Law countries, although somewhat similar forms for the taking down of testimony exist there.[34] Under the influence of Anglo-American conceptions, affidavits have been used to some extent in international procedure.[35] Still, it is not surprising that the Mexican Agents attempted to resist the use of forms so unfamiliar to them. No question of the admissibility of affidavits could be raised before the United States-Mexican Commissions since the Conventions expressly stipulated that they might be introduced, and both of these Commissions reaffirmed that affidavits would be freely admitted, their evidential value being for the Commission to determine.[36] These Commissions

---

Commission may deem proper in the circumstances of each case. Copies of all such printed or published documents, when filed with the Commission, shall also be furnished or made available to the opposing Agent for his use. Official publications of law, statutes, and judicial decisions and published works of recognized authority on subjects within the cognizance of the Commission may be referred to without being formally proven."

[33] Case of the Mazapil Copper Co., Ltd., British-Mexican Commission, Decisions and Opinions of Commissioners, p. 132, at 135: notice taken that a certain officer operated as a Maderista leader; Case of Augustin Melliar Ward, British-Mexican Commission, Further Decisions and Opinions, p. 107, at 109; notice taken that the Zapatistas formed part of the Constitutionalist Army in August 1914; Rep. française (Hélène Bimar) v Etats-Unis mexicains, French-Mexican Commission, Sentence No. 31 (unpublished): notice taken that the forces which occupied Mexico City from August 14 to 17, 1914, were Constitutionalists; Rep. française (Pierre Petri) v. Etats-Unis mexicains, French-Mexican Commission, Sentence No. 41: notice taken that on March 2, 1915, Coyoacán was occupied by Zapatistas.

[34] Thus §377 of the German *Zivilprozessordnung* provides: "If the object of the testimony is information which the witness would probably furnish on the basis of his books or other documents, the Court may order that the witness need not appear at the trial, provided that he furnish a written answer to the questions under oath. The same may be followed in other cases in so far as the Court, according to the circumstances, in particular under consideration of the nature of the questions, considers a written declaration of the witness as sufficient and the parties are in accord therewith."

[35] See Ralston, Law and Procedure of International Tribunals, p. 215. Affidavits were received by the Permanent Court of International Justice in the Mavrommatis Case. See Publications of the Court, Series C, No. 13—III, pp. 488, 490.

[36] *United States-Mexican General Claims Commission:* U. S. A. (William A. Parker) v. United Mexican States, Opinions of Commissioners, 1927, p. 35, at 37: "Under the provisions of the Treaty and the rules of this Commission, the affidavits of the claimant himself, his brother, and his friend are clearly admissible in evidence in this case. Their

went further and admitted unsworn statements.[36a] The British-Mexican Convention provided for the introduction of "documents, interrogatories or other evidence," and it was argued by the Mexican agent that the omission of the word "affidavits" meant that such documents were not admissible. All the members of the Commission agreed that this contention must be rejected.[37] The opinion of the Commission is based on the necessity of using affidavits.[38] The Mexican Commissioner based his opinion on the principle of freedom in the admission of evidence which he conceived to be "universally accepted, both in Municipal and International Law." [39] The British Commissioner, in a lengthy separate opinion,[40] answered the contentions of the Mexican agent. He denied that the wording of the United States-Mexican Conventions had anything to do with the interpretation of the British-Mexican Convention since the texts of the former had not been put before the British government during the negotiations. The rule of *ejusdem generis* must be invoked with the result that "other evidence" would cover any kind of evidence in documentary form. If it was the intention of the Mexican government, in concluding the Convention, to exclude the use of affidavits, then the text was ambiguous and under the rule of *contra preferentes* Mexico could not take advantage of the ambiguity.

After these three Commissions had decided in favor of the admissibility of affidavits, the Mexican agents argued that even though admissible, affidavits were entitled to no probative force whatever. The most elaborate exposition of this view is the separate opinion of

---

evidential value—the weight to be given them—is for this Commission to determine and in so determining their pecuniary interest and family ties will be taken into account." *United States-Mexican Special Claims Commission:* U. S. A. (Naomi Russell) *v.* United Mexican States, Opinions of Commissioners, 1926–1931, p. 44.

[36a] U. S. A. (William A. Parker) *v.* United Mexican States, *supra,* note 36, at p. 38.

[37] Case of Virginia Lessard Cameron, Decisions and Opinions of Commissioners, p. 33.

[38] "Most of the claims originate in acts of violence, of which documentary evidence will seldom, if ever, be available. The most recent of the facts have been committed nearly 10 years ago and the most remote nearly twenty years ago. It is clear that oral testimonial evidence in most cases cannot be obtained owing to the death or disappearance of witnesses, and that, if available, one would hesitate to attach much weight to the evidence of witnesses who spoke of events which happened so many years ago.

"If, the evidence already being so scarce, the Commissioners were to be deprived of the light of truth, dim as it may be, that may shine out of some affidavits, it would mean that their task would be attended by greater difficulties than seems avoidable, and that the position of one party to the Convention would be seriously prejudiced." *Ibid.,* at pp. 35–36.

[39] *Ibid.,* at p. 48.   [40] *Ibid.,* at pp. 40–44.

Mexican Commissioner Roa in the *Russell* case before the United
States-Mexican Special Claims Commission.[41] The fundamental ob
jection which he finds to the use of affidavits is that they are taken
ex parte, without notice to the opposite party and without opportunity
for cross-examination. This, he considers, makes them valueless in a
contested action. No decision was made by the Special Claims Com
mission on this point. In a case before the General Claims Commission
in which a contention of this nature was made, the Commission (opin
ion by the American Commissioner) held that the express stipulation
of affidavits in the Convention made it impossible to regard them as
being without any probatory force,[42] and went on to say:

> "Unquestionably it is true . . . that affidavits used before domestic
> courts have contained false statements, but it does not follow that, because
> false testimony may be revealed in a given case that there is a presumption
> that all testimony is false, and that a form of evidence sanctioned by the
> arbitral agreement and by international practice cannot be used profitably
> When sworn statements instead of unsworn statements are employed in an
> international arbitration it is undoubtedly because the use of an affidavit in an
> arbitration is to some extent an approach to testimony given before do
> mestic tribunals with the prescribed sanctions of judicial procedure. When
> sworn testimony is submitted by either party the other party is of course
> privileged to undertake to impeach it, and, further, to analyze its value, as
> the Commission must do." [43]

The British-Mexican Commission also refused to hold that affida
vits were not entitled to any weight whatever, though stating that they
"must and will be weighed with the greatest caution and circumspec
tion." [44]

A certain merit must be conceded to both sides of the controversy
If any use at all is to be made of affidavits then they must be weighed
together with all the other evidence. The circumstances of the case
the contents of the affidavit itself, the corroborating evidence, may
in many cases, show that the affidavit under consideration is worthy
of credence. In addition, the sanction of punishment for perjury in
the municipal law under which the affidavit was sworn to may be

[41] U. S. A. (Naomi Russell) *v.* United Mexican States, Opinions of Commissioner
1926–1931, p. 44, at 104–110.
[42] U. S. A. (G. L. Solis) *v.* United Mexican States, Opinions of Commissioner
1929, p. 48.   [43] *Ibid.,* at p. 49.
[44] Case of Virginia Lessard Cameron, *supra,* note 37 at p. 35.

considered as offering some guarantee of the truth of the statements made.[45] On the other hand, it must be admitted that the practice of some of the Commissions in placing great reliance on affidavit evidence is not advisable. The absence of cross-examination is a factor of considerable importance. The solution lies in an extension of the practice of taking testimony on deposition reinforced by conventional stipulation permitting testimonial compulsion by the tribunal. Depositions or "interrogatories" [46] were extensively used in the German-Mexican and French-Mexican Commissions instead of affidavits, with generally satisfactory results.

§243. Interrogation of Agents. In three cases before the Italian-Mexican Commission,[47] the Italian agent, being unable to present proof with the memorial, asked the Commission to permit him to interrogate the Mexican agent with respect to the facts. In Mexican procedure this is known as *"poner posiciones"* or *"diferir el juramento."* The Commission held that such mode of proof was not admissible in a procedure where the governments were litigants. It was only to be applied to a defendant who had personal knowledge of the facts.[47a]

[45] In several cases before the British-Mexican Commission, the Mexican agent argued that no weight should be given to certain affidavits because the affiants were not liable to prosecution for perjury. In all these cases the Commission made use of the affidavits in arriving at its decision without adverting to the Mexican contention. Mexico City Bombardment Claims, Decisions and Opinions of Commissioners, p. 100, at 101: affidavit sworn to before American Vice-Consul in Mexico City; Case of Norman Tucker Tracy, *ibid.*, p. 118, at 120: affidavit of Mexican national sworn to before British consul at El Paso, Texas; Case of Frederick W. Stacpoole, *ibid.*, p. 124, at 125: affidavit of American citizen sworn to before British Vice-Consul in Mexico City.

[46] In the Case of Virginia Lessard Cameron, British-Mexican Commission, *supra,* note 37, at p. 43, the British Commissioner described the interrogatory thus: ". . . a plaintiff or defendant who wishes to interrogate a witness has the right to put to him certain questions in writing, and the questions are put and the answers given by the witness in the presence of a judge. A copy of the questions is furnished beforehand to the other side, who have the right, if they so choose, to frame certain cross-questions which are enclosed in a sealed envelope and handed to the judge, and the judge apparently puts these questions to the witnesses at the time when the interrogatories are taken." This, the British Commissioner said, is not true cross-examination and therefore interrogatories should carry not much more weight than the statements of a witness in an affidavit. The present writer has had no experience with interrogatories, but *a priori* he finds it difficult to agree with this conclusion.

[47] Case of Pietro Gebbia, Decision No. 46 (unpublished); Case of Rosa Spada, Decision No. 48 (unpublished); Case of Francesco Osti y Hermanos, Decision No. 81 (unpublished).

[47a] "La posición o el juramento diferido es recurso probatorio que procede cuando se trata de una demanda dirigida contre una persona en su calidad individual y sus declaraciones pueden contribuir a ilustrar la materia controvertida, pero no lo estimo procedente cuando la demanda va dirigida, no contra el agente en su calidad personal, sino contra un Gobierno del cual el agente es un simple personero." Case of Rosa Spada, *supra,* note 47.

§244. **Evidence of the Claimant.** Since no exclusionary rule
existed, the Commissions readily received evidence given by the
claimant himself in the form of affidavits or depositions. A clear
difference is evident, however, in the manner in which different Com
missions evaluated such evidence. The United States-Mexican Gen
eral Claims Commission treated the statements of a claimant exactly
like any other evidence, taking into account, of course, his pecuniary
interest,[48] and rendered awards on such statements even when uncor
roborated.[49] The British-Mexican Commission, on the other hand
laid down the rule that "only in cases of the rarest exception" could
unsupported affidavits of claimants be accepted as sufficient evidence
"Such documents are sworn without the guarantee of cross-examina
tion by the other party; in nearly all cases a false statement will
remain without penalty, and, as they are signed by the party most
interested in the judgment, they can not have the value of unbiased
and impartial outside evidence." [50] This rule was enforced with the
utmost strictness and a considerable number of claims were dismissed
because they rested on the uncorroborated statements of claimants.[51]
In the only case of the kind presented, the French-Mexican Commission followed the same rule.[52] The rule of the British-Mexican Com-

[48] U. S. A. (William A. Parker) *v.* United Mexican States, Opinions of Commissioners
1927, p. 35, at 37; U. S. A. (Walter H. Faulkner) *v.* United Mexican States, *ibid.,* p. 86
at 95.
[49] "An arbitral tribunal cannot, in my opinion, refuse to consider sworn statement
of a claimant, even when contentions are supported solely by his own testimony. I
must give such testimony its proper value for or against such contentions. Unim
peached testimony of a person who may be the best informed person regarding trans
actions and occurrences under consideration can not properly be disregarded because
such a person is interested in a case. No principle of domestic or international law
would sanction such an arbitrary disregard of evidence.
"It seems to me that whatever may be said with regard to the desirability or neces
sity of having testimony to corroborate the testimony of a claimant, a statement need
not be regarded in the legal sense as unsupported even though it is unaccompanied by
other statements. Statements of claimants may be impeached by information showing
them to be incorrect, and they may be corroborated by statements showing them to be
correct. Evidence produced by one party in a litigation may be supported by legal
presumptions which arise from the non-production of information exclusively in the
possession of another party. . . ." American Commissioner Nielsen concurring in U. S. A
(Daniel Dillon) *v.* United Mexican States, Opinions of Commissioners, 1929, p. 61, at 65
[50] Mexico City Bombardment Claims, Decisions and Opinions of Commissioners
p. 100, at 103.
[51] Case of Annie Engelheart, Further Decisions and Opinions, p. 65; Case of W. A
Odell, *ibid.,* p. 61; Case of John C. J. Leigh, *ibid.,* p. 80; Case of Henry Payne, *ibid.*
p. 110; Case of George R. Read, *ibid.,* p. 154; Case of George Creswell Delamain, *ibid.*
p. 222; Case of Alfred Mackenzie and Thomas Harvey, *ibid.,* p. 277; Case of the
Debenture Holders of the New Parral Mines Syndicate, *ibid.,* p. 281; Case of Sarah
Bryant, Countess d'Etchegoyen, *ibid.,* p. 361.
[52] Rep. française (Marcel Gomes) *v.* Etats-Unis mexicains, Sentence No. 44 (unpub-

mission has much to commend it, particularly where affidavits are used. It is exceedingly difficult to establish the credibility of statements from a written document, and where the statements emanate from the claimant himself they should be considered with the greatest caution. Yet, it is inadvisable to lay down an all but inflexible rule of this nature. In many cases of the kind which come before international tribunals, the evidence of the claimant is the only evidence obtainable. It is often possible to make a reasonable estimate of the credibility of a claimant's statements from the surrounding circumstances. In such a case, the words of Sir John Percival [53] may well be applied:

"If the Commissioners, acting as reasonable men of the world and bearing in mind the facts of human nature, do feel convinced that a particular event occurred or state of affairs existed, they should accept such things as established, regardless of the method of proof established."

Closely related to this problem is the question as to the effect on the weight to be given to the claimant's evidence when it is found that the latter had been guilty of misrepresentation in some particular. Here again the General Claims Commission and the British-Mexican Commission differed. The former held that "exaggeration and even misrepresentation of facts on the part of claimants are not so uncommon as to destroy the value of their contentions," [54] while the British-Mexican Commission stated that: "The Commissioners do not feel at liberty to base an award on the signature of a man who swears that 'the facts are true and correct' and who, by the same instrument in and under which his name appears, is shown not to have been present when the greater part of 'the facts' occurred." [55]

§245. Qualifications of Witnesses. No definite rules for determining the relative merit of testimony given by witnesses were evolved

---

lished, Mexican Commissioner absent): "[La Commission] ne se croit pas justifiée à admettre la materialité d'un vol, sur la simple declaration de l'intéressé, non appuyée par aucune preuve documentaire ou testimoniale."

In several cases the Italian-Mexican Commission held that the testimony of the claimant alone was not sufficient to establish the value of articles alleged to have been destroyed. Case of Alessandro Robbioni, Decision No. 5 (unpublished); Case of Caterina Capiteruccio viuda de Rafael Bello, Decision No. 62 (unpublished).

[53] Dissenting in Mexico City Bombardment Claims, British-Mexican Commission, Decisions and Opinions of Commissioners, p. 100, at 109.

[54] United Mexican States (Francisco Mallén) v. U. S. A., Opinions of Commissioners, 1927, p. 254, at 256. Accord: U. S. A. (Walter H. Faulkner) v. United Mexican States, ibid., p. 86, at 90.

[55] Case of Joseph Shone, Decisions and Opinions of Commissioners, p. 136, at 140.

by the Commissions. Each case was decided upon the basis of the circumstances involved: the evidence of a witness testifying as from his own knowledge was given more weight than one who recounted hearsay or merely confirmed the evidence of another; [56] testimony given a considerable length of time after the event was not regarded as entitled to very great weight.[57] A few statements with regard to the weight to be given to evidence furnished by public officials are to be found. Evidence furnished by a receiver with respect to the assets of a company in liquidation was said to be worthy of special credence.[58] On the other hand, reports furnished by consuls were to be treated like the evidence of any other witness.[59] The Italian-Mexi-

[56] "It is not denied that the statement of a person who confirms what another states in detail may have some value, but it is unquestionably true that in order to form a definite opinion each witness must set forth in his own manner the things he saw or knew since the comparison of different statements throws a light upon the facts equivalent to a confrontation of witnesses." U. S. A. (Pomeroy's El Paso Transfer Co.) v. United Mexican States, United States-Mexican General Claims Commission, Opinions of Commissioners, 1931, p. 1, at 5.

"The Commission, confronted with conflicting evidence, do not hesitate to accept as the more valuable the deposition of the witnesses Martinez and Salazar. That those witnesses were the servants of the claimant has not been established, but even if they were, this would not be a sufficient reason to reject utterly the testimony of persons who had first-hand knowledge of the events and who had been heard under affirmation a few months after they occurred. The account given by them makes more impression than the purely negative assertions of persons who lived a kilometre away and who were, after fourteen years had elapsed, asked to declare what they thought they remembered." Case of Gervase Scrope, British-Mexican Commission, Further Decisions and Opinions of Commissioners, p. 269, at 270.

[57] "The majority of the Commission cannot regard [the affidavit of Señor Carrillo] as possessing such force as to support in a convincing manner the claimant's deposition. The affidavit of Señor Carrillo has been drawn up more than fifteen years after the events; the declarations have been made without interrogation by the other party, and he does not say how the many minute details, about which the affidavit gives evidence, came to his knowledge." Mexico City Bombardment Claims, British-Mexican Commission, Decisions and Opinions of Commissioners, p. 100, at 107.

[58] "This information furnished by the receiver we regard as important. The receiver occupies a position of high public trust for the discharge of which he is answerable under Mexican law." U. S. A. (William A. Parker) v. United Mexican States, United States-Mexican General Claims Commission, Opinions of Commissioners, 1927, p. 82, at 85.

[59] "The Commission has frequently had occasion to consider testimony furnished by Consular officers. Generally speaking, such testimony should be valuable. It is the important duty of officials of this character to search out and report facts to their governments. However, their testimony must of course be considered in the light of tests applicable to witnesses generally, the tests as to a person's sources of information and his capacity to ascertain and his willingness to tell the truth. The Commission has considered reports of Consuls in the light of those tests, giving weight to those which have revealed the ascertainment of facts which opportunity and effort have made possible and of course attaching little importance to reports based on scanty information." U. S. A. (Lillie S. Kling) v. United Mexican States, United States-Mexican General Claims Commission, Opinions of Commissioners, 1931, p. 36, at 47. Reports of consuls were considered by this Commission in the following cases: U. S. A. (Walter H. Faulkner) v. United Mexican States, Opinions of Commissioners, 1927, p. 86; U. S. A. (Harry

can Commission placed great weight on evidence furnished by public officials.[59a]

§246. **Evidence of the Nationality of the Claimant.** There has never been any general agreement among arbitral tribunals as to the rules relating to the sufficiency of evidence necessary to establish the nationality of the claimant. The practice of the Mexican Claims Commission is no exception. The first problem presented was as to whether it was necessary for the claimant government to produce convincing proof of nationality or whether it was sufficient for it to make out a *prima facie* case. The first alternative was accepted by the United States-Mexican General Claims Commission.[60] The nationality of the claimant is one of the conditions of the exercise of jurisdiction; convincing proof of nationality is a jurisdictional requirement. Even the admissions of the respondent government cannot in all cases take the place of adequate proof of nationality.[61] The British-Mexican Commission, on the other hand, was impressed with the difficulty of tracing the life of the claimant from day to day in order to determine whether he had continued to preserve his nationality at all times.

"Such conclusive proof is impossible and would be nothing less than *probatio diabolica*. All that an international commission can reasonably require in the way of proof of nationality is *prima facie* evidence sufficient to

---

Roberts) *v.* United Mexican States, *ibid.*, p. 100; U. S. A. (Laura M. B. Janes) *v.* United Mexican States, *ibid.*, p. 108; U. S. A. (Thomas H. Youmans) *v.* United Mexican States, *ibid.*, p. 150; U. S. A. (L. J. Kalklosch) *v.* United Mexican States, Opinions of Commissioners, 1929, p. 126; U. S. A. (Alexander St. J. Corrie) *v.* United Mexican States, *ibid.*, p. 133; U. S. A. (F. M. Smith) *v.* United Mexican States, *ibid.*, p. 208; U. S. A. (Lily J. Costello, *et al.*) *v.* United Mexican States, *ibid.*, p. 252; U. S. A. (Helen O. Mead) *v.* United Mexican States, Opinions of Commissioners, 1931, p. 150.

[59a] In the Case of Alessandro Robbioni, Decision No. 5 (unpublished), a letter written by the Governor of the Federal District in 1916, stating that certain objects belonging to the claimant were in his office, was admitted in evidence. It was said that this would not be sufficient proof before a tribunal of strict law but that it could be accepted by a tribunal of equity. In the Case of Sucesion del Señor Alfredo Campanella, Decision No. 74 (unpublished), the statement of an official of a government department that he had seen a receipt which was subsequently lost was accepted as evidence. In several cases the statements of public officials of the Secretariat of War were accepted as evidence of the character of forces alleged to have committed injurious acts. Case of José Labatelli, Decision No. 65 (unpublished); Case of Biagio Limongi, Decision No. 68 (unpublished).

[60] U. S. A. (William A. Parker) *v.* United Mexican States, Opinions of Commissioners, 1927, p. 35; U. S. A. (Edgar A. Hatton) *v.* United Mexican States, Opinions of Commissioners, 1929, p. 6.

[61] But *cf.* this statement from Ralston, Law and Procedure of International Tribunals, p. 173: "In many commissions the mere presentation of the claim by the accredited representative of the claimant country has, in the absence of dispute or circumstances of suspicion, been treated by the commission as satisfactory."

satisfy the Commissioners and to raise the presumption of nationality, leaving it open to the respondent State to rebut the presumption by producing evidence to show that the claimant has lost his nationality through his own act or some other cause." [62]

Superficially, there seems to be a considerable difference between the positions of these two Commissions. Yet, the difference is no more than superficial. The General Claims Commission required "convincing" or "adequate" proof; the British-Mexican Commission *"prima facie* evidence sufficient to satisfy the Commissioners." In practice both Commissions arrived at the same result; the claimant government need not make out an ironclad case of nationality but it must present fairly good evidence thereof.

The second problem relates to the rules governing the manner in which proof of nationality must be made. It was argued by Mexico that since nationality is determined by the municipal law of the country whose nationality is claimed, proof must be made in the manner prescribed by that municipal law. [63] Thus, if the law of the State of X prescribes that the nationality by birth can be established only by the production of an entry in the Civil Register, then an international tribunal must require the same proof even though there is convincing evidence of some other character. [64] Only the German-

---

[62] Case of Robert John Lynch, Decisions and Opinions of Commissioners, p. 20, at 21.

[63] "While the Agent of the United States deems that this question falls within the general criteria that must govern the evidence, the Mexican Agent thinks that a proof must be rendered in conformity with the special legislation of the United States in order to prove the civil state and consequently the nationality. The undersigned believes that the soundest doctrine according to International Law is the one expressed by Fiore in his 'Private International Law' (Vol. II, sec. 354). According to that author proof "must be rendered in accordance with the law of the country where the interested party pretends to have acquired the citizenship, when the acquisition of same must be established, and according to the country of origin, when the loss of same must be proved." Separate Opinion of Mexican Commissioner Roa in U. S. A. (Naomi Russell) *v.* United Mexican States, United States-Mexican Special Claims Commission, Opinions of Commissioners, 1926-1931, p. 44, at 110.

[64] Another theory which has been advanced is that proof of nationality must be made in accordance with the forms prescribed by the law of the *respondent* state. This position seems to have been taken by a tribunal of the Permanent Court of Arbitration in the Case of the Religious Properties in Portugal between Great Britain, France and Spain on the one hand and Portugal on the other. In respect of several claims advanced on behalf of persons claimed to be Spanish nationals, the claims were dismissed because the claimant did not prove "in the manner prescribed by the Spanish Civil Code and by the Portuguese Civil Code that he belonged to one of the nationalities mentioned [*i.e.*, British, French or Spanish]." Compromis, Protocoles des Séances et Sentences du Tribunal d'Arbitrage constituée en vertu du compromis signée à Lisbonne le 31 juillet 1913 (The Hague, 1920), p. 24. This holding seems to be unique in international jurisprudence, and is so bizarre as to make any comment unnecessary.

Mexican Commission accepted this point of view.[65] The other Commissions, before which the problems arose, refused to hold themselves bound by the provisions of any municipal law and accepted any form of proof which, in the opinion of the Commissioners, was sufficient to establish nationality.[66] The view of the German-Mexican Commission seems to rest on a confusion between substance and procedure. Nationality is a legal status arising because a municipal law attaches certain legal consequences to a fact situation. This status arises irrespective of any rules relating to proof. Thus, if the law of the State of X provides that a person acquires its nationality by virtue of birth in its territory, then the proof of the fact of birth there establishes that the person in question acquired the nationality of X at birth. The law of X may provide that proof of nationality before its courts may be made only by showing an entry in the Civil Register. But it is not the entry in the Register which creates the status of nationality, it is the fact of birth within the territory. If, on the other hand,

---

[65] Case of Carlos Klemp, 24 Amer. Journal of International Law (1930), p. 610.

[66] *United States-Mexican General Claims Commission:* U. S. A. (William A. Parker) *v.* United Mexican States, Opinions of Commissioners, 1927, p. 35, at 38: "While the nationality of an individual must be determined by rules prescribed by municipal law, still the facts to which such rules of municipal law must be applied in order to determine the fact of nationality must be proven as any other facts are proven." But *cf.* American Commissioner Nielsen speaking for the Commission in U. S. A. (G. L. Solis) *v.* United Mexican States, Opinions of Commissioners, 1929, p. 48, at 49-50: "It has sometimes been said that, since obviously nationality of a claimant must be determined in the light of the law of the claimant government, proof adequate to establish citizenship under that law must be considered sufficient for an international tribunal. Even if this view be not accepted without qualification, it is certain that an international tribunal should not ignore local law and practices with regard to proof of nationality. The liberal practice in the United States in the matter of proving nationality in the absence of written, official records is shown by numerous judicial decisions." This is the reverse of the rule contended for by Mexico. The latter rule is intended to be restrictive. Nielsen's contention amounts to saying that even if the proof is insufficient to satisfy the Commission it should be considered adequate if it would be so considered by American courts. *Quaere* as to whether a laxity of procedural requirements in municipal law should be made use of to give a government an advantage in international proceedings.

British-Mexican Commission: Case of Virginia Lessard Cameron, Decisions and Opinions of Commissioners, p. 33.

French-Mexican Commission: Rep. française (Georges Pinson) *v.* Etats-Unis mexicains, Jurisprudence de la Commission franco-mexicaine des réclamations, p. 1, at 48, Presiding Commissioner Verzijl: "A mon avis, un tribunal international a le devoir de déterminer la nationalité des réclamants d'une façon telle, que pour lui ladite nationalité est certaine, indépendament, en principe, de ce que prescrit le droit national de chaque réclamant individuel. Les dispositions nationals ne sont pas pour lui sans valeur, mais il ne se trouve pas lié par elles; il peut poser des exigences plus rigoureuses que la législation nationale, par exemple pour pouvoir démasquer des naturalisations obtenues *in fraudem legis,* mais il peut également se contenter d'exigences moins séveres, dans des cas où raisonnablement, il ne lui paraît pas nécessaire, afin de former son opinion, de mettre en action l'appareil entier de preuves formelles."

the law of X provides that nationality is acquired only by entry in the Civil Register, then an international tribunal would have to require proof of that fact.[67]

§247. The Same: Consular Certificates of Immatriculation. The most important practical consequence of this divergence of opinion as to the rules governing proof of nationality was with respect to the weight to be given to consular certificates of immatriculation. These are certificates attesting that the claimant has been entered into the register of nationals kept by a consul. The German-Mexican [68] and the Italian-Mexican [68a] Commissions held that such a certificate had no probative force whatever. The British-Mexican [69] and French-Mexican [70] Commissions held otherwise and accepted such certificates as *prima facie* proof. This is a problem on which a number of international tribunals have rendered conflicting decisions,[71] but it is not one for which a categorical solution is possible. A consul is an official charged with keeping a register of nationals, and as such his certificate is entitled to credence. Just how much weight should be given to the certificate depends, it is submitted, on the consular regulations prescribing the requisites for inscription in the consular register. If these regulations provide that the production of a passport is sufficient to enable a person to secure registration, then the consul's certificate is evidence only of the fact that the person inscribed had a passport at the time. If the consular regulations require the production of a birth certificate or a naturalization certificate, then the consul's certificate should be received as evidence of the existence of one of these documents.[72] These considerations formed the basis of the decision of the

[67] The Permanent Court of International Justice has taken the same view as that of the Commissions cited in the previous note: "In the opinion of the Polish government, proof of the acquisition of Czechoslovak nationality can only be established by means of a certificate from the Czechoslovak Government recording the fact. The Court cannot take this view. . . . The Court is entirely free to estimate the value of statements made by the Parties." German Interests in Polish Upper Silesia (Merits), Publications of the Court, Series A, No. 7, p. 72.

[68] Case of Carlos Klemp, 24 Amer. Journal of International Law (1930), p. 610.

[68a] Case of Giovanni Battista Massetto, Decision No. 51 (unpublished).

[69] Case of Robert John Lynch, Decisions and Opinions of Commissioners, p. 20.

[70] Rep. française (Georges Pinson) *v.* Etats-Unis mexicains, *supra,* note 66, at 32–56.

[71] Such certificates were held admissible in the Esteves Case, Spanish-Venezuelan Commission of 1903, Ralston Venezuelan Arbitrations of 1903, p. 922, at 923, Garay Case, U. S.-Mexican Commission of 1868, 3 Moore, International Arbitrations, p. 2532. *Contra:* Case of the Religious Properties in Portugal, Tribunal of the Permanent Court of Arbitration, *supra,* note 64, at 75, 76.

[72] See Camille Jordan, *"Des preuves de la nationalité et de l'immatriculation,"* 9 *Revue de droit international et de législation comparée* (2nd series, 1907), p. 267.

French-Mexican Commission.[73] The British-Mexican Commission seems to have gone further in stating that, "a consular certificate is a formal acknowledgment by the agent of a sovereign State that the legal relationship of nationality subsists between that State and the subject of the certificate." [74] This statement is surely inaccurate. The inscription of a person in a consular register is not a judicial act; it is a mere listing of a name. Certain prerequisites must exist before this listing can be made by the consul. His certificate then can mean nothing more than that these prerequisites existed at the time. It is not, therefore, the consular certificate which is proof of nationality, but the documents not submitted to the tribunal whose existence the consular certificate attests.[75]

§248. The Same: Birth and Baptismal Certificates. The Mexican agents before the various Commissions attached great importance to the production of birth certificates.[76] Baptismal certificates, consular certificates, affidavits were, they contended, merely secondary evidence and should not be admitted in evidence unless birth certificates were not procurable. The United States-Mexican General Claims Commission gave partial countenance to this view in stating that:

"In those jurisdictions where the local laws require registration of births a duly certified copy of such registration is evidence of birth in establishing either American or Mexican nationality by birth; but such evidence is not exclusive, and while ordinarily it is desirable that certificates of registrations of birth, which are usually contemporaneous with the fact of birth, should be produced when practicable in support of a claim of nationality by birth,

[73] ". . . la législation française en matière d'immatriculation consulaire est très stricte et contient toutes les garanties possibles que le consul n'immatricule pas des personnes qui ne possèdent pas la nationalité de son pays." Rep. française (Georges Pinson) v. Etats-Unis mexicains, supra, note 66, at p. 55.

[74] Case of Robert John Lynch, supra, note 69, at 21.

[75] Cf. Case of Herbert Carmichael, British-Mexican Commission, Further Decisions and Opinions of Commissioners, p. 45, wherein a certificate of nationality issued by a Canadian notary public was held not to be proof of nationality. "A notary public, although a public servant, cannot be considered as an agent working under the permanent control of, nor as being in continuous touch with, the Government. The keeping of a register of British subjects does not form part of his official duties. Neither does his normal professional work, nor his previous training therefor, include frequent contacts with questions of nationality. His function gravitates in civil law, not in public or international law. To his declarations in matters of citizenship no preponderating value can be attached." But cf. case of William M. Bowerman and Messrs. Burberry, Ltd., ibid., p. 17, where a notary's certificate was accepted as evidence of the nationality of a company.

[76] See particularly Rep. française (Georges Pinson) v. Etats-Unis mexicains, supra, note 66, at 41, where the Presiding Commissioner pointed out the relative unimportance of a birth certificate as proof of nationality in countries of the jus sanguinis.

or the absence of such certificate explained, it by no means follows that proof of birth cannot be made in any other way." [77]

In several cases both the General Claims Commission [78] and the British-Mexican Commission [79] readily gave weight to baptismal certificates without requiring an explanation of the failure to produce birth certificates, contenting themselves with the assumption that registration of births was probably not in effect at the time in the territory in which birth was claimed.[80] Neither of these Commissions attached much importance to the Mexican contention that the claimant might have been born in another country than the one in which he was baptized. The Spanish-Mexican Commission admitted baptismal certificates as evidence of nationality on the narrow ground that under Spanish law they were entitled to the same status as birth certificates. [80a]

§249. The Same: Other Evidence of Nationality. Before the United States-Mexican and British-Mexican Commissions affidavits of relatives and acquaintances of the claimant were often used in proof of nationality where birth certificates were not available. The British-Mexican Commission stated that: "From one point of view an affidavit sworn by a father concerning the birth of his child has more value than the statement he may make to the Registrar of Births, since the latter statements are not made upon oath." [81] The General

---

[77] U. S. A. (William A. Parker) v. United Mexican States, Opinions of Commissioners, 1927, p. 35, at 37.

[78] U. S. A. (G. L. Solis) v. United Mexican States, Opinions of Commissioners, 1929, p. 48, at 50.

[79] Case of Robert John Lynch, Decisions and Opinions of Commissioners, p. 20, at 22; Case of Robert O. Renaud, Further Decisions and Opinions of Commissioners, p. 114, at 115.

[80] Case of the Lynch case, supra, note 79, the baptismal certificate evidenced a baptism in Cape Colony in 1868. The Commission said: "In view of the date of compulsory birth registration in England, it can safely be assumed that compulsory registration of births was not in existence in Cape Colony in 1868." In the Solis case, supra, note 78, the baptism had taken place in Texas in 1883. The Commission said: "It is doubtless well known that birth certificates are often not available among official records in the United States."

[80a] Case of Santos Bárcena, Decision No. 7 (unpublished).

[81] Case of Annie B. G. Kidd, Decisions and Opinions of Commissioners, p. 50, at 51. The following paragraph from the same opinion illustrates the sort of facts which this Commission considered to be corroborative evidence: "There is first of all the consular certificate, which was delivered a few months after the murder of the late Mr. Kidd and at a moment when the Consul-General must have realized that he was imposing on his government the serious obligation of protecting the interests of the widow and children. Furthermore, the day after Mr. Kidd's murder, there were proceedings before the Constitutionalist Court of First Instance, and in the course of the interrogatories all the witnesses described Mr. Kidd as a native of Canada. Two

Claims Commission, in one case, considered that the fact that a person had occupied public office in the United States was "pertinent" evidence of American citizenship,[82] and in other cases gave weight to the fact that claimants had voted in the United States and had served on juries.[83] On one occasion, the same Commission held that an entry of a birth in a family bible was sufficient to establish birth.[84]

§250. "Best Evidence Rule." The discussion of birth and baptismal certificates above, illustrates an application of what might be called the best evidence rule on an analogy with Anglo-American law. The one general statement of this rule was made by the British-Mexican Commission.

"The Commission . . . realize that the weighing of outside evidence, if any such be produced, may be influenced by the degree to which it was possible to produce proof of a better quality. In cases where it is obvious that everything has been done to collect stronger evidence and where all efforts to do so have failed, a court can be more easily satisfied than in cases where no such endeavor seem to have been made. This consideration has guided and will guide the Commission in other cases, for instance, as regards the fixing of the amount of the award. But in the claim now before them the Commission cannot believe that it would have been impracticable to produce at least some corroboration of the statement of the claimant." [85]

The Rules of several of the Commissions provided that copies of documents in governmental archives might be produced only where there were difficulties in the way of obtaining the originals from such archives.[86]

§251. The Quantum of Evidence Necessary to Establish Certain Facts. In general, the Commissions followed the ordinary rules

---

weeks after the murder of Mr. Kidd, the British Chargé d'Affaires at Mexico City reported to the Governor-General of Canada that 'a Canadian, Mr. W. A. Kidd' had been killed. Moreover there is the further fact that Mrs. Kidd returned to Canada after she lost her husband and that she was at once appointed as tutor of her minor children with the approval of the relatives on both sides."

[82] U. S. A. (Daniel R. Archuleta) v. United Mexican States, Opinions of Commissioners, 1929, p. 73, at 75.

[83] U. S. A. (Adolph and Charles Deutz) v. United Mexican States, Opinions of Commissioners, 1929, p. 213, at 214.

[84] U. S. A. (Mary E. A. Munroe) v. United Mexican States, Opinions of Commissioners, 1929, p. 314, at 316.

[85] Case of W. Allan Odell, Further Decisions and Opinions of the Commissioners, p. 61, at 63. See also Mexico City Bombardment Claims, Decisions and Opinions of Commissioners, p. 100, at 107.

[86] British-Mexican Rule 24; French-Mexican Rules, Art. 26; German-Mexican Rules, Art. 26.

with respect to the quantum of proof. However, with respect to certain facts a heavier burden was laid on the claimant government.

(1) *Evidence necessary to establish international delinquency.* It is a serious matter to charge a government with a violation of international law. Quite properly, many international tribunals have posited a presumption of the lawfulness of governmental acts. Something more than a *prima facie* case is therefore required to sustain such a charge.[87] The General Claims Commission stated that such evidence must be "convincing"[88] and again that it must be "of the highest and most conclusive character."[89] Is it ever possible to produce "conclusive" evidence of an international delinquency? The present writer is inclined to doubt it. "Convincing" is perhaps as strong an adjective as can be applied to the quantum of proof necessary in these cases. The British-Mexican Commission laid down a rather more definite rule of proof of negligence of authorities in failing to suppress or punish for injuries to aliens.

". . . a strong *prima facie* evidence can be assumed to exist in these cases in which *first* the British Agent will be able to make it acceptable that the facts were known to the competent authorities, either because they were of public notoriety or because they were brought to their knowledge in due time, and *second* the Mexican Agent does not show any evidence as to action taken by the authorities."[90]

(2) *Evidence necessary to establish a contract with a government.* The United States-Mexican General Claims Commission had before it one case involving the question as to whether there was a special rule of evidence with regard to the proof of the existence of a contract with a government.[91] It was alleged that the claimant had conveyed mail for the Mexican government and had stabled horses be-

---

[87] See Ralston, Law and Procedure of International Tribunals, pp. 223–224.
[88] U. S. A. (Daniel R. Archuleta) v. United Mexican States, Opinions of Commissioners, 1929, p. 73, at 77.
[89] U. S. A. (Walter J. N. McCurdy) v. United Mexican States, Opinions of Commissioners, 1929, p. 137, at 141. Perhaps this language was used because of the endeavor to prove "misconduct, in a grave degree," of Mexican officials. See also U. S. A. (Charles E. Tolerton) v. United Mexican States, Opinions of Commissioners, 1927, p. 402.
[90] Mexico City Bombardment Claims, Decisions and Opinions of Commissioners, p. 100, at 101. The dissenting opinion of the Mexican Commissioner stresses the necessity of "conclusive" proof. See also his dissenting opinion in the Case of the Santa Gertrudis Jute Mill Co., Ltd., *ibid.*, p. 147, at 153.
[91] U. S. A. (Pomeroy's El Paso Transfer Co.) v. United Mexican States, Opinions of Commissioners, 1931, p. 1.

longing to the Mexican Post Office, during the Madero revolution in 1911, at the request of Mexican postal authorities. The claimant did not produce any written evidence of the alleged contract. The Commission adverted to this fact in disallowing the claim, saying:

"It is known that the same contracts which, when made between persons, require little or no formality, upon being entered into with governments, require special formalities adapted to the character of the latter, which are that of entities, exercising their functions through agencies. Such formalities are necessary as well for the transaction as for exacting from the government compliance with its obligations. From the foregoing it is clear that to establish before any tribunal the existence of a contract with a government, the requirements are more rigorous and exacting than when the contract is between private persons." [92]

This may seem to set up an international "Statute of Frauds" with respect to governmental contracts. Yet it is to be noted that the Commission proceeded largely on the ground that the evidence of the existence of an oral contract was not convincing. Had this not been the case, it is believed that the Commission would have given an award as it had done in an earlier case involving an oral contract.[93] Still, it is difficult to understand why the requirements for proving a governmental contract should be "more rigorous and exacting" than when the contract is between private persons. If the governmental authorities violated their regulations in failing to give a written order, the private claimant should not be penalized therefor. The latter should be required to show some cause why a written order was not asked for. Once the tribunal is satisfied that such cause existed, it should apply the ordinary rules of proof to the existence of the contract.

(3) *Evidence necessary to establish amount of damages to property*. It is often a difficult task for a tribunal to establish the amount of property damages. In the case of movable property, particularly, the facts are peculiarly within the knowledge of the claimant and the tribunal must exercise great caution to guard against exaggeration of the amount of loss. Several of the Commissions therefore followed the practice of awarding an arbitrary amount on equitable grounds

[92] *Ibid.*, at 10.
[93] U. S. A. (Joseph E. Davies) *v.* United Mexican States, Opinions of Commissioners, 1927, p. 197.

where they were not satisfied that the amount claimed was not exaggerated.[94] This practice apparently did not satisfy the Mexican Government, and the British-Mexican Supplementary Convention of 1931 amended Article 2 of the original Convention by adding the words "that its amount be proved" [*i.e.*, the amount of the alleged damage]. In a case arising subsequently [95] the Mexican agent contended that this meant that the claim had to be rejected unless there were proof of the amount claimed in the memorial, the Commission no longer enjoying discretion to fix the amount of the award. The Commission rejected this contention. In its view it still enjoyed discretion to fix the amount, and the only meaning which the amendment had was that the British agent could no longer leave the amount entirely to the Commission's discretion but was obliged to furnish all available evidence as to the amount.[96] This is probably as sen-

---

[94] *British-Mexican Commission*—Mexico City Bombardment Claims, Decisions and Opinions of Commissioners, p. 100, at 104–105: "The majority of the Commissioners are convinced that losses have been suffered and that, according to the Convention, they are to be compensated by the United Mexican States, and the mere fact that their amount has not yet been established cannot deprive the claimants of their right. . . . But it seems equally wrong to accept, in the absence of convincing evidence, the figures calculated by each of the claimants. . . . To this dilemma the Commission sees only one solution, *i.e.*, to lay down its own rule for the judging of the award. . . . This rule adopted by the majority of the Commissioners is that the Mexican Government, in the absence of clear evidence, cannot be obliged to pay more to each claimant than the amount representing the value of such objects as may be safely supposed to constitute the average portable property of young, unmarried men of the social class for which the Hostels of the Y.M.C.A. are particularly destined. Arbitrary as this amount may seem, it is more in conformity with the spirit of the Convention than either the denial of all award whatever or the granting of sums for which no reliable evidence exists." Followed in Case of Frederick W. Stacpoole, *ibid.*, p. 124.

    German-Mexican Commission—Rep. Alemana (Waldemar Julsrud) *v.* Estados Unidos Mexicanos, Decision No. 41 (unpublished): "No hay antecedents bastantes . . . para apreciar el monto de los daños y sobre muchas partidas de la reclamación no existe prueba alguna. Procede, en consecuencia, hacer una avaluación global, en equidad, de los daños sufridos en sus bienes por el reclamante." *Accord:* Rep. Alemana (Carlos F. Haerter y Otto Guthaes) *v.* Estados Unidos Mexicanos, Decision No. 15 (unpublished); Rep. Alemana (Adolfo Luedecke) *v.* Estados Unidos Mexicanos, Decision No. 16 (unpublished).

    French-Mexican Commission—Rep. française (Hélène Bimar) *v.* Etats-Unis mexicains, Sentence No. 31 (unpublished). Claim was made in the amount of 63,427.02 pesos, and 15,000 pesos were awarded because the Commission was not convinced that the loss was as great as claimed. The Commission required proof of loss to be made in exact detail, stating in the *motifs:* "Attendu que la réclamante n'a pu produire qu'une liste des meubles, bijoux, marchandises et valeurs dont elle a été dépouillé sans pouvoir produire à l'appui les factures d'achat ou telle autre preuve; Attendu que, pour ce qui concerne les bijoux, la réclamante n'a pu fournir avec toute précision le poids des perles et des diamants; Attendu que pour ce qui concerne les actions de la Banque Nationale et de la Banque de Londres y México, la réclamante n'a pu apporter les numéros de ces titres, . . ."

[95] Case of John Gill, Further Decisions and Opinions of Commissioners, p. 85.

[96] "*By whom it is to be proved?* The answer is: by the British Agent, who is no longer—as he was before the change in the Convention—allowed to leave the amount

sible an interpretation of the cryptic language of the amendment as
is possible. Certainly, the interpretation of the Mexican agent would
have resulted in great injustice. Yet it comes as something of a shock
to hear that without such a provision the agent for the claimant
government could forego producing any evidence as to the amount of
damages and throw himself on the discretion of the Commission.

§252. **Some Examples of the Kinds of Evidence Made Use of
by the Commissions.** It may be interesting to catalogue briefly some
of the kinds of evidence which were introduced. Balance sheets authenticated under oath by a public accountant were admitted as competent evidence of the assets of a company.[97] Photographs were used
to show the ruinous condition of a building after occupation by revolutionary forces.[98] A certified copy of a will was accepted to prove
that the claimant was sole heir of her deceased husband and executrix
of his will.[99] The British-Mexican Commission permitted proof of
the national character of a company to be made by the production
either of a certificate of incorporation [100] or of a notary's certificate.[101]
In accordance with the general practice of international tribunals receipts for military requisitions issued by military authorities in the
field were admitted in evidence.[102]

---

entirely to the discretion of the Commission, but who is now obliged to show everything in his possession and everything which may be available, and to do everything
in his power, in order to make the amount of the damage acceptable. A claim for
an obviously exaggerated amount, asked by a claimant, cannot be exposed to him
while leaving the final determination to the Commission. He is to create the conviction that he has earnestly tried to place all existing evidence at our disposal. In
other words, he has to produce such evidence and to use such arguments as to enable
the Commission to award a fair and reasonable amount." *Ibid.,* at 90.

[97] U. S. A. (William A. Parker) *v.* United Mexican States, United States-Mexican
General Claims Commission, Opinions of Commissioners, 1927, p. 82, at 84.

[98] Case of James Hammet Howard, British-Mexican Commission, Further Decisions
and Opinions, p. 226. In the Case of Alfredo Attolini, Italian-Mexican Commission,
Decision No. 17 (unpublished), photographs of a sacked house were given no weight in
the absence of testimony as to when the photographs were taken.

[99] Case of Mrs. J. H. Henderson, British-Mexican Commission, Further Decisions
and Opinions, p. 30, at 31.

[100] Case of the Madera Co., Ltd., Further Decisions and Opinions, p. 67.

[101] Case of William M. Bowerman and Messrs. Burberry's, Ltd., Further Decisions
and Opinions, p. 17. *Cf.* Case of Herbert Carmichael, *supra,* note 72a, in which the
same Commission refused to consider a notary's certificate as evidence of the nationality of an individual.

[102] U. S. A. (Edgar A. Hatton) *v.* United Mexican States, United States-Mexican
General Claims Commission, Opinions of Commissioners, 1929, p. 6; Case of the Mazapil
Copper Co., British-Mexican Commission, Decisions and Opinions of Commissioners,
p. 132. Case of Denis J. and Daniel Spillane, British-Mexican Commission, Further
Decisions and Opinions, p. 330; Case of Robert Henderson, *ibid.,* p. 332; Rep. Alemana
(Waldemar Julsrud) *v.* Estados Unidos Mexicanos, German-Mexican Commission, De-
cision No. 41 (unpublished); Case of Sucesion de Giacomo Spada, Italian-Mexican

§253. **Time Limits for the Presentation of Evidence.** In none of the Conventions was any provision made for limiting the introduction of evidence to any time before the close of the proceedings. Nor was any attempt made to impose any limits in the Rules of the General or Special Claims Commissions, or of the French-Mexican, British-Mexican or German-Mexican Commissions. The absence of any express limitations on the introduction of new evidence seems to have occasioned difficulties in at least two of the Commissions. In 1928 the French-Mexican Rules were amended so as to permit expressly the introduction of new evidence during the oral hearings, the adverse party being allowed ten days in which to answer such evidence.[103] Previously, in 1926, the General Claims Rules had been amended in a contrary sense: Each memorial, answer or reply had to be accompanied, at the time of filing, by copies of all the proof on which the party presenting it intended to rely. Proof presented at a later date was to be rejected by the Commission, unless the agents, by stipulation confirmed by the Commission, agreed upon the admission of further evidence.[104] Similar provisions were incorporated into the Spanish-Mexican[105] and Italian-Mexican[106] Rules when these were adopted.

The amended provision of the General Claims Rules accords with the severe criticism which has recently been made of the practice of admitting new evidence at any stage of the proceedings. It has been suggested that future conventions "should contain stipulations which would allow the introduction of new evidence, after the issues of fact have first been shaped, only after a showing that its introduction is

Commission, Decision No. 16 (unpublished); Case of Mme. Villamil de Mansigny, reorganized French-Mexican Commission, Sentence No. 36 (unpublished). *Cf.* U. S. A. (Macedonio J. García) *v.* United Mexican States, United States-Mexican General Claims Commission, Opinions of Commissioners, 1927, p. 146.

For the practice of other international tribunals see Ralston, Law and Procedure of International Tribunals, pp. 217–218.

[103] Art. 38.

[104] Rule IV 8. The United States-Mexican General Claims Protocol of April 24, 1934, provided that all evidence on behalf of the claimant government should be filed with the memorial, and all evidence on behalf of the respondent government with the answer. No further evidence was to be filed, except such evidence with the brief as would rebut evidence filed with the answer.

[105] Art. 20.

[106] Art. 18. The Italian-Mexican Rules differed somewhat from the General Claims and Spanish-Mexican Rules. There was no express statement that proof presented subsequent to the filing of pleadings was to be rejected, and if the agents failed to agree on the admission of new evidence the Commission could decide.

In the Case of María de Jesús Picaso viuda de Visconti, Decision No. 57 (unpublished), the Italian-Mexican Commission refused to receive proof of nationality presented after the time for filing claims had expired.

necessary to a proper adjudication of the case and also after a showing of real inability to have produced it before." [107]   The considerations which can be marshalled in support of this suggestion are compelling,[108] and there can be little doubt that some limitation of the
time is necessary.[109]

[107] American and Panamanian General Claims Arbitration, Report of Bert L. Hunt,
Washington (1934), p. 22.

[108] "Issues of law arise from properly proven facts. The essential facts should
therefore be established before an effort is made definitely to apply the law thereto,
and if the basic facts are to be changed or modified after the development of the law,
not only is much time wasted in such development but the real issues are thereby
confused and the work of the tribunal made more difficult. Moreover, it is not incon-
ceivable that, on occasion, vital evidence may be withheld until the time for the collection of counter-evidence shall have passed. . . . It is much more important that
all evidence be introduced with the earliest pleadings in arbitration cases because, unlike
in domestic proceedings, the matter of obtaining counter evidence is often a very difficult and dilatory one, and consequently the development of new issues of fact and
law at late stages of the arbitral pleadings unduly prolong the proceedings." *Loc. cit.*

[109] Art. 52 of the Statute of the Permanent Court of International Justice provides:
"After the Court has received the proofs and evidence within the time specified for
the purpose, it may refuse to accept any further oral or written evidence that one party
may desire to present unless the other side consent."

The Court's interpretation of this provision was set forth in the Peter Pázmany
University Case as follows: "According to the Court's previous practice, if there is no
special decision fixing the time limit contemplated by Article 52 of the State for the
production of new documents, this time limit has been regarded as expiring upon the
termination of the written proceedings; if, after a case is ready for hearing, new documents are produced by one party, the consent referred to in that Article has been presumed unless the other party, after receiving copies of such documents, lodges an
objection; but in the absence of that party's consent, the Statute allows the Court
to refuse to accept the documents in question but does not oblige it to do so.

"In these circumstances, it is desirable that, at the opening of the oral proceedings,
the Court should know the views of the two parties with regard to the intended production of new documents by one of them. For this reason, such an intention should,
if possible, be expressed early enough to enable the other party to intimate, before
the hearings, whether it gives or withholds its consent." Publications of the Court,
Series A/B, No. 61, p. 215.

CHAPTER 16

AGENTS AND COUNSEL

§254. Agents and Counsel Distinguished. In all international arbitrations carried on in judicial form the governments are represented by agents.[1] Rarely are the functions of agents set forth with any clarity in *compromis* or claims conventions.[2] Nevertheless, custom has developed to such an extent that the agent has achieved a fairly well defined status.[3] In the hands of the agent are the general management and control of the case. He is the intermediary between the tribunal and the government he represents and his powers are exceptionally wide. He may engage the responsibility of his government in connection with matters before the tribunal, and his government may be bound by his declarations or conduct.[4] The position of counsel or advocates of a government is to be sharply differentiated from that of the agent. Counsel act under the direction and control of the agent and their chief function is to address arguments to the tribunal.[5] They cannot take decisions regarding questions of procedure which will bind the government [6] which they represent and

---

[1] "Without reference to [an agent] in the protocol the governments are universally represented by such an officer." Ralston, Law and Procedure of International Tribunals, p. 192.

[2] An unusually detailed provision for the functions of agents and counsel is Art. 2 of the United States-British Claims Convention of Feb. 8, 1853. U. S. Treaty Series No. 123.

[3] See Ralston, *op. cit., supra*, note 1, pp. 192–197.

[4] In a case before the Permanent Court of International Justice, the court stated in regard to certain declarations made to it by an agent that it was "in no doubt as to the binding character of all these declarations." Case Concerning German Interests in Upper Silesia, Publications of the Court, Series A, No. 7, p. 13. In another case, a declaration by an agent was recorded in the operative part of the judgment. Case of the Free Zones, Series A/B, No. 46, p. 172.

[5] In the Fur Seal Arbitration between the United States and Great Britain, the tribunal refused to recognize the right of agents to argue on motions. The agents presented the motions and counsel argued them. This is clearly out of line with the usual practice of tribunals. Agents may always argue before the tribunal.

[6] See Publications of the Permanent Court of International Justice, Series E, No. 7, p. 294.

284

their declarations or conduct will not engage the responsibility of that government.

§255. **Provisions in the Conventions.** These are the rules evolved by the practice of international tribunals. They furnish the background for the application of the provisions of the Mexican Claims Commissions where no differentiation was made between agents and counsel. Thus, the Conventions with the United States provided:

Each Government may nominate and appoint agents and counsel,[7] who will be authorized to present to the Commission, orally or in writing, all the arguments deemed expedient in favor of or against any claim. The agents or counsel of either Government may offer to the Commission any documents, affidavits, interrogatories, or other evidence desired in favor of or against any claim and shall have the right to examine witnesses under oath or affirmation before the Commission, in accordance with such rules of procedure as the Commission shall adopt.[8]

This form was followed, with some changes in wording, in the British-Mexican Convention.[9] The other Conventions were considerably less detailed. They were in this form:

Each Government may appoint an agent and counsel who shall present to the Commission, orally or in writing, the evidence and arguments which they may deem desirable to invoke in support of the claims or against them.[10]

§256. **Provisions in the Rules of Procedure.** While the Conventions indiscriminately placed agents and counsel on the same footing, the Rules of Procedure showed a clear differentiation between the two. The agent was required to subscribe or countersign every

[7] The Conventions with the United States employ the plural, all the other Conventions provide for the appointment of "an agent and counsel." The Spanish version of the Conventions with the United States employs the terms *"agentes y abogados."* In all the other Conventions the terms are: *"un agente y consejeros."* Versions in other languages are as follows: French—*"un agent et des conseils"*; German—*"einen Vertreter"* and *"Berater"*; Italian—*"un agente e dei consiglieri."*

[8] General Claims Convention, Art. III; Special Claims Convention, Art. IV.

[9] "Each government may appoint an Agent and Counsel to present to the Commission either orally or in writing the evidence and arguments they may deem it desirable to adduce either in support of the claims or against them.

"The Agent or Counsel of either Government may offer to the Commission any documents, interrogatories or other evidence desired in favour of or against any claim and shall have the right to examine witnesses under affirmation before the Commission, in accordance with Mexican Law and such rules of procedure as the Commission shall adopt." British-Mexican Convention, Art. IV.

[10] French-Mexican Convention, Art. IV; German-Mexican Convention, Art. V; Italian-Mexican Convention, Art. IV; Spanish-Mexican Convention, Art. IV.

memorial.[11] He was required to file notice with the secretaries that a case was ready to be submitted.[12] An agent was obliged to take notice of all orders of the Commission [13] and was entitled to receive copies of all pleadings and documents filed with the secretaries.[14] Agents of the two Governments might stipulate to extend the date on which an answer [15] or reply [16] was to be filed. They might stipulate an amendment to pleadings,[17] and might agree, subject to revision in the discretion of the Commission, on the order in which cases should come on for submission before the Commission.[18] Most important of all they might settle claims by agreement.[19]

While the Conventions all provided for the presentation of evidence by agents *and counsel,* the Rules of all the Commissions except one provided that the Commission would receive and consider evidence presented to it by the *agents.*[20] Even the one exception, the Rules of the United States-Mexican General Claims Commission, placed counsel in a subordinate role: the Commission would receive evidence "presented to it by the respective agents or in the name of such agents by an assistant agent or counsel." [21] The same Rules pro-

[11] U. S.-Mexican General Rule IV 2; U. S.-Mexican Special Rule IV 2; British-Mexican Rule 10; French-Mexican Rules, Art. 11; German-Mexican Rules, Art. 11; Spanish-Mexican Rules, Art. 13; Italian-Mexican Rules, Art. 11.

[12] U. S.-Mexican General Rule X 2; U. S.-Mexican Special Rule X 2; British-Mexican Rule 41; French-Mexican Rules, Art. 37; German-Mexican Rules, Art. 37; Spanish-Mexican Rules, Art. 40; Italian-Mexican Rules, Art. 35.

[13] U. S.-Mexican General Rule VI; no parallel provisions in the Rules of other Commissions.

[14] U. S.-Mexican General Rule XII 1 (f); U. S.-Mexican Special Rule XII 1 (f); British-Mexican Rule 53 (e); French-Mexican Rules, Art. 51 (e); German-Mexican Rules, Art. 51 (e); Spanish-Mexican Rules, Art. 52 (g); Italian-Mexican Rules, Art. 48 (e).

[15] U. S.-Mexican General Rule IV 3 (a); U. S.-Mexican Special Rule IV 3 (a); British-Mexican Rule 12 (a); French-Mexican Rules, Art. 14; German-Mexican Rules, Art. 14 (a); Spanish-Mexican Rules, Art. 14 (a); Italian-Mexican Rules, Art. 12 (a).

[16] U. S.-Mexican General Rule IV 4 (a); U. S.-Mexican Special Rule IV 4 (a); British-Mexican Rule 12 (b); French-Mexican Rules, Art. 15; German-Mexican Rules, Art. 15 (a); Spanish-Mexican Rules, Art. 15 (a); Italian-Mexican Rules, Art. 13 (a).

[17] U. S.-Mexican General Rule 5 (a); U. S.-Mexican Special Rule 5 (a); British-Mexican Rule 15; French-Mexican Rules, Art. 17; German-Mexican Rules, Art. 17; Spanish-Mexican Rules, Art. 17; Italian-Mexican Rules, Art. 15.

[18] U. S.-Mexican General Rule X 1; U. S.-Mexican Special Rule X 1; British-Mexican Rule 40; French-Mexican Rules, Art. 36; German-Mexican Rules, Art. 36; Spanish-Mexican Rules, Art. 42; Italian-Mexican Rules, Art. 36.

[19] U. S.-Mexican General Rule XI 3; U. S.-Mexican Special Rule XI 3; British-Mexican Rules 33-35; French-Mexican Rules, Art. 45; German-Mexican Rules, Art. 45; Spanish-Mexican Rules, Art. 47; Italian-Mexican Rules, Art. 41.

[20] U. S.-Mexican Special Rule VIII 1; British-Mexican Rule 23; French-Mexican Rules, Art. 25; German-Mexican Rules, Art. 25; Italian-Mexican Rules, Art. 27. The Spanish-Mexican Rules, Art. 28, speak of the presentation of evidence "by each of the Governments."

[21] Rule VIII 1.

vided that: "No such statement, documents or other evidence will be received or considered by the Commission if presented through any other channel."

Similarly, all the Rules of Procedure gave the agents the right to call witnesses.[22] Under the Rules of the British-Mexican, French-Mexican, German-Mexican and United States-Mexican General and Special Claims Commissions, an agent might examine a witness on direct, but cross-examination might be conducted either by an agent or by counsel. The Rules of the Spanish-Mexican Commission permitted examination of witnesses to be conducted only by interrogatories submitted by the agents to the secretaries. Cross-examination might be conducted by the agents.

§257. Position of Counsel under the Rules. On the whole, then, the Rules placed counsel in a rather subordinate position. The one function which they retained under all the Rules (excepting those of the Italian-Mexican Commission which contained no mention whatever of counsel) was that of arguing before the Commission [23] and cross-examining witnesses.[24] Only the Rules of the United States-Mexican General Claims Commission gave them some further functions: they might sign memoranda and memorials in the name of the agent,[25] present evidence in the name of the agent [26] and prepare briefs.[27] This subordination of counsel may seem to be in contradiction with the Conventions which apparently placed agents and counsel on the same footing, but in reality it is an indication of the manner in which the meagre terms of a treaty are filled out and clarified by reliance upon customary international procedural law.

§258. Power to Settle Claims. One of the most important powers of the agents before the Mexican Claims Commission was that of settling or compromising claims. None of the Conventions contained any provisions with regard to this. Yet all of the Rules of Procedure made some reference to it. The Rules of most of the Commissions provided that "in the event that the agents of the two governments should stipulate any award, or the disposition of any claim, such

[22] U. S.-Mexican General Rule VIII 2; U. S.-Mexican Special Rule VIII 2; British-Mexican Rule 27; French-Mexican Rules, Art. 29; German-Mexican Rules, Art. 29; Spanish-Mexican Rules, Art. 33; Italian-Mexican Rules, Art. 30.
[23] U. S.-Mexican General Rule X 3; U. S.-Mexican Special Rule X 3; British-Mexican Rule, Art. 38; German-Mexican Rules, Art. 38; Spanish-Mexican Rules, Art. 43.
[24] *Supra*, note 22.
[25] Rule III 2.
[26] Rule VIII 1.
[27] Rule X 2.

stipulation shall be presented to the Commission for confirmation and award in accordance therewith or other proper order thereon." [28] The Rules of the British-Mexican Commission were more elaborate in this respect, providing that the agents might meet as often as they thought necessary for discussion of a claim with a view to reaching an agreement, that such discussion should be on a confidential basis and should not deprive an agent of the right to contest the case without reference to any offers exchanged or concessions made in negotiations if no settlement was arrived at, and providing for the filing of agreements to settle with the secretaries and adjudication thereon by the Commission.[29] This procedure of settlement by agreement of the agents was used to a considerable extent in the British-Mexican Commission.[30]

§259. **Practice of the Commissions with Respect to Agents.** The French-Mexican Commission stated that agents were to be considered "not as simple advocates, at liberty to announce any kind of personal opinion even though these opinions be contrary to the opinion of their government, but as the official representative of the latter. If it were otherwise, one would never know whether the agent was setting forth his own personal opinions or the official point of view of the government, and the arguments would assume a hybrid and indefinable character. This interpretation of the rôle of the agents is the only one which is in conformity with customary international law in matter of arbitral procedure." [31] This statement is clearly in conformity with the spirit of the Rules of Procedure, and the practice of the various Commissions, in the few cases which reveal interesting instances of the powers of agents, bears it out. In a case before the United States-Mexican General Claims Commission, the American agent waived his right to a hearing on a motion to reject the Mexican answer, and subsequently announced, on behalf of the American Agency and of the private claimant, a disclaimer of title in the claimant to various locomotives which were the subject-matter of a contract before the Commission.[32] In a case before the French-Mexican

---

[28] U. S.-Mexican General Rule XI 3; U. S.-Mexican Special Rule XI 3; French-Mexican Rules, Art. 45; German-Mexican Rules, Art. 45; Spanish-Mexican Rules, Art. 47; Italian-Mexican Rules, Art. 41.

[29] Rules 33–35.

[30] See *supra*, p. 80.

[31] Rep. française (Georges Pinson) *v.* Etats-Unis mexicains, Jurisprudence de la Commission franco-mexicaine des réclamations, at p. 31.

[32] U. S. A. (Ill. Cent. R. R. Co.) *v.* United Mexican States, United States-Mexican General Claims Commission, Opinions of Commissioners, 1927, pp. 187, 188.

Commission, the French agent made a declaration, with the consent of the Mexican agent, that the French government would divide the proceeds of the award in conformity with the evidence as to the various French interests existing when the claim arose. The Commission took note of this declaration in rendering its decision.[33] A series of cases before the same Commission demonstrate the power of agents to agree on the receivability of claims. Considerable difficulty was experienced in interpreting a provision of the Convention relating to the "allotment" (*cession*) of a proportionate share of the damages suffered by a Mexican company where claim was made on behalf of French shareholders. The agents of the two governments concluded a series of agreements in twenty-eight cases to the effect that these claims should be admissible because more than 50% of the capital in the companies involved belonged to French citizens, these agreements being confirmed by the Commission.[34] In effect, this was an agreement by the Mexican agent to waive the requirement of "allotment" stipulated by the Convention.

§260. **Counsel for Private Claimants.** In practice, counsel for private claimants play an important part in the preparation of claims for submission. But, in view of the traditional theory that the claim is that of the state, they have no standing before the tribunal. Only in the Rules of the United States-Mexican, Spanish-Mexican and Italian-Mexican Commissions was any mention made of them, it being required that the memorial "shall be subscribed by solicitor or counsel, if any, of the claimant." [35] Under the Rules of the United States-Mexican Commissions briefs prepared by the claimant or his attorney might be presented if countersigned by the agent or his counsel.[36]

---

[33] République française (Intérêts français dans la Cía. Azucarera del Paraiso Novello) *v.* Etats-Unis mexicains, Sentence No. 4–B (unpublished, Mexican Commissioner absent).

[34] Sentences Nos. 2–A to 29–A, Sept. 11, 1928 (unpublished).

[35] U. S.-Mexican General Rule IV 2; U. S.-Mexican Special Rule IV 2; Spanish-Mexican Rules, Art. 13; Italian-Mexican Rules, Art. 11.

[36] U. S.-Mexican General Rule X 2; U. S.-Mexican Special Rule X 2.

CHAPTER 17

THE MEASURE OF DAMAGES
AND PAYMENT OF AWARDS

MEASURE OF DAMAGES [1]

§261. Introductory. No part of the law of international claims is more fragmentary or confused than that relating to the measure of damages. Doctrinal writings [2] are few and most arbitral tribunals have given little consideration to the necessity of working out consistent principles.[3] Compromise behind the closed doors of the conference chamber has often been the rule and the awards of many tribunals present a patchwork of seemingly arbitrary determinations on this subject. Much of the difficulty arises from the failure to reach agreement on a sound theory of state responsibility. Undeniably, a satisfactory practice with respect to the measure of damages can never be wholly achieved until such an agreement is reached. Nevertheless, much can be done to improve the practice within the present inadequate theoretical framework.

§262. Provisions in the Conventions. The Conventions contain only the most meagre of provisions relating to damages. The United States-Mexican General Claims Commission contained a provision to the following effect (Article IX):

In any case the Commission may decide that international law, justice and equity require that a property right be restored to the claimant in addition to the amount awarded in any such case for all loss or damage sustained prior to the restitution. In any case where the Commission so decides the restitution of the property or right shall be made by the Government affected

---

[1] Problems relating to the proof of the amount of damages are considered in the chapter on "Evidence," *supra*, p. 279 *et seq.*

[2] The most satisfactory study is Eagleton, "Measure of Damages in International Law," 39 Yale Law Journal, p. 52 (1929).

[3] A notable exception is the opinion of Umpire Parker in the Lusitania Cases, U. S.-Germany Mixed Claims Commission, Consolidated Edition of Decisions and Opinions, p. 17.

after such decision has been made, as hereinbelow provided. The Commission, however, shall at the same time determine the value of the property or right decreed to be restored and the Government affected may elect to pay the amount so fixed after the decision is made rather than to restore the property or right to the claimant.

In the event the Government affected should elect to pay the amount fixed as the value of the property or right decreed to be restored, it is agreed that notice will be filed with the Commission within thirty days after the decision and the amount fixed as the value of the property or right shall be paid immediately. Upon failure so to pay the amount the property or right shall be restored immediately.

This interesting provision for *restitutio in integrum* was undoubtedly inserted in order to provide for possible claims for the restoration of oil or agrarian lands held by Americans in Mexico. No use was ever made of this provision since no such claims were ever passed upon by the Commission. Nevertheless, the provision is one which might well be embodied in all claims conventions. Precedents for *restitutio in integrum* are exceedingly rare in international law,[4] and it is a subject which should be dealt with explicitly in conventions.

The United States-Mexican Special Claims Commission contained no provision at all on damages but each of the Conventions with the European States contained a provision similar to the following in the British-Mexican Convention (Article VI):

In order to determine the amount of compensation to be granted for damage to property, account shall be taken of the value declared by the interested parties for fiscal purposes, except in cases which in the opinion of the Commission are really exceptional.

The amount of the compensation for personal injuries shall not exceed that of the most ample compensation granted by Great Britain in similar cases.

---

[4] "The essential principle contained in the actual notion of an illegal act—a principle which seems to have been established by international practice and in particular by the decisions of arbitral tribunals—is that reparation must, as far as possible, wipe out all the consequences of the illegal act and re-establish the situation which would, in all probability, have existed if that act had not been committed. Restitution in kind, or if this is not possible, payment of a sum corresponding to the value which a restitution in kind would bear; the award, if need be, of loss sustained which would not be covered in kind or payment in place of it,—such are the principles which should serve to determine the amount of compensation due for an act contrary to international law." The Factory at Chorzów, Permanent Court of International Justice, Series A, No. 17, p. 29.

The provision requiring the Commission to take account of declaration of the value of property for fiscal purposes in determining property damages is unexceptionable. It furnishes a possible check on inflated or arbitrarily determined awards, and a few instances of its application by Commissions are recorded.[5] The provision regarding damages for personal injuries seems altogether meaningless. It is impossible to ascertain whether it refers to compensation awarded by municipal courts in suits between individuals, or by administrative authorities in proceedings against the government, or by the Foreign Office in international claims. The words "most ample compensation" constitute so vague a standard that the field is left altogether open. It is not surprising to find that no decision of any of the Commissions gives any indication that this provision was taken into account in fixing damages.

§263. **Practice of the Commissions.** Only one of the Commissions ever considered the problem of damages at length. This was the General Claims Commission in the *Janes* case.[6] Aside from this one exception, the decisions give only the barest hints of the reasons why damages were fixed at the particular figure. Indeed, in most cases, even this hint is lacking. A coherent picture of the practice of the Commissions must therefore be pieced together out of innumerable fragments.

§264. **The Janes Case.** The *Janes* case has already become classic, and it deserves extended discussion. Claim was made by the United States on behalf of the widow and the four children of an American engineer who had been murdered by a Mexican. It was claimed that the Mexican authorities had been lax in failing to apprehend and punish the murderer. Damages of $25,000 were asked for. The American agent took the position that the measure of damages should be the measure of injury suffered by the claimants as a result of the wrongful death because Mexico in failing to apprehend the murderer had condoned and ratified the wrongful act, thereby making the act its own. The Mexican agent argued that damages could be ascertained in money only if it could be shown that the negligence of the government and not the crime itself had directly caused damage.

---

[5] *E.g.*, Republica Alemana (Delires y Cía.) *v.* Estados Unidos Mexicanos, German-Mexican Commission, Decision No. 31 (unpublished).

[6] U. S. A. (Laura M. B. Janes) *v.* United Mexican States, Opinions of Commissioners, 1927, p. 108.

The Commission definitely rejected the theory of complicity or condonation in convincing fashion. In particular it pointed out the unsatisfactory consequences of what it called the "old conception."

"If the murdered man had been poor, or if, in a material sense, his death had meant little to his relatives, the satisfaction given these relatives should be confined to a small sum, though the grief and indignity suffered may have been great. On the other hand, if the old theory is sustained and adhered to, it would, in cases like the present one, be to the pecuniary benefit of a widow and her children if a Government did not measure up to its international duty of providing justice, because in such a case the Government would repair the pecuniary damage caused by the killing, whereas she practically never would have obtained such reparation if the state had succeeded in apprehending and punishing the culprit." [7]

It then went on to say that the rejection of the theory of complicity does not force the assumption of the opposite extreme, that if the government is not liable for the crime itself, then it can only be responsible, in a punitive way, to another government, not to a private claimant.

"There again, the solution in other cases of improper governmental action shows the way out. It shows that, apart from reparation or compensation for material losses, claimants always have been given substantial satisfaction for serious dereliction of duty on the part of a Government, and this world-wide international practice was before the Governments of the United States and Mexico when they framed the Convention concluded September 8, 1923. . . . The indignity done the relatives of Janes by nonpunishment in the present case is, as that in other cases of improper governmental action, a damage directly caused by an individual by a Government. If this damage is different from the damage caused by the killing, it is quite different from the wounding of material honor and national feeling of the State of which the victim was a national." [8]

Thus, the claimants are to be compensated, not for the damage caused by the murder of Janes, *i.e.*, the property damage, loss of support, etc., resulting from his death, but for the damage caused to them by the government by reason of its failure to prosecute. Here indeed is a type of injury most difficult to assess in terms of money. The language of the Commission on this question of assessment is worth quoting *in extenso*.

[7] *Ibid.*, at 115–116.   [8] *Ibid.*, at 117–118.

"As to the measure of such a damage caused by the delinquency of a Government, the nonpunishment, it may readily be granted that its computation is more difficult and uncertain than that of the damage caused by the killing itself. The two delinquencies being different in their origin, character, and effect, the measure of damages for which the Government should be liable cannot be computed by merely stating the damages caused by the private delinquency of Carbajal [the murderer]. But a computation of this character is not more difficult than computations in other cases of denial of justice such as illegal encroachments on one's liberty, harsh treatment in jail, insults and menaces of prisoners, or even nonpunishment of the perpetrator of a crime which is not an attack on one's property or one's earning capacity, for instance a dangerous assault or an attack on one's reputation and honor. Not only the individual grief of the claimants should be taken into account, but a reasonable and substantial redress should be made for the mistrust and lack of safety, resulting from the Government's attitude. If the nonprosecution and nonpunishment of crimes (or of specific crimes) in a certain period and place occurs with regularity, such nonrepression may even assume the character of nonprevention and be treated as such. One among the advantages of severing the Government's dereliction of duty from the individual's crime is in that it grants an opportunity to take into account several shades of denial of justice, more serious ones and lighter ones (no prosecution at all; prosecution and release; prosecution and light punishment; prosecution, punishment, and pardon), whereas the old system operates automatically and allows for the numerous forms of such a denial one amount only, that of full and total reparation.

"Giving careful consideration to all elements involved, the Commission holds that an amount of $12,000 without interest, is not excessive as satisfaction for the personal damage caused the claimants by the nonapprehension and nonpunishment of the murderer of Janes." [9]

Superficially this is a most attractive statement of principles for the assessment of damages. But closer study reveals some difficult problems. Granted that assessment to correspond with the injury caused by the crime is based on a false theoretical assumption (condonation), such a method of assessment at least has the advantage of a certain definiteness. The probable life expectancy of the murdered man, his earning capacity, the amount of his contributions to his relatives, may all be taken into account. But here damages are to be assessed on the basis of grief and indignity caused and the extent of government dereliction, and "reasonable and substantial redress

[9] *Ibid.*, at 118–119.

should be made for the misconduct and lack of safety, resulting from the Government's attitude." All these are highly indefinite quantities. Supposing that it were shown that the claimant wife and her murdered husband were estranged and that the wife suffered no grief and indignity because of the failure to prosecute. Would Mexico be relieved of the duty to pay damages on this score just as, in American law, there can be no recovery for alienation of affections when the defendant shows that there was in fact no affection? [10] If it is proper to increase recovery by taking into account "mistrust and lack of safety," why should the individual receive damages on this score? The "mistrust and lack of safety" is a matter of concern to all aliens in the country and not to this particular claimant.

Perhaps these questions would not press upon us so insistently, if the Commission had shown us just how these various elements were used in determining the precise amount of damages. Instead we are told that "giving careful consideration to all elements involved," the Commission holds that $12,000 "is not excessive." The suspicion that this amount may have been decided upon by the old method of compromise and guess is not dispelled when it is noted that Commissioner Nielsen who concurred in this award based his opinion on the theory of condonation which the majority expressly rejected.

§265. **Practice of the General Claims Commission.** The *Janes* case established the principle that damages are to be assessed on the basis of the injury caused to the individual claimant by the acts of the respondent government itself. It would follow that in cases of "indirect responsibility" recovery would be allowed only for the grief and indignity caused by a failure to prosecute the assailant, whereas in cases of "direct responsibility" recovery would be allowed as if the claimant had been injured by a private individual. The latter conclusion is not expressed by the Commission but it seems to follow logically from the decision. To what extent did the General Claims Commission abide by these principles in its decisions?

§266. **The Same: Personal Injuries.** It will be remembered that in the *Janes* case the Commission stated that the various degrees of improper governmental action would be taken into account in determining the amount of damages for grief and indignity suffered. In that case, which was one of a failure to apprehend a murderer, the

[10] Servio *v.* Servio, 172 N. Y. 438, 65 N. E. 270 (1902).

amount of damages was fixed at $12,000. Apparently, then, the seriousness of the degree of governmental misconduct is the one criterion which we can rely on in tracing the practice of the Commission in cases involving "indirect responsibility." We find some striking inconsistencies in practice.

In two cases of "indirect responsibility" the Commission exceeded the amount awarded in the *Janes* case. In the *Chapman* case [11] $15,000 was awarded. The claimant was a consul and the award is to be explained as based on breach of the duty of special protection owed to consuls. The same sum was also awarded in the *Massey* case [12] in which the murderer of Massey had been allowed to escape from jail by a jailer. While this was a case of "indirect responsibility," the fact of the negligence of the jailer gave it a flavor of "direct responsibility" and probably explains the unusual size of the award. In two cases, $10,000 was awarded for failure to prosecute a murder; in one of the cases the murderer had been rendered immune from prosecution under a general amnesty; [13] in the other, the murderer had been indicted but never brought to trial.[14] In the *Richards* case,[15] $9,000 was awarded. Here the alleged murderers had been tried and acquitted and deficiencies occurred in the procedure on appeal. In two cases, $8,000 was awarded; one involved an inadequate sentence (four years' imprisonment),[16] the other a failure to prosecute at all.[17] Awards amounting to $7,000 were made in five cases; two of these were cases of failure to apprehend the murderers; [18] in the other three the murderers had been tried in a lax manner.[19] In four cases the

[11] U. S. A. (William E. Chapman) *v.* United Mexican States, Opinions of Commissioners, 1927, p. 228.

[12] U. S. A. (Gertrude Parker Massey) *v.* United Mexican States, Opinions of Commissioners, 1927, p. 228.

[13] U. S. A. (F. R. West) *v.* United Mexican States, Opinions of Commissioners, 1927, p. 404.

[14] United Mexican States (Salomé Lerma de Galván) *v.* U. S. A., Opinions of Commissioners, 1927, p. 408.

[15] U. S. A. (George David Richards) *v.* United Mexican States, Opinions of Commissioners, 1927, p. 412.

[16] U. S. A. (Ethel Morton) *v.* United Mexican States, Opinions of Commissioners, 1929, p. 151.

[17] U. S. A. (Helen O. Mead) *v.* United Mexican States, Opinions of Commissioners, 1931, p. 150.

[18] U. S. A. (Richard A. Newman) *v.* United Mexican States, Opinions of Commissioners, 1929, p. 284; U. S. A. (Sarah Ann Gorham) *v.* United Mexican States, Opinions of Commissioners, 1931, p. 132.

[19] U. S. A. (Elvira Almaguer) *v.* United Mexican States, Opinions of Commissioners, 1929, p. 291; U. S. A. (Lillian Greenlaw Sewell) *v.* United Mexican States, Opinions of Commissioners, 1931, p. 112; U. S. A. (Minnie East) *v.* United Mexican States, *ibid.*, 1931, p. 140.

Commission awarded $5,000; in two of these there was a failure to apprehend the murderers; [20] in one an inadequate sentence (two months' imprisonment) had been imposed; [21] in another, the prisoners had been allowed to escape.[22] Four cases involved awards of $5,000; one of these was a case where the murderer had not been apprehended; [23] in two there were undue delays in prosecution.[24] The fourth of these cases is indeed extraordinary—a claimant who had been wounded in the arm by bandits was awarded $5,000 because his alleged assailants had been released without trial after being arrested.[25] In two cases of wrongful death only $2,500 was awarded. These were the *Waterhouse* and *Connolly* cases [26] in which the assailants had been subjected to evidently adequate punishment for homicide, but awards were granted because of a failure to prosecute for theft.

Only a most indulgent eye would see any reasonable consistency in the foregoing record. If there be any reason for awarding $12,000 in one case of failure to apprehend a murderer and for awarding $5,000 in another case of the same kind it does not appear in the decisions. It may be that the subtleties implicit in the formula of the *Janes* case could not be conveyed in print, or perhaps the *Janes* formula was found a convenient verbal cloak for the old practice of compromise.

Superficially, it would seem that a more consistent practice could be followed in cases of "direct responsibility" for here the damages would, in the first instance, be measured by the pecuniary loss suffered by the claimant. But, "grief and indignity" was often involved in cases of "direct responsibility." To take a typical case: an American citizen is murdered by a policeman. Mexico may then become liable for the pecuniary loss suffered by the dependents of the murdered man. If

---

[20] U. S. A. (Hazel M. Corcoran) *v.* United Mexican States, Opinions of Commissioners, 1929, p. 211; U. S. A. (Martha Ann Austin) *v.* United Mexican States, Opinions of Commissioners, 1931, p. 108.

[21] U. S. A. (George Adams Kennedy) *v.* United Mexican States, Opinions of Commissioners, 1927, p. 289.

[22] U. S. A. (Ida R. S. Putnam) *v.* United Mexican States, Opinions of Commissioners, 1927, p. 222. The concurring opinion of Commissioner Nielsen suggests that the award might have been fixed at a higher figure if there had been more convincing evidence of negligence in permitting the escape.

[23] U. S. A. (Louise O. Canahl) *v.* United Mexican States, Opinions of Commissioners, 1929, p. 90.

[24] U. S. A. (John D. Chase) *v.* United Mexican States, Opinions of Commissioners, 1929, p. 17; U. S. A. (J. J. Boyd) *v.* United Mexican States, *ibid.*, 1929, p. 78.

[25] U. S. A. (Frank L. Clark) *v.* United Mexican States, Opinions of Commissioners, 1929, p. 300.

[26] U. S. A. (George M. Waterhouse) *v.* United Mexican States, Opinions of Commissioners, 1929, p. 221; U. S. A. (Norman T. Connolly) *v.* United Mexican States, *ibid.*, 1929, p. 87.

the policeman has not been adequately punished, these dependents are also entitled to damages for grief and indignity. One would assume then, that in such cases of double governmental responsibility, the damages would be cumulated. Such, however, was not the practice of the Commission. In the *Swinney* case,[27] claim was made on behalf of the parents of Swinney who had been shot by Mexican border guards. The latter were released without punishment. The Commission "considering among other things the financial support the deceased man gave the claimants, their prospects of life and the character of the delinquency involved," held that the claimants had suffered damages to the extent of $7,000. Here was a double responsibility and yet the recovery was substantially the same as in a case of "indirect responsibility" alone.

When this case is compared with other cases of double responsibility it appears that damages for grief and indignity were ignored by the Commission to a considerable extent if not altogether. In the *Kling* case[28] involving a claim on behalf of the mother of Kling, shot by Mexican soldiers who were never punished, $9,000 was awarded. Kling was 22 years old and had been earning $400 a month. The *Roper*,[29] *Brown*,[30] and *Small*[31] cases involved the deaths of three American seamen who had been drowned while running from shots fired at them by Mexican policemen. The latter were never punished. The Commission took into account, "among other things" which were not explained, the earning capacity of each of the deceased and the financial support given to the claimants. It awarded $6,000 to the mother of Roper, $8,000 to the widow of Brown, and $5,000 to the sisters of Small.

In these cases only direct pecuniary damage seems to have been calculated,[32] but, when direct pecuniary damage was not present the

[27] U. S. A. (J. W. and N. L. Swinney) v. United Mexican States, Opinions of Commissioners, 1927, p. 131.
[28] U. S. A. (Lillie S. Kling) v. United Mexican States, Opinions of Commissioners, 1931, p. 36.
[29] U. S. A. (Margaret Roper) v. United Mexican States, Opinions of Commissioners, 1927, p. 205.
[30] U. S. A. (Mamie Brown) v. United Mexican States, Opinions of Commissioners, 1927, p. 211.
[31] U. S. A. (Rosetta Small) v. United Mexican States, Opinions of Commissioners, 1927, p. 212.
[32] In only one case can it be definitely said that both direct pecuniary damages and damages for grief and indignity were awarded. The amount of the award was $20,000 for a wrongful death. U. S. A. (Thomas A. Youmans) v. United Mexican States, Opinions of Commissioners, 1927, p. 150.

Commission was willing to award damages for grief and indignity. The *Stephens* case [33] involved a claim by the brothers of Stephens who had been shot by a soldier. The soldier was sentenced to imprisonment but was allowed to escape by a jailer. The latter was acquitted after trial. The only pecuniary loss shown was that one of the brothers joined the deceased in contributing $75 a month to an aged aunt. None the less, the Commission, although holding that direct pecuniary damage was too remote, awarded $7,000 for grief and indignity. The *Connelly* [34] and *Munroe* [35] cases involved the murder of several Americans by a mob in which Mexican soldiers had participated. The participants were not punished. The Commission awarded $18,000 to four brothers and two sisters of Connelly, and $11,000 to the sister and surviving next of kin of Arnold, apparently for grief and indignity alone, there being little evidence of material support.

It is well to compare these extraordinarily large awards with the award in the *Teodoro García* case.[36] This was the case in which a little child was killed by shots fired by American soldiers while the child and her family were on a raft on the Rio Grande. Claim was made on behalf of her father and mother. The Commission held that the shooting was in violation of international law but that there had been no "denial of justice" though a decision of a court-martial punishing the soldiers had been reversed by the President of the United States. Only $2,000 was awarded and in fixing this amount the Commission did not "consider reparation of pecuniary loss only, but also satisfaction for indignity suffered." [37] Thus, both the pecuniary loss and indignity resulting to the parents from the death of a child were held to amount to $2,000, while in the *Connelly* case [38] indignity alone was held to entitle brothers and sisters to $18,000. It is true that in the *Teodoro García* case the United States had carried through a judicial proceeding against the soldiers who had fired the shots; but in the

---

[33] U. S. A. (Charles S. Stephens) *v.* United Mexican States, Opinions of Commissioners, 1927, p. 397.

[34] U. S. A. (Agnes Connelly) *v.* United Mexican States, Opinions of Commissioners, 1927, p. 159.

[35] U. S. A. (Mary E. A. Munroe) *v.* United Mexican States, Opinions of Commissioners, 1929, p. 314.

[36] U. S. A. (Teodoro García) *v.* United Mexican States, Opinions of Commissioners, 1927, p. 163. For a discussion of the merits of this case see *supra*, p. 138.

[37] The Commission said that the knowledge of the claimants that they were crossing the river in violation of law "ought to influence" the amount of damages. *Ibid.*, at 169. This seems more like rationalization than a reason.

[38] *Supra*, note 34.

Stephens case [39] Mexico had actually sentenced the guilty soldier and had carried through a judicial proceeding against the jailer who had allowed him to escape, and yet the brothers of Stephens were held to have suffered indignity to the extent of $7,000.

In short, we are forced to the conclusion that the Commission failed to work out any consistent policy either with respect to "indirect" or to "direct responsibility." Formulae were announced and perhaps even applied on a few occasions. But, generally speaking, the policy of compromise seems to have ruled with but little restraint.

§267. **The Same: Unlawful Arrest and Imprisonment.** In awarding damages for unlawful arrest and imprisonment, the Commission seems to have started out with a firm intention of establishing a definite measure of recovery. In the *Faulkner* case,[40] the Commission relied on the *Topaze* case [41] decided by one of the Venezuelan Commissions of 1903 in which $100 for each day of detention was awarded. The General Claims Commission increased this by 50% to take account of the change in the value of money and awarded $1,050 for seven days' detention. This may seem a somewhat arbitrary manner of assessing damages, but it has the great merit of certainty and definiteness. Unfortunately, the Commission never again adhered to this standard. In the *Chazen* case [42] it awarded $500 for five days' detention, while in the *Dujay* case [43] it awarded $500 for 28 hours' detention. The latter decision relied upon a decision of another tribunal in which $3,000 had been awarded for a detention of one and a half months.[44] In the *Dillon* case [45] $2,500 was awarded for twelve days' detention, but the added factor that the claimant had been held *incommunicado* was taken into account. Where longer periods of detention were involved, the Commission seems not to have applied any

[39] *Supra,* note 33.
[40] U. S. A. (Walter H. Faulkner) *v.* United Mexican States, Opinions of Commissioners, 1927, p. 86.
[41] British-Venezuelan Commission, Ralston, Venezuelan Arbitrations of 1903, p. 329.
[42] U. S. A. (Louis Chazen) *v.* United Mexican States, Opinions of Commissioners, 1931, p. 20.
[43] U. S. A. (Fannie P. Dujay) *v.* United Mexican States, Opinions of Commissioners, 1929, p. 180.
[44] Case of George F. Underhill, United States-Venezuelan Commission of 1903, Ralston Venezuelan Arbitrations of 1903, p. 49. The Commission also cited the payment of $2,200 for one month's detention of three seamen by the United States in the Case of the Ingrid. 42 Stat. 610.
[45] U. S. A. (Daniel Dillon) *v.* United Mexican States, Opinions of Commissioners, 1929, p. 61.

definite standard. In the *Roberts* [46] and *Strother* [47] cases it awarded $8,000 for nineteen months' detention; in the *Turner* case,[48] $4,000 for five months' detention; in the *Dyches* case,[49] $8,000 for eighteen months' detention.

§268. The Same: Property Damage. In contrast with the cases heretofore discussed, the Commission showed an admirable consistency in calculating damages for injuries to property. In almost every case in which an award was made, the claimant received exactly the sum he had requested. One of the exceptions, the *Deutz* case,[50] illustrates the scrupulous adherence of the Commission to an exact calculation of damages. Claim was made for $103,540.32 for breach of contract arising out of the refusal of the Mexican Government to receive certain deliveries of goods and out of the cancellation of further orders. With respect to goods which had been delivered but returned the Commission awarded $44,902.57, calculated by subtracting the cost price from the contract price and adding thereto the loss sustained by the claimants in reselling the goods below cost price. With respect to the undelivered portion of the goods, the Commission awarded $36,764.60 which was calculated to be the loss of profits suffered by the claimants as a result of the failure of Mexico to complete its contract.[51] In only a very few cases did the Commission award what might be considered a compromise sum. One of these cases was the *Melczer* case [52] in which $175,000 was claimed to be the value of a confiscated pipe line. The Commission found the evidence as to value to be very vague and awarded $15,000.

[46] U. S. A. (Harry Roberts) *v.* United Mexican States, Opinions of Commissioners, 1927, p. 100.

[47] U. S. A. (Russell Strother) *v.* United Mexican States, Opinions of Commissioners, 1927, p. 392.

[48] U. S. A. (Mary Ann Turner) *v.* United Mexican States, Opinions of Commissioners, 1927, p. 416.

[49] U. S. A. (Clyde Dyches) *v.* United Mexican States, Opinions of Commissioners, 1929, p. 193.

[50] U. S. A. (Adolph Deutz) *v.* United Mexican States, Opinions of Commissioners, 1929, p. 213.

[51] It is to be noted that the Commission had no hesitancy in awarding damages for loss of profits. There has been considerable doubt as to whether such damages can be awarded. For a discussion of the subject see Eagleton, "Measure of Damages in International Law," *supra,* note 2, who concludes (at p. 73): "To summarize, it is very rare that an international tribunal has denied in principle the right to award indirect damages. That such damages should be refused in particular instances is quite natural, and it would be absurd to offer such cases as proof of a rule forbidding indirect damages. On the contrary, the evidence is overwhelming that indirect damages are permissible and have frequently been allowed by international tribunals."

[52] U. S. A. (Melczer Mining Co.) *v.* United Mexican States, Opinions of Commissioners, 1929, p. 228.

§269. **Practice of the British–Mexican Commission: Personal Injuries.** The Commissions dealing with revolutionary claims were relieved of the difficulties arising from the distinction between "direct" and "indirect responsibility." Under the Conventions, Mexico's responsibility was always direct. As a result, these Commissions had the opportunity of following a fairly consistent practice with respect to damages for personal injuries, *i.e.*, the amount of pecuniary loss suffered by the claimant. The British-Mexican Commission did not take the opportunity. In a number of cases it did attempt an approximate calculation of the loss suffered. In the *Clapham* case [53] the claimant was a mining engineer who had lost a leg as a result of injuries received from revolutionary forces. His salary had been £1,000 a year and as a consequence of his disability he found it difficult to secure employment. The Commission awarded 20,000 pesos upon the following reasoning:

"It seems just and equitable . . . that an award be granted him, that will set off, by means of an annuity, the lifelong injury which was the result of the wound. The Commission have found no guidance in any law or decree for the determination of the annuity, the less so as in nearly all other cases the annuity begins very soon after the accident, whereas in this case sixteen years and probably more will have elapsed before any payment can follow. The Commission, also taking into account the station in life of the claimant, think an annuity of 2,000 pesos, Mexican gold, fair and reasonable, and as, in order to purchase such annuity a man of the age of Mr. Clapham will have to pay about 20,000 pesos, Mexican gold, they fix the award at that figure." [54]

This was the nearest that the Commission came to approximating an exact calculation of damages for personal injuries. In another case [55] involving personal injuries the Commission awarded 6,000 pesos taking "the view that the compensation to be awarded to the claimant must take into account his station in life, and be in just proportion to the extent and to the serious nature of the personal injury which he sustained"; and in a case involving wrongful death a widow received 29,000 pesos, "taking into consideration the age of the murdered man, his position, and [the widow's] age and position." [56] A much more

[53] Case of George Henry Clapham, Further Decisions and Opinions, p. 159.
[54] *Ibid.*, at 162.
[55] Case of William MacNeill, Further Decisions and Opinions, p. 96.
[56] Case of Edith Henry, Further Decisions and Opinions, p. 299, at 303.

striking deviation from sound principle occurred in the *Buckingham* case.[57] Claim was made on behalf of the widow of Buckingham, who had been killed by bandits, in the amount of 100,000 pesos. It was shown that Buckingham was 48 years old at the time of his death, that his probable term of service was twelve years, and that his salary had been 700 pesos a month. Thus the loss suffered by his widow would be at least 100,800 pesos. No claim was made for personal loss or suffering. Nevertheless, the Commission awarded a sum of 31,000 pesos, thinking this "in accordance with the principles of justice and equity."

§270. **The Same: Property Damage.** The scrupulous exactness which the General Claims Commission attempted to attain in calculating property damages has been noted above. The British-Mexican Commission was not nearly as strict on this matter. While, in many cases, the amount of damages claimed was awarded, other cases show plainly the effects of compromise. For this, however, blame should not be laid at the doors of the Commission. In many cases, convincing proof of the amount of damages was lacking and the Commission was forced to resort to a kind of rough justice. A few examples will suffice. In the *Mexico City Bombardment* cases [58] the Commission held that Mexico was liable for damage done to the property of the claimants who had resided in a Y.M.C.A. hostel. It was said that the mere fact that the amount of the losses had not been established could not deprive the claimants of their right. The Commission then went on to say:

"But it seems equally wrong to accept, in the absence of convincing evidence, the figures calculated by each of the claimants. . . .

"To this dilemma the Commission sees only one solution, *i.e.*, to lay down its own rule for the adjudging of the award. This rule must be established independently of the individual claims. It cannot grant to the one more than to the other because it rejects the figures which each of the claimants puts forward. It must constitute the nearest approach to justice and equity which the case admits.

"This rule, adopted by the majority of the Commissioners, is that the Mexican Government, in the absence of clear evidence, cannot be obliged to pay more to each claimant than the amount representing the value of such objects as may be safely supposed to constitute the average portable prop-

---

[57] Case of Leonor Buckingham, Further Decisions and Opinions, p. 323.
[58] Decisions and Opinions of Commissioners, p. 100.

erty of young, unmarried men of the social class for which the Hostels of the Y.M.C.A. are particularly destined. Arbitrary as this amount may seem, it is more in conformity with the spirit of the Convention than either the denial of all award whatever or the granting of sums for which no reliable evidence exists." [59]

This same thought is apparent in other cases, though not as fully expressed. In the *Bowerman* case [60] where £233–9–0 was claimed, the Commission was "of opinion that £180–0–0 would be a fair sum to allow." In the *Urmston* case [61] 570,000 pesos was claimed for destruction of property. The Commission awarded only 100,000 pesos, stating:

"It . . . has not been made possible to the Commission to decide with absolute exactness whether the sums, claimed for the specific items, do or do not exceed the value thereof. The Commission do not, therefore, feel at liberty to award the full amount claimed under this head, but they are convinced that 100,000 pesos is well justified." [62]

In the *Merrow* case [63] a claim of 177,026 pesos for property damage appeared to the Commission to be "fantastically exaggerated" and 3,000 pesos was awarded as "a nearer approach to the truth."

Contrary to the practice of the General Claims Commission as exemplified in the *Deutz* case,[64] the British-Mexican Commission refused to allow any damages for loss of profits.[65] It also refused to allow awards for expenditure incurred in keeping property in good order, this expenditure being regarded not as a loss but as a means of avoiding loss.[66]

§271. **Practice of the French–Mexican Commission.** Nearly all the claims presented to the French-Mexican Commission were for property damage. Hence, the chief problem in assessing damages arose out of the frequent lack of convincing evidence of loss. In the

---

[59] *Ibid.*, at 105.
[60] Case of William E. Bowerman, Decisions and Opinions of Commissioners, p. 141.
[61] Case of A. B. Urmston, Further Decisions and Opinions, p. 337.
[62] *Ibid.*, p. 340.
[63] Case of Frank Scribner Merrow, Further Decisions and Opinions, p. 343.
[64] See *supra*, p. 301.
[65] Case of the Sonora (Mexico) Land and Timber Co., Further Decisions and Opinions, p. 292.
[66] Case of Mrs. James W. Hambleton, Further Decisions and Opinions, p. 311; Case of Webster Welbanks, *ibid.*, p. 334; Case of the Palmerejo and Mexican Gold Fields, Ltd., *ibid*, p. 347.

argument of the *Pinson* case [67] the Mexican and French agents advanced directly contrary theses as to what should be done in such cases. The Mexican agent argued that since Mexico's promise to indemnify was one of grace, the principle of equity should be applied to keep damages to a minimum where there was doubt of the character of the force which had committed the acts or a failure of exact proof of loss suffered. The French agent took the position that since proof of loss was very difficult because of the disturbed condition of Mexico, therefore the principles of equity should be applied to allow the greatest compensation possible for the victims of the revolution. The Commission thereupon stated that:

"La vraie équité qui doit inspirer les sentences de la Commission ne pourra consister qu'à tenir en equilibre, autant que possible, les considérations d'équité invoquées par les deux agences, chacune en faveur des intérêts dont la gestion lui est confiée." [68]

In practice, the Commission, both in its original composition and after its reorganization, showed itself very willing to reduce the amount of damages claimed unless the most exact proof was produced. The reorganized French-Mexican Commission followed the rule laid down by earlier tribunals to the effect that damages cannot be awarded for loss of growing crops.[69] The rule was first established on the ground that such damages are speculative because it is problematical whether a crop can ever be harvested.[70] This is hardly a reason for refusing to award damages, since there is nothing inherently impossible in fixing a sum for the loss of a crop taking into account the probability of loss through natural causes.[71] The French-Mexican Commission reached its decision by employing what can only be described as a

[67] Rep. française (Georges Pinson) *v.* Etats-unis mexicains, Jurisprudence de la commission franco-mexicaine des réclamations, at p. 132.

[68] *Ibid.,* at p. 133.

[69] Case of the Compañia Azucarera del Paraiso Novello, Sentence No. 70 (unpublished).

[70] Thus in the Valentiner Case, German-Venezuelan Commission, Ralston, Venezuelan Arbitrations of 1903, p. 562, it was said: ". . . there are so many elements of uncertainty dependent upon conditions of weather, health and industry of laborers preparing the crop for shipment and transportation, and ultimate realization on the crop, that the umpire is inclined to the opinion that the damage would be too remote."

[71] When the French-Mexican Commission was under the presidency of M. Verzijl it took the view that loss of growing crops is a *damnum emergens* and that compensation therefore could be awarded, but that the greatest caution must be observed in fixing damages because of the vicissitudes to which growing crops are exposed. République française (Louis et Joseph Feuillebois) *v.* Etats-unis mexicains, Sentence No. 45 (unpublished, Mexican Commissioner absent).

verbalism. The loss of crops was said to be a *"préjudice"* or *"manque à gagner"* rather than a *"perte"* or *"dommage"* and since the Convention provided for compensation for *"pertes ou dommages"* no recovery could be allowed.

§272. **Practice of the German–Mexican Commission.** The German-Mexican Commission made even less of an attempt to establish a consistent policy with respect to assessing damages than the Commissions we have considered heretofore. Indeed, this Commission frankly stated that it would make an award on equitable principles where sufficient proof of amount of damages was not submitted.[72] In no case was an award made for the full amount claimed, even in cases where it would appear that a more or less exact computation of damages was possible. In one case the Commission, while holding that it could not award damages, recommended to the Mexican Secretariat of Foreign Relations that compensation should be paid as an act of grace.[73] In a case involving damages for wrongful death, account was taken of the expectancy of life and of the past earnings of the deceased; an award of 20,000 pesos was made when it was shown that the deceased had earned 250 pesos a month.[74] This Commission also adopted the rule that damages could not be allowed for destruction of growing crops.[75]

§273. **Practice of the Italian–Mexican Commission.** The Italian-Mexican Commission followed the same practice as the German-Mexican Commission.[76] A striking example of the application of equitable principles is the *Orio* case [77] which involved a claim for wrongful death. The claimants were the widow and children of the deceased, and 85,510 pesos were asked. The damages were elaborately detailed on the basis of a life expectancy of 28 years and specific sums were asked for living expenses for the wife and for support and

---

[72] Republica Alemana (Testamentaria del Señor Hugo Bell) *v.* Estados Unidos Mexicanos No. 41 (unpublished).

[73] Republica Alemana (Testamentaria del Señor Hugo Bell) *v.* Estados Unidos Mexicanos, Decision No. 67 (unpublished).

[74] Republica Alemana (Laura Vda. de Plehn) *v.* Estados Unidos Mexicanos, Decision No. 13 (unpublished).

[75] Republica Alemana (E. Puttkamer, S. en C.) *v.* Estados Unidos Mexicanos, Decision No. 29 (unpublished); Republica Alemana (Max Müller) *v.* Estados Unidos Mexicanos, Decision No. 37 (unpublished).

[76] Thus in the case of Alessandro Robbioni, Decision No. 5 (unpublished), the Commission held that it could not make an award because of insufficient proof of damage, but recommended, on the basis of equity, that the Mexican government pay 700 pesos.

[77] Case of Ventura Torres viuda de Antonio Orio, Decision No. 98 (unpublished).

education of the children. The Commission held this excessive and awarded 19,000 pesos on equitable grounds. This Commission also followed the rule of refusing to award damages for destruction of growing crops.[78]

§274. **A Theory of Damages.** We have said earlier that the fundamental postulate underlying the law of claims is the interest in maintaining a reasonable freedom of international intercourse. If this postulate were to be followed logically all damages awarded in international claims would be punitive; *i.e.*, they would be directed towards stigmatizing a state for failing to maintain an adequate governmental system and towards encouraging the maintenance of such a system in the future. Superficially, the historic practice of international tribunals of calculating damages on the basis of the loss suffered by the individual claimant,[79] seems inconsistent with the fundamental postulate. This practice is of such long standing that it would be futile to attempt to eradicate it. Nor would it be desirable to do so. The loss suffered by the individual furnishes some measure of definiteness in an otherwise highly indefinite field. Yet reconciliation of principle and practice is not impossible.

If the fundamental postulate is followed then any damages which are awarded are in the nature of a sanction for the maintenance of freedom of intercourse. It is suggested that this sanction may consist of two elements, one in the nature of reparation, measured in accordance with the loss suffered by the individual claimant, the other punitive, measured by the degree of inadequacy of the governmental system. This would mean that every award would contain a punitive element.[80] Indeed, if the necessity for punitive damages were not present, *i.e.*, if inadequacy of the governmental system were not shown, there would be no basis for any award at all. On the other hand,

---

[78] Case of Luis Occelli, Decision No. 66 (unpublished).

[79] In the Chorzów Factory Case it was said by the Permanent Court of International Justice: "It is a principle of international law that the reparation of a wrong may consist in an indemnity corresponding to the damage which the nationals of the injured state have suffered as a result of the act which is contrary to international law. This is even the most usual form of reparations. . . ." Series A, No. 17, p. 27.

[80] There has been some difference of opinion as to whether punitive damages can be awarded by arbitral tribunals. See Lusitania Cases, United States-German Mixed Claims Commission, Consolidated Edition of Decisions and Opinions, at p. 25; Borchard, Diplomatic Protection of Citizens Abroad, §174; Eagleton, "Measure of Damages in International Law," *supra*, note 2, at p. 62; Ralston, Law and Procedure of Arbitral Tribunals, p. 267. The latter two writers are of the opinion that, generally speaking, arbitral tribunals have admitted that punitive damages are allowable in international law, but have often refused to grant them because of the limitations of the *compromis*.

punitive damages would be awarded even where it was shown that the pecuniary interests of the individual claimant were remote, or where no individual claimant could be found as, for example, where the original claimant had died without leaving an heir. The distribution of the award would of course be within the discretion of the claimant state. Presumably, the compensatory portion of the award would normally go to the individual. The punitive portion might well be retained in the treasury of the state as a recovery on behalf of all its nationals.

The advantages of such a practice would be twofold. On the one hand it would clearly demonstrate the nature of the award as a sanction for the enforcement of principles of international law. On the other hand, it would do away with the tendency to make awards for "grief and indignity" of the sort exemplified in the *Janes* case. The objections to such awards are obvious. It is a pure fiction to suppose that the relatives of a deceased man suffer any greater grief or indignity by reason of the failure of a government to prosecute his murderer. In fact, under the present practice, it is all to their interest if the murderer is not prosecuted since they can then recover substantial damages. Failure to prosecute is a delinquency which injures all nationals of the claimant state and not merely the relatives of the deceased. It is important that the award should reflect this undeniable fact.

It must, of course, be understood that the theory here set forth could not have been applied by the Mexican Claims Commissions. The Conventions with which we have dealt provided for the settlement of the claims "of citizens," these claims being "for losses or damages suffered by persons or by their properties." Admittedly this language is too narrow to have permitted the application of any such theory of damages as has been suggested. However, it is submitted that future claims conventions could be rested on a more satisfactory and rational basis if they were to be drawn up in accordance with the theory here advanced.

INTEREST ON AWARDS

§275. **Introductory.** The negotiators of the Mexican Claims Conventions committed the obvious error of failing to make any provision for the calculation of interest on awards. However, the

negotiators have the excuse of acting in the tradition of claims arbitrations: provisions for interest are rarely included in claims conventions.[81] Just why this should be so cannot easily be answered. Perhaps it is due to force of habit. It seems obvious that suitable provisions for this purpose should be included in all claims conventions.[82] As a result of this omission, several of the Commissions were forced to work out their own solutions.

§276. **Practice of the French–Mexican Commission.** An extended discussion of the problem is to be found in the opinion of presiding Commissioner Verzijl in the *Pinson* case [83] before the French-Mexican Commission. The Presiding Commissioner held that the silence of the Convention meant that in claims where Mexico's liability rested solely on its *ex gratia* promise no interest could be awarded, but where Mexico's liability was based upon principles of international law then interest could be awarded in accordance with international law practice. After a brief review of international practice he laid down the following principles: (1) Interest would not be granted on awards which Mexico was bound to pay only because of her *ex gratia* promise, excepting that if Mexico did not pay the awards after a reasonable time (to be determined in accordance with the provisions of the Convention) interest at the rate of 6% per annum was to be added. (2) On awards for requisitions and for *"délits internationaux"* interest at the rate of 6% [84] would be awarded. The running of interest should in principle commence on the date when the award is rendered, but, in view of the fact that the various claims must be considered as part of a whole and since it would be unfair to the claimants to award them more or less interest depending on the accident of the order of decision, an arbitrary date should be fixed. This date was to be May 1, 1929, which, it was thought, would

[81] Provisions for awarding interest were contained in the following Conventions: U. S.-British Treaty of November 19, 1794 (the Jay Treaty), U. S. Treaty Series No. 105; U. S.-Venezuelan Convention of December 5, 1885, U. S. Treaty Series No. 371; U. S.-Chilean Convention of August 7, 1892, U. S. Treaty Series No. 42; U. S.-British Special Agreement of August 18, 1910, U. S. Treaty Series No. 573.

[82] For example of awards of interest in the absence of a provision therefore in the convention see Administrative Decision No. III, U. S.-German Mixed Claims Commission, Consolidated Edition of Decisions and Opinions, p. 62; Ralston, Law and Procedure of International Tribunals, pp. 128–131; Eagleton, Responsibility of States, p. 205.

[83] République française (Georges Pinson) *v.* Etats-unis mexicains, Jurisprudence de la commission franco-mexicaine des réclamations, pp. 134–140.

[84] This rate was said not to be exaggerated "dans les circonstances actuelles et tenu compte de la productivité du capital au Mexique." *Ibid.,* at p. 139.

be about the middle of period during which the Commission would be rendering awards. (3) With respect to awards for contractual debts for a sum certain and for forced loans, interest at the rate of 6% would be awarded commencing from the date at which the claim had been brought to the attention of the Mexican government or filed before the National Claims Commission.

Some of the details of these rules are open to argument, but, on the whole, they represent a thoughtful attempt to settle all possible phases of a difficult and confused problem. During the Presidency of M. Verzijl these rules were followed, but after the reorganization of the Commission interest was not awarded in any cases.

§277. **Practice of the General Claims Commission.** The United States-Mexican General Claims Commission first touched the problem in a curious fashion. During the first ten months of the period during which decisions were handed, the Commission did not discuss the question as to whether or not interest could be awarded. However, interest at the rate of 6% was awarded without discussion in three cases.[85] All of these cases involved contractual claims and interest was to commence from the date of the breach of the contract. The terminal date of the interest period was to be fixed by the Commission subsequently. In one case involving breach of contract interest was not awarded.[86] Finally in the *Illinois Central* case,[87] the Commission considered the problem and said the following:

"Unfortunately the Convention of September 8, 1923, contains no specific stipulation with respect to the inclusion of interest in pecuniary awards. Allowances of interest have been made from time to time by international tribunals acting under arbitral agreements which, like the Agreement of September 8, 1923, have made no mention of this subject. . . . Other Agreements have contained stipulations authorizing awards of interest under specific conditions and for more or less definitely prescribed periods. . . . None of the opinions rendered by tribunals created under those agreements with respect to a variety of cases appears to be at variance with the principle to which we deem it proper to give effect that interest must be regarded

[85] U. S. A. (John B. Okie) *v.* United Mexican States, Opinions of Commissioners, 1927, p. 61; U. S. A. (William A. Parker) *v.* United Mexican States, *ibid.*, 1927, p. 82; U. S. A. (J. Parker Kirlin) *v.* United Mexican States, *ibid.*, 1927, p. 162.

[86] U. S. A. (Home Insurance Co.) *v.* United Mexican States, Opinions of Commissioners, 1927, p. 86.

[87] U. S. A. (Illinois Central R. R. Co.) *v.* United Mexican States, Opinions of Commissioners, 1927, p. 187, at 189.

as a proper element of compensation. It is the purpose of the Convention of September 8, 1923, to afford the respective nationals of the High Contracting Parties, in the language of the convention, 'just and adequate compensation for their losses or damages.' In our opinion just compensatory damages in this case would include not only the sum due, as stated in the Memorial, under the aforesaid contract, but compensation for the loss of the use of that sum during a period within which the payment thereof continues to be withheld. However, the Commission will not award interest beyond the date of the termination of the labors of the Commission in the absence of specific stipulations in the Agreement of September 8, 1923, authorizing such action."

Following this opinion, the Commission awarded interest at the rate of 6% [88] in cases involving contractual claims and forced loans.[89] In each case interest was to run from the date of the breach to the date of the rendition of the last award by the Commission.[90] Interest was not allowed on any claims for personal injuries or wrongful death.

§278. **Practice of Other Commissions.** A decision of the German-Mexican Commission revealed sharply differing views on the question of interest on awards.[91] The Mexican Commissioner contended that no interest could be awarded. The German Commissioner took the view of the *Pinson* case, *viz.*, that no interest could be awarded in cases where the liability of Mexico was *ex gratia*, but that it could be awarded in claims based on international law. The Presiding Commissioner (Cruchaga) was of the opinion that interest might be awarded whenever the Commission should consider it equitable, but as a matter of fact, interest was not awarded in any case. When the problem arose before the Italian-Mexican Commission, of

[88] In U. S. A. (American Bottle Co.) *v.* United Mexican States, Opinions of Commissioners, 1929, p. 162, which involved a contract claim for an amount due from a brewery which had been seized by the government, it appeared that the claimant had informed the brewery company that it would charge the account with interest at the rate of 5%. Notwithstanding this fact, the Commission awarded 6% interest since the claim was against the government and not against the brewery company.

[89] For example of an award of interest in a claim for a forced loan see U. S. A. (Laura A. Mecham) *v.* United Mexican States, Opinions of Commissioners, 1929, p. 168.

[90] An exception to this rule was made in U. S. A. (United Dredging Co.) *v.* United Mexican States, Opinions of Commissioners, 1927, p. 394. The claim was for services rendered. The Commission remarked that the sum might be considered to have become due when the work was interrupted. However, because of the inadequacy of the evidence with regard to the arrangement under which the services were rendered, interest was computed from the date on which the memorandum of the claim was filed with the Commission.

[91] Republica Alemana (Frederico Griese) *v.* Estados Unidos Alemanos, Decision No. 8 (unpublished).

which Señor Cruchaga was also Presiding Commissioner, it was held
that the Commission had no power to award interest, but this statement was qualified by the statement that this was not to be taken to
mean that when the responsibility of Mexico should be established in
conformity with the rules of international law that the Commission
could not order the payment of such interest as appeared to it justified.[92] In fact, interest was never awarded. The British-Mexican and
Spanish-Mexican Commissions did not award interest in any cases and
no discussion of the problem appears to have taken place.

Payment of Awards

§279. **Modes of Payment.** Elaborate provisions with respect to
the payment of awards were contained in the General Claims Convention.[93] The total amount awarded to the citizens of one country
was to be deducted from the total awarded to the citizens of the
other, and the balance paid in gold coin or its equivalent at Washington
or at Mexico City. In any case the Commission might decide that
a property or right be restored to the claimant in addition to the
amount awarded for loss or damage sustained. At the same time the
Commission was required to determine the value of such property
or right, and the government affected was given an election to pay
this amount rather than to restore the property or right. If that government chose to pay the amount fixed it was agreed that notice was to
be given within thirty days after the decision and the amount fixed
was to be paid immediately.

The Special Claims Convention [94] and the French-Mexican Convention [95] provided that payment was to be made to the claimant
government in gold or its equivalent. The other Conventions provided
that the form in which the Mexican Government should make payment was to be determined by both governments after termination of

---

[92] " . . . la Comisión carese de atribuciones para imponer el pago de intereses al
Gobierno demando, en virtua de que la Convención sólo habla de 'pérdidas o daños'
y en parte alguna se refiere a lucro cessantes, como son los perjuicios y los intereses.
No imputa lo anterior, en modo alguno, una declaración de que cuando la responsibilidad
de México se haya establecido de conformidad a los principios del Derecho Internacional, no pueda esta Comisión ordenar el pago de intereses que aparezcan justificados;
pues cabe distinguir, entre las reclamaciones presentadas a nuestro estudio, aquellas
tienen por unica base la promesa graciosa del Gobierno demando y las que derivan de
obligaciones fundadas en preceptos juridicos reconocidos por la comunidad internacional."
Case of Alessandro Bayardini, Decision No. 6 (unpublished).
[93] Article IX.   [94] Article IX.   [95] Article IX.

the work of the Commission, such payment to be made in gold or its equivalent to the claimant government.[96]

§280. **Currency of Awards.** No provision was made in the Conventions with respect to the currency in which awards should be expressed. The General Claims Commission adopted the practice of rendering awards in United States currency "having in mind the purpose of avoiding future uncertainties with respect to rates of exchange which it appears the two Governments also had in mind in framing the first paragraph of Article IX of the Convention of September 8, 1923, with respect to the payment of the balance therein mentioned 'in gold coin or its equivalent.' "[97] In contractual claims, the Commission applied the rate of exchange as of the date of the breach of the contract.[98]

The early practice of the British-Mexican Commission with respect to the currency of awards was not consistent. Of the first five awards which were made three were expressed to be payable in Mexican gold pesos [99] and two in pounds sterling.[100] Finally, in the *Watson* case,[101] the Commission stated:

"It seems arbitrary to let such currency be dependent upon what is asked in the claim. There is no reason why gold pesos should be awarded in one case, silver pesos in another, Pounds Sterling in a third, and United States dollars in a fourth. The Commission, having also regard to article 9 of the Convention, are of the opinion that the awards can be based upon no other money than the national and legal money of the State to be held liable for the payment. Awards will, for that reason, in the future be made in Mexican national gold." [102]

The Italian-Mexican Commission refused to follow this decision. It held that all awards should be made in current Mexican money (*i.e.*,

---

[96] Article X, German-Mexican Convention; Article IX, British-Mexican, Italian-Mexican and Spanish-Mexican Conventions.

[97] U. S. A. (Peerless Motor Car Co.) *v.* United Mexican States, Opinions of Commissioners, 1927, p. 303, at 305.

[98] U. S. A. (George W. Cook) *v.* United Mexican States, *ibid.*, 1927, p. 318; U. S. A. (Francis J. Acosta) *v.* United Mexican States, Opinions of Commissioners, 1929, p. 121; U. S. A. (Singer Sewing Machine Co.) *v.* United Mexican States, *ibid.*, 1929, p. 123.

[99] Mexican City Bombardment Claim, Decisions and Opinions of Commissioners, p. 100; Case of the Mazapil Copper Co., Ltd., *ibid.*, p. 132; Case of C. E. McFadden, *ibid.*, p. 155.

[100] Case of William E. Bowerman, Decisions and Opinions of Commissioners, p. 141; Case of John Gill, Further Decisions and Opinions, p. 85.

[101] Case of Mrs. Jessie Watson, Further Decisions and Opinions, p. 92.

[102] *Ibid.*, p. 95.

silver pesos) and that Article IX of the Convention referred only to intergovernmental settlement subsequent to the work of the Commission and not to the determination of awards.[103]

All awards of the French-Mexican, German-Mexican and Spanish-Mexican Commissions were expressed to be payable in gold pesos.

[103] "Todas las sentencias dictadas por esta Comisión, se entendarán fijadas en pesos plata, con exclusión de cualquiera otra divisa y expecialmente del peso oro, porque las indemnizaciones acordadas se han calculado, en todos los casos resueltos por las Comisión, relacionado el daño sufrido con el peso plata, por lo que cualquier cambio en la moneda significaría una alteración de la sentencia.

"Por 'moneda corriente' entiende la Comisión por unanimidad el peso mexicano a que se refiere la Ley Monetaria de los Estados Unidos Mexicanos de 27 de julio de 1931." Case of Fernando Scagno, Decision No. 12 (unpublished).

CHAPTER 18

CONCLUSION

Now that we have finished our travels through the minutiae of the history and practice of the Mexican Claims Commissions, we may pause to consider the results achieved by the Commissions and the bearing of the matters which we have studied on the future of international adjudication. It cannot be doubted that most of the Commissions are to be credited with the accomplishment of substantial results—the final disposition of a great mass of claims. While it cannot be said that any Commission proceeded with the expedition which might have been expected, four of them, the British-Mexican, German-Mexican, Spanish-Mexican and Italian-Mexican Commissions, were able to avoid any serious friction. Significantly, all of these with the exception of the British-Mexican Commission, had as Presiding Commissioner Señor Miguel Cruchaga of Chile. On the other side of the balance must be entered the complete failure of the United States-Mexican Special Claims Commission and the serious difficulties encountered in the work of the United States-Mexican General Claims Commission and of the French-Mexican Commission.

It is not easy to apportion the blame for failure or difficulties. From one point of view it might be said that particular Commissioners were responsible. The United States could say, conceivably, that the difficulties of the Special and General Claims Commissions were due to Señores Octavio and Alfaro, while the Mexican government might feel that Mr. Nielsen was more to blame. So the Mexican government might charge Mr. Verzijl with responsibility for the unfortunate history of the French-Mexican Commission. On the other hand, any one of these gentlemen could, with more or less justification, retort that they were being accused mainly because they had taken a view of the law which they conceived to be the proper one. Unquestionably, the choice of the personnel of a Commission is of the greatest importance

and governments have often been entirely too casual in making these choices. Yet some of the gentlemen mentioned above had enjoyed high reputations as international lawyers.

Again, the blame might be fastened upon the shoulders of those who negotiated the Conventions. We have noted numerous instances of ambiguities which were productive of controversy. The most bitter controversies raged about the interpretation of the jurisdictional articles of the Conventions dealing with revolutionary claims. Some of the Commissioners believed that these articles were clear and unambiguous and would say, perhaps, that the difficulties encountered were due to what they would consider the intransigent position of the Mexican government.

Even when we consider the four Commissions which had relatively peaceful histories, we find some fundamental weaknesses. The British-Mexican Convention was amended in several important respects while the Commission was functioning. The German-Mexican and Italian-Mexican Commissions functioned smoothly, but it is noteworthy that these Commissions applied equitable principles in the broadest possible fashion so that many of their decisions can hardly be said to be based on law. The Spanish-Mexican Commission rendered all of its awards without opinions, with the exception of five opinions on points of procedure. We may infer that compromise played a large part in the determination of claims by this Commission. The desire to compromise and adjust is apparent in the opinions of the other three "successful" Commissions. Perhaps this was the reason for their success; if so, it is a sad commentary on the effort to settle international disputes by adjudication.

It may well be that the difficulties presented by the history of the Mexican Claims Commissions are inherent in the system of adjudication through *ad hoc* tribunals. The fundamental defects in this system would appear to be the casual choice of the members and their limited tenure, the fragmentary character of international procedural law, and the close connection of the litigating governments with the tribunal.

These defects suggest that the proper forum for the adjudication of claims is not an evanescent tribunal but the Permanent Court of International Justice. Only a few changes would be necessary in the Statute of the Court to adapt it to this purpose. The court could be

divided into a number of *"Chambres de Réclamations,"* each to consist of three judges. These Chambers would sit for the hearing and adjudication of claims submitted by special agreement at times when the full Court was not in session. The Registry of the Court would fulfill admirably the functions now served by joint secretaries of Commissions. The problem of securing evidence could be taken care of by amending the Statute so as to require states to recognize and give effect to letters rogatory issued by the Court. The business of the Court heretofore has not been of such volume as to make the suggested jurisdiction over claims too great a burden on the judges. With a Court composed of fifteen members, it should not be too difficult a task to apportion the business of claims adjudication in a convenient manner. It may be pointed out that not the least of the advantages to be procured from using the Permanent Court would be the saving of a considerable part of the expense which claims commissions now entail.

While the substitution of the Permanent Court for *ad hoc* tribunals may be the ideal solution, it is hardly likely to occur within the foreseeable future. Governments will doubtless continue to conclude claims conventions for a considerable time to come. For these governments the history of the Mexican Claims Commissions holds many lessons. We can only select the most important of these.

1. It is a grave mistake to construct a tribunal out of two national members and one neutral member. Few men are capable of holding the balance between two contending national commissioners. If the governments do not object to the possibility of decision by compromise rather than by adjudication, they should provide for two national commissioners with an umpire in case of disagreement. Otherwise they should provide either for one, or better still three, neutral commissioners. Incidentally, it would be well for governments considering the appointment of a neutral commissioner to ponder not only his reputation for learning and impartiality, but also the legal views which he has expressed in the past.

2. Agents should be severely discouraged from submitting every possible claim to the tribunal. The agent of a government stands in a much different position from the attorney of a private litigant. He should consider himself, to a certain extent, as a judicial officer, and pass upon all claims before their submission so that only such claims as are truly meritorious are presented for decision. The failure to scru-

tinize claims before submission is undoubtedly the chief reason for the unduly long periods required for the termination of claims adjudications. At the same time, agents should be scrupulous in claiming damages which approximate the losses suffered. The agents of the governments in the United States-Mexican General Claims Commission were particularly at fault in permitting highly exaggerated claims for damages to be filed.

3. Rules of procedure are a most important factor in the functioning of a tribunal. Under the system established by the Mexican Claims Conventions they were drawn up by the Commissions themselves. This entailed considerable delay and many of the Commissions did not begin to hear claims until many months after their organization. It would be advisable for the governments themselves to draw up a set of rules which could be annexed to the Convention. The Commission should, of course, be given full liberty to amend these rules as occasion should warrant.

4. It need hardly be said that the claims convention should be drawn up with the most scrupulous clarity. Those who have participated in the drafting of treaties or legislation will know that draftsmen are often tempted to permit a difficult or controverted point to remain intentionally ambiguous. Such a temptation should never be indulged in when drafting a claims convention. Ambiguities cause conflict and delay, and may often wreck the whole structure of settlement.

5. It is important for Commissioners to bear in mind that expeditiousness of adjudication is of prime importance. A practice which can contribute much towards that end is the determination of fundamental questions at the outset. The United States-German Mixed Claims Commission adopted the practice of laying down fundamental rules of decision in a series of "Administrative Decisions" before taking up individual claims. The Mexican Claims Commissions might well have operated with greater efficiency if they had also adopted such a practice.

These are the major considerations which emerge from a study of the Mexican Claims Commissions. The many minor improvements of practice which might be made have been indicated at various places in this volume.

APPENDICES

I. UNITED STATES–MEXICAN GENERAL CLAIMS COMMISSION

A. CONVENTION OF SEPTEMBER 8, 1923 [1]

The United States of America and the United Mexican States, desiring to settle and adjust amicably claims by the citizens of each country against the other since the signing on July 4, 1868, of the Claims Convention entered into between the two countries (without including the claims for losses or damages growing out of the revolutionary disturbances in Mexico which form the basis of another and separate Convention), have decided to enter into a Convention with this object, and to this end have nominated as their Plenipotentiaries:

The President of the United States of America:

The Honorables Charles Evans Hughes, Secretary of State of the United States of America, Charles Beecher Warren and John Barton Payne, and

The President of the United Mexican States:

Señor Don Manuel C. Téllez, Chargé d'Affaires ad interim of the United Mexican States at Washington;

Who, after having communicated to each other their respective full powers found to be in due and proper form, have agreed upon the following Articles:

Los Estados Unidos de América y los Estados Unidos Mexicanos, deseando arreglar y ajustar amigablemente las reclamaciones de los ciudadanos de cada uno de los dos países en contra del otro desde la firma, el 4 de julio de 1868, de la Convención de Reclamaciones celebrada entre los dos países (sin incluir las reclamaciones por pérdidas o daños provenientes de los trastornos revolucionarios en México que constituyen la base de distinta y separada Convención), han resuelto celebrar una Convención con tal fin, y al efecto han nombrado como sus Plenipotenciarios:

El Presidente de los Estados Unidos de América:

Los Honorables Charles Evans Hughes, Secretario de Estado de los Estados Unidos de América, Charles Beecher Warren y John Barton Payne, y

El Presidente de los Estados Unidos Mexicanos:

Señor Don Manuel C. Téllez, Encargado de Negocios ad interim de los Estados Unidos Mexicanos en Wáshington;

Quienes, después de haberse comunicado mutuamente sus respectivos plenos poderes y encontrándolos en buena y debida forma, han convenido en los artículos siguientes:

[1] Text from U. S. Treaty Series No. 678.

Article I

All claims (except those arising from acts incident to the recent revolutions) against Mexico of citizens of the United States, whether corporations, companies, associations, partnerships or individuals, for losses or damages suffered by persons or by their properties, and all claims against the United States of America by citizens of Mexico, whether corporations, companies, associations, partnerships or individuals, for losses or damages suffered by persons or by their properties; all claims for losses or damages suffered by citizens of either country by reason of losses or damages suffered by any corporation, company, association or partnership in which such citizens have or have had a substantial and bona fide interest, provided an allotment to the claimant by the corporation, company, association or partnership of his proportion of the loss or damage suffered is presented by the claimant to the Commission hereinafter referred to; and all claims for losses or damages originating from acts of officials or others acting for either Government and resulting in injustice, and which claims may have been presented to either Government for its interposition with the other since the signing of the Claims Convention concluded between the two countries July 4, 1868, and which have remained unsettled, as well as any other such claims which may be filed by either Government within the time hereinafter specified, shall be submitted to a

Artículo I

Todas las reclamaciones (exceptuando aquellas provenientes de actos incidentales a las recientes revoluciones) en contra de México, de cuidadanos de los Estados Unidos, ya sean corporaciones, compañías, asociaciones, sociedades o individuos particulares, por pérdidas o daños sufridos en sus personas o en sus propiedades, y todas las reclamaciones en contra de los Estados Unidos de América, de ciudadanos mexicanos, ya sean corporaciones, compañías, asociaciones, sociedades o individuos particulares, por pérdidas o daños sufridos en sus personas o en sus propiedades; todas las reclamaciones por pérdidas o daños sufridos por ciudadanos de cualquiera de los dos países en virtud de pérdidas o daños sufridos por alguna corporación, compañía, asociación o sociedad en que dichos ciudadanos tengan o hayan tenido un interés sustancial y bona fide, siempre que el reclamante presente a la Comisión que más adelante se menciona, una asignación hecha al mismo reclamante por la corporación, compañía, asociación, o sociedad, de su parte proporcional de la pérdida o daño sufrido; y todas las reclamaciones por pérdidas o daños provenientes de actos de funcionarios u otras personas que obren por cualquiera de los dos Gobiernos y que resulten en injusticia, y las cuales reclamaciones puedan haber sido presentadas a cualquiera de los dos Gobiernos para su interposición con el otro desde la firma de la Conven-

Commission consisting of three members for decision in accordance with the principles of international law, justice and equity.

Such Commission shall be constituted as follows : one member shall be appointed by the President of the United States; one by the President of the United Mexican States; and the third, who shall preside over the Commission, shall be selected by mutual agreement between the two Governments. If the two Governments shall not agree within two months from the exchange of ratifications of this Convention in naming such third member, then he shall be designated by the President of the Permanent Administrative Council of the Permanent Court of Arbitration at The Hague described in Article XLIX of the Convention for the pacific settlement of international disputes concluded at The Hague on October 18, 1907. In case of the death, absence or incapacity of any member of the Commission, or in the event of a member omitting or ceasing to act as such, the same procedure shall be followed for filling the vacancy as was followed in appointing him.

ción de Reclamaciones celebrada entre los dos países el 4 de julio de 1868 y que han quedado pendientes de arreglo, asi como cualesquiera otras reclamaciones semejantes que puedan ser presentadas por cualquiera de los dos Gobiernos dentro del período especificado más adelante, seran sometidas a una Comisión integrada por tres miembros, para su fallo de acuerdo con los principios del Derecho Internacional, de la justicia y de la equidad.

Dicha Comisión quedará constituida como sigue : un miembro será nombrado por el Presidente de los Estados Unidos; otro por el Presidente de los Estados Unidos Mexicanos; y el tercero, quien presidirá la Comisión, será escogido por acuerdo mutuo de los dos Gobiernos. Si los dos Gobiernos no se pusieren de acuerdo en la designación de dicho tercer miembro dentro de los dos meses siguientes al canje de ratificaciones de esta Convención, éste será entonces designado por el Presidente del Consejo Administrativo Permanente de la Corte Permanente de Arbitraje de La Haya a que se refiere el Artículo XLIX de la Convención para el arreglo pacífico de las disputas internacionales concluída en La Haya en 18 de octubre de 1907. En caso del fallecimiento, ausencia o incapacidad de cualquier miembro de la Comisión, o en caso de que alguno de ellos omita obrar como tal o cese de hacerlo, se empleará para llenar la vacante el mismo método que se siguió para nombrarlo.

Article II

The Commissioners so named shall meet at Washington for organization within six months after the exchange of the ratifications of this Convention, and each member of the Commission, before entering upon his duties, shall make and subscribe a solemn declaration stating that he will carefully and impartially examine and decide, according to the best of his judgment and in accordance with the principles of international law, justice and equity, all claims presented for decision, and such declaration shall be entered upon the record of the proceedings of the Commission.

The Commission may fix the time and place of its subsequent meetings, either in the United States or in Mexico, as may be convenient, subject always to the special instructions of the two Governments.

Article III

In general, the Commission shall adopt as the standard for its proceedings the rules of procedure established by the Mixed Claims Commission created under the Claims Convention between the two Governments signed July 4, 1868, in so far as such rules are not in conflict with any provision of this Convention. The Commission, however, shall have authority by the decision of the majority of its members to establish such other rules for its proceedings as may be deemed expedient and necessary, not in conflict with any of the provisions of this Convention.

Articulo II

Los Comisionados así nombrados se reunirán en Washington para organizarse, dentro de un plazo de seis meses después del canje de las ratificaciones de esta Convención; y cada miembro de la Comisión, antes de comenzar sus labores, hará y suscribirá una declaración solemne de que cuidadosa e imparcialmente examinará y decidirá, según su mejor saber, y de acuerdo con los principios del Derecho Internacional, de la justicia y de la equidad, todas las reclamaciones presentadas para su fallo y dicha declaración deberá asentarse en el registro de actas de la Comisión.

La Comisión podrá fijar el tiempo y lugar de sus juntas subsecuentes, ya sea en los Estados Unidos o en México, según convenga, sujeta siempre a las instrucciones especiales de los dos Gobiernos.

Artículo III

En general, la Comisión adoptará como norma de sus actuaciones las reglas de procedimiento establecidas por la Comisión Mixta de Reclamaciones creada por la Convención de Reclamaciones entre los dos Gobiernos, firmada el 4 de julio de 1868, en cuanto dichas reglas no estén en pugna con cualquiera de las disposiciones de esta Convención. La Comisión tendrá poder, sin embargo, por resolución de la mayoría de sus miembros, para establecer en sus actuaciones las otras reglas que se estimen convenientes y necesarias, que no estén en pugna con cualquiera

Each Government may nominate and appoint agents and counsel who will be authorized to present to the Commission, orally or in writing, all the arguments deemed expedient in favor of or against any claim. The agents or counsel of either Government may offer to the Commission any documents, affidavits, interrogatories or other evidence desired in favor of or against any claim and shall have the right to examine witnesses under oath or affirmation before the Commission, in accordance with such rules of procedure as the Commission shall adopt.

The decision of the majority of the members of the Commission shall be the decision of the Commission.

The language in which the proceedings shall be conducted and recorded shall be English or Spanish.

ARTICLE IV

The Commission shall keep an accurate record of the claims and cases submitted, and minutes of its proceedings with the dates thereof. To this end, each Government may appoint a Secretary; these Secretaries shall act as joint Secretaries of the Commission and shall be subject to its instructions. Each Government may also appoint and employ any necessary assistant secretaries and such other assistance as deemed necessary. The Commission may also appoint and employ any persons necessary

de las disposiciones de esta Convención.

Cada Gobierno podrá nombrar y designar agentes y abogados que quedarán autorizados para presentar a la Comisión, oralmente o por escrito, todos los argumentos que consideren oportunos, en pro o en contra de cualquiera reclamación. Los agentes o abogados de cualquiera de los dos Gobiernos, podrán presentar a la Comisión cualesquiera documentos, affidavits, interrogatorios o cualquiera otra prueba que se desee, en pro o en contra de alguna reclamación, y tendrán el derecho de examinar testigos, bajo juramento o protesta, ante la Comisión, de acuerdo con las reglas de procedimiento que lar Comisión adoptaré.

La decisión de la mayoría de los miembros de la Comisión será la decisión de la Comisión.

El idioma en que se llevarán y registrarán las actuaciones será el inglés o el español.

ARTÍCULO IV

La Comisión llevará un registro exacto de las reclamaciones y de los casos sometidos y minutas de sus actuaciones con sus fechas respectivas. Con tal fin, cada Gobierno podrá nombrar un Secretario; estos secretarios actuarán conjuntamente como secretarios de la Comisión y estarán sujetos a sus instrucciones. Cada Gobierno podrá también nombrar y emplear los secretarios adscritos que sean necesarios, así como los demás empleados que se consideren necesarios. La Comisión podrá,

to assist in the performance of its duties.

ARTICLE V

The High Contracting Parties, being desirous of effecting an equitable settlement of the claims of their respective citizens thereby affording them just and adequate compensation for their losses or damages, agree that no claim shall be disallowed or rejected by the Commission by the application of the general principle of international law that the legal remedies must be exhausted as a condition precedent to the validity or allowance of any claim.

ARTICLE VI

Every such claim for loss or damage accruing prior to the signing of this Convention, shall be filed with the Commission within one year from the date of its first meeting, unless in any case reasons for the delay, satisfactory to the majority of the Commissioners, shall be established, and in any such case the period for filing the claim may be extended not to exceed six additional months.

The Commission shall be bound to hear, examine and decide, within three years from the date of its first meeting, all the claims filed, except as hereinafter provided in Article VII.

Four months after the date of the first meeting of the Commissioners,

igualmente, nombrar y emplear cualesquiera otras personas necesarias para que la ayuden en el desempeño de sus deberes.

ARTÍCULO V

Las Altas Partes Contratantes, deseosas de efectuar un arreglo equitativo de las reclamaciones de sus respectivos ciudadanos, y concederles mediante ello compensación justa y adecuada por sus pérdidas o daños, convienen en que la Comisión no negará o rechazará ninguna reclamación alegando la aplicación del principio general de Derecho Internacional, de que han de agotarse los remedios legales como condición precedente a la validez o admisión de cualquiera reclamación.

ARTÍCULO VI

Todas y cada una de tales reclamaciones por pérdida o daño originadas antes de la firma de esta Convención, serán presentadas a la Comisión dentro del primer año de la fecha de su primera junta, a menos de que en algún caso se comprueben para la tardanza, razones satisfactorias para la mayoría de los Comisionados y en cualquiera de estos casos, el período para presentar la reclamación podrá ser prorrogado hasta por un plazo que no exceda de seis meses más.

La Comisión estará obligada a oír, examinar y fallar, dentro de los tres años subsiguientes a la fecha de su primera junta, todas las reclamaciones presentadas, salvo en los casos previstos en el Artículo VII.

Cuatro meses después de la fecha de la primera junta de los Comisiona-

and every four months thereafter, the Commission shall submit to each Government a report setting forth in detail its work to date, including a statement of the claims filed, claims heard and claims decided. The Commission shall be bound to decide any claim heard and examined within six months after the conclusion of the hearing of such claim and to record its decision.

Article VII

The High Contracting Parties agree that any claim for loss or damage accruing after the signing of this Convention, may be filed by either Government with the Commission at any time during the period fixed in Article VI for the duration of the Commission; and it is agreed between the two Governments that should any such claim or claims be filed with the Commission prior to the termination of said Commission, and not be decided as specified in Article VI, the two Governments will by agreement extend the time within which the Commission may hear, examine and decide such claim or claims so filed for such a period as may be required for the Commission to hear, examine and decide such claim or claims.

Article VIII

The High Contracting Parties agree to consider the decision of the Commission as final and conclusive upon each claim decided, and to give full

dos, y cada cuatro meses después, la Comisión habrá de rendir a cada Gobierno un informe dando cuenta en detalle de sus trabajos hasta la fecha, incluyendo un estado de las reclamaciones presentadas, de las oídas y de las falladas. La Comisión estará obligada a decidir cualquier reclamación oída y examinada dentro de los seis meses siguientes a la terminación de la audiencia de dicha reclamación, y a hacer constar su fallo.

Artículo VII

Las Altas Partes Contratantes convienen en que cualquiera reclamación por pérdida o daño que se origine después de la firma de esta Convención, puede ser presentada a la Comisión por cualquiera de los Gobiernos en cualquier tiempo durante el período señalado en el Artículo VI para la duración de la Comisión; y los dos Gobiernos convienen en que si se presentaré a la Comisión alguna o algunas de dichas reclamaciones antes de que terminen las labores de dicha Comisión, y no sean falladas de conformidad con lo establecido en el Artículo VI, los dos Gobiernos de común acuerdo prorrogarán el tiempo dentro del cual la Comisión pueda oír, examinar y fallar tal reclamación o reclamaciones así presentadas, por el plazo que pueda ser necesario para que la Comisión oiga, examine y decida tal reclamación o reclamaciones.

Artículo VIII

Las Altas Partes Contratantes convienen en considerar como finales y concluyentes las decisiones de la Comisión que recaigan sobre cada una

effect to such decisions. They further agree to consider the result of the proceedings of the Commission as a full, perfect and final settlement of every such claim upon either Government, for loss or damage sustained prior to the exchange of the ratifications of the present Convention (except as to claims arising from revolutionary disturbances and referred to in the preamble hereof). And they further agree that every such claim, whether or not filed and presented to the notice of, made, preferred or submitted to such Commission shall from and after the conclusion of the proceedings of the Commission be considered and treated as fully settled, barred and thenceforth inadmissible, provided the claim filed has been heard and decided.

de las reclamaciones falladas, y dar pleno efecto a tales decisiones. Convienen además en considerar el resultado de las actuaciones de la Comisión como un arreglo pleno, perfecto y final de todas y cada una de tales reclamaciones en contra de cualquiera de los Gobiernos, por pérdida o daño sufrido antes del canje de ratificaciones de la presente Convención (exceptuando aquellas reclamaciones provenientes de trastornos revolucionarios y a las cuales se hace mención en el preámbulo de esta Convención). Y convienen, además, en que todas y cada una de tales reclamaciones, hayan sido o nó presentadas o llevadas a conocimiento, hechas, propuestas o sometidas a dicha Comisión, deberán, a partir y después de la terminación de las actuaciones de la Comisión, ser consideradas y tratadas como plenamente ajustadas, excluídas y de allí en adelante inadmisibles, siempre que la reclamación presentada haya sido oida y fallada.

ARTICLE IX

The total amount awarded in all the cases decided in favor of the citizens of one country shall be deducted from the total amount awarded to the citizens of the other country and the balance shall be paid at Washington or at the City of Mexico, in gold coin or its equivalent to the Government of the country in favor of whose citizens the greater amount may have been awarded.

In any case the Commission may decide that international law, justice

ARTÍCULO IX

La cantidad total adjudicada en todos los casos decididos, en favor de los ciudadanos de uno de los países, será deducida de la cantidad total adjudicada a los ciudadanos del otro país y el saldo será pagado en Washington o en la Ciudad de México, en moneda de oro o su equivalente, al Gobierno del país en favor de cuyos ciudadanos se haya adjudicado la cantidad mayor.

En cualquier caso la Comisión puede decidir que el Derecho Inter-

and equity require that a property or right be restored to the claimant in addition to the amount awarded in any such case for all loss or damage sustained prior to the restitution. In any case where the Commission so decides the restitution of the property or right shall be made by the Government affected after such decision has been made, as herein below provided. The Commission, however, shall at the same time determine the value of the property or right decreed to be restored and the Government affected may elect to pay the amount so fixed after the decision is made rather than to restore the property or right to the claimant.

In the event the Government affected should elect to pay the amount fixed as the value of the property or right decreed to be restored, it is agreed that notice thereof will be filed with the Commission within thirty days after the decision and that the amount fixed as the value of the property or right shall be paid immediately. Upon failure so to pay the amount the property or right shall be restored immediately.

ARTICLE X

Each Government shall pay its own Commissioner and bear its own expenses. The expenses of the Commission including the salary of the third Commissioner shall be defrayed in equal proportions by the two Governments.

nacional, la justicia y la equidad requieren que una propiedad o un derecho sea restituído al reclamante, además de la cantidad que se le adjudique en cualquiera de tales casos por toda la pérdida o daño sufrido antes de la restitución. En cualquier caso en que la Comisión así lo resuelva, la restitución de la propiedad o del derecho será hecha por el Govierno afectado después de que tal decisión haya sido dictada, según se previene más adelante. La Comisión, no obstante, fijará al mismo tiempo el valor de la propiedad o del derecho cuya restitución se ha decretado y el Gobierno afectado tendrá opción de pagar la cantidad así fijada después de la resolución, en vez de restituir la propiedad o el derecho al reclamante.

En el caso de que el Gobierno afectado opte por pagar la cantidad fijada como valor de la propiedad o el derecho cuya restitución sea decretada, se conviene en que se dará el correspondiente aviso a la Comisión dentro de los treinta días siguientes a la resolución y que la cantidad fijada como valor de la propiedad o del derecho, será pagada inmediatamente. En defecto del pago inmediato, la propiedad o el derecho será restituido inmediatamente.

ARTÍCULO X

Cada Gobierno pagará su propio Comisionado y erogará sus propios gastos. Los gastos de la Comisión, inclusive el sueldo del tercer Comisionado, se cubrirán por partes iguales por los dos Gobiernos.

Article XI	Artículo XI
The present Convention shall be ratified by the High Contracting Parties in accordance with their respective Constitutions. Ratifications of this Convention shall be exchanged in Washington as soon as practicable and the Convention shall take effect on the date of the exchange of ratifications.	La presente Convención será ratificada por las Altas Partes Contratantes de acuerdo con sus respectivas Constituciones.
	Las ratificaciones de esta Convención serán canjeadas en Washington tan pronto como sea practicable y la Convención empezará a surtir sus efectos en la fecha del canje de ratificaciones.
In witness whereof, the respective Plenipotentiaries have signed and affixed their seals to this Convention.	En testimonio de lo cual, los Plenipotenciarios respectivos firmaron esta Convención y fijaron en ella su sello.
Done in duplicate at Washington this eighth day of September, 1923.	Hecha por duplicado en Washington el día ocho de Septiembre de 1923.

CHARLES EVANS HUGHES   [SEAL]
CHARLES BEECHER WARREN   [SEAL]
JOHN BARTON PAYNE   [SEAL]
MANUEL C. TÉLLEZ   [SEAL]

B. SUPPLEMENTARY CONVENTION OF AUGUST 16, 1927 [1]

WHEREAS a convention was signed on September 8, 1923, between the United States of America and the United Mexican States for the settlement and amicable adjustment of certain claims therein defined; and	CONSIDERANDO que el 8 de septiembre de 1923 se firmó una convención entre los Estados Unidos de Norte América y los Estados Unidos Mexicanos para el arreglo y ajuste amistoso de las reclamaciones que en ella se definen;
WHEREAS under Article VI of said convention the Commission constituted pursuant thereto is bound to hear, examine and decide within three years from the date of its first meeting	CONSIDERANDO que según el Artículo VI de dicha convención la Comisión que según aquélla se constituyó está obligada a oír, examinar y decidir dentro de los tres años

[1] Text from U. S. Treaty Series No. 758.

ll the claims filed with it, except as
provided in Article VII; and

WHEREAS it now appears that
the said Commission cannot hear,
examine and decide such claims
within the time limit thus fixed;

The President of the United States
of America and the President of the
United Mexican States are desirous
that the time originally fixed for
the duration of the said Commission
should be extended, and to this end
have named as their respective plenipotentiaries, that is to say:

The President of the United States
of America, Honorable Frank B.
Kellogg, Secretary of State of the
United States; and

The President of the United
Mexican States, His Excellency Señor
Don Manuel C. Téllez, Ambassador
Extraordinary and Plenipotentiary
of the United Mexican States at
Washington;

Who, after having communicated
to each other their respective full
powers found in good and due form,
have agreed upon the following
articles:

ARTICLE I

The High Contracting Parties agree
that the term assigned by Article VI
of the Convention of September 8,
1923, for the hearing, examination and
decision of claims for loss or damage
accruing prior to September 8, 1923,
shall be and the same hereby is extended for a time not exceeding two
years from August 30, 1927, the day

después de la fecha de su primera
junta todas las reclamaciones presentadas ante ella, excepto lo que
previene el Artículo VIII; y

CONSIDERANDO que ahora resulta
que dicha Comisión no puede oír,
examinar y decidir tales reclamaciones
dentro de ese plazo;

El Presidente de los Estados Unidos
de Norte América, y el Presidente
de los Estados Unidos Mexicanos,
deseando que se prorrogue el plazo
fijado originariamente para la duración de dicha Comisión, han nombrado como a sus Plenipotenciarios
respectivos:

El Presidente de los Estados Unidos
de Norte América, Honorable Frank
B. Kellogg, Secretario de Estado de
los Estados Unidos de América; y

El Presidente de los Estados Unidos
Mexicanos, Su Excelencia Señor Don
Manuel C. Téllez, Embajador Ex-
traordinario y Plenipotenciario de los
Estados Unidos Mexicanos en Wásh-
ington;

Quienes, después de haberse
comunicado mutuamente sus Plenos
Poderes respectivos, hallándolos en
buena y debida forma, han convenido
en los siguientes Artículos:

ARTÍCULO I

Las Altas Partes Contratantes convienen en que el plazo designado por
el Artículo VI de Convención del
8 de septiembre de 1923, para la
audiencia, examen y decisión de
reclamaciones por pérdida o daños
acaecidos antes del 8 de septiembre
de 1923, se prorrogue, y por la presente se prorroga, durante un plazo

when, pursuant to the provisions of the said Article VI, the functions of the said Commission would terminate in respect of such claims; and that during such extended term the Commission shall also be bound to hear, examine and decide all claims for loss or damage accruing between September 8, 1923, and August 30, 1927, inclusive, and filed with the Commission not later than August 30, 1927.

It is agreed that nothing contained in this Article shall in any wise alter or extend the time originally fixed in the said Convention of September 8, 1923, for the presentation of claims to the Commission, or confer upon the Commission any jurisdiction over any claim for loss or damage accruing subsequent to August 30, 1927.

ARTICLE II

The present Convention shall be ratified and the ratifications shall be exchanged at Washington as soon as possible.

In witness whereof the above-mentioned Plenipotentiaries have signed the same and affixed their respective seals.

Done in duplicate at the City of Washington, in the English and Spanish languages, this sixteenth day of August in the year one thousand nine hundred and twenty-seven.

que no exceda de dos años contados desde el 30 de agosto de 1927, día en que, según las disposiciones de dicho Artículo VI, terminarían las funciones de tal Comisión por lo que toca a esas reclamaciones; y que durante el término de esta prorroga, la Comisión continuará obligada a oír, examinar y decidir cualesquiera reclamaciones por pérdida o daños acaecidos entre el 8 de septiembre de 1923 y el 30 de agosto de 1927, inclusive, siempre que hayan sido presentadas a la Comisión en Fecha no posterior al 30 de agosto de 1927.

Se conviene, además, en que nada de lo contenido en este Artículo altera o prorroga, en modo alguno, el plazo fijado originariamente en dicha Convención del 8 de septiembre de 1923 para la presentación de reclamaciones a la Comisión, ni confiere a ésta jurisdicción alguna sobre reclamaciones por pérdida o daños ocurridos con posterioridad al 30 de agosto de 1927.

ARTÍCULO II

Esta Convención se ratificará en cuanto sea posible, canjeándose las ratificaciones en Wáshington.

En testimonio de lo cual, los supra-dichos Plenipotenciarios la han firmado, fijando en ella sus sellos respectivos.

Hecha por duplicado, en inglés y en castellano, en la ciudad de Wáshington el día diez y seis de agosto del año de mil novecientos veintisiete.

FRANK B. KELLOGG   [SEAL]

MANUEL C. TÉLLEZ   [SEAL]

C. SUPPLEMENTARY CONVENTION OF SEPTEMBER 2, 1929 [1]

WHEREAS a convention was signed on September 8, 1923, between the United States of America and the United Mexican States for the settlement and amicable adjustment of certain claims therein defined; and

WHEREAS under Article VI of said Convention the Commission constituted pursuant thereto is bound to hear, examine and decide within three years from the date of its first meeting all the claims filed with it, except as provided in Article VII; and

WHEREAS by a convention concluded between the two Governments on August 16, 1927, the time for hearing, examining and deciding the said claims was extended for a period of two years; and

WHEREAS it now appears that the said Commission can not hear, examine and decide such claims within the time limit thus fixed;

The President of the United States of America and the President of the United Mexican States are desirous that the time thus fixed for the duration of the said Commission should be further extended, and to this end have named as their respective plenipotentiaries, that is to say:

The President of the United States of America, Herschel V. Johnson, Chargé d'Affaires ad interim of the United States of America in Mexico; and

CONSIDERANDO que el 8 de septiembre de 1923 se firmó una convención entre los Estados Unidos de Norte América y los Estados Unidos Mexicanos para el arreglo y ajuste amistoso de las reclamaciones que en ella se definen; y

CONSIDERANDO que según el Artículo VI de dicha convención la Comisión que según aquélla se constituyó está obligada a oír, examinar y decidir dentro de los tres años después de la fecha de su primera junta todas las reclamaciones presentadas ante ella, excepto lo que previene el Artículo VII; y

CONSIDERANDO que el día 16 de agosto de 1927 se concluyó una convención entre ambos Gobiernos extendiendo por un período de dos años el plazo para oír, examinar y decidir dichas reclamaciones; y

CONSIDERANDO que ahora resulta que dicha Comisión no puede oír, examinar y decidir tales reclamaciones dentro de ese plazo;

El Presidente de los Estados Unidos de Notre América y el Presidente de los Estados Unidos Mexicanos, deseando que se prorrogue nuevamente el plazo así fijado para la duración de dicha Comisión, ha nombrado como a sus Plenipotenciarios respectivos:

El Presidente de los Estados Unidos de Norte América al Señor Herschel V. Johnson, Chargé d'Affaires ad-ínterim de los Estados Unidos de Norte América en México; y

[1] Text from U. S. Treaty Series No. 801.

The President of the United Mexican States, Señor Genaro Estrada, Under Secretary of State in charge of Foreign Affairs;

Who, after having communicated to each other their respective full powers found in good and due form, have agreed upon the following Articles:

ARTICLE I

The High Contracting Parties agree that the term assigned by Article VI of the convention of September 8, 1923, as extended by Article I of the convention concluded between the two Governments on August 16, 1927, for the hearing, examination and decision of claims for loss or damage accruing prior to September 8, 1923, shall be and the same hereby is further extended for a time not exceeding two years from August 30, 1929, the day when, pursuant to the provisions of the said Article I of the convention concluded between the two Governments on August 16, 1927, the functions of the said Commission would terminate in respect of such claims; and that during such extended term the Commission shall also be bound to hear, examine and decide all claims for loss or damage accruing between September 8, 1923, and August 30, 1927, inclusive, and filed with the Commission not later than August 30, 1927.

It is agreed that nothing contained in this Article shall in any wise alter

El Presidente de los Estados Unidos Mexicanos al Señor Genaro Estrada, Sub-secretario de Relaciones Exteriores, Encargado el Despacho;

Quienes, después de haberse comunicado mutuamente sus Plenos Poderes respectivos, hallándolos en buena y debida forma, han convenido en los siguientes Artículos;

ARTÍCULO I

Las Altas Partes Contratantes convienen en que el plazo designado por el Artículo VI de la convención del 8 de septiembre de 1923, según quedó extendido por el Artículo I de la convención concluída entre los dos Gobiernos el 16 de agosto de 1927, para la audiencia, examen y decisión de reclamaciones por pérdida o daños acaecidos antes del 8 de septiembre de 1923, se prorrogue, y por la presente nuevamente se prorroga, durante un plazo que no exceda de dos años, contados desde el 30 de agosto de 1929, día en que, según las disposiciones de dicho Artículo I de la convención concluída entre los dos Gobiernos el 16 de agosto de 1927, terminarían las funciones de tal Comisión, por lo que toca a esas reclamaciones; y que durante el término de esta prórroga, la Comisión continuará obligada a oír, examinar y decidir cualesquiera reclamaciones por pérdida o daños acaecidos entre el 8 de septiembre de 1923 y el 30 de agosto de 1927, inclusive, siempre que hayan sido presentadas a la Comisión en fecha no posterior al 30 de agosto de 1927.

Se conviene, además, en que nada de lo contenido en este Artículo altera

or extend the time originally fixed in the said convention of September 8, 1923, for the presentation of claims to the Commission, or confer upon the Commission any jurisdiction over any claim for loss or damage accruing subsequent to August 30, 1927.

o prorroga en modo alguno, el plazo fijado originariamente en dicha Convención del 8 de septiembre de 1923 para la presentación de reclamaciones a la Comisión, ni confiere a ésta jurisdicción alguna sobre reclamaciones por pérdida o daños ocurridos con posterioridad al 30 de agosto de 1927.

Article II

The Present Convention shall be ratified and the ratifications shall be exchanged in the City of Mexico as soon as possible.

In witness whereof the above mentioned Plenipotentiaries have signed the same and affixed their respective seals.

Done in duplicate in the City of Mexico in the English and Spanish languages, this second day of September in the year one thousand nine hundred and twenty nine.

Artículo II

Esta Convención se ratificará en cuanto sea posible, canjeándose las ratificaciones en la ciudad de México.

En testimonio de lo cual, los supradichos Plenipotenciarios la han firmado, fijando en ella sus sellos respectivos.

Hecha por duplicado, en inglés y en castellano, en la ciudad de México el día dos de septiembre del año de mil novecientos veintinueve.

HERSCHEL V. JOHNSON   [SEAL]

G. ESTRADA   [SEAL]

D. SUPPLEMENTARY CONVENTION OF JUNE 18, 1932 [1]

WHEREAS a convention was signed on September 8, 1923, between the United States of America and the United Mexican States for the settlement and amicable adjustment of certain claims therein defined; and

WHEREAS under Article VI of said Convention the Commission constituted pursuant thereto was required to hear, examine and decide

CONSIDERANDO que el 8 de septiembre de 1923 se firmó una Convención entre los Estados Unidos de América y los Estados Unidos Mexicanos, para el arreglo y ajuste amistoso de ciertas reclamaciones que en ella se definen; y

CONSIDERANDO que según el Artículo VI de dicha Convención, la Comisión que según aquélla se constituyó, está obligada a oír, examinar

[1] Text from U. S. Treaty Series No. 883.

within three years from the date of its first meeting all the claims filed with it, except as provided in Article VII; and

WHEREAS by a convention concluded between the two Governments on August 16, 1927, the time for hearing, examining and deciding the said claims was extended for a period of two years; and

WHEREAS by a convention concluded between the two Governments on September 2, 1929, the time for hearing, examining and deciding the said claims was extended for a further period of two years; and

WHEREAS it has been found that the said Commission could not hear, examine, and decide such claims within the limit thus fixed;

The President of the United States of America and the President of the United Mexican States are desirous that the time thus fixed for the duration of the said Commission should be further extended, and to this end have named as their respective plenipotentiaries, that is to say:

The President of the United States of America, J. Reuben Clark, Jr., Ambassador Extraordinary and Plenipotentiary of the United States of America to Mexico; and

The President of the United Mexican States, Manuel C. Téllez, Secretary of State for Foreign Affairs;

Who, after having communicated to each other their respective full powers found in good and due form, have agreed upon the following articles:

y decidir dentro de los tres años después de la fecha de su primera junta, todas las reclamaciones presentadas ante ella, excepto lo que previene el Artículo VII; y

CONSIDERANDO que el día 16 de agosto de 1927 se concluyó una Convención entre ambos Gobiernos extendiendo por un período de dos años el plazo para oír, examinar y decidir dichas reclamaciones; y

CONSIDERANDO que por la Convención firmada entre los dos Gobiernos el 2 de septiembre de 1929 el plazo para oir, examinar y decidir dichas reclamaciones fue prorrogado por un período adicional de dos años; y

CONSIDERANDO que dicha Comisión no pudo oír, examinar y decidir tales reclamaciones dentro del plazo convenido;

El Presidente de los Estados Unidos de América y el Presidente de los Estados Unidos Mexicanos, deseando que se prorrogue nuevamente el plazo así fijado para la duración de dicha Comisión, han nombrado para ese objeto como sus Plenipotenciarios respectivos:

El Presidente de los Estados Unidos de América, al Señor J. Reuben Clark, Jr., Embajador Extraordinario y Plenipotenciario de los Estados Unidos de América en México; y

El Presidente de los Estados Unidos Mexicanos, al Señor Manuel C. Téllez, Secretario de Relaciones Exteriores;

Quienes, después de haberse comunicado sus Plenos Poderes respectivos, hallándolos en buena y debida forma, han convenido en los siguientes artículos:

Article I

The High Contracting Parties agree that the term assigned by Article VI of the Convention of September 8, 1923, as extended by Article I of the Convention concluded between the two Governments on September 2, 1929, for the hearing, examination, and decision of claims for loss or damage accruing prior to August 30, 1927, and filed with the Commission prior to said date, shall be, and the same is hereby extended from August 30, 1931, the date on which, pursuant to the provisions of the said Article I of the Convention of 1929, the functions of the said Commission terminated in respect to such claims, for a further period which shall expire in two full years from the date of the exchange of ratifications of this Convention.

It is agreed that nothing contained in this Article shall in any wise alter or extend the time originally fixed in the said Convention of September 8, 1923, for the presentation of claims to the Commission, or confer upon the Commission any jurisdiction over any claim for loss or damage accruing subsequent to August 30, 1927.

Article II

The present Convention shall be ratified and the ratifications shall be exchanged at Washington as soon as possible.

In witness whereof the above-mentioned Plenipotentiaries have signed

Artículo I

Las Altas Partes Contratantes convienen en que el plazo designado por el Artículo VI de la Convención del 8 de septiembre de 1923, según quedó extendido por el Artículo I de la Convención concluída entre los dos Gobiernos el 2 de septiembre de 1929 para la audiencia, examen y decisión de reclamaciones por pérdida o daños acaecidos antes del 30 de agosto de 1927 y presentadas a la Comisión antes de dicha fecha, se prorrogue, y por la presente nuevamente se prorroga, del 30 de agosto de 1931, día en que, según las disposiciones de dicho Artículo I de la Convención de 1929 antes mencionada, terminarían las funciones de tal Comisión por lo que toca a esas reclamaciones, por un período adicional que terminará en dos años contados desde la fecha del canje de ratificaciones de la presente Convención.

Se conviene, además, en que nada de lo contenido en este Artículo altera o prorroga, en modo alguno, el plazo fijado originariamente en dicha Convención del 8 de septiembre de 1923, para la presentación de reclamaciones a la Comisión, ni confiere a ésta jurisdicción alguna sobre reclamaciones por pérdida o daños ocurridos con posterioridad al 30 de agosto de 1927.

Artículo II

Esta Convención se ratificará en cuanto sea posible, canjeándose las ratificaciones en la ciudad de Wáshington.

En testimonio de lo cual, los supradichos Plenipotenciarios la han

the same and affixed their respective seals.

Done in duplicate at the City of Mexico, in the English and Spanish languages, this eighteenth day of June in the year one thousand nine hundred and thirty-two.

firmado, fijando en ella sus sellos respectivos.

Hecha por duplicado, en inglés y en español, en la ciudad de México, el día diez y ocho de junio del año de mil novecientos treinta y dos.

J. REUBEN CLARK JR.

[SEAL]

MANUEL C. TÉLLEZ

[SEAL]

E. PROTOCOL OF JUNE 18, 1932 [1]

J. Reuben Clark, Jr., Ambassador Extraordinary and Plenipotentiary of the United States of America to Mexico and Manuel C. Téllez, Secretary of State for Foreign Affairs, duly authorized, have agreed to sign the following Protocol:

In proceeding to the signature of the Convention providing for a further extension of the General Claims Convention (signed September 8, 1923) for a period which shall expire two years from the date of the exchange of ratifications of the Convention signed this date, it is expressly agreed between the two Governments as follows:

1. The two Governments will proceed to an informal discussion of the agrarian claims now pending before the General Claims Commission, with a view to making an adjustment thereof that shall be consistent with the rights and equities of the claimants and the rights and obligations of the Mexican Government. Pending such discussion no agrarian claims will be presented to the Commission for decision, but memorials of cases not yet memorialized may be filed in order to regularize the awards of the Commission made upon the agreed adjustments.

2. The meetings of the General Claims Commission shall be held partly in the City of Mexico, and partly in the City of Washington. The Commission shall, in fixing the place of future meetings pursuant to the terms of Article II of the General Claims Convention, have in mind the convenience, for the Mexican Government, of hearing in Mexico City the claims against Mexico, and the convenience, for the Government of the United States, of hearing in Washington the claims against the United States.

3. The Presiding Commissioner shall be requested to have the Commission sit continuously, with only short and occasional vacations.

[1] Text furnished by Department of State.

4. The Agents of the respective Governments shall be instructed to amend, with the approval of the Commission, the rules of procedure to the following effect:

A. As to the memorializing of claims:

(*a*) Within one year from the date on which the joint secretariat begins its work, under the renewed Convention, memorials shall be filed on all claims to be memorialized, provided the joint secretariat shall remain open for the filing of memorials for a continuous year from the date on which it opens for work.

(*b*) At the expiration of said year, claims that have not been memorialized shall be adjudicated by decisions based only on the memoranda filed, and on no other document, it being understood that in each of said cases the defendant Government denies all responsibility upon the facts alleged or arguments made in the various memoranda.

B. At the expiration of the year provided for the memorialization of cases, either Agent may ask the Commission to dispose of any case on which a memorial has not been filed.

C. With a view to curtailing oral arguments as much as may be possible, having in mind an adequate presentation of the facts and of the principles of law involved in the cases, so as to expedite the work of the Commission, a plan shall be elaborated by which:

(*a*) General oral arguments shall be curtailed as much as possible, consistent with the due and adequate presentation of the cases:

(*b*) Oral arguments in cases involving points of law already determined by the Commission, shall be omitted and the case be decided upon the written record, except in those cases in which either Government, through its Agent or otherwise, shall request permission for the making of a further oral argument, and in such an instance the request shall specify the particular points on which oral argument is desired.

D. Where there are a group of claims which, as to their facts and as to the points of law involved, are the same, and where one of such cases has been dismissed by the Commission, the two Agents will consult together with a view to having the other claims of the group determined by the Commission, without argument. When the Agents are unable to agree on any given case, either Government may, if it wishes, bring that case directly to the attention of the other Government with a view to reaching an agreement as to its disposition. If an agreement as to the dismissal of any claim be reached, either by the Agents or by the two Governments, such agreement shall be reported to the Commission with a request that the case be dismissed by the Commission in accordance with the terms of the agreement. The two Governments will request their respective Commissioners to give effect to such agreements by making awards in accordance with the terms of such agreements. If the two Agents are unable to agree, and neither of the two Governments intervenes, or

if either or both of the two Governments intervene and are unable to agree, the case shall go before the Commission for decision.

E. Where one of a group of claims, that as to their facts and as to the points of law involved are the same, has been decided affirmatively by the Commission, the two Agents will consult together regarding all the other claims of the group, with a view to reaching an agreement as to the amount of the award which should be made in each of such cases. If the Agents are unable, as to any such case, to agree upon an award, either Government may, if it desires, bring such case to the attention of the other Government with a view to reaching an agreement on an award thereon. If an agreement as to an award be reached either by the Agents or by the Governments, such an agreement shall be reported to the Commission with a request that an award be made in such case in consonance with the agreement. The two Governments will request their respective Commissioners to give effect to such agreements by making awards in accordance with the terms of such agreements. If no agreement is reached regarding any case, the case shall then go before the Commission in due course.

Done in duplicate in the City of Mexico in the English and Spanish languages this eighteenth day of June one thousand nine hundred and thirty-two.

[SEAL]　　　　　　　　　　J. REUBEN CLARK, JR.

[SEAL]　　　　　　　　　　MANUEL C. TÉLLEZ

F. PROTOCOL OF APRIL 24, 1934 [1]

Josephus Daniels, Ambassador Extraordinary and Plenipotentiary of the United States of America to the Government of Mexico, and José Manuel Puig Casauranc, Secretary for Foreign Affairs of the United Mexican States, duly authorized, have agreed on behalf of their two Governments to conclude the following Protocol:

Whereas, It is the desire of the two Governments to settle and liquidate as promptly as possible those claims of each Government against the other which are comprehended by, and which have been filed in pursuance of,

Josephus Daniels, Embajador Extraordinario y Plenipotenciario de los Estados Unidos de América ante el Gobierno de México, y José Manuel Puig Casauranc, Secretario de Relaciones Exteriores de los Estados Unidos Mexicanos, debidamente autorizados, convienen en firmar, en nombre de sus respectivos Gobiernos, el siguiente Protocolo:

Considerando que es el deseo de ambos Gobiernos arreglar y liquidar, tan pronto como sea posible, las reclamaciones de cada uno de los dos Gobiernos en contra del otro, comprendidas en la Convención General

[1] Text from U. S. Executive Agreement Series No. 57.

the General Claims Convention between the two Governments, concluded on September 8, 1923;

Whereas, It is not considered expedient to proceed, at the present time, to the formal arbitration of the said claims in the manner provided in that Convention;

Whereas, It is considered to be conducive to the best interests of the two Governments, to preserve the *status quo* of the General Claims Convention above mentioned and the Convention extending the duration thereof, which latter was concluded on June 18, 1932, as well as the agreement relating to agrarian claims under Article I of the additional Protocol of June 18, 1932;

Whereas, It is advisable to endeavor to effect a more expeditious and more economical disposition of the claims, either by means of an *en bloc* settlement or a more simplified method of adjudication, and

Whereas, In the present state of development of the numerous claims the available information is not such as to permit the two Governments to appraise their true value with sufficient accuracy to permit of the successful negotiation of an *en bloc* settlement thereof at the present time;

Therefore, It is agreed that:
First. — The two Governments will proceed to an informal discussion of the agrarian claims now pending before the General Claims Commis-

de Reclamaciones celebrada el 8 de septiembre de 1923 entre los dos Gobiernos y registradas de acuerdo con la misma;

Considerando que no se juzga viable, en los momentos actuales, proceder al arbitraje formal de dichas reclamaciones mediante el procedimiento que establece la Convención mencionada;

Considerando que se juzga conducente para los mejores intereses de ambos Gobiernos conservar el *"statu quo"* de la Convención General de Reclamaciones arriba mencionada y de la Convención de Prórroga celebrada el 18 de junio de 1932, así como de lo convenido para las reclamaciones agrarias en el Artículo I del Protocolo adicional de 18 de junio de 1932;

Considerando que conviene intentar la resolución más rápida y más económica de las reclamaciones, ya sea por medio de un arreglo global o de un método más simplificado para fallarlas, y

Considerando que en el presente estado de tramitación de las numerosas reclamaciones, los datos de que se dispone son de tal naturaleza que no permiten a los dos Gobiernos estimar el verdadero valor de ellas con exactitud suficiente para permitir la negociación con éxito de un arreglo global de las mismas en los momentos actuales;

Por tanto, queda convenido que:
Primero. — Los dos Gobiernos procederán a discutir, de manera informal, las reclamaciones agrarias pendientes en la actualidad ante la

sion, with a view to making an adjustment thereof that shall be consistent with the rights and equities of the claimants and the rights and obligations of the Mexican Government, as provided by the General Claims Protocol of June 18, 1932. Pending such discussion no agrarian claims will be presented to the Commissioners referred to in Clause Third nor, in turn, to the Umpire referred to in Clause Fifth of this Protocol; but memorials of cases not yet memorialized may be filed in order to regularize the awards made upon the agreed adjustments.

Consequently, the subsequent provisions of this Protocol shall apply to agrarian claims only insofar as they do not conflict with the status thereof, as exclusively fixed by the terms of the agreed Article I of the additional protocol to the extension of the General Claims Convention, signed June 18, 1932.

Second. — The two Governments shall proceed, in accordance with the provisions of Clause Sixth below, promptly to complete the written pleadings and briefs in the remaining unpleaded and incompletely pleaded cases.

Third. — Each Government shall promptly designate, from among its own nationals, a Commissioner, who shall be an outstanding jurist and

Comisión General de Reclamaciones, con el propósito de llegar a un arreglo con respecto a ellas, en consonannancia con la equidad y con los derechos de los reclamantes y con los derechos y obligaciones del Gobierno Mexicano, según lo establecido por el Protocolo de la Comisión General de 18 de junio de 1932. Mientras esté pendiente esta discusión, no se presentarán reclamaciones agrarias a los Comisionados a que se refiere la Cláusula Tercera, ni, en su caso, al Arbitro a que alude la Cláusula Quinta de este Protocolo; pero podrán presentarse Memoriales de los casos en que aun no se hayan presentado, con objeto de formalizar los fallos que se dicten sobre los arreglos propalados.

Por consiguiente, las disposiciones subsecuentes de este Protocolo serán aplicables a las reclamaciones agrarias únicamente en lo que no se opongan a la situación de dichas reclamaciones, como está fijada exclusivamente por los términos del Artículo I pactado en el Protocolo adicional a la Convención de Prórroga de la Convención General de Reclamaciones, firmada en 18 de junio de 1932.

Segundo. — Los dos Gobiernos de acuerdo con las disposiciones de la Cláusula Sexta de este Protocolo, procederán desde luego a completar los escritos y alegatos en los casos en que éstos no se hayan presentado o estén incompletos.

Tercero. — Cada uno de los dos Gobiernos designará en breve plazo a un Comisionado de su propia nacionalidad, quien deberá ser un

whose function it shall be to appraise, on their merits, as rapidly as possible, the claims of both Governments which have already been fully pleaded and briefed and those in which the pleadings and briefs shall be completed in accordance herewith.

Fourth. — Six months before the termination of the period herein agreed upon for the completion of the pleadings and briefs referred to in Clause Sixth or at an earlier time should they so agree, the said Commissioners shall meet, at a place to be agreed upon by them, for the purpose of reconciling their appraisals. They shall, as soon as possible, and not later than six months from the date of the completion of the pleadings and briefs, submit to the two Governments a joint report of the results of their conferences, indicating those cases in which agreement has been reached by them with respect to the merits and the amount of liability, if any, in the individual cases and also those cases in which they shall have been unable to agree with respect to the merits or the amount of liability, or both.

Fifth. — The two Governments shall, upon the basis of such joint report, and with the least possible delay, conclude a convention for the final disposition of the claims, which convention shall take one or the other of the two following forms, namely, first, an agreement for an *en bloc* settle-

destacado jurisconsulto y cuyas funciones serán las de estimar en cuanto a sus fundamentos y tan rápidamente como sea posible, las reclamaciones de ambos Gobiernos, en las cuales hayan sido completados todos los escritos y alegatos, así como aquellas en que hayan de completarse tales escritos y alegatos según lo dispuesto por este Protocolo.

Cuarto. — Seis meses antes de vencer el plazo para completar los escritos y alegatos a que se refiere la Cláusula Sexta, o en alguna fecha anterior, en caso de que así lo convengan, los referidos Comisionados se reunirán en el lugar que designen de común acuerdo con el objeto de armonizar sus estimaciones. Tan pronto como sea posible y dentro de los seis meses contados desde la fecha en que se completen los escritos y alegatos, presentarán a los dos Gobiernos un dictamen conjunto sobre el resultado de sus conferencias, en el que indicarán los casos en que hayan llegado a un acuerdo en cuanto a los fundamentos y al monto de la responsabilidad, si alguna resultare, en cada caso, indicando asímismo los casos en que no hayan podido ponerse de acuerdo, ya sea respecto a los fundamentos o al monto de la responsabilidad, o a ambas cosas.

Quinto. — Los dos Gobiernos, sobre la base del referido dictamen conjunto, y con el menor retardo posible, celebrarán una Convención para la resolución definitiva de las reclamaciones, debiendo en dicha Convención adoptarse una u otra de las dos formas siguientes, a saber : primero, la de un

ment of the claims wherein there shall be stipulated the net amount to be paid by either Government and the terms upon which payment shall be made; or, second, an agreement for the disposition of the claims upon their individual merits. In this latter event, the two above-mentioned Commissioners shall be required to record their agreements with respect to individual claims and the bases upon which their conclusions shall have been reached, in the respective cases.

The report shall be accepted, by the convention to be concluded by the two Governments, as final and conclusive dispositions of those cases. With respect to those cases in which the Commissioners shall not have been able to reach agreements, the two Governments shall, by the said convention, agree that the pleadings and briefs in such cases, together with the written views of the two Commissioners concerning the merits of the respective claims, be referred to an Umpire, whose written decisions shall also be accepted by both Governments as final and binding. All matters relating to the designation of an Umpire, time within which his decisions should be rendered and general provisions relating to his work shall be fixed in a Convention to be negotiated under provisions of this Clause.

Sixth. — The procedure to be followed in the development of the pleadings and briefs, which procedure shall be scrupulously observed by the

convenio para un arreglo global de las reclamaciones, en el que se estipulará la cantidad líquida que habrá de pagar alguno de los dos Gobiernos y las condiciones en que se habrá de efectuar tal pago; o, segundo, la de un convenio para la resolución de las reclamaciones sobre los fundamentos de cada una. En este último caso, se exigirá a los dos Comisionados arriba mencionados, que hagan constar los acuerdos celebrados por ellos con respecto a cada una de las reclamaciones y los fundamentos en que se basen sus conclusiones, en el caso respectivo.

El dictamen que rindan será aceptado, por medio de la Convención que celebren los dos Gobiernos, como la resolución definitiva y final de dichos casos. Con respecto a los casos en que los Comisionados no hayan podido ponerse de acuerdo, los dos Gobiernos, en esa misma Convención, estipularán que los escritos y alegatos presentados en ellos, juntamente con las opiniones escritas de los dos Comisionados sobre los fundamentos de las reclamaciones respectivas, se someterán a un Arbitro cuyos fallos escritos serán aceptados también por ambos Gobiernos como definitivos y obligatorios. Todo lo que se refiere a designación de Arbitro, período de tiempo de que dispondrá para fallar y modalidades de su trabajo, serán fijados en la Convención de que habla esta Cláusula.

Sexto. — El procedimiento que se seguirá en el desarrollo de los escritos y alegatos, procedimiento que observarán escrupulosamente los Agen-

Agents of the two Governments, shall be the following :

(*a*) The time allowed for the completion of the pleadings and briefs shall be two years counting from a date hereafter to be agreed upon by the two Governments by an exchange of notes, which shall not be later than November 1, 1934.

(*b*) The pleadings and briefs of each Government shall be filed at the Embassy of the other Government.

(*c*) The pleadings and briefs to be filed shall be limited in number to four, namely, Memorial, Answer, Brief and Reply Brief. Only three copies of each need be presented to the other Agent, but four additional copies shall be retained by the filing Agency for possible use in future adjudication. Each copy of Memorial, Answer and Brief shall be accompanied by a copy of all evidence filed with the original thereof. The pleadings and briefs, which may be in either English or Spanish at the option of the filing Government, shall be signed by the respective Agents or properly designated substitutes.

(*d*) With the Memorial the claimant Government shall file all the evidence on which it intends to rely. With the Answer the respondent Government shall file all the evidence upon which it intends to rely. No further evidence shall be filed by either side except such evidence, with the Brief, as rebuts evidence filed with

tes de los dos Gobiernos, será el siguiente :

(*a*) El plazo concedido para completar los escritos y alegatos será de dos años contados desde la fecha en que posteriormente convengan los dos Gobiernos por medio de un cambio de notas, que no se efectuará más tarde del 1° de noviembre de 1934.

(*b*) Los escritos y alegatos de cada uno de los dos Gobiernos serán presentados en la Embajada del otro Gobierno.

(*c*) Los escritos y alegatos que se presenten quedan limitados a cuatro, a saber : el Memorial, la Contestación, el Alegato y el Alegato de Réplica. Sólo será necesario presentar tres copias de cada uno al otro Agente, pero la Agencia que los presente conservará cuatro ejemplares adicionales para que se puedan usar al resolverse los casos en el futuro. Cada una de las copias de tales Memoriales, Contestaciones y Alegatos irá acompañada de una copia de todas las pruebas presentadas con el escrito original. Los escritos y alegatos, que podrán presentarse en inglés o en español, a voluntad del Gobierno que los presente, estarán firmados por los Agentes respectivos o por substitutos de éstos designados en debida forma.

(*d*) Con el Memorial, el Gobierno demandante presentará todas las pruebas en que se funde. Con su Contestación, el Gobierno demandado presentará todas las pruebas en que piense apoyarse. No se presentará prueba adicional alguna por ninguna de las dos partes exceptuando las pruebas que se presenten con el

the Answer. Such evidence shall be strictly limited to evidence in rebuttal and there shall be explained at the beginning of the Brief the alleged justification for the filing thereof. If the other side desires to object to such filing, its views may be set forth in the beginning of the Reply Brief, and the Commissioners, or the Umpire, as the case may require, shall decide the point, and if it is decided that the evidence is not in rebuttal to evidence filed with the Answer, the additional evidence shall be entirely disregarded in considering the merits of the claim.

The Commissioners may at any time order the production of further evidence.

(e) In view of the desire to reduce the number of pleadings and briefs to a minimum in the interest of economy of time and expense, it shall be the obligation of both Agents fully and clearly to state in their Memorials the contention of the claimant Government with respect to both the factual bases of the claims in question and the legal principles upon which the claims are predicated and, in the Answer, the contentions of the respondent Government with regard to the facts and legal principles upon which the defense of the case rests. In cases in which Answers already filed do not sufficiently meet this provision so as to afford the claimant Government an adequate basis for preparing its legal Brief with full general knowledge of the factual and legal defenses of the respondent Gov-

Alegato para refutar las pruebas presentadas con la Contestación. Tales constancias se limitarán a pruebas de refutación y se expresará al principio del Alegato las justificaciones que se tengan para presentar dichas pruebas. Si la otra parte deseare objetar su presentación, sus objeciones pueden manifestarse al principio del Alegato de Réplica, y los Comisionados o el Arbitro, según sea el caso, decidirán el punto. Si se resolviera que las pruebas no refutan las presentadas con la Contestación, las adicionales no se tomarán en cuenta al considerarse los fundamentos de la reclamación.

Los Comisionados podrán en cualquier tiempo pedir que se presenten pruebas adicionales.

(e) En vista del deseo que hay de reducir el número de los escritos y alegatos al mínimo, en provecho de la economía de tiempo y gastos, será obligación de ambos Agentes exponer amplia y claramente en sus Memoriales los argumentos nel Gobierno demandante con respecto tanto a los hechos en que se base alguna reclamación como a los principios jurídicos en que se funde, y, en la Contestación, los argumentos del Gobierno demandado relativos a los hechos y principios jurídicos en que se apoye la defensa del caso. En los casos en que las Contestaciones ya presentadas no se ajusten exactamente a esta disposición para dar al Gobierno reclamante una base adecuada para la preparación de su Alegato con perfecto conocimiento de los hechos y excepciones legales del Gobierno

ernment, it shall have the right to file a Counter Brief within thirty days following the date of filing the Reply Brief.

(*f*) For the purposes of the above pleadings and briefs, as well as the appraisals and decisions of the two Commissioners and the decisions of the Umpire, above mentioned, the provisions of the General Claims Convention of September 8, 1923, shall be considered as fully effective and binding upon the two Governments, except insofar as concerns the matter of procedure, which shall be that provided for herein.

(*g*) Whenever practicable, cases of a particular class shall be grouped for memorializing and/or for briefing.

(*h*) In order that the two Agents may organize their work in the most advantageous manner possible and in order that the two-year period allowed for pleadings and briefs may be utilized in a manner which shall be most equitable to both sides, each Agent shall, within thirty days from the beginning of the two-year pleading period, submit to the other Agent a tentative statement showing the total number of Memorials and Briefs such Agent intends to file. Six months after the beginning of the two-year pleading period, the two Agents shall respectively submit in the same manner statements setting out definitely by name and docket number the claims in which it is proposed to complete the pleadings and briefs,

demandado, tendrá el derecho de presentar un Contraalegato dentro de los trienta días siguientes a la fecha de la presentación del Alegato de Réplica.

(*f*) Por lo que respecta a los escritos y alegatos arriba mencionados, así como a las estimaciones y fallos de los dos Comisionados y los fallos del Arbitro, se considerarán como plenamente efectivas y obligatorias para ambos Gobiernos la disposiciones de la Convención General de Reclamaciones de 8 de septiembre de 1923, salvo en lo que respecta a la materia de procedimientos, la cual se regirá por el presente Protocolo.

(*g*) Siempre que sea factible, se agruparán los casos de una clase determinada, para la presentación de los Memoriales y de los Alegatos, o de cualquiera de los dos.

(*h*) Para que los dos Agentes puedan organizar sus trabajos en la forma más eficiente que sea posible, y para que el período de dos años concedido para la presentación de escritos y alegatos se pueda aprovechar del modo más equitativo para ambas partes, cada uno de los dos Agentes, dentro de los treinta días siguientes al comienzo de dicho período de dos años para la presentación de tales escritos, deberá presentar al otro Agente un estado previo que demuestre el número total de Memoriales y Alegatos que piense presentar. A los seis meses contados desde el comienzo del referido período de dos años para la presentación de escritos, los dos Agentes presentarán respectiva-

indicating those in which they intend to combine cases in the manner indicated in paragraph (g) above. The number of pleadings and briefs so indicated shall not, except by later agreement between the two Governments, be exceeded by more than ten per cent.

(i) In order to enable the Agencies to distribute their work equally over the two-year pleading period, each Agency shall be under the obligation to file its Memorials at approximately equal intervals during the first seventeen months of the two-year period, thus allowing the remaining seven months of the period for the completion of the pleadings and briefs in the last case memorialized. The same obligation shall attach with respect to the filing of the pleadings and briefs referred to in paragraph (k) below.

(j) The time to be allowed for filing Answers shall be seventy days from the date of filing Memorials. The time to be allowed for filing Briefs shall be seventy days from the date of filing the Answers. The time to be allowed for filing Reply Briefs shall be seventy days from the date of filing the Briefs.

(k) In those cases in which some

mente, en la misma forma, estados que expongan definitivamente, especificando los nombres y números de registro, las reclamaciones en las que se propongan completar los escritos y alegatos con la indicación de los casos en que piensen agruparlos del modo indicado en el inciso (g) anterior. El número de escritos y alegatos mencionados no deberá, salvo acuerdo posterior entre los dos Gobiernos, excederse en más de un diez por ciento.

(i) Para que las Agencias puedan distribuir sus trabajos uniformemente en todo el período de dos años para presentación de escritos, cada una de ellas estará obligada a presentar sus Memoriales a intervalos más o menos iguales durante los primeros diecisiete meses del referido período, a efecto de que durante los siete meses restantes se completen los escritos y alegatos en el último caso en que se hubiere presentado Memorial. Esta misma obligación existirá con respecto a la presentación de los escritos y alegatos a que se refiere el inciso (k) más adelante.

(j) El plazo que se concede para la presentación de Contestaciones será de setenta días contados desde la fecha de la presentación de los Memoriales. El plazo para la presentación de Alegatos será de setenta días contados desde la fecha de la presentación de las Contestaciones. El plazo para la presentación de Alegato de Réplica será de setenta días, contados desde la fecha de la presentación de los Alegatos.

(k) En aquellos casos en que se

pleadings or briefs were filed with the General Claims Commission before the date of signature hereof, the Agency which has the right to file the next pleading or brief shall be allowed to determine when that document shall be filed, taking into consideration the necessity of complying with the provisions of paragraph (*i*) above.

(*l*) In counting the seventy-day periods mentioned in paragraph (*j*) above, no deductions shall be made for either Sundays or holidays. The date of filing the above described pleadings and briefs shall be considered to be the date upon which they shall be delivered at the Embassy of the other Government. If the due date shall fall on Sunday or a legal holiday, the pleading or brief shall be filed upon the next succeeding business day. The two Governments shall, for this purpose, instruct their respective Embassies to receive and give receipts for such pleadings and briefs any weekday between the hours of 10 and 16 (4 P.M.) except on the following legal holiday of both countries:

hayan presentado algunos escritos o alegatos ante la Comisión General de Reclamaciones con anterioridad a la fecha de la firma del presente Protocolo, la Agencia que tenga derecho a presentar el escrito a alegato siguiente estará autorizada para determinar la fecha en que se haya de presentar tal documento, tomando en consideración la necesidad que hay de cumplir las disposiciones del inciso (*i*) anterior.

(*l*) Al contar los períodos de setenta días de que habla el inciso (*j*) anterior, no se harán deducciones por concepto de domingos ni días de fiesta. La fecha de la presentación de los escritos y alegatos antes mencionados se considerará que es la fecha en que sean entregados en la Embajada del otro Gobierno. Si la fecha de vencimiento cayere en algún domingo o día de fiesta oficial, el escrito o alegato se presentará en el día hábil siguiente. Los dos Gobiernos, con este objeto, darán instrucciones a sus Embajadas respectivas de recibir y dar recibos por tales escritos y alegatos en todos los días hábiles, entre las 10 y las 16 horas, exceptuando los siguientes días de fiesta oficiales de ambos países:

Of the United States	Of Mexico	De los Estados Unidos	De Mexico
January 1	January 1	1° de enero	1° de enero
February 22	February 5	22 de febrero	5 de febrero
May 30	May 1	30 de mayo	1° de mayo
July 4	May 5	4 de julio	5 de mayo
First Monday in September	September 14	Primer lunes de septiembre	14 de septiembre
	September 15		15 de septiembre
Last Thursday in November	September 16	Ultimo jueves de noviembre	16 de septiembre
	October 12		12 de octubre
December 25	November 20	25 de diciembre	20 de noviembre
	December 25		25 de diciembre
	December 31.		31 de diciembre.

(*m*) In view of the herein prescribed limitations upon the time allowed for the completion of the work of the Agencies and the Commissioners, it is recognized that the success of this simplified plan of procedure depends fundamentally upon the prompt and regular filing of the pleadings and briefs in accordance with the provisions of this Protocol. It is agreed, therefore, that any pleading or brief which shall be filed more than thirty days after the due date for the filing thereof, shall be disregarded by the Commissioners and the Umpire, and that the respective case shall be considered by them upon the pleadings and briefs preceding the tardy pleadings and briefs, unless, by agreement of the two Governments, the continued pleading of the respective case shall be resumed.

(*n*) It shall not be necessary to present original evidence but all documents hereafter submitted as evidence shall be certified as true and complete copies of the original if they be such. In the event that any particular document filed is not a true and complete copy of the original, that fact shall be so stated in the certificate.

(*o*) The complete original of any document filed, either in whole or in part, shall be retained in the Agency filing the document and shall be made available for inspection by

(*m*) En vista de las limitaciones prescritas en este protocolo respecto al período de tiempo fijado para la terminación de las labores de las Agencias y de los Comisionados, se reconoce que el éxito de este plan simplificado de procedimiento depende, fundamentalmente, de la presentación puntual y regular de los escritos y alegatos en los términos establecidos por las disposiciones de este Protocolo. Se conviene, por consiguiente, que cualquier escrito o alegato que se entregue más de treinta días después de la fecha fijada para su presentación, no será tomado en cuenta por los Comisionados y el Árbitro, y que el caso de que se trate será considerado por ellos únicamente sobre la base de los escritos y alegatos que precedan al que se hubiere presentado extemporáneamente, a menos de que, por acuerdo entre ambos Gobiernos, se autorice la continuación de las alegaciones en el caso respectivo.

(*n*) No será necesario presentar las pruebas originales, pero todos los documentos que de hoy en adelante se presenten en calidad de pruebas, serán certificados como copias fieles y completas de sus originales si así lo fueren. En el caso de que algún documento determinado que se presente no sea copia fiel y completa del original, ese hecho se hará constar en la certificación.

(*o*) El original completo de cualquier documento presentado, ya sea total o parcialmente, será conservado en la Agencia que lo presente y estará disponible para su inspección por

any authorized representative of the Agent of the other side.

(*p*) Where the original of any document or other proof is filed at any Government office on either side, and cannot be conveniently withdrawn, and no copy of such document is in the possession of the Agent of the Government desiring to present the same to the Commissioners in support of the allegations set out in his pleadings or briefs, he shall notify the Agent of the other Government in writing of his desire to inspect such document. Should such inspection be refused, then the action taken in response to the request to inspect, together with such reasons as may be assigned for the action taken, shall be reported to the Commissioners and, in turn, to the Umpire mentioned in Clause Fifth of this Protocol, so that due notice thereof may be taken.

Done in duplicate in Mexico, D.F., in the English and Spanish languages this twenty-fourth day of the month of April one thousand nine hundred and thirty-four.

cualquier representante autorizado del Agente de la otra parte.

(*p*) Cuando el original u otra prueba esté archivado en las oficinas de cualquiera de los dos Gobiernos, y no pueda ser retirado facilmente, ni exista copia de tal documento en poder del Agente del Gobierno que desee presentarlo a los Comisionados, en apoyo de los punto contenidos en sus escritos o alegatos, entonces notificará por escrito al Agente de la parte contraria acerca de su deseo de examinar el referido documento. Si a una solicitud de examen se rehusa la exhibición del documento de que se trata, tal actitud, junto con las razones que se dieren para excusarla, serán puestas en conocimiento de los Comisionados y, en su caso, del Arbitro a que se refiere la Cláusula Quinta de este Protocolo, y ésto será tomado en cuenta por ellos.

Hecho por duplicado, en inglés y en español, en la Ciudad de México, el día veinticuatro del mes de abril del año de mil novecientos treinta y cuatro.

JOSEPHUS DANIELS   [SEAL]

PUIG   [SEAL]

G. RULES OF PROCEDURE, AS ADOPTED SEPTEMBER 4, 1924[1]

I

PLACE AND TIME OF HEARINGS

1. The office of the Commission shall be maintained at the City of

I

FECHA Y LUGAR DE LAS AUDIENCIAS

1. La Oficina de la Comisión será establecida y mantenida en la ciudad

---

[1] Text from Rules and Regulations Approved and Established by the Commission by Order Entered September 4, 1924 (Washington, 1925).

Washington, where its records shall be kept.

2. The time and place of meetings shall be fixed by orders of the Commission.

II
DOCKETS AND RECORDS

1. A duplicate docket shall be provided, one to be kept by each of the two secretaries in his own language, in which shall be promptly entered the name of each claimant and the amount claimed when the claim is formally filed with the Commission, and in which shall be recorded all the proceedings had in relation thereto.

2. Each claim shall constitute a separate case before the Commission and be docketed as such. Claims shall be numbered consecutively, beginning with that first filed as Number 1.

3. A duplicate minute book shall be kept in like manner by the secretaries in which shall be entered a chronological record of all proceedings of the Commission. The minute book shall at each sitting of the Commission be signed by the Commissioners and countersigned by the secretaries.

4. Such additional records shall be kept by the secretaries as shall be required by these Rules or prescribed from time to time by the Commission.

III
FILING AND DOCKETING OF CLAIMS

1. All claims must be filed by the respective Governments through

de Wáshington a donde se guardarán sus archivos.

2. La fecha y lugar de las juntas se fijarán por acuerdo de la Comisión.

II
EXTRACTOS, REGISTROS Y ACTAS

1. Se llevarán dos libros iguales de registro, uno por cada Secretario en su idioma propio, y en ellos se asentará inmediatamente al presentarse formalmente la reclamación ante la Comisión, el nombre de cada reclamante y la cantidad reclamada; y, además, se registrarán en los mismos todos los trámites que se vayan dando.

2. Cada reclamación constituirá un caso separado ante la Comisión y se registrará como tal. Se enumerarán progresivamente todas las reclamaciones, empezando por la que se presente primero, que llevará el número uno.

3. Se llevarán de la misma manera, dos libros iguales de actas, uno por cada Secretario en su idioma propio, y en ellos se asentará una relación cronológica de todas las actuaciones de la Comisión. En cada sesión de la Comisión firmarán el libro de actas los Comisionados y lo refrendarán los Secretarios.

4. Los Secretarios llevarán los registros adicionales que ordena el presente Reglamento o que la Comisión disponga cuando lo estime conveniente.

III
PRESENTACION Y REGISTRO DE LAS RECLAMACIONES

1. Toda reclamación deberá ser presentada por los Gobiernos res-

or in the name of the agents thereof.

2. A claim shall be deemed to have been formally filed with the Commission —

(a) Upon there being presented to the secretaries a Memorandum or statement, in duplicate, one in English and one in Spanish, countersigned or signed by the agent of the United States or of Mexico, as the case may be, or in the name of such agent by an assistant agent or counsel duly qualified before this Commission, setting forth as to each claim contained in said Memorandum or statement the name of the claimant, a brief statement of the nature of the claim and the amount thereof: or

(b) Upon there being presented to the secretaries (without such preliminary Memorandum or statement) by the agent of the United States or of Mexico, as the case may be, or in the name of such agent by an assistant agent or counsel duly qualified before this Commission, a memorial in duplicate, one in English and the other in Spanish, conforming to these rules and executed and verified as hereinafter provided, accompanied by copies of all documents and other proofs in support of the claim then in possession of the agent of the Government filing the same. Documents and proofs may be filed in the language of the claimant, subject to the further orders of the Commission.

pectivos por conducto o a nombre de sus Agentes.

2. Cualquiera reclamación se considerará como formalmente presentada ante la Comisión:

(a) Al presentarse a los Secretarios un Memorándum o declaración en dos ejemplares, uno en inglés y el otro en español, firmados o refrendados por el Agente de los Estados Unidos, o por el de México, según sea el caso, o en nombre de esos Agentes, por los Sub-Agentes y Consejeros debidamente acreditados ante la Comisión, exponiendo con respecto a cada reclamación contenida en dicho Memorándum o declaración, el nombre del reclamante, una relación breve de lanatura leza de la reclamación, y el monto de la misma; o bien,

(b) Al presentarse a los Secretarios (sin Memorándum o declaración preliminar) por el Agente de los Estados Unidos o por el de México, según el caso, o en nombre de esos Agentes, por los Sub-Agentes y Consejeros debidamente acreditados ante la Comisión, un Memorial en dos ejemplares, uno en inglés y otro en español, conforme a este Reglamento, hecho y autenticado como se dispone más adelante, a los que se acompañarán todos los documentos y demás pruebas en que se funde la reclamación y que ya estén en poder del Agente del Gobierno que la presente. Los documentos y pruebas deben ser presentados en la lengua del reclamante, y quedarán sujetos a lo que sobre ellos disponga la Comisión.

3. Upon receipt of the Memorandum or statement mentioned in clause (a) of section 2 hereof, or of the memorial mentioned in clause (b), an endorsement of filing, with the date thereof, shall be made thereon and signed by the secretaries, and the claim shall be immediately docketed under the appropriate number.

4. At any time after August 30, 1925, on motion of the agent of either Government, the Commission, for good cause shown, will fix a time as short as may be reasonable for presenting memorials as to claims filed as provided in clause (a) of section 2 hereof then pending and as to which memorials have not theretofore been presented.

5. Any claim for loss or damage accruing prior to September 8, 1923, shall be filed with the Commission either in the manner mentioned in clause (a) or in clause (b) of section 2 hereof, before the 30th day of August, 1925, unless in any case reasons for the delay satisfactory to the majority of the Commissioners shall be established, and in such case the period for filing may be extended by the Commission to any date prior to March 1, 1926.

6. Any claim for loss or damage accruing on or after September 8, 1923, shall be filed in a similar manner before the 30th day of August, 1927.

3. Al recibirse el Memorándum o declaración a que se refiere la cláusula (a) del artículo 2 de esta regla o el Memorial a que se refiere la cláusula (b), se hará en él una anotación de su presentación, con la fecha de la misma, por los Secretarios y suscrita por los mismos e inmediatamente se registrará la reclamación con su número correspondiente.

4. En cualquier momento después del 30 de agosto de 1925, la Comisión fijará, a moción del Agente de cualesquier de los dos Gobiernos, si hay causa suficiente para ello, un plazo tan corto como sea prudente, para la presentación de Memoriales referentes a reclamaciones ya presentadas de acuerdo con la cláusula (a) del artículo 2 de esta regla, que se encuentren pendientes y de las que no se haya presentado aún el Memorial.

5. Todas las reclamaciones por pérdidas o daños acaecidos antes del 8 de septiembre de 1923, se presentarán a la Comisión, ya sea de la manera dispuesta en la cláusula (a), o en la cláusula (b) a que se refiere el artículo 2 de esta regla, antes del 30 de agosto de 1925, a no ser que en algún caso se pruebe que hubo causas que justifiquen la demora, a satisfacción de la mayoría de los Comisionados, y, en este caso, el período para su presentación podrá ser ampliado por la Comisión por un término no posterior al 1° de marzo de 1926.

6. Todas las reclamaciones por pérdidas o daños acaecidos en o después del 8 de septiembre de 1923, serán presentadas de un modo semejante antes del 30 de agosto de 1927.

IV

PLEADINGS

1. The written pleadings shall consist of the memorial, the answer, the reply if desired, amendments and motions, unless by agreement between the agents, confirmed by the Commission, or by order of the Commission other pleadings are allowed. Either party may have the right to plead to new matter.

2. *The Memorial.*

The memorial shall be signed and verified by the claimant, or, upon good cause shown, by his attorney in fact, which cause shall be averred by such attorney, and it shall be subscribed by solicitor or counsel, if any, of the claimant. Every memorial shall also be subscribed or countersigned by the agent of the Government filing the same.

The Memorial shall contain a clear and concise statement of the facts upon which the claim is based. It shall set forth the information enumerated below in such detail as may be practicable in each particular case, or explain the absence thereof:

(a) Facts showing that the losses or damages for which the claim is made resulted from some one or more of the causes specified in the General Claims Convention between the United States and Mexico dated September 8, 1923, which became effective by exchange of ratifications

IV

ESCRITOS FUNDAMENTALES

1. Los escritos fundamentales consistirán en el Memorial, la Contestación, la Réplica, si se deseare presentar, las reformas a estos escritos y las mociones, a no ser que por convenio entre los Agentes, confirmado por la Comisión, o por acuerdo de la Comisión, puedan presentarse otros escritos. Cualquiera de las partes podrá tener el derecho de contestar sobre materias nuevas.

2. *El Memorial.*

El Memorial deberá estar firmado y verificado por el reclamante, o por su apoderado, cuando para ello se demuestre causa justificada, lo que hará constar dicho apoderado; y, además, deberá firmarlo el abogado o patrono del reclamante, en caso de tenerlo. Todo Memorial deberá, además, estar firmado o refrendado por el Agente del Gobierno que lo presente.

El Memorial contendrá una relación clara y concisa de los hechos en que se funde la reclamación. Expondrá, con el mayor detalle cuanto fuere factible en cada caso, los informes que a continuación se requieren; y, a falta de alguno de ellos, explicará los motivos de la omisión;

(a) Los hechos que demuestren que la pérdida o daño por los cuales se hace la reclamación, resultaron de alguna o algunas de las causas especificadas en la Convención General de Reclamaciones entre México y los Estados Unidos, fechada el 8 de septiembre de 1923, que entró en

on March 1, 1924, and that the same occurred subsequent to July 4, 1868.

(b) The amount of the claim; the time when and place where it arose; the kind or kinds and amount and value of property lost or damaged itemized so far as practicable; personal injuries, if any, and losses or damages resulting therefrom; the facts and circumstances attending the loss or damage to person or property out of which the claim arises, and upon which the claimant intends to rely to establish his claim.

(c) For and on behalf of whom the claim is preferred, and if in a representative capacity, the authority of the person preferring the claim.

(d) The citizenship of the owner or owners of the claim from the time of its origin to the date of the filing thereof; whether such citizenship was derived from birth, naturalization, or other act, and all facts in relation thereto; and where in any case it shall appear that there has entered into the chain of title to the claim the rights or interests of any person or corporation of any country other than that of the claimant, then the facts in relation to such right or interest must be fully set forth.

(e) If the claimant sets out as a basis of his claim loss or damage

vigor por el canje de ratificaciones de marzo 1° de 1924; y que dicha pérdida o daño ocurrió después del 4 de julio de 1868.

(b) El monto de la reclamación; la fecha y lugar en donde se originó; la clase o clases y cantidad y valor de la propiedad perdida o dañada, en relación pormenorizada hasta donde sea factible; los daños sufridos en la persona si los hubiere habido, y las pérdidas o daños que resultaren de los mismos; los hechos y demás circunstancias concomitantes con la pérdida o daño a la persona o a la propiedad por los que se origina la reclamación y sobre los cuales el reclamante pretende fundarse para establecer su reclamación.

(c) Por quién y a nombre de quién se presenta la reclamación; y si la persona que la presenta lo hace con carácter de representante, la comprobación de su personalidad.

(d) La nacionalidad del dueño o dueños de la reclamación desde la fecha del origen de ésta hasta la fecha de la presentación de tal reclamación; si la nacionalidad proviene de nacimiento, de naturalización o de algún otro acto, y todos los hechos concernientes a este respecto; y, cuando en algún caso apareciese que se han introducido en la serie de títulos de derecho a la reclamación, derechos o intereses de alguna persona o compañía de nacionalidad distinta de la del reclamante, entonces se tendrán que exponer en su totalidad los hechos relacionados con ese derecho o interés.

(e) Si el reclamante expone, como la base de su reclamación, la pérdida

suffered by any corporation, company, association, or partnership in which the claimant or person on whose behalf the claim is made has or had a substantial and *bona fide* interest, then the memorial shall set forth the nature and extent of that interest and all facts or equitable considerations in connection with or in support of such claim. In event an allotment is claimed, there shall be presented to the Commission documentary evidence thereof executed by some person authorized to contract generally on behalf of such corporation, company, association, or partnership, or there shall be clearly stated reasons valid in law for failure to present the same. The Commission will, in any such exceptional case determine as to the validity of such reasons under the convention and deal with the case accordingly.

(*f*) Whether the entire amount of the claim does now, and did at the time when it had its origin, belong solely and absolutely to the claimant, and if any other person is or has been interested therein or in any part thereof, then who is such other person and what is or was the nature and extent of his interest; and how, when, and by what means and for what consideration the transfer of rights and interests, if any, took place between the parties.

(*g*) Whether the claimant, or any other who may at any time have been entitled to the amount claimed, or any part thereof, has ever received

o daño sufrido por alguna corporación, compañía, asociación o sociedad en la cual el reclamante o la persona a nombre de quien se hace la reclamación, tiene o tuvo un interés substancial y *bona fide*, entonces el Memorial expondrá la naturaleza y extensión de dicho interés, y todos los hechos o consideraciones equitativos relacionados con dicha reclamación o en apoyo de ella. En caso de que se alegue una asignación se presentará a la Comisión la prueba documental de tal acto, ejecutado por alguna persona con poder general para contratar en nombre de la corporación, compañía, asociación o sociedad de que se trata, o se expondrán claramente las causas legales que puedan fundar la ausencia de tal prueba. La Comisión podrá, en estos casos excepcionales, decidir sobre la validez de tales causas de acuerdo con la Convención y proceder en el caso de acuerdo con esa decisión.

(*f*) Si el monto total de la reclamación pertenece ahora, y perteneció en la fecha en que se originó, única y absolutamente al reclamante, y si alguna otra persona está o ha estado interesada en la misma o en parte alguna de ella. En este último caso quién es esa otra persona y cuál es o fué la naturaleza y la extensión de su interés; y cómo, cuándo, por qué medios y por qué compensación se hizo el traspaso de derechos o intereses entre las partes, si lo hubo.

(*g*) Si el reclamante, o cualquiera otra persona que en cualquier tiempo haya tenido derecho a la cantidad reclamada, o de alguna parte de ella,

any, and if any, what sum of money, or equivalent or indemnification in any form, for the whole or part of the loss or damage upon which the claim is founded; and if so, when and from whom the same was received.

(*h*) Whether the claim has ever been presented or complaint with respect to it been lodged with the Mexican Government, or any official or agency thereof, acting either *de jure* or *de facto*, or with the Government of the United States or any official or agency thereof, and, if so, the facts in relation thereto.

(*i*) Claims put forward on behalf of a claimant who is dead, either for injury to person or loss of or damage to property, shall be presented by the personal or legal representative of the estate of the deceased. The memorial shall set out with respect to both the claimant and such representative the facts which, under these Rules, would be required of the former were he alive and presenting his claim before the Commission; and the claim shall be accompanied by documentary evidence properly certified of the authority of such representative.

(*j*) Where more than one claim arises out of the same set of facts, all or any of such claims may be included in the same memorial.

ha recibido alguna suma de dinero; y, en caso afirmativo, qué suma, o qué equivalencia o indemnización en cualquiera forma que sea, ya por el monto total o por parte del importe de la pérdida o daño en que se funde la reclamación; y de ser así, cuándo y de quién se recibió.

(*h*) Si alguna vez se ha presentado la reclamación o si se ha depositado alguna queja respecto a la misma ante el Gobierno Mexicano, o bien ante cualquier funcionario o dependencia del mismo, ya sea que haya actuado *de jure* o *de facto* o bien ante el Gobierno de los Estados Unidos o ante cualquier funcionario o dependencia del mismo; y en caso de ser así, los hechos relativos a dicha presentación.

(*i*) Las reclamaciones que se presenten a nombre de un reclamante fallecido, ya sea por daños a la persona; o pérdida o daño a la propiedad, se presentarán por el representante personal o legal de la sucesión del finado; y el Memorial expondrá, con respecto, tanto al reclamante como a dicho representante, los hechos que, conforme a este Reglamento, se le exigirían al primero si estuviese vivo y presentase su reclamación ante la Comisión; y, además, se acompañarán a la reclamación las pruebas documentales, debidamente certificadas, de la autorización de dicho representante.

(*j*) En los casos en que varias reclamaciones se deriven de un mismo grupo de hechos, se podrán incluir, todas o cualquiera de ellas, en el mismo Memorial.

3. The Answer.

(a) The answer in each case shall be filed with the secretaries in duplicate in English and Spanish within sixty (60) days from the date on which the memorial is filed, unless the time be extended in any case by stipulation between the agents of the respective Governments filed in like manner with the secretaries, or by the Commission in its discretion for good cause shown, on motion after due notice.

(b) The answer shall be directly responsive to each of the allegations of the memorial and shall clearly announce the attitude of the respondent Government with respect to each of the various elements of the claim. It may in addition thereto contain any new matter or affirmative defense which the respondent Government may desire to assert within the scope of the convention.

(c) The answer shall be accompanied by copies of the documents and other proof on which the respondent Government will rely in defense of the claim.

4. The Reply.

(a) Where a reply is deemed necessary in any case on behalf of the claimant, it may be filed with the secretaries in duplicate in English and Spanish within thirty (30) days from the date on which the answer is filed, unless the time be extended in any case by stipulation between the agents of the respective Governments filed in like manner with the secretaries, or by the Commission in its

3. La Contestación.

(a) La Contestación, en cada caso, se presentará a los Secretarios, en dos ejemplares, uno en español y otro en inglés, dentro de sesenta (60) días contados a partir de la fecha en que se presente el Memorial, a no ser que en cualquier caso se prorrogue el plazo por convenio entre los Agentes de los Gobiernos respectivos, notificando en la misma forma a los Secretarios, o por la Comisión cuando lo juzgue conveniente, y se demuestre justa causa, a moción debidamente notificada.

(b) La Contestación se referirá directamente a cada uno de los puntos del Memorial y manifestará claramente la actitud del Gobierno que contesta respecto a cada uno de los diversos elementos de la reclamación. Puede, además, presentar todas aquellas materias nuevas o defensas de carácter afirmativo que el Gobierno que conteste desee hacer constar dentro del alcance de la Convención.

(c) La Contestación llevará anexas las copias de los documentos y otras pruebas en que se fundare el Gobierno que contesta a la reclamación.

4. La Réplica.

(a) Cuando en algún caso se considere necesaria una Réplica por parte del reclamante, podrá presentarse en dos ejemplares, uno en inglés y otro en español, ante los Secretarios, dentro de treinta días contados a partir de la fecha en que fué presentada la Contestación, a menos que se prorrogue el plazo en cualquier caso por convenio entre los Agentes de los Gobiernos respectivos, debidamente presentado,

discretion for good cause shown, on motion after due notice.

(b) The Reply, if any be filed, shall deal only with the allegations in the answer which present facts or contentions not adequately met and dealt with in the memorial and with new matter or affirmative defenses, if any, set up in the answer.

(c) The Reply shall be accompanied by copies of documents and other proofs upon which the claimant relies in support thereof not filed with the memorial.

5. *Amendments to Pleadings.*

(a) The Memorial, answer, and/or reply may be amended at any time before final award either (1) by stipulation between the agents of the respective Governments, confirmed by the Commission, agreeing to the filing of any amendment set out in such stipulation, which shall be filed with the secretaries as in the case of original pleadings, or (2) by leave of the Commission in its discretion, such leave to be granted only upon motion, after due notice and upon such terms as the Commission shall impose.

(b) All motions for leave to amend pleadings shall be in writing, filed with the secretaries in duplicate in English and Spanish, and shall set

en forma semejante, ante los Secretarios, o por orden de la Comisión a juicio de ella, en vista de haberse probado causa suficiente, a moción debidamente notificada.

(b) La Réplica, caso de presentarse, se concretará a los argumentos consignados en la Contestación que se refieran a hechos o a argumentos que no hayan sido debidamente tratados en el Memorial, y a materias nuevas o a hechos afirmativos alegados en la defensa, si los hubiere, contenidos en la Contestación.

(c) A la Réplica, se acompañarán copias de los documentos y de las otras pruebas en que se haya basado el reclamante para apoyarla y que no hayan sido presentados en el Memorial.

5. *Reformas de los Escritos Fundamentales.*

(a) El Memorial, la Contestación y la Réplica, o cualesquier de ellos, podrán reformarse en cualquier momento antes del fallo definitivo, ya sea, (1) por acuerdo entre los Agentes de los Gobiernos respectivos confirmado por la Comisión, en el que convengan en la presentación de cualquiera reforma consignada en dicho acuerdo que se depositará con los Secretarios como si se tratara de los escritos fundamentales originales, o (2) por permiso que la Comisión estime conveniente conceder, el cual sólo podrá concederse mediante moción, previa notificación, y conforme a las condiciones que la Comisión imponga.

(b) Todas las mociones solicitando permiso para reformar los escritos fundamentales se presentarán por escrito, en dos ejemplares, uno en

out the amendments desired to be made and the reasons in support thereof.

(c) Amendments to pleadings shall be accompanied by copies of documents and other proofs which will be relied upon in support thereof, unless the same have been filed with the original pleadings.

(d) Answer or Reply may be filed to amendments, if desired, in like manner as in the case of original pleadings, within such time as may be stipulated by the agents of the respective parties, or fixed in the orders of the Commission allowing the amendment as the case may be.

6. The Commission will not consider any matter of claim or defense not set up in appropriate pleadings or amendments thereto made as herein provided; and pleadings or amendments thereto not complying with this rule may, at any time before final award, be rejected by the Commission of its own motion, and on stated grounds, with leave to amend within such time as may be fixed by the Commission within its discretion.

V

PRINTING AND COPIES OF
PLEADINGS

1. In cases where the amount or value of the claim exceeds the sum of

español y otro en inglés, ante los Secretarios, y contendrán las reformas que deseen hacerse y las razones en que se funden.

(c) Las reformas a los escritos fundamentales deberán acompañarse de las copias de los documentos y otras pruebas que se aduzcan en su apoyo, a menos que éstos hayan sido presentados con los escritos fundamentales originales.

(d) Podrán presentarse Contestaciones o Réplicas a los escritos de reforma, si se desea, de la misma manera que cuando se trate de escritos fundamentales originales, dentro del plazo que convengan los Agentes de las respectivas partes, o que se fije en los acuerdos de la Comisión que conceden la reforma, según sea el caso.

6. La Comisión no tomará en consideración nada relativo a la reclamación o a la defensa que no esté debidamente consignado en los escritos fundamentales o en las reformas relativas a la misma reclamación como dispone este Reglamento; y tales escritos fundamentales o sus reformas que no se ajusten a esta regla podrán ser desechados por la Comisión, por su propia autoridad, y siempre que exprese las razones que tiene para ello, pero dejando al reclamante la opción de enmendarlos dentro del plazo que la misma Comisión fijará discrecionalmente.

V

IMPRESION Y COPIAS DE LOS
ESCRITOS

1. En los casos en que la suma o valor de la reclamación, exceda de la

$25,000 (United States currency) the memorial and other pleadings and amendments shall be printed in quarto form at the expense of the party filing the same, and twenty-five (25) copies thereof in English and twenty-five (25) copies in Spanish shall be delivered to the secretaries at the time of filing for use of the Commission and agents.

2. Where the amount or value of the claim is for the sum of $25,000 (United States currency) or less, then the pleadings need not be printed, but at the time of filing of the originals there shall be delivered to the secretaries five (5) additional typewritten copies in English and five (5) additional typewritten copies in Spanish for use of the Commission and agents.

3. As to documents and other proofs filed with the secretaries in support of claims or defenses, only such portion thereof as shall be relied upon need be printed, with such explanatory note as may enable the Commission or counsel to understand the same.

4. The provisions of this rule may be modified in any case so as to dispense with or require printing, as the case may be, in the discretion of the Commission.

VI

NOTICE TO PARTIES

The filing with the secretaries of the Commission of any pleadings, amendments, documents, or notice by

cantidad de $25,000.00 (moneda de los Estados Unidos), el Memorial y los demás escritos fundamentales y reformas, serán impresos en cuarto a expensas de la parte que los presenta, y veinticinco (25) ejemplares de los mismos en inglés, así como veinticinco (25) ejemplares en español, se entregarán a los Secretarios, al hacerse la presentación, para uso de la Comisión y de los Agentes.

2. Cuando el monto o valor de la reclamación, sea por la cantidad de $25,000.00 (moneda de los Estados Unidos), o menos, entonces no será necesario imprimir los escritos fundamentales, sino que, al tiempo de presentar los, se entregarán a los Secretarios cinco (5) copias mecanográficas adicionales en inglés y cinco (5) copias mecanográficas adicionales en español, para uso de la Comisión y de los Agentes.

3. En cuanto a los documentos y pruebas presentadas ante los Secretarios en apoyo de reclamaciones o de defensa, sólo se imprimirá aquella parte que se aduzca, con una nota explicativa que permita su comprensión a la Comisión o a los Consejeros.

4. Las disposiciones de esta regla se podrán modificar en cualquier caso, ya sea dispensando o exigiendo la impresión, a discreción de la Comisión, según las circunstancias.

VI

NOTIFICACIONES

La presentación a los Secretarios de la Comisión de cualesquier escritos fundamentales, reformas, documentos

the respective agents or counsel shall constitute notice thereof to the opposite party and shall be deemed a compliance with these rules as to any notice required to be given hereunder. The agents will be required to take notice of all orders of the Commission, and copies of such orders, certified by the secretaries, shall be furnished to the agents promptly upon the entry thereof.

o a visos por los Agentes o Consejeros respectivos, constituirá la notificación a la parte contraria y será considerada como el cumplimiento de estas Reglas con relación a cualquiera notificación requerida conforme a las mismas. Los Agentes tendrán obligación de tomar conocimiento de todos los acuerdos de la Comisión, y los Secretarios les proporcionarán copias certificadas de ellos inmediatamente que se dicten.

VII

Motions to Dismiss or Reject

1. A motion to dismiss a claim may be made at any time after the docketing thereof and before final submission to the Commission for good cause shown in the motion, and apparent on the face of the record, going to the jurisdiction of the Commission or the merits of the claim.

2. A motion to reject or strike out any pleading may be made at any time after the filing thereof and before submission of the claim to the Commission for any cause apparent on the face of the pleading.

3. Should any such motion be sustained, the Commission may in its discretion permit amendments to the end that each claim within the jurisdiction of the Commission shall be disposed of upon its merits in accord-

VII

Promociones para Desechar Reclamaciones o Rechazar Escritos

1. Podrá hacerse moción para desechar una reclamación en cualquier tiempo, después de que ésta se haya registrado y antes de someterse finalment a la Comisión, por alguna causa justificada que se demuestre en la moción y que se desprenda claramente de las constancias de los autos, ya sea por lo que atañe a la jurisdicción de la Comisión o a la naturaleza de la reclamación.

2. Puede hacerse una moción para rechazar o eliminar cualquier escrito fundamental en cualquier tiempo después de haber sido presentado y antes de que sea sometida la reclamación a la Comisión, por cualquiera causa que se desprenda claramente del escrito fundamental.

3. En caso de que se apruebe una de estas mociones, la Comisión podrá, a su discreción, permitir que se hagan las reformas necesarias con el fin de que cada reclamación, dentro de la jurisdicción de la Comisión, sea re-

ance with international law, justice, and equity.

4. All motions shall be in writing and shall set forth concisely the grounds of the motion. They shall be filed with the secretaries as in the case of original pleadings and shall be promptly brought on for hearing before the Commission.

VIII

EVIDENCE

1. The Commission will receive and consider all written statements, documents, affidavits, interrogatories, or other evidence which may be presented to it by the respective agents or in the name of such agents by an assistant agent or counsel in support of or against any claim, and will give such weight thereto as in its judgment such evidence is entitled in the circumstances of the particular case. No such statement, documents, or other evidence will be received or considered by the Commission if presented through any other channel.

2. The agent of either party shall have the right, after due notice given within the time and in the manner prescribed in these Rules or in any order of the Commission, to produce witnesses and examine them under oath or affirmation before the Commission, and in such event any witness introduced on behalf of one party shall be subject to cross-examination by the agent for the opposite party, or his counsel.

suelta conforme a sus méritos y de acuerdo con el Derecho Internacional, con la justicia y con la equidad.

4. Todas las mociones se harán por escrito y contendrán de manera concisa los fundamentos en que estén basadas. Serán presentadas a los Secretarios de la misma manera que los escritos fundamentales originales y serán llevadas prontamente al acuerdo de la Comisión.

VIII

PRUEBAS

1. La Comisión recibirá y considerará todas las declaraciones, los documentos, los "affidavits," los interrogatorios u otras pruebas que por escrito le sean presentadas, por conducto de los respectivos Agentes o en nombre de ellos por los Sub-Agentes y Consejeros, en apoyo de, o en contra de cualquiera reclamación, concediéndoles el valor que a su juicio tengan tales pruebas, según las circunstancias de cada caso particular. Ninguno de estos documentos, declaraciones u otras pruebas, serán recibidas o consideradas por la Comisión, si se presentaren por cualquier otro conducto.

2. El Agente de cualesquiera de las partes tendrá el derecho, previa la debida notificación al Agente de la parte contraria, hecha dentro del término y en la forma prescrita en estas Reglas, o en cumplimiento de cualquier acuerdo de la Comisión, para presentar testigos y examinarlos bajo juramento o protesta ante la Comisión; y, en tal caso, cualquier testigo presentado por una de las partes estará sujeto a repreguntas por

3. When an original paper on file in the archives of the United States or Mexico can not be conveniently withdrawn, duly certified copies, with the English or Spanish translation thereof, if requested, may be received in evidence in lieu thereof.

4. Where the original of any document or other proof is filed at any Government office on either side, and can not be conveniently withdrawn, and no copy of such document is in the possession of the agent of the Government desiring to present the same to the Commission in support of the allegations set out in his pleadings, he shall notify the agent of the the other Government in writing of his desire to inspect such document. Should such inspection be refused, then the action taken in response to the request to inspect, together with such reasons as may be assigned for the action taken, shall be reported to the Commission, and the Commission will take note thereof.

5. The right to inspect the original of such document when granted shall extend to the whole of the document of which part only is brought forward in support of or in answer to a claim, but shall not extend to any enclosures therein, or annexes thereto, or minutes, or endorsements thereon, if such enclosures, annexes, minutes, or endorsements are not adduced as evidence or specifically referred to in the pleadings.

el Agente de la parte contraria o por su Consejero.

3. Cuando un documento original que se encuentre en los archivos de México, o de los Estados Unidos, no pueda ser retirado fácilmente, entonces podrán recibirse como pruebas en su lugar, si así se solicitare, copias debidamente certificadas, con su correspondiente traducción al inglés o al español.

4. Cuando el original u otra prueba esté archivada en las oficinas de cualesquier de los dos Gobiernos, y no pueda ser retirado fácilmente, ni exista copia de tal documento en poder del Agente del Gobierno que desee presentarlo a la Comisión, en apoyo de los puntos contenidos en sus escritos fundamentales, entonces notificará por escrito al Agente de la parte contraria, acerca de su deseo de examinar el referido documento. Si a una solicitud de examen, se rehusa la exhibición del documento de que se trata, tal conducta junto con las razones que se dieren para excusarla, serán puestas en conocimiento de la Comisión, y esto será tomado en cuenta por ella.

5. El derecho concedido para examinar el original de tales documentos, cuando se conceda, se extenderá a todo el documento, del cual sólo una parte sea presentada en apoyo de o en contestación a una reclamación; pero no se extenderá a ninguno de sus anexos, apéndices, actas o anotaciones que contenga, si tales anexos, apéndices, actas o anotaciones no son aducidas como prueba o explícitamente señalados en los escritos fundamentales.

IX

Taking of Oral Testimony

1. Should the agent of either Government desire to take oral testimony before the Commission in any case he shall, within fifteen (15) days from the expiration of the time for filing the reply of the claimant in such case, give notice to that effect by filing such notice in writing with the secretaries, as in these rules provided, stating the number and the names and addresses of the witnesses whom he desires to examine and the date on which application will be made to the Commission to fix a time and place to hear such oral testimony. No oral testimony will be heard in any case, except in pursuance of notice given within the time and in the manner herein stated, unless it be allowed by the Commission in its discretion for good cause shown.

2. The examination of witnesses shall be within the control and discretion of the Commission. Any member of the Commission may, in his discretion and in the interest of justice, question any witness at any point in the giving of his testimony. Where oral testimony is taken before the Commission, it shall be reported verbatim in writing by a stenographer appointed by the Commission, or otherwise as it may direct. Such report or a transcript in both English and Spanish shall be made a part of the record and copy in English and Spanish furnished to the agents of the respective Governments.

IX

Del Examen de los Testigos

1. En cualquier caso en que uno de los Agentes desee presentar testimonio oral ante la Comisión, dará aviso a ese efecto dentro de quince (15) días contados desde la fecha en que expire el plazo para presentar la Réplica del reclamante, haciéndolo por escrito ante los Secretarios, conforme a lo prevenido en estas Reglas, manifestando el número, los nombres y las direcciones de los testigos que se desee examinar y la fecha en que se hará solicitud a la Comisión para que ésta fije el día y lugar en que deberá recibirse dicho testimonio oral. No se tomará ningún testimonio oral en ningún caso, sino de acuerdo con la notificación dada dentro del término y en la forma antes prescritos, a menos que así lo permita la Comisión a su juicio, siempre que para ello se demuestre causa justificada.

2. El examen de testigos estará sujeto a las órdenes y al criterio de la Comisión. Cualquier miembro de la Comisión podrá, conforme a su criterio y para los fines de la justicia, interrogar a cualquier testigo sobre cualquier punto al rendir su testimonio. Siempre que se rindan testimonios orales ante la Comisión, éstos se harán constar *verbatim*, por escrito, por un estenógrafo nombrado por la Comisión, o en cualquiera otra forma que ésta disponga. Dicho informe o versión taquigráfica, tanto en español como en inglés, se hará constar en los autos, y se proporcionará copia del mismo informe o ver-

3. A witness may testify either in English or Spanish, or, if necessary, in any other language; but in any case the language used shall be that best adapted to the understanding of the witness. Oral testimony shall be translated under the direction of the Commission into Spanish, English, or both languages.

X

HEARINGS

1. The order in which cases shall come on for submission before the Commission shall be determined (a) by agreement between the agents of the United States and of Mexico, subject to revision in the discretion of the Commission, or (b) by order of the Commission.

2. When the agent of the Government presenting the claim is ready to submit a case to the Commission, he shall file notice with the secretaries, and may file together with such notice a brief prepared by himself or his counsel (or a brief prepared by the claimant or his attorney if countersigned by the agent or his counsel) and such documentary proofs in support thereof in addition to those already filed by him, as he may desire. On the filing of notice and brief, the agent of the other Government may within twenty (20) days file with the secretaries a reply brief, together with such written proofs in addition to those already filed by him as he may care to present. Within ten (10) days

sión en español y en inglés, al Agente de cada Gobierno.

3. Todo testigo podrá rendir su declaración ya sea en inglés o en español, o si es necesario en cualquier otro idioma, pero en cualquier caso el idioma que se use será el que mejor se adapte a la comprensión del testigo. Los testimonios orales se traducirán bajo la dirección de la Comisión, al inglés, al español o a ambos idiomas.

X

AUDIENCIAS

1. El orden en que los casos deberán llegar ante la Comisión, para su conocimiento, se determinará: (a) por medio de convenios entre el Agente de México y el Agente de los Estados Unidos, sujetos a revisión conforme al criterio de la Comisión, y (b) por orden de la propia Comisión.

2. Cuando el Agente del Gobierno que presente la reclamación esté preparado para presentar un caso a la Comisión, notificará a los Secretarios, y podrá presentar juntamente con dicha notificación un alegato preparado por él mismo o por su Consejero, o un alegato formulado por el reclamante, o su abogado si va refrendado por el Agente o su Consejero, así como las pruebas documentales en que se funde, además de las que previamente haya presentado, según su deseo. Al presentarse la notificación y el alegato, el Agente del otro Gobierno podrá, dentro de los veinte (20) días siguientes, presentar a los Secretarios un alegato en contestación, juntamente con las pruebas escritas que desee rendir, además de las que previa-

the agent of the Government presenting the claim may reply thereto by a counter brief, accompanied by additional written proofs, if any. Any new matter presented in or with the reply brief may be answered by the agent of the other Government within five (5) days.

3. When a case comes on for submission to the Commission, the agents or their respective counsel shall be heard on either side. The agent of the Government presenting the claim, or his counsel, shall open the case, and the agent of the other Government or his counsel may reply, in which event further discussion shall be within the discretion of the Commission. The time allowed for oral argument will be fixed by the Commission.

4. When a case is submitted in pursuance of the foregoing provisions, the proceedings before the Commission in that case shall be deemed closed unless opened by order of the Commission.

XI

AWARDS

1. The award of the Commission in respect of each claim shall be rendered at a public session of the Commission.

2. The award shall set out fully the grounds on which it is based, and shall be signed by at least two members of the Commission. The award shall state in each case whether the English or Spanish text shall con-

mente haya presentado. Dentro de diez (10) días el Agente del Gobierno que presente la reclamación podrá replicar por medio de un nuevo alegato, acompañado de pruebas adicionales escritas, si las hubiere. El Agente del Gobierno contrario podrá contestar sobre cualquiera materia nueva presentada en o con el alegato de réplica, dentro de cinco (5) días.

3. Cuando llegue el momento de presentar algún caso a la Comisión, los Agentes de cualesquiera de las dos partes o sus consejeros respectivos serán oídos. El Agente del Gobierno que presente la reclamación o su Consejero abrirá la discusión del caso, y el Agente del otro Gobierno o su Consejero podrá contestar, y en ese caso cualquiera discusión adicional estará sujeta al criterio de la Comisión. La duración de los argumentos orales se fijará por la Comisión.

4. Cuando el caso se haya sometido de acuerdo con las disposiciones anteriores, se considerarán como terminados los trámites ante la Comisión en ese caso, a no ser que vuelvan a abrirse por acuerdo de la misma.

XI

SENTENCIAS

1. La sentencia de la Comisión con respecto a cada reclamación, deberá darse en una sesión pública de la Comisión.

2. La sentencia consignará ampliamente todos los fundamentos en que esté basada, y deberá ser firmada por dos miembros de la Comisión cuando menos. La sentencia deberá expresar en cada caso cuál de los dos

trol in event of doubt as to the construction thereof.

3. In the event that the agents of the two Governments shall stipulate any award, or the disposition of any claim, such stipulation shall be presented to the Commission for confirmation and award in accordance therewith or other proper order thereon.

4. Any member of the Commission who dissents from the award may make and sign a dissenting report setting out the grounds upon which he dissents and the award which in his opinion should have been made.

5. Four signed copies of the award, and of a dissenting opinion, if any, two in English and two in Spanish, shall be filed in the office of the Commission, and forty printed copies, twenty in English and twenty in Spanish, shall be given to each of the agents.

6. Upon the application of either agent made within sixty days after the rendition of an award, and after giving the other agent an opportunity to be heard, the Commission may interpret or rectify a judgment which is obscure or incomplete or contradictory or which contains any error in expression or calculation.

7. Two copies, one in Spanish and one in English, of each award rendered by the Commission shall be entered in a book entitled "Register

idiomas, el español o el inglés, debe hacer fe en caso de duda, respecto a su interpretación.

3. En caso de que los Agentes de los dos Gobiernos convengan en cuanto a la cantidad que debe ser reconocida a favor de algún reclamante, o respecto a cualquiera otra determinación que deba tomarse en relación con cualquiera reclamación, este acuerdo se presentará a la Comisión para que lo confirme y dicte sentencia de conformidad con el mismo o para que acuerde lo que proceda.

4. Cualquier miembro de la Comisión que no esté conforme con una sentencia, podrá hacer y firmar un escrito de inconformidad, exponiendo las razones de su inconformidad y la sentencia que a su juicio debería haberse dado.

5. Se presentarán en las oficinas de la Comisión, cuatro (4) copias firmadas de la sentencia, así como de los escritos de inconformidad, si los hubiere, dos serán en español y dos en inglés, y se entregarán a cada Agente, cuarenta ejemplares impresos, veinte en español y veinte en inglés.

6. A petición de cualesquier de los Agentes, hecha dentro de los sesenta días después de dictada una sentencia, y oyendo al otro Agente, la Comisión puede interpretarla o ratificarla, si es oscura, incompleta, contradictoria o si contiene algún error de expresión o numérico.

7. Se asentarán en un libro llamado "Registro de Sentencias" dos (2) copias, una en español y otra en inglés, de cada sentencia dada por la Comi-

of Awards." Awards shall be entered in the Register in the order in which they are rendered by the Commission. Any dissenting report of any member of the Commission shall be entered in the Register of Awards, in English and in Spanish, immediately following the award actually rendered in a given case.

8. The secretaries shall forward two printed copies of both texts of all awards to the International Bureau of the Permanent Court of Arbitration at The Hague.

XII

Duties of the Secretaries

1. The Secretaries shall —

(a) Be subject to the directions of the Commission.

(b) Be the custodians of all documents and records of the Commission, and keep them systematically arranged in safe files. While affording every reasonable facility to the agents and their respective counsel to inspect and make excerpts therefrom, no documents or records shall be withdrawn from the files of the Commission save by its order duly entered of record.

(c) Make and keep in the English and Spanish languages the Docket, Minute Book, Notice Book, Order Book, Register of Awards, and such other books and documents as the Commission may from time to time order.

(d) Indorse on each document presented to the Commission the date of

sión. Dicho asiento se hará en el Registro en el orden cronológico de la rendición de las sentencias. Los votos de inconformidad de los miembros de la Comisión también se registrarán en este libro, en inglés y en español, inmediatamente después de las sentencias que los provocaron.

8. Los Secretarios mandarán a la Oficina Internacional de la Corte Permanente de Arbitraje de La Haya dos (2) copias impresas de los dos (2) textos de cada sentencia.

XII

Obligaciones de los Secretarios

1. Los Secretarios deberán:

(a) Estar supeditados a las órdenes de la Comisión.

(b) Guardar todos los documentos y registros de la Comisión y conservarlos sistemáticamente arreglados en archiveros de seguridad. Aun cuando deban prestarse todas las facilidades que sean razonables a los Agentes y a sus respectivos consejeros para examinar y tomar notas de ellos, no deberán permitir que se retire de los archivos ningún documento o registro excepto por acuerdo de la Comisión debidamente registrado.

(c) Formar tanto en inglés como en español un Registro, un Libro de Actas, un Libro de Notificaciones, un Libro de Acuerdos y un Libro de Registro de Sentencias y todos los demás libros y documentos que la Comisión disponga cuando lo estime conveniente.

(d) Anotar en cada documento que se presente a la Comisión la fecha de

filing, and enter a minute thereof in the docket.

(*e*) Enter in the Notice Book in Spanish and English all notices required by these rules to be filed by the respective agents with the secretaries; and promptly give notice thereof to the agent required to be notified thereby. Entry shall also be made in said Notice Book of the date on which said notice is given, and all proceedings in respect and in pursuance of said notice.

(*f*) Furnish promptly to the agent of the opposite party copies of all pleadings, motions, notices, and other papers filed with the secretaries by the agent of either Government, and make due record thereof.

(*g*) Perform such other duties as may from time to time be prescribed by the Commission.

2. Persons employed in making translations for the Commission, and interpreters employed at the hearings before the Commission, shall be placed under the exclusive control and direction of the secretaries.

XIII

Computation of Time

Wherever in these rules a period of days is mentioned for the doing of any act, the date from which the period begins to run shall not be counted and the last day of the period shall be counted, and Sundays shall be excluded.

su presentación y hacer la anotación correspondiente en el Libro de Registro.

(*e*) Asentar en los dos Libros iguales de Notificaciones, uno en español y otro en inglés, todas las notificaciones que conforme a estas Reglas deberán dar los respectivos Agentes a los Secretarios; y dar inmediato aviso de ello al Agente a quien deba notificarse. Se asentará en dichos Libros de Notificaciones, la fecha en que se haga cada notificación así como todos los trámites relativos y originados en el cumplimiento de esa notificación.

(*f*) Proporcionar sin demora al Agente de la parte contraria, copias de todos los escritos fundamentales, mociones, notificaciones y otros documentos presentados a los Secretarios por el Agente de cualquier Gobierno, registrándolos debidamente.

(*g*) Desempeñar todas las demás obligaciones que les señale la Comisión, cuando lo estime conveniente.

2. Las personas empleadas como traductores y los intérpretes empleados en las audiencias, estarán bajo el exclusivo control de los Secretarios.

XIII

Del Computo de los Terminos

Siempre que en estas Reglas se mencione un período de días para la ejecución de un acto, no se contará el día a partir del cual comienza a computarse el plazo y sí se contará el último día y se excluirán los domingos.

<table>
<tr><td>

XIV

Amendments to Rules

The agents of the respective Governments shall be heard on any proposed amendment to these rules before action is taken thereon by the Commission.

XV

Silence of Rules

In, or in reference to, any matter as to which express provision is not made in these rules, the Commission will proceed as international law, justice, and equity require.

Approved:

C. van Vollenhoven,
President.

Joseph R. Baker,
Commissioner.

G. Fernandez MacGregor,
Commissioner.

Thomas A. Simpson,
United States Secretary.

José Romero,
Mexican Secretary.

</td><td>

XIV

De las Reformas a las Reglas

Los Agentes de los respectivos Gobiernos deberán ser oídos cuando se trate de reformar estas Reglas, antes de que la Comisión decida sobre la materia.

XV

Del Silencio de las Reglas

En cualquiera materia no tratada expresamente en este Reglamento, la Comisión procederá de acuerdo con el Derecho Internacional, con la justicia y con la equidad.

Aprobado: [1]

C. van Vollenhoven,
Presidente.

G. Fernández MacGregor,
Comisionado.

Joseph R. Baker,
Comisionado.

José Romero,
Secretario Mexicano.

Thomas A. Simpson,
Secretario Americano.

</td></tr>
</table>

H. RULES OF PROCEDURE, AS AMENDED OCTOBER 25, 1926 [2]

I

Office and Meetings

1. The office of the Commission shall be maintained at the City of Washington, where its records shall be kept.

2. The time and place of meetings shall be fixed by orders of the Commission.

---

[1] El texto en inglés fué aprobado por la Comisión en sesión celebrada el 4 de septiembre de 1924, designando a los señores licenciados Genaro Fernández MacGregor, C. L. Bouvé y José Romero para hacer la traducción correspondiente al castellano. [Note in orginal text.]

[2] Text from mimeographed copy furnished by the Department of State.

II

DOCKETS AND RECORDS

1. A duplicate docket shall be provided, to be kept by the Joint Secretaries in both English and Spanish, in which shall be promptly entered the name of each claimant and the amount claimed when the claim is formally filed with the Commission, and in which shall be recorded all the proceedings had in relation thereto.

2. Each claim shall constitute a separate case before the Commission and be docketed as such. Claims shall be numbered consecutively, beginning with that first filed as Number 1.

3. A duplicate minute book shall be kept in like manner by the Joint Secretaries in which shall be entered a chronological record of all proceedings of the Commission. The minute book shall at each sitting of the Commission be signed by the Commissioners and countersigned by the Joint Secretaries.

4. Such additional records shall be kept by the Joint Secretaries as shall be required by these rules or prescribed from time to time by the Commission.

III

FILING AND DOCKETING OF CLAIMS

1. All claims must be filed by the respective Governments through or in the name of the Agents thereof.

2. A claim shall be deemed to have been formally filed with the Commission —

(a) Upon there being presented to the Joint Secretaries a memorandum or statement, in duplicate, one in English and one in Spanish, setting forth as to the claim asserted in said memorandum or statement the name of the claimant, a brief statement of the nature of the claim and the amount thereof; or

(b) Upon there being presented to the Joint Secretaries a memorial in duplicate, one in English and one in Spanish, complying with the provisions of Rule IV, Section 2.

3. Upon receipt of the memorandum or statement mentioned in clause (a) of section 2 hereof, or of the memorial mentioned in clause (b), an endorsement of filing, with the date thereof, shall be made thereon and signed by the Joint Secretaries, and the claim shall be immediately docketed under the appropriate number.

4. The Commission, on motion of the agent of either Government, or on its own motion, after consultation with the Agents, will, for good cause shown, fix such time as to it may seem reasonable within which Memorials shall be filed in claims filed as provided in clause (a) of section 2 hereof.

5. Any claim for loss or damage accruing prior to September 8, 1923, shall

be filed with the Commission either in the manner mentioned in clause (*a*) or in clause (*b*) of section 2 hereof, before the 30th day of August, 1925, unless in any case reasons for the delay satisfactory to the majority of the Commissioners shall be established, and in such case the period for filing may be extended by the Commission to any date prior to February 28, 1926.

6. Any claim for loss or damage accruing on or after September 8, 1923, shall be filed in a similar manner before the 30th day of August, 1927.

IV

PLEADINGS

1. The written pleadings shall consist of the Memorial, the Answer, and the Reply if desired, unless by agreement between the Agents, confirmed by the Commission, or by order of the Commission, other pleadings are allowed. The pleadings shall be accompanied by copies of all documents and other proofs upon which either Government relies in support or in defense of a claim. All statements concerning and discussion of matters of law shall be confined to such briefs as may be filed or oral arguments as may be made in support or in defense of a claim.

2. *The memorial.*

The memorial shall contain a clear and concise statement of the facts upon which the claim is based. The memorial shall set forth the information enumerated below in such detail as may be practicable in each particular case :

(*a*) Facts showing that the losses or damages for which the claim is made resulted from some one or more of the causes specified in the General Claims Convention concluded between the United States and Mexico September 8, 1923.

(*b*) The amount of the claim ; the time when and place where it arose ; the kinds and amount and value of property lost or damaged itemized so far as practicable ; personal injuries, if any, and losses or damages resulting therefrom ; the facts and circumstances attending the loss or damage to person or property out of which the claim arises, and upon which the claimant government intends to rely to establish the claim.

(*c*) On behalf of whom the claim is preferred, and if in a representative capacity, the authority of the person preferring the claim.

(*d*) The citizenship of the owner or owners of the claim from the time of its origin to the date of the filing thereof ; whether such citizenship was derived from birth, naturalization, or other act, and all facts in relation thereto ; and where in any case it shall appear that there has entered into the chain of title to the claim the rights or interests of any person or corporation of any country other than that of the claimant, then the facts in relation to such right or interest must be fully set forth.

(*e*) If the claimant sets out as a basis of his claim loss or damage suffered

by any corporation, company, association, or partnership in which the claimant or person on whose behalf the claim is made has or had a substantial and *bona fide* interest, then the memorial shall set forth the nature and extent of that interest and all facts of equitable considerations in connection with or in support of such claim.   In event an allotment is claimed, there shall be presented to the Commission documentary evidence thereof executed by some person authorized to contract generally on behalf of such corporation, company, association, or partnership, or there shall be clearly stated reasons for failure to present such allotment.   The Commission will, in any such exceptional case determine as to the validity of such reasons under the Convention and deal with the case accordingly.

(*f*) Whether the entire amount of the claim does now, and did at the time when it had its origin, belong solely and absolutely to the claimant, and if any other person is or has been interested therein or in any part thereof, then who is such other person and what is or was the nature and extent of his interest; and how, when, and by what means and for what consideration the transfer of rights and interests, if any, took place between the parties.

(*g*) Whether the claimant, or any other who may have been entitled to the amount claimed, or any part thereof, has ever received any, and if any, what sum of money, or equivalent or indemnification in any form, for the whole or part of the loss or damage upon which the claim is founded; and if so, when and from whom the same was received.

(*h*) Whether the claim has ever been presented, or complaint with respect to it been lodged with either Government, and if so, the facts in relation thereto.

(*i*) A claim arising from loss or damage alleged to have been suffered by a national who is dead may be filed on behalf of an heir or legal representative of the deceased.

(*j*) Where more than one claim arises out of the same set of facts, all or any of such claims may be included in the same memorial.

3. *The answer.*

(*a*) The answer in each case shall be filed with the Joint Secretaries within sixty (60) days from the date on which the memorial is filed, unless prior to the termination of that period the time be extended by stipulation between the Agents, duly filed with the Joint Secretaries and confirmed by the Commission.   Where an extension is desired by either Agent, and the Agents fail to enter into a stipulation with regard thereto, the Commission may, after due notice and hearing, order an extension for good cause shown on motion made prior to the termination of the aforesaid period of sixty (60) days.

(*b*) The answer shall be directly responsive to each of the allegations of the memorial and shall clearly announce the attitude of the respondent Government with respect to each of the various elements of the claim.   It may in

addition thereto contain any new matter which the respondent Government may desire to assert within the scope of the Convention.

4. *The reply.*

(*a*) Where a reply is deemed necessary in any case, it may be filed with the Joint Secretaries within thirty (30) days from the date on which the Answer is filed, unless prior to the termination of that period the time be extended by stipulation between the Agents, duly filed with the Joint Secretaries and confirmed by the Commission. Where an extension is desired by either Agent, and the Agents fail to enter into a stipulation with regard thereto, the Commission may, after due notice and hearing, order an extension for good cause shown on motion made prior to the termination of the aforesaid period of thirty (30) days.

(*b*) The Reply, if any be filed, shall deal only with matters contained in the Answer.

5. *Amendments to pleadings.*

(*a*) The Memorial, Answer, and/or Reply may be amended at any time before final award either (1) by stipulation between the Agents confirmed by the Commission, which shall be filed with the Joint Secretaries as in the case of original pleadings, or (2) by leave of the Commission in its discretion, such leave to be granted only upon motion, after due notice and upon such terms as the Commission shall impose.

(*b*) All motions for leave to amend pleading shall be in writing, filed with the Joint Secretaries, and shall set out the amendments desired to be made and the reasons in support thereof.

(*c*) Amendments to pleadings shall be accompanied by copies of documents and other proofs which will be relied upon in support thereof, unless the same have been filed with the original pleadings.

(*d*) Answer or Reply may be filed to amendments, if desired, in like manner as in the case of original pleadings within such time as may be stipulated by the Agents and confirmed by the Commission or fixed in the orders of the Commission allowing the amendment, as the case may be.

(*e*) No amendment shall be made to any Memorial, Answer or Reply filed on or after October 25, 1926.

6. The Commission will not consider any matters of claim or defense which have not been set up in the pleadings or are not supported by evidence.

7. On motion of either Agent, or on its own motion, the Commission, after hearing the Agents, may, in its discretion, order the consolidation of claims, the separation of claims, or the rectification of the names of claimants and of other obvious errors in the wording of claims.

8. Each Memorial, Answer and Reply must be accompanied, at the time of filing, by copies of all the proof on which the party presenting it intends to rely. Proof presented at a later date will be rejected by the Commission.

The Agents may by stipulation, confirmed by the Commission, agree upon the admission of further evidence at any time after the filing of pleadings.

9. Documents or the copies thereof and other proofs submitted in support of or in opposition to any claim may be filed in the language of the party submitting them subject to the further orders of the Commission, but copies of all documents and other proofs so submitted must be filed as hereinafter provided.

V

COPIES AND TRANSLATIONS OF PLEADINGS AND OTHER PAPERS

1. At the time of filing Memorials and other pleadings, the Agent filing them shall file with the Joint Secretaries five (5) additional copies thereof in English and five (5) additional copies thereof in Spanish for the use of the Commission and Agents.

2. As to documents and other proof filed in support of or in opposition to claims, and in connection with pleadings herein provided for, only such portions thereof as shall be relied upon need be copied, with such explanatory note as may enable the Commission or Agents to understand them : *Provided*, however, that on the request of the opposing Agent the complete document or a certified copy thereof shall be made available in the office of the Commission. Except it is otherwise stipulated by the Agents and confirmed by the Commission, five (5) copies of all documents and other proof presented in support of the pleadings shall be filed with the Joint Secretaries for the use of the Commission and Agents, subject to the provisions of Rule VIII, section 6.

3. Papers filed by either Agent with the Joint Secretaries may be typewritten or printed in quarto form in the discretion of the Agent filing them; but the Commission may in its discretion direct that they be printed.

VI

NOTICES TO PARTIES

The filing with the Joint Secretaries of any pleadings, documents, or notice by either Agent shall constitute notice thereof to the other Agent upon being furnished to him by the Joint Secretaries and shall be deemed a compliance with these rules as to any notice required to be given thereunder. The agents shall be required to take notice of all orders of the Commission, and copies of each of such orders, certified by the Joint Secretaries, shall be furnished to the Agents on the day on which it is made or the following day.

VII

MOTIONS TO DISMISS OR REJECT

1. A motion to dismiss a claim may be made at any time after the docketing thereof and before final submission to the Commission for good cause shown in

the motion, and apparent on the face of the record, going to the jurisdiction of of the Commission or the merits of the claim. In all cases in which one of the parties has made a motion to dismiss a claim filed by the other, the running of the periods of time provided in the rules for the filing of the Answer to the Memorial or to any other pleadings relative to the claim concerned and which may have been presented prior to the date of the motion, shall be suspended.

2. A motion to reject or strike out any pleading may be made at any time after the filing thereof and before submission of the claim to the Commission for any cause apparent on the face of the pleading.

3. In any decision rendered by the Commission sustaining a motion filed in pursuance of either of the two preceding sections it will prescribe what, if any, amendment to a pleading may be filed by the party against which such motion is directed and the conditions upon which such amendment, if any, may be filed.

4. All motions shall be in writing and shall set forth concisely the grounds of the motion. They shall be filed with the Joint Secretaries as in the case of original pleadings, and shall be promptly brought on for hearing before the Commission at such time as it may prescribe.

5. A motion to dismiss a claim once filed may be withdrawn only by leave of the Commission first had and obtained. In its order (1) granting such leave, or (2) denying a motion to withdraw and overruling the motion to dismiss, the Commission will prescribe such terms as it may see fit, including the time within which an Answer may be filed and the time within which the case will be heard on its merits, any provision in these rules to the contrary notwithstanding.

6. On and after October 25, 1926, no motion shall be made by one Government to dismiss a claim or to reject or strike out a pleading submitted by the other.

VIII

EVIDENCE

1. The Commission will receive and consider all written statements, documents, affidavits, interrogatories, or other evidence which may be presented by either Government in support of or against any claim, and will give to such evidence the weight to which it is entitled in the judgment of the Commission.

2. Either Agent shall have the right, after due notice given within the time and in the manner prescribed in these rules, to produce witnesses and examine them under oath or affirmation before the Commission, and in such event any witness introduced on behalf of either Government shall be subject to cross-examination by the other Government.

3. When an original paper on file in the archives of the United States or Mexico can not be conveniently withdrawn, duly certified copies, with the

English or Spanish translation thereof, if requested, may be received in evidence in lieu thereof.

4. Where the original of any document or other proof is filed at any Government office on either side, and can not be conveniently withdrawn, and no copy of such document is in the possession of the Agent of the Government desiring to present the same to the Commission in support of the allegations set out in his pleadings, he shall notify the other Agent in writing of his desire to inspect such document. Should such inspection be refused, then the action taken in response to the request to inspect, together with such reasons as may be assigned for the action taken, shall be reported to the Commission, and the Commission will take note thereof.

5. The right to inspect the original of such document when granted shall extend to the whole of the document of which part only is brought forward in support of or in answer to a claim, but shall not extend to any enclosures therein, or annexes thereto, or minutes, or endorsements thereon, if such enclosures, annexes, minutes or endorsements are not adduced as evidence or specifically referred to in the pleadings.

6. Printed or published copies of any public documents, reports, and evidence taken in connection therewith, and printed or published under or by authority of either Government may be filed with the Commission and referred to from time to time by either Agent in support of or defense to claims without being copied into the record, printed, or otherwise proved, where the portion thereof so relied upon is properly identified in the pleadings or briefs. Matter so filed and referred to will be given such weight as the Commission may deem proper in the circumstances of each case. Copies of all such printed or published documents, when filed with the Commission, shall also be furnished or made available to the opposing Agent for his use. Official publications of law, statutes, and judicial decisions and published works of recognized authority on subjects within the cognizance of the Commission may be referred to without being formally proven.

IX

TAKING OF ORAL TESTIMONY

1. Should either Agent desire to take oral testimony before the Commission in any case he shall, within fifteen (15) days from the expiration of the time for filing the reply of the claimant in such case, give notice to that effect by filing such notice in writing with the Joint Secretaries, as in these rules provided, stating the number and the names and addresses of the witnesses whom he desires to examine and the date on which application will be made to the Commission to fix a time and place to hear such oral testimony. No oral testimony will be heard in any case, except in pursuance of notice given within

the time and in the manner herein stated, unless it be allowed by the Commission in its discretion for good cause shown.

2. The examination of witnesses shall be within the control and discretion of the Commission. Any member of the Commission may, in his discretion and in the interest of justice, question any witness at any point in the giving of his testimony. Where oral testimony is taken before the Commission, it shall be reported verbatim in writing by a stenographer appointed by the Commission, or otherwise as it may direct. Such report or a transcript in both English and Spanish shall be made a part of the record and copies in English and Spanish furnished to the respective Agents.

3. A witness may testify either in English or Spanish, or, if necessary, in any other language; but in any case the language used shall be that best adapted to the understanding of the witness. Oral testimony shall be translated under the direction of the Commission into Spanish, English, or both languages.

X

HEARINGS

1. *Trial Calendar*

The Joint Secretaries shall prepare and keep a trial calendar in duplicate, one in English and one in Spanish, in which shall be listed for hearing all cases which either Government shall submit for this purpose. The cases so listed shall be numbered consecutively in the order in which they are submitted, beginning with number 1. In addition, the trial calendar shall set out the dates on which the briefs mentioned in section (3) of this rule become due, as well as the dates on which they are filed.

2. *Listing in Trial Calendar*

When the Agent presenting a claim desires to proceed to the hearing of a case, he shall file notice to such effect with the Joint Secretaries and may file, together with such notice, a brief in support of the claim. On receipt of such notice the Joint Secretaries shall list such claim on the trial calendar.

3. *When a Case is Ready for Hearing*

Upon the listing of cases as provided in section 2 hereof, the respondent Government shall have twenty (20) days in which to file a brief, or reply brief, as the case may be. The claimant Government shall have ten (10) days from the filing of such brief or reply brief in which to file a counter-brief with the Joint Secretaries. Upon the filing of the counter-brief, or at the expiration of the time for filing that brief or any earlier brief, if such earlier brief is not filed on the due date, the case shall be ready for hearing.

4. *Order of Hearings*

The order in which cases shall come up for hearing shall be determined by their position in numerical sequence on the trial calendar, unless the Agents

by stipulation made before or during any hearing and confirmed by the Commission, change the order. The Joint Secretaries shall make the necessary entries, recording any change in the numerical order.

In the event that there are no cases ready for hearing on the trial calendar, cases may be listed on the calendar by order of the Commission. Such action may be taken only after the Commission has consulted the Agents with respect to the cases which may be so listed on the calendar and with respect to the procedure to be followed in trying them. An order by the Commission listing cases may be made not less than twenty (20) days (1) after the expiration of the time within which an Answer may be filed or (2) in cases where an Answer shall be filed then after the filing of a Reply or the expiration of the time within which a Reply may be filed.

5. *Conduct of Hearings*

When a case comes on for hearing before the Commission, the Agents or counsel shall be heard on either side. The Agent or counsel of the claimant Government shall open the case, and the Agent or counsel of the respondent Government may reply. The right to close the case rests with the claimant Government. The time allowed for oral argument shall be fixed by the Commission.

6. When a case has been heard in pursuance of the foregoing provisions, the proceedings before the Commission shall be deemed closed unless otherwise ordered by the Commission.

XI

Awards and Decisions

1. The award or any other judicial decision of the Commission in respect of each claim shall be rendered at a public sitting of the Commission.

2. The award or other decision shall set out fully the grounds on which it is based, and shall be signed by at least two members of the Commission.

3. In the event that the Agents enter into a stipulation with respect to any adjustment of a claim, such stipulation shall be presented to the Commission with an application for an award in accordance with the stipulation.

4. Any member of the Commission may render a dissenting opinion.

5. The Joint Secretaries shall furnish to each of the Agents four (4) typewritten copies, (two (2) in English and two (2) in Spanish), or in cases where the Commission orders them printed, ten (10) copies (five (5) in English and five (5) in Spanish), of each award or other decision and of each dissenting opinion.

6. Upon the application of either Agent made within sixty (60) days after the Joint Secretaries have furnished the Agents copies of the awards or other decisions, and after giving the other Agent an opportunity to be heard, the

Commission may interpret or rectify a decision which is obscure or incomplete or contradictory or which contains any error in expression or calculation or in which the two texts do not correspond.

7. Two (2) copies, one (1) in English and one (1) in Spanish, of each award or other decision rendered by the Commission and of each dissenting opinion shall be entered in a book entitled "Register of Awards and Decisions."

8. The Joint Secretaries shall forward two (2) printed copies of both texts of all printed awards and other decisions and dissenting opinions to the International Bureau of the Permanent Court of Arbitration at The Hague.

XII

Duties of the Joint Secretaries

1. The Joint Secretaries shall —

(a) Be subject to the directions of the Commission.

(b) Be the custodians of all documents and records of the Commission, and keep them systematically arranged in safe files. While affording every reasonable facility to the Agents and their respective counsel to inspect and make excerpts therefrom, no documents or records shall be withdrawn from the files of the Commission save by its order duly entered of record.

(c) Make and keep in the English and Spanish languages the Docket, Trial Calendar, Minute Book, Notice Book, Order Book, Register of Awards and Decisions and such other books and documents as the Commission may from time to time order.

(d) Indorse on each document presented to the Commission the date of filing, and enter a minute thereof in the Docket.

(e) Enter in the Notice Book in Spanish and English all notices required by these rules to be filed by the respective Agents with the Joint Secretaries; and promptly give notice thereof to the Agent required to be notified thereby. Entry shall also be made in said Notice Book of the date on which said notice is given, and all proceedings in respect and in pursuance of said notice.

(f) Furnish to each Agent on the day of filing or the following day copies of all pleadings, notices, and other papers filed with the Joint Secretaries by the other Agent and make due record thereof.

(g) Perform such other duties as may from time to time be prescribed by the Commission.

2. Persons employed in making translations for the Commission, and interpreters and reporters of testimony employed at the hearings before the Commission, shall be placed under the exclusive control and direction of the Joint Secretaries, subject to the direction of the Commission.

XIII

COMPUTATION OF TIME

Wherever in these rules a period of days is mentioned for the doing of any act, the date from which the period begins to run shall not be counted and the last day of the period shall be counted, and Sundays shall be excluded.

XIV

AMENDMENTS TO RULES

The respective Agents shall be heard on any proposed amendment to these rules before action is taken thereon by the Commission.

XV

SILENCE OF RULES

In, or in reference to, any matter as to which express provision is not made in these rules, the Commission will proceed as international law, justice, and equity require.

XVI

TRANSITORY ARTICLE

1. *Concerning Evidence*

(a) When as to any claim memorialized prior to October 25, 1926, the claimant government has not presented all the evidence that it desires to present in support of such claim in connection with the pleadings filed with such claim prior to October 25, 1926, and that it has not had an opportunity to present in connection with pleadings duly filed subsequent to the foregoing date, it shall file the same with the Joint Secretaries at least sixty-five (65) days before the date on which it intends to notice the case for hearing as provided in these rules. The respondent government shall within thirty days (30) from the date such evidence is so filed, present to the Joint Secretaries such evidence as it may desire in its own behalf and which it has not had an opportunity to present in connection with pleadings duly filed as aforesaid. The claimant government shall have thirty (30) days in which to submit evidence in reply to the evidence so submitted by the respondent government, and shall within five (5) days thereafter notice the case for hearing.

(b) When as to any claim memorialized prior to October 25, 1926, the claimant government has already presented all the evidence it desires to present in connection with the pleadings already filed in such claim prior to October 25, 1926, or in connection with pleadings filed subsequent thereto, the claimant

government shall notify the respondent government, through the Joint Secretaries, of its desire to notice the case for hearing. The respondent government shall within thirty (30) days from the receipt of such notice by the Joint Secretaries, file with the Joint Secretaries such evidence as it may desire to present in connection with such claim and which it has not had an opportunity to present in connection with pleadings duly filed. The claimant Government shall within thirty (30) days from the date such evidence is so filed, submit through the Joint Secretaries such evidence as it may desire in reply to the evidence submitted by the respondent Government. The claimant Government shall notice the claim for hearing within thirty-five (35) days from the date the respondent Government submits its evidence.

(c) No evidence shall be filed or admitted in any case covered by this rule after the case has been listed on the trial docket, except by stipulation between the Agents confirmed by the Commission.

(d) All evidence submitted under the terms of this Article must be furnished in the manner and form in these rules provided.

2. *Concerning Briefs*

(a) Wherever, prior to October 25, 1926, a brief and reply brief have been filed, a counter-brief may be filed before November 15, 1926.

(b) Wherever, prior to October 25, 1926, a counter-brief has been filed, the respondent Government may before November 15, 1926, file a brief in response thereto.

II. UNITED STATES–MEXICAN SPECIAL CLAIMS COMMISSION

A. CONVENTION OF SEPTEMBER 10, 1923 [1]

The United States of America and the United Mexican States, desiring to settle and adjust amicably claims arising from losses or damages suffered by American citizens through revolutionary acts within the period from November 20, 1910, to May 31, 1920, inclusive, have decided to enter into a Convention for that purpose, and to this end have nominated as their Plenipotentiaries:

The President of the United States:

George F. Summerlin, Chargé d'Affaires ad interim of the United States of America in Mexico.

The President of the United Mexican States:

Alberto J. Pani, Secretary of State for Foreign Affairs.

Who, after having communicated to each other their respective full powers found to be in due and proper form, have agreed upon the following Articles:

ARTICLE I

All claims against Mexico of citizens of the United States, whether corpora-

Los Estados Unidos Mexicanos y los Estados Unidos de América, deseosos de arreglar y ajustar amigablemente las reclamaciones provenientes de pérdidas o daños sufridos por ciudadanos americanos por actos revolucionarios dentro del período comprendido del 20 de noviembre de 1910 al 31 de mayo de 1920, inclusive, han resuelto celebrar una Convención con tal fin, y al efecto han nombrado como sus Plenipotenciarios:

El Presidente de los Estados Unidos Mexicanos:

A Alberto J. Pani, Secretario de Estado y del Despacho de Relaciones Exteriores.

El Presidente de los Estados Unidos:

A George F. Summerlin, Encargado de Negocios ad-interim de los Estados Unidos de América en México.

Quienes, después de haberse comunicado mutuamente sus respectivos plenos poderes encontrándolos en buena y debida forma, han convenido en los artículos siguientes:

ARTÍCULO I

Todas las reclamaciones en contra de México hechas por ciudadanos de

[1] Text from U. S. Treaty Series No. 676.

tions, companies, associations, partnerships or individuals, for losses or damages suffered by persons or by their properties during the revolutions and disturbed conditions which existed in Mexico, covering the period from November 20, 1910, to May 31, 1920, inclusive, including losses or damages suffered by citizens of the United States by reason of losses or damages suffered by any corporation, company, association or partnership in which citizens of the United States have or have had a substantial and bona fide interest, provided an allotment to the American claimant by the corporation, company, association or partnership of his proportion of the loss or damage is presented by the claimant to the Commission hereinafter referred to, and which claims have been presented to the United States for its interposition with Mexico, as well as any other such claims which may be presented within the time hereinafter specified, shall be submitted to a Commission consisting of three members.

Such Commission shall be constituted as follows: one member shall be appointed by the President of the United States; one by the President of the United Mexican States; and the third, who shall preside over the Commission, shall be selected by mutual agreement between the two Governments. If the two Governments shall not agree

los Estados Unidos, ya sean corporaciones, compañías, asociaciones, sociedades o individuos particulares, por pérdidas o daños sufridos en sus personas o en sus propiedades durante las revoluciones y disturbios que existieron en México durante el período comprendido del 20 de noviembre de 1910 al 31 de mayo de 1920, inclusive, incluyendo pérdidas o daños sufridos por ciudadanos de los Estados Unidos en virtud de pérdidas o daños sufridos por cualquier corporación, compañía, asociación o sociedad en las que los ciudadanos de los Estados Unidos tengan o hayan tenido un interés sustancial y bona fide, siempre que el reclamante americano presente á la Comisión que más adelante se menciona, una asignación hecha al mismo reclamante por la corporación, compañía, asociación o sociedad, de su parte proporcional de la pérdida o daño, y las cuales reclamaciones hayan sido presentadas a los Estados Unidos para su interposición con México, así como cualesquiera otras reclamaciones semejantes que puedan ser presentadas dentro del plazo especificado más adelante, serán sometidas a una Comisión integrada por tres miembros.

Dicha Comisión quedará constituida como sigue: un miembro será nombrado por el Presidente de los Estados Unidos Mexicanos; otro por el Presidente de los Estados Unidos; y el tercero, quien presidirá la Comisión, será escogido por acuerdo mutuo de los dos Gobiernos. Si los dos Gobiernos no se pusieren de acuerdo en la designación de dicho tercer

within two months from the exchange of ratifications of this Convention in naming such third member, then he shall be designated by the President of the Permanent Administrative Council of the Permanent Court of Arbitration at The Hague described in Article 49 of the Convention for the Pacific Settlement of International Disputes concluded at The Hague on October 18, 1907. In case of the death, absence or incapacity of any member of the Commission, or in the event of a member omitting or ceasing to act as such, the same procedure shall be followed for filling the vacancy as was followed in appointing him.

ARTICLE II

The Commissioners so named shall meet at Mexico City within six months after the exchange of the ratifications of this Convention, and each member of the Commission, before entering upon his duties, shall make and subscribe a solemn declaration stating that he will carefully and impartially examine and decide, according to the best of his judgment and in accordance with the principles of justice and equity, all claims presented for decision, and such declaration shall be entered upon the record of the proceedings of the Commission.

The Mexican Government desires that the claims shall be so decided because Mexico wishes that her responsibility shall not be fixed according to the generally accepted rules and principles of international

miembro dentro de los dos meses siguientes al canje de ratificaciones de esta Convención, éste será entonces designado por el Presidente del Consejo Administrativo Permanente de la Corte Permanente de Arbitraje de la Haya, descrito en el Artículo 49 de la Convención para el Arreglo Pacífico de los Conflictos Internacionales, celebrada en la Haya en octubre 18 de 1907. En caso de fallecimiento, ausencia o incapacidad de cualquier miembro de la Comisión, o en caso de que alguno de ellos omita obrar como tal o cese de hacerlo, se empleará para llenar la vacante el mismo método que se siguió para nombrarlo.

ARTÍCULO II

Los Comisionados así nombrados se reunirán en la Ciudad de México dentro de un plazo de seis meses después del canje de ratificaciones de esta Convención, y cada miembro de la Comisión, antes de comenzar sus labores, hará y subscribirá una declaración solemne de que cuidadosa e imparcialmente examinará y decidirá, según su mejor saber y de acuerdo con los principios de la justicia y de la equidad, todas las reclamaciones presentadas para su fallo, y dicha declaración deberá asentarse en el registro de actas de la Comisión.

El Gobierno Mexicano desea que las reclamaciones sean falladas de esa manera, porque México quiere que su responsabilidad no se fije según las reglas y principios generalmente aceptados de Derecho Internacional, sino

law, but *ex gratia* feels morally bound to make full indemnification and agrees, therefore, that it will be sufficient that it be established that the alleged loss or damage in any case was sustained and was due to any of the causes enumerated in Article III hereof.

The Commission may fix the time and place of its subsequent meetings, as may be convenient, subject always to the special instructions of the two Governments.

ARTICLE III

The claims which the Commission shall examine and decide are those which arose during the revolutions and disturbed conditions which existed in Mexico covering the period from November 20, 1910, to May 31, 1920, inclusive, and were due to any act by the following forces:

(1) By forces of a Government *de jure* or *de facto*.

(2) By revolutionary forces as a result of the triumph of whose cause governments *de facto* or *de jure* have been established, or by revolutionary forces opposed to them.

(3) By forces arising from the disjunction of the forces mentioned in the next preceding paragraph up to the time when the government *de jure* established itself as a result of a particular revolution.

(4) By federal forces that were disbanded, and

(5) By mutinies or mobs, or insurrectionary forces other than those referred to under subdivisions (2),

que *ex gratia* se siente moralmente obligado a dar completa indemnización y conviene, por consiguiente, en que bastará que se compruebe que el daño o pérdida que se alega en cualquier caso fué sufrido y que fué ocasionado por alguna de las causas enumeradas en el Artículo III de esta Convención.

La Comisión puede fijar el tiempo y lugar de sus juntas subsecuentes, según convenga, sujeta siempre a las instrucciones especiales de los dos Gobiernos.

ARTÍCULO III

Las reclamaciones que la Comisión examinará y decidirá son las surgidas durante las revoluciones y disturbios que existieron en México durante el período comprendido del 20 de noviembre de 1910 al 31 de mayo de 1920, inclusive, y que provinieron de cualquier acto de las siguientes fuerzas:

(1) Por fuerzas de un Gobierno *de jure* o *de facto*.

(2) Por fuerzas revolucionarias que hayan establecido al triunfo de su causa gobiernos *de jure* o *de facto*, o por fuerzas revolucionarias contrarias a aquellas.

(3) Por fuerzas procedentes de la disgregación de las mencionadas en el párrafo anterior, hasta el momento de establecerse el Gobierno *de jure* emanado de una revolución determinada.

(4) Por fuerzas federales que fueron disueltas y

(5) Por motines o tumultos o fuerzas insurrectas distintas de las mencionadas en las subdivisiones

(3) and (4) above, or by bandits, provided in any case it be established that the appropriate authorities omitted to take reasonable measures to suppress insurrectionists, mobs or bandits, or treated them with lenity or were in fault in other particulars.

ARTICLE IV

In general, the Commission shall adopt as the standard for its proceedings the rules of procedure established by the Mixed Claims Commission created under the Claims Convention between the two Governments signed July 4, 1868, in so far as such rules are not in conflict with any provision of this Convention. The Commission, however, shall have authority by the decision of the majority of its members to establish such other rules for its proceedings as may be deemed expedient and necessary, not in conflict with any of the provisions of this Convention.

Each Government may nominate and appoint agents and counsel who will be authorized to present to the Commission, orally or in writing, all the arguments deemed expedient in favor of or against any claim. The agents or counsel of either Government may offer to the Commission any documents, affidavits, interrogatories or other evidence desired in favor of or against any claim and shall have the right to examine witnesses under oath or affirmation before the Commission, in accordance with such

(2), (3) y (4) de este artículo, o por bandoleros, siempre que en cualquier caso se compruebe que las autoridades competentes omitieron tomar las medidas apropiadas para reprimir a los insurrectos, tumultos o bandoleros, o que los trataron con lenidad o fueron negligentes en otros respectos.

ARTÍCULO IV

En general, la Comisión adoptará como norma de sus actuaciones las reglas de procedimento establecidas por la Comisión Mixta de Reclamaciones creada por la Convención de Reclamaciones entre los dos Gobiernos, firmada el 4 de julio de 1868, en cuanto dichas reglas no estén en pugna con cualquiera de las disposiciones de esta Convención. La Comisión tendrá poder, sin embargo, por resolución de la mayoría de sus miembros, para establecer en sus actuaciones las otras reglas que se estimen convenientes y necesarias, que no estén en pugna con cualquiera de las disposiciones de esta Convención.

Cada Gobierno podrá nombrar y designar agentes y abogados que quedarán autorizados para presentar a la Comisión, oralmente o por escrito, todos los argumentos que consideren oportunos, en pro o en contra de cualquiera reclamación. Los agentes o abogados de cualquiera de los dos Gobiernos, podrán presentar a la Comisión cualesquiera documentos, affidavits, interrogatorios o cualquiera otra prueba que se desee en pro o en contra de alguna reclamación, y tendrá el derecho de examinar testi-

rules of procedure as the Commission shall adopt.

The decision of the majority of the members of the Commission shall be the decision of the Commission.

The language in which the proceedings shall be conducted and recorded shall be Spanish or English.

ARTICLE V

The Commission shall keep an accurate record of the claims and cases submitted, and minutes of its proceedings with the dates thereof. To this end, each Government may appoint a Secretary; these Secretaries shall act as joint Secretaries of the Commission and shall be subject to its instructions. Each Government may also appoint and employ any necessary assistant secretaries and such other assistance as deemed necessary. The Commission may also appoint and employ any persons necessary to assist in the performance of its duties.

ARTICLE VI

Since the Mexican Government desires to arrive at an equitable settlement of the claims of the citizens of the United States and to grant them a just and adequate compensation for their losses or damages, the Mexican Government agrees that the Commission shall not disallow or reject any claim by the application of the general principle of international law that the

gos, bajo juramento o protesta, ante la Comisión, de acuerdo con las reglas de procedimiento que la Comisión adoptare.

La decisión de la mayoría de los miembros de la Comisión será la decisión de la Comisión.

El idioma en que se llevarán y registrarán las actuaciones será el español o el inglés.

ARTÍCULO V

La Comisión llevará un registro exacto de las reclamaciones y de los casos sometidos y minutas de sus actuaciones con sus fechas respectivas. Con tal fin, cada Gobierno podrá nombrar un Secretario; estos Secretarios actuarán conjuntamente como Secretarios de la Comisión y estarán sujetos a sus instrucciones. Cada Gobierno podrá también nombrar y emplear los Secretarios adscritos que sean necesarios, así como los demás empleados que se consideren necesarios. La Comisión podrá, igualmente, nombrar y emplear cualesquiera otras personas necesarias para que la ayuden en el desempeño de sus deberes.

ARTÍCULO VI

Como el Gobierno de México desea llegar a un arreglo equitativo de las reclamaciones de los ciudadanos de los Estados Unidos, y concederles una compensación justa y adecuada por sus pérdidas o daños, el Gobierno Mexicano conviene en que la Comisión no negará o rechazará reclamación alguna alegando la aplicación del principio general de Derecho Inter-

legal remedies must be exhausted as a condition precedent to the validity or allowance of any claim.

ARTICLE VII

Every claim shall be filed with the Commission within two years from the date of its first meeting, unless in any case reasons for the delay, satisfactory to the majority of the Commissioners, shall be established, and in any such case the period for filing the claim may be extended not to exceed six additional months.

The Commission shall be bound to hear, examine and decide, within five years from the date of its first meeting, all the claims filed.

Four months after the date of the first meeting of the Commissioners, and every four months thereafter, the Commission shall submit to each Government a report setting forth in detail its work to date, including a statement of the claims filed, claims heard and claims decided. The Commission shall be bound to decide any claim heard and examined within six months after the conclusion of the hearing of such claim and to record its decision.

ARTICLE VIII

The High Contracting Parties agree to consider the decision of the Commission as final and conclusive upon each claim decided, and to give

nacional, de que han de agotarse los remedios legales como condición precedente a la validez o admisión de cualquiera reclamación.

ARTÍCULO VII

Todas las reclamaciones serán presentadas a la Comisión dentro de los dos años contados desde la fecha de su primera junta, a menos de que en algún caso se compruebe para la tardanza, razones satisfactorias para la mayoría de los Comisionados y en cualquiera de estos casos, el período para presentar la reclamación podrá ser prorrogado hasta por un plazo que no exceda de seis meses más.

La Comisión estará obligada a oír, examinar y decidir dentro de los cïnco años siguientes a la fecha de su primera junta, todas las reclamaciones presentadas.

Cuatro meses después de la fecha de la primera junta de los Comisionados, y cada cuatro meses después, la Comisión habrá de rendir a cada Gobierno, un informe dando cuenta en detalle de sus trabajos hasta la fecha, incluyendo un estado de las reclamaciones presentadas, de las oídas y de las decididas. La Comisión estará obligada a decidir cualquiera reclamación oída y examinada dentro de los seis meses siguientes a la terminación de la audiencia de tal reclamación y a hacer constar su fallo.

ARTÍCULO VIII

Las Altas Partes Contratantes convienen en considerar como finales y concluyentes las decisiones de la Comisión que recaigan sobre cada

full effect to such decisions. They further agree to consider the result of the proceedings of the Commission as a full, perfect and final settlement of every such claim upon the Mexican Government, arising from any of the causes set forth in Article III of this Convention. And they further agree that every such claim, whether or not filed and presented to the notice of, made, preferred or submitted to such Commission shall from and after the conclusion of the proceedings of the Commission be considered and treated as fully settled, barred and thenceforth inadmissible, provided the claim filed has been heard and decided.

ARTICLE IX

The total amount awarded to claimants shall be paid in gold coin or its equivalent by the Mexican Government to the Government of the United States at Washington.

ARTICLE X

Each Government shall pay its own Commissioner and bear its own expenses. The expenses of the Commission including the salary of the third Commissioner shall be defrayed in equal proportions by the two Governments.

ARTICLE XI

The present Convention shall be ratified by the High Contracting

una de las reclamaciones falladas, y dar pleno efecto a tales decisiones. Convienen además en considerar el resultado de las actuaciones de la Comisión como un arreglo pleno, perfecto y final de todas y cada una de tales reclamaciones contra el Gobierno Mexicano provenientes de cualquiera de las causas enumeradas en el Artículo III de esta Convención. Y convienen, además, en que todas y cada una de tales reclamaciones, hayan sido o no presentadas o llevadas a conocimiento, hechas, propuestas o sometidas a dicha Comisión, deberán, a partir y después de la terminación de las actuaciones de la Comisión, ser consideradas y tratadas como plenamente ajustadas, excluidas, y de allí en adelante inadmisibles, siempre que la reclamación presentada haya sido oída y fallada.

ARTÍCULO IX

La cantidad total adjudicada a los reclamantes será pagada en moneda de oro o su equivalente por el Gobierno Mexicano al Gobierno de los Estados Unidos, en Wáshington.

ARTÍCULO X

Cada Gobierno pagará su propio Comisionado y erogará sus propios gastos. Los gastos de la Comisión, inclusive el sueldo del tercer Comisionado, se cubrirán por partes iguales por los dos Gobiernos.

ARTÍCULO XI

La presente Convención será ratificada por las Altas Partes Contra-

Parties in accordance with their respective Constitutions. Ratifications of this Convention shall be exchanged in Mexico City as soon as practicable and the Convention shall take effect on the date of the exchange of ratifications.

In witness whereof, the respective Plenipotentiaries have signed and affixed their seals to this Convention.

Done in duplicate at Mexico City this tenth day of September, 1923.

GEORGE F. SUMMERLIN.   [SEAL]
A. J. PANI.   [SEAL]

tantes de acuerdo con sus respectivas Constituciones. Las ratificaciones de esta Convención serán canjeadas en la ciudad de México tan pronto como sea practicable y la Convención ems pezará a surtir sus efectos en la fecha del canje de ratificaciones.

En testimonio de lo cual, los Plenipotenciarios respectivos firmaron esta Convención y fijaron en ella su sello.

Hecha por duplicado en la ciudad de México, el día diez de septiembre de mil novecientos veintitres.

GEORGE F. SUMMERLIN.   [SEAL]
A. J. PANI.   [SEAL]

B. SUPPLEMENTARY CONVENTION OF AUGUST 17, 1929 [1]

WHEREAS a convention was signed on September 10, 1923, between the United States of America and the United Mexican States for the settlement and amicable adjustment of certain claims therein defined; and

WHEREAS Article VII of said convention provided that the Commission constituted pursuant thereto should hear, examine and decide within five years from the date of its first meeting all the claims filed with it; and

WHEREAS it now appears that the said Commission can not hear, examine and decide such claims within the time limit thus fixed;

The President of the United States of America and the President of the

CONSIDERANDO que los Estados Unidos de Norte América y los Estados Unidos Mexicanos firmaron, el 10 de septiembre de 1923, una Convención para el arreglo y ajuste amistoso de ciertas reclamaciones que allí se definen; y

CONSIDERANDO que el Artículo VII de dicha Convención dispone que la Comisión constituída de acuerdo con ella debería oír, examinar y decidir, dentro de los cinco años subsecuentes a la fecha de su primera junta, todas las reclamaciones que se le hubieren presentado; y

CONSIDERANDO que ahora resulta que dicha Comisión no puede oír, examinar y decidir tales reclamaciones dentro de ese plazo;

El Presidente de los Estados Unidos de Norte América y el Presidente de

[1] Text from U. S. Treaty Series No. 802.

United Mexican States are desirous that the time originally fixed for the duration of the said Commission should be extended, and to this end have named as their respective plenipotentiaries, that is to say:

The President of the United States of America, Honorable William R. Castle, junior, Acting Secretary of State of the United States; and

The President of the United Mexican States, His Excellency Señor Don Manuel C. Téllez, Ambassador Extraordinary and Plenipotentiary of the United Mexican States at Washington;

Who, after having communicated to each other their respective full powers found in good and due form, have agreed upon the following articles:

ARTICLE I

The High Contracting Parties agree that the term assigned by Article VII of the Convention of September 10, 1923, for the hearing, examination and decision of claims for loss or damage accruing during the period from November 20, 1910, to May 31, 1920, inclusive, shall be and the same hereby is extended for a time not exceeding two years from August 17, 1929, the day when pursuant to the provisions of the said Article VII, the functions of the said Commission would terminate in respect of such claims.

It is agreed that nothing contained in this Article shall in any

los Estados Unidos Mexicanos están deseosos de que el plazo fijado originalmente para la duración de dicha Comisión se prorrogue, y con este fin han nombrado como plenipotenciarios respectivos:

El Presidente de los Estados Unidos de Norte América, al Honorable William R. Castle, junior, Secretario de Estado en funciones de los Estados Unidos; y

El Presidente de los Estados Unidos Mexicanos, a Su Excelencia Señor Don Manuel C. Téllez, Embajador Extraordinario y Plenipotenciario de los Estados Unidos Mexicanos en Wáshington;

QUIENES, después de haberse comunicado mutuamente sus plenos poderes respectivos, hallándolos en buena y debida forma, han convenido en los siguientes Artículos:

ARTÍCULO I

Las Altas Partes Contratantes convienen en que el plazo fijado por el Artículo VII de la Convención del 10 de septiembre de 1923, para la audiencia, examen y decisión de reclamaciones por pérdida o daños acaecidos durante el período del 20 de noviembre de 1910 al 31 de mayo de 1920, inclusive, se prorrogue, y por la presente se prorroga, durante un plazo que no exceda de dos años contados desde el 17 de agosto de 1929, día en que, según las disposiciones de dicho ArtículoVII, terminarían las funciones de tal Comisión por lo que toca a esas reclamaciones.

Se conviene en que nada de lo contenido en este Artículo altera o pro-

wise alter or extend the time originally fixed in the said Convention of September 10, 1923, for the presentation of claims to the Commission, or confer upon the Commission any jurisdiction over any claim for loss or damage accruing prior to November 20, 1910, or subsequent to May 31, 1920.

rroga en modo alguno el plazo fijado originariamente en dicha Convención de 10 de septiembre de 1923 para la presentación de reclamaciones a la Comisión, ni confiere a ésta jurisdicción alguna sobre reclamaciones por pérdida o daños acaecidos con anterioridad al 20 de noviembre de 1910 o posterioridad al 31 de mayo de 1920.

Article II

The present Convention shall be ratified and the ratifications shall be exchanged at Washington as soon as possible.

In witness whereof the above mentioned Plenipotentiaries have signed the same and affixed their respective seals.

Done in duplicate at the city of Washington, in the English and Spanish languages, this seventeenth day of August in the year one thousand nine hundred and twenty-nine.

Artículo II

Esta Convención se ratificará en cuanto sea posible canjeándose las ratificaciones en Wáshington.

En testimonio de lo cual, los supradichos Plenipotenciarios la han firmado fijando en ella sus sellos respectivos.

Hecha por duplicado, en inglés y en castellano, en la ciudad de Wáshington, el día diez y siete de agosto del año de mil novecientos veintinueve.

W. R. Castle, Jr.   [seal]
Manuel C. Téllez   [seal]

C. CONVENTION OF APRIL 24, 1934 [1]

The United States of America and the United Mexican States, desiring to settle and adjust amicably the claims comprehended by the terms of the Special Claims Convention concluded by the two Governments on the 10th day of September, 1923, without resort to the method of international adjudication provided by the

Los Estados Unidos de América y los Estados Unidos Mexicanos, deseando arreglar y ajustar amigablemente las reclamaciones comprendidas dentro de las disposiciones de la Convención Especial de Reclamaciones celebrada entre ambos Gobiernos el día 10 de septiembre de 1923, sin recurrir al sistema de arbitraje inter-

[1] Text from U. S. Treaty Series No. 878.

said agreement, have decided to enter into a Convention for that purpose, and to this end have nominated as their Plenipotentiaries:

The President of the United States:

The Honorable Josephus Daniels, Ambassador Extraordinary and Plenipotentiary of the United States of America in Mexico, and

The President of the United Mexican States:

The Honorable José Manuel Puig Casauranc, Secretary of State for Foreign Affairs,

Who, after having communicated to each other their respective full powers, found to be in due and proper form, have agreed upon the following articles:

ARTICLE I

The claims of the United States of America covered by the Special Claims Convention of September 10, 1923, shall be adjusted, settled and forever thereafter barred from further consideration, by the payment by the Government of Mexico to the Government of the United States of a sum of money which shall equal the same proportion of the total amount claimed by the United States in all such cases (after the deductions provided for in Article IV hereof), as the proportion represented — in respect to the total sum claimed by the Governments of Belgium, France, Germany, Great Britain, Italy and Spain — by the total amount found to be due from the Mexican Government in the settle-

nacional establecido en dicho Convenio, han resuelto celebrar una Convención con tal fin, y al efecto han nombrado como sus Plenipotenciarios:

El Presidente de los Estados Unidos:

Al Honorable Josephus Daniels, Embajador Extraordinario y Plenipotenciario de los Estados Unidos en México, y

El Presidente de los Estados Unidos Mexicanos:

Al Honorable José Manuel Puig Casauranc, Secretario de Relaciones Exteriores,

Quienes, después de haberse comunicado mutuamente sus respectivos plenos poderes y encontrándolos en buena y debida forma, han convenido en los Artículos siguientes:

ARTÍCULO I

Las reclamaciones de los Estados Unidos de América comprendidas en la Convención Especial de 10 de septiembre de 1923, quedarán ajustadas, arregladas y para siempre excluidas de toda consideración ulterior, mediante el pago por el Gobierno de México al Gobierno de los Estados Unidos de una suma de dinero que representará la misma proporción de la suma total reclamada por los Estados Unidos en todos los casos (después de las deducciones que establece el Artículo IV de esta Convención), que la proporción que significa — respecto de la suma total reclamada por los Gobiernos de Bélgica, Francia, Alemania, Gran Bretaña, Italia y España — el monto total que se halló debe el Gobierno de

ment of similar claims and under the conventions concluded with those Governments by the Government of Mexico during the years from September 25, 1924 to December 5, 1930.

To determine said general average percentage resulting from the settlements with said countries for similar claims, the classic arithmetical procedure shall be used, that is to say, the total amount awarded to Belgium, France, Germany, Great Britain, Italy and Spain shall be multiplied by one hundred and the product shall be divided by the total amount claimed by said countries.

Having thus determined the general average percentage, in order to ascertain the amount that Mexico should pay to the United States, said percentage shall be multiplied by the total amount claimed by the United States (after the deductions provided for in Article IV of this Convention) and the resulting products shall be divided by one hundred.

ARTICLE II

The amount provided for in Article I above shall be paid at Washington, in dollars of the United States, at the rate of $500,000.00 (five hundred thousand dollars) per annum, beginning January 1, 1935, and continuing until the whole amount thereof shall have been paid.

ARTICLE III

Deferred payments, by which term is meant all payments made

México en el arreglo de esas reclamaciones similares y de acuerdo con los términos de las convenciones concluidas con esos Gobiernos por el de México durante el período de tiempo comprendido entre el 25 de septiembre de 1924 y el 5 de diciembre de 1930.

Para hallar ese porcentaje promedio general que resulte de los arreglos con dichos países en reclamaciones similares, se usará el procedimiento aritmético clasico, es decir, se multiplicará el monto total de las cantidades concedidas a Bélgica, Francia, Alemania, Gran Bretaña, Italia y España, por cien y el producto se dividirá entre el monto total de las cantidades reclamadas por esos países.

Encontrado así el porcentaje promedio general, para determinar la cantidad que deberá pagar México a los Estados Unidos, se multiplicará este porcentaje por la cantidad total reclamada por los Estados Unidos (después de las deducciones que establece el artículo IV de esta Convención) y el producto así encontrado se dividirá entre cien.

ARTÍCULO II

La cantidad de que habla el Artículo I que precede será pagada en Wáshington, en dólares de los Estados Unidos, a razón de 500.000.00 (quinientos Mil) dólares por año, comenzando el primero de enero de 1935, y continuando hasta que aquella cantidad haya sido pagada totalmente.

ARTÍCULO III

Los pagos a plazo, expresión que significa todos los pagos que se efec-

after January 2, 1935, shall bear interest at the rate of one-fourth of one per cent per annum for the first year counting from January 1, 1935, and an additional one-fourth of one per cent for each additional year until the maximum of one per cent is reached which shall be applied beginning January 1, 1939. In the event of failure to make annual payments when due, however, this rate shall be increased at the rate of one-fourth of one per cent per annum on the amount of deferred payments during the period of any such delay until a maximum additional rate of three per cent on such overdue amounts is reached.

ARTICLE IV

In computing the total amount of claims mentioned in Article I above, there shall be deducted from the total amount of all special claims filed by the United States under the terms of the Special Claims Convention of September 10, 1923, the following items:

First: Claims decided.

Second: One-half of the amount represented by the total claimed in all cases in which the same claim has been filed twice, either for the same or for different amounts, with the Special Claims Commission.

Third: From the claims registered for the same reason with both Com-

túen después del 2 de enero de 1935, causarán interés a razón de un cuarto de uno por ciento por año, para el primer año contado a partir del primero de enero de 1935, y un cuarto de uno por ciento adicional para cada año subsiguiente, hasta llegar a uno por ciento, rédito máximo que se alpicará a partir del 1.º de enero de 1939. Sin embargo, en caso de que no se efectuaren los pagos anuales a su vencimiento, dicho rédito será aumentado a razón de un cuarto de uno por ciento por año sobre la cantidad de pagos diferidos durante el período de cualesquiera de esas demoras, hasta llegar a un máximo de rédito adicional de tres por ciento sobre tales pagos retrasados.

ARTÍCULO IV

Al computar el importe total de las reclamaciones a que se refiere el Artículo I anterior, se deducirán del importe total de todas las reclamaciones registradas en la Comisión Especial por los Estados Unidos de conformidad con lo dispuesto por la Convención Especial de Reclamaciones de 10 de septiembre de 1923, las siguientes partidas:

Primero: Las reclamaciones falladas:

Segundo: La mitad de la cantidad correspondiente al importe total reclamado en todos los casos en los que una misma reclamación ha sido registrada dos veces, ya sea por la misma cantidad o por sumas distintas, ante la Comisión Especial de Reclamaciones.

Tercero: De las reclamaciones registradas en ambas Comisiones por

missions, there shall be deducted the total amount of all claims that in fact or apparently should have been registered only with the General Claims Commission established by the Convention of September 8, 1923.

The determination, by the representatives of both Governments referred to in Article V of this Convention, of claims that ought to be withdrawn from the Special Commission because in fact or apparently they should have been registered only with the General Commission for presentation and adjudication, does not prejudge the jurisdiction in and validity of said claims, which shall be determined in each case when examined and adjudicated by the Commissioners or Umpire in accordance with the provisions of the General Claims Convention of September 8, 1923 and the Protocol of April 24, 1934, or the Special Claims Convention of September 10, 1923, and the Protocol of June 18, 1932, in the event it shall be found by the Commissioners or Umpire to have been improperly eliminated from the Special Claims settlement. In the latter event, the claims improperly eliminated in the opinion of the Commissioners or Umpire, shall be settled and adjusted by the same *en bloc* procedure prescribed by this Convention for all claims registered with the Special Commission.

el mismo concepto, se deducirá el importe total de todas las reclamaciones que debida o aparentemente debieron registrarse sólo en la Comisión General de Reclamaciones creada por la Convención de 8 de septiembre de 1923.

La determinación por los Representantes de ambos Gobiernos a que se refiere el Artículo V de esta Convención, de las reclamaciones que deben retirarse de la Comisión Especial, porque debida o aparentemente sólo debieron haberse registrado ante la Comisión General para su tramitación y fallo, no prejuzga de la competencia en dichas reclamaciones ni de su validez, lo cual se determinará en cada una de ellas al ser consideradas y falladas por los Comisionados o el Arbitro de acuerdo con lo establecido en la Convención General de Reclamaciones de 8 de septiembre de 1923 y en el Protocolo de abril 24 de 1934, o en la Convención Especial de Reclamaciones de 10 de septiembre de 1923 y el Protocolo de 18 de junio de 1932, si es que los Comisionados o el Arbitro encontraren que las referidas reclamaciones fueron indebidamente eliminadas del arreglo global de las reclamaciones presentadas ante la Comisión Especial. En este último caso, las reclamaciones indebidamente eliminadas a juicio de los Comisionados o del Arbitro, se arreglarán y ajustarán mediante el mismo procedimiento de arreglo global que para todas las reclamaciones registradas ante la Comisión Especial establece esta Convención.

Article V

The total amount of the special claims of the United States, as well as the deductions to be made therefrom, in accordance with Article IV above, and the proportionate [amount thereof to be paid in accordance with Article I above, shall be determined by a Joint Committee consisting of two members, one to be appointed by each Government, whose joint report, after due conference and consideration, shall be accepted as final.

Article VI

It is agreed that, for the purpose of facilitating a proper distribution by the United States to the respective claimants of the amount to be paid as provided for herein, the Mexican Government shall deliver to the United States, upon request, all evidence in its possession bearing upon the merits of particular claims and to procure, at the cost of the United States, such additional evidence as may be available in Mexico and as may be indicated by the Government of the United States to be necessary to the proper adjudication of particular claims, leaving to the judgment of the Mexican Government the furnishing of originals or certified copies thereof and with the specific reservation that no documents shall be delivered which

Artículo V

El importe total de las reclamaciones presentadas por los Estados Unidos ante la Comisión Especial, así como las deducciones que deben hacerse de dicha cantidad de acuerdo con el Artículo IV anterior y la cantidad proporcional de dicha suma que deberá pagarse según el Artículo I de esta Convención, serán determinadas por un Comité Unido compuesto de dos miembros, cada uno nombrado por su respectivo Gobierno, cuyo dictamen, que se emitirá conjuntamente, después de discutido y considerado debidamente, será aceptado como definitivo.

Artículo VI

Se conviene en que, con objeto de facilitar la debida distribución por los Estados Unidos entre los reclamantes respectivos de la cantidad que deberá pagarse de acuerdo con esta Convención, el Gobierno Mexicano entregará al de los Estados Unidos, a solicitud de este último, todas las pruebas que obren en su poder relativas a los fundamentos de determinadas reclamaciones en particular y recabar, a costa de los Estados Unidos, todas aquellas pruebas adicionales que puedan obtenerse en México y que manifieste el Gobierno de los Estados Unidos ser necesarias para la debida adjudicación de determinados casos, quedando a juicio del Gobierno Mexicano proporcionar los originales o copias certificadas de ellos y con la salvedad expresa de que no se entre-

owing to their nature cannot be furnished by said Government.	garán documentos que por su propia naturaleza no puedan ser suministrados por este Gobierno.

### Article VII	### Artículo VII
The present Convention shall be ratified by the High Contracting Parties in accordance with their respective Constitutions, such ratifications being exchanged in Mexico City as soon as practicable, and the Convention shall take effect on the date of the exchange of ratifications.	La presente Convención será ratificada por las Altas Partes Contratantes de acuerdo con sus respectivas Constituciones, ratificaciones que serán canjeadas en la ciudad de México tan pronto como sea factible, y empezará a surtir sus efectos en la fecha del canje de ratificaciones.
In witness whereof, the respective Plenipotentiaries have signed and affixed their seals to this Convention.	En testimonio de lo cual, los Plenipotenciarios respectivos firmaron esta Convención y fijaron en ella sus sellos.
Done in duplicate, in English and Spanish, at Mexico City this 24th day of April 1934.	Hecha por duplicado en inglés y en español en la Ciudad de México, el día 24 de abril de 1934.
JOSEPHUS DANIELS [SEAL]	PUIG [SEAL]

D. RULES OF PROCEDURE ADOPTED AUGUST 22, 1924, AS AMENDED [1]

I

PLACE AND TIME OF HEARINGS

1. The Commission shall sit at the City of Mexico, where its office shall be maintained and its records kept.

2. The Commission may fix the time and place of its subsequent meetings, as may be convenient, subject always to the special instructions of the two Governments. The time and place of such meetings shall be fixed by orders of the Commission.

II

DOCKETS AND RECORDS

1. A duplicate docket shall be provided, one to be kept by each of the two secretaries in his own language, in which shall be promptly entered the name

[1] Text from Rules of the Special Claims Commission, United States and Mexico (Washington, 1925).

of each claimant and the amount claimed when the claim is formally filed with the Commission, and in which shall be recorded all the proceedings had in relation thereto.

2. Each claim shall constitute a separate case before the Commission and be docketed as such. Claims shall be numbered consecutively, beginning with that first filed as Number 1.

3. A duplicate minute book shall be kept in like manner by the secretaries, in which shall be entered a chronological record of all proceedings of the Commission. The minute book shall at each sitting of the Commission be signed by the Commissioners and countersigned by the secretaries.

4. Such additional records shall be kept by the secretaries as shall be required by these rules or prescribed from time to time by the Commission.

III

FILING AND DOCKETING OF CLAIMS

1. A claim shall be deemed to have been formally filed with the Commission —

(a) Upon there being presented to the secretaries a memorandum or statement, in duplicate, one in English and one in Spanish, signed or countersigned by the agent of the United States, or some one authorized by him to sign on his behalf, setting forth as to each claim contained in said memorandum or statement the name of the claimant, a brief statement of the nature of the claim, and the amount thereof; but the Mexican Government shall not be required to answer and the Commission will not consider any claim so filed by a memorandum unless and until a memorial thereon is filed as in these rules provided; or

(b) Upon there being presented to the secretaries (without such preliminary memorandum or statement) by or on behalf of the agent of the United States a memorial in duplicate, one in English and the other in Spanish, accompanied by copies of all documents and other proofs in support of the claim then in possession of the agent of the United States.

2. Upon receipt of the memorandum or statement mentioned in clause (a) of section 1 hereof, or of the memorial mentioned in clause (b), an endorsement of filing, with the date thereof, shall be made thereon and signed by the secretaries, and the claim shall be immediately docketed under the appropriate number.

3. Every claim shall be filed with the Commission whether in the manner mentioned in clause (a) or in clause (b) of section 1 hereof before the 18th day of August, 1926, unless in any case the reasons for the delay satisfactory to the majority of the Commissioners shall be established, and in such case the period

for filing may be extended by the Commission not to exceed six additional months.

4. At any time after August 18, 1926, the Commission will, on motion of the Mexican agent, fix a time for filing memorials as to claims filed as provided in clause (*a*) of section 1 hereof then pending and as to which memorials have not theretofore been filed.

IV

THE PLEADINGS

1. The written pleadings shall consist of the memorial, the answer, the reply if desired, amendments and motions, unless by agreement between the agents or by order of the Commission other pleadings are allowed. Either party may have the right to plead to new matter.

2. *The memorial.*

The memorial shall be signed and verified by the claimant, or upon good cause shown by his attorney in fact, which cause shall be averred by such attorney; and it shall be subscribed by solicitor or counsel, if any, of the claimant. Every memorial shall also be subscribed or countersigned by the agent of the United States.[1]

The memorial shall contain a clear and concise statement of the facts upon which the claim is based. It shall set forth the information enumerated below in such detail as may be practicable in each particular case, or explain the absence thereof —

(*a*) Facts showing that the losses or damages for which the claim is made resulted from some one or more of the causes specified in Article III of the Special Claims Convention between the United States and Mexico dated September 10, 1923, which became effective by exchange of ratifications on February 19, 1924, and that the same occurred between November 20, 1910, and May 31, 1920, inclusive.

(*b*) The amount of the claim; the time when and place where it arose; the kind or kinds and amount and value of property lost or damaged itemized so far as practicable; personal injuries, if any, and losses or damages resulting therefrom; the facts and circumstances attending the loss or damage to person or property out of which the claim arises, and upon which the claimant intends to rely to establish his claim.

(*c*) For and on behalf of whom the claim is preferred, and if in a representative capacity, the authority of the person preferring the claim.

---

[1] On January 24, 1925, this paragraph was amended to read as follows:
The memorial shall be signed and verified by the claimant, or upon good cause shown, by his attorney in fact, which cause shall be averred by such attorney; or signed by the agent of the United States presenting the same in his discretion; and it shall be subscribed by solicitor or counsel, if any, of the claimant. Every memorial shall also be subscribed or countersigned by the agent of the United States.

(*d*) The citizenship of the owner or owners of the claim from the time of its origin to the date of the memorial; whether such citizenship was derived from birth, naturalization, or other act, and all facts in relation thereto; and where in any case it shall appear that there has entered into the chain of title to the claim the rights or interests of any person or corporation of any country other than that of the claimant, then the facts in relation to such right or interest must be fully set forth.

(*e*) If the claimant sets out as a basis of his claim loss or damage suffered by any corporation, company, association, or partnership in which the claimant or person on whose behalf the claim is made has or had a substantial and *bona fide* interest, then the memorial shall set forth the nature and extent of that interest and all facts or equitable considerations in connection with or in support of such claim.

(*f*) Whether the entire amount of the claim does now, and did at the time when it had its origin, belong solely and absolutely to the claimant, and if any other person is or has been interested therein or in any part thereof, then who is such other person and what is or was the nature and extent of his interest; and how, when, and by what means and for what consideration the transfer of rights and interests, if any, took place between the parties.

(*g*) Whether the claimant, or any other who may at any time have been entitled to the amount claimed, or any part thereof, has ever received any; and if any, what sum of money or equivalent or indemnification in any form for the whole or part of the loss or damage upon which the claim is founded; and if so, when and from whom the same was received.

(*h*) Whether the claim has ever been presented, or complaint with respect to it been lodged with the Mexican Government, or any official or agency thereof, acting either *de jure* or *de facto*, or with the Government of the United States or any official or agency thereof; and if so, the facts in relation thereto.

(*i*) Claims put forward on behalf of a claimant who is dead, either for injury to person or loss of or damage to property, shall be presented by the personal or legal representative of the estate of the deceased; and the memorial shall set out with respect to both the claimant and such representative the facts which, under these rules, would be required of the former were he alive and presenting his claim before the Commission; and the claim shall be accompanied by documentary evidence, properly certified, of the authority of such representative.

(*j*) Where more than one claim arises out of the same set of facts, all or any of such claims may be included in the same memorial.

3. *The answer.*

(*a*) The answer in each case shall be filed with the secretaries in duplicate in English and Spanish within sixty (60) days from the date on which the memo-

rial is filed, unless the time be extended in any case by stipulation between the agents of the respective Governments filed in like manner with the secretaries, or by the Commission in its discretion for good cause shown, on motion after due notice.

(b) The answer shall be directly responsive to each of the allegations of the memorial and shall clearly announce the attitude of the respondent Government with respect to each of the various elements of the claim. It may in addition thereto contain any new matter or affirmative defense which the respondent Government may desire to assert within the scope of the convention.

(c) The answer shall be accompanied by copies of the documents and proof on which the respondent Government will rely in defense of the claim.

4. *The reply.*

(a) Where a reply is deemed necessary in any case on behalf of the claimant, it may be filed with the secretaries in duplicate in English and Spanish within thirty (30) days from the date on which the answer is filed, unless the time be extended in any case by stipulation between the agents of the respective Governments filed in like manner with the secretaries, or by the Commission, in its discretion, for good cause shown on motion after due notice.

(b) The reply, if any be filed, shall deal only with the allegations in the answer which present facts or contentions not adequately met or dealt with in the memorial, and with new matter or affirmative defenses, if any, set up in the answer.

(c) The reply shall be accompanied by copies of documents and other proofs upon which the claimant relies in support thereof not filed with the memorial.

5. *Amendments to pleadings.*

(a) The memorial, answer, and/or reply may be amended at any time before final award either (1) by stipulation between the agents of the respective Governments agreeing to the filing of any amendment set out in such stipulation, which shall be filed with the secretaries as in the case of original pleadings, or (2) by leave of the Commission in its discretion, such leave to be granted only upon motion, after due notice to the opposite party given as herein provided, and upon such terms as the Commission shall impose.

(b) All motions for leave to amend pleadings shall be in writing, filed with the secretaries in duplicate in English and Spanish, and shall set out the amendments desired to be made and the reasons in support thereof.

(c) Amendments to pleadings shall be accompanied by copies of documents and proofs which will be relied upon in support thereof, unless the same have been filed with the original pleadings.

(d) Answer or reply may be filed to amendments, if desired, in like manner as in the case of originals within such time as may be stipulated by the agents of the respective parties, or fixed in the orders of the Commission allowing the amendment, as the case may be.

(*e*) The Commission will not consider any matter of claim or defense not set up in appropriate pleadings or amendment thereto made as herein provided; but the Commission may in its discretion at any time before final award direct or advise amendments to pleadings which it may deem essential to a proper consideration of any claim or to meet the ends of justice.

V

PRINTING AND COPIES OF PLEADINGS

1. In cases where the amount or value of the claim exceeds the sum of $25,000 (United States currency) the memorial and other pleadings and amendments shall be printed in quarto form at the expense of the party filing the same, and twenty-five (25) copies thereof in English and twenty-five (25) copies in Spanish shall be delivered to the secretaries at the time of filing for use of the Commission and agents.

2. Where the amount or value of the claim is for the sum of $25,000 (United States currency) or less, then the pleadings need not be printed, but at the time of filing of the originals there shall be delivered to the secretaries five (5) additional copies in English and five (5) additional copies in Spanish for use of the Commission and agents.

3. As to documents and proofs filed with the secretaries in support of claims or defenses, only such portion thereof as shall be relied upon need be printed with such explanatory note as may enable the Commission or counsel to understand the same.[1]

4. The provisions of this rule will be modified in any case so as to dispense with or require printing, as the case may be, in the discretion of the Commission.

VI

NOTICE TO PARTIES

The filing with the secretaries of the Commission of any pleadings, amendments, documents, or notice by the respective agents or counsels shall constitute notice thereof to the opposite party and shall be deemed a compliance with these rules as to any notice required to be given hereunder.

---

[1] On January 24, 1925, this paragraph was amended to read as follows:
As to documents and other proofs filed in support of claims or defenses, only such portion thereof as shall be relied upon need be translated and printed or copied, with such explanatory note as may enable the Commission or counsel to understand the same; provided, however, that the complete document or a certified copy thereof shall be filed with the Commission and shall also be made available to the agent for the opposing party on request upon the agent filing the same.

VII

MOTIONS TO DISMISS OR REJECT

1. A motion to dismiss a claim may be made at any time after the docketing hereof and before final submission to the Commission for good cause shown in he motion, and apparent on the face of the record, going to the jurisdiction of the Commission or the merits of the claim.

2. A motion to reject or strike out any pleading may be made at any time after the filing thereof and before submission of the claim to the Commission or any cause apparent on the face of the pleading.

3. Should any such motion be sustained, the Commission may in its discreion permit amendments to the end that each claim within the jurisdiction of he Commission shall be disposed of upon its merits in accordance with justice and equity.

4. All motions shall be in writing and shall set forth concisely the grounds of the motion. They shall be filed with the secretaries as in the case of original pleadings and shall be promptly brought on for hearing before the Commission.

VIII

EVIDENCE

1. The Commission will receive and consider all written statements, documents, affidavits, interrogatories, or other evidence which may be presented to : by or on behalf of the respective agents in support of or against any claim, and will give such weight thereto as in its judgment such evidence is entitled in the circumstances of the particular case. No such statement, documents, or other evidence will be received or considered by the Commission if presented through any other channel.

2. The agent of either party shall have the right, after due notice to the agent of the other party given within the time and in the manner prescribed in hese rules or in any order of the Commission, to produce witnesses and examine hem under oath or affirmation before the Commission, and in such event any witness introduced on behalf of one party shall be subject to cross-examination y the agent for the opposite party or his counsel.

3. When an original paper on file in the archives of the United States or Mexico can not be conveniently withdrawn, duly certified copies, with the English or Spanish translation thereof, if requested, may be received in evidence in lieu thereof.

4. Where the original of any document or other proof is filed at any Government office on either side, and can not be conveniently withdrawn, and no copy of such document is in the possession of the party desiring to present the same to the Commission in support of the allegations set out in his pleadings,

he shall notify the agent of the other party in writing of his desire to inspect such document. The action taken in response to the request to inspect, together with such reasons as may be assigned for the action taken, shall be reported to the Commission, and the Commission will take note thereof.

5. The right to inspect the original of such documents when granted shall extend to the whole of the document of which part only is brought forward in support of or in answer to a claim, but shall not extend to any enclosures therein, or annexes thereto, or minutes, or endorsements thereon, if such enclosures, annexes, minutes, or endorsements are not adduced as evidence or specifically referred to in the pleadings.

6. [1] Printed or published copies of any public documents, reports, and evidence taken in connection therewith and printed or published under or by authority of either Government may be filed with the Commission and referred to from time to time by the agent of either Government in support of or defense to claims without being copied into the record, printed, or otherwise proved, where the portion thereof so relied upon is properly identified in the pleadings or briefs. Matter so filed and referred to will be given such weight as the Commission may deem proper in the circumstances of each case. Copies of all such printed or published documents, when filed with the Commission, shall also be furnished or made available to the agent of the opposing Government for his use.

Official publications of laws, statutes, and judicial decisions and published works on subjects within the cognizance of the Commission may be referred to without being formally proven when the last are of recognized authority.

IX

Taking of Oral Testimony

1. Should the agent of either Government desire to take oral testimony before the Commission in any case, he shall within fifteen (15) days from the expiration of the time for filing the reply of the claimant in such case give notice to that effect by filing such notice in writing with the secretaries as in these rules provided, stating the number and the names and addresses of the witnesses which he desires to examine and the date on which application will be made to the Commission to fix a time and place to hear such oral testimony. No oral testimony will be heard in any case except in pursuance of notice given within the time and in the manner herein stated, unless it be allowed by the Commission in its discretion for good cause shown.

2. The examination of witnesses shall be within the control and discretion of the Commission. Any member of the Commission may, in his discretion

---

[1] This section was added by an order of January 24, 1925.

and in the interest of justice, question any witness at any point in the giving of his testimony.   Where oral testimony is taken before the Commission, the same shall be reported verbatim in writing by a stenographer appointed by the Commission, or otherwise as it may direct.   Such report or a transcript in both English and Spanish shall be made a part of the record, and copy in English and Spanish furnished to the agents of the respective Governments.

3. A witness may testify either in English or Spanish, but in any case the language used shall be that best adapted to the understanding of the witness. Where oral testimony is given in English or in Spanish, the same shall be translated under the direction of the Commission into the other language.

X

Hearings

1. The order in which cases shall come on for submission before the Commission shall be determined (a) by agreement between the agent of the United States and the Mexican agent, subject to revision in the discretion of the Commission, or (b) by order of the Commission.

2. When the agent of the United States is ready to submit a case to the Commission he shall file notice with the secretaries, which notice shall be notice to the agent of Mexico to that effect, and the agent of the United States may file together with such notice a brief prepared by himself or his counsel, or a brief prepared by the claimant if countersigned by the agent, and such documentary proofs in support thereof, in addition to those already filed by him, as he may desire.   On the filing of notice and brief, the Mexican agent may within twenty (20) days file with the secretaries a reply brief, together with such written proofs in addition to those already filed by him as he may care to present.   Within ten (10) days the agent of the United States may reply thereto by a counter brief, accompanied by additional written proofs, if any. Any new matter presented in or with the reply brief may be answered by the Mexican Government within five (5) days.

3. When a case comes on for submission to the Commission, the agents or their respective counsel shall be heard on either side.   The agent of the United States or his counsel shall open the case and the Mexican agent or his counsel may reply, in which event further discussion shall be within the discretion of the Commission.   The time allowed for oral argument will be fixed from time to time by the Commission.

4. When a case is submitted in pursuance of the foregoing provisions, the proceedings before the Commission in that case shall be deemed closed unless opened by order of the Commission.

XI

AWARDS

1. The award of the Commission in respect of each claim shall be delivered at a public session of the Commission as soon after the hearing of such claim has been concluded as may be possible.

2. The award shall set out fully the grounds on which it is based, and shall be signed by the members of the Commission concurring therein.

3. In the event that the agents of the two Governments should stipulate any award, or the disposition of any claim, such stipulation shall be presented to the Commission for confirmation and award in accordance therewith or other proper order thereon.

4. Any member of the Commission who dissents from the award shall make and sign a dissenting report setting out the grounds upon which he dissents and the award which in his opinion should have been made.

5. Four signed copies of the award, and of a dissenting opinion if any, two in English and two in Spanish, shall be filed in the office of the Commission, and forty printed copies, twenty in English and twenty in Spanish, shall be given to each of the Agents.

XII

DUTIES OF THE SECRETARIES

1. The secretaries shall—

(a) Be subject to the directions of the Commission.

(b) Be the custodians of all documents and records of the Commission, and keep them systematically arranged in safe files. While affording every reasonable facility to the American and Mexican agents and their respective counsel to inspect and make excerpts therefrom, no documents or records shall be withdrawn from the files of the Commission save by its order duly entered of record.

(c) Make and keep in the English and Spanish languages the Docket, Minute Book, and such other books and documents as the Commission may from time to time order.

(d) Indorse on each document presented to the Commission the date of filing, and enter a minute thereof in the Docket.

(e) Keep a duplicate Notice Book in Spanish and English in which entry shall be made of all notices required by these rules to be filed by the respective agents with the secretaries; and promptly give notice thereof to the agent required to be notified thereby. Entry shall be made in said Notice Book of the date on which said notice is given, and all proceedings in respect and in pursuance of said notice.

(*f*) Furnish promptly to the agent of the opposite party copies of all pleadings, motions, notices, and other papers filed with the secretaries by the agent of either Government, and make due record thereof.

(*g*) Provide duplicate books, in which shall be recorded all awards and decisions of the Commission signed by the Commissioners, including dissenting opinions, if any, and countersigned by the secretaries.

(*h*) Perform such other duties as may from time to time be prescribed by the Commission.

XIII

COMPUTATION OF TIME

Wherever in these rules a period of days is mentioned for the doing of any act, the day from which the period begins to run shall not be counted and the last day of the period shall be counted, and Sundays and legal holidays shall be excluded.

XIV

AMENDMENTS TO RULES

After five (5) days' notice in writing to each of them, these rules may be amended at any time at a meeting participated in by the Presiding Commissioner and the American and Mexican Commissioners, and by the affirmative vote of not less than two. The agents of the respective Governments shall be heard on any proposed amendment to these rules before action is taken thereon by the Commission.

RODRIGO OCTAVIO,
President.

F. GONZÁLEZ ROA,
Commissioner.

ERNEST B. PERRY,
Commissioner.

Countersigned:

J. ASPE SUINAGA,
Mexican Secretary.

NOBLE WARRUM,
United States Secretary.

III. FRENCH–MEXICAN CLAIMS COMMISSION

A. CONVENTION OF SEPTEMBER 25, 1924[1]

Les Etats-Unis du Mexique et la République française, désireux de régler définitivement et d'une manière amicale toutes les réclamations pécuniaires provoquées par des pertes ou dommages subis par des Français ou des protégés français à raison d'actes révolutionnaires commis pendant la période comprise entre le 20 novembre 1910 et le 31 mai 1920 inclus, ont décidé de conclure une Convention à cet effet et ont nommé pour leurs Plénipotentiaires, savoir :

Le Président des Etats-Unis du Mexique, M. Alberto J. Pani, Secrétaire d'Etat aux Finances ;

et le Président de la République Française, M. Jean Baptiste Périer, Envoyé Extraordinaire et Ministre Plénipotentiaire de la République Française au Mexique, Officier de l'Ordre National de la Légion d'Honneur ;

Lesquels, après s'être communiqué leurs pleins pouvoirs trouvés en bonne et due forme, sont convenus des articles suivants :

Los Estados Unidos Mexicanos y la República Francesa, deseosos de arreglar definitiva y amigablemente todas las reclamaciones pecuniarias motivadas por las pérdidas o daños que resintieron los ciudadanos o protegidos franceses, a causa de actos revolucionarios ejecutados durante el período comprendido entre el 20 de noviembre de 1910 y el 31 de mayo de 1920, inclusive, han decidido celebrar una Convención con tal fin, y al efecto han nombrado como sus Plenipotenciarios :

El Presidente de los Estados Unidos Mexicanos al C. Ingeniero don Alberto J. Pani, Secretario de Hacienda y Crédito Público ;

El Presidente de la República Francesa al señor Jean-Baptiste Périer, Enviado Extraordinario y Ministro Plenipotenciario de Francia en México, Oficial de la Orden Nacional Francesa de la Legión de Honor ;

Quienes, después de comunicarse sus Plenos Poderes, y de hallarlos en buena y debida forma, convinieron en los artículos siguientes :

[1] Text from Convención de Reclamaciones celebrada entre los Estados Unidos Mexicanos y la República Francesa (Mexico 1925).

Article I

Toutes les réclamations définies à l'article III de la présente Convention seront soumises à une Commission de trois membres; un membre de cette Commission sera nommé par le Président des Etats-Unis du Mexique; un autre membre sera nommé par le Président de la République française; le troisième membre, qui présidera la Commission, sera désigné à la suite d'un accord entre les deux Gouvernements. A défaut de cet accord dans le délai de deux mois à compter de l'échange des ratifications, le Président de la Commission sera désigné par le Président du Conseil Administratif Permanent de la Cour d'Arbitrage de la Haye; la requête aux fins de nomination du Président de la Commission sera adressée au Président de ce Conseil par les deux Gouvernements dans un nouveau délai d'un mois, ou, passé ce délai, par le Gouvernement le plus diligent. En tout cas, le tiers-arbitre ne pourra être ni mexicain, ni français, non plus que national d'un pays qui ait à faire valoir, à l'encontre du Mexique, des réclamations identiques à celles qui forment l'objet de la présente Convention.

En cas de décès d'un membre de la Commission, ainsi qu'au cas où un membre de la Commission serait empêché, ou, pour une raison quelconque, s'abstiendrait, de remplir ses fonctions, il serait remplacé immédiatement suivant la procédure employée pour pourvoir à sa nomination.

Artículo I

Todas las reclamaciones especificadas en el artículo III de esta Convención se someterán a una Comisión compuesta de tres miembros: uno de ellos será nombrado por el Presidente de los Estados Unidos Mexicanos; otro por el Presidente de la República Francesa; y el tercero, que presidirá la Comisión, será designado de acuerdo por los dos Gobiernos. Si éstos no llegan a dicho acuerdo en un plazo de dos meses contados desde el día en que se haga el canje de las ratificaciones, el Presidente del Consejo Administrativo Permanente de la Corte Permanente de Arbitraje de La Haya, será quien designe al Presidente de la Comisión. La solicitud de este nombramiento se dirigirá por ambos Gobiernos al Presidente del citado Consejo, dentro de un nuevo plazo de un mes o, pasado este plazo, por el Gobierno más diligente. En todo caso, el tercer árbitro no podrá ser mexicano ni francés, ni ciudadano de nación que tenga contra México reclamaciones iguales a las que son objeto de esta Convención.

En caso de muerte de alguno de los miembros de la Comisión, o en caso de que alguno de ellos esté impedido para cumplir sus funciones o se abstenga por cualquier causa de hacerlo, será reemplazado inmediatamente siguiendo el mismo procedimiento que se haya empleado para nombrarlo.

Article II

Les Commissaires ainsi désignés se réuniront à Mexico dans les six mois à compter de l'échange des ratifications de la présente Convention. Chaque membre de la Commission, avant de commencer ses travaux, fera et signera une déclaration solennelle, par laquelle il s'engagera à examiner avec soin et à juger avec impartialité, d'après les principes de l'équité, toutes les réclamations présentées, attendu que le Mexique a la volonté de réparer gracieusement les dommages subis, et non de voir sa responsabilité établie conformément aux principes généraux du droit international. Il suffira, par conséquent, de prouver que le dommage allégué a été subi et qu'il est dû à quelqu'une des causes énumérées à l'article III de la présente Convention, pour que le Mexique se sente, *ex-gratia*, décidé à indemniser.

Ladite déclaration sera enregistrée dans les procés-verbaux de la Commission.

La Commission fixera la date et le lieu de ses audiences.

Article III

La Commission connaîtra de toutes les réclamations contre le Mexique à raison des pertes ou dommages subis par des Français ou des protégés français, ou par des sociétés, compagnies, associations ou personnes morales françaises ou sous la protection française ; ou des pertes ou

Artículo II

Los Comisionados así designados se reunirán en la ciudad de México dentro de los seis meses contados a partir de la fecha del canje de ratificaciones de la presente Convención. Cada uno de los miembros de la Comisión, antes de dar principio a sus trabajos hará y firmará una declaración solemne en que se comprometa a examinar con cuidado y a fallar con imparcialidad, conforme a los principios de la equidad, todas las reclamaciones presentadas, supuesto que la voluntad de México es la de reparar graciosamente a los damnificados, y no que su responsabilidad se establezca de conformidad con los principios generales del Derecho Internacional ; siendo bastante, por tanto, que se pruebe que el daño alegado haya existido y se deba a alguna de las causas enumeradas en el artículo III de esta Convención, para que México se sienta "ex gratia." decidido a indemnizar.

La citada declaración se registrará en las actas de la Comisión.

La Comisión fijará la fecha y el lugar de sus sesiones.

Artículo III

La Comisión conocerá de todas las reclamaciones contra México por las pérdidas o daños resentidos por ciudadanos franceses o protegidos franceses, y por sociedades, compañías, asociaciones o personas morales francesas, o sujetas a la protección francesa ; o por las pérdi-

dommages causés aux intérêts de Français ou de protégés français dans des sociétés, compagnies, associations ou autres groupements d'intérêts, pourvu que l'intérêt du lésé, dès avant l'époque du dommage ou de la perte, soit supérieur à cinquante pour cent du capital total de la société ou association dont il fait partie, et qu'en outre, le dit lésé présente à la Commission une cession, consentie à son profit, de la proportion qui lui revient dans les droits à indemnité dont peut se prévaloir ladite société ou association. Les pertes ou dommages dont il est question dans le présent article sont ceux qui ont été causés pendant la période comprise entre le 20 novembre 1910 et le 31 mai 1920 inclus, par quelqu'une des forces ci-après énumérées :

1. par les forces d'un Gouvernement *de jure* ou *de facto;*

2. par les forces révolutionnaires, qui, à la suite de leur triomphe, ont établi des Gouvernements *de jure* ou *de facto*, ou par les forces révolutionnaires qui leur étaient opposées ;

3. par les forces provenant de la désagrégation de celles qui sont définies à l'alinéa précédent, jusqu'au moment où le Gouvernement *de jure* aurait été établi à la suite d'une révolution déterminée ;

4. par les forces provenant de la dissolution de l'armée fédérale ;

5. du fait de mutineries ou soulèvements, ou par des forces insurrectionnelles autres que celles qui sont indiquées aux alinéas 2, 3 et 4 ci-dessus, ou par des brigands à condition que, dans chaque cas, il soit

das o daños causados a los intereses de ciudadano franceses o de protegidos franceses en sociedades, compañías, asociaciones u otros grupos de intereses, siempre que, en este caso, el interés del damnificado sea de más de un cincuenta por ciento del capital total de la sociedad o asociación de que forma parte, anterior a la época en que se resintió el daño o pérdida, y que, además, se presente a la Comisión una cesión hecha al reclamante de la parte proporcional de la pérdida o daño que le toque en tal compañía o asociación. Las pérdidas o daños de que se habla en este artículo deberán haber sido causados durante el período comprendido entre el 20 de noviembre de 1910 y el 31 de mayo de 1920, inclusive, por las fuerzas siguientes:

1. Por fuerzas de un Gobierno *de jure* o *de facto;*

2. Por fuerzas revolucionarias que hayan establecido al triunfo de su causa Gobiernos *de jure* o *de facto*, o por fuerzas revolucionarias contrarias a aquéllas ;

3. Por fuerzas procedentes de la disgregación de las que se mencionan en el párrafo precedente, hasta el momento en que el Gobierno de jure hubiere sido establecido después de una revolución determinada ;

4. Por fuerzas procedentes de la disolución del Ejército Federal.

5. Por motines o levantamientos, o por fuerzas insurrectas distintas de las indicadas en los párrafos 2, 3 y 4 de este artículo, o por bandoleros, con tal de que, en cada caso, se pruebe que las autoridades competentes omi-

établi que les autorités compétentes ont omis de prendre des mesures raisonnables pour réprimer les insurrections, soulèvements, mutineries ou actes de brigandage dont il s'agit, ou pour en punir les auteurs, ou bien qu'il soit établi que les dites autorités ont été en faute de quelque autre manière.

La Commission connaîtra aussi des réclamations relatives aux pertes ou dommages dûs aux actes des autorités civiles, à condition que ces actes aient leur cause dans des événements ou des troubles révolutionnaires survenus dans la période prévue ci-dessus et qu'ils aient été exécutés par quelqu'une des forces définies aux alinéas 1, 2 et 3 du présent article.

tieron dictar medidas razonables para reprimir las insurrecciones, levantamientos, motines o actos de bandolerismo de que se trata, o para castigar a sus autòres; o que se pruebe, asimismo, que las autoridades incurrieron en falta de alguna otra manera.

La Comisión conocerá también de las reclamaciones por pérdidas o daños causados por actos de autoridades civiles, siempre que dichos actos se originen en sucesos y trastornos revolucionarios, dentro de la época a que alude este artículo y que hayan sido ejecutados por alguna de las fuerzas descritas en los párrafos 1, 2 y 3 del presente artículo.

Article IV

La Commission réglera sa procédure tout en se conformant aux dispositions de la présente Convention.

Chaque Gouvernement pourra nommer un Agent et des Conseils qui présenteront à la Commission, oralement ou par écrit, les preuves et arguments qu'ils jugeront bon d'invoquer à l'appui des réclamations ou contre elles.

La décision de la majorité des membres de la Commission sera celle de la Commission. A défaut de majorité, la voix du Président prévaudra.

La langue employée tant dans la procédure que dans les sentences sera l'espagnol ou le français.

Artículo IV

La Comisión decretará sus propios procedimientos, pero ciñéndose a las disposiciones de la presente Convención.

Cada Gobierno podrá nombrar un Agente y Consejeros que presenten a la Comisión, ya sea oralmente o por escrito, las pruebas y argumentos que juzguen conveniente aducir en apoyo de las reclamaciones o en contra de ellas.

La decisión de la mayoría de los miembros de la Comisión, será la de la Comisión. Si no hubiere mayoria prevalecerá la decisión del Presidente.

Tanto en los procedimientos como en los fallos se empleará el español o el francés.

Article V

La Commission tiendra un registre où seront enregistrés, en toute exactitude et à leur date respective, toutes les réclamations et les cas divers qui lui seront soumis, ainsi que les minutes des débats.

A cet effet, chaque Gouvernement pourra désigner un Secrétaire. Ces Secrétaires dépendront de la Commission et seront soumis à ses instructions.

Chaque Gouvernement pourra aussi nommer et employer autant de Secrétaires-adjoints qu'il jugera convenable. La Commission pourra, elle aussi, nommer et employer autant d'aides qu'elle jugera nécessaire en vue de mener à bien sa mission.

Article VI

Le Gouvernement du Mexique étant désireux d'arriver à un réglement équitable des réclamations définies à l'article III ci-dessus, et d'accorder aux intéressés une indemnité juste, qui corresponde aux pertes et dommages subis, il est convenu que la Commission ne devra écarter ou rejeter aucune réclamation pour le motif que les recours légaux n'auraient pas été épuisés avant présentation de ladite réclamation.

Lorsqu'il s'agira de fixer le montant des indemnités à accorder pour des dommages à des biens, il sera tenu compte de la valeur de ces biens, telle qu'elle aura été déclarée au fisc par les intéressés, sauf dans les cas que la Commission estimera vraiment exceptionnels.

Artículo V

La Comisión irá registrando con exactitud todas las reclamaciones y los diversos casos que le fueren sometidos, así como las actas de los debates, con sus fechas respectivas.

Para tal fin, cada Gobierno podrá designar un Secretario. Dichos Secretarios dependerán de la Comisión y estarán sometidos a sus instrucciones.

Cada Gobierno podrá nombrar, asimismo, y emplear los Secretarios adjuntos que juzgare prudente. La Comisión podrá nombrar y emplear, igualmente, los ayudantes que juzgue necesarios para llevar a cabo su misión.

Artículo VI

Deseando el Gobierno de México llegar a un arreglo equitativo sobre las reclamaciones especificadas en el artículo III, y conceder a los reclamantes una indemnización justa que corresponda a las pérdidas o daños que hayan sufrido, queda convenido que la Comisión no habrá de descartar o rechazar ninguna reclamación por causa de que no se hubieren agotado, antes de presentar dicha reclamación, todos los recursos legales.

Para fijar el importe de las indemnizaciones que habrán de concederse por daños a los bienes, se tendrá en cuenta el valor declarado al fisco por los interesados, salvo en casos verdaderamente excepcionales, a juicio de la Comisión.

Le montant des indemnités pour des dommages aux personnes ne dépassera pas celui des indemnités les plus larges accordées en France dans des cas analogues.

El importe de las indemnizaciones por daños personales no excederá al de las indemnizaciones más amplias concedidas por Francia en casos semejantes.

Article VII

Toute réclamation devra être présentée à la Commission dans le délai de neuf mois à partir du jour de la première réunion de la Commission, à moins que, dans des cas exceptionnels, la majorité des membres de ladite Commission ne juge satisfaisantes les raisons données pour justifier le retard. La période pendant laquelle ces réclamations exceptionnelles pourront être enregistrées sera de trois mois au plus, après l'expiration du délai normal.

La Commission devra entendre, examiner et régler, dans le délai de deux ans à partir du jour de sa première réunion, toutes les réclamations qui lui auront été présentées.

Trois mois après le jour de la première réunion des membres de la Commission et ensuite, tous les deux mois, la Commission devra soumettre à chacun des Gouvernements intéréssés un rapport détaillé relatant les travaux accomplis, et exposant, en outre, les réclamations présentées, celles qui auront été entendues et celles sur lesquelles il aura été statué.

La Commission devra statuer sur toute réclamation qui lui sera présentée, dans les six mois à compter de la clôture des débats relatifs à ladite réclamation.

Artículo VII

Toda reclamación habrá de presentarse ante la Comisión dentro del plazo de nueve meses contados desde el día de la primera reunión de ella, a menos que, en casos excepcionales, la mayoría de los miembros de esa Comisión juzgue satisfactorias las razones que se den para justificar el retardo; el período dentro del cual podrán registrarse dichas reclamaciones excepcionales no se extenderá a más de tres meses después del término de expiración del plazo normal.

La Comisión oirá, examinará y resolverá dentro del plazo de dos años, contados desde el día de su primera sesión, todas las reclamaciones que le fueren presentadas.

Tres meses después del día de la primera reunión de los miembros de la Comisión, y luego bimestralmente, la Comisión someterá a cada uno de los Gobiernos interesados un informe donde queden establecidos pormenorizadamente los trabajos realizados, y que comprenda también una exposición de las reclamaciones presentadas de las oídas y de las resueltas.

La Comisión dará su fallo sobre toda reclamación que se le presente, dentro del plazo de seis meses, contados desde la clausura de los debates relativos a dicha reclamación.

Article VIII

Les Hautes Parties Contractantes conviennent de considérer comme définitive la décision de la Commission sur chaque affaire réglée par elle et de donner plein effet auxdites décisions. Elles conviennent, aussi, de considérer le résultat des travaux de la Commission comme un règlement complet, parfait et définitif de toutes les réclamations contre le Gouvernement du Mexique procédant de quelqu'une des causes énumérées à l'article III de la présente Convention. Elles conviennent, en outre, qu'à partir de la fin des travaux de la Commission, sera désormais considérée comme entièrement et irrévocablement réglée toute réclamation de cet ordre, qu'elle ait été ou non présentée à ladite Commission, à condition, pour celles qui auraient été présentées à la Commission, que cette dernière les ait examinées et ait statué sur elles.

Article IX

Les paiements seront faits en or ou en une monnaie équivalente et ils seront versés directement par le Gouvernement mexicain au Gouvernement français.

Article X

Chaque Gouvernement paiera les honoraires de son propre Commissaire, ainsi que ceux du personnel qu'il lui aura adjoint.

Les dépenses de la Commission et les honoraires du tiers arbitre seront supportés par moitié par chaque Gouvernement.

Artículo VIII

Las altas Partes Contratantes convienen en considerar como definitiva la decisión de la Comisión sobre cada uno de los asuntos que juzgue, y en dar pleno efecto a las rrefeidas decisiones. Convienen también en considerar el resultado de los trabajos de la Comisión como un arreglo pleno, perfecto y definitivo, de todas las reclamaciones que contra el Gobierno de México provengan de alguna de las causas enumeradas en el artículo III de la presente Convención. Convienen, además, en que desde el momento en que terminen los trabajos de la Comisión, toda reclamación de esa especie, haya o no sido presentada a dicha Comisión, habrá de considerarse como arreglada absoluta e irrevocablemente para lo sucesivo; a condición de que, las que hubieren sido presentadas a la Comisión, hayan sido examinadas y resueltas por ella.

Artículo IX

Los pagos se efectuarán en oro o en moneda equivalente, y se harán por el Gobierno mexicano al Gobierno francés.

Artículo X

Cada Gobierno pagará los honorarios de su Comisionado y los de su personal.

Los gastos de la Comisión, lo mismo que los honorarios correspondientes al tercer Comisionado, los sufragarán por mitad ambos Gobiernos.

ARTICLE XI

La présente Convention est rédigée en espagnol et en français, étant entendu que le texte français fera foi en cas de divergence.

ARTICLE XII

Les Hautes Parties Contractantes ratifieront la présente Convention conformément à leur constitution respective. Les ratifications en seront échangées à Mexico le plus tôt que faire se pourra. Dés la date de cet échange, la Convention entrera en vigueur.

ARTICLE XIII

En foi de quoi, les Plénipotentiaires susnommés ont signé la présente Convention et y ont apposé leurs cachets.

Fait en double à Mexico, le vingt-cinq septembre mil neuf cent vingt-quatre.

[Signé] A. J. PANI.
[Signé] JEAN PÉRIER.

ARTÍCULO XI

Esta Convención está redactada en cada una de las lenguas española y francesa, quedando convenido que cualquiera duda sobre su interpretación será dilucidada por el texto francés.

ARTÍCULO XII

Las altas partes Contratantes ratificarán la presente Convención, de conformidad con sus respectivas Constituciones. El canje de las ratificaciones se efectuará en la ciudad de México tan pronto como fuere posible, y la Convención entrará en vigor desde el momento en que se haga el cambio de ratificaciones.

En fe de lo cual, los Plenipotenciarios respectivos firmaron la presente Convención, poniendo en ella sus sellos.

Hecha por duplicado en la ciudad de México, el día veinticinco de septiembre de mil novecientos veinticuatro.

(L. S.) A. J. PANI. Rúbrica.
(L. S.) JEAN PÉRIER. Rúbrica.

B. SUPPLEMENTARY CONVENTION OF MARCH 12, 1927 [1]

LA RÉPUBLIQUE FRANÇAISE et LES ETATS-UNIS DU MEXIQUE, considérant que la commission créée en vertu de la Convention du 25 septembre 1924, n'a pas pu terminer ses travaux

LA REPÚBLICA FRANCESA Y LOS ESTADOS UNIDOS MEXICANOS considerando que la Comisión creada en virtud de la Convención de 25 de septiembre de 1924 no pudo terminar

[1] Text from 79 League of Nations Treaty Series, p. 424.

dans le délai fixé par ladite convention, sont tombés d'accord pour conclure la présente convention, et à cet effet, ont nommé comme plénipotentiaires :

LE PRÉSIDENT DE LA RÉPUBLIQUE FRANÇAISE :

Monsieur Jean-Baptiste PÉRIER, envoyé extraordinaire et ministre plénipotentiaire de la République française au Mexique, officier de l'ordre national de la Légion d'honneur ;

LE PRÉSIDENT DES ETATS-UNIS DU MEXIQUE :

Monsieur Aarón SÁENZ, secrétaire d'Etat aux Relations extérieures ;

Lesquels, après s'être communiqué leurs pleins pouvoirs trouvés en bonne et due forme, sont convenus des articles suivants :

ARTICLE I

La Commission, en vertu de la présente convention, entendra, examinera et résoudra, dans le délai de neuf mois à compter de sa première réunion, les réclamations qui font l'objet de la Convention du 25 septembre 1924 et qui ont été présentées conformément à ladite convention. Si, dans ce délai, la Commission ne pouvait pas terminer ses travaux, ce délai serait prorogé pour une durée n'excédant pas neuf mois, par simple échange de notes entre les Hautes Parties contractantes. La commission devra tenir sa première séance dans les deux mois qui suivront la

sus trabajos en el plazo fijado por la mencionada Convención, han convenido en celebrar la presente Convención y al efecto han nombrado como Plenipotenciarios :

EL PRESIDENTE DE LA REPÚBLICA FRANCESA :

al Señor Jean-Baptiste PÉRIER, Enviado Extraordinario y Ministro Plenipotenciario de la República Francesa en Mexico, Oficial de la Orden Nacional de la Legión de Honor.

EL PRESIDENTE DE LOS ESTADOS UNIDOS MEXICANOS :

al Señor Licenciado don Aarón SÁENZ, Secretario de Relaciones Exteriores.

Quienes, después de comunicarse sus Plenos Poderes y de hallarlos en buena y debida forma, convinieron en los artículos siguientes :

ARTÍCULO I

La Comisión en virtud de la presente Convención, oirá, examinará y resolverá en el plazo de nueve meses contados desde su primera reunión, las reclamaciones que son objeto de la Convención de 25 de septiembre de 1924 y que fueron presentadas conforme a la mencionada Convención. Si dentro de este plazo la Comisión no pudiere terminar sus trabajos, aquel sera prorogado por un lapso que no exceda de neuve meses mediante un simple cambio de notas entre las Altas Partes Contratantes. La Comisión celebrará su primera sesión dentro de los dos meses siguientes al

nomination du président de la commission.

ARTICLE II

Aussitôt après l'échange des ratifications, il sera procédé à la désignation du président de la commission. Si les Hautes Parties contractantes ne parviennent pas, dans un délai de quatre mois comptés du jour où auront été échangées lesdites ratifications, à le désigner d'un commun accord, ils prieront le président du Conseil administratif de la Cour permanente d'arbitrage de La Haye de faire lui-même ce choix. Les Hautes Parties contractantes se réservent le droit de remplacer les arbitres actuellement en fonctions en vertu de la Convention du 25 septembre 1924.

ARTICLE III

Les délais de procédure fixés par le Règlement du 23 mars 1925 seront suspendus le 14 mars 1927 et recommenceront à courir à partir de la date la première réunion de la commission.

ARTICLE IV

Toutes les dispositions de la Convention du 25 septembre 1924 et du Règlement de procédure du 23 mars 1925 qui né sont pas modifiées par les dispositions de la présente convention restent en vigueur.

ARTICLE V

La présente convention est rédigée en français et en espagnol.

nombramiento del Presidente de la Comisión.

ARTÍCULO II

Tan pronto como se haya efectuado el canje de ratificaciones, se procederá a la designación del Presidente de la Comisión. Si las Altas Partes Contratantes en un plazo de cuatro meses contados desde el día en que se haga el canje de las mencionadas ratificaciones, no llegaren de un común acuerdo a designarlo, recurrirán al Presidente del Consejo Administrativo de la Corte Permanente de Arbitraje de La Haya, para que éste haga la eleccion. Las Altas Partes Contratantes se reservan el derecho de reemplazar los árbitros actualmente en funciones en virtud de la Convención de 25 de septiembre de 1924.

ARTÍCULO III

Los plazos de procedimiento fijados por el Reglamento de 23 de marzo de 1925, quedarán suspendidos el 14 de marzo de 1927 y se reanudarán a partir de la fecha de la primera reunión de la Comisión.

ARTÍCULO IV

Todas las disposiciones de la Convención de 25 de septiembre de 1924 y de su Reglamento de 23 de marzo de 1925 que no son modificadas por las disposiciones de la presente Convención, quedan en vigor.

ARTÍCULO V

La presente Convención está redactada en cada una de las lenguas francesa y española.

ARTICLE VI

Les Hautes Parties contractantes ratifieront la présente convention conformément aux dispositions de leur constitution respective. L'échange des ratifications aura lieu à Mexico aussitôt que faire se pourra et, dès cet échange, la convention entrera en vigueur.

En foi de quoi les plénipotentiaires susnommés ont signé la présente convention et y ont apposé leurs cachets.

Fait en double à Mexico, le douze mars mil neuf cent vingt-sept.

(L. S.) JEAN PÉRIER.
(L. S.) AARÓN SÁENZ.

ARTÍCULO VI

Las Altas Partes Contratantes ratificarán la presente Convención de conformidad con las disposiciones de su Constitución respectiva. El canje de ratificaciones se efectuará en la Ciudad de México tan pronto como posible fuere y la Convención entrará en vigor desde el momento en que se haga el canje de ratificaciones.

En fe de lo cual los Plenipotenciarios respectivos firmaron la presente Convención poniendo en ella sus sellos.

Hecha por duplicado en la ciudad de México, a los doce dias del mes de marzo de mil novecientos veintisiete.

(L. S.) JEAN PÉRIER.
(L. S.) AARÓN SÁENZ.

Copie certifiée conforme :
Le Ministre plénipotentiaire,
Chef du Service du Protocole:
P. de Fouquières.

C. SUPPLEMENTARY CONVENTION OF AUGUST 2, 1930 [1]

Los Estados Unidos Mexicanos y la República Francesa considerando :

Que el plazo establecido por la Convención de 25 de septiembre de 1924 y la Convención Adicional del 12 de marzo de 1927, no fue suficiente para que la Comisión Mixta de Reclamaciones, creada por la primera de dichas Convenciones, terminara sus trabajos ;

Que el funcionamiento de esta Comisión mostró la conveniencia de expresar con más claridad algunas de las disposiciones de las convenciones ya mencionadas ; para precisar los términos según los cuales ha debido y debe fijarse la responsabilidad que el Gobierno de México ha asumido *ex gratia*, para indemnizar a los ciudadanos o compañías franceses por pérdidas que sufrieron durante la revolución en el período comprendido entre el 20 de noviembre de 1910 al a 31 de mayo de 1930, inclusive ;

[1] Text from Memoria de la Secretaría de Relaciones Exteriores, 1929–1930, p. 36.

Que en estas condiciones es posible simplificar el procedimiento y aún la composición del tribunal arbitral;

Han convenido en celebrar la presente Convención y al efecto han nombrado como sus Plenipotenciarios:

El Presidente de los Estados Unidos Mexicanos al Señor Don Genaro Estrada, Secretario de Relaciones Exteriores, y el Presidente de la República Francesa al Señor Jean Baptiste Périer, Enviado Extraordinario y Ministro Plenipotenciario de Francia en México, Comendador de la Orden Nacional Francesa de la Legión de Honor;

Quienes, después de comunicarse sus Plenos Poderes, y de hallarlos en buena y debida forma, convinieron en los artículos siguientes:

Artículo I

Una Comisión Arbitral compuesta de dos miembros designados uno por el Gobierno mexicano y otro por el Gobierno francés, terminará el estudio de todas las reclamaciones por pérdidas o daños sufridos en México por ciudadanos franceses, sociedades francesas o intereses franceses en sociedades mexicanas y que quedan enumeradas en la lista que obra anexa a la presente Convención. Esta lista comprende las reclamaciones que fueron presentadas debidamente ante la Comisión Mixta de Reclamaciones, creada por la Convención de 25 de septiembre de 1924, y que estaban pendientes de resolución al terminar los trabajos de la Comisión mencionada.

Artículo II

La Comisión tendrá su sede en la ciudad de México y se reunirá una vez efectuado el canje de ratificaciones de la presente Convención. Juzgará las reclamaciones en lista de acuerdo con los principios de la equidad, a condición, sin embargo, de que quede probado que el daño ha existido; de que se debe a una de las causas enumeradas en el Artículo III; y de que no sea la consecuencia de un acto legítimo y sea comprobado su monto.

Artículo III

La Comisión conocerá de todas las reclamaciones contenidas en la lista que obra anexa, por las pérdidas o daños resentidos por ciudadanos franceses o por sociedades, compañías o asociaciones o personas morales francesas; o las pérdidas o daños causados a los intereses de ciudadanos franceses en sociedades, compañías, asociaciones u otros grupos de intereses, siempre que en este caso, el interés del damnificado sea de más de un cincuenta por ciento del capital total de la sociedad o asociación de que forma parte, anterior a la época en que se resintió el daño o pérdida y que, además, se presente a la Comisión una cesión hecha al reclamante de la parte proporcional de la pérdida o daño que

le toquen en tal compañía o asociación. Las pérdidas o daños de que se habla en este Artículo deberán haber sido causados durante el período comprendido entre el 20 de noviembre de 1910 y el 31 de mayo de 1930, inclusive, por la fuerzas siguientes:

I. Por fuerzas de un Gobierno *de jure* o *de facto.*

II. Por fuerzas revolucionarias que hayan establecido, al triunfo de su causa, un Gobierno *de jure* o *de facto.*

III. Por fuerzas procedentes de la disolución del Ejército Federal.

IV. Por motines y levantamientos o por fuerzas insurrectas distintas de las indicadas en los párrafos 2 y 3 de este Artículo o por bandoleros, con tal de que en cada caso se pruebe que las autoridades competentes omitieron dictar medidas razonables para reprimir las insurrecciones, levantamientos, motines, o actos de bandolerismo de que se trata o para castigar a sus autores o bien que quede establecido que las autoridades mencionadas son responsables de cualquiera otra manera.

La Comisión conocerá también de las reclamaciones por pérdidas o daños causados por actos de autoridades civiles, siempre que dichos actos se originen en sucesos y trastornos revolucionarios, dentro de la época a que alude este Artículo, y que hayan sido ejecutados por alguna de las fuerzas descritas en los párrafos 1 y 2 del presente Artículo.

Entre las reclamaciones de la competencia de la Comisión no están comprendidas las originadas por fuerzas de Victoriano Huerta o por actos de su régimen.

La Comisión no será competente para conocer de reclamaciones relativas a la circulación o aceptación, voluntaria o forzosa, de papel moneda.

Artículo IV

La Comisión, y en su caso el árbitro de que se hablará más adelante, tendrán facultad para rechazar en todo o en parte cualquiera de las reclamaciones contenidas en la lista que obra anexa, si no caen bajo la competencia de la Comisión, tal como ha sido definida en el Artículo anterior.

Artículo V

Los expedientes de las reclamaciones enumeradas en la lista anexa con todos los documentos canjeados hasta el presente y comprendiendo las conclusiones de las dos Partes en cuanto al fondo, que existen en los archivos de la Secretaría de la Comisión Mixta creada por la Convención de 25 de septiembre de 1924, serán puestos a disposición de los miembros de la Comisión, tan pronto como ésta quede constituída, la que deberá estudiarlos y pronunciar el fallo respectivo en un lapso de nueve meses, a partir del canje de ratificaciones de esta Convención. En el caso de que uno de los miembros de la Comisión esté impedido de

participar activamente en los trabajos por razón de enfermedad, ausencia de la ciudad de México o cualquiera otra causa, será designado inmediatamente un suplente a pedimento del otro miembro de la Comisión, y el tiempo durante el cual los trabajos hayan estado por esa causa prácticamente interrumpidos, no será contado en el lapso de nueve meses previsto.

Artículo VI

Cada miembro de la Comisión tendrá derecho de solicitar como prueba cualquier documento relativo que obre en los archivos del Gobierno de México o del Gobierno de Francia, los que deberán suministrarlo original o en copia. Excepcionalmente la Comisión podrá solicitar y recibir cualquiera otra clase de prueba.

Artículo VII

Las decisiones dadas de común acuerdo por los dos miembros de la Comisión serán definitivas para ambos Gobiernos. Si los dos comisionados no hubieren podido ponerse de acuerdo sobre una o más reclamaciones, se proveerá por ambos Gobiernos, de común acuerdo y a pedimento de cualquiera de los comisionados, a la designación de un árbitro. Si no es posible que los dos Gobiernos lleguen a un acuerdo sobre el particular en el plazo de un mes, se procederá de la siguiente manera:

Cada Parte designará un miembro de la Corte Permanente de Arbitraje de La Haya, que no sea de su nacionalidad, y las dos personas así designadas elegirán el árbitro. En caso de que no lleguen los dos miembros de la Corte Permanente de Arbitraje de La Haya a ponerse de acuerdo para la elección del árbitro, la hará el Presidente del Consejo de Administración de la misma Corte, a solicitud de los dos Gobiernos o a la del que sea más diligente.

El árbitro no podrá ser mexicano ni francés ni nacional de un país que tenga reclamaciones contra México, semejantes a las establecidas en el Artículo III de esta Convención.

Al árbitro así designado se le entregarán los expedientes de las reclamaciones en que no hayan podido ponerse de acuerdo los comisionados y deberá pronunciar su fallo en un plazo de seis meses a partir de la recepción del expediente.

El árbitro actuará en la ciudad de México y en unión de los comisionados decidirá en cada caso.

Las sentencias pronunciadas por el árbitro serán definitivas y obligatorias para ambos Gobiernos.

Artículo VIII

Para fijar el importe de las indemnizaciones que habrán de concederse por daños a los bienes, se tendrá en cuenta el valor declarado al Fisco por los intere-

sados, salvo en casos verdaderamente excepcionales, a juicio de la Comisión
o del árbitro.

El importe de las indemnizaciones por daños personales no excederá al de
las indemnizaciones más amplias concedidas por Francia en casos semejantes.

Artículo IX

La forma en que el Gobierno mexicano pagará las indemnizaciones se fijará
por ambos Gobiernos una vez terminadas las labores de la Comisión. Los
pagos se efectuarán en oro o en moneda equivalente, y se harán al Gobierno
francés por el Gobierno mexicano.

Artículo X

Cada Gobierno pagará los honorarios de su Comisionado y los del personal
que le sea asignado. Ambos Gobiernos pagarán por mitad los gastos de la
Comisión y los honorarios correspondientes al árbitro.

Artículo XI

Las Altas Partes Contratantes convienen en dar pleno efecto a las decisiones,
tanto de los comisionados, dadas por unanimidad, como a las dictadas por el
árbitro. Convienen también en considerar las decisiones de la Comisión y del
árbitro, así como las pronunciadas por la Comisión Mixta creada por la Convención de 25 de septiembre de 1924, como un arreglo pleno, perfecto y definitivo de todas las reclamaciones que contra el Gobierno de México provengan de
daños causados por la revolución en el período comprendido del 20 de noviembre
de 1910 al 31 de mayo de 1920. Convienen, además, en que desde el momento
en que terminen los trabajos de la Comisión y del árbitro, toda reclamación
de esa especie, inscrita o no en la lista anexa, habrá de considerarse como
arreglada absoluta e irrevocablemente para lo sucesivo, a condición de que, las
que figuran en la lista hayan sido examinadas y resueltas por la Comisión o el
árbitro.

Artículo XII

Las Altas Partes Contratantes ratificarán la presente Convención, de conformidad con sus respectivas Constituciones. El canje de las ratificaciones se
efecturán en la ciudad de México tan pronto como fuere posible, y la Convención entrará en vigor desde el momento en que se haga el cambio de ratificaciones.

En fe de lo cual, los Plenipotenciarios respectivos firmaron la presente Convención, poniendo en ella sus sellos.

Hecho en dos originales en las lenguas española y francesa, que hacen igualmente fe, en México, a los dos días del mes de agosto de mil novecientos treinta.

Firmado: G. Estrada.

Firmado: Jean Périer.

Lista de las reclamaciones en tramitación a que se refieren los Artículos I, III
y IV de esta Convención

a) Reclamaciones consideradas admisibles por lo que se refiere a la nacionalidad por sentencia de la Comisión:

N.º 11.   Bourillon, Jacques & Cie. — Sentencia 2-A.

N.º 109.   Lombard Hermanos. — Sentencia 3-A.

N.º 181 a 183.   Cía. Azucarera de Paraíso Novillero, S. A. — Sentencia 4-A.

N.º 72.   Allegre & Cía. (Albert Allegre.) — Sentencia 5-A.

N.º 175.   Audiffred Hermanos y Cía. — Sentencia 16-A.

N.º 129.   Barry & Cie. (León Barry y Cía.) — Sentencia 7-A.

N.º 173.   Bonavit Hermanos (Viuda Bonavit.) — Sentencia 8-A.

N.º 68/69.   Chabot & Cie. (Felicien Chabot.) — Sentencia 9-A.

N.º 208.   Coblentz & Cía. — Sentencia 10-A.

N.º 228 a 230.   Etchart Hermanos. — Sentencia 11-A.

N.º 19.   Fourton & Cía. — Sentencia 12-A

N.º 20/21/22.   Garcin & Cie. — Sentencia 13-A.

N.º 242.   Giraud Margaillan & Cie.   (Henri Margaillan Reynaud.) — Sentencia 14-A.

N.º 26/27/28.   Groues & Cie. — Sentencia 15-A.

N.º 186 a 188.   Augustin Jacques & Cie. Sucs. — Sentencia 16-A.

N.º 96 a 99.   Clement Jacques & Cie. — Sentencia 17-A.

N.º 53 a 56.   Pascal Rome & Cie. — Sentencia 18-A.

N.º 116.   Philipp Proal & Beraud (Beraud y Philip.) — Sentencia 19-A.

N.º 177/178.   Pinoncelly Margaillan & Cie. — Sentencia 20-A.

N.º 60.   Reinier & Cie.   (Henri Reinier.) — Sentencia 21-A.

N.º 159.   A. Save & Cie. — Sentencia 22-A.

N.º 122 a 124.   Signoret Honnorat & Cie.   (Signoret, Allegre y Cía.) — Sentencia 23-A.

N.º 138.   Signoret & Reynaud Sucs. — Sentencia 24-A.

N.º 136.   Tardan Hermanos. — Sentencia 25-A.

N.º 140/141.   Thome & Cie. — Sentencia 26-A.

N.º 143 a 147.   Veyan Jean & Cie. — Sentencia 27-A.

N.º 2 y 3.   La Abeja, S. A. — Sentencia 28-A.

N.º 219/345.   Cía. Agrícola Francesa de Ojo de Agua Grande. — Sentencia 29-A.

N.º 198.   Pablo Nájera. — Sentencia 1-A.

b) Reclamaciones consideradas admisibles por lo que se refiere a la nacionalidad por acuerdo entre los Agentes:

N.º 225.   Obligataires du Credit Foncier Mexicain. — Acuerdo del 5 de septiembre de 1928.

N.º 37. S. & J. Jacques Sucs. — Acuerdo del 5 de septiembre de 1928.

N.º 112. May Hermanos. — Acuerdo del 5 de septiembre de 1928.

N.º 115. Pons & Cie. (Pons Hermanos.) — Acuerdo del 5 de septiembre de 1928.

N.º 63. Ricaud Hermanos. — Acuerdo del 5 de septiembre de 1928.

N.º 4. Alphand Baptistin. — Acuerdo del 5 de septiembre de 1928.

N.º 179 y 180. André Pascal. — Acuerdo del 5 de septiembre de 1928.

N.º 74 a 76. Armieux Paul. — Acuerdo del 5 de septiembre de 1928.

N.º 256. Astruc Herederos. — Acuerdo del 5 de septiembre de 1928.

N.º 184. Bartheneuf Louis. — Acuerdo del 5 de septiembre de 1928.

N.º 150. Bedian Theodore. — Acuerdo del 5 de septiembre de 1928.

N.º 32. Belescablet Michel. — Acuerdo del 5 de septiembre de 1928.

N.º 258. Bergez Lucien. — Acuerdo del 5 de septiembre de 1928.

N.º 10. Bourlon Albert. — Acuerdo del 5 de septiembre de 1928.

N.º 148. Brunet Lidome. — Acuerdo del 5 de septiembre de 1928.

N.º 9. Borel Jacques. — Acuerdo del 5 de septiembre de 1928.

N.º 171. Celso y Meynet. — Acuerdo del 5 de septiembre de 1928.

N.º 190. Cornillón Dr. — Acuerdo del 5 de septiembre de 1928.

N.º 275/340. Crenier Viuda. — Acuerdo del 5 de septiembre de 1928.

N.º 164. Dorcasberro Carlos y Miguel & Juanet Jules. — Acuerdo del 5 de septiembre de 1928.

N.º 13. Dreyeus Edgard. — Acuerdo del 5 de septiembre de 1928.

N.º 226. Esclangon Viuda. — Acuerdo del 5 de septiembre de 1928.

N.º 263. Ferre Herederos. — Acuerdo del 5 de septiembre de 1928.

N.º 304. Fix Viuda de L. — Acuerdo del 5 de septiembre de 1928.

N.º 94. Garcin Herederos de Emile. — Acuerdo del 5 de septiembre de 1928.

N.º 149. Gas León. — Acuerdod el 5 de septiembre de 1928.

N.º 127–128. Gastinel Agustín. — Acuerdo del 5 de septiembre de 1928.

N.º 36. Hocquart de Turtot. — Acuerdo del 5 de septiembre de 1928.

N.º 23. Horvilleur Herederos. — Acuerdo del 5 de septiembre de 1928.

N.º 3. Lacaud Raoul. — Acuerdo del 5 de septiembre de 1928.

N.º 307. Lacour Herederos. — Acuerdo del 5 de septiembre de 1928.

N.º 309. Lenoir Maximiliano. — Acuerdo del 5 de septiembre de 1928.

N.º 41. Manuel Víctor. — Acuerdo del 5 de septiembre de 1928.

N.º 110. Manuel Isidore Herederos. — Acuerdo del 5 de septiembre de 1928.

N.º 111. Markassuza Herederos de Carlos. — Acuerdo del 5 de septiembre de 1928.

N.º 43 a 49 y 70. Maurer Herederos. — Acuerdo del 5 de septiembre de 1928.

N.º 267. Milloux Herederos. — Acuerdo del 5 de septiembre de 1928.

N.º 50. Moniet Claude. — Acuerdo del 5 de septiembre de 1928.

N.º 57. Peyrat Paul Pierre. — Acuerdo del 5 de septiembre de 1928.

N.º 246. Reynaud Vve. — Acuerdo del 5 de septiembre de 1928.

N.º 269 y 131 a 135. Ricaud Alexander Herederos. — Acuerdo del 5 de septiembre de 1928.

N.º 202. Signoret Joseph A. — Acuerdo del 5 de septiembre de 1928.

N.º 252/286. Spitalier Herederos de Aduen. — Acuerdo del 5 de septiembre de 1928.

N.º 271. Troncoso Viuda. — Acuerdo del 5 de septiembre de 1928.

N.º 247. Villemin Viuda de F. — Acuerdo del 5 de septiembre de 1928.

N.º 244/245. La Orilla Compañía de. — Acuerdo del 5 de septiembre de 1928.

N.º 237-238. Inguaran Compañía de. — Acuerdo del 5 de septiembre de 1928.

c) Reclamaciones consideradas admisibles por lo que se refiere a la nacionalidad por medio de conclusiones:

N.º 71. Albrand Esteban.

N.º 80. Audifred Víctor.

N.º 174. Vve. Bastien.

N.º 257. Heritiers Bellon.

N.º 291. Emile Bellon.

N.º 7. Beraud Henri.

N.º 151. Bernard Pedro.

N.º 294. Blanc André.

N.º 212. Boisrouvray A. de.

N.º 8. Blum Samuel.

N.º 259. Caire Heritiers.

N.º 88. Caire Gustave.

N.º 297/313. Chaurand Andre.

N.º 224/280. Dancre Roger.

N.º 14. Dibildox Louis.

N.º 90. Elissetche Lorenzo.

N.º 231/262. Estrayer Viuda.

N.º 93. Fenelon.

N.º 17/18. Feuillebais Joseph et Louis.

N.º 197. Gendrop Teófilo.

N.º 117. Ssion H. Geraud Rives.

N.º 235. Gomes Marcel Jean.

N.º 104. Hermitte Desire.

N.º 86. Hubard & Bourlon (Alfred Bourlon.)

N.º 108. Julien-Levy Marcel.

N.º 105. Lacouture Eugene.

N.º 65. Laguens Louis.

N.º 107. G. Lanneluc Sanson.

N.º 106. Lambreton Pierre.

N.º 167. Larrassiette Pierre.

N.º 278/240. Lecrit Viuda.

N.º 194. Lions Emile.

N.º 40. Malaboeuf Abbe.

N.º 203/204. Matty Viuda.

N.º 266. Maurin Casimir.

N.º 42. Meriniac Edouard.

N.º 319. Ollivier Hermanos y Cía.

N.º 155/156. Pellat Herederos.

N.º 30. Peitri Pierre.

N.º 51. Pradeau Albert Antoine.

N.º 61. Renaud Amelie.

N.º 248. Louis Reynaud.

N.º 249. Louis Reynaud.

N.º 250. Manuel Reynaud.

N.º 251. Louis Reynaud.

N.º 62. Ricaud Cyprier.

N.º 279. Saint Jean.

N.º 205. Simon Joseph.

N.º 327. Talavero Antoine.

N.º 137. Turin Herederos.

N.º 142. Veron Louis.

N.º 166. Villamil de Mansigny.

N.º 170. Villamil d'Ivry.

N.º 12. Dreyfus Frères.

N.º 161/162. Fabre Frères.

d) Reclamaciones pendientes de aceptarse por lo que se refiere a la nacionalidad :

N.º 209. Cía. Agrícola Franco Mexicana.

N.º 214/218. Durand Hermanos.

N.º 227. Esclangon & Cie.

N.º 339. Loubet Alexandre.

N.º 58. Peyri Louis.

N.º 213. De la Torre Herederos.

N.º 191. F. Lebre Vda. de Bernal Hortence.

D. RULES OF PROCEDURE ADOPTED MARCH 23, 1925, AS AMENDED [1]

Chap. I. — Des Audiences de la Commission

Art. 1.[2] La Commission siègera á Mexico[, á moins qu'elle n'en décide autrement]. Elle fixera [la date de ses sessions et] la date et le lieu de ses audiences.

Chap. II. — Des Registres et Procès-verbaux

Art. 2. Il sera tenu deux registres identiques, un pour chaque Secrétaire dans sa langue respective, sur lesquels seront portés, dès la présentation d'une réclamation á la Commission, le nom du demandeur et la somme réclamée, ainsi que tous les actes de procédure auxquels cette réclamation donnera lieu.

Art. 3. Chaque réclamation constituera une cause distincte et sera enregistrée comme telle. Les réclamations seront numérotées dans l'ordre de leur présentation, la première devant porter le numéro *un*.

Art. 4. Il sera tenu deux registres identiques de procès-verbaux, un par chaque Secrétaire dans sa langue respective, sur lesquels seront transcrit tous les actes de la Commission suivant leur ordre de date. Les Commissaires et les Secrétaires signeront tous les procès-verbaux.

Art. 5. Les Secrétaires tiendront aussi les autres registres que prévoit le présent règlement ou ceux dont la Commission prescrira la tenue.

Chap. III. — De la Présentation et de l'Enregistrement des Réclamations

Art. 6. Une réclamation sera considérée comme formellement présentée à la Commission :

(*a*) par la remise aux Secrétaires d'un memorandum ou déclaration, établi en deux originaux signés par l'Agent français ou par une autre personne dûment désignée par celui-ci pour signer en ses lieu et place, et contenant le nom du demandeur, l'exposition sommaire de la réclamation et le montant de cette dernière. Toutefois, l'Agent mexicain ne sera pas tenu de repondre, et la Commission n'examinera aucune réclamation ainsi présentée par voie de memorandum, jusqu'à ce qu'ait été remis le mémoire prévu par le présent règlement ;

(*b*) lorsque, sans memorandum ou déclaration préliminaire, l'Agent français remettra aux Secrétaires un mémoire en deux originaux, accompagné des

---

[1] Text from Règlement de Procédure de la Commission franco-mexicaine des Reclamations (Mexico City 1925). Amendments from manuscript copy furnished by Prof. J. W. H. Verzijl. Brackets indicate matter added by amendments.
[2] Amended Oct. 19, 1928.

documents à l'appui de la réclamation, qui, en ce moment seront entre les mains dudit Agent.

Art. 7. Dès que les Secrétaires recevront le memorandum ou déclaration dont il est question au paragraphe (*a*) de l'article précédent ou le mémoire prévu au paragraphe (*b*) du même article, ils y porteront la date de sa remise, mention qui devra être signée par eux ; ensuite ils enregistreront la réclamation sous le numéro qui lui revient.

Art. 8. Toutes les réclamations devront être présentées à la Commission dans la forme prescrite au paragraphe (*a*) ou au paragraphe (*b*) de l'article 6, avant le 14 décembre 1925, sauf dans les cas où la Commission jugera satisfaisante les raisons invoquées pour justifier un retard ; dans ces cas, la Commission pourra proroger de trois mois au plus le délai fixé ci-dessus.

Art. 9. En tout temps après le 14 décembre 1925, la Commission fixera, sur la réquisition de l'Agent mexicain, un délai pour la remise des mémoires relatifs aux réclamations déjà présentées en la forme prévue au paragraphe (*a*) de l'article 6.

CHAP. IV. — DES PIÈCES FONDAMENTALES

Art. 10. Les pièces fondamentales seront le mémoire, le contremémoire, les pièces relatives aux exceptions, la réplique et la duplique, si les Agents désire présenter ces dernières, les modifications à ces diverses pièces, et les conclusions. D'autre pièces pourront cependant être présentées, si les Agents en conviennent, ou si la Commission en décide ainsi. Chaque partie aura le droit de répondre sur faits nouveaux.

DU MÉMOIRE

Art. 11. Le mémoire devra être signé par le demandeur ou par son mandataire et par l'Agent français. Il contiendra une relation claire et concise des faits sur lesquels la réclamation est fondée, et l'exposition, aussi détaillée, sauf, en cas d'omission de l'un d'entre eux, à donner les motifs de cette omission :

(*a*) la nationalité en raison de laquelle le demandeur s'estime en droit de se prévaloir personnellement des dispositions de la Convention. Si, dans la série des titres invoqués à propos d'une réclamation donnée, il se trouve des droits ou intérêts appartenant à une personne ou compagnie de nationalité distincte de celle du demandeur, il y aura lieu d'exposer complètement les faits concernant ces droits ou intérêts ;

(*b*) si le demandeur invoque, comme fondement de sa réclamation, la perte ou les dommages subis par une société, compagnie, association ou autre groupe d'intérêts, dans lesquels lui ou la personne au nom de qui le réclamation est présentée, a ou a eu un intérêt supérieur à cinquante pour cent du capital de ladite société ou association ; le mémoire devra indiquer la nature et l'impor-

tance de cet intérêt ainsi que tous faits et considérations relatifs á cette réclamation ou l'appuyant;

(c) les faits prouvant que la perte ou les dommages, fondement de la réclamation, procèdent de l'une ou de plusieurs des causes définies à l'article III
de la Convention conclue entre la République française et les Etats-Unis du
Mexique le 25 septembre 1924 et entrée en vigeur par l'échange des ratifications le 29 décembre 1924, et que la perte ou les dommages en questions sont
survenus au cours de la période comprise entre le 20 novembre 1910 et le 31 mai
1920 inclus;

(d) le montant de la réclamation, la date et le lieu où se sont produits les
faits sur lesquels elle se fonde; la nature, l'importance et la valeur de la
propriété perdue ou endommagée, exposées de façon aussi détaillée que possible; les dommages qui en resultent; les faits et autres circonstances con-
comitants des dommages à la personne ou bien de la perte de ou des dommages
à la propriété.

(e) par qui et au nom de qui la réclamation est présentée, et, si la personne
qui la présente agit à titre de mandataire, la preuve de sa qualité;

(f) si le demandeur, ou bien toute autre personne qui, à un moment donné,
a eu droit à la somme réclamée ou à une part de celle-ci, a reçu une somme
d'argent ou une compensation équivalente, et, dans l'affirmative, quelle somme
ou quelle compensation, quelle qu'en ait été la forme; et s'il en est ainsi, quand
et de qui cette somme ou compensation a été reçue;

(g) si la réclamation a été déjà présentée, ou si une requête y relative a été
déjà présentée au Gouvernement Mexicain ou à l'un de ses fonctionnaires,
ayant agi, l'un ou l'autre, *de jure* ou *de facto*, ou bien au Gouvernement de la
République Française ou à l'un de ses fonctionnaires, et, dans l'affirmative,
tout ce qui concerne cette présentation.

Art. 12. Les réclamations présentées au nom d'une personne décédée, soit
pour dommages à la personne, soit pour perte de ou dommages à la propriété,
devront être présentées par celui ou ceux qui ont qualité pour représenter la
succession et le mémoire exposera, quant au *de cujus* et à celui qui le répresente,
les faits qui conforméments au présent règlement, seraient exigés du premier,
s'il était en vie et présentait lui-même sa réclamation à la Commission; enfin,
la réclamation sera accompagnée de la preuve que celui ou ceux qui présentent
la réclamation au nom du défunt, ont qualité pour représenter la succession.

Art. 13. Lorsque plusieurs réclamations seront fondées sur un même
ensemble de faits, elles pourront, toutes ou quelques une d'entre elles, faire
l'objet d'un seul mémoire.

Du Contre-mémoire

Art. 14. Le contre-mémoire sera remis aux Secrétaires en deux originaux,
dans les soixante jours de la remise du mémoire, à moins que ce délai n'ait été

prorogé par accord des Agents, signifié aux Secrétaires, ou par décision de la Commission, sur conclusions dûment signifiées.

Le contre-mémoire répondra précisement et clairement à chacun des points du mémoire. Il pourra, en outre, contenir des faits nouveaux et autres moyens, à la condition que leur connaissance n'excède pas la compétence de la Commission, telle qu'elle est définie par la Convention.

Le contre-mémoire sera accompagné des documents que l'Agent mexicain jugera utile de produire à l'appui de ses assertions.

DE LA RÉPLIQUE

Art. 15. Lorsque le demandeur désirera répliquer, il remettra aux Secrétaires sa réplique, en deux originaux, dans les trente jours comptés à partir du jour où a été remis le contre-mémoire, à moins que ce délai ne soit prorogé par accord des Agents, ou par décision de la Commission, sur conclusions dûment signifiées.

La réplique sera limité à la discussion des arguments exposés dans le contre-mémoire, et aux faits nouveaux ou autres moyens contenus dans le contre-mémoire.

La réplique sera accompagné des documents que le demandeur jugera utile de produire à l'appui de sa réclamation et qu'il n'aura pas du remettre en même temps que le mémoire.

DE LA DUPLIQUE

Art. 16. Lorsque l'Agent mexicain désirera dupliquer, il remettra aux Secrétaires sa duplique, en deux originaux, dans les quinze jours comptés à partir du jour où a été remise la réplique, à moins que ce délai ne soit prorogé par accord des Agents, dûment signifié aux Secrétaires, ou par décision de la Commission, sur conclusions dûment signifiées. La duplique sera soumise aux mêmes règles que la réplique.

DES MODIFICATIONS AUX PIÈCES FONDAMENTALES

Art. 17. Les pièces fondamentales pourront être modifiées en tout état de cause avant la sentence définitive, soit par décision de la Commission, sur conclusions dûment signifiées à la partie adverse ; la décision enoncera les modifications à apporter.

Les conclusions aux fins de modifications des pièces fondamentales seront remises, en deux originaux, aux Secrétaires et indiqueront les modifications désirés et les raisons pour cela.

Les modifications aux pièces fondamentales seront accompagnées des documents jugés utiles, autres que ceux qui auront déjà été joints aux pièces fondamentales, dont la modification est demandée.

Il pourra être répondu aux pièces modifiées, en la même forme que s'il s'agissait des pièces primitives, dans le délai convenu entre les Agents, ou fixé par la Commission, si c'est cette dernière qui a autorisé la modification.

La Commission ne prendra en considération, quant à la demande ou à la défense, que les points contenus dans les pièces fondamentales ou dans les modifications a celles-ci. Toutefois, la Commission pourra, d'office et en tout état de cause avant le sentence définitive, ordonner des modifications aux pièces fondamentales, lorsqu'elle l'estimera indispensable, pour qu'il soit dûment procédé à l'examen d'une réclamation donnée, ou bien dans l'intérêt de la justice.

Chap. V. — Des Exceptions

Art. 18. Lorsque l'Agent mexicain désirera proposer une exception ou une fin de non-recevoir tendant à ce qu'une affaire ne soit pas discutée au fond, il pourra proposer le déclinatoire à cet effet, soit préalablement à toute défense relative au fond et dans le délai fixé pour la remise du contre-mémoire, soit au moment de répondre sur le fond. S'il y a plusieurs exceptions ou fins de non-recevoir de cette nature, elles seront proposées conjointement. Toute autre exception ou fin de non-recevoir sera proposée dans le contre-mémoire.

Art. 19. Si les exceptions ou fins de non-recevoir, auxquelles se rapporte l'article précédent, sont proposées par voie déclinatoire, la procédure relative au fond sera suspendue. Dans ce cas, il n'y aura pas d'autres pièces fondamentales que le mémoire, le déclinatoire et la réplique a celui-ci. Si le déclinatoire est rejeté, l'Agent mexicain sera tenu de remettre le contre-mémoire dans les trente jours de la décision de rejet.

Chap. VI. — De la Jonction et de la Séparation de Plusieurs Réclamations

Art. 20. La Commission pourra toujours ordonner la jonction ou la séparation de plusieurs réclamations. Avant de statuer, la Commission entendra les Agents dans le délai qu'elle leur aura fixé.

Chap. VII. — Des Conclusions de Rejet

Art. 21. Les conclusions tendant au rejet d'une réclamation pourront être déposées en tout état de cause avant la sentence définitive; elles devront être fondées sur un ou des motifs tirés des actes de procédure relatifs a ladite réclamation.

Art. 22. Les conclusions tendant au rejet d'une pièce fondamentale pourront être déposées en tout état de cause avant la sentence définitive; elles devront être fondées sur un ou des motifs tirés de ladite pièce fondamentale.

Art. 23. En cas d'approbation d'une partie ou de l'ensemble de ces conclusions, la Commission pourra, à sa discretion, prescrire les modifications néces-

saires, afin qu'elle puisse, dans les limites de sa compétence, statuer dûment sur chaque réclamation.

Art. 24. Toutes les conclusions seront écrites et exposeront d'une manière concise les points sur lesquels elles se fondent. Elles seront remises aux Secrétaires en la même forme que les pièces fondamentales et seront promptement soumises à l'examen de la Commission.

CHAP. VIII. — DE LA PREUVE

Art. 25. La Commission examinera les documents qui seront produits par les Agents.

Art. 26. Si un document que l'une des parties désire invoquer comme preuve, se trouve dans les archives de la République Française ou des Etats-Unis du Mexique, il conviendra, autant que possible, d'obtenir la production de l'original. Si l'original ne peut être déplacé que difficilement, une expédition pourra en tenir lieu.

Art. 27. Si une partie a l'intention de produire un document qui, se trouvant dans les archives de la République Française ou des Etats-Unis du Mexique, n'en puisse facilement être retiré, et dont elle ne possède pas copie, cette partie notifiera à l'Agent de la partie adverse son désir de prendre connaissance dudit document. Les mesures que cet Agent prendra comme suite à ladite requête, ainsi que les raisons par lesquelles il justifiera ces mesures, seront portées à la connaissance de la Commission qui, au moment de statuer, devra en tenir compte.

Art. 28. En cas d'autorisation de prendre connaissance d'un tel document, l'autorisation portera sur le document en entier, même si une partie seulement en doit être produite, mais elle ne s'étendra pas aux documents annexes, minutes et annotations qu'il pourra contenir, si ces documents, minutes et annotations ne sont pas invoquées comme preuves, ou s'il n'y est pas explicitement fait allusion dans les pièces fondamentales.

Art. 29. Chaque Agent aura le droit, en exécution d'une décision de la Commission, dûment signifiée à la partie adverse, de produire des témoins à la Commission et de les interroger sous serment devant elle ; dans ce cas, chaque témoin produit par une des parties pourra être également interrogé par l'Agent de la partie adverse ou par l'avocat de cet Agent.

Art. 30. Dans tous les cas où l'un des Agents désirera produire des témoins à la Commission, il le notifiera aux Secrétaires dans les quinze jours de la date à laquelle expire le délai prévu pour la remise de la réplique par le demandeur. Il fera connaître le nombre, les noms et les adresses des témoins qu'il désire interroger, afin que la Commission fixe le jour et le lieu où seront reçues la ou les dispositions. Il ne sera entendu aucun témoin autre que celui ou ceux dont il aura été question dans la notification prévue ci-dessus, sauf décision contraire de la Commission.

Art. 31. La Commission fixera la procédure suivant laquelle aura lieu l'audition des témoins. Les dépositions seront consignées sur les procésverbaux et il en sera remis copie à chacun des Agents.

Art. 32. Les Agents pourront établir un questionnaire conformément auquel les témoins devront être interrogés par la Commission. Dans ce cas, l'audition aura lieu après la remise de la dernière pièce fondamentale, et la Commission fixera un délai raisonnable pour la comparution du témoin, lequel sera assigné par les soins de l'Agent qui invoque son témoignage.

Art. 33. Le demandeur pourra, à la requête des Agents ou de l'un d'eux, ou bien d'office, être cité à comparaître devant la Commission ; il sera entendu suivant la procédure prévue à l'article précédent.

Art. 34. Après la remise de la dernière pièce fondamentale, et en tout état de cause avant la sentence définitive, la Commission pourra décider de prendre l'avis d'un ou de plusieurs experts sur les matières qui exigent des connaissances spéciales, et elle pourra ordonner également des descentes sur les lieux.

Art. 35. Si un témoin ou le demandeur ne peut pas comparaître devant la Commission, il pourra être entendu par l'autorité judiciaire compétente de sa résidence, sur commission rogatoire adressée à cette autorité par la voie des Agents. La déposition sera reçue suivant les formes prescrites par la loi du lieu.

CHAP. IX. — DES AUDIENCES

Art. 36. La Commission fixera l'ordre dans lequel les affaires seront portées devant elle, soit en tenant compte des accords intervenus entre les Agents, soit en décidant elle-même de son propre chef.

Art. 37. Lorsque l'Agent français sera prêt à soumettre une affaire à la Commission, il le notifiera aux Secrétaires ; il pourra en même temps, déposer des conclusions accompagnées des documents qu'il désire produire en plus de ceux qu'il aura déjà remis. Dans les vingt jours qui suivront le dépôt des conclusions, l'Agent mexicain pourra, de son côté, déposer ses conclusions accompagnées des documents qu'il désire produire, en plus de ceux qu'il aura déjà remis. Dans les dix jours, l'Agent français pourra répliquer par de nouvelles conclusions, avec preuves supplémentaires à l'appui. L'Agent mexicain pourra dans les cinq jours, répondre sur tous les faits nouveaux contenus dans les conclusions de réplique.

Art. 38.[1] La Commission entendra les Agents ou leurs avocats respectifs sur les affaires qui lui seront soumises[; mais de nouvelles preuves pourront être soumises au cours des audiences, et à dater de leur transmission, la partie adverse aura un délai de 10 jours pour présenter les conclusions qui conviendrait a ses droits]. L'Agent [de la République] Française ou son avocat ouvrira la discussion et l'Agent mexicain ou son avocat pourra répondre ; il

[1] Amended May 18, 1928.

appartiendra à la Commission d'apprécier s'il y a lieu de poursuivre les débats.

Art. 39.[1] [Quand un cas aura été soumis d'accord avec les dispositions précédentes] la procédure sera considérée comme terminée et la Commission déclarera les débats clos. Nonobstant cette décision, la Commission pourra rouvrir les débats et poursuivre l'examen de la cause[, en tenant compte de toutes les preuves et documents nouveaux qui auront été produits].

Art. 40. Les Agents pourront renoncer à assister aux audiences.

Art. 41. Les personnes étrangères à la Commission ne pourront assister aux audiences qu'avec l'assentiment du Président.

CHAP. X. — DES SENTENCES

Art. 42.[1] Les sentences seront publiques; elles seront signifiées aux Agents [par l'intermédiaire des Secrétaires].

Art. 43.[2] La sentence énoncera les motifs sur lesquels elle est fondée; elle devra être signée par les membres de la Commission qui l'approuvent. Toute membre de la Commission qui n'approuvera pas une sentence, établira et signera une déclaration de non-conformité où il [pourra exposer et motiver] la solution qui, à son avis, aurait dû être adoptée.

[*Art. 44.*[3] La Commission se réserve toute liberté pour la procédure à suivre pour la préparation et rédaction de ses sentences.]

Art. 45. Lorsque les Agents seront d'accord, soit sur un point de procédure, soit sur le fond, leur proposition conjointe sera soumise à l'homologation de la Commission, qui, toutefois restera libre de prendre telle décision qui lui paraîtra convenable.

Art. 46. La Commission pourra, d'office ou bien à la requête des Agents ou de l'un d'eux, éclaircir ou rectifier une sentence, dont le texte serait obscur, incomplet ou contradictoire, ou bien contiendrait une erreur matérielle. Si l'éclaircissement ou la rectification est requis par l'un des Agents, la requête à cet effet, laquelle devra être soumise à la Commission dans les quinze jours de la signification de la sentence, sera communiquée à l'autre Agent, qui aura quinze jours pour y répondre.

[1] Amended Oct. 19, 1928.
[2] Amended April 23, 1928.
[3] This whole article amended April 23, 1928 to read as above. As originally adopted this article was as follows:
Art. 44. Le Président désignera, pour chaque affaire, un Commissaire qui devra en faire rapport. Le Rapporteur établira une liste des points sur lesquels la Commission devra se prononcer. Ce questionnaire sera communiqué aux autres Commissaires. Si la Commission adopte unanimant l'opinion du Rapporteur, la sentence sera rédigée par lui. S'il se forme deux opinions, la sentence sera rédigée par le Rapporteur ou par l'autre Commissaire, suivant que ce sera le premier ou le second qui fera partie de la majorité. S'il se forme trois opinions, la sentence sera rédigée par le Président.

Chap. XI. — Des Langues qui Devront Être Employées et des Formes qui Devront Être Observées dans l'Etablissement des Pièces, Documents, Décisions et Sentences

Art. 47. Les pièces et documents remis par les Agents devront être rédigés en français ou en espagnol. Les pièces seront établies en deux originaux signés, accompagnés de quatre copies, et les autres documents, en un seul original signé, accompagné de quatre copies.

Art. 48. A la requête de l'un des Agents, dûment signifiée à l'autre, celui-ci sera tenu de fournir dans un délai raisonnable la traduction complète ou partielle d'une pièce ou d'un document remis par lui ; en attendant la remise de cette traduction, les délais fixés par le présent règlement seront suspendus. La Commision pourra ordonner, d'office, la traduction complète ou partielle d'une pièce ou d'un document.

Art. 49.[1] Les décisions et sentences de la Commission seront rédigées en français et en espagnol. [La Commission indiquera dans chaque sentence celui des deux textes qui fera foi. Elle se réserve la liberté de ne publier d'abord qu'un seul des textes.]

Chap. XII. — Des Significations

Art. 50. La remise par les Agents aux Secrétaires des pièces fondamentales, modifications à ces pièces, documents ou avis vaudra signification à la partie adverse et sera considérée comme l'exécution des dispositions du présent règlement à ce sujet.

Chap. XIII. — Des Obligations des Secrétaires

Art. 51. Les Secrétaires devront :

(*a*) assurer la garde de tous les documents et registres de la Commission, lesquels devront être rangés et conservés dans les armoires de sûreté. Ils devront donner toutes les facilités raisonnables aux Agents français et mexicain et à leurs avocats respectifs pour leur permettre d'examiner les documents et registre et d'en prendre des extraits ; toutefois, les documents et registres ne devront pas être retirés des archives, sauf sur décision, dûment enregistrée de la Commission ;

(*b*) tenir, respectivement en français et en espagnol, un registre sur lequel seront mentionnées, à leur date, toutes les significations faites en vertu du présent règlement, ainsi que toutes les formalités relatives et consécutives aux dites significations ;

(*c*) délivrer sans retard à la partie adverse des expéditions des pièces fondamentales, conclusions et autres documents remis par l'une des parties ;

[1] Amended April 23, 1928.

(*d*) tenir chacun, respectivement en français et en espagnol, un registre sur lequel seront transcrites les sentences et décisions de la Commission.

Chap. XIV. — De la Computation des Délais

Art. 52. Pour le calcul des delais fixés par le présent règlement, le jour à partir duquel le délai court, sera compté, mais non celui où il expire. Les dimanches et jours fériés officiels seront déduits.

Chap. XV. — Des Modifications au Réglement de Procédure

Art. 53. La Commission pourra réformer le présent règlement de procédure, après avoir entendu les Agents.

Fait à Mexico, le 23 mars 1925

R. Octavio

E. Lagarde   F. González Roa

IV. GERMAN–MEXICAN CLAIMS COMMISSION

A. CONVENTION OF MARCH 16, 1925[1]

Der Praesident der Vereinigten Staaten von Mexico einerseits und der Praesident des Deutschen Reiches andererseits, beide im Namen ihrer Laender, haben anlaesslich der freiwilligen Aufforderung die der Erstere am 14. Juli 1921 in der Absicht an die Deutsche Regierung gerichtet hat, die deutschen Reichsangehoerigen durch Geld fuer Schaeden und Verluste zu entschaedigen, die sie durch revolutionaere Handlungen, begangen in der Zeit vom 20. November 1910 bis 31. Mai 1920 einschliesslich, erlitten haben, beschlossen, ein Abkommen hierueber zu treffen. Zu diesem Zwecke haben als Bevollmaechtigte ernannt:

Der Praesident der Vereinigten Staaten von Mexico Herrn Lizentiaten Aarón Sáenz, Staatssekretaer und Leiter des Staatssekretariats der Auswaertigen Angelegenheiten.

Der Praesident des Deutschen Reiches Herrn Eugen Will, ausserordentlichen Gesandten und bevollmaechtigten Minister in Mexico. Diese sind, nachdem sie ihre Vollmachten ausgetauscht und sie in guter und gehoeriger Form befunden haben, ueber die folgenden Artikel uebereingekommen:

El Presidente de los Estados Unidos Mexicanos, de una parte, y de la otra el Presidente de la República Alemana, ambos en nombre de sus respectivos países, dando cumplimiento a la graciosa invitación que el primero hizo al Gobierno Alemán el 14 de julio de 1921 para indemnizar pecuniariamente por las pérdidas o daños que hubieren resentido los ciudadanos alemanes a causa de actos revolucionarios ejecutados durante el período comprendido entre el 20 de noviembre de 1910 y el 31 de mayo de 1920, inclusive, han decidido celebrar una Convención con tal fin y al efecto han nombrado como sus Plenipotenciarios:

El Presidente de los Estados Unidos Mexicanos al señor licenciado don Aarón Sáenz, Secretario de Estado y del Despacho de Relaciones Exteriores.

El Presidente de la República Alemana al Excelentísimo señor Eugen Will, su Enviado Extraordinario y Ministro Plenipotenciario en México.

Quienes, después de comunicarse sus Plenos Poderes, y de hallarlos en buena y debida forma, convinieron en os artículos siguientes:

[1] Text from Convención de Reclamaciones entre los Estados Unidos Mexicanos y Alemania y su Reglamento (Mexico 1926).

Artikel I

Alle im Artikel IV dieses Abkommens naeher bezeichneten Reklamationen werden einer aus drei Mitgliedern bestehenden Kommission unterbreitet, von der je ein Mitglied von dem Praesidenten der Vereinigten Staaten von Mexico und von dem Praesidenten des Deutschen Reiches und das dritte, das den Vorsitz uebernehmen soll, von den beiden Praesidenten gemeinsam ernannt wird. Im Falle, dass die beiden Praesidenten in einem Zeitraum von zwei Monaten von Tage des Austausches der Ratificationsurkunden an gerechnet zu einem solchen Uebereinkommen nicht gelangen sollten, wird der Praesident des Verwaltungsrates des staendigen Schiedsgerichtshofes im Haag den Praesidenten der Kommission bezeichnen. Das Ersuchen um diese Ernennung ist von den beiden Praesidenten an den Praesidenten des genannten Rates innerhalb Monatsfrist zu richten, nach Ablauf dieses Zeitraumes von dem daran am meisten interessierten Praesidenten. Auf alle Faelle darf der dritte Schiedsrichter weder Mexikaner noch Deutscher sein, auch kein Angehoeriger einer Nation, die gegen Mexico Reklamationen hat, wie sie Gegenstand dieses Abkommens sind.

Im Falle des Ablebens eines Mitgliedes der Kommission oder falls ein Mitglied an der Ausuebung seines Amtes verhindert sein sollte oder sich damit aus irgend einem Grunde nicht zu befassen vermag, wird es sofort ersetzt und zwar durch das gleiche

Artículo I

Todas las reclamaciones especificadas en el artículo IV de esta Convención se someterán a una Comisión compuesta de tres miembros : uno de ellos será nombrado por el Presidente de los Estados Unidos Mexicanos, otro por el Presidente de la República Alemana, y el tercero, que presidirá la Comisión, será designado de acuerdo por los dos Presidentes. Si éstos no llegan a dicho acuerdo, en un plazo de dos meses contados desde el día en que se haga el canje de las ratificaciones, el Presidente del Consejo Administrativo Permanente de la Corte Permanente de Arbitraje de La Haya, será quien designe al Presidente de la Comisión. La solicitud de este nombramiento se dirigirá por ambos Presidentes al Presidente del citado Consejo, dentro de un plazo de un mes, pasado este plazo, por el Presidente más diligente. En todo caso, el tercer árbitro no podrá ser mexicano ni alemán, ni ciudadano de nación que tenga contra México reclamaciones iguales a las que son objeto de este Convención.

En caso de muerte de alguno de los miembros de la Comisión, o en caso de que alguno de ellos esté impedido para cumplir sus funciones o se abstenga por cualquier causa de hacerlo, será reemplazado inmediatamente, siguiendo el mismo proce-

Verfahren durch das seine Ernennung erfolgt ist.

dimiento que se haya empleado para nombrarlo.

ARTIKEL II

Die so bestellten Kommissionsmitglieder werden in der Stadt Mexico innerhalb von vier Monaten nach Austausch der Ratifikationsurkunden des vorliegenden Abkommens zusammentreten. Jedes Kommissionsmitglied wird vor Beginn seiner Arbeiten eine feierliche Erklaerung abgeben und unterzeichnen, in der es sich verpflichtet, alle vorgelegten Reklamationen mit Sorgfalt zu pruefen und mit Unparteilichkeit nach den Grundsaetzen der Billigkeit zu entscheiden, angesichts des Umstandes, dass Mexico willens ist, den Geschaedigten den Schaden freiwillig zu ersetzen, und nicht etwa deswegen, weil seine Verpflichtung aus den Bestimmungen des Artikels XVIII des in Kraft befindlichen Freundschafts, Handels, und Schiffahrtsvertrags zwischen den Vereinigten Staaten von Mexico und dem Deutschen Reich hergeleitet werden koennte. Es genuegt daher nachzuweisen, dass der behauptete Schaden entstanden ist und sich auf eine der in Artikel IV dieses Abkommens aufgefuehrten Ursachen zurueckfuehren laesst, damit Mexico sich "ex gratia" geneigt sieht, eine Entschaedigung zu leisten.

Die oben angefuehrte Erklaerung wird zu den Akten der Kommission genommen werden.

Die Kommission wird den Tag und den Ort ihrer weiteren Sitzungen festsetzten.

ARTÍCULO II

Los Comisionados así designados se reunirán en la ciudad de México dentro de los cuatro meses contados a partir de la fecha del canje de ratificaciones de la presente Convención. Cada uno de los miembros de la Comisión, antes de dar principio a sus trabajos, hará y firmará una declaración solemne en que se comprometa a examinar con cuidado y a fallar con imparcialidad, conforme a los principios de la equidad, todas las reclamaciones presentadas supuesto que la voluntad de México es la de reparar graciosamente a los damnificados y no que su responsabilidad se establezca de conformidad con lo preceptuado en el artículo XVIII del Tratado de Amistad, Comercio y Navegación vigente, entre los Estados Unidos Mexicanos y la República Alemana; siendo bastante, por tanto, se pruebe que el daño alegado haya existido y se deba a alguna de las causas enumeradas en el artículo IV de esta Convención, para que México se sienta "ex gratia," inclinado a indemnizar.

La citada declaración se registrará en las actas de la Comisión.

La Comisión fijará la fecha y el lugar de sus sesiones ulteriores.

Artikel III

Das Deutsche Reich erkennt das Entgegenkommen an, das die Vereinigten Staaten von Mexico zeigen, indem sie zugeben, dass ihre Verantwortlichkeit, ausschliesslich fuer die Zwecke dieses Abkommens, gemaess den Grundsaetzen der Billigkeit festgestellt wird, und sich nicht auf den Artikel XVIII des zwischen den beiden Laendern bestehenden, am 5. Dezember 1882 in der Stadt Mexico unterzeichneten Freundschafts, Handels, und Schiffahrtsvertrages berufen, um diese Reklamationen abzuweisen. Das Deutsche Reich erklaert deshalb feierlich sein Einverstaendnis damit, das dieses Abkommen den genannten Vertrag weder ganz noch teilweise, weder stillschweigend noch ausdruecklich abaendert, und dass es sich verpflichtet, sich nicht auf dieses Abkommen als Praezedenzfall zu berufen.

Artikel IV

Die Kommission wird in allen Reklamationen gegen Mexico wegen Verlusten oder Schaeden erkennen, die deutsche Reichsangehoerige oder Gesellschaften, Unternehmungen, Vereinigungen oder deutsche juristische Personen erlitten haben, ebenso wegen Verlusten oder Schaeden, die deutschen Reichsangehoerigen in Gesellschaften, Vereinigungen oder anderen Interessentengruppen verursacht worden sind, vorausgesetzt, dass in diesem Fall der Anteil des Geschaedigten an dem Gesamtkapital der Gesellschaft oder Vereinigung, der er angehoert hat, vor dem Zeitpunkt, an

Artículo III

La República Alemana aprecia la graciosa actitud adoptada por los Estados Unidos Mexicanos al permitir que su responsabilidad se fije, para los efectos de esta única Convención, conforme a los principios de la equidad y al no invocar, para descartar estas reclamaciones, el artículo XVlII del Tratado de Amistad, Comercio y Navegación vigente entre los dos países, firmado el 5 de diciembre de 1882 en la ciudad de México; por lo tanto, la República Alemana solemnemente declara que reconoce que esta Convención no modifica en todo o en parte, tácita o expresamente dicho Tratado, y que se compromete a no invocar esta misma Convención como precedente.

Artículo IV

La Comisión conocerá de todas las reclamaciones contra México por las pérdidas o daños resentidos por ciudadanos alemanes y por sociedades, compañías, asociaciones o personas morales alemanas; o por pérdidas o daños causados a ciudadanos alemanes, en sociedades, asociaciones u otros grupos de intereses, siempre que, en este caso, el interés del damnificado sea de más de un cincuenta por ciento del capital total de la sociedad o asociación de que forma parte, anterior a la época en que se resintió el daño o pérdida, y que además se presente a la Comisión una cesión hecha al recla-

dem der Schaden oder Verlust erlitten wurde, mehr als 50% betragen hat und dass ausserdem der Kommission die Urkunde ueber die Abtretung des dem Reklamanten zustehenden verhaeltnismaessigen Anteils des Verlustes oder Schadens, der ihn als Mitglied einer derartigen Gesellschaft oder Vereinigung trifft, vorgelegt wird. Die Verluste oder Schaeden, von denen dieser Artikel handelt, muessen in der Zeit vom 20. November 1910 bis zum 31. Mai 1920 einschliesslich von folgenden Streitkraeften verursacht worden sein:

1. von Streitkraeften einer Regierung, die *de jure* oder *de facto* bestanden hat,

2. von revolutionaeren Streitkraeften, die beim Siege ihrer Sache eine Regierung *de jure* oder *de facto* eingesetzt haben, oder von den gegnerischen revolutionaeren Streitkraeften,

3. von Streitkraeften, die von den im vorigen Absatz genannten Truppen abgesprengt worden sind, bis zu dem Augenblick, an dem die Regierung, nach einer entschiedenen Revolution, *de jure* eingesetzt worden ist,

4. von versprengten Streitkraeften des Bundesheeres,

5. durch Aufstaende oder Erhebungen oder von anderen als den in den Absaetzen 2, 3 und 4 dieses Artikels angegebenen aufstaendischen Streitkraeften oder von Raeuberbanden und zwar, wenn in jedem Fall nachgewiesen werden kann, dass die zustaendigen Behoerden es unterlassen haben, die erforderlich erscheinenden Massnahmen zu treffen, um derartige Aufstaende, Erhebungen, Meutereien

mante de la parte proporcional de la pérdida o daño que le toque en tal compañía o asociación. Las pérdidas o daños de que se habla en este artículo deberán haber sido causados durante el período comprendido entre el 20 de noviembre de 1910 y el 31 de mayo de 1920, inclusive, por las fuerzas siguientes:

1.º Por fuerzas de un Gobierno *de jure* o *de facto;*

2.º Por fuerzas revolucionarias que hayan establecido al triunfo de su causa Gobierno *de jure* o *de facto*, o por fuerzas revolucionarias contrarias a aquéllas;

3.º Por fuerzas procedentes de la disgregación de las que se mencionan en el párrafo precedente, hasta el momento en que el Gobierno *de jure* hubiere sido establecido después de una revolución determinada;

4.º Por fuerzas procedentes de la disolución del Ejército Federal;

5.º Por motines o levantamientos, o por fuerzas insurrectas distintas de las indicadas en los párrafos 2º, 3º y 4º de este artículo, o por bandoleros, con tal que, en cada caso, se pruebe que las autoridades competentes omitieron dictar medidas razonables para reprimir las insurrecciones, levantamientos, motines, o actos de bandolerismo de que se trata, o para castigar a sus actores; o que se pruebe,

oder raeuberische Handlungen zu unterdruecken oder die Urheber zu bestrafen oder, falls nachgewiesen wird, dass den Behoerden irgend eine andere Unterlassung zur Last faellt.

Die Kommission wird ebenfalls in den Reklamationen wegen Verlusten oder Schaeden erkennen, die durch Handlungen von Zivilbehoerden verursacht worden sind, jedoch nur, falls sie auf revolutionaere Ereignisse und Stoerungen zurueckzufuehren sind, die in den Zeitraum fallen, der in diesem Artikel vorgesehen ist, und falls sie einer der in den Absaetzen 1, 2 und 3 des vorstehenden Artikels genannten Streitkraefte zur Last gelegt werden koennen.

asimismo, que las autoridades incurrieron en falta de alguna otra manera.

La Comisión conocerá también de las reclamaciones por pérdidas o daños causados por actos de autoridades civiles, siempre que dichos actos se originen en sucesos y trastornos revolucionarios, dentro de la épcca a que alude este artículo y que hayan sido ejecutadas por alguna de las fuerzas descritas en los párrafos 1º, 2º y 3º del presente artículo.

Artikel V

Die Kommission wird sich innerhalb der Bestimmungen dieses Abkommens ihre eigne Geschaeftsordnung geben.

Jede Regierung kann einen Vertreter sowie Berater ernennen, die der Kommission, sei es muendlich oder schriftlich, die Beweismittel und Tatsachen unterbreiten koennen, die sie zur Unterstuetzung der Reklamationen oder dagegen vorzubringen fuer zweckmaessig halten.

Die Kommission entscheidet mit Stimmenmehrheit. Bei Stimmengleichheit gibt der Praesident den Ausschlag.

Sowohl bei den Verhandlungen als auch bei den Entscheidungen wird die spanische oder englische Sprache angewandt.

Artículo V

La Comisión decretará sus propios procedimientos, pero ciñéndose a las disposiciones de la presente Convención.

Cada Gobierno podrá nombrar un Agente y Consejeros que presenten a la Comisión, ya sea oralmente o por escrito, las pruebas y argumentos que juzguen conveniente aducir en apoyo de las reclamaciones o en contra de ellas.

La decisión de la mayoría de los miembros de la Comisión, será la de la Comisión. Si no hubiere mayoría prevalecerá la decisión del Presidente.

Tanto en los procedimientos como en los fallos, se empleará el español o el inglés.

Artikel VI

Die Kommission wird alle Reklamationen und die verschiedenen Faelle, die ihr unterbreitet werden, genau eintragen, ebenso die Niederschriften ueber die Verhandlungen mit den entsprechenden Daten.

Fuer diesen Zweck wird jede Regierung einen Sekretaer bestimmen. Die genannten Sekretaere werden der Kommission unterstehen und sind ihren Weisungen unterworfen.

Jede Regierung kann ebenfalls die ihr erforderlich erscheinenden Hilfssekretaere ernennen und anstellen. Die Kommission kann gleichfalls die Hilfskraefte bestimmen und anstellen, die sie benoetigt, um ihre Aufgaben erfuellen zu koennen.

Artikel VII

Da die Mexikanische Regierung gewillt ist, zu einer entgegenkommenden Regelung der im Artikel IV naeher bezeichneten Reklamationen zu gelangen und den Reklamanten eine gerechte Entschaedigung entsprechend den Schaeden und Verlusten, die sie erlitten haben, zu bewilligen, wird bestimmt, dass die Kommission keine Reklamation abweisen oder verwerfen darf nur aus dem Grunde, dass vor Einreichung der Reklamation noch nicht alle Rechtsmittel erschoepft sind.

Bei der Feststellung der Summe, die fuer Entschaedigungen von Sachschaeden zugestanden werden sollen, wird der von den Beteiligten dem Steuerfiskus angegebene Wert zu Grunde gelegt werden, mit Ausnahme von ganz besonderen Faellen, die die

Artículo VI

La Comisión irá registrando con exactitud todas las reclamaciones y los diversos casos que le fueren sometidos, así como las actas de los debates, con sus fechas respectivas.

Para tal fin, cada Gobierno designará un Secretario. Dichos Secretarios dependerán de la Comisión y estarán sometidos a sus instrucciones.

Cada Gobierno podrá nombrar, asimismo, y emplear los Secretarios adjuntos que juzgare prudente. La Comisión podrá nombrar y emplear, igualmente, los ayudantes que juzgue necesarios para llevar a cabo su misión.

Artículo VII

Deseando el Gobierno de México llegar a un arreglo gracioso sobre las reclamaciones especificadas en el artículo IV, y conceder a los reclamantes una indemnización justa que corresponda a las pérdidas y daños que hayan sufrido, queda convenido que la Comisión no habrá de descartar o rechazar ninguna reclamación por causa de que no se hubiere agotado, antes de presentar dicha reclamación, todos los recursos legales.

Para fijar el importe de las indemnizaciones que habrán de concederse por daños a los bienes, se tendrá en cuenta el valor declarado al Fisco por los interesados, salvo en casos verdaderamente excepcionales a juicio de la Comisión.

Kommission auf Grund ihres Gutachtens als solche bezeichnet.

Der Betrag der Entschaedigungen fuer persoenliche Schaeden soll die weitestgehenden Entschaedigungen, die Deutschland fuer solche Faelle bewilligt hat, nicht uebersteigen.

Artikel VIII

Jede Reklamation muss der Kommission innerhalb von 6 Monaten, von dem Zeitpunkt ihrer ersten Zusammenkunft an gerechnet, eingereicht werden, abgesehen von Ausnahmefaellen, in denen die Mehrzahl der Mitglieder der Kommission die Gruende billigen sollte, die eine Verzoegerung rechtfertigen; der Zeitraum, innerhalb dessen solche ausserordentlichen Reklamationen eingetragen werden koennen, darf die ordentliche Frist nicht um mehr als 2 Monate uebersteigen.

Die Kommission wird alle ihr eingereichten Reklamationen innerhalb eines Zeitraumes von 2 Jahren von dem Zeitpunkt ihrer ersten Zusammenkunft an gerechnet anhoeren, pruefen und entscheiden.

Drei Monate nach der ersten Zusammenkunft der Kommissions-Mitglieder und nachher alle 2 Monate wird die Kommission jeder Regierung einen Bericht unterbreiten, in dem die erledigten Arbeiten im einzelnen aufgefuehrt werden und in dem auch eine Zusammenstellung der eingereichten, verhandelten und entschiedenen Reklamationen enthalten sein soll.

Die Kommission wird ihre Entscheidung ueber jede ihr vorgelegte Reklamation innerhalb von 6 Mona-

El importe de las indemnizaciones por daños personales no excederá al de las indemnizaciones más amplias concedidas por Alemania en casos semejantes.

Artículo VIII

Toda reclamación habrá de presentarse ante la Comisión dentro del plazo de seis meses contados desde el día de su primera reunión, a menos que, en casos excepcionales, la mayoría de los miembros de la misma Comisión juzgue satisfactorias las razones que se den para justificar el retardo; el período dentro del cual podrán registrarse dichas reclamaciones excepcionales no se extenderá a más de dos meses después del término de expiración del plazo normal.

La Comisión oirá, examinará y resolverá dentro del plazo de dos años, contados desde el día de su primera reunión, todas las reclamaciones que le fueren presentadas.

Tres meses después del día de la primera reunión de los miembros de la Comisión, y luego bimestralmente, la Comisión someterá a cada uno de los Gobiernos un informe donde queden establecidos pormenorizadamente los trabajos realizados, y que comprenda también una exposición de las reclamaciones presentadas, de las oídas y de las resueltas.

La Comisión dará su fallo sobre toda reclamación que se le presente, dentro del plazo de seis meses, con-

ten geben, von dem Tage an gerechnet, an dem die Verhandlung ueber die betreffende Reklamation geschlossen ist.

Artikel IX

Die Hohen Vertragschliessenden Teile verpflichten sich, den Spruch der Kommission ueber jeden von ihr behandelten Fall als endgueltig anzusehen und ihren einzelnen Entscheidungen volle Rechtskraft zuzubilligen. Sie kommen auch dahin ueberein, dass das Ergebnis der Arbeiten der Kommission als eine vollkommene, umfassende und endgueltige Regelung aller gegen die Mexikanische Regierung geltend gemachten Reklamationen anzusehen ist, aus welchen der in dem Artikel IV des gegenwaertigen Abkommens aufgezaehlten Gruende auch immer sie entstanden sein moegen. Sie kommen schliesslich dahin ueberein, dass von dem Augenblick an, in dem die Kommission ihre Arbeiten beendigt hat, jede Reklamation der angegebenen Art, sei sie der Kommission unterbreitet oder nicht, zukuenftig fuer endgueltig und unwiderruflich erledigt anzusehen ist, jedoch unter der Voraussetzung, dass diejenigen, welche der Kommission vorgelegt wurden, von ihr auch wirklich geprueft und entschieden worden sind.

Artikel X

Die Zahlungsweise, in der die Mexikanische Regierung die Entschaedigungssumme entrichten wird, soll von beiden Regierungen festgesetzt werden, sobald die Arbeiten der Kommission beendigt sind.

tados desde la clausura de los debates relativos a dicha reclamación.

Artículo IX

Las Altas Partes Contratantes convienen en considerar como definitiva la decisión de la Comisión sobre cada uno de los asuntos que juzgue, y en dar pleno efecto a las referidas decisiones. Convienen también en considerar el resultado de los trabajos de la Comisión como un arreglo pleno, perfecto y definitivo, de todas las reclamaciones que contra el Gobierno de México, provengan de alguna de las causas enumeradas en el artículo IV de la presente Convención. Convienen además, en que desde el momento en que terminen los trabajos de la Comisión, toda reclamación de esa especie, haya o no sido presentada a dicha Comisión, habrá de considerarse como arreglada absoluta e irrevocablemente para lo sucesivo ; a condición de que, las que hubieren sido presentadas a la Comisión, hayan sido examinadas y resueltas por ella.

Artículo X

La forma en que el Gobierno Mexicano pagará las indemnizaciones se fijará por ambos Gobiernos, una vez terminadas las labores de la Comisión.

Die Zahlungen werden in Gold oder in gleichwertiger Muenze entrichtet werden und zwar an die Deutsche Regierung von der Mexikanischen Regierung.

Artikel XI

Jede Regierung bezahlt die Gehaelter ihres Kommissionsmitglieds und des dazu gehoerigen Personals.

Die allgemeinen Ausgaben der Kommission, ebenso wie das dem dritten Kommissionsmitglied zugestandene Gehalt, tragen die beiden Regierungen je zur Haelfte.

Artikel XII

Die von Deutschen Reichsangehoerigen der Nationalen Reklamations-Kommission gemaess Dekret vom 30. August 1919 und dessen Ausfuehrungsbestimmungen eingereichten Schadenersatzansprueche unterliegen folgenden Vorschriften :

I. Soweit sie entschieden und von den Reklamanten in dem gesetzlich vorgeschriebenen Zeitraum nicht angefochten worden sind, fallen sie unter den Artikel IX dieses Abkommens, und ihre Zahlung richtet sich nach den Bestimmungen des Artikels X.

II. Soweit sie entschieden, jedoch von den Reklamanten gemaess Artikel XII des erwaehnten Dekrets angefochten worden sind, werden sie in dessen Ausfuehrung der gemaess diesem Abkommen ernannten Kommission zur Bestaetigung, Abaenderung oder Aufhebung des gefaellten Spruches vorgelegt.

III. Soweit sie sich in Bearbeitung befinden und noch nicht entschieden

Artículo XI

Cada Gobierno pagará los honorarios de su Comisionado y los de su personal.

Los gastos comunes de la Comisión, lo mismo que los honorarios correspondientes al tercer Comisionado, los sufragarán por mitad ambos Gobiernos.

Artículo XII

Las reclamaciones presentadas por los ciudadanos alemanes a la Comisión Nacional de Reclamaciones de acuerdo con el decreto de 30 de agosto de 1919 y sus reglamentos, se someten a las reglas siguientes :

I. Las que hubieren sido falladas y no objetadas por los reclamantes dentro de los términos de la ley respectiva, quedan comprendidas en el artículo IX de esta Convención y su pago se regirá por lo dispuesto en el artículo X de la misma.

II. Las resueltas y objetadas por los reclamantes conforme al artículo XII del decreto mencionado, serán sometidas para los efectos del mismo decreto, a la Comisión nombrada conforme a esta Convención para la confirmación, modificación o revocación del fallo.

III. Las que se hallen en tramitación y no estén resueltas, serán some-

sind, werden sie der durch dieses Abkommen eingesetzten Kommission vorgelegt und den Bestimmungen des Abkommens unterworfen.

tidas a la Comisión que crea esta Convención y se sujetarán a los términos de la misma Convención.

Artikel XIII

Dieses Abkommen wird in spanischer und in deutscher Sprache abgefasst und es besteht Einverstaendnis darueber, dass im Zweifelsfalle bei der Auslegung der spanische Text massgebend sein soll.

Artículo XIII

Esta Convención está redactada en español y en alemán, y queda convenido que cualquier duda sobre su interpretación será dilucidada por el texto español.

Artikel XIV

Die Hohen Vertragschliessenden Teile werden das gegenwaertige Abkommen in Uebereinstimmung mit ihren Verfassungen ratifizieren. Der Austausch der Ratifikationsurkunden findet in der Stadt Mexico sobald als moeglich statt, und das Abkommen tritt mit der Veroeffentlichung des Austausches der Urkunden in Kraft.

Zu Urkund dessen haben die betreffenden Bevollmaechtigten das gegenwaertige Abkommen unterschrieben und ihre Siegel beigedrueckt.

Doppelt ausgefertigt in der Stadt Mexico am sechzehnten Maerz Eintausend neunhundert und fuenfundzwanzig.

Artículo XIV

Las Altas Partes Contratantes ratificarán la presente Convención, de conformidad con sus respectivas Constituciones. El canje de las ratificaciones se efectuará en la Ciudad de México tan pronto como fuere posible, y la Convención entrará en vigor desde el momento en que se publique el cambio de ratificaciones.

En fe de lo cual, los Plenipotenciarios respectivos firmaron la presente Convención poniendo en ella sus sellos.

Hecha por duplicado en la ciudad de México, a los dieciséis días del mes de marzo de mil novecientos veinticinco.

(L. S.) gez. Aarón Sáenz.
(L. S.) gez. Eugen Will.

(L. S.) Aarón Sáenz.
(L. S.) Eugen Will.

B. SUPPLEMENTARY CONVENTION OF DECEMBER 20, 1927 [1]

Das Deutsche Reich und die Vereinigten Staaten von Mexiko sind

El Reich Alemán y los Estados Unidos Mexicanos considerando que

[1] Text from Reichsgesetzblatt, 1928, II, p. 375.

in der Erwägung, dass die gemäss dem Abkommen vom 16. März 1925 gebildete Kommission ihre Arbeiten innerhalb des in dem genannten Abkommen festgesetzten Zeitraums nicht beendigen konnte, übereingekommen, das gegenwärtige Abkommen zu treffen, und haben zu diesem Zwecke als Bevollmächtigte ernannt:

der Deutsche Reichspräsident
den Ausserordentlichen Gesandten und Bevollmächtigten Minister in Mexiko, Herrn *Eugen Will;*
der Präsident der Vereinigten Staaten von Mexiko
den Unterstaatssekretär und Leiter des Staatssekretariats der Auswärtigen Angelegenheiten, Herrn *Genaro Estrada.*

Diese sind, nachdem sie ihre Vollmachten ausgetauscht und sie in guter und gehöriger Form befunden haben, über die folgenden Artikel übereingekommen:

Art. 1. Die Kommission wird auf Grund des gegenwärtigen Abkommens innerhalb des Zeitraums von neun Monaten, gerechnet vom 6. März 1928 an, die Reklamationen anhören, prüfen und entscheiden, welche den Gegenstand des Abkommens vom 16. März 1925 bilden und welche eingereicht worden sind in Gemässheit dieses Abkommens und in Übereinstimmung und unter den Bedingungen, die festgesetzt sind in den Artikeln VIII und XII desselben.

Art. 2. Alle Bestimmungen des Abkommens vom 16. März 1925 und der Vorschrift über das Verfahren vom 6. März 1926, insofern sie nicht

la Comisión creada en virtud de la Convención de 16 de marzo de 1925 no pudo terminar sus trabajos en el plazo fijado por la mencionada Convención, han convenido en celebrar la presente Convención y al efecto han nombrado como Plenipotenciarios:

el Presidente del Reich Alemán
al Excelentísimo señor *Eugen Will*, su Enviado Extraordinario y Ministro Plenipotenciario en México;
el Presidente de los Estados Unidos Mexicanos
al señor don *Genaro Estrada*, Subsecretario de Relaciones Exteriores, Encargado del Despacho.

Quienes, después de comunicarse sus Plenos Poderes y de hallarlos en buena y debida forma, convinieron en los artículos siguientes:

Art. 1.° La Comisión en virtud de la presente Convención, oirá, examinará y resolverá en el plazo de nueve meses contados desde el 6 de marzo de 1928, las reclamaciones que son objeto de la Convención de 16 de marzo de 1925, y que fueron presentadas conforme a la misma Convención de acuerdo y en las condiciones fijadas por los artículos VIII y XII de la misma.

Art. 2.° Todas las disposiciones de la Convención de 16 de marzo de 1925 y de su Reglamento de 6 de marzo de 1926 que no son modificadas por las

abgeändert werden durch die Vorschriften des gegenwärtigen Abkommens, bleiben in Kraft.

Art. 3. Das gegenwärtige Abkommen ist sowohl in deutscher als in spanischer Sprache abgefasst. Es besteht Einverständnis darüber, dass im Zweifelsfalle bei der Auslegung der spanische Text massgebend sein soll.

Art. 4. Die Hohen Vertragschliessenden Teile werden das gegenwärtige Abkommen in Übereinstimmung mit den Vorschriften ihrer Verfassungen ratifizieren.

Der Austausch der Ratifikationsurkunden findet in der Stadt Mexiko so bald als möglich statt, und das Abkommen tritt mit dem Zeitpunkt des Austausches der Ratifikationsurkunden in Kraft.

Zu Urkund dessen werden die beiderseitigen Bevollmächtigten das gegenwärtige Abkommen unterschreiben und ihr Siegel beidrücken.

Doppelt ausgefertigt in der Stadt Mexiko am zwanzigsten Dezember eintausendneunhundertsiebenundzwanzig.

disposiciones de la presente Convención, quedan en vigor.

Art. 3.° La presente Convención está redactada en cada una de las lenguas alemana y española, y queda convenido que cualquier duda sobre su interpretación, será dilucidada por el texto español.

Art. 4.° Las Atlas Partes Contratantes ratificarán la presente Convención de conformidad con las disposiciones de su Constitución respectiva.

El Canje de ratificaciones se efectuará en la Ciudad de México, tan pronto que fuere posible y la Convención entrará en vigor desde el momento en que se haga el Canje de Ratificaciones.

En fe de lo cual los Plenipotenciarios respectivos firmarán la presente Convención, poniendo en ella sus sellos.

Hecha por duplicado en la Ciudad de México, a los veinte días del mes de diciembre de mil novecientos veintisiete.

(Siegel)	Eugen Will
(Sello)	G. Estrada

C. SUPPLEMENTARY CONVENTION OF DECEMBER 15, 1928 [1]

Los Estados Unidos Mexicanos y el Reich Alemán, en vista de que el plazo fijado por la Convención Adicional de 20 de diciembre de 1927, en su artículo 1.°, no fue bastante a la Comisión para concluir sus trabajos, han convenido en celebrar la presente Convención y, al efecto, han nombrado como Plenipotenciarios:

[1] Text from Diario Oficial, July 23, 1929.

El Presidente de los Estados Unidos Mexicanos, al señor don Genaro Estrada, Subsecretario de Relaciones Exteriores, Encargado del Despacho.

El Presidente del Reich Alemán, al Excelentísimo Señor Eugen Will, su Enviado Extraordinario y Ministro Plenipotenciario en México.

Quienes, después de comunicarse sus Plenos Poderes y de hallarlos en buena y debida forma, convinieron en los artículos siguientes:

Art. 1.° — Se prorroga por nueve meses, contados a partir del 6 de diciembre de 1928, la Convención Adicional a la Convención de Reclamaciones celebrada entre los Estados Unidos Mexicanos y el Reich Alemán el 16 de marzo de 1925, quedando en vigor todas las disposiciones de la Convención mencionada, que no sean modificadas por la presente.

Art. 2.° La presente Convención está redactada en cada una de las lenguas española y alemana, y queda convenido que cualquiera duda sobre su interpretación, será dilucidada por el texto español.

Art. 3.° Las Altas Partes Contratantes ratificarán la presente Convención de conformidad con las disposiciones de su Constitución respectiva.

El canje de ratificaciones se efectuará en la ciudad de México, tan pronto como fuere posible, y la Convención entrará en vigor desde el momento en que se haga el Canje de Ratificaciones.

En fe de lo cual los Plenipotenciarios respectivos firmarán la presente Convención, poniendo en ella sus sellos.

Hecha por duplicado en la ciudad de México, a los quince días del mes de diciembre de mil novecientos veintiocho.

(F. S.) G. Estrada.   (F. S.) Eugen Will.

D. SUPPLEMENTARY CONVENTION OF AUGUST 14, 1929 [1]

Los Estados Unidos Mexicanos y el Reich Alemán en vista de que el plazo fijado por la Convención Adicional del 15 de diciembre de 1928, en su artículo 1.° no fue bastante a la comisión para concluir sus trabajos, han convenido en celebrar la presente Convención y al efecto, han nombrado como Plenipotenciarios:

El Presidente de los Estados Unidos Mexicanos, al señor don Genaro Estrada, Subsecretario de Relaciones Exteriores, Encargado del Despacho;

El Presidente del Reich Alemán, al Encargado de Negocios de Alemania, señor Erwin Poensgen.

Quienes, después de comunicarse sus Plenos Poderes y hallarlos en buena y debida forma, convinieron en los artículos siguientes:

[1] Text from Diario Oficial, November 9, 1929.

Art. 1.° Se prorroga por seis meses contados a partir del 6 de septiembre de 1929, la Convención Adicional a la Convención de Reclamaciones celebrada entre los Estados Unidos Mexicanos y el Reich Alemán, el 16 de marzo de 1925, quedando en vigor todas las disposiciones de la Convención mencionada que no sean modificadas por la presente.

Art. 2.° La presente Convención está redactada en cada una de las lenguas, española y alemana, y queda convenido que cualquier duda sobre su interpretación, será dilucidada por el texto español.

Art. 3.° Las Altas Partes Contratantes ratificarán la presente Convención de conformidad con las disposiciones de su Constitución respectiva.

El canje de ratificaciones se efectuará en la ciudad de México, tan pronto como fuere posible.

En fe de lo cual, los Plenipotenciarios respectivos firmarán la presente Convención, poniendo en ella sus sellos.

Hecha por duplicado en la ciudad de México, a los catorce días del mes de agosto de mil novecientos veintinueve.

(L. S.) G. Estrada.   (L. S.) Erwin Poensgen.

E. RULES OF PROCEDURE ADOPTED MARCH 6, 1926[1]

Capítulo I

AUDIENCIAS DE LA COMISIÓN

Art. 1. La Comisión tendrá su asiento en la ciudad de México, en donde se fijará y determinará tiempo y lugar de sus juntas.

Capítulo II

REGISTROS Y ACTAS

Art. 2. Se llevarán dos libros iguales de registro, uno por cada Secretario en español o en inglés y en ellos se asentará inmediatamente, al presentarse formalmente la reclamación ante la Comisión, el nombre de cada reclamante y la suma reclamada ; y, además, se registrarán en los mismos, todos los trámites que se vayan dando.

Art. 3. Cada reclamación constituirá un caso separado ante la Comisión y se registrará como tal. Se numerarán progresivamente todas las reclamaciones, empezando por la que se presente primero, que llevará el número 1.

[1] Text from Convención de Reclamaciones entre los Estados Unidos Mexicanos y Alemania y su Reglamento (Mexico 1926).

Art. 4. Se llevarán, de la misma manera, dos libros iguales de actas, uno por cada Secretario en español o en inglés, y en ellos se asentará una relación cronológica de todas las actuaciones de la Comisión. Los Comisionados y los Secretarios firmarán todas las actas.

Art. 5. Los Secretarios llevarán los registros adicionales que ordena el presente reglamento o que la Comisión disponga.

Capítulo III

Presentación y registro de las reclamaciones

Art. 6. Cualquiera reclamación se considerará como formalmente presentada ante la Comisión :

(*a*) Al presentarse a los Secretarios un memorándum o declaración en dos ejemplares firmados por el Agente de la República Alemana, o por alguna persona autorizada por él para firmar en su nombre, exponiendo, con respecto a cada reclamación contenida en dicho memorándum o declaración, el nombre del reclamante, una relación breve de la naturaleza de la reclamación, y el monto de la misma ; pero el Agente Mexicano no estará obligado a contestar, y la Comisión no considerará ninguna reclamación así presentada por memorándum, hasta que se haya presentado un Memorial sobre dicha reclamación, conforme a la dispuesto en estas Reglas ;

(*b*) Al presentarse a los Secretarios (sin memorándum o declaración preliminar) por el Agente de la República Alemana, un Memorial, en dos ejemplares, al que se acompañarán todos los documentos y demás pruebas en que se funde la reclamación, y que ya estén en poder del Agente de la República Alemana.

Art. 7. Al recibirse el memorándum o declaración a que se refiere el inciso (*a*) del artículo 6 del presente Reglamento, o el Memorial a que se refiere el inciso (*b*) del mismo artículo, se hará en él una anotación de su presentación, con la fecha de la misma, subscrita por los Secretarios e inmediatamente se registrará la reclamación con su número correspondiente.

Art. 8. Todas las reclamaciones se presentarán a la Comisión, ya sea de la manera dispuesta en el inciso (*a*), o en el inciso (*b*) del artículo 6, antes del 4 de septiembre de 1926, a no ser que en algún caso se pruebe que hubo causas que justifiquen la demora, a satisfacción de la Comisión, pues, en este caso, el período para su presentación podrá ser ampliado por la Comisión por un término que no exceda de dos meses más.

Art. 9. En cualquier momento, después del 4 de septiembre de 1926, la Comisión fijará, a moción del Agente Mexicano, un plazo para la presentación de Memoriales relativos a reclamaciones ya presentadas, de acuerdo con el inciso (*a*) del artículo 6.

Capítulo IV

ESCRITOS FUNDAMENTALES

Art. 10. Los escritos fundamentales consistirán en el Memorial, la Contestación, los relativos a excepciones, la Réplica y la Dúplica (si estos dos últimos se desearen presentar), las reformas a estos escritos y las mociones, a no ser que por convenio entre los Agentes o por acuerdo de la Comisión, puedan presentarse otros escritos. Cualquiera de las partes podrá tener el derecho de contestar sobre materias nuevas.

Art. 11. El Memorial.

El Memorial deberá estar firmado por el reclamante, o por su apoderado y también por el Agente de la República Alemana.

El Memorial contendrá una relación clara y concisa de los hechos en que se funda la reclamación. Expondrá, con el mayor detalle posible en cada caso, los informes que a continuación se requieren (y, a falta de alguno de ellos, explicará los motivos de la omisión).

(*a*) La nacionalidad en razón de la cual el reclamante se considera con derecho a invocar personalmente las disposiciones de la Convención. Cuando en algún caso apareciese que se han introducido en la serie de títulos de derecho a la reclamación, derechos o intereses de alguna persona o compañía de nacionalidad distinta de la del reclamante, entonces se tendrán que exponer en su totalidad los hechos relacionados con ese derecho o interés.

(*b*) Si el reclamante expone, como base de su reclamación, la pérdida o daño sufrido por alguna sociedad, compañía, asociación u otro grupo de intereses en el cual el reclamante o la persona a nombre de quien se hace la reclamación, tiene o tuvo un interés superior al cincuenta por ciento del capital total de la sociedad o asociación de que forma parte, entonces el Memorial expondrá la naturaleza y extensión de dicho interés, y todos los hechos o consideraciones relacionados con dicha reclamación o en apoyo de ella.

(*c*) Los hechos que demuestren que la pérdida o daño por el cual se hace la reclamación, resultó de alguna o de algunas de las causas especificadas en el artículo IV de la Convención de Reclamaciones celebrada entre los Estados Unidos Mexicanos y la República Alemana, fechada el 16 de marzo de 1925, que entró en vigor por el canje de ratificaciones de 1.º de febrero de 1926; y que dicha pérdida o daño ocurrió entre el 20 de noviembre de 1910 y el 31 de mayo de 1920, inclusive.

(*d*) El monto de la reclamación; la fecha y lugar en donde se originó; la clase o clases y cantidad y valor de la propiedad perdida o dañada, en relación pormenorizada hasta donde sea posible; las lesiones sufridas en la persona, si las hubiere habido, y las pérdidas o daños que resultaron de las mismas; los hechos y demás circunstancias concomitantes con la pérdida o daño a la persona

o a la propiedad por los que se origina la reclamación y sobre las cuales el reclamante pretenda fundarse para establecer su reclamación.

(*e*) Por quién y a nombre de quién se presenta la reclamación; y, si la persona que la presenta lo hace con carácter de representante, la comprobación de su personalidad.

(*f*) Si el derecho a la reclamación pertenece ahora, y perteneció en la fecha en que se originó, única y absolutamente al reclamante, o si alguna otra persona está o ha estado interesada en la misma o en parte alguna de ella. En este último caso quién es esa otra persona y cuál es o fué la naturaleza y la extensión de su interés; y cómo, cuándo, por qué medios y por qué compensación se hizo el traspaso de derechos e intereses entre las partes.

(*g*) Si el reclamante, o cualquiera otra persona que en cualquier tiempo haya tenido derecho a la cantidad reclamada, o a alguna parte de ella, ha recibido alguna suma de dinero; y, en caso afirmativo, qué suma, o qué equivalencia o indemnización en cualquier forma que sea, ya por el monto total o por parte del importe de la pérdida o daño en que se funde la reclamación; y, de ser así cuándo y de quién se recibió.

(*h*) Si alguna vez se ha presentado la reclamación, o si se ha depositado alguna queja respecto de la misma ante el Gobierno Mexicano, o bien ante cualquier funcionario del mismo, ya sea que haya actuado *de jure* o *de facto*, o bien ante el Gobierno de la República Alemana o ante cualquier funcionario del mismo; y, en caso de ser así, los hechos relativos a dicha presentación.

Art. 12. Las reclamaciones que se presenten en nombre de un reclamante fallecido, ya sea por daños a la persona, ya sea por pérdida de la propiedad o daño a la misma, se presentarán por el representante personal o legal de la sucesión del finado; y el Memorial expondrá, con respecto, tanto al reclamante como a dicho representante, los hechos que, conforme a este Regalmento, se le exigirían al primero si estuviese vivo y presentase su reclamación ante la Comisión; y, además, se acompañarán a la reclamación las pruebas documentales, debidamente certificadas, de la autorización de dicho representante.

Art. 13. En los casos en que varias reclamaciones se deriven de un mismo grupo de hechos, se podrán incluir todas o cualesquiera de ellas, en el mismo Memorial.

Art. 14. La Contestación.

(*a*) La Contestación se presentará a los Secretarios, en dos ejemplares, dentro de sesenta (60) días contados a partir de la fecha en que se presente el Memorial, a no ser que en cualquier caso se prorrogue el plazo por convenio entre los Agentes, notificado a los Secretarios, o por la Comisión, a moción debidamente notificada.

(*b*) La Contestación se referirá directamente a cada uno de los puntos del Memorial y manifestará claramente la actitud del Gobierno que contesta respecto a cada uno de los diversos elementos de la reclamación. Puede, además,

presentar las materias nuevas o hechos de defensa que el Gobierno que contesta desee hacer constar dentro del alcance de la Convención.

(c) La Contestación llevará anexas las copias de los documentos y pruebas en que se fundará el Gobierno que contesta a la reclamación.

Art. 15. La Réplica.

(a) Cuando en algún caso se considere necesaria una Réplica por parte del reclamante, podrá presentarse, en dos ejemplares, a los Secretarios dentro de treinta (30) días contados a partir de la fecha en que fué presentada la Contestación, a menos que se prorrogue el plazo por convenio entre los Agentes, debidamente presentado, en forma semejante, a los Secretarios, o por orden de la Comisión, a moción debidamente notificada.

(b) La Réplica, caso de presentarse, se concretará a los argumentos consignados en la Contestación, y que se refieran a hechos o a puntos que no hayan sido debidamente tratados en el Memorial, y a aquellas materias nuevas o hechos de defensa, si los hubiere, contenidos en la Contestación.

(c) A la Réplica se acompañarán copias de los documentos y de las otras pruebas en los que se haya basado el reclamante y que no hayan sido presentados con el Memorial.

Art. 16. La Dúplica.

Cuando el Agente Mexicano considere necesario duplicar, podrá hacerlo presentando dos ejemplares de la Dúplica, dentro de quince (15) días contados desde el día en que fué presentada la Réplica, a menos que por convenio entre los Agentes, debidamente presentado a los Secretarios, o por orden de la Comisión, se prorrogue el plazo, a moción debidamente notificada. La Dúplica se sujetará a las mismas reglas que la Réplica.

Art. 17. Reformas de los escritos fundamentales.

(a) Los escritos fundamentales podrán reformarse en cualquier momento antes del fallo definitivo, ya sea (1) por acuerdo entre los Agentes, presentado a los Secretarios como si se tratara de los escritos fundamentales, o (2) por permiso de la Comisión, que sólo podrá concederse mediante moción y después de la notificación a la otra parte, conforme a las condiciones que la Comisión imponga.

(b) Todas las mociones solicitando permiso para reformar los escritos fundamentales se presentarán en dos ejemplares, a los Secretarios, y contendrán las reformas que deseen hacerse y las razones en que se fundan.

(c) Las reformas a los escritos fundamentales deberán acompañarse de las copias de los documentos y pruebas que se aduzcan en su apoyo, a menos que éstos hayan sido presentados con los escritos fundamentales originales.

(d) Podrán presentarse contestaciones a los escritos de reforma, de la misma manera que cuando se trate de escritos originales, dentro del plazo que convengan los Agentes, o que se fije en los acuerdos de la Comisión que concedan la reforma, según sea el caso.

(e) La Comisión no tomará en consideración nada relativo a la reclamación o a la defensa que no esté debidamente consignado en los escritos fundamentales o en las reformas relativas a los mismos, como lo dispone este Reglamento; pero la Comisión podrá, de oficio y en cualquier fecha anterior a su fallo definitivo, ordenar que se hagan reformas a los escritos fundamentales cuando lo estime esencial para la debida consideración de cualquier reclamación o para los fines de la justicia.

Capítulo V

EXCEPCIONES

Art. 18. La excepción que oponga el Agente Mexicano para no entrar a discutir el fondo del asunto, puede ser presentada en forma de contestación especial, antes de toda defensa relativa al fondo, y en el plazo fijado para la Contestación, o al responder sobre el fondo, según elija el mismo Agente. Si hay varias excepciones de esta naturaleza, deben ser presentadas conjuntamente. Cualquiera otra excepción debe ser presentada en la Contestación.

Art. 19. Si las excepciones a que se refiere el artículo anterior son presentadas en forma de contestación especial, la tramitación por lo que se refiere al estudio del fondo de la cuestión, se suspenderá. En este caso no habrá más escritos fundamentales que el Memorial, la Excepción y su Réplica. Inmediatamente después de la audiencia, si la excepción es desechada, el demandado estará obligado a contestar el Memorial dentro del plazo de treinta (30) días.

Capítulo VI

ACUMULACIÓN O SEPARACIÓN DE AUTOS

Art. 20. La Comisión tiene siempre derecho de ordenar la acumulación o la separación de las reclamaciones. Antes de resolver, la Comisión oirá a los Agentes dentro del plazo que les fije.

Capítulo VII

MOCIONES PARA DESECHAR

Art. 21. Podrá hacerse moción para desechar una reclamación en cualquie tiempo, después de que ésta se haya registrado y antes de someterse finalmente a la Comisión, por alguna causa justificada que se demuestre en la moción y que se desprenda claramente de las constancias de los autos, ya sea por lo que atañe a la jurisdicción de la Comisión o a la naturaleza de la reclamación.

Art. 22. Puede hacerse una moción para rechazar o eliminar cualquier escrito fundamental cualquier tiempo después de haber sido presentado y antes de que sea sometida la reclamación a la Comisión, por cualquiera causa que se desprenda claramente del escrito fundamental.

Art. 23. En caso de que se apruebe una de estas mociones, la Comisión podrá, a su discreción, permitir que se hagan las reformas necesarias con el fin de que cada reclamación, dentro de la jurisdicción de la Comisión, sea resuelta.

Art. 24. Todas las mociones se harán por escrito y presentarán de manera concisa los fundamentos en que estén basadas. Serán presentadas a los Secretarios de la misma manera que los escritos fundamentales, y serán prontamente llevadas ante la Comisión para su consideración.

Capítulo VIII

PRUEBA

Art. 25. La Comisión recibirá y considerará todas las declaraciones, los documentos y demás pruebas que por escrito le sean presentadas, por conducto de los Agentes.

Art. 26. En caso de que un documento que se desee aducir como prueba se encuentre en los archivos de los Estados Unidos Mexicanos o de la República Alemana, se procurará presentar el original; y solamente cuando en los archivos haya dificultades para facilitar el original, podrá presentarse copia certificada del mismo, total o parcial.

Art. 27. Cuando un documento original que esté archivado en las oficinas de cualquier a de los dos Gobiernos, no pueda ser retirado fácilmente, ni exista copia de tal documento en la parte que desee presentarlo a la Comisión, en apoyo de los puntos contenidos en sus escritos fundamentales, entonces notificará por escrito al Agente de la parte contraria, acerca de su deseo de examinar el referido documento. Las medidas que este último tome en respuesta a la solicitud de examen, así como las razones que se señalaren para ello, serán puestas en conocimiento de la Comisión para que ésta resuelva.

Art. 28. El derecho concedido para examinar el original de tales documentos, se estenderá a todo el documento, del cual sólo una parte sea presentada; pero no se extenderá a ninguno de sus inclusos, anexos, minutas o anotaciones que contenga, si tales inclusos, anexos, minutas o anotaciones no son aducidos como prueba o explícitamente señalados en los escritos fundamentales.

Art. 29. El Agente de cualquiera de las partes, tendrá el derecho, previa la debida notificación al Agente de la parte contraria, en cumplimiento de cualquier acuerdo de la Comisión, para presentar testigos y examinarlos bajo protesta ante la Comisión; y, en tal caso, cualquier testigo presentado por una de las partes, estará sujeto a repreguntas por el Agente de la parte contraria o por el Abogado del Agente.

Art. 30. En cualquier caso en que uno de los Agentes desee presentar testigos para ser examinados ante la Comisión, dará aviso por escrito a los Secretarios dentro de quince (15) días contados desde al fecha en que expire el plazo para presentar la réplica del reclamante, manifestando el número, los nombres

y las direcciones de los testigos que desee examinar, para que la Comisión fije día y lugar en que deberá recibirse dicho testimonio oral. No se tomará ningún testimonio oral, sino de acuerdo con la notificación dada dentro del término y en la forma antes prescritos, a menos que así lo permita la Comisión.

Art. 31. El examen de testigos estará sujeto al procedimiento y a la forma que fije la Comisión. La declaración se hará constar en los autos, y se proporcionará copia de la misma al Agente de cada Gobierno.

Art. 32. Los Agentes pueden solicitar que los testigos sean examinados por la Comisión, conforme a los interrogatorios que presenten.

En tal caso, el examen se hará después del último escrito fundamental, concediéndose un plazo prudente para que el testigo comparezca, y será citado por medio del Agente que invocó su testimonio.

Art. 33. El reclamante puede ser citado a petición de los Agentes o de oficio, y se le examinará siguiéndose los mismos procedimientos a que se refiere el artículo anterior.

Art. 34. Después del último escrito fundamental y en cualquier tiempo antes del fallo, la Comisión puede ordenar que se oiga el parecer de uno o más peritos sobre materias que exijan conocimientos especiales, e igualmente puede ordenar vistas de ojos.

Art. 35. En caso de que no pudiere presentarse un testigo o un reclamante ante la Comisión, puede ser examinado por exhorto dirigido por conducto de los Agentes a la autoridad judicial competente del lugar del domicilio o de la residencia del testigo o del reclamante. La declaración será recibida con las formalidades de la ley local.

Capítulo IX

AUDIENCIAS

Art. 36. El orden en que los casos deberán llegar ante la Comisión, para su conocimiento, se determinará: (*a*) por medio de convenio entre el Agente Mexicano y el Agente Alemán, sujeto a decisión de la Comisión; o (*b*), por acuerdo de la propia Comisión.

Art. 37. Cuando el Agente de la República Alemana esté preparado para presentar un caso a la Comisión, notificará a los Secretarios; y podrá presentar juntamente con dicha notificación, un alegato, así como las pruebas documentales en que se funde, además de las que previamente haya presentado. Al presentarse el alegato, el Agente Mexicano podrá, dentro de los veinte (20) días siguientes, presentar a los Secretarios un alegato en contestación, juntamente con las pruebas escritas que desee invocar, además de las que previamente haya presentado. Dentro de diez (10) días el Agente de la República Alemana podrá replicar por medio de un nuevo alegato, acompañado de pruebas adicionales. El Agente Mexicano podrá contestar sobre cualquier materia nueva presentada en el alegato de réplica, dentro de cinco (5) días.

Art. 38. Cuando llegue el momento de someter algún caso a la Comisión, los Agentes o sus Abogados respectivos serán oídos. El Agente de la República Alemana o su Abogado, abrirá la discusión del caso, y el Agente Mexicano o su Abogado, podrá contestar, y en ese caso, cualquier discusión adicional estará sujeta al criterio de la Comisión.

Art. 39. Cuando un caso se haya sometido de acuerdo con las disposiciones anteriores, se considerarán como terminados los trámites ante la Comisión en ese caso, para lo cual la Comisión declarará cerrado el caso. No obstante este acuerdo, la Comisión podrá volver a abrir el caso para que se verifique nueva audiencia.

Art. 40. La concurrencia a las audiencias puede ser renunciada por uno o por los dos Agentes.

Art. 41. Para concurrir a las audiencias se necesita el permiso del Presidente de la Comisión cuando se trate de personas ajenas a la misma Comisión.

Capítulo X

SENTENCIAS

Art. 42. Las sentencias de la Comisión serán públicas y se notificarán a los Agentes.

Art. 43. La sentencia consignará ampliamente todos los fundamentos en que esté basada, y deberán firmarla los miembros de la Comisión que convengan en ella. Cualquier miembro de la Comisión que no esté conforme con una sentencia, hará y firmará un escrito de inconformidad, exponiendo sus razones y la resolución que a su juicio debería haberse dado.

Art. 44. El Presidente designará al Comisionado que deba estudiar cada asunto, el cual presentará un interrogatorio sobre los puntos que deban decidirse. Dicho interrogatorio será comunicado a los otros Comisionados. El autor del interrogatorio redactará la sentencia, si su opinión hubiere prevalecido, y, en caso contrario, la redactará el otro Comisionado, si su propia opinión es la que ha prevalecido.

En caso de que no hubiera mayoría, el Presidente dictará la sentencia.

Art. 45. En el caso de que los Agentes estipulen alguna solución, o el trámite de alguna reclamación, esa estipulación se presentará a la Comisión para que la confirme y dicte sentencia de conformidad con la misma, o para que acuerde lo que proceda.

Art. 46. La Comisión puede, de oficio o a petición de cualquiera de los Agentes, aclarar o rectificar una sentencia cuya parte resolutiva sea obscura, incompleta o contradictoria, o contenga un error de escritura o de cálculo. En el caso de que la aclaración se haga a petición de uno de los Agentes, la promoción será dada a conocer al otro Agente para que la conteste dentro de quince (15) días.

La petición de aclaración debe presentarse dentro de quince (15) días contados desde la notificación de la sentencia, cuando el recurso se introduzca por uno de los Agentes.

Capítulo XI

IDIOMAS Y COPIAS

Art. 47. Todos los escritos y documentos presentados por los Agentes, deberán serlo en español o en inglés. De todos los escritos se presentarán dos originales firmados y cuatro copias, y de los demás documentos el original y cuatro copias.

Art. 48. A petición de cualquiera de los Agentes, debidamente notificada al otro, este último estará obligado a presentar dentro de un plazo razonable, la traducción completa o parcial de un escrito o documento, quedando entre tanto suspenso el término que esté corriendo. La Comisión podrá ordenar la traducción completa o parcial de un escrito o documento.

Art. 49. Todas las resoluciones de la Comisión deberán ser redactadas en español o en inglés.

Capítulo XII

NOTIFICACIONES

Art. 50. La presentación a los Secretarios de cualesquiera escritos fundamentales, reformas, documentos o avisos por los Agentes, constituirá la notificación a la parte contraria y será considerada como el cumplimiento de estas Reglas con relación a cualquiera notificación requerida conforme a las mismas.

Capítulo XIII

OBLIGACIONES DE LOS SECRETARIOS

Art. 51. Los Secretarios deberán:

(*a*) Guardar todos los documentos y registros de la Comisión sistemáticamente arreglados en archiveros de seguridad. Aun cuando deben presentarse todos las facilidades que sean razonables a los Agentes Mexicano y Alemán y a sus respectivos Abogados para examinar y tomar notas de ellos, no deberá retirarse de los archivos ningún documento o registro sino por acuerdo de la Comisión debidamente anotado.

(*b*) Formar en español o en inglés, cada uno, un registro, un libro de actas y todos los demás libros y documentos que la Comisión disponga.

(*c*) Anotar en todos los escritos que se les presenten, la fecha de su presentación y hacer una relación de los mismos en el libro de registro.

(*d*) Llevar cada uno, un libro de notificaciones, en español o en inglés, en los cuales se asentarán todas las notificaciones que conforme a estas Reglas deberán

hacerse. Se asentará en dichos libros de notificaciones la fecha en que se haga cada notificación, así como todos los trámites relativos y originados en el cumplimiento de esa notificación.

(*e*) Proporcionar sin demora al Agente de la parte contraria, copias de todos los escritos fundamentales, mociones, notificaciones y otros documentos presentados a los Secretarios por los Agentes.

(*f*) Llevar cada uno un libro de registro, en el que deberán asentarse todas las sentencias y decisiones de la Comisión.

Capítulo XIV

COMPUTO DE LOS TERMINOS

Art. 52. Siempre que en estas Reglas se menciona un período de días para la ejecución de un acto, no se contará el día a partir del cual comienza a computarse el plazo, y sí se contará el último día y se excluirán los domingos y días oficialmente festivos.

Capítulo XV

REFORMAS A LAS REGLAS

Art. 53. La Comisión podrá reformar en cualquier tiempo estas Reglas, oyendo a los Agentes.

V. BRITISH–MEXICAN CLAIMS COMMISSION

A. CONVENTION OF NOVEMBER 19, 1926[1]

His Majesty the King of the United Kingdom of Great Britain and Ireland, and of the British Dominions beyond the Seas, Emperor of India and the President of the United Mexican States, desiring to adjust definitively and amicably all pecuniary claims arising from losses or damages suffered by British subjects or persons under British protection, on account of revolutionary acts which occurred during the period comprised between the 20th of November 1910 and the 31st of May 1920 inclusive, have decided to enter into a Convention for that purpose, and to this end have appointed as their Plenipotentiaries:

His Majesty the King of the United Kingdom of Great Britain and Ireland, and of the British Dominions beyond the Seas, Emperor of India:

Esmond Ovey, Esq., Companion of the Order of St. Michael and St. George, Member of the Royal Victorian Order, His Envoy Extraordinary and Minister Plenipotentiary in Mexico.

Su Majestad el Rey del Reino Unido de la Gran Bretaña e Irlanda, y de los Dominios Británicos allende los Mares, Emperador de la India, y el Presidente de los Estados Unidos Mexicanos, deseosos de arreglar definitiva y amigablement todas las reclamaciones pecuniarias motivadas por las pérdidas o daños que resintieron los súbditos o protegidos británicos, a causa de actos revolucionarios ejecutados durante el período comprendido entre el 20 de noviembre de 1910 y el 31 de mayo de 1920, inclusive, han decidido celebrar una Convención con tal fin, y al efecto han nombrado como sus Plenipotenciarios:

Su Majestad el Rey del Reino Unido de la Gran Bretaña e Irlanda y de los Dominios Británicos allende los Mares, Emperador de la India:

al señor Esmond Ovey, Compañero de la Orden de San Miguel y San Jorge, Miembro de la Real Orden Victoriana, Su Enviado Extraordinario y Ministro Plenipotenciario en México.

[1] Text from 85 League of Nations Treaty Series, p. 51.

467

The PRESIDENT OF THE UNITED MEXICAN STATES:

Señor Licenciado Don Aarón SÁENZ, Secretary of State for Foreign Relations;

Who, having communicated to each other their respective Full Powers, found to be in good and due form, have agreed upon the following articles:

ARTICLE I

All the claims specified in Article 3 of this Convention shall be submitted to a Commission composed of three members; one member shall be appointed by His Britannic Majesty; another by the President of the United Mexican States; and the third, who shall preside over the Commission, shall be designated by mutual agreement between the two Governments. If the Governments should not reach the aforesaid agreement within a period of four months counting from the date upon which the exchange of ratifications is effected, the President of the Permanent Administrative Council of the Permanent Court of Arbitration at The Hague shall designate the President of the Commission. The request for this appointment shall be addressed by both Governments to the President of the aforesaid Council, within a further period of one month, or after the lapse of that period, by the Government which may first take action in the matter. In any case the third arbitrator shall be neither British nor Mexican, nor a national of

EL PRESIDENTE DE LOS ESTADOS UNIDOS MEXICANOS:

al señor Licenciado Don Aarón SÁENZ, Secretario de Estado y del Despacho de Relaciones Exteriores.

Quienes, después de comunicarse sus respectivos Plenos Poderes, y de hallarlos en buena y debida forma, convinieron en los artículos siguientes:

ARTÍCULO I

Todas las reclamaciones especificadas en el artículo 3 de esta Convención, se someterán a una Comisión compuesta de tres miembros; uno de ellos será nombrado por Su Majestad Británica; otro por el Presidente de los Estados Unidos Mexicanos; y el tercero, que presidirá la Comisión, será designado de acuerdo por los dos Gobiernos. Si éstos no llegan a dicho acuerdo en un plazo de cuatro meses contados desde el día en que se haga el canje de las ratificaciones, el Presidente del Consejo Administrativo Permanente de la Corte Permanente de Arbitraje de La Haya, será quien designe al Presidente de la Comisión. La solicitud de este nombramiento se dirigirá por ambos Gobiernos al Presidente del citado Consejo, dentro de un nuevo plazo de un mes, o pasado este plazo, por el Gobierno más diligente. En todo caso el tercer árbitro no podrá ser ni británico ni mexicano, ni nacional de un país que tenga contra México reclamaciones iguales a las que son objeto de esta Convención.

a country which may have claims against Mexico similar to those which form the subject of this Convention.

In the case of the death of any member of the Commission, or in case a member should be prevented from performing his duties, or for any reason should abstain from performing them, he shall be immediately replaced according to the procedure set forth above.

En caso de muerte de alguno de los miembros de la Comisión, o en caso de que alguno de ellos esté impedido para cumplir sus funciones o se abstenga por cualquiera causa de hacerlo, será reemplazado inmediatamente, de acuerdo con el mismo procedimiento detallado arriba.

ARTICLE 2

The Commissioners thus designated shall meet in the City of Mexico within six months counting from the date of the exchange of ratifications of this Convention. Each member of the Commission, before entering upon his duties, shall make and subscribe a solemn declaration in which he shall undertake to examine with care, and to judge with impartiality, in accordance with the principles of justice and equity, all claims presented, since it is the desire of Mexico *ex gratia* fully to compensate the injured parties, and not that her responsibility should be established in conformity with the general principles of International Law; and it is sufficient therefore that it be established that the alleged damage actually took place, and was due to any of the causes enumerated in Article 3 of this Convention, for Mexico to feel moved *ex gratia* to afford such compensation.

The aforesaid declaration shall be entered upon the record of the proceedings of the Commissions.

ARTÍCULO 2

Los Comisionados así designados se reunirán en la ciudad de México dentro de los seis meses contados a partir de la fecha del canje de ratificaciones de esta Convención. Cada uno de los miembros de la Comisión, antes de dar principio a sus trabajos, hará y firmará una declaración solemne en que se comprometa a examinar con cuidado y a fallar con imparcialidad, conforme a los principios de la justicia y de la equidad, todas las reclamaciones presentadas, supuesto que la voluntad de México es la de reparar plenamente, *ex gratia*, a los damnificados, y no que su responsabilidad se establezca de conformidad con los principios generales del Derecho Internacional; siendo bastante, por tanto, que se pruebe que el daño alegado haya existido y se deba a alguna de las causas enumeradas en el artículo 3 de esta Convención, para que México se sienta *ex gratia*, decidido a hacer tal indemnización.

La citada declaración se registrará en las actas de la Comisión.

The Commission shall fix the date and place of their sessions.

ARTICLE 3

The Commission shall deal with all claims against Mexico for losses or damages suffered by British subjects or persons under British protection, British partnerships, companies, associations or British juridical persons or those under British protection; or for losses or damages suffered by British subjects or persons under British protection, by reason of losses or damages suffered by any partnership, company or association in which British subjects or persons under British protection have or have had an interest exceeding fifty per cent, of the total capital of such partnership, company or association, and acquired prior to the time when the damages or losses were sustained. But in view of certain special conditions in which some British concerns are placed in such societies which do not possess that nationality it is agreed that it will not be necessary that the interest above mentioned shall pertain to one single individual, but it will suffice that it pertains jointly to various British subjects, provided that the British claimant or claimants shall present to the Commission an allotment to the said claimant or claimants of the proportional part of such losses or damages pertaining to the claimant or claimants in such partnership, company or association. The losses or damages mentioned in this article must have been caused during the period included be-

La Comisión fijará la fecha y el lugar de sus sesiones.

ARTÍCULO 3

La Comisión conocerá de todas las reclamaciones contra México por las pérdidas o daños resentidos por súbditos británicos o protegidos británicos, y por sociedades, compañías, asociaciones o personas morales británicas, o sujetas a la protección británica; o por las pérdidas o daños sufridos por súbditos británicos o protegidos británicos, en virtud de pérdidas o daños sufridos por cualesquier sociedad, compañía o asociación en las que los súbditos o protegidos británicos tengan o hayan tenido un interés de más del cincuenta por ciento del capital total de la sociedad, compañía o asociación, y adquirido anteriormente a la época en que se resintió el daño o pérdida. Pero en vista de ciertas condiciones especiales en que se encuentran algunos negocios británicos en sociedades que no tienen la misma nacionalidad, se conviene en que no será necesario que el interés expresado corresponda a un solo individuo, sino que bastará que en conjunto corresponda a varios súbditos británicos, siempre que el reclamante o reclamantes británicos presenten a la Comisión una cesión hecha al mismo reclamante o reclamantes de la parte proporcional de tales pérdidas o daños que les corresponda en dicha sociedad, compañía o asociación. Las pérdidas o daños de que se habla en este artículo deberán haber sido causados durante el período comprendido entre el 20 de noviembre de 1910 y el

tween the 20th of November, 1910, and the 31st May, 1920, inclusive, by one or any of the following forces:

1. By the forces of a Government *de jure* or *de facto;*

2. By revolutionary forces, which after the triumph of their cause, have established Governments *de jure* or *de facto*, or by revolutionary forces opposed to them;

3. By forces arising from the disjunction of those mentioned in the next preceding paragraph up to the time when a *de jure* Government had been established, after a particular revolution;

4. By forces arising from the disbandment of the Federal Army;

5. By mutinies or risings or by insurrectionary forces other than those referred to under subdivisions 2, 3 and 4 of this Article, or by brigands, provided that in each case it be established that the competent authorities omitted to take reasonable measures to suppress the insurrections, risings, riots or acts of brigandage in question, or to punish those responsible for the same; or that it be established in like manner that the authorities were blamable in any other way.

The Commission shall also deal with claims for losses or damages caused by acts of civil authorities, provided such acts were due to revolutionary events and disturbed conditions within the period referred

31 de mayo de 1920, inclusive, por una o cualquiera de las fuerzas siguientes:

1. Por fuerzas de un Gobierno *de jure* o *de facto;*

2. Por fuerzas revolucionarias que hayan establecido al triunfo de su causa Gobiernos *de jure* o *de facto*, o por fuerzas revolucionarias contrarias a aquéllas;

3. Por fuerzas procedentes de la disgregación de las que se mencionan en el párrafo precedente hasta el momento en que el Gobierno *de jure* hubiere sido establecido después de una revolución determinada;

4. Por fuerzas procedentes de la disolución del Ejército Federal;

5. Por motines o levantamientos, o por fuerzas insurrectas distintas de las indicadas en los párrafos 2, 3 y 4 de este artículo, o por bandoleros, con tal de que, en cada caso, se pruebe que las autoridades competentes omitieron dictar medidas razonables para reprimir las insurrecciones, levantamientos, motines o actos de bandolerismo de que se trata o para castigar a sus autores; o que se pruebe, asimismo, que las autoridades incurrieron en falta de alguna otra manera.

La Comisión conocerá también de las reclamaciones por pérdidas o daños causados por actos de autoridades civiles, siempre que dichos actos se originen en sucesos y trastornos revolucionarios dentro de la época a que

to in this Article, and that the said acts were committed by any of the forces specified in subdivisions 1, 2 and 3 of this Article.

ARTICLE 4

The Commission shall determine their own methods of procedure, but shall not depart from the provisions of this present Convention.

Each Government may appoint an Agent and Counsel to present to the Commission either orally or in writing the evidence and arguments they may deem it desirable to adduce either in support of the claims or against them.

The Agent or Counsel of either Government may offer to the Commission any documents, interrogatories or other evidence desired in favour of or against any claim and shall have the right to examine witnesses under affirmation before the Commission, in accordance with Mexican Law and such rules of procedure as the Commission shall adopt.

The decision of the majority of the members of the Commission shall be the decision of the Commission. If there should be no majority, the decision of the President shall be final.

Either the English or Spanish languages shall be employed, both in the proceedings and in the judgments.

ARTICLE 5

The Commission shall keep an accurate and up-to-date record of all the claims and the various cases

alude este artículo y que hayan sido ejecutados por alguna de las fuerzas descritas en los párrafos 1, 2 y 3 del presente artículo.

ARTÍCULO 4

La Comisión determinará sus propios procedimientos, pero ciñéndose a las disposiciones de la presente Convención.

Cada Gobierno podrá nombrar un Agente y consejeros que presenten a la Comisión, ya sea oralmente o por escrito, las pruebas y argumentos que juzguen conveniente aducir en apoyo de las reclamaciones o en contra de ellas.

El Agente o consejeros de cualquiera de los dos Gobiernos, podrán presentar a la Comisión cualesquiera documentos, interrogatorios o cualquiera otra prueba que se desee en pro o en contra de alguna reclamación, y tendrán el derecho de examinar testigos, bajo protesta, ante la Comisión, de acuerdo con las leyes mexicanas y con las reglas de procedimiento que la Comisión adoptare.

La decisión de la mayoría de los miembros de la Comisión será la de la Comisión. Si no hubiere mayoría prevalecerá la decisión del Presidente.

Tanto en los procedimientos como en los fallos, se empleará el inglés o el español.

ARTÍCULO 5

La Comisión llevará un registro actual y exacto de todas las reclamaciones y los diversos casos que le

which shall be submitted to them, as also the minutes of the debates, with the dates thereof.

For such purpose each Government may appoint a Secretary. These Secretaries shall be attached to the Commission and shall act as joint Secretaries and shall be subject to the Commission's instructions.

Each Government may likewise appoint and employ such assistant Secretaries as they may deem advisable. The Commission may also appoint and employ the assistants they may consider necessary for carrying on their work.

ARTICLE 6

The Government of Mexico being desirous of reaching an equitable agreement in regard to the claims specified in Article 3 and of granting to the claimants just compensation for the losses or damages they may have sustained, it is agreed that the Commission shall not set aside or reject any claim on the grounds that all legal remedies have not been exhausted prior to the presentation of such claim.

In order to determine the amount of compensation to be granted for damage to property, account shall be taken of the value declared by the interested parties for fiscal purposes, except in cases which in the opinion of the Commission are really exceptional.

The amount of the compensation for personal injuries shall not exceed that of the most ample compensation granted by Great Britain in similar cases.

fueren sometidos, así como las actas de los debates, con sus fechas respectivas.

Para tal fin, cada Gobierno podrá designar un Secretario. Dichos Secretarios dependerán de la Comisión y actuarán como Secretarios conjuntos, y estarán sometidos a las instrucciones de la Comisión.

Cada Gobierno podrá nombrar, asimismo, y emplear los Secretarios adjuntos que juzgare prudente. La Comisión podrá nombrar y emplear igualmente los ayudantes que juzgue necesarios para llevar a cabo su misión.

ARTÍCULO 6

Deseando el Gobierno de México llegar a un arreglo equitativo sobre las reclamaciones especificadas en el artículo 3 y conceder a los reclamantes una indemnización justa que corresponda a las pérdidas o daños que hayan sufrido, queda convenido que la Comisión no habrá de descartar o rechazar ninguna reclamación por causa de que no se hubieren agotado, antes de presentar dicha reclamación, todos los recursos legales.

Para fijar el importe de las indemnizaciones que habrán de concederse por daños a los bienes, se tendrá en cuenta el valor declarado al fisco por los interesados, salvo en casos verdaderamente excepcionales, a juicio de la Comisión.

El importe de las indemnizaciones por daños personales no excederá al de las indemnizaciones más amplias concedidas por la Gran Bretaña en casos semejantes.

ARTICLE 7

All claims must be formally filed with the Commission within a period of nine months counting from the date of the first meeting of the Commission; but this period may be prolonged for a further six months in special and exceptional cases, and provided that it be proved to the satisfaction of the majority of the Commission that justifiable causes existed for the delay.

The Commission shall hear, examine and decide within a period of two years counting from the date of their first session, all claims which may be presented to them.

Four months after the date of the first meeting of the members of the Commission and every four months thereafter, the Commission shall submit to each of the interested Governments a report setting forth in detail the work which has been accomplished, and comprising a statement of the claims filed, claims heard and claims decided.

The Commission shall deliver judgment on every claim presented to them within a period of six months from the termination of the hearing of such claim.

ARTICLE 8

The High Contracting Parties agree to consider the decision of the Commission as final in respect of each matter on which they may deliver judgment, and to give full effect to such decisions. They likewise agree to consider the result of the labours

ARTÍCULO 7

Toda reclamación habrá de presentarse formalmente ante la Comisión dentro del plazo de nueve meses contados desde el día de la primera reunión de ella; pero este plazo podrá extenderse por seis meses más en casos especiales y excepcionales y siempre que se pruebe a juicio de la mayoría de la Comisión que hubo causas para justificar el retardo.

La Comisión oirá, examinará y resolverá dentro del plazo de dos años, contados desde el día de su primera sesión, todas las reclamaciones que le fueren presentadas.

Cuatro meses después del día de la primera reunión de los miembros de la Comisión, y luego cada cuatro meses, la Comisión someterá a cada uno de los Gobiernos interesados un informe donde queden establecidos pormenorizadamente los trabajos realizados, y que comprenda también una exposición de las reclamaciones presentadas, de las oídas y de las resueltas.

La Comisión dará su fallo sobre toda reclamación que se le presente, dentro del plazo de seis meses, contados desde la clausura de los debates relativos a dicha reclamación.

ARTÍCULO 8

Las Altas Partes Contratantes convienen en considerar como definitiva la decisión de la Comisión sobre cada uno de los asuntos que juzgue, y en dar pleno efecto a las referidas decisiones. Convienen también en considerar el resultado de los trabajos de

of the Commission as a full, perfect and final settlement of all claims against the Mexican Government arising from any of the causes set forth in Article 3 of this present Convention. They further agree that from the moment at which the labours of the Commission are concluded, all claims of that nature, whether they have been presented to the Commission or not, are to be considered as having been absolutely and irrevocably settled for the future; provided that those which have been presented to the Commission have been examined and decided by them.

ARTICLE 9

The form in which the Mexican Government shall pay the indemnities shall be determined by both Governments after the work of the Commission has been brought to a close. The payments shall be made in gold or in money of equivalent value and shall be made to the British Government by the Mexican Government.

ARTICLE 10

Each Government shall pay the emoluments of their Commissioner and those of his staff.

Each Government shall pay half of the expenses of the Commission, and of the emoluments of the third Commissioner.

ARTICLE 11

This Convention is drawn up in English and in Spanish.

---

la Comisión como un arreglo pleno, perfecto y definitivo, de todas las reclamaciones que contra el Gobierno de México provengan de alguna de las causas enumeradas en el artículo 3 de la presente Convención. Convienen, además, en que desde el momento en que terminen los trabajos de la Comisión, toda reclamación de esa especie, haya o no sido presentada a dicha Comisión, habrá de considerarse como arreglada absoluta e irrevocablemente para lo sucesivo; a condición de que, las que hubieren sido presentadas a la Comisión, hayan sido examinadas y resueltas por ella.

ARTÍCULO 9

La forma en que le Gobierno Mexicano pagará las indemnizaciones se fijará por ambos Gobiernos, una vez terminadas las labores de la Comisión. Los pagos se efectuarán en oro o en moneda equivalente, y se harán al Gobierno Británico por el Gobierno Mexicano.

ARTÍCULO 10

Cada Gobierno pagará los honorarios de su Comisionado y los de su personal.

Ambos Gobiernos pagarán por mitad los gastos de la Comisión y los honorarios correspondientes al tercer Comisionado.

ARTÍCULO 11

Esta Convención está redactada en cada una de las lenguas inglesa y española.

ARTICLE 12

The High Contracting Parties shall ratify this present Convention in conformity with their respective Constitutions. The exchange of ratifications shall take place in the City of Mexico as soon as possible and the Convention shall come into force from the date of the exchange of ratifications.

In witness whereof, the respective Plenipotentiaries have signed the present Convention, and have affixed thereto their Seals.

Done in duplicate, in the City of Mexico, on the nineteenth day of November, 1926.

ARTÍCULO 12

Las Altas Partes Contratantes ratificarán la presente Convención, de conformidad con sus respectivas Constituciones. El canje de las ratificaciones se efectuará en la ciudad de México tan pronto como fuere posible, y la Convención entrará en vigor desde el momento en que se haga el cambio de ratificaciones.

En fe de lo cual, los Plenipotenciarios respectivos firmaron la presente Convención, poniendo en ella sus sellos.

Hecha por duplicado en la ciudad de México, a los diecinueve días del mes de noviembre de 1926.

(*L. S.*)   Esmond OVEY.

(*L. S.*)   Aarón SÁENZ.

B. SUPPLEMENTARY CONVENTION OF DECEMBER 5, 1930 [1]

HIS MAJESTY THE KING OF GREAT BRITAIN, IRELAND AND THE BRITISH DOMINIONS BEYOND THE SEAS, EMPEROR OF INDIA and THE PRESIDENT OF THE UNITED MEXICAN STATES, considering on the one hand : that the Commission created by virtue of the Convention of the 19th November, 1926, could not complete its labours within the period fixed by the said Convention, and that furthermore the work of the said Commission showed the desirability of expressing with greater clarity certain of the provisiols of the said Convention in order to determine the methods by which should have been and must

SU MAJESTAD EL REY DE LA GRAN BRETAÑA, IRLANDA Y DE LOS DOMINIOS BRITÁNICOS ALLENDE LOS MARES, EMPERADOR DE LA INDIA y EL PRESIDENTE DE LOS ESTADOS MEXICANOS, considerando por una parte : que la Comisión creada en virtud de la Convención de 19 de noviembre de 1926, no pudo terminar sus trabajos en el plazo fijado por la mencionada Convención y que, además, el funcionamiento de esta Comisión mostró la conveniencia de expresar con mayor claridad algunas de las disposiciones de la Convención mencionada, para precisar los términos según los cuales ha debido y

[1] Text from 119 League of Nations Treaty Series, p. 261.

now be decided the responsibility, held by the Mexican Government to be *ex gratia*, to indemnify British subjects and British-protected persons for losses arising from revolutionary acts done during the period comprised between the 20th November, 1910, and the 31st May, 1920, inclusive, have agreed to sign the present Convention, and to that effect have named as their Plenipotentiaries:

HIS MAJESTY THE KING OF GREAT BRITAIN, IRELAND AND THE BRITISH DOMINIONS BEYOND THE SEAS, EMPEROR OF INDIA:

Mr. Edmund St. J. D. J. MONSON, His Envoy Extraordinary and Minister Plenipotentiary in Mexico;

THE PRESIDENT OF THE UNITED MEXICAN STATES:

Señor Don Genaro ESTRADA, Secretary of State and of the Department of Foreign Relations;

Who have communicated their respective full powers, and having found them in due and proper form, have agreed on the following Articles:

ARTICLE 1

The High Contracting Parties agree that the period fixed by Article 7 of the Convention of the 19th November, 1926, for the hearing, examination and decision of the claims already presented in accordance with the terms of the said Article 7, shall be extended by the present Convention for a period not exceeding nine months as from the 22nd August, 1930; this

debe fijarse la responsabilidad que el Gobierno de México estima *ex gratia* para indemnizar a los súbditos o protegidos británicos, por pérdidas a causa de actos revolucionarios ejecutados durante el período comprendido entre el 20 de noviembre de 1910 y el 31 de mayo de 1920, inclusive, han convenido en celebrar la presente Convención, y al efecto han nombrado como Plenipotenciarios:

SU MAJESTAD EL REY DE LA GRAN BRETAÑA, IRLANDA Y DE LOS DOMINIOS BRITÁNICOS ALLENDE LOS MARES, EMPERADOR DE LA INDIA:

Al señor Edmund St. J. D. J. MONSON, Su Enviado Extraordinario y Ministro Plenipotenciario en México;

EL PRESIDENTE DE LOS ESTADOS UNIDOS MEXICANOS:

Al señor don Genaro ESTRADA, Secretario de Estado y del Despacho de Relaciones Exteriores;

Quienes después de comunicarse sus respectivos Plenos Poderes, y de hallarlos en buena y debida forma, convinieron en los artículos siguientes:

ARTÍCULO 1

Las Altas Partes Contratantes convienen en que el plazo fijado por el Artículo 7 de la Convención de 19 de noviembre de 1926, para la audiencia, examen y decisión de las reclamaciones ya presentadas de acuerdo con los términos del mismo Artículo 7, por la presente se prorroga durante un plazo de nueve meses contados desde el 22 de agosto de 1930. Si dentro de

may, however, be extended for a period not exceeding nine months by a simple exchange of notes between the High Contracting Parties, should the Commission have failed to complete its labours within this period.

ARTICLE 2

Article 2 of the Convention of the 19th November, 1926, shall be amended as follows:

The Commissioners so nominated shall meet in the City of Mexico within the six months reckoned from the date of the exchange of ratifications of this Convention. Each member of the Commission, before entering upon his duties, shall make and subscribe a solemn declaration in which he shall undertake to examine with care, and to judge with impartiality, in accordance with the principles of justice and equity, all claims presented, since it is the desire of Mexico *ex gratia* fully to compensate the injured parties, and not that her responsibility should be established in conformity with the general principles of International Law; and it is sufficient therefore that it be established that the alleged damage actually took place, and was due to any of the causes enumerated in Article 3 of this Convention, that it was not the consequence of a lawful act and that its amount be proved for Mexico to feel moved *ex gratia* to afford such compensation.

The aforesaid declaration shall be entered upon the record of the proceedings of the Commission.

ARTÍCULO 2

Se modifica el Artículo 2 de la Convención de 19 de noviembre de 1926, en la siguiente forma:

Los Comisionados así designados se reunirán en la ciudad de México, dentro de los seis meses, contados a partir de la fecha del canje de ratificaciones de esta Convención. Cada uno de los miembros de la Comisión, antes de dar principio a sus trabajos, hará y firmará una declaración solemne en que se comprometa a examinar con cuidado y a fallar con imparcialidad, conforme a los principios de la justicia y de la equidad, todas las reclamaciones presentadas, supuesto que la voluntad de México es la de reparar plenamente, *ex gratia*, a los damnificados, y no que su responsabilidad se establezca de conformidad con los principios generales del Derecho Internacinal; siendo bastante, por tanto, que se pruebe que el daño alegado haya existido y se deba a alguna de las causas enumeradas en el Artículo 3 de esta Convención; de que no sea la consecuencia de un acto legítimo y sea comprobado su monto, para que México se sienta *ex gratia*, decidido a hacer tal indemnización.

La citada declaración se registrará en las actas de la Comisión.

The Commission shall fix the date and place of their sessions in Mexico.

La Comisión fijará la fecha y el lugar de sus sesiones en México.

ARTICLE 3

Article 3 of the Convention of the 19th November, 1926, shall be amended as follows:

The Commission shall deal with all claims against Mexico for losses or damages suffered by British subjects, British partnerships, companies, associations or British juridical persons; or for losses or damages suffered by British subjects, by reason of losses or damages suffered by any partnership, company or association in which British subjects have or have had an interest exceeding fifty per cent of the total capital of such partnership, company or association and acquired prior to the time when the damages or losses were sustained. But in view of certain special conditions in which some British concerns are placed in such societies which do not possess that nationality, it is agreed that it will not be necessary that the interest above mentioned shall pertain to one single individual, but it will suffice that it pertains jointly to various British subjects, provided that the British claimant or claimants shall present to the Commission an allotment to the said claimant or claimants of the proportional part of such losses or damages pertaining to the claimant or claimants in such partnership, company or association. The losses or damages mentioned in this article must have been caused during the period included between the 20th November,

ARTÍCULO 3

Se modifica el Artículo 3 de la Convención de 19 de noviembre de 1926, en la siguiente forma:

La Comisión conocerá de todas las reclamaciones contra México, por las pérdidas o daños resentidos por súbditos británicos, por sociedades compañías, asociaciones o personas morales británicas, o por las pérdidas o daños sufridos por cualquier sociedad, compañía o asociación en las que los súbditos británicos tengan o hayan tenido un interés de más del cincuenta por ciento del capital total de la sociedad, compañía o asociación, y adquirido anteriormente a la época en que se resintió el daño o pérdida. Pero en vista de ciertas condiciones especiales en que se encuentran algunos negocios británicos en sociedades que no tienen la misma nacionalidad, se conviene en que no será necesario que el interés expresado corresponda a un solo individuo, sino que bastará que en conjunto corresponda a varios súbditos británicos, siempre que el reclamante o reclamantes británicos presenten a la Comisión una cesión hecha al mismo reclamante o reclamantes, de la parte proporcional de tales pérdidas o daños que les corresponda en dicha sociedad, compañía o asociación. Las pérdidas o daños de que se habla en este Artículo, deberán haber sido causados durante el período comprendido entre el 20 de noviembre de 1910 y el 31 de mayo de 1920, inclu-

1910, and the 31st May, 1920, inclusive, by one or any of the following forces:

    1. By the forces of a Government *de jure* or *de facto;*

    2. By revolutionary forces which, after the triumph of their cause, have established a Goverment *de jure* or *de facto;*

    3. By forces arising from the disbandment of the Federal Army;

    4. By mutinies or risings or by insurrectionary forces other than those referred to under subdivisions 2 and 3 of this Article, or by brigands, provided that in each case it be established that the competent authorities omitted to take reasonable measures to suppress the insurrections, risings, riots or acts of brigandage in question, or to punish those responsible for the same; or that it be established in like manner that the said authorities were blameable in any other way.

The Commission shall also deal with claims for losses or damages caused by acts of civil authorities, provided such acts were due to revolutionary events and disturbances within the period referred to in this Article, and that the said acts were committed by any of the forces specified in subdivisions 1 and 2 of this Article.

The claims within the competence of the Commission shall not include those caused by the forces of Victoriano Huerta or by the acts of his régime.

sive, por una o cualquiera de las fuerzas siguientes:

    1. Por fuerzas de un Gobierno *de jure* o *de facto.*

    2. Por fuerzas revolucionarias, que hayan establecido, al triunfo de su causa, un Gobierno *de jure* o *de facto.*

    3. Por fuerzas procedentes de la disolución del Ejército Federal.

    4. Por motines y levantamientos o por fuerzas insurrectas distintas de las indicadas en los párrafos 2 y 3 de este Artículo o por bandoleros, con tal de que en cada caso se pruebe que las autoridades competentes omitieron dictar medidas razonables para reprimir las insurrecciones, levantamientos, motines o actos de bandolerismo de que se trata o para castigar a sus autores o bien que quede establecido que las autoridades mencionadas son responsables de cualquiera otra manera.

La Comisión conocerá también de las reclamaciones por pérdidas o daños causados por actos de autoridades civiles, siempre que dichos actos se originen en sucesos y trastornos revolucionarios, dentro de la época a que alude este Artículo, y que hayan sido ejecutados por alguna de las fuerzas descritas en los párrafos 1 y 2 del presente Artículo.

Entre las reclamaciones de la competencia de la Comisión no están comprendidas las originadas por fuerzas de Victoriano Huerta o por actos de su régimen.

The Commission shall not be competent to admit claims concerning the circulation or acceptance, voluntary or forced, of paper money.

La Comisión no será competente para conocer de reclamaciones relativas a la circulación o aceptación, voluntaria o forzosa, de papel moneda.

ARTICLE 4

The terms of procedure fixed by the said Convention and by its rules of procedure which were suspended on the 21st August, 1930, shall re-enter into force as from the date of exchange of ratifications of the present Convention.

All the provisions of the Convention of the 19th November, 1926, and its rules of procedure approved at the session of the 1st September, 1928, which are not modified by the provisions of the present Convention, remain in force.

ARTÍCULO 4

Los plazos de procedimiento fijados por la misma Convención y sus Reglas de Procedimiento, que quedaron suspendidos en 21 de agosto de 1930, se reanudan a partir del canje de ratificaciones de la presente Convención.

Todas las disposiciones de la Convención de 19 de noviembre de 1926 y de sus Reglas de Procedimiento aprobadas en la Sesión del 1.° de septiembre de 1928, que no son modificadas por las disposiciones de la presente Convención, quedan en vigor.

ARTICLE 5

The present Convention is drawn up in English and Spanish.

ARTÍCULO 5

La presente Convención está redactada en cada una de las lenguas inglesa y española.

ARTICLE 6

The High Contracting Parties shall ratify this present Convention in conformity with their respective Constitutions. The exchange of ratifications shall take place in the City of Mexico as soon as possible and the Convention shall come into force from the date of the exchange of ratifications.

In witness whereof, the respective Plenipotentiaries have signed the present Convention, and have affixed thereto their seals.

ARTÍCULO 6

Las Altas Partes Contratantes ratificarán la presente Convención, de conformidad con las disposiciones de sus Constituciones respectivas. El canje de ratificaciones se efectuará en la ciudad de México, tan pronto como fuere posible, y la Convención entrará en vigor desde el momento en que se haga el canje de ratificaciones.

En fé de lo cual, los Plenipotenciarios respectivos firmaron la presente Convención, poniendo en ella sus sellos.

Done in duplicate, in the City of Mexico, on the fifth day of December, nineteen hundred and thirty.

Hecha por duplicado en la ciudad de México, a los cinco días del mes de diciembre de mil novecientos treinta.

(*L. S.*) E. MONSON.

(*L. S.*) G. ESTRADA.

C. RULES OF PROCEDURE ADOPTED SEPTEMBER 1, 1928[1]

CAPÍTULO I

I. PLACE OF HEARING

LUGAR DE LAS AUDIENCIAS

1. The Commission shall sit at the City of Mexico, unless it be otherwise determined.

Art. 1. La Comisión tendrá su asiento en la Ciudad de México, a menos que determine otro lugar.

CAPÍTULO II

II. REGISTER AND MINUTES

REGISTROS Y ACTAS

2. A duplicate register shall be provided, one to be kept by each of the two Secretaries in his own language, in which shall be promptly entered the name of each claimant and the amount claimed at the time that a claim is formally filed with the Commission, whereupon in addition shall be recorded all the proceedings held in relation thereto.

Art. 2. Los Secretarios llevarán dos libros iguales de registro, cada uno en su propio idioma, y en ellos se asentarán inmediatamente, al presentarse formalmente una reclamación ante la Comisión, el nombre de cada reclamante y la suma reclamada; y, además, se registrarán en los mismos todos los trámites que se vayan dando.

3. Each claim shall constitute a separate case before the Commission and be registered as such. Claims shall be numbered consecutively, beginning with that first filed as number 1.

Art. 3. Cada reclamación constituirá un caso separado ante la Comisión y se registrará como tal. Se numerarán progresivamente todas las reclamaciones, empezando por la que se presente primero, que llevará el número uno.

4. A duplicate minute book shall be kept in like manner by the Secretaries, each in his own language,

Art. 4. Los Secretarios llevarán de la misma manera, dos libros iguales de actas, cada uno en su propio idioma, y

---

[1] English text from Decisions and Opinions of Commissioners, p. 9. Spanish text from Reglas de Procedimiento de la Comisión de Reclamaciones entre los Estados Unidos Mexicanos y la Gran Bretaña (Mexico City, 1928).

in which shall be entered a chronological record of all proceedings of the Commission. All the minutes shall be signed by the Commissioners and the Secretaries.

5. Such additional books and records shall be kept by the Secretaries as shall be required by these rules or prescribed by the Commission.

III. FILING AND REGISTRATION OF CLAIMS

6. A claim shall be deemed to have been formally filed with the Commission upon delivery to the Secretaries by the Agent of Great Britain of a memorial in duplicate, one in English and the other in Spanish, accompanied by all documents and other proofs in support of the claim then in possession of the Agent of Great Britain.

7. Upon receipt of the memorial mentioned in Article 6 hereof, an endorsement of filing, with the date thereof, shall be made thereon and signed by the Secretaries, and the claim shall be immediately registered under the appropriate number.

8. Every claim shall be filed with the Commission before the 22nd May, 1929, unless in any case reasons for the delay satisfactory to the Commission shall be established, and in such case the period for filing may be extended by the Commission not to exceed six additional months.

en ellos se presentará una relación cronológica de todas las actuaciones de la Comisión. Los Comisionados y los Secretarios firmarán todas las actas.

Art. 5. Los Secretarios llevarán los libros y registros adicionales que ordena el presente Reglamento o que la Comisión disponga.

CAPÍTULO III
PRESENTACIÓN Y REGISTRO DE LAS RECLAMACIONES

Art. 6. Toda reclamación se considerará como formalmente presentada ante la Comisión al entregar el Agente de la Gran Bretaña a los Secretarios un Memorial, en dos ejemplares, uno en español y otro en inglés, al que se acompañarán todos los documentos y demás pruebas en que se funde la reclamación, y que ya estén en poder del Agente de la Gran Bretaña.

Art. 7. Al recibirse el Memorial a que se refiere el artículo 6 del presente Reglamento, se hará en él una anotación de su presentación, con la fecha de la misma, subscrita por los Secretarios e inmediatamente se registrará la reclamación con su número correspondiente.

Art. 8. Todas las reclamaciones se presentarán a la Comisión antes del 22 de mayo de 1929, a no ser que en algún caso se pruebe que hubo causas que justifiquen la demora, a satisfacción de la Comisión, pues, en este caso, el período para su presentación podrá ser ampliado por la Comisión por un término que no exceda de seis meses más.

CAPÍTULO IV

IV. THE PLEADINGS

ESCRITOS FUNDAMENTALES

9. The written pleadings shall consist of the memorial, the answer, demurrers, the reply and the rejoinder, amendments and motions, unless by agreement between the Agents or by order of the Commission other pleadings are allowed.

Art. 9. Los escritos fundamentales serán el Memorial, la Contestación, los relativos a excepciones dilatorias, la Réplica y la Dúplica, las reformas a estos escritos y las mociones, a no ser que por convenio entre los Agentes o por acuerdo de la Comisión, puedan presentarse otros escritos.

10. The memorial.

The memorial shall be signed by the claimant or by his attorney in fact and further by the British Agent or only by the British Agent, but in this case a signed statement of the claim by the claimant shall be included in the memorial.

Art. 10. El Memorial.

El Memorial deberá estar firmado por el reclamante, o por su apoderado y también por el Agente Británico, o solamente por éste último, pero en este caso se incluirá en el Memorial una exposición de los hechos que motivan la reclamación, firmada por el reclamante.

The memorial shall contain a clear and concise statement of the facts upon which the claim is based. It shall set forth the information enumerated below in such detail as may be practicable in each particular case, or explain the absence thereof.

El Memorial contendrá una relación clara y concisa de los hechos en que se funda la reclamación. Expondrá, con el mayor detalle posible en cada caso, los informes que a continuación se requieren, y, a falta de alguno de ellos, explicará los motivos de la omisión.

(*a*) The nationality in virtue of which the claimant considers himself entitled to invoke the provisions of the Convention. Where in any case it shall appear that there has entered into the chain of title to the claim the rights or interests of any person or corporation of any country other than that of the claimant, then the facts in relation to such right or interest must be fully set forth.

(*a*) La nacionalidad en razón de la cual el reclamante se considera con derecho a invocar las disposiciones de la Convención. Cuando en algún caso apareciere que se han introducido en la serie de títulos que dan derecho a la reclamación, derechos o participaciones de alguna persona o compañía de nacionalidad distinta de la del reclamante, entonces se tendrán que exponer de una manera completa los hechos relacionados con ese derecho o participación.

(*b*) If the claimant sets out as a basis of his claim loss or damage

(*b*) Si el reclamante expone, como base de su reclamación, la pérdida o

suffered by any partnership, company, association or other joint interests in which the claimant has or had an interest, exceeding 50 per cent of the whole capital of the company or association of which he is a member, then the memorial shall set forth the nature and extent of that interest and all facts or considerations in connection with or in support of such claim.

(c) Facts showing that the losses or damages for which the claim is made resulted from some one or more of the causes specified in Article III of the Claims Convention between Great Britain and the United Mexican States dated the 19th November, 1926, which became effective by exchange of ratifications the 8th March, 1928, and that the same occurred between the 20th November, 1910, and the 31st May, 1920, inclusive.

(d) The amount of the claim; the time when and place where it arose; the kind or kinds and amount and value of property lost or damaged itemized so far as practicable; personal injuries, if any, and losses or damages resulting therefrom; the facts and circumstances attending the loss or damage to person or property out of which the claim arises, and upon which the claimant intends to rely to establish his claim.

(e) For and on behalf of whom the claim is preferred, and, if in a repre-

daño sufrido por alguna sociedad, compañía, asociación u otro grupo de intereses en el cual el reclamante tiene o tuvo una participación superior al cincuenta por ciento del capital total de la sociedad o asociación de que forma parte, entonces el Memorial expondrá la naturaleza y extensión de dicha participación, y todos los hechos o consideraciones relacionados con dicha reclamación o que le sirvan de apoyo.

(c) Los hechos que demuestren que la pérdida o daño por el cual se hace la reclamación resultó de alguna o de algunas de las causas especificadas en el artículo III de la Convención de Reclamaciones celebrada entre los Estados Unidos Mexicanos y la Gran Bretaña, fechada el 19 de noviembre de 1926, que entró en vigor por el canje de ratificaciones de 8 de marzo de 1928, y que dicha pérdida o daño ocurrió entre el 20 de noviembre de 1910 y el 31 de mayo de 1920, inclusive.

(d) El monto de la reclamación; la fecha y lugar en que se originó; la clase, cantidad y valor de la propiedad perdida o dañada, en relación promenorizada hasta donde sea posible; las lesiones sufridas en la persona, si las hubiere habido, y las pérdidas o daños que resultaron de las mismas; los hechos y demás circunstancias concomitantes con la pérdida o daño a la persona o a la propiedad por los que se origina la reclamación y sobre las cuales el reclamante pretenda fundarse para establecer su reclamación.

(e) Por quién y a nombre de quién se presenta la reclamación; y, si la

sentative capacity, the authority of the person preferring the claim.

(f) Whether the right to the claim does now, and did at the time when it had its origin, belong solely and absolutely to the claimant, and if any other person is or has been interested therein or in any part thereof, then who is such other person and what is or was the nature and extent of his interest.

(g) Whether the claimant, or any other person who may at any time have been entitled to the amount claimed, or any part thereof, has ever received any, and, if any, what sum of money or equivalent or indemnification in any form for the whole or part of the loss or damage upon which the claim is founded; and, if so, when and from whom the same was received.

(h) Whether the claim has ever been presented, or complaint with respect to it been lodged with the Mexican Government, or any official thereof, acting either *de jure* or *de facto*, or with the Government of Great Britain or any official thereof; and, if so, the facts in relation thereto.

11. Claims presented solely for the death of a British subject shall be filed on behalf of those British subjects considering themselves personally entitled to present them. Any claims presented for damage to a British subject already deceased at

persona que la presenta lo hace con carácter de representante, la comprobación de su personalidad.

(f) Si el derecho a la reclamación pertenece ahora, y perteneció en la lecha en que se originó, única y absofutamente al reclamante, o si alguna otra persona está o ha estado interesada en la misma o en parte alguna de ella. En este último caso quién es esa otra persona y cuál es o fue la naturaleza y la extensión de su participación.

(g) Si el reclamante o cualquiera otra persona que en cualquier tiempo haya tenido derecho a la cantidad reclamada, o a alguna parte de ella, ha recibido alguna suma de dinero; y, en caso afirmativo, qué suma, o qué equivalente o indemnización en cualquier forma que sea, ya por el monto total o por parte del importe de la pérdida o daño en que se funde la reclamación; y, de ser así, cuándo y de quién se recibió.

(h) Si alguna vez se ha presentado la reclamación o alguna queja respecto de la misma ante el Gobierno Mexicano o bien ante cualquier funcionario del mismo, ya sea que haya actuado *de jure* o *de facto*, o bien ante el Gobierno de la Gran Bretaña o ante cualquier funcionario del mismo; y, en caso de ser así, los hechos relativos a dicha presentación.

Art. 11. Las reclamaciones que se hicieren exclusivamente por el homicidio de algún británico se presentarán a nombre personal de los británicos que se creyeren con derecho a presentarlas. Las que se presentaren por daños causados a un británico que ya

the time of filing such claim, if for damage to property, shall be filed on behalf of his estate and through his legal representative, who shall duly establish his legal capacity therefor.

12. The answer.

(a) The answer in each case shall be filed with the Secretaries in duplicate in English and Spanish within one hundred and eighty days from the date on which the memorial is filed, unless the time be extended in any case by agreement between the Agents filed with the Secretaries, or by order of the Commission on motion after due notice.

(b) The answer shall refer directly to each of the allegations of the memorial and shall clearly indicate the attitude of the respondent Government with respect to each of the various elements of the claim. It may, in addition thereto, contain any new matter or affirmative defence which the respondent Government may desire to assert within the scope of the Convention.

(c) The answer shall be accompanied by the documents and proofs on which the respondent Government will rely in their defence to the claim.

13. The reply.

(a) Where a reply is deemed necessary in any case on behalf of the claimant, it may be filed with the Secretaries in duplicate in English and Spanish within thirty (30) days from the date on which the answer is filed, unless the time be extended in any case by agreement between

hubiere fallecido al tiempo de la reclamación, deberán presentarse, si esos daños fueron en sus propiedades, en nombre de la Sucesión respectiva y por medio de su representante legal, cuya personalidad se acreditará debidamente.

Art. 12. La Contestación.

(a) La Contestación se presentará a los Secretarios, en dos ejemplares, uno en español y otro en inglés, dentro de ciento ochenta días contados a partir de la fecha en que se presente el Memorial, a no ser que en cualquier caso se prorrogue el plazo por convenio entre los Agentes, notificado a los Secretarios, o por la Comisión, a moción debidamente notificada.

(b) La Contestación se referirá directamente a cada uno de los puntos del Memorial y manifestará claramente la actitud del Gobierno que contesta respecto a cada uno de los diversos elementos de la reclamación. Puede, además, presentar las materias nuevas o puntos de defensa que el Gobierno que contesta desee hacer constar, dentro de los límites de la Convención.

(c) La Contestación llevará anexos los documentos y pruebas en que se funde el Gobierno que contesta la reclamación.

Art. 13. La Réplica.

(a) Cuando en algún caso se considere necesaria una Réplica por parte del reclamante, podrá presentarse, en dos ejemplares, uno en español y otro en inglés, a los Secretarios dentro de treinta (30) días contados a partir de la fecha en que fue presentada la Contestación, a menos que se pro-

the Agents filed in like manner with the Secretaries, or by order of the Commission on motion after due notice.

(*b*) The reply shall deal only with the allegations in the answer which present facts or contentions not adequately dealt with in the memorial and with new matter, if any, set up in the answer.

(*c*) The reply shall be accompanied by the documents and other proofs upon which the claimant relies in support thereof not filed with the memorial.

14. The rejoinder.

Whenever the Mexican Agent shall deem it necessary to file a rejoinder, he may do so by filing the same in duplicate, in English and Spanish, within thirty (30) days from the date on which the reply is filed, unless the time be extended in any case by agreement between the Agents, filed in like manner with the Secretaries, or by order of the Commission on motion after due notice. The rejoinder shall be subject to the same rules as the reply.

15. Amendments to pleadings.

(*a*) The pleadings may be amended at any time before final award either (1) by agreement between the Agents which shall be filed with the Secretaries as in the case of original pleadings, or (2) by leave of the Commission, such leave to be granted only upon motion after due notice to the

rrogue el plazo por convenio entre los Agentes, debidamente presentado, en forma semejante, a los Secretarios, o por orden de la Comisión, a moción debidamente notificada.

(*b*) La Réplica se concretará a los argumentos consignados en la Contestación y que se refieran a hechos o puntos que no hayan sido debidamente tratados en el Memorial, y a aquellos nuevos puntos de vista que hubieren sido aducidos en la Contestación.

(*c*) A la Réplica se acompañarán los documentos y demás pruebas en los que se haya basado el reclamante y que no hayan sido presentados con el Memorial.

Art. 14. La Dúplica.

Cuando el Agente Mexicano considere necesario duplicar, podrá hacerlo presentando dos ejemplares de la Dúplica, uno en español y otro en inglés, dentro de treinta (30) días contados desde el día en que fue presentada la Réplica, a menos que por convenio entre los Agentes, debidamente presentado a los Secretarios, o por orden de la Comisión se prorrogue el plazo, a moción debidamente notificada. La Dúplica se sujetará a las mismas reglas que la Réplica.

Art. 15. Reformas de los escritos fundamentales.

(*a*) Los escritos fundamentales podrán reformarse en cualquier momento antes del fallo definitivo, ya sea (1) por acuerdo entre los Agentes, presentado a los Secretarios como si se tratara de los escritos fundamentales originales o (2) por permiso de la Comisión, que sólo podrá conce-

opposite party and upon such terms as the Commission shall impose.

(b) All motions for leave to amend pleadings shall be in writing, filed with the Secretaries in duplicate in English and Spanish, and shall set out the amendments desired to be made and the reasons in support thereof.

(c) Amendments to pleadings shall be accompanied by the documents and proofs which will be relied upon in support thereof, unless the same have been filed with the original pleadings.

(d) Answer may be filed to amendments in like manner as in the case of originals within such time as may be stipulated by the Agents or fixed in the orders of the Commission allowing the amendment, as the case may be.

(e) The Commission will not consider any matter of claim or defence not set up in appropriate pleadings or amendment thereto made as herein provided; but the Commission may in its discretion at any time before final award direct amendments to pleadings which it may deem essential to a proper consideration of any claim or to meet the ends of justice.

derse mediante moción después de la notificación a la otra parte, conforme a las condiciones que la Comisión imponga.

(b) Todas las mociones en que se solicite permiso para reformar los escritos fundamentales se presentarán a los Secretarios, en dos ejemplares, uno en español y otro en inglés, y contendrán las reformas que deseen hacerse y las razones en que se funden.

(c) Las reformas a los escritos fundamentales irán acompañadas de los escritos y pruebas que se aduzcan en su apoyo, a menos que éstos hayan sido presentados con los escritos fundamentales originales.

(d) Podrán presentarse contestaciones a los escritos de reforma de la misma manera que cuando se trate de escritos originales, dentro del plazo que convengan los Agentes, o que se fije en los acuerdos de la Comisión que concedan la reforma, según sea el caso.

(e) La Comisión no tomará en consideración nada relativo a la reclamación o a la defensa que no esté debidamente consignado en los escritos fundamentales o en las reformas relativas a los mismos como lo dispone este Reglamento; pero la Comisión podrá, de oficio y en cualquier fecha anterior a su fallo definitivo, ordenar que se hagan reformas a los escritos fundamentales cuando lo estime esencial para la debida consideración de cualquier reclamación o para los fines de la justicia.

V. DEMURRERS

16. Any demurrers interposed by the Mexican Agent so as not to take up discussion of the merits of the claim may be filed in the form of a special answer prior to any pleading in defence upon the merits of the claim, and within the term fixed for the answer, or when answering the claim upon its merits, at the choice of the said Agent. Should there be various demurrers of this nature in any one claim, they shall be filed together.

17. Should the demurrers referred to in the preceding Article be filed in the form of a special answer, the course of the proceedings shall be stayed in so far as concerns the study of the merits of the claim. In that event there will be no pleadings other than the memorial, the demurrer and the reply thereto. Should the demurrer be overruled, the respondent shall be obliged to answer the memorial within a term of thirty (30) days after the date on which the decision to that effect is notified.

VI. JOINDER OR SEPARATION OF CLAIMS

18. The Commission shall have at all times the right to order the joinder or separation of claims. Before deciding thereon, the Commission shall hear the Agents within such time as it may fix therefor.

CAPÍTULO V

EXCEPCIONES DILATORIAS

Art. 16. La excepción dilatoria que oponga el Agente Mexicano para no entrar a discutir el fondo del asunto, puede ser presentada en forma de contestación especial antes de toda defensa relativa al fondo, y en el plazo fijado para la Contestación, o al responder sobre el fondo, según elija el mismo Agente. Si hay varias excepciones de esta naturaleza en una misma reclamación, deberán ser presentadas conjuntamente.

Art. 17. Si las excepciones dilatorias a que se refiere al artículo anterior son presentadas en forma de contestación especial, la tramitación por lo que se refiere al estudio del fondo de la cuestión, se suspenderá. En este caso no habrá más escritos fundamentales que el Memorial, la Excepción Dilatoria y su Réplica. Si la Excepción Dilatoria es desechada, el demandado estará obligado a contestar el Memorial dentro del plazo de treinta (30) días, a partir de la fecha en que se notifique la resolución respectiva.

CAPÍTULO VI

ACUMULACIÓN O SEPARACIÓN DE RECLAMACIONES

Art. 18. La Comisión tiene siempre derecho de ordenar la acumulación o la separación de las reclamaciones. Antes de resolver, la Comisión oirá a los Agentes dentro del plazo que les fije.

VII. MOTIONS TO DISMISS OR REJECT

MOCIONES PARA DESECHAR O RECHAZAR

19. A motion to dismiss a claim may be made at any time after registration thereof and before final submission to the Commission for good cause shown in the motion.

Art. 19. Podrá presentarse moción para desechar una reclamación en cualquier tiempo, después de que ésta se haya registrado y antes de someterse definitivamente a la Comisión, fundada en causa que se justifique debidamente en la moción.

20. A motion to reject or strike out any pleading may be made at any time after the filing thereof and before submission of the claim to the Commission for any cause apparent on the face of the pleading.

Art. 20. Puede presentarse una moción pidiendo que se rechace o elimine cualquier escrito fundamental, en cualquier tiempo después de haber sido presentado y antes de que se someta la reclamación a la Comisión, por cualquiera causa que conste en el escrito fundamental.

21. Should any such motion be sustained, the Commission may in its discretion permit amendments to the end that each claim within the jurisdiction of the Commission shall be disposed of.

Art. 21. En caso de que se apruebe una de estas mociones, la Comisión podrá a su discreción permitir que se hagan las reformas necesarias con el fin de que se resuelvan todas las reclamaciones que estén dentro de la jurisdicción de la Comisión.

22. All motions shall be in writing and shall set forth concisely the grounds of the motion. They shall be filed with the Secretaries as in the case of original pleadings and shall be promptly brought on for hearing before the Commission.

Art. 22. Todas las mociones se harán escrito y presentarán de manera concisa los fundamentos en que estén basadas. Serán presentadas a los Secretarios de la misma manera que los escritos fundamentales, y se dará inmediatamente cuenta de ellas a la Comisión para que sean resueltas.

VIII. EVIDENCE

PRUEBA

23. The Commission will receive and consider all written statements, documents and other evidence which may be presented to it by the respective Agents.

Art. 23. La Comisión recibirá y tomará en cuenta todas las declaraciones, documentos y demás pruebas que por escrito le presenten cualquiera de los Agentes.

24. Should any document that it is desired to produce as evidence be on file in the archives of Great Britain or the United Mexican States, the endeavour shall be made to produce the original; and only when there are difficulties in the way of obtaining the originals from such archives, will it be permissible to produce certified copies of the whole or any part thereof.

25. When the original of any document filed at any Government office on either side cannot be conveniently withdrawn, and no copy of such document can be made, the party desiring to present the same to the Commission in support of the allegations set out in his pleadings shall notify the Agent of the other party in writing of his desire to inspect such document. The action taken in response to the request to inspect, together with such reasons as may be assigned for the action so taken, shall be reported to the Commission so that the Commission may decide thereon.

26. The right to inspect the original of such documents, when granted, shall extend to the whole of the documents of which part only is produced, but shall not extend to any enclosures therein, or annexes thereto, or minutes, or endorsements thereon, if such enclosures, annexes, minutes or endorsements are not adduced as evidence or specifically referred to in the pleadings.

27. The Agent of either party

Art. 24. En caso de que un documento que se desee aducir como prueba se encuentre en los archivos de los Estados Unidos Mexicanos o de la Gran Bretaña, se procurará presentar el original; y solamente cuando en los archivos haya dificultades para facilitar el original, podrá presentarse copia certificada del mismo, total o parcial.

Art. 25. Cuando un documento original que esté archivado en las oficinas de cualquiera de los dos Gobiernos, no pueda ser retirado fácilmente, ni pueda sacarse copia de tal documento, la parte que desee presentarlo a la Comisión, en apoyo de los puntos contenidos en sus escritos fundamentales, notificará por escrito al Agente de la parte contraria, su deseo de examinar el referido documento. Las medidas que este último tome en respuesta a la solicitud de examen, así como las razones que se señalaren para ello, serán puestas en conocimiento de la Comisión para que ésta resuelva.

Art. 26. El derecho concedido para examinar el original de tales documentos, comprenderá el de examinar todo el documento, aun cuando sólo una parte haya sido presentada; pero no comprenderá el de examinar ninguno de los inclusos, anexos, minutas o anotaciones que contenga, si tales inclusos, anexos, minutas o anotaciones no han sido pedidos ni aducidos como prueba o explícitamente señalados en los escritos fundamentales.

Art. 27. El Agente de cualquiera

shall be entitled, upon due notice to the Agent of the opposing party and pursuant to any order of the Commission, to produce witnesses and examine them under affirmation before the Commission; and in that event any witness produced by one of the parties may be subjected to cross-examination by the Agent or Counsel of the opposing party.

28. Should the Agent of either Government desire to produce witnesses for examination by the Commission in any case, he shall within fifteen (15) days from the expiration of the time for filing of the last pleading in such case give notice to that effect by filing such notice in writing with the Secretaries, stating the number and the names and addresses of the witnesses whom he desires to examine so that the Commission may fix a time and place to hear such oral testimony. No oral testimony will be heard in any case except in pursuance of notice given within the time and in the manner herein stated, unless allowed by the Commission.

29. The examination of witnesses shall be conducted in accordance with the procedure and in such manner as the Commission may determine. Their testimony shall be made a part of the record, and a copy shall be furnished to the Agent of each Government.

30. The claimant may be called upon to appear on request of the Agents or in the discretion of the Commission, and he shall in that event be examined in accordance with the procedure referred to in the preceding paragraph.

de las partes tendrá el derecho, previa la debida notificación al Agente de la parte contraria, en cumplimiento de cualquier acuerdo de la Comisión, de presentar testigos y examinarlos bajo protesta ante la Comisión; y, en tal caso, cualquier testigo presentado por una de las partes podrá ser repreguntado por el Agente o abogado de la parte contraria.

Art. 28. En cualquier caso en que uno de los Agentes desee presentar testigos para ser examinados ante la Comisión dará aviso por escrito a los Secretarios dentro de quince (15) días contados desde la fecha en que expire el plazo para presentar el último escrito fundamental, manifestando el número, los nombres y las direcciones de los testigos que desee examinar, para que la Comisión fije día y lugar en que deberá recibirse dicho testimonio oral. No se tomará ningún testimonio oral, sino de acuerdo con la notificación dada dentro del término y en la forma antes prescritos, a menos que así lo permita la Comisión.

Art. 29. El examen de testigos estará sujeto al procedimiento y a la forma que fije la Comisión. La declaración se hará constar en los autos, y se proporcionará copia de la misma al Agente de cada Gobierno.

Art. 30. El reclamante puede ser citado a petición de los Agentes o de oficio, y se le examinará siguiéndose los mismos procedimientos a que se refiere el artículo anterior.

31. The Commission may, after filing of the last pleading and at any time prior to the award, order that the opinion of one or more experts be heard on matters requiring special knowledge, and it may likewise order views of premises.

32. Should it not be possible for any witness or claimant to appear before the Commission, he may be examined by means of letters rogatory issued by the Commission or any competent judicial authorities at the seat of the Commission and addressed to competent judicial authorities at the place of residence of such witness or claimant. Such testimony shall be received in accordance with the formalities required by law at that particular place.

IX. SETTLEMENT BY AGREEMENT BETWEEN THE AGENTS

33. The Agents may, prior to the hearing of any claim, meet as often as they may think necessary for discussion of such claim, with a view to reaching some agreement in regard thereto.

34. This discussion shall be on a confidential basis and should no satisfactory settlement be arrived at, either Agent shall have the right to contest the case before the Commission without reference to any offers exchanged or concessions made in his negotiations with the other Agent.

35. Should a satisfactory settlement be arrived at, copies of the agreement shall be sent to the Secre-

Art. 31. Después del último escrito fundamental y antes del fallo, la Comisión puede ordenar que se oiga el parecer de uno o más peritos sobre materias que exijan conocimientos especiales, e igualmente puede ordenar vistas de ojos.

Art. 32. En caso de que no pudiere presentarse un testigo o un reclamante ante la Comisión, puede ser examinado por exhorto dirigido por la Comisión o la autoridad judicial competente de la sede de la Comisión a la del lugar del domicilio o de la residencia del testigo o del reclamante. La declaración será recibida con las formalidades de la ley local.

CAPÍTULO IX

ARREGLO POR CONVENIO DE LOS AGENTES

Art. 33. Antes de celebrarse audiencia sobre cualquiera reclamación los dos Agentes podrán celebrar las juntas que estimen necesarias para discutir la reclamación, con la mira de llegar a un acuerdo.

Art. 34. Esta discusión será en un terreno confidencial y de no llegarse a una solución satisfactoria cualquiera de los Agentes tendrá el derecho de discutir el caso ante la Comisión sin que pueda hacer referencia a las ofertas cruzadas o a las concesiones hechas en sus negociaciones con el otro Agente.

Art. 35. De llegarse a un arreglo satisfactorio, se enviarán copias del Convenio a la Secretaría de la Co-

taries of the Commission. The Commission will then adjudicate upon the agreement and approve same or otherwise and order notice of its decision to be served pursuant to article 46 hereof.

misión. La Comisión resolverá sobre el convenio aprobándolo o no y su resolución la mandará notificar, de acuerdo con el artículo 46 de este Reglamento.

X. DECISIONS ON MATTERS OF PROCEDURE

36. All applications to the Commission to make orders pursuant to Articles 15, 18, 25, 28, 29, 32 and 50 hereof, or on other matters of procedure, shall be in writing.

37. The joint Secretaries shall advise the Agent of the opposing party of any such application, and both parties may argue before the Commission, for which purpose a day and hour shall be set for the hearing.

38. Any orders of the Commission made pursuant to the two preceding Articles shall be entered in a special book, and copies of such orders shall be sent to the Agents.

39. When the Commission is in recess, the Commissioner or Commissioners residing at the seat of the Commission may make any orders as referred to in Article 36 hereof, with the exception of the methods ordered by Article 15, subject to the formalities provided by Articles 37 and 38 hereof. Any such order or orders made by them, which shall be immediately enforceable, shall be submitted to the Commission for ratification at the following session.

CAPÍTULO X

RESOLUCIONES DE TRÁMITE

Art. 36. Toda solicitud que se dirija a la Comisión para que dicte órdenes de acuerdo con los artículos 15, 18, 25, 28, 29, 32 y 50 de este Reglamento, o sobre cualquier otro asunto de trámite, se hará por escrito.

Art. 37. Los Secretarios darán aviso de la solicitud al Agente de la otra parte, pudiendo alegar cada una de las partes ante la Comisión, a cuyo efecto se señalará día y hora para la audiencia.

Art. 38. Los acuerdos que la Comisión dicte conforme a los dos artículos anteriores, se asentarán en un libro especial de Acuerdos, y se enviará copia de ellos a los Agentes.

Art. 39. Durante los recesos de la Comisión, el Comisionado o Comisionados que residan en el lugar de asiento de la Comisión, podrán dictar las resoluciones a que se refiere el artículo 36 con excepción de los casos a que se refiere el artículo 15 de este Reglamento, sujetándose a las formalidades establecidas en los artículos 37 y 38. Los acuerdos así dictados, que podrán ejecutarse desde luego, serán sometidos a la Comisión en su siguiente reunión para ser ratificados.

CAPÍTULO XI

XI. HEARINGS

AUDIENCIAS

40. The order in which cases shall come on for submission before the Commission shall be determined (*a*) by agreement between the Agent of Great Britain and the Mexican Agent, subject to revision in the discretion of the Commission, or (*b*) by order of the Commission.

41. When the Agent of Great Britain is ready to submit a case to the Commission for decision, he shall file notice with the Secretaries, and he may file together with such notice a brief and documentary proofs in support thereof, in addition to those already filed by him. On the filing of the brief, the Mexican Agent may within thirty (30) days file with the Secretaries a reply brief, together with such written proofs in addition to those already filed by him as he may care to invoke. Within fifteen (15) days, the Agent of Great Britain may reply thereto by a counter brief, accompanied by additional proofs. Any new matter in the reply brief may be answered by the Mexican Agent within fifteen (15) days.

42. When a case comes on for submission to the Commission, the Agents or their respective counsel shall be heard. The Agent of Great Britain or his counsel shall open the case and the Mexican Agent or his counsel may reply. Any further dis-

Art. 40. El orden en que los casos deberán llegar ante la Comisión para su conocimiento, se determinarán:

(*a*) por medio de convenio entre el Agente Mexicano y el Agente Británico sujeto a decisión de la Comisión: o (*b*) por acuerdo de la propia Comisión.

Art. 41. Cuando el Agente de la Gran Bretaña esté preparado para presentar un caso a la Comisión para resolución, lo notificará a los Secretarios; y podrá presentar juntamente con dicha notificación, un alegato, así como las pruebas documentales en que se funde, además de las que previamente haya presentado. Al presentarse el alegato, el Agente Mexicano podrá dentro de los treinta (30) días siguientes, presentar a los Secretarios un alegato en contestación, juntamente con las pruebas escritas que desee invocar, además de las que previamente haya presentado. Dentro de quince (15) días el Agente de la Gran Bretaña podrá replicar por medio de un nuevo alegato, acompañado de pruebas adicionales. El Agente Mexicano podrá contestar sobre cualquiera materia nueva presentada en el alegato de réplica, dentro de quince (15) días.

Art. 42. Cuando llegue el momento de someter algún caso a la Comisión, los Agentes o sus abogados respectivos podrán alegar verbalmente. El Agente de la Gran Bretaña o su abogado, abrirá la discusión del caso, y el Agente Mexicano

cussion shall be within the discretion of the Commission.

43. When a case is submitted in pursuance of the foregoing provisions, the proceedings before the Commission in that case shall be deemed closed. Notwithstanding this order, the Commission may again hear the Agents on any points it may deem necessary.

44. Attendance at the hearings may be waived by either one or both Agents.

45. In the case of persons having no connection with the Commission, permission from the Presiding Commissioner will be required before they can be present at any hearing or hearings.

XII. AWARDS

46. The award of the Commission in respect of each claim shall be delivered at a public session of the Commission as soon after the hearing of such claim has been concluded as may be possible.

47. The award shall set out fully the grounds on which it is based, and shall be signed by the members of the Commission concurring therein. Any member of the Commission who dissents from the award shall make and sign a dissenting report setting out the grounds upon which he dissents and the award which in his opinion should have been made.

48. The Commission may in its discretion or on request of either Agent make clear or correct any award the decision in which may

o su abogado, podrá contestar. Cualquiera discusión adicional estará sujeta al criterio de la Comisión.

Art. 43. Cuando un caso se haya sometido de acuerdo con las disposiciones anteriores, se considerarán como terminados los trámites ante la Comisión. No obstante este acuerdo, la Comisión podrá oír de nuevo a los Agentes en los puntos en que lo estime necesario.

Art. 44. La concurrencia a las audiencias puede ser renunciada por uno o por los dos Agentes.

Art. 45. Para concurrir a las audiencias se necesita el permiso del Presidente de la Comisión cuando se trate de personas ajenas a la misma Comisión.

CAPÍTULO XII
SENTENCIAS

Art. 46. La sentencia de la Comisión en cada reclamación se entregará en una sesión pública de la Comisión, tan pronto como sea posible después de que hayan terminado las audiencias respectivas.

Art. 47. La sentencia consignará ampliamente todos los fundamentos en que está basada, y deberán firmarla los miembros de la Comisión que convengan en ella. Cualquier miembro de la Comisión que no esté conforme con una sentencia, redactará y firmará un voto particular, exponiendo sus razones y la resolución que a su juicio debería haberse dado.

Art. 48. La Comisión puede de oficio o a petición de cualquiera de los Agentes, aclarar o rectificar una sentencia cuya parte resolutiva sea

be obscure, incomplete or contradictory, or contain any error in writing or of calculation. Should such declaratory order be made on request of one of the Agents, his motion thereof shall be notified to the other Agent, who may answer same within fifteen (15) days.

Any request for a declaratory order as above shall be filed within fifteen (15) days from notice of the award, whenever one of the Agents shall have recourse thereto.

XIII. LANGUAGES AND COPIES

49. All documents filed by the Agents must be in English or in Spanish. Duplicate originals, duly signed, and four copies of all pleadings shall be filed, and one original and five copies in the case of other documents.

50. On request of either Agent, duly notified to the other Agent, the latter shall file within a reasonable time a complete or partial translation of any document, any period then running being suspended for the time being. The Commission may order a complete or partial translation of any documents to be made.

51. All decisions of the Commission shall be written in English and Spanish.

XIV. NOTICE TO PARTIES

52. The filing with the Secretaries of the Commission of any plead-

obscura, incompleta o contradictoria, o contenga un error de escritura o de cálculo. En el caso de que la aclaración se haga a petición de uno de los Agentes, la promoción será dada a conocer al otro Agente para que la conteste dentro de quince (15) días.

La petición de aclaración debe presentarse dentro de quince (15) días, contados desde la notificación de la sentencia, cuando el recurso se introduzca por uno de los Agentes.

CAPÍTULO XIII
IDIOMAS Y COPIS

Art. 49. Todos los documentos presentados por los Agentes, deberán serlo en español o en inglés. De todos los escritos se presentarán dos originales firmados y cuatro copias, y de los demás documentos el original y cinco copias.

Art. 50. A petición de cualquiera de los Agentes, debidamente notificada al otro, este último estará obligado a presentar dentro de un plazo razonable, la traducción completa o parcial de un documento, quedando entre tanto suspenso el término que esté corriendo. La Comisión podrá ordenar la traducción completa o parcial de un escrito o documento.

Art. 51. Todas las resoluciones de la Comisión deberán ser redactadas en español y en inglés.

CAPÍTULO XIV
NOTIFICACIONES

Art. 52. La presentación a los Secretarios de cualesquiera escritos

ings, amendments, documents, or notice by the respective Agents (or counsel) shall constitute notice thereof to the opposite party and shall be deemed a compliance with these rules as to any notice required to be given hereunder. To that end the Secretaries shall notify the Agents of any pleading or documents on the same day as received by them.

XV. DUTIES OF THE SECRETARIES

53. The Secretaries shall —

(a) Be the custodians of all documents and records of the Commission, and keep them systematically arranged in safe files. While affording every reasonable facility to the British and Mexican Agents and their respective counsel to inspect and make excerpts therefrom, no documents or records shall be withdrawn from the files of the Commission save by its order duly entered on record.

(b) Make and keep, in the English and Spanish languages respectively, the Register, Minute Book and such other books and documents as the Commission may order.

(c) Endorse on each document the date of filing, and enter a minute thereof in the Register.

(d) Each keep a notice book respectively in English and Spanish, in which entry shall be made of all notices required by these rules to be filed. Entry shall be made in said notice book of the date on which said

---

fundamentales, reformas, documentos o avisos por los Agentes o sus Abogados, constituirá la notificación a la parte contraria y será considerada como el cumplimiento de estas Reglas con relación a cualquiera notificación que se necesite conforme a las mismas. A ese efecto los Secretarios tienen la obligación de notificar a los Agentes el mismo día que reciban cualquier escrito o documento.

CAPÍTULO XV

OBLIGACIONES DE LOS SECRETARIOS

Art. 53. Los Secretarios deberán:

(a) Guardar todos los documentos y registros de la Comisión sistemáticamente arreglados en archivos de seguridad. Aún cuando deben presentarse todas las facilidades que sean razonables a los Agentes Mexicano y Británico y a sus respectivos Abogados para examinar y tomar notas de ellos, no deberá retirarse de los archivos ningún documento o registro, sino por acuerdo de la Comisión debidamente anotado.

(b) Formar en español y en inglés, cada uno respectivamente, un registro, un libro de actas y todos los demás libros y documentos que la Comisión disponga.

(c) Anotar en todos los escritos que se presenten, la fecha de su presentación y hacer una relación de los mismos en el libro de registro.

(d) Llevar cada uno, un libro de notificaciones, respectivamente en español y en inglés, en los cuales asentarán todas las notificaciónes que conforme a estas Reglas deberán hacerse. Se asentará en dichos libros

notice is given, and all proceedings in respect and in pursuance of said notice.

(*e*) Furnish promptly to the Agent of the opposite party and to each Commissioner copies of all pleadings, motions, notices, and other papers filed with the Secretaries by the Agents.

(*f*) Each keep a Register in which shall be recorded all awards and decisions of the Commission, including the dissenting opinions signed by the Commissioners and Secretaries. They shall likewise each keep a book in which shall be entered all orders made by the Commission.

(*g*) Perform such other duties as may from time to time be prescribed by the Commission.

(*h*) Render reports, as laid down in Article VII of the Convention, to their respective Governments at such a time as the Commission may not be sitting, and send copies of such reports to each Commissioner.

XVI. COMPUTATION OF TIME

54. Whenever in these rules a period of days is mentioned for the doing of any act, such period shall begin to run as from the day following that on which notice is served and the date on which said period terminates shall be counted, and Sundays and the legal holidays of both countries shall be excluded.

de notificaciones la fecha en que se haga cada notificación, así como todos los trámites relativos y originados en el cumplimiento de esa notificación.

(*e*) Proporcionar sin demora al Agente de la parte contraria y a cada Comisionado, copias de todos los escritos fundamentales, mociones, notificaciones y otros documentos presentados a los Secretarios por los Agentes.

(*f*) Llevar cada uno un libro, en el que deberán asentarse todas las sentencias y decisiones de la Comisión, incluyendo los votos particulares firmados por los Comisionados y los Secretarios. Además llevarán cada uno un libro en que asienten los acuerdos de la Comisión.

(*g*) Rendir los informes a que se refiere el artículo VII de la Convención a sus respectivos Gobiernos, cuando la Comisión no esté reunida, enviando copia de ellos a cada Comisionado.

(*h*) Ejecutar los trabajos que de tiempo en tiempo ordene la Comisión.

CAPÍTULO XVI
CÓMPUTO DE TÉRMINOS

Art. 54. Siempre que en estas Reglas se mencione un término para la ejecución de un acto, dicho término comenzará a correr desde el día siguiente a aquél en que se hubiese hecho la notificación, y se contará en él el día del vencimiento, y se excluirán los domingos y días oficialmente festivos de ambos países.

Capítulo XVII

XVII. AMENDMENTS TO RULES	REFORMA DE LAS REGLAS

55. The Commission may at any time amend these rules after hearing the Agents.

Art. 55. La Comisión podrá reformar en cualquier tiempo estas Reglas, oyendo a los Agentes.

(SIGNED) Dr. A. R. Zimmerman,
     President of the Commission.

(SIGNED) Artemus Jones, K. C.,
     British Commissioner.

(SIGNED) Lic. Benito Flores,
     Mexican Commissioner.

VI. ITALIAN–MEXICAN CLAIMS COMMISSION

A. CONVENTION OF JANUARY 13, 1927 [1]

Il Presidente degli Stati Uniti Messicani e Sua Maestá il Re d'Italia, desiderosi di regolare definitivamente ed amichevolmente tutti i reclami pecuniarii motivati per le perdite o danni sofferti da sudditi Italiani in causa di atti rivoluzionari compiuti nel periodo compreso fra il 20 Novembre 1910 ed il 31 Maggio 1920, inclusivo, hanno deciso di conchiudere una Convenzione a tal effetto ed hanno nominato perció a Loro Plenipotenziari:

Il Presidente degli Stati Uniti Messicani: il signore Avvocato Aarón Sáenz, Ministro degli Affari Exteri.

Sua Maestá il Re d'Italia: il signore Dottor Gino Macchioro Vivalba, Grande Ufficiale della Corona d'Italia, Commendatore dei Santi Maurizio e Lazzaro, Commendatore della Stella d'Italia, Suo Inviato Straordinario e Ministro Plenipotenziario in Messico.

I quali dopo aver scambiato i Loro Pieni Poteri ed averli trovati in buona e debita forma, hanne convenuto negli articoli seguenti:

El Presidente de los Estados Unidos Mexicanos y Su Majestad el Rey de Italia, deseosos de arreglar definitiva y amigablemente todas las reclamaciones pecuniarias motivadas por las pérdidas o daños que resintieron los súbditos italianos a causa de actos revolucionarios ejecutados durante el período comprendido entre el 20 de noviembre de 1910 y el 31 de mayo de 1920, inclusive, han decidido celebrar una Convención con tal fin, y al efecto, han nombrado como sus Plenipotenciarios:

El Presidente de los Estados Unidos Mexicanos al señor licenciado don Aarón Sáenz, Secretario de Estado y del Despachode Relaciones Exteriores.

Su Majestad el Rey de Italia, al señor doctor Gino Macchioro Vivalba, Gran Oficial de la Corona de Italia, Comendador de los Santos Mauricio y Lázaro, Comendador de la Estrella de Italia, su Enviado Extraordinario y Ministro Plenipotenciario en México.

Quienes, después de comunicarse sus Plenos Poderes y de hallarlos en buena y debida forma, convinieron en los artículos siguientes:

[1] Text from Convención de Reclamaciones celebrada entre los Estados Unidos Mexicanos y el Gobierno de Italia (Mexico City, 1929).

Articolo I

Tutti i reclami indicati nell'Articolo III di questa Convenzione saranno sottoposti ad una Commissione composta de tre Membri: uno di essi sará nominato dal Presidente degli Stati Uniti Messicani; un altro sará nominato da Sua Maestá il Re d'Italia; ed el terzo, che presiederá la Commissione, sará designato di comune accordo dai due Governi. Se essi non pervengano a detto accordo nel termine quattro mesi a partire dal giorno dello scambio delle ratifiche, il Presidente del Consiglio Amministrativo Permanente della Corte Permanente dell'Aja, designerá il Presidente della Commissione. La richiesta di tale nomina sará rivolta da entrambi i Governi al Presidente del detto Consiglio entro un nuovo termine di un mese, o trascorso tale termine, dal Governo piú diligente. In ogni caso, il terzo Arbitro non potrá essere né Messicano né Italiano, né suddito di un Paese che abbia contró el Messico dei reclami uguali a quelli che formano oggetto di questa Convenzione.

In caso di decesso di uno dei Membri della Commissione o qualora uno di essi sia impedito di compiere le sue funzioni o si astenga dal compierle per qualsiasi motivo, egli sará immediatamente sostituito, con lo atesso procedimento stabilito in questa Convenzione.

Articolo II

I Membri della Commissione cosi nominati si riuniranno nella Cittá di

Artículo I

Todas las reclamaciones especificadas en el artículo III de esta Convención, se sometarán a una Comisión, compuesta de tres miembros: uno de ellos será nombrado por el Presidente de los Estados Unidos Mexicanos; otro, por Su Majestad el Rey de Italia, y el tercero, que presidirá la Comisión, será designado de acuerdo por los dos Gobiernos. Si éstos no llegan a dicho acuerdo en un plazo de cuatro meses, contados desde el día en que se haga el canje de las ratificaciones, el Presidente del Consejo Administrativo Permanente de la Corte Permanente de Arbitraje de La Haya, será quien designe al Presidente de la Comisión. La solicitud de este nombramiento se dirigirá por ambos Gobiernos al Presidente del citado Consejo, dentro de un nuevo plazo de un mes, o pasado este plazo por el Gobierno más diligente. En todo caso, el tercer árbitro no podrá ser mexicano ni italiano, ni nacional de un país que tenga contra México reclamaciones iguales a las que son objeto de esta Convención.

En caso de muerte de alguno de los miembros de la Comisión, o en caso de que alguno de ellos esté impedido para cumplir sus funciones o se abstenga por cualquiera causa de hacerlo, será reemplazado inmediatamente, siguiendo el mismo procedimiento establecido en esta Convención.

Artículo II

Los comisionados así designados, se reunirán en la ciudad de México,

Messico entro sei mesi dalla data dello scambio delle ratifiche della presente Convenzione. Ciascuno dei Membri della Commissione, prima di iniziare i suoi lavori, fará e firmerá una solenne dichiarazione, nella quale egli si obbligherá ad essaminare con cura ed a risolvere con imparzialitá — secondo i principi della giustizia e dell'equitá — tutti i reclami presentati, poiché la volontá del Messico e quella d'indennizzare graziosamente i danneggiati e non che la sua responsabilitá si stabilisca in conformitá ai principi generali del Diritto Internazionale, bastando pertanto si provi che il danno affermato abbia esistito e sia dovuto ad alcuna delle cause enumerate nell'articolo III di questa Convenzione, perché il Messico si senta disposto "ex gratia" ad indennizzare.

La predetta dichiarazione verrá registrata negli Atti della Commissione.

La Commissione fisserá la data ed il luogo delle sue sedute.

Articolo III

La Commissione conoscerá di tutti i reclami contro il Messico per la perdite od i danni sofferti da sudditi italiani o da società, compagnie, associazione o persone morali italiane ; o per perdite o danni causati a sudditi italiani, in società ed associazioni, purché, in questo caso, l'interesse del danneggiato sia superiore al cinquanta per cento del capitale totale della società o de la associazione di cui egli fa parte ed anteriore all'epoca in cui

dentro de los seis meses, contados a partir de la fecha del canje de ratificaciones de la presente Convención. Cada uno de los miembros de la Comisión, antes de dar principio a sus trabajos, hará y firmará una declaración solemne en que se comprometa a examinar con cuidado y a fallar con imparcialidad, conforme a los principios de la justicia y de la equidad, todas las reclamaciones presentadas, supuesto que la voluntad de México es la de reparar graciosamente a los damnificados y no que su responsabilidad se establezca de conformidad con los principios generales del Derecho Internacional ; siendo bastante, por tanto, se pruebe que el daño alegado haya existido y se deba a alguna de las causas enumeradas en el artículo III de esta Convención, para que México se sienta, "ex-gratia," inclinado a indemnizar.

La citada declaración se registrará en las actas de la Comisión.

La Comisión fijará la fecha y el lugar de sus sesiones.

Artículo III

La Comisión conocerá de todas las reclamaciones contra México, por pérdidas o daños resentidos por súbditos italianos y por sociedades, compañías, asociaciones o personas morales italianas, o por pérdidas o daños causados a súbditos italianos, en sociedades y asociaciones, siempre que, en este caso, el interés del damnificado sea de más de un cincuenta por ciento del capital total de la sociedad o asociación de que forme

la perdita od il danno sono stati sofferti e purché inoltre si presenti alla Commissione un atto di cessione fatta al reclamante della parte proporzionale della perdita o del danno che gli spetti in detta compagnia od associazione. Le perdite od i dani di cui si parla in questo articolo dovranno esser stati causati durante il periodo compreso fra il 20 Novembre 1910 ed il 31 Maggio 1920, inclusivo, dalle forze seguenti:

1.º Da forze di un Governo *de jure* o *de facto;*

2.º Da forze rivoluzionarie che abbiano costituito, al trionfo della loro causa, un Governo *de jure* o *de facto* o da forze rivoluzionarie contrarie alle predette;

3.º Da forze derivanti dalla disgregazione di quelle indicate nel paragrafo precedente, fino al momento in cui il Governo *de jure* sia stato stabilito dopo una determinata rivoluzione;

4.º Da forze derivanti della dissoluzione dell'Esercito Federale;

5.º Da ammutinamenti od insurrezione o da forze insorte, diverse da quelle indicate nei paragrafi 2.º, 3.º e 4.º di questo articolo, o da banditi purché, in ogni caso, si provi che le competenti Autoritá abbiano trascurato di prendere ragionevoli misure per reprimere l'insurrezione, gli ammutinamenti e le sollevazioni o gli atti di brigantaggio di cui si tratta, o per punire i loro autori; o che la Autoritá siano incorse in qualche manchevolezza di altra natura.

La Commissione conoscerá ugualmente dei reclami per perdite o danni

parte, anterior a la época en que se resintió el daño o pérdida y que además se presente a la Comisión una cesión hecha al reclamante de la parte proporcional de la pérdida o daño que le toque en tal compañía o asociación. Las pérdidas o daños de que se habla en este artículo, deberán haber sido causados durante el período comprendido entre el 20 de noviembre de 1910 y el 31 de mayo de 1920, inclusive, por las fuerzas siguientes:

1.º Por fuerzas de un Gobierno *de jure* o *de facto:*

2.º Por fuerzas revolucionarias que hayan establecido al triunfo de su causa un Gobierno *de jure* o *de facto*, o por fuerzas revolutionarias contrarias a aquéllas;

3.º Por fuerzas procedentes de la disgregación de las que se mencionan en el párrafo precedente, hasta el momento en que el Gobierno *de jure* hubiere sido establecido después de una revolución determinada;

4.º Por fuerzas procedentes de la disolución del Ejército Federal;

5.º Por motines o levantamientos, o por fuerzas insurrectas distintas de las indicadas en las párrafos 2.º, 3.º y 4.º de este artículo, o por bandoleros, con tal que, en cada caso, se pruebe que las autoridades competentes omitieron dictar medidas razonables para reprimir las insurrecciones, levantamientos, motines o actos de bandolerismo de que se trata, o para castigar a sus autores; o que se pruebe, asimismo, que las autoridades incurrieron en falta de alguna otra manera.

La Comisión conocerá también de las reclamaciones por pérdidas o daños

causati da atti di Autoritá Civili, purché detti atti abbiano la loro origine da avvenimenti e disordini rivoluzionari, entro l'epoca alla quale allude questo articolo e siano stati eseguiti da alcuna delle forze indicate nei paragrafi 1.º, 2.º e 3.º del presente articolo.

causados por actos de autoridades civiles, siempre que dichos actos se originen en sucesos y trastornos revolucionarios, dentro de la época a que alude este artículo y que hayan sido ejecutados por alguna de las fuerzas descritas en los párrafos 1.º, 2.º y 3.º del presente artículo.

Articolo IV

La Commissione determinerá la sua propria procedura, atenendosi peró alle disposizioni della presente Convenzione.

Ciascun Governo potrá nominare un Agente e dei consiglieri che presentino alla Commissione, verbalmente o per iscritto, le prove e gli argomenti che giudichino opportuno di addurre in appoggio ai reclami o contro gli stessi.

La decisione della maggioranza dei Membri della Commissione sará quella della Commissione. Qualora non si formasse una maggioranza, prevarrá la decisione del Presidente.

Tanto ni procedimenti come nelle sentenze, si userá la lingua spagnuola o la italiana.

Artículo IV

La Comisión decretará sus procedimientos, pero ciñéndose a las disposiciones de la presente Convención.

Cada Gobierno podrá nombrar un Agente y Consejeros que presenten a la Comisión, ya sea oralmente o por escrito, las pruebas y argumentos que juzguen conveniente aducir en apoyo de las reclamaciones o en contra de ellas.

La decisión de la mayoría de los miembros de la Comisión, será la de la Comisión. Si no hubiere mayoría, prevalecerá la decisión del Presidente.

Tanto en los procedimientos como en los fallos, se empleará el español o el italiano.

Articolo V

La Commissione registrerá con esatteza tutti i reclami ed i adversi casi che le fossero sottoposti, come pure i verbali delle discussioni, in ordine di data.

A tal fine, ciascun Governo designerá un Segretario. Questi Segretari dipenderanno dalla Commissione e saranno soggetti alle sue istruzioni.

Ciascun Governo potrá nominare, ugualmente, ed impiegare i Segretari

Artículo V

La Comisión irá registrando con exactitud todas las reclamaciones y los diversos casos que le fueren sometidos, así como las actas de los debates, con sus fechas respectivas.

Para tal fin, cada Gobierno designará un Secretario. Dichos Secretarios dependerán de la Comisión y estarán sometidos a sus instrucciones.

Cada Gobierno podrá nombrar, asimismo, y emplear los Secretarios

aggiunti che giudicasse del caso. La Commissione potrá ugualmente nominare ed impiegare gli assistenti che giudicasse necessari per condurre a termine la sua missione.

Articolo VI

Poiché il Governo del Messico desidera di giungere ad una definizione equitativa dei reclami specificati all'articolo III e concedere ai reclamanti una giusta indennitá che corrisponda alle perdite od ai danni da loro sofferti, resta inteso che la Commissione non scarterá o respingerá alcun reclamo per il fatto che non siano state esaurite, prima della presentazione del reclamo, tutta le vie di ricorso legale.

Per fissare l'ammontare delle indennitá da concedersi per danni arrecati ai beni, si terrá in conto il valore dichiarato al Fisco dagli interessati, salvo che per i casi veramente eccezionale, a giudizio della Commissione.

L'ammontare dell'indennitá per danni personali non eccederá quello delle maggiori indennitá concesse in casi simili dall'Italia.

Articolo VII

Ogni reclamo dovrá presentarsi assolutamente dinnazi la Commissione entro il termine di quattro mesi dal giorno della sua prima riunione, a meno che, in casi eccezionali, la maggioranza dei Membri della Commissione giudichi soddisfacenti i motivi addotti in ciascun caso per giustificare il ritardo; il periodo

adjuntos que juzgare prudente. La Comisión podrá nombrar y emplear, igualmente, los ayudantes que juzgue necesarios para llevar a cabo su misión.

Artículo VI

Deseando el Gobierno de México llegar a un arreglo equitativo sobre las reclamaciones especificadas en el artículo III, y conceder a los reclamantes una indemnización justa que corresponda a las pérdidas o daños que hayan sufrido, queda convenido que la Comisión no habrá de descartar o rechazar ninguna reclamación por causa de que no se hubieren agotado, antes de presentar dicha reclamación, todos los recursos legales.

Para fijar el importe de las indemnizaciones que habrán de concederse por los daños a los bienes, se tendrá en cuenta el valor declarado al Fisco por los interesados, salvo en casos verdaderamente excepcionales, a juicio de la Comisión.

El importe de las indemnizaciones por daños personales no excederá al de las indemnizaciones más amplias concedidas por Italia en casos semejantes.

Artículo VII

Toda reclamación habrá de presentarse formalmente ante la Comisión, dentro del plazo de cuatro meses, contados desde el día de su primer reunión, a menos que, en casos excepcionales, la mayoría de los miembros de la misma Comisión juzgue satisfactorias las razones que se den en cada caso para justificar el retardo;

entro il quale potrano essere registrati simili reclami eccezionali non potrá estendersi a piú di due mesi al di lá della scandenza del termine normale.

La Commissione ascolterá, esaminerá e risolverá entro il termine di un anno, dal giorno della sua prima riunione, tutti i reclami che le fossero presentati.

Due mesi dopo il giorno della prima riunione dei Membri della Commissione, e successivamente ad ogni bimestre, la Commissione sottoporrá a ciascuno dei Governi una Relazione, in cui risultino dettagliatamente descritti i lavori compiuti e che contenga ugualmente un'esposizione dei reclami presentati, di quelli trattati e di quelli risolti.

La Commissione emetterá la sua decisione in ordine a ciascun reclamo che le sia stato presentato, entro il termine di tre mesi, a partire dalla chiasura delle discussione concernenti il reclamo stesso.

Articolo VIII

Le Alte Parti Contraenti convengone nel considerare come definitiva la decisione della Commissione su ciascuno degli affari che essa giudichi e nel dar piena esecuzione alle predette decisioni. Esse convengono pure nel considerare il risultato dei lavori della Commissione come un regolamento pieno, perfetto e definitivo di tutti i reclami contro il Governo del Messico che provengano da alcuna delle cause enumerate allo articolo III della presente Convenzione. Esse convengono infine nel

el período dentro del cual podrán registrarse dichas reclamaciones excepcionales, no se extenderá a más de dos meses, después del término de expiración del plazo normal.

La Comisión oirá, examinará y resolverá, dentro del plazo de un año, contado desde el día de su primera reunión, todas las reclamaciones que le fueren presentadas.

Dos meses después del día de la primera reunión de los miembros de la Comisión, y luego bimestralmente, la Comisión someterá a cada uno de los Gobiernos, un informe donde queden establecidos, pormenorizadamente, los trabajos realizados y que comprenda también una exposición de las reclamaciones presentadas, de las oídas y de las resueltas.

La Comisión dará su fallo sobre toda reclamación que se le presente, dentro del plazo de tres meses, contados desde la clausura de los debates relativos a dicha reclamación.

Artículo VIII

Las Altas Partes Contratantes, convienen en considerar como definitiva la decisión de la Comisión, sobre cada uno de los asuntos que juzgue, y en dar pleno efecto a las referidas decisiones. Convienen también en considerar el resultado de los trabajos de la Comisión, como un arreglo pleno, perfecto y definitivo, de todas las reclamaciones que contra el Gobierno de México, provengan de alguna de las causas enumeradas en el artículo III de la presente Convención. Convienen, además, en que

senso che, dal momento in cui finiscano i lavori della Commissione, qualsiasi reclamo di tale natura sia esso state presentato, o no, alla Commissione, debba considerarsi come regolato assolutamente ed irrevocabilmente nell'avvenire; a condizione che i reclami presentati alla Commissione siano stati esaminati e risolti dalla stessa.

desde el momento en que terminen los trabajos de la Comisión, toda reclamación de esa especie, haya o no sido presentada a dicha Comisión, habrá de considerarse como arreglada absoluta e irrevocablemente para lo sucesivo, a condición de que, las que hubieren sido presentadas a la Comisión, hayan sido examinadas y resueltas por ella.

Articolo IX

La forma in cui il Governo Messicano pagherá la indennitá sará fissata da entrambi i Governi, dopo terminati i lavori della Commissione. I pagamenti sarano effetuati in oro od in moneta equivalente e saranno fatti del Governo Messicano al Governo Italiano.

Artículo IX

La forma en que el Gobierno Mexicano pagará las indemnizaciones, se fijará por ambos Gobiernos, una vez terminadas las labores de la Comisión. Los pagos se efectuarán en oro o en moneda equivalente, y se harán por el Gobierno Mexicano al Gobierno Italiano.

Articolo X

Ciascun Governo pagherá gli onorari del suo Commissario e quelli del suo personale.

Alle spesse comuni della Commissione, nonché agli onarari spettanti al terzo Commissario, contribuiranno in parti uguali entrambi i Governi.

Artículo X

Cada Gobierno pagará los honorarios de su Comisionado y los de su personal.

Los gastos comunes de la Comisión, lo mismo que los honorarios correspondientes al tercer Comisionado, los sufragarán por mitad ambos Gobiernos.

Articolo XI

La presente Convenzione é redatta in lingua spagnuola ed in lingua italiana e resta inteso che per qualsiasi dubbio intorno alla sua interpretazione dará norma il testo espagnuolo.

Artículo XI

Esta Convención está redactada en español y en italiano, y queda convenido que cualquiera duda sobre su interpretación, será dilucidada por el texto español.

Articolo XII

Le Alte Parti Contraenti ratificheranno la presente Convenzione, in

Artículo XII

Las Altas Partes Contratantes ratificarán la presente Convención, de

conformitá alle loro rispetive Costituzioni. Lo scambio delle ratifiche avrá luogo in Cittá di Messico non appena possibili e la Convenzione entrerá in vigore dal momento in cui lo scambio delle ratifiche sia pubblicato.

In fe di che, i rispettive Plenipotenziari hanno firmato la presente Convenzione apponendovi i loro sigilli.

Fatta, in doppio originale, nella Cittá di Messico, il giorno tredici del mese di Genaio dell'anno millenovecento ventisette.

L. S.) FIRMATO. AARÓN SÁENZ.

(L. S.) FIRMATO. G. MACCHIORO VIVALBA.

conformidad con sus respectivas Constituciones. El canje de las ratificaciones se efectuará en la ciudad de México, tan pronto como fuere posible, y la Convención entrará en vigor desde el momento en que se publique el cambio de ratificaciones.

En fe de lo cual, los Plenipotenciarios respectivos firmaron la presente Convención, poniendo en ella sus sellos.

Hecha por duplicado, en la ciudad de México, a los trece días del mes de enero de mil novecientos veintisiete.

(L. S.) FIRMADO, AARÓN SÁENZ.

(L. S.) FIRMADO, G. MACCHIORO VIVALBA.

B. RULES OF PROCEDURE ADOPTED DECEMBER 6, 1930 [1]

CAPÍTULO I

OFICINAS Y JUNTAS

Art. 1. La Oficina de la Comisión será establecida y mantenida en la Ciudad de México, en donde se guardarán sus archivos.

Art. 2. La fecha y local de las reuniones se fijarán por acuerdo de la Comisión.

CAPÍTULO II

LIBROS DE REGISTRO Y ACTAS

Art. 3. Se llevarán dos libros iguales de registro, uno por cada Secretario en su propio idioma, donde se asentarán, al presentarse formalmente la reclamación, el nombre de cada reclamante y la cantidad reclamada; y además, se registrarán, en los mismos, todos los trámites que se vayan produciendo en cada reclamación.

Art. 4. Cada reclamación constituirá un caso separado ante la Comisión y se registrará como tal. Se numerarán progresivamente todas las reclamaciones en el orden en que se presenten.

[1] Text from Reglas de Procedimiento de la Comisión de Reclamaciones entre los Estados Unidos Mexicanos y el Gobierno de Italia (Mexico City, 1931).

Art. 5. Los Secretarios llevarán los Registros adicionales que ordena el presente reglamento o que la Comisión disponga.

Art. 6. Se llevarán dos libros iguales de actas, uno por cada Secretario en su propio idioma, y en ellos se asentará una relación cronológica de todos los trámites y acuerdos de la Comisión. En las sesiones que ésta celebre se firmará el libro de actas por los Comisionados.

Las actas serán también firmadas por los Secretarios.

Capítulo III
PRESENTACIÓN Y REGISTRO DE LAS RECLAMACIONES

Art. 7. La reclamación se considerará como formalmente presentada ante la Comisión :

(*a*) Al presentarse en siete ejemplares a los Secretarios un Memorándum que contendrá el nombre del reclamante, una relación breve de la naturaleza de la reclamación y el monto de la misma ; o bien,

(*b*) Al presentarse a los Secretarios un Memorial, en siete ejemplares, conforme a las disposiciones del Artículo 11.

Art. 8. Al recibirse el Memorándum a que se refiere el inciso (*a*), o el Memorial a que se refiere el inciso (*b*) del artículo anterior, se hará en ellos una nota de su presentación, con la fecha de la misma, por los Secretarios y suscrita por ellos ; e inmediatamente se registrará la reclamación con su número correspondiente.

Art. 9. Todas las reclamaciones por pérdidas o daños acaecidos durante el período comprendido entre el 20 de Noviembre de 1910 y el 31 de Mayo de 1920, sean las que se formulen en forma de Memorándum o las que se formulen en forma de Memoriales, deberán presentarse antes de vencer el término de cuatro meses, contados desde el 29 de noviembre de 1930, fecha en que se instaló la Comisión.

Sólo podrá ampliarse este plazo por acuerdo especial de la Comisión cuando, a su juicio, esté justificada la demora para la presentación de algún Memorial o Memorándum. Esta ampliación de plazo no podrá exceder de dos meses.

En cualquier momento, después de vencidos los cuatro meses de que habla el primer párrafo de este Artículo, la Comisión fijará, a moción del Agente Mexicano, un plazo para la presentación de Memoriales relativos a las reclamaciones que se hubieren presentado en forma de Memorándum. Los Memorándums no serán materia de contestación.

Capítulo IV
ESCRITOS

Art. 10. Los escritos principales serán : el Memorial, la Contestación, la Réplica y la Dúplica, si los Agentes las presentaren, las Reformas a estos escritos

y los relativos a excepciones y mociones. Por convenio entre los Agentes, confirmado por la Comisión, o por acuerdo de ésta, los Agentes podrán presentar escritos complementarios, o sea, que se refieran a las materias tratadas en el Memorial y la Contestación.

Art. 11. El Memorial.

Para ser admitido a tramitación, cada Memorial deberá ser firmado por el reclamante o por su apoderado, y podrá estar suscrito por el abogado o patrono del reclamante, si lo hubiere.

Todos los Memoriales deberán también ser suscritos o refrendados con su firma por el Agente del Gobierno Italiano.

El Memorial contendrá una relación de los hechos en que se funde la reclamación. Expondrá en cada caso:

(*a*) Los hechos que demuestren que la pérdida o daño por los cuales se hace la reclamación, resultaron de alguna o algunas de las causas especificadas en el Artículo 3.º de la Convención de Reclamaciones entre México e Italia, suscrita en la ciudad de México el 13 de enero de 1927.

(*b*) El monto de la reclamación; la fecha y lugar en donde se originó el daño o pérdida; la clase, cantidad y valor de la propiedad perdida o dañada; una relación, pormenorizada hasta donde sea posible, de los agravios sufridos en la persona, si los hubiere; y las pérdidas o daños que resultaron de los mismos; los hechos y demás circunstancias concurrentes con la pérdida o daño, ya sea en la persona, ya en la propiedad, por los que se origina la reclamación y sobre los cuales el reclamante se funda para establecerla.

(*c*) A nombre de quién se formula la reclamación. Si la persona que la presenta lo hace con el carácter de representante, comprobará su personalidad.

(*d*) La nacionalidad del dueño o dueños de la reclamación en la fecha en que se causó el daño o pérdida y en la fecha en que se presenta la reclamación. Si la nacionalidad proviene de nacimiento, de naturalización o de algún otro acto, deberán exponerse y comprobarse todos los hechos concernientes a este respecto.

(*e*) Si el reclamante alega, como base de su reclamación, la pérdida o daño sufrido por alguna sociedad, compañía, asociación o persona moral, en la cual es parte el reclamante o la persona a nombre de quien se hace la reclamación, comprobará que su interés es de más de un cincuenta por ciento (50%) del capital social de la sociedad o asociación de que forma parte, y que ese interés fué adquirido con anterioridad a la época en que se resintió el daño o pérdida. Además, se presentará a la Comisión una cesión hecha al reclamante de la parte proporcional de la pérdida o daño que le toque en tal compañía o asociación. En tal caso, el Memorial expondrá todos los hechos o consideraciones de equidad relacionados con dicha reclamación o en apoyo de ella. En caso de que el título del reclamante sea traslativo de dominio en su favor, presentará a la Comisión la prueba documental en que se funde, o se expondrán las causas que puedan fundar la ausencia de tal prueba.

(*f*) Si el derecho a la reclamación pertenece ahora, y perteneció en la fecha en que se originó, única y absolutamente al reclamante, o si alguna otra persona está o ha estado interesada en la misma o en parte alguna de ella. En este último caso quién es esa otra persona y cuál es o fué la naturaleza y la extensión de su interés; y cómo, cuándo, por qué medios y por qué compensación se hizo el traspaso de derechos o intereses entre las partes, si lo hubo.

(*g*) Si el reclamante, o cualquiera otra persona que en cualquier tiempo haya tenido derecho a la cantidad reclamada, o a alguna parte de ella, ha recibido alguna suma de dinero; y, en caso afirmativo, qué suma, o qué equivalencia o indemnización en cualquiera forma que sea, ya por el monto total o por parte del importe de la pérdida o daño en que se funde la reclamación; y de ser así, cuándo y de quién se recibió.

(*h*) Si alguna vez se ha presentado la reclamación o si se ha depositado alguna queja respecto a la misma ante cualquiera de los Gobiernos; y en caso de ser así, los hechos relativos a dicha presentación.

(*i*) Cualquiera reclamación derivada de daño o pérdida que se alegue que, fué sufrida por un italiano fallecido, deberá ser presentada por los representantes legales de la sucesión. Cuando haya habido escritura de adjudicación, la reclamación podrá ser presentada por los adjudicatarios.

(*j*) En los casos en que varias reclamaciones se deriven de un mismo grupo de hechos, se podrán incluir todas o cualesquiera de ellas en un mismo Memorial.

(*k*) La omisión de cualquiera de estos requisitos deberá ser justificada ante la Comisión.

Art. 12.   La Contestación.

(*a*) La Contestación, en cada caso, se presentará a los Secretarios, dentro de sesenta días contados a partir de la fecha en que se presente el Memorial, a no ser que antes de que se termine el plazo, éste se prorrogue: (1) por convenio entre los Agentes notificado a los Secretarios y confirmado por la Comisión; o (2) por la Comisión cuando considere que hay causa suficiente para ello, a solicitud del Agente Mexicano, siempre que la moción respectiva sea hecha con anterioridad al vencimiento del plazo de sesenta días. Mientras se resuelve este punto se suspenderán los términos.

(*b*) La Contestación se referirá a cada uno de los puntos del Memorial, y manifestará la actitud del Gobierno que contesta respecto a los diversos elementos de la reclamación. Puede, además, contener todas aquellas materias neuvas que el Gobierno que contesta desee hacer constar dentro del alcance de la Convención.

Art. 13.   La Réplica.

(*a*) En los casos en que se estime necesario presentar una Réplica, podrá ser entregada a los Secretarios dentro de treinta (30) días contados a partir de la fecha en que se presente la Contestación, a menos que, antes de terminar el

plazo, éste se prorrogue: (1) por convenio entre los Agentes respectivos, presentado en la misma forma a los Secretarios y confirmado por la Comisión; o (2) por la Comisión, cuando considere que hay causa suficiente para ello a solicitud del Agente Italiano, siempre que la moción respectiva sea hecha con anterioridad al vencimiento del plazo de treinta (30) días. También en este caso, mientras se resuelve, se suspenderán los términos.

(*b*) La Réplica, caso de presentarse, se concretará a las materias contenidas en la Contestación.

Art. 14. La Dúplica.

Cuando un Agente considere necesario duplicar, podrá hacerlo dentro de treinta (30) días contados desde la fecha en que fuere presentada la Réplica. La Dúplica y su tramitación se sujetarán a las mismas reglas de la Réplica.

Art. 15. Reformas a los escritos presentados.

(*a*) El Memorial y la Contestación, como también la Réplica y la Dúplica, podrán reformarse en cualquier momento antes del fallo definitivo, ya sea: (1) por acuerdo entre los Agentes confirmado por la Comisión; o (2) por permiso de la Comisión, a solicitud de alguno de los Agentes previo traslado al otro, y conforme a las condiciones que la Comisión establezca.

(*b*) Todas las mociones solicitando permiso para reformar los escritos indicados en la letra (*a*) se presentarán por escrito ante los Secretarios, y contendrán las reformas que deseen hacerse y las razones en que se funden.

(*c*) Las reformas a los escritos a que se refieren los incisos anteriores deberán acompañarse de las copias de los documentos o pruebas que se aduzcan en su apoyo.

(*d*) Podrán presentarse Contestaciones, Réplicas o Dúplicas a los escritos de reforma, de la misma manera que si se tratara de escritos principales, dentro del plazo que convengan los Agentes y confirme la Comisión, o que se fije por ésta.

Art. 16. La Comisión no tomará en cuenta hechos relativos a la reclamación o a la defensa, que no estén debidamente consignados en los escritos principales o que no estén apoyados con pruebas. Las consideraciones de derecho serán atendidas hasta la terminación de las audiencias.

Art. 17. A moción de cualquiera de los Agentes, o por propia iniciativa, la Comisión, después de oír a los Agentes podrá acordar la acumulación o separación de las reclamaciones.

Art. 18. Cada Memorial, Contestación, Réplica y Dúplica, al presentarse, irán acompañados de los documentos correspondientes.

Los Agentes podrán, por convenio entre ellos, confirmado por la Comisión, ponerse de acuerdo sobre la admisión de nuevos documentos en cualquier fecha posterior a la presentación de los escritos principales. A falta de acuerdo entre los Agentes, resolverá la Comisión.

Capítulo V

EXCEPCIONES DILATORIAS

Art. 19. Las Excepciones Dilatorias que opongan los Agentes para no entrar a discutir el fondo del asunto, pueden ser presentadas en forma de contestación especial, antes de toda defensa relativa al fondo, y en el plazo fijado para la Contestación las del Agente Mexicano, y en el fijado para la Réplica, las del Agente Italiano; o al responder sobre el fondo, según elija el Agente respectivo. Si hay varias excepciones de esta naturaleza, deben ser presentadas conjuntamente. Cualquiera otra excepción debe ser presentada en la Contestación.

Art. 20. Si las excepciones a que se refiere el artículo anterior son presentadas en forma de contestación especial, la tramitación, por lo que se refiere al estudio del fondo de la cuestión, se suspenderá. Si la excepción es desechada, el recurrente deberá evacuar el trámite pendiente dentro del plazo de treinta (30) días.

Capítulo VI

COPIAS Y TRADUCCIONES DE ESCRITOS PRINCIPALES Y OTROS DOCUMENTOS

Art. 21. De todos los escritos presentados a la Comisión el Agente respectivo deberá entregar a los Secretarios siete copias.

Art. 22. En las copias a que se refiere el artículo anterior sólo será necesario insertar, en cuanto a los documentos y pruebas que se acompañan a los escritos, aquella parte que se aduzca. Sin embargo, a petición del Agente de la parte contraria, el documento íntegro o copia certificada del mismo deberá ser proporcionado a la Comisión.

Art. 23. La Comisión podrá mandar imprimir los documentos que se presenten.

Capítulo VII

NOTIFICACIONES

Art. 24. Las Notificaciones de cualquier escrito se considerarán hechas con la entrega que los Secretarios harán a los Agentes de la copia respectiva.

Capítulo VIII

MOCIONES SOBRE INADMISIBILIDAD DE RECLAMACIONES

Art. 25. En cualquier tiempo, después de registrada una reclamación, el Agente Mexicano podrá presentar moción por escrito pidiendo que se la declare inadmisible por causa justificada, dando las pruebas de su moción.

Admitida la moción, se suspenderán los términos que estén corriendo.

Las Mociones de Inadmisibilidad podrán ser retiradas por consentimiento de la Comisión, en las condiciones que ella fije.

Art. 26. Las Mociones de Inadmisibilidad se someterán a la misma tramitación señalada para las Mociones de reforma.

Capítulo IX

DE LA PRUEBA

Art. 27. La Comisión recibirá y considerará todas las declaraciones, documentos, interrogatorios u otras pruebas que por escrito le sean presentadas por conducto de los Agentes, dentro de los términos que señala este Reglamento, en apoyo de o en contra de cualquier reclamación. Ninguno de estos documentos, declaraciones u otras pruebas serán recibidos o considerados por la Comisión, si se presentaren por cualquier otro conducto.

Art. 28. Cuando un documento original que se encuentre en los archivos de alguno de los Gobiernos interesados no pueda ser retirado, podrán recibirse como pruebas en su lugar copias debidamente certificadas.

Art. 29. Cuando un documento u otra prueba esté archivada en las oficinas de cualesquiera de los dos Gobiernos, y no pueda ser retirada fácilmente, ni exista copia en poder del Agente que desee presentarlo a la Comisión, hará saber por escrito al Agente contrario su deseo de examinar el referido documento o prueba. Si esa solicitud de examen no es obsequiada por el Agente requerido, tal conducta, junto con las razones que se dieren en su apoyo, será puesta en conocimiento de la Comisión, para que ésta adopte la resolución que estime conveniente.

El derecho concedido para examinar tales piezas se extenderá a todo el documento del cual sólo se haya presentado una parte.

Art. 30. Los Agentes tendrán derecho a presentar testigos bajo las siguientes condiciones :

(*a*) Los testigos serán examinados bajo juramento o protesta por la Comisión, al tenor de los interrogatorios presentados por los Agentes. Cualquier testigo presentado por uno de los Agentes estará sujeto a preguntas o repreguntas por el Agente de la parte contraria, o por los miembros de la Comisión.

(*b*) En cualquier caso en que uno de los Agentes desee presentar testimonio oral, dará aviso dentro de diez (10) días, contados desde la fecha en que expire el plazo para presentar la Réplica o la Dúplica en su caso, haciéndolo por escrito, ante ambos Secretarios y manifestando los nombres y las direcciones de los testigos que desea examinar. No se tomará ningún testimonio oral sino de acuerdo con la notificación dada dentro del término y en la forma antes prescritos, a menos que así lo permita la Comisión.

(*c*) La Comisión fijará la fecha y el lugar en que recibirán las declaraciones testimoniales, las cuales se harán constar por escrito proporcionándose copias de ellas a los Agentes.

(*d*) Las declaraciones se rendirán en español, a menos que el testigo no posea ese idioma ; en tal caso se empleará el idioma que mejor se adapte a la comprensión del testigo. Las declaraciones en idioma extranjero se traducirán bajo la dirección de la Secretaría.

(*e*) En caso de que no pudiera presentarse un testigo ante la Comisión, podrá ser examinado por exhorto dirigido por conducto de los Agentes a la autoridad judicial competente del lugar del domicilio o de la residencia del testigo. La declaración será recibida con las formalidades de la Ley local.

Art. 31. La Comisión, cuando lo juzgue conveniente, podrá recibir testimonios orales en cualquier estado del juicio.

La Comisión, o cualquiera de sus miembros, podrá hacer comparecer, antes de la vista de la causa, a cualquiera de los testigos que hayan declarado.

Art. 32. Después del último escrito principal y en cualquier tiempo antes del fallo, la Comisión podrá ordenar que se oiga el parecer de uno o más peritos sobre materias que exijan conocimientos especiales, e igualmente podrá ordenar vistas de ojos.

Capítulo X

AUDIENCIAS

Art. 33. Las audiencias se verificarán ante la Comisión reunida en pleno.

Art. 34. Cada Secretario llevará su Agenda de Audiencias en su propio idioma, en la cual serán apuntados para la vista todos los casos que cada Agente someta coneste propósito. Los casos así puestos en lista serán numerados consecutivamente en el orden en que sean sometidos. Además, en las Agendas de Audiencias se anotarán las fechas en que se vence el término para los Alegatos escritos mencionados en el Artículo 35, así como la fecha en que éstos deban presentarse.

Art. 35. Cuando el Agente del Gobierno de Italia desee que se proceda a la vista de un caso, lo notificará a los Secretarios; y podrá presentar, juntamente con dicha notificación, un alegato escrito, así como las pruebas documentales en que se funde, además de las que previamente haya presentado. El Agente Mexicano podrá, dentro de diez (10) días, contados desde la fecha en que reciba la copia del alegato de referencia, presentar alegato escrito de contestación juntamente con las pruebas escritas que desee. El Agente Italiano podrá presentar, dentro de diez (10) días de que reciba la contestación referida, un alegato de Réplica unido a nuevas pruebas, si las hubiere, y finalmente el Agente Mexicano podrá presentar dentro de diez (10) días de que reciba la Réplica, un alegato de Dúplica unido a nuevas pruebas, si las hubiere.

Art. 36. Los casos serán examinados en el orden en que estén registrados en la Agenda de Audiencias, a menos que se cambie ese orden por convenio de los Agentes o acuerdo de la Comisión. Ambos Secretarios harán los asientos respectivos, registrando cualquier cambio que se hiciese en el orden numérico.

Si no hubiere en la Agenda ningún caso listado para vista, se podrán listar los casos que ordene la Comisión, después de oír a los Agentes. Cualquiera orden de la Comisión, para examinar casos. tendrá que dictarse por lo menos

pasados diez (10) días después del vencimiento del plazo para presentar Contestación, Réplica o Dúplica, según el caso.

Art. 37. Con los alegatos escritos termina el procedimiento. Sólo habrá alegatos orales cuando lo pidan de común acuerdo los Agentes o lo determine la Comisión a solicitud de alguno de ellos.

La Comisión fijará, en cada caso, las reglas a que estarán sometidas las alegaciones orales.

Art. 38. Terminado el proceso de una reclamación, los tres Comisionados examinarán el caso conjuntamente, y la Comisión dictará su fallo.

Capítulo XI

SENTENCIAS Y DECISIONES

Art. 39. Las sentencias o cualquiera otra decisión judicial de la Comisión con respecto a cada reclamación, deberá darse a conocer en sesión pública de la Comisión.

Art. 40. La sentencia o cualquiera otra decisión judicial consignará los fundamentos en que está basada, y deberá estar firmada por dos miembros de la Comisión, cuando menos. El Comisionado disidente, si lo hubiere, podrá formular su voto particular.

Art. 41. Si los Agentes celebran un convenio con respecto a cualquier reclamación, tal convenio será presentado a la Comisión para que ésta pueda tomarlo en cuenta en la sentencia que dicte.

Art. 42. Ambos Secretarios proporcionarán a cada uno de los Agentes cuatro (4) copias, o, en los casos en que la Comisión ordene que se impriman, diez (10) copias de cada sentencia o de cualquiera otra decisión, y de cada una de las opiniones disidentes, si se hubieren formulado en voto particular y el Comisionado disidente lo autoriza.

Art. 43. A solicitud de cualquiera de los Agentes, hecha dentro de los quince (15) días subsiguientes a la fecha en que ambos Secretarios hayan proporcionado a los Agentes las copias de las sentencias o de cualquiera otra decisión, y después de dar al otro Agente una oportunidad para ser oído, la Comisión podrá aclarar una decisión que en su parte resolutiva sea obscura, incompleta o contradictoria, o que contenga cualquier error de expresión o de cálculo.

Art. 44. En un libro intitulado "Registro de Sentencias y Decisiones" será archivada una copia de cada una de las sentencias o de cualquiera otra decisión dictada por la Comisión y de cada opinión disidente.

Ambos Secretarios enviarán a la Oficina Internacional de la Corte Permanente de Arbitraje de La Haya, dos (2) copias de todas las sentencias y de las opiniones disidentes que se hayan impreso, si se hubiesen formulado en voto particular, siempre que el Comisionado disidente así lo autorice.

Capítulo XII

IDIOMAS

Art. 45. Todos los documentos presentados por los Agentes deberán serlo en español o en italiano.

Art. 46. A petición de cualquiera de los Agentes, debidamente notificada al otro, este último estará obligado a presentar dentro de un plazo razonable, la traducción completa o parcial de un documento, quedando entretanto suspenso el término que esté corriendo. La Comisión podrá ordenar la traducción completa o parcial de un documento.

Art. 47. Todas las resoluciones de la Comisión deberán ser redactadas en español y en italiano.

Capítulo XIII

OBLIGACIONES DE LOS SECRETARIOS

Art. 48. Los Secretarios, que en el desempeño de las atribuciones y deberes que les señala el presente Reglamento procedieren conjuntamente, deberán :

(*a*) Estar supeditados a las órdenes de la Comisión.

(*b*) Guardar todos los documentos y registros de la Comisión y conservarlos sistemáticamente arreglados en archiveros de seguridad. Aun cuando deben prestarse todas las facilidades que sean razonables a los Agentes y a los respectivos Consejeros para examinar y tomar nota de ellos, no deberán permitir que se retire de los archivos ningún documento o registro, excepto por acuerdo de la Comisión, debidamente registrado.

(*c*) Formar un Registro, una Agenda de Audiencias, un Libro de Actas, un Libro de Notificaciones, un Libro de Acuerdos, un Libro de "Sentencias y Decisiones" y todos los demás libros y documentos que la Comisión disponga.

(*d*) Anotar en cada documento que se presente a la Comisión la fecha de su presentación y hacer la anotación correspondiente en el Libro de Registro.

(*e*) Asentar en los dos Libros de Notificaciones, todas las que conforme a estas Reglas deberán hacerse; y dar inmediato aviso de ello al Agente a quien deba notificarse. Se asentará en dichos libros la fecha en que se haga cada notificación, así como todos los trámites a que ella dé lugar.

(*f*) Proporcionar dentro de veinticuatro (24) horas al Agente de la parte contraria, copia de todos los escritos principales, mociones y otros documentos presentados a los Secretarios por el otro Agente, registrándolos debidamente. De esta entrega se dará recibo por el Agente.

(*g*) Desempeñar todas las demás obligaciones que les señale la Comisión.

(*h*) Rendir los informes a que se refiere el Artículo VII de la Convención a sus respectivos Gobiernos, cuando la Comisión no esté reunida, enviando copias de ellos a cada Comisionado. Estos informes serán provisionales y sujetos a la ratificación de la Comisión.

Art. 49. Las personas empleadas como traductores, intérpretes y taquígrafos, estarán bajo la jurisdicción de los Secretarios, y sujetos también a las instrucciones de la Comisión.

Capítulo XIV

DEL CÓMPUTO DE LOS TÉRMINOS

Art. 50. Siempre que en estas reglas se mencione un período de tiempo para la ejecución de un acto, no se contará el día a partir del cual comienza a computarse el plazo y sí se contará el último día y se excluirán los domingos y días oficialmente festivos en ambos países.

Capítulo XV

DE LAS REFORMAS DE LAS REGLAS

Art. 51. La Comisión podrá reformar en cualquier tiempo estas Reglas, oyendo a los Agentes. La discusión sobre reformas no suspenderá los términos, ni las reformas tendrán efecto retroactivo.

Art. 52. En cualquiera materia no tratada expresamente en este Reglamento, la Comisión procederá de acuerdo con la Convención, el Derecho Internacional, la justicia y la equidad.

(F) Miguel Cruchaga,
Comisionado Presidente.

(F) Isidro Fabela,
Comisionado Mexicano.

(F) Mario Serra di Cassano,
Comisionado Italiano.

VII. SPANISH–MEXICAN CLAIMS COMMISSION

A. CONVENTION OF NOVEMBER 25, 1925 [1]

El Presidente de los Estados Unidos Mexicanos y Su Majestad el Rey de España, deseosos de arreglar definitiva y amigablemente todas las reclamaciones pecuniarias motivadas por las pérdidas o daños que resintieron los súbditos españoles a causa de actos revolucionarios ejecutados durante el período comprendido entre el 20 de noviembre de 1910 y el 31 de mayo de 1920, inclusive, han decidido celebrar una Convención con tal fin, y al efecto han nombrado como sus Plenipotenciarios:

El Presidente de los Estados Unidos Mexicanos, al señor licenciado don Aarón Sáenz, Secretario de Estado y del Despacho de Relaciones Exteriores.

Su Majestad el Rey de España, al Excelentísimo señor don José Gil Delgado y Olazábal, Marqués de Berna, su Enviado Extraordinario y Ministro Plenipotenciario en México.

Quienes, después de comunicarse sus Plenos Poderes, y de hallarlos en buena y debida forma, convinieron en los artículos siguientes:

Artículo Primero

Todas las reclamaciones especificadas en el Artículo Tercero de esta Convención, se someterán a una Comisión compuesta de tres miembros: uno de ellos será nombrado por el Presidente de los Estados Unidos Mexicanos; otro por Su Majestad el Rey de España, y el tercero, que presidirá la Comisión, será designado de común acuerdo por los dos Gobiernos. Si éstos no llegan a dicho acuerdo, en un plazo de dos meses, contados desde el día en que se verifique el canje de las ratificaciones, el Presidente del Consejo Administrativo Permanente del Tribunal Permanente de Arbitraje de El Haya, será quien designe al Presidente de la Comisión. La solicitud de este nombramiento se dirigirá por ambos Gobiernos al Presidente del citado Consejo, dentro de un nuevo plazo de un mes, o pasado este plazo por el Gobierno más diligente. En todo caso, el tercer árbitro no podrá ser mexicano ni español, ni ciudadano de nación que tenga contra México reclamaciones iguales a las que son objeto de esta Convención.

[1] Text from Convención que crea una Comisión especial de Reclamaciones entre los Estados Unidos Mexicanos y España (Mexico City, 1926).

521

En caso de muerte de alguno de los miembros de la Comisión, o en caso de que alguno de ellos esté imposibilitado de cumplir sus funciones o se abstenga por cualquiera causa de hacerlo, será reemplazado inmediatamente, siguiendo el mismo procedimiento detallado arriba.

Artículo Segundo

Los Comisionados así designados, se reunirán en la ciudad de México, dentro de los seis meses contados a partir de la fecha del canje de ratificaciones de la presente Convención. Cada uno de los miembros de la Comisión, antes de dar principio a sus trabajos, hará y firmará una declaración solemne en que se comprometa a examinar con cuidado y fallar con imparcialidad, conforme a los principios de la equidad, todas las reclamaciones presentadas, supuesto que la voluntad de México es la de reparar graciosamente a los damnificados, y no que su responsabilidad se establezca de conformidad con los principios generales del Derecho Internacional; siendo bastante, por tanto, que se pruebe que el daño alegado haya existido y se deba a alguna de las causas enumeradas en el Artículo Tercero de esta Convención, para que México se sienta, "ex gratia," decidido a indemnizar.

La citada declaración se registrará en las actas de la Comisión.

La Comisión fijará la fecha y el lugar de sus sesiones.

Artículo Tercero

La Comisión conocerá de todas las reclamaciones contra México por las pérdidas o daños sufridos en sus personas o en sus bienes por súbditos o protegidos españoles, y por sociedades, compañías, asociaciones o personas morales españolas; o por las pérdidas o daños causados a los intereses de súbditos españoles o protegidos españoles en sociedades, compañías, asociaciones u otros grupos de intereses, siempre que, en este caso, el interés del damnificado sea de más de un cincuenta por ciento del capital total de la sociedad o asociación de que forma parte, y adquirido anteriormente a la época en que se resintió el daño o pérdida, y que, además, se presente a la Comisión una cesión hecha al reclamante de la parte proporcional de la pérdida o daños que le toquen en tal compañía o asociación. Las pérdidas o daños de que se habla en este artículo, deberán haber sido causados durante el período comprendido entre el 20 noviembre de 1910 y el 31 de mayo de 1920, inclusive, por las fuerzas siguientes:

1. Por fuerzas de un Gobierno *de jure* o *de facto;*
2. Por fuerzas revolucionarias que hayan establecido al triunfo de su causa Gobiernos *de jure* o *de facto,* o por fuerzas revolucionarias contrarias a aquéllas;
3. Por fuerzas procedentes de la disgregación de las que se mencionan en el párrafo precedente, hasta el momento en que el Gobierno *de jure* hubiere sido establecido después de una revolución determinada;
4. Por fuerzas procedentes de la disolución del Ejército Federal;

5. Por motines o levantamientos, o por fuerzas insurrectas distintas de las indicadas en los párrafos 2, 3 y 4 de este artículo, o por bandoleros, con tal de que, en cada caso, se pruebe que las autoridades competentes omitieron dictar medidas razonables para reprimir las insurrecciones, levantamientos, motines o actos de bandolerismo de que se trata, o para castigar a sus autores; o que se pruebe, asimismo, que las autoridades incurrieron en falta de alguna otra manera.

Artículo Cuarto

La Comisión decretará sus propios procedimientos, pero ciñéndose a las disposiciones de la presente Convención.

Cada Gobierno podrá nombrar un Agente y Consejeros que presenten a la Comisión, ya sea oralmente o por escrito, las pruebas y argumentos que juzguen conveniente aducir en apoyo de las reclamaciones o en contra de ellas.

La decisión de la mayoría de los miembros de la Comisión, será la de la Comisión. Si no hubiere mayoría, prevalecerá la decisión del Presidente.

Artículo Quinto

La Comisión irá registrando con exactitud todas las reclamaciones y los diversos casos que le fueren sometidos, así como las actas de los debates, con sus fechas respectivas.

Para tal fin, cada Gobierno podrá designar un Secretario. Dichos Secretarios dependerán de la Comisión y estarán sometidos a sus instrucciones.

Cada Gobierno podrá nombrar, asimismo, y emplear los Secretarios adjuntos que juzgare prudente. La Comisión podrá obrar y emplear, igualmente, los ayudantes que juzgue necesarios para llevar a cabo su misión.

Artículo Sexto

Deseando el Gobierno de México llegar a un arreglo equitativo sobre las reclamaciones especificadas en el Artículo Tercero, y conceder a los reclamantes una indemnización justa que corresponda a las pérdidas o daños que hayan sufrido, queda convenido que la Comisión no habrá de descartar o rechazar ninguna reclamación por causa de que no se hubieren agotado, antes de presentar dicha reclamación, todos los recursos legales.

Para fijar el importe de las indemnizaciones que habrán de concederse por daños a los bienes, se tendrá en cuenta el valor declarado al Fisco por los interesados, salvo en casos verdaderamente excepcionales, a juicio de la Comisión.

El importe de las indemnizaciones por daños personales, no excederá al de las indemnizaciones más amplias concedidas por España en casos semejantes.

Artículo Septimo

Toda reclamación habrá de presentarse ante la Comisión dentro del plazo de nueve meses, contados desde el día de la primera reunión de ella; pero este

plazo podrá extenderse por tres meses más, en casos especiales y excepcionales, y siempre que se pruebe, a juicio de la mayoría de la Comisión, que hubo causas para justificar el retardo.

La Comisión oirá, examinará y resolverá dentro del plazo de tres años y medio, contados desde el día de su primera sesión, todas las reclamaciones que le fueren presentadas.

Seis meses después del día de la primera reunión de los miembros de la Comisión, y luego bimestralmente, la Comisión someterá a cada uno de los Gobiernos interesados, un informe detallado de los trabajos realizados, y que comprenda también una exposición de las reclamaciones presentadas, de las oídas y de las resueltas.

La Comisión dará su fallo sobre toda reclamación que se le presente, dentro del plazo de seis meses, contados desde la clausura de los debates relativos a dicha reclamación.

Artículo Octavo

Las Altas Partes Contratantes convienen en considerar como definitiva la decisión de la Comisión sobre cada uno de los asuntos que juzgue, y en dar pleno efecto a las referidas decisiones. Convienen también en considerar el resultado de los trabajos de la Comisión como un arreglo pleno, perfecto y definitivo, de todas las reclamaciones que contra el Gobierno de México provengan de alguna de las causas enumeradas en el Artículo Tercero de la presente Convención. Convienen, además, en que desde el momento en que terminen los trabajos de la Comisión, toda reclamación de esa especie, haya o no sido presentada a dicha Comisión, habrá de considerarse como arreglada absoluta e irrevocablemente para lo sucesivo; a condición de que, las que hubieren sido presentadas a la Comisión, hayan sido examinadas y resueltas por ella.

Artículo Noveno

La forma en que el Gobierno mexicano pagará las indemnizaciones, se fijará por ambos Gobiernos, una vez terminadas las labores de la Comisión. Los pagos se efectuarán en oro o en moneda equivalente, y se harán al Gobierno Español por el Gobierno Mexicano.

Artículo Decimo

Cada Gobierno pagará los honorarios de su Comisionado y los de su personal.

Ambos Gobiernos pagarán por mitad los gastos de la Comisión y los honorarios correspondientes al tercer Comisionado.

Artículo Decimoprimero

Las Atlas Partes Contratantes ratificarán la presente Convención, de conformidad con sus respectivas Constituciones. El canje de las ratificaciones se

efectuará en la ciudad de México tan pronto como fuere posible, y la Convención entrará en vigor desde el momento en que dicho cambio de ratificaciones se haya verificado.

En fe de lo cual, los Plenipotenciarios respectivos firmaron la presente Convención, poniendo en ella sus sellos.

Hecha por duplicado en la ciudad de México el día veinticinco de noviembre de mil novecientos veinticinco.

(L. S.) Firmado: (L. S.) Firmado:

Aarón Sáenz.   El Marqués de Berna.

B. SUPPLEMENTARY CONVENTION OF DECEMBER 5, 1930 [1]

Su Majestad el Rey de España y el Presidente de los Estados Unidos Mejicanos, considerando, por una parte, que la Comisión creada por la Convención de 25 de Noviembre de 1925 no pudo terminar sus trabajos en el plazo fijado por la mencionada Convención y que, además, el funcionamiento de esta Comisión mostró la conveniencia de expresar con mayor claridad algunas de las disposiciones de la Convención mencionada para precisar los términos según los cuales ha debido y debe fijarse la responsabilidad que el Gobierno de Méjico ha asumido "ex gratia" para indemnizar a los súbditos españoles por pérdidas a causa de actos revolucionarios ejecutados durante el período comprendido entre el 20 de Noviembre de 1910 y el 31 de Mayo de 1920, inclusive, han convenido en celebrar la presente Convención, y al efecto han nombrado como Plenipotenciarios:

Su Majestad el Rey de España, al Sr. D. Francisco Martínez de Galinsoga y de la Serna, Vizconde de Gracia Real, Gran Cruz de Isabel la Católica, etc., etc., Su Enviado Extraordinario y Ministro Plenipotenciario en Méjico;

El Presidente de los Estados Unidos Mejicanos, al Sr. D. Genaro Estrada, Secretario de Estado y del Despacho de Relaciones Exteriores,

Quienes, después de comunicarse sus respectivos plenos poderes, y de hallarlos en buena y debida forma, convinieron en los artículos siguientes:

Artículo 1.º Las Altas Partes contratantes convienen en que el plazo fijado por el artículo 7.º de la Convención de 25 de Noviembre de 1925 para la audiencia, examen y decisión de las reclamaciones ya presentadas, de acuerdo con los términos del mismo artículo 7.º, por la presente se prorroga durante un plazo de diez y ocho meses, contados desde el 6 de Julio de 1930. Si dentro de este plazo la Comisión no pudiere terminar sus trabajos, aquél será prorrogado por un lapso que no exceda de un año, mediante un simple cambio de Notas entre las Partes contratantes.

[1] Text from Colección legislativa de España, 1931, p. 418.

Artículo 2.º   Se modifica el artículo 2.º de la Convención de 25 de Noviembre de 1925, en la siguiente forma :

Los comisionados así designados se reunirán en la ciudad de Méjico dentro de los seis meses, contados a partir de la fecha del canje de ratificaciones de esta Convención.   Cada uno de los miembros de la Comisión, antes de dar principio a sus trabajos, hará y firmará una declaración solemne en que se comprometa a examinar con cuidado y a fallar con imparcialidad, conforme a los principios de la equidad, todas las reclamaciones presentadas, supuesto que la voluntad de Méjico es la de reparar plenamente, "ex gratia," a los damnificados, y no que su responsabilidad se establezca de conformidad con los principios generales del Derecho internacional ; siendo bastante, por tanto, que se pruebe que el daño alegado haya existido y se deba a alguna de las causas enumeradas en el artículo 3.º de esta Convención ; de que no sea la consecuencia de un acto legítimo y sea comprobado su monto para que Méjico se sienta, "ex gratia," decidido a hacer tal indemnización.

La citada declaración se registrará en las actas de la Comisión.

La Comisión fijará la fecha y el lugar de sus sesiones en Méjico.

Artículo 3.º   Se modifica el artículo 3.º de la Convención de 25 de Noviembre de 1925, en la siguiente forma :

La Comisión conocerá de todas las reclamaciones contra Méjico por las pérdidas o daños resentidos por súbditos españoles, por Sociedades, Compañías, Asociaciones o personas morales españolas o por las pérdidas o daños causados a los intereses de ciudadanos españoles en Sociedades, Compañías, asociaciones u otros grupos de interesês, siempre que en este caso el interés del damnificado sea de más de un 50 por 100 del capital total de la Sociedad o Asociación de que forma parte, anterior a la época en que se resintió el daño o pérdida, y que, además, se presente a la Comisión una cesión hecha al reclamante de la parte proporcional de la pérdida o daño que le toque en tal Compañía o Asociación.   Las pérdidas o daños de que se habla en este artículo deberán haber sido causados en el período comprendido del 20 de Noviembre de 1910 al 31 de Mayo de 1920 por las fuerzas siguientes :

1. Por fuerzas de un Gobierno *de jure* o *de facto*.

2. Por fuerzas revolucionarias que hayan establecido al triunfo de su causa un Gobierno de "jure" o de "facto."

3. Por fuerzas procedentes de la disolución del Ejército federal.

4. Por motines y levantamientos o por fuerzas insurrectas distintas de las indicadas en los párrafos 2 y 3 de este artículo y por bandoleros, con tal de que en cada caso se pruebe que las Autoridades competentes omitieron dictar medidas razonables para reprimir las insurrecciones, levantamientos, motines o actos de bandolerismo de que se trata, o para castigar a sus autores, o bien que quede establecido que las Autoridades mencionadas son responsables de cualquier otra manera.

La Comisión conocerá también de las reclamaciones por pérdidas o daños causados por actos de autoridades civiles, siempre que dichos actos se originen en sucesos y trastornos revolucionarios, dentro de la época a que alude este artículo y que hayan sido ejecutados por alguna de las fuerzas descritas en los párrafos 1 y 2 del presente artículo.

Entre las reclamaciones de la competencia de la Comisión no están comprendidas las originadas por fuerzas de Victoriano Huerta o por actos de su régimen.

La Comisión no será competente para conocer de reclamaciones relativas a la circulación o aceptación voluntaria o forzosa de papel moneda.

Artículo 4.º Los plazos de procedimiento fijados por la misma Convención y su Reglamento que quedaron suspendidos el 6 de Julio de 1930, se reanudan a partir de la fecha del canje de ratificaciones de la presente Convención.

Todas las disposiciones de la Convención de 25 de Noviembre de 1925 y de su Reglamento, que no sean modificadas por las disposiciones de la presente Convención, quedan en vigor.

Artículo 5.º Las Altas Partes Contratantes ratificarán la presente Convención, de conformidad con lo que establecen sus respectivas Constituciones.

El canje de las ratificaciones se efectuará en la ciudad de Méjico tan pronto como fuere posible y la Convención entrará en vigor desde el momento en que dicho canje de ratificaciones se haya efectuado.

En fe de lo cual los Plenipotenciarios respectivos firman la presente.

Hecha por duplicado en la ciudad de Méjico el día cinco de Diciembre de mil novecientos treinta.

Vizconde de Gracia Real.
Genaro Estrada.

C. RULES OF PROCEDURE [1]

TÍTULO I
OFICINA Y JUNTAS

Artículo 1. La Oficina de la Comisión será establecida y mantenida en la ciudad de México en donde se guardarán sus archivos.

Artículo 2. La fecha y lugar de las reuniones se fijarán por acuerdo de la Comisión.

TÍTULO II
EXTRACTOS, REGISTROS Y ACTAS

Artículo 3. Se llevarán dos libros iguales de registro por los Secretarios y en ellos se asentarán, al presentarse formalmente la reclamación ante la Comisión,

[1] Text from Reglas de Procedimiento (Mexico City, 1927).

el nombre de cada reclamante y la cantidad reclamada; y, además, se registrarán en los mismos todos los trámites que se vayan produciendo.

Artículo 4. Cada reclamación constituirá un caso separado ante la Comisión y se registrará como tal. Se numerarán progresivamente todas las reclamaciones en el orden en que se presenten.

Artículo 5. Se llevarán de la misma manera dos libros iguales de actas, por los Secretarios, y en ellos se asentará una relación cronológica de todos los trámites de la Comisión. En cada sesión de la Comisión firmarán el libro de actas los Comisionados y lo refrendarán los Secretarios.

Artículo 6. Los Secretarios llevarán los registros adicionales que ordena el presente reglamento o que la Comisión disponga cuando lo estime conveniente.

TÍTULO III

PRESENTACIÓN Y REGISTRO DE LAS RECLAMACIONES

Artículo 7. Toda reclamación deberá ser presentada por los Gobiernos respectivos, por conducto o a nombre de sus Agentes.

Artículo 8. La reclamación se considerará como formalmente presentada ante la Comisión:

(*a*) Al presentarse a los Secretarios un Memorándum o Declaración en dos ejemplares, el cual contendrá, con respecto a la reclamación, el nombre del reclamante, una relación breve de la naturaleza de la reclamación y el monto de la misma; o bien,

(*b*) Al presentarse a los Secretarios un Memorial en dos ejemplares conforme a las disposiciones del Artículo 13.

Artículo 9. Al recibirse el Memorándum o Declaración a que se refiere la cláusula (*a*) del Artículo 8 o el Memorial a que se refiere la cláusula (*b*) del mismo Artículo, se hará en él una anotación de su presentación, con la fecha de la misma, por los Secretarios y suscrita por los mismos e inmediatamente se registrará la reclamación con su número correspondiente.

Artículo 10. La Comisión, a moción de cualquiera de los Agentes o por sí misma, después de oír a aquéllos, fijará, si hay causa suficiente, el plazo que juzgue razonable para que se presenten los Memoriales referentes a reclamaciones ya presentadas, de acuerdo con la cláusula (*a*) del Artículo 8.

Artículo 11. Todas las reclamaciones por pérdidas o daños acaecidos durante el período comprendido entre el 20 de noviembre de 1910 y el 31 de mayo de 1920, se presentarán a la Comisión, ya sea de la manera dispuesta en la cláusula (*a*) o en la cláusula (*b*) del Artículo 8, antes del 7 de octubre de 1927, a no ser que en algún caso se pruebe que hubo causas que justifiquen la demora, a satisfacción de la mayoría de la Comisión, y, si así acaeciere, el período para su presentación podrá ser ampliado por la Comisión por un plazo de tres meses más.

Título IV
ESCRITOS FUNDAMENTALES

Artículo 12. Los escritos fundamentales serán el Memorial y la Contestación. Si las partes lo desean, pueden presentar una Réplica y una Dúplica. Por convenio entre los Agentes, confirmado por la Comisión, o por acuerdo de ésta las partes podrán presentar escritos suplementarios. Los escritos fundamentales deberán ir acompañados de copias de los documentos y pruebas en que se apoyen. Concluída la tramitación podrán las partes presentar Alegatos escritos o hacer alegaciones orales en la vista de la causa.

Artículo 13. El Memorial.

El Memorial deberá ser firmado por el reclamante o por su apoderado y deberá estar suscrito por el abogado o patrono del reclamante, si lo hubiere. Todos los Memoriales deberán también ser suscritos o refrendados por el Agente respectivo.

El Memorial contendrá una relación clara y concisa de los hechos en que se funde la reclamación. Expondrá en cada caso, con el mayor detalle posible:

(*a*) Los hechos que demuestren que la pérdida o daño por los cuales se hace la reclamación, resultaron de alguna o algunas de las causas especificadas en la Convención Especial de Reclamaciones entre México y España, suscrita en la ciudad de México el 25 de noviembre de 1925.

(*b*) El monto de la reclamación; la fecha y lugar en donde se originó; el daño o perjuicio, la clase, cantidad y valor de la propiedad perdida o dañada, en relación pormenorizada hasta donde sea factible; los agravios sufridos en la persona, si los hubiere, y las pérdidas o daños que resultaren de los mismos; los hechos y demás circunstancias concurrentes con la pérdida o daño, ya en la persona o ya en la propiedad, por los que se origina la reclamación y sobre los cuales el reclamante pretende fundarse para establecerla.

(*c*) A nombre de quién se formula la reclamación. Si la persona que la presenta lo hace con carácter de representante, comprobará su personalidad.

(*d*) La nacionalidad del dueño o dueños de la reclamación desde la fecha del origen de ésta hasta la fecha de su presentación. Si la nacionalidad proviene de nacimiento, de naturalización o de algún otro acto, deberán exponerse y comprobarse todos los hechos concernientes a este respecto. Igualmente se procederá cuando en algún caso apareciese que, en la serie de títulos de derecho a la reclamación, se hayan introducido derechos o intereses de alguna persona o compañía de nacionalidad distinta de la del reclamante.

(*e*) Si el reclamante alega, como base de su reclamación, la pérdida o daño sufrido por alguna corporación, compañía, asociación o sociedad en la cual el reclamante o la persona a nombre de quien se hace la reclamación, manifestará que su interés es de más de un cincuenta por ciento (50%) del capital social de la sociedad o asociación de que forma parte, adquirido anteriormente a la

época en que se resintió el daño o pérdida, y que, además, se presente a la Comisión una cesión hecha al reclamante de la parte proporcional de la pérdida o daño que le toque en tal compañía o asociación. En tal caso, el Memorial expondrá todos los hechos o consideraciones equitativos relacionados con dicha reclamación o en apoyo de ella. En caso de que el título del reclamante sea traslaticio de dominio en su favor, presentará a la Comisión la prueba documental en que se funde y acreditará que fue otorgada por alguna persona con poder para contratar en nombre de la corporación, compañía, asociación o sociedad de que se trata, o se expondrán claramente las causas legales que puedan fundar la ausencia de tal prueba. La Comisión podrá, en estos casos excepcionales, decidir sobre la validez de tales causas de acuerdo con la Convención.

(f) Si el monto total de la reclamación pertenece ahora, y perteneció en la fecha en que se originó, única y absolutamente al reclamante, y si alguna otra persona está o ha estado interesada en la misma o en parte alguna de ella. En este último caso quién es esa otra persona y cuál es o fue la naturaleza y la extensión de su interés; y cómo, cuándo, por qué medios y por qué compensación se hizo el traspaso de derechos o intereses entre las partes, si lo hubo.

(g) Si el reclamante, o cualquiera otra persona que en cualquier tiempo haya tenido derecho a la cantidad reclamada, o a alguna parte de ella, ha recibido alguna suma de dinero; y, en caso afirmativo, qué suma, o qué equivalencia o indemnización enc ualquiera forma que sea, ya por el monto total o por parte del importe de la pérdida o daño en que se funde la reclamación; y de ser así, cuándo y de quién se recibió.

(h) Si alguna vez se ha presentado la reclamación o si se ha depositado alguna queja respecto a la misma ante cualquiera de los Gobiernos; y en caso de ser así, los hechos relativos a dicha presentación.

(i) Cualquier reclamación derivada de daño o pérdida que se alegue fue sufrida por un nacional fallecido podrá ser presentada por el representante legal de la sucesión.

(j) En los casos en que varias reclamaciones se deriven de un mismo grupo de hechos, se podrán incluir, todas o cualquiera de ellas, en el mismo Memorial.

(k) La omisión de cualquiera de estos requisitos deberá ser justificada ante la Comisión.

Artículo 14. La Contestación.

(a) La Contestación en cada caso, se presentará a los Secretarios, dentro de sesenta (60) días contados a partir de la fecha en que se presente el Memorial, a no ser que antes de que se termine el plazo, éste se prorrogue (1) por convenio entre los Agentes notificado a los Secretarios y confirmado por la Comisión, o (2) por la Comisión, cuando considere que hay causa suficiente para ello, a pedido de cualquiera de los Agentes en caso de no producirse acuerdo

entre ellos, siempre que la moción respectiva sea hecha con anterioridad al vencimiento del plazo de sesenta días.

(*b*) La Contestación se referirá directamente a cada uno de los puntos del Memorial y manifestará claramente la actitud del Gobierno que contesta respecto a cada uno de los diversos elementos de la reclamación. Puede, además, contener todas aquellas materias nuevas que el Gobierno que contesta desee hacer constar dentro del alcance de la Convención.

Artículo 15. La Réplica.

(*a*) En los casos en que se estime necesario presentar una Réplica en nombre de algún reclamante, podrá ser ésta entregada a los Secretarios dentro de treinta (30) días contados a partir de la fecha en que se presente la Contestación, a menos que, antes de terminar el plazo éste se prorrogue (1) por convenio entre los Agentes respectivos, presentado en la misma forma a los Secretarios y confirmado por la Comisión, o (2) por la Comisión cuando considere que hay causa suficiente para ello a pedido de cualquiera de los Agentes, en caso de no producirse acuerdo entre ellos, siempre que la moción respectiva sea hecha con anterioridad al vencimiento del plazo de treinta días.

(*b*) La Réplica, caso de presentarse, se concretará a las materias contenidas en la Contestación.

Artículo 16. La Dúplica.

Cuando un Agente considere necesario duplicar, podrá hacerlo presentando dos ejemplares de la Dúplica, dentro de quince (15) días contados desde el día en que fue presentada la Réplica. La Dúplica se sujetará a las mismas reglas de la Réplica.

Artículo 17. Reformas de los Escritos Presentados.

(*a*) El Memorial y la Contestación, como también la Réplica y la Dúplica, podrán reformarse en cualquier momento antes del fallo definitivo, ya sea (1) por acuerdo entre los Agentes, confirmado por la Comisión, en el que convengan en la presentación de cualquiera reforma consignada en dicho acuerdo que se depositará ante los Secretarios como si se tratara de los escritos fundamentales originales, o (2) por permiso que la Comisión estime conveniente conceder, el cual sólo podrá otorgarse mediante moción, previa notificación, y conforme a las condiciones que la Comisión imponga.

(*b*) Todas las mociones solicitando permiso para reformar los escritos fundamentales se presentarán por escrito ante los Secretarios, y contendrán las reformas que deseen hacerse y las razones en que se funden.

(*c*) Las reformas a los escritos fundamentales deberán acompañarse de las copias de los documentos y otras pruebas que se aduzcan en su apoyo, a menos que éstos hayan sido presentados con los escritos fundamentales originales.

(*d*) Podrán presentarse Contestaciones, Réplicas o Dúplicas a los escritos de reforma, si se desea, de la misma manera que cuando se trata de escritos

fundamentales originales, dentro del plazo que convengan los Agentes y que confirme la Comisión, o que se fije en los acuerdos de la Comisión que concedan la reforma, según sea el caso.

Artículo 18. La Comisión no tomará en consideración hechos relativos a la reclamación o a la defensa que no estén debidamente consignados en los escritos fundamentales o que no estén apoyados con pruebas. Las observaciones de derecho serán atendidas hasta la terminación de las audiencias.

Artículo 19. A moción de cualquiera de los Agentes, o por propia iniciativa, la Comisión, después de oír a los Agentes, podrá acordar la acumulación o separación de reclamaciones.

Artículo 20. Cada Memorial Contestación, Réplica y Dúplica, al ser presentada, debe acompañarse con los documentos en los cuales intenta basarse el Gobierno que lo presenta. Los documentos presentados en fecha posterior serán rechazados por la Comisión. Los Agentes podrán, por convenio confirmado por la Comisión, ponerse de acuerdo sobre la admisión de nuevos documentos, en cualquiera fecha posterior a la presentación de los Escritos fundamentales.

Título V

COPIAS Y TRADUCCIONES DE ESCRITOS FUNDAMENTALES Y OTROS DOCUMENTOS

Artículo 21. Al presentarse los Memoriales y otros escritos fundamentales y reformas, el Agente que los presente deberá entregar a los Secretarios diez (10) copias adicionales para uso de la Comisión y de los Agentes.

Artículo 22. De los documentos y otras pruebas que se acompañen en apoyo de reclamaciones o de defensas, sólo será necesario copiar, en su caso, aquella parte que se aduzca, con una nota explicativa que permita su comprensión a la Comisión o a los Agentes. Sin embargo, a pedido del Agente de la parte contraria, el documento íntegro o copia certificada del mismo, deberá ser proporcionado a la Comisión. Deberán presentarse diez (10) copias de estos documentos y pruebas.

Artículo 23. La Comisión podrá ordenar la publicación de los documentos que se presenten.

Título VI

NOTIFICACIONES

Artículo 24. La presentación a los Secretarios de cualquier escrito fundamental, reformas, documentos o avisos por los Agentes, constituirá la notificación a la parte contraria y será considerada como el cumplimiento de estas Reglas con relación a cualquiera notificación requerida conforme a las mismas. Los Agentes tendrán obligación de tomar conocimiento de todos los acuerdos de la Comisión, y los Secretarios les proporcionarán copias certificadas de ellos inmediatamente que se dicten.

Título VII

MOCIONES SOBRE INADMISIBILIDAD DE RECLAMACIONES

Artículo 25. Podrá hacerse moción para declarar inadmisible una reclamación en cualquier tiempo, después de que ésta se haya registrado y antes de someterse finalmente a la Comisión, por alguna causa justificada y que se desprenda claramente de los autos, ya sea por lo que atañe a la jurisdicción de la Comisión o a la naturaleza de la reclamación. En todos los casos en que una de las partes haga moción para que se declare inadmisible una reclamación presentada por la otra, se suspenderán los términos que estén corriendo para la Contestación del Memorial, o de cualquiera otro de los escritos fundamentales relativos a la reclamación de que se trate y que se hayan presentado con anterioridad a la fecha de la moción.

Artículo 26. Todas las Mociones se harán por escrito y contendrán de manera concisa los fundamentos en que estén basadas. Serán presentadas a los Secretarios de la misma manera que los escritos fundamentales originales.

Artículo 27. Una vez que una Moción para declarar inadmisible una reclamación haya sido presentada, podrá ser retirada únicamente previa autorización de la Comisión. En su acuerdo, ya sea dando tal consentimiento, ya sea negando lugar a la declaración de inadmisibilidad o de retiro, la Comisión prescribirá las condiciones que le parezcan convenientes, tales como el término dentro del cual deba presentarse la Contestación, y el término dentro del cual será vista la reclamación en cuanto a sus propios méritos, quedando sin efecto cualquiera otra prescripción en contrario en estas Reglas.

Título VIII

DE LA PRUEBA

Artículo 28. La Comisión recibirá y considerará todas las declaraciones, los documentos, los "affidavits," los interrogatorios u otras pruebas que por escrito le sean presentadas, por cualquiera de los Gobiernos en las oportunidades que señala este Reglamento en apoyo de, o en contra de cualquier reclamación, concediéndole el valor que a su juicio tengan tales pruebas. Ninguno de estos documentos, declaraciones u otras pruebas, serán recibidos o considerados por la Comisión, si se presentaren por cualquier otro conducto.

Artículo 29. Cuando un documento original que se encuentre en los archivos de alguno de los Gobiernos interesados no pueda ser retirado fácilmente, podrán recibirse como pruebas en su lugar, si así se solicitare, copias debidamente certificadas.

Artículo 30. Cuando el original u otra prueba esté archivado en las oficinas de cualesquiera de los dos Gobiernos, y no pueda ser retirado fácilmente, ni exista copia de tal documento en poder del Agente del Gobierno que desee presentarlo a la Comisión, en apoyo de los puntos contenidos en sus escritos

fundamentales, notificará por escrito al Agente de la parte contraria, acerca de su deseo de examinar el referido documento. Si a una solicitud de examen se rehusa la exhibición del documento de que se trata, tal conducta junto con las razones que se dieren para excusarla, serán puestas en conocimiento de la Comisión, y esto será tomado en cuenta por ella.

Artículo 31. El derecho concedido para examinar el original de tales documentos, cuando se otorgue, se extenderá a todo el documento, del cual sólo se haya presentado una parte en apoyo o en contestación a una reclamación; pero no se extenderá a ninguno de sus anexos, apéndices, actas o anotaciones que contenga, si tales anexos, apéndices, actas o anotaciones no son aducidos como prueba o explícitamente señalados en los escritos fundamentales.

Artículo 32. Las copias impresas o publicadas de cualquier documento o informe oficial, así como las pruebas que consten en los mismos y que hayan sido impresas o publicadas por cualquiera de los dos Gobiernos, o con su autorización, podrán ser presentadas a la Comisión, pudiendo los Agentes respectivos hacer referencia a las mismas, llegado el caso, en apoyo de las reclamaciones presentadas por una de las partes o en defensa contra las presentadas por la parte contraria, sin necesidad de insertarlas en los autos o comprobar su existencia en ninguna otra forma, siempre que la parte de dichos documentos que se aduzca pueda ser fácilmente identificada en los escritos fundamentales o en los alegatos. La Comisión dará a los documentos presentados de este modo o a los cuales se haga referencia de la manera indicada, el valor que crea conveniente, según las circunstancias de cada caso. Se proporcionarán igualmente, al Agente del Gobierno contrario, o se pondrán a su disposición, para que haga uso de ellos, ejemplares de todos estos documentos impresos o publicados, cuando se hayan presentado ante la Comisión.

Se podrá hacer referencia a las publicaciones oficiales de códigos, leyes, decisiones judiciales y otras publicaciones, que traten de materias que sean del conocimiento de la Comisión, sin que sea necesario comprobar la existencia de dichas obras cuando sean de reconocida autoridad.

Artículo 33. El Agente de cualquiera de las partes tendrá el derecho, previa la debida notificación al Agente de la parte contraria, hecha dentro del término y en la forma prescrita en el Artículo siguiente, o en cumplimiento de cualquier acuerdo de la Comisión, para presentar testigos. Los testigos serán examinados bajo juramento o protesta por ambos Secretarios al tenor de los interrogatorios presentados por los Agentes. Cualquier testigo presentado por una de las partes estará sujeto a repreguntas por el Agente de la parte contraria.

Artículo 34. En cualquier caso en que uno de los Agentes desee presentar testimonio oral, dará aviso dentro de quince (15) días contados desde la fecha en que expire el plazo para presentar la Réplica o la Dúplica en su caso, haciéndolo por escrito ante ambos Secretarios y manifestando el número, los nombres y las direcciones de los testigos que desee examinar. No se tomará ningún

testimonio oral sino de acuerdo con la notificación dada dentro del término y en la forma antes prescritos, a menos que así lo permita la Comisión, siempre que para ello se demuestre causa justificada.

Ambos Secretarios fijarán la fecha y lugar en que, procediendo conjuntamente, recibirán las pruebas testimoniales, las cuales se harán constar por escrito o en cualquiera otra forma que dispongan. Dicha declaración, que será firmada por el testigo, se hará constar en los autos, y se proporcionará copia de ella al Agente de cada Gobierno.

Artículo 35. Las declaraciones se rendirán en español, a menos que el testigo no posea ese idioma; en tal caso se empleará el idioma que mejor se adapte a la comprensión del testigo. Las declaraciones en idioma extranjero se traducirán bajo la dirección de la Secretaría de la Comisión.

Artículo 36. Después del último escrito fundamental y en cualquier tiempo antes del fallo, la Comisión puede ordenar que se oiga el parecer de uno o más peritos sobre materias que exijan conocimientos especiales, e igualmente puede ordenar vistas de ojos.

Artículo 37. En caso de que no pudiere presentarse un testigo o un reclamante ante la Comisión, puede ser examinado por exhorto dirigido por conducto de los Agentes a la autoridad judicial competente del lugar del domicilio o de la residencia del testigo o del reclamante. La declaración será recibida con las formalidades de la ley local.

Artículo 38. La Comisión, cuando lo juzgue conveniente, podrá recibir testimonios orales en cualquier estado del juicio.

La Comisión, o cualquiera de sus miembros, podrá hacer comparecer antes de la vista de la causa a cualquiera de los testigos que hayan declarado ante los Secretarios.

TÍTULO IX

AUDIENCIAS

Artículo 39.   Agenda de Audiencias.

Ambos Secretarios prepararán y conservarán una Agenda de Audiencias, en dos ejemplares, en la cual serán apuntados para la vista todos los casos que el Gobierno reclamante somete con este propósito. Los casos así puestos en lista serán numerados consecutivamente en el orden en que sean sometidos, empezando con el número 1. Además, la Agenda de Audiencias expresará las fechas en que se vence el término para los Alegatos mencionados en el Artículo 41, así como la fecha en que éstos se presenten.

Artículo 40.   Anotación en la Agenda de Audiencias.

Cuando el Agente que presenta una reclamación desee que se proceda a la vista del caso, notificará a ese efecto a ambos Secretarios, y podrá presentar, juntamente con dicha notificación, un Alegato en apoyo de la reclamación. Al recibir tal notificación, ambos Secretarios consignarán dicha reclamación en la Agenda de Audiencias.

Artículo 41. Epoca en que un Caso está listo para la Vista.

Al hacerse la anotación en la lista de los casos de acuerdo con lo estipulado en el artículo 40, el Gobierno que contesta tendrá veinte (20) días para la presentación de un Alegato o de un Contra-Alegato, según sea el caso. El Gobierno reclamante tendrá diez (10) días, a contar de la fecha de tal Alegato o Contra-Alegato, para presentar una Dúplica ante ambos Secretarios. Al presentarse la Dúplica, o al vencerse el plazo, para presentar tal documento, si éste no se ha presentado, el caso quedará listo para ser visto.

Artículo 42. Orden de las Vistas.

El orden en el cual serán oídos los casos, será determinado por su posición en la sección numérica de la Agenda de Audiencias, a menos que los Agentes cambien el orden por convenio celebrado antes o durante una audiencia y que tal convenio sea confirmado por la Comisión. Ambos Secretarios harán los asientos necesarios, registrando cualquier cambio que se haga en el orden numérico.

Si no hay en la Agenda ningún caso listo para la vista, se podrán listar en aquélla los casos que ordene la Comisión. Tal procedimiento podrá seguirse solamente después de que la Comisión haya consultado a los Agentes sobre los casos que pudieran ser apuntados en la Agenda y sobre el procedimiento que se seguirá para juzgarlos. Cualquiera orden de la Comisión alistando casos tendrá que dictarse por lo menos pasados veinte (20) días (1) después del vencimiento del plazo dentro del cual pueda presentarse una Contestación, o (2) en los casos en que sea presentada una Contestación, después de la presentación de una Dúplica o del vencimiento del plazo dentro del cual pueda presentarse una Dúplica. Excepcionalmente, la Comisión podrá alterar el orden de las audiencias.

Artículo 43. Procedimiento para las Vistas.

Cuando un caso llegue ante la Comisión para audiencia, serán oídos los Agentes o los consejeros de ambas partes. El Agente o el Consejero del Gobierno reclamante deberá abrir el caso, y el Agente o el Consejero del Gobierno demandado podrá contestar. El tiempo concedido para la argumentación oral será fijado por la Comisión.

Artículo 44. Cuando un caso haya sido visto de acuerdo con las estipulaciones anteriores, se considerarán terminados los procedimientos ante la Comisión a no ser que ésta ordene otra cosa.

TÍTULO X

SENTENCIAS Y DECISIONES

Artículo 45. La Sentencia o cualquiera otra decisión judicial de la Comisión con respecto a cada reclamación, deberá dictarse en una sesión pública de la Comisión.

Artículo 46. La sentencia o cualquiera otra decisión judicial consignará ampliamente todos los fundamentos en que esté basada, y deberá ser firmada por dos miembros de la Comisión, cuando menos.

Artículo 47. En caso de que los Agentes celebren un convenio con respecto a cualquier ajuste de una reclamación, tal convenio será presentado a la Comisión con una solicitud, para que aquélla dicte una sentencia de acuerdo con el convenio.

Artículo 48. Cualquier miembro de la Comisión puede expresar una opinión disidente.

Artículo 49. Ambos Secretarios proporcionarán a cada uno de los Agentes cuatro (4) copias, o, en los casos en que la Comisión ordene que se impriman, diez (10) copias de cada sentencia o de cualquiera otra decisión y de cada una de las opiniones disidentes.

Artículo 50. A solicitud de cualquiera de los Agentes, hecha dentro de los sesenta (60) días subsiguientes a la fecha en que ambos Secretarios hayan proporcionado a los Agentes las copias de las sentencias o de cualquiera otra decisión, y después de dar al otro Agente una oportunidad para ser oído, la Comisión podrá interpretar o rectificar una decisión que en su parte resolutiva no sea clara, que sea incompleta o contradictoria o que contenga cualquier error de expresión o cálculo.

Artículo 51. En un libro intitulado "Registro de Sentencias y Decisiones" será archivada una copia de cada una de las sentencias o de cualquiera otra decisión dictada por la Comisión, y de cada opinión disidente.

Ambos Secretarios enviarán a la Oficina Internacional de la Corte Permanente de Arbitraje de La Haya dos (2) copias de todas las sentencias y opiniones disidentes que se hayan impreso.

TÍTULO XI

OBLIGACIONES DE LOS SECRETARIOS

Artículo 52. Los Secretarios que en el desempeño de las atribuciones y deberes que les señala el presente Reglamento procederán conjuntamente, deberán:

(*a*) Estar supeditados a las órdenes de la Comisión.

(*b*) Guardar todos los documentos y registros de la Comisión y conservarlos sistemáticamente arreglados en archiveros de seguridad. Aun cuando deban prestarse todas las facilidades que sean razonables a los Agentes y a sus respectivos Consejeros para examinar y tomar notas de ellos, no deberán permitir que se retire de los Archivos ningún documento o registro excepto por acuerdo de la Comisión debidamente registrado.

(*c*) Recibir la prueba a que se refiere el Título VIII, Artículo 33.

(*d*) Formar un Registro, una Agenda de Audiencias, un Libro de Actas, un

Libro de Notificaciones, un Libro de Acuerdos y un Libro de Sentencias y Decisiones y todos los demás libros y documentos que la Comisión disponga cuando lo estime conveniente.

(*e*) Anotar en cada documento que se presente a la Comisión la fecha de su presentación y hacer la anotación correspondiente en el Libro de Registro.

(*f*) Asentar en los dos Libros iguales de Notificaciones, todas las notificaciones que conforme a estas Reglas deberán dar los respectivos Agentes a los Secretarios; y dar inmediato aviso de ello al Agente a quien deba notificarse. Se asentará en dichos Libros de Notificaciones, la fecha en que se haga cada Notificación, así como todos los trámites relativos y originados en. el cumplimiento de esa Notificación.

(*g*) Proporcionar sin demora al Agente de la parte contraria, copia de todos los escritos fundamentales, mociones, notificaciones y otros documentos presentados a los Secretarios por el Agente de cualquier Gobierno, registrándolos debidamente.

(*h*) Desempeñar todas las demás obligaciones que les señale la Comisión, cuando lo estime conveniente.

Artículo 53. Las personas empleadas como traductores, intérpretes y taquígrafos, estarán bajo la exclusiva jurisdicción de los Secretarios, y sujetos también a las instrucciones de la Comisión.

TÍTULO XII
DEL CÓMPUTO DE LOS TÉRMINOS

Artículo 54. Siempre que en estas Reglas se mencione un período de días para la ejecución de un acto, no se contará el día a partir del cual comienza a computarse el plazo y sí se contará el último día y se excluirán los domingos y días de fiestas nacionales de los dos países.

TÍTULO XIII
DE LAS REFORMAS A LAS REGLAS

Artículo 55. Los Agentes respectivos deberán ser oídos cuando se trate de reformar estas Reglas, antes de que la Comisión decida sobre la materia.

TÍTULO XIV
DEL SILENCIO DE LAS REGLAS

Artículo 56. En cualquiera materia no tratada expresamente en este Reglamento, la Comisión procederá de acuerdo con el Derecho Internacional, con la justicia y con la equidad.

VIII. SPECIAL MEXICAN CLAIMS COMMISSION OF THE UNITED STATES

A. ACT OF APRIL 10, 1935[1]

Be it enacted by the Senate and House of Representatives of the United States of America in Congress assembled, That (*a*) there is hereby established a commission to be known as the "Special Mexican Claims Commission" (hereinafter referred to as the "Commission") which shall be composed of three commissioners, learned in the law, to be appointed by the President. Such Commission shall have jurisdiction to hear and determine, as hereinafter provided, conformable to the terms of the Convention of September 10, 1923, and justice and equity, all claims against the Republic of Mexico, notices of which were filed with the Special Claims Commission, United States and Mexico, established by said Convention of September 10, 1923, in which the said Commission failed to award compensation, except such claims as may be found by the Committee provided for in the special claims Convention of April 24, 1934, to be General Claims and recognized as such by the General Claims Commission. For the purpose of this Act, claims which were brought to the attention of the American agency charged with the prosecution of claims before the aforesaid Commission, prior to the expiration of the periods specified in the convention of September 10, 1923, for the filing of claims, but which, because of error or inadvertance, were not filed with or brought to the attention of the Commission within the said periods, shall be deemed to have been filed with the Commission within such periods.

(*b*) The President shall designate one of such commissioners as chairman of the Commission. Not more than two of such commissioners shall be members of the same political party. Each commissioner shall be a citizen of the United States, shall hold office until the functions of the Commission are terminated, and shall receive a salary at the rate of $7,500 a year. Any vacancy that may occur in the membership of the Commission shall be filled in the same manner as in the case of an original appointment. Two members of the Commission shall constitute a quorum for the transaction of its business.

SEC. 2. The Commission shall have a secretary, and such additional legal, clerical, and technical assistants as may be approved and appointed by the Secretary of State, and at the rates of compensation fixed by him.

[1] Text from Public No. 30, 74th Congress.

SEC. 3. (*a*) Before taking up his duties, each commissioner shall make and subscribe a solemn oath or declaration that he will carefully and impartially examine and decide all claims according to the best of his judgment and in accordance with the evidence and the applicable principles of justice and equity, and the terms of the said convention of September 10, 1923. All decisions by the Commission, which shall be by majority vote, shall constitute a full and final disposition of the cases decided. Such decisions shall be based upon the present records in the cases and such additional evidence and written legal contentions as may be presented within such period as may be prescribed therefor by the Commission.

(*b*) The Commission shall have authority, in its discretion, to make independent investigations of cases. For the purpose of all investigations which, in the opinion of the Commission, are necessary and proper for carrying out the provisions of this Act, each commissioner is empowered to administer oaths and affirmations, subpena witnesses, take evidence, and require the production of books, papers, or other documents which the commissioner or the Commission deems relevant to the inquiry.

(*c*) Such attendance of witnesses and the production of such documentary evidence may be required from any place in the United States at any designated place of hearing. In case of disobedience to a subpena the Commission may invoke the aid of any district or territorial court of the United States or the Supreme Court of the District of Columbia in requiring the attendance and testimony of witnesses and the production of documentary evidence, and the court within the jurisdiction of which such inquiry is carried on may, in case of contumacy or refusal to obey a subpena issued to any person, issue an order requiring such person to appear before the Commission, or to produce documentary evidence if so ordered or to give evidence touching the matter in question; and any failure to obey such order of the court may be punished by such court as a contempt thereof.

(*d*) For the purpose of assisting the Commission in carrying out the provisions of this Act, the heads of the various departments and independent agencies and establishments of the Government are hereby directed to coöperate with the Commission and to place at its disposal such information as the Commission may from time to time request.

SEC. 4. If, after all claims have been passed upon and all awards have been entered, the Commission shall find that the total amount of such awards is greater than the amount that the Government of Mexico has agreed to pay to the Government of the United States in satisfaction of the claims, less the expenses of the Commission, it shall reduce the awards on a percentage basis to such amount, and shall enter final awards in such reduced amounts.

SEC. 5. The said Commission shall perform its duties in the city of Washington, beginning within fifteen days after its appointment. It shall, as soon as

practicable, make all needful rules and regulations not contravening the laws of the United States, or the provisions of this Act, for regulating the mode of procedure by and before it and for carrying into full and complete effect the provisions of this Act; it shall also, as soon as practicable, notify all claimants of record of the establishment of the Commission and of the rules of procedure adopted by it for the adjudication of the claims, including the time allowed for the filing of additional evidence and written legal contentions.

SEC. 6. The Commission shall complete its work within two years from the date on which it undertakes the performance of its duties, at which time all powers, rights, and duties conferred by this Act upon the Commission shall terminate.

SEC. 7. The Commission shall be allowed the necessary actual expenses of office rent, furniture, stationery, books, printing and binding, and other necessary incidental expenses, to be certified as necessary by the Commission and approved by the Secretary of State.

SEC. 8. The Commission shall, at the time of entering an award on any claim, allow counsel or attorneys employed by the claimant or claimants, out of the amount awarded, such fees as it shall determine to be just and reasonable for the services rendered the claimant or claimants in prosecuting such claim, which allowance shall be entered as a part of said award: *Provided, however*, That the Commission shall determine just and reasonable fees, where there is a contract or agreement for services in connection with the proceedings before the Commission and with the preparations therefor, only upon the written request of the claimant or claimants, or of the counsel or attorneys, made to the Commission within ninety days after notice of the entry of an award and notice of the provisions of this section shall have been mailed by the Commission to the claimant or claimants; and payment shall be made by the Secretary of the Treasury to the person or persons to whom such allowance shall be made in the same manner as payments are made to claimants under section 9 of this Act, which shall constitute payment in full to the counsel or attorneys for prosecuting such claim; and whenever such allowance shall be made all other liens upon, or assignments, sales, or transfers of the claim or the award thereon, whether absolute or conditional, for services rendered or to be rendered by counsel or attorneys in the preparation or presentation of any claim or part or parcel thereof, shall be absolutely null and void and of no effect.

SEC. 9. The said Commission shall, upon the completion of its work, submit a report to the Secretary of State, attaching thereto the following documents in duplicate: (*a*) a statement of the expenses of the Commission; (*b*) a list of all claims rejected; (*c*) a list of all claims allowed in whole or in part, together with the amount of each claim and the amount awarded by the Commission; and (*d*) its decisions in writing showing the reasons for the allowance

or disallowance of the respective claims. Certified copies of lists (*a*) and (*c*) shall be transmitted by the Secretary of State to the Secretary of the Treasury, who shall, after making the deduction provided for in section 11 hereof, distribute in ratable proportions, among the persons in whose favor awards shall have been made, or their assignees, heirs, executors, or administrators of record, according to the proportions which their respective awards shall bear to the whole amount then available for distribution, such moneys as may have been received into the Treasury in virtue of the convention of April 24, 1934. The Secretary of the Treasury shall follow like procedure with reference to any amounts that may thereafter be received from the Government of Mexico under the convention of April 24, 1934.

SEC. 10. As soon as the adjudication of the claims shall have been completed, the records, books, documents, and all other papers in the possession of the Commission, or members of its staff, shall be deposited with the Department of State.

SEC. 11. For the expenses of the Commission in carrying out the duties as aforesaid, the sum of $90,000, or so much thereof as may be necessary, is hereby authorized to be appropriated out of any money in the Treasury not otherwise appropriated, including personal services in the District of Columbia, or elsewhere, without regard to the provisions of any statute relating to employment, rent in the District of Columbia, furniture, office supplies, and equipment, including law books and books of reference, stenographic reporting and translating services, without regard to section 3709 of the Revised Statutes; traveling expenses; printing and binding; and such other necessary expenses as may be authorized by the Secretary of State: *Provided*, That any expenditures from the amount herein authorized to be appropriated shall become a first charge upon any moneys received from the Government of Mexico in settlement of these claims, and the amount of such expenditures shall be deducted from the first payment by the Government of Mexico and deposited in the Treasury of the United States as miscellaneous receipts.

SEC. 12. After a fee has been fixed under section 8, any person accepting any consideration (whether or not under a contract or agreement entered into prior or subsequent to the enactment of this Act) the aggregate value of which (when added to any consideration previously received) is in excess of the amount so fixed, for services in connection with the proceedings before the Commission, or any preparations therefor, shall, upon conviction thereof, be punished by a fine of not more than four times the aggregate value of the consideration accepted by such person therefor.

B. RULES AND REGULATIONS, ADOPTED SEPTEMBER 16, 1935[1]

I. NOTIFICATION TO CLAIMANTS

Notification of the establishment of this Commission and of these rules shall be sent as soon as practicable to all persons who appear from the records of the former Special Claims Commission, United States and Mexico, or from the records of the former Agency of the United States before that Commission, to be proper parties to —

(1) Claims against the Republic of Mexico, notices of which were filed with the former Special Claims Commission, with the exception of claims which were found by the Joint Committee established under the Convention of April 24, 1934, between the United States and Mexico, to be General claims; and

(2) Claims which were brought to the attention of the former Agency before the expiration of the periods specified in the Convention of September 10, 1923, between the United States and Mexico, for the filing of claims, but which, because of error or inadvertence, were not filed with or brought to the attention of the former Special Claims Commission within the said periods.

The notification herein provided for shall be without prejudice to the subsequent determination of the rights of the persons so notified, or of other persons claiming as assignees, heirs, executors, administrators, or otherwise, with respect to the prosecution of claims before this Commission.

In the absence of a showing satisfactory to this Commission that the interests of claimants of record before the former Special Claims Commission have passed into other hands, no change in the title of any claim, as registered with the former Commission, will be made by this Commission.

II. BASIS OF DECISIONS

In conformity with the provisions of the act of April 10, 1935, the decisions of the Commission shall be made in accordance with the applicable principles of justice and equity and the terms of the convention of September 10, 1923, article III of which reads as follows:

"The claims which the Commission shall examine and decide are those which arose during the revolutions and disturbed conditions which existed in Mexico covering the period from November 20, 1910, to May 31, 1920, inclusive, and were due to any act by the following forces:

"(1) By forces of a government de jure or de facto.

[1] Text from Rules and Regulations of the Special Mexican Claims Commission (Washington, 1935).

"(2) By revolutionary forces as a result of the triumph of whose cause governments de facto or de jure have been established, or by revolutionary forces opposed to them.

"(3) By forces arising from the disjunction of the forces mentioned in the next preceding paragraph up to the time when the government de jure established itself as a result of a particular revolution.

"(4) By federal forces that were disbanded and

"(5) By mutinies or mobs, or insurrectionary forces other than those referred to under subdivisions (2), (3) and (4) above, or by bandits, provided in any case it be established that the appropriate authorities omitted to take reasonable measures to suppress insurrectionists, mobs, or bandits, or treated them with enity or were in fault in other particulars."

The decisions of the Commission shall, except in such cases as it may consider to require independent investigation, be based upon the present records in the cases and such additional evidence and written legal contentions as may be presented within such period as may be prescribed therefor by the Commission.

III. Period for Filing Additional Evidence and Written Legal Contentions

The period for the filing of additional evidence and written legal contentions shall be 45 days from the date of the mailing of the above-mentioned notification: *Provided*, That the Commission may, for good cause shown on behalf of any claimant, extend the said period for such time as it may deem necessary in connection with any claim.

IV. Form of Additional Evidence and Written Legal Contentions

Documentary evidence may consist of naturalization papers, deeds, contracts, wills, letters of administration, letters testamentary, bills of sale, foreign laws, decrees or regulations, sequestration orders, birth, death, and marriage certificates, affidavits, manifests, invoices, bills of lading, ships' papers, charter parties, insurance policies, receipts, letters, photographs, etc. Papers bearing signatures should be accompanied (*a*) by the addresses of the signers, or (*b*) by a statement that they are deceased, or (*c*) by a statement that their whereabouts is unknown and cannot be ascertained, as the case may be. Public documents or records (whether originals or copies) exhibited in evidence should, if possible, be authenticated by the certificate of their official custodian or recorder. Private papers or documents (whether originals or copies) should, if possible, be verified as to their contents and signatures by the affidavit of a person familiar with and competent to testify as to their verity, such as the

person who issued or signed the documents or who saw them issued or signed and is familiar with their contents. Verification may not be made by the magistrate or other person administering the oath, nor may it be made by the claimant himself unless the facts are within his exclusive knowledge. All testimony, papers, or documents in a foreign language which may be produced in evidence should be accompanied by a translation thereof in the English language.

Testimonial evidence must be set forth in writing upon the oath or affirmation of the deponent or affiant, who should in every instance state —

(*a*) His age, place of birth, nationality, present residence and occupation, and residence and occupation at the time the events occurred in regard to which he testifies.

(*b*) Facts and circumstances showing that he is familiar with, and competent to testify about, the matters to which his deposition or affidavit relates.

(*c*) Whether he has any interest, direct or indirect, and if so what interest, in the claim and, if he has any contingent interest therein, to what extent and upon the happening of what event he will be entitled to share in any indemnification which may be received in settlement of the claim.

(*d*) Whether he is the agent, attorney, or relative (and if a relative, what relation) of the claimant, or of any person having an interest in the claim.

The oath (affirmation) to any document or paper filed as evidence should meet the following requirements:

(*a*) The oath (affirmation) should be duly administered according to the laws of the place where it is taken by a magistrate or other person competent by such laws to administer oaths, having no interest in the claim to which the evidence relates and not being the agent or attorney of any person having such interest, and it must be certified by him that such is the case. An oath (affirmation) may be taken outside of the United States before a diplomatic or consular officer, or any other officer of the United States authorized to administer oaths by the laws of the United States, having no interest and not being the agent or attorney of any person having an interest in the claim, and it must be certified by him that such is the case. If the magistrate, officer, or other person administering the oath is a relative of any person having an interest in the claim, the degree of relationship must also be certified by the person administering the oath.

(*b*) In all cases the authority of the magistrate or other person to administer the oath (affirmation), whether outside or within the United States, must be certified, unless that person be a notary public, or a diplomatic, consular, or other officer having a seal of office, in which case an impression of the seal will be sufficient certification. In the case of a notary public the date of the expiration of his or her commission should be stated.

No particular form is prescribed for written legal contentions which may be submitted to the Commission.

V. BOOKS OF THE COMMISSION

The books of the Commission shall comprise the following:

(1) A Docket Book, which shall contain —

(a) The names and addresses of all claimants of record before the former Special Claims Commission, United States and Mexico, as defined in section I hereof, or of the persons satisfactorily shown to have succeeded to the interests of such claimants of record.

(b) The names and addresses of the attorneys of record.

(c) The docket numbers of the claims, which, with respect to claims filed with the former Special Claims Commission, shall be the same as the former docket numbers.

(d) The dates of notification to claimants in pursuance of section 5 of the act of April 10, 1935, and the dates of all subsequent correspondence between claimants or their attorneys and the Commission.

(e) A notation of every act or proceeding of the Commission with respect to any claim.

(f) A notation of every document received by the Commission with respect to any claim.

(2) A Minute Book, in which shall be recorded all proceedings and orders of the Commission.

(3) A Decision Book, which shall contain all decisions of the Commission regarding the claims presented.

(4) An Account Book, in which shall be recorded all expenditures by the Commission.

VI. ACCESS TO FILES AND WITHDRAWAL OF DOCUMENTS

Within the periods specified for the presentation of additional evidence and written legal contentions, claimants or their duly authorized representatives may be permitted, in the discretion of the Commission, to examine in the offices of the Commission the files relating to the claims in which they are directly interested. Papers or documents may be withdrawn from the files only with the express approval of the Commission and upon a written undertaking for the return of such papers or documents within a period to be specified in each instance.

VII. CORRESPONDENCE BETWEEN THE COMMISSION AND CLAIMANTS OF RECORD

Under the law establishing the Commission, the burden of proving claims rests upon the claimants, and the Commission has the judicial function of

deciding the claims. The Commissioners and the officials connected with the Commission are therefore unable to assist claimants or their attorneys in the prosecution of claims or to discuss the merits of claims with claimants or their representatives. They will, however, upon request, advise claimants or their representatives of the status of the claims in which they are interested and of the procedure for perfecting such claims. No person will be recognized as a representative of a claimant in the absence of a power of attorney or other document duly authorizing him to act on the claimant's behalf.

VIII. Presentation of Claims for Decision

Upon the expiration of the periods prescribed for the submission of additional evidence and written legal contentions, the staff of the Commission will proceed to prepare for the consideration of the Commission reports with respect to the claims which are ready for decision. The Commission may, in its discretion, issue administrative decisions grouping claims or formulating general principles applicable to the disposition of claims.

IX. Decisions

The decisions of the Commission shall set forth the reasons for the allowance or disallowance of the claims presented. In every instance in which an award is made express reference shall be made to section 4 of the act of April 10, 1935, which reads as follows:

"If, after all claims have been passed upon and all awards have been entered, the Commission shall find that the total amount of such awards is greater than the amount that the Government of Mexico has agreed to pay to the Government of the United States in satisfaction of the claims, less the expenses of the Commission, it shall reduce the awards on a percentage basis to such amount, and shall enter final awards in such reduced amounts."

The Commission, moreover, in the absence of satisfactory evidence that the amount of the fees of counsel or attorneys employed by the claimant or claimants is the subject of a contract between such counsel or attorneys and the claimant or claimants, shall, at the time of entering an award on any claim, enter as a part of the said award an allowance to such counsel or attorneys of such fees as it shall determine to be just and reasonable for the services rendered the claimant or claimants in the prosecution of the claim.

X. Period for Application to Commission for Allowance of Fees Where There Is a Contract or Agreement for Services

In any case in which it is shown to the satisfaction of the Commission that the fees of counsel or attorneys have been fixed by contract or agreement, the

Commission will not enter an allowance of fees unless so requested in writing by the claimant or claimants, or the counsel or attorneys, within 90 days after notice of the entry of an award and notice of the provisions of section 8 of the act shall have been mailed by the Commission to the claimant or claimants.

EDGAR E. WITT, *Chairman.*
J. H. SINCLAIR, *Commissioner.*
D. T. LANE, *Commissioner.*

BARR BUILDING,
Washington, D. C., September 16, 1935.

TABLE OF CASES

TABLE OF REFERENCES TO TREATIES, RULES OF PROCEDURE AND LEGISLATION

TREATIES

RULES OF PROCEDURE

LEGISLATION

TABLE OF REFERENCES TO AUTHORS

INDEX